The Status of Women in Librarianship

Historical, Sociological, and Economic Issues

Edited by Kathleen M. Heim

Neal-Schuman Publishers, Inc.

Z
668
.S75
1983

Published by Neal-Schuman Publishers, Inc.
23 Cornelia Street
New York, New York 10014

Copyright ©1983 by Neal-Schuman Publishers, Inc.

All rights reserved. Reproduction of this book,
in whole or in part, without written permission
of the publisher is prohibited.

Printed and bound in the United States of America.

Library of Congress Cataloging in Publication Data

Main entry under title:

The Status of Women in librarianship.

   Bibliography: p. 443
   Includes index.
   1. Library science—Vocational guidance—Addresses,
essays, lectures. 2. Women librarians—Addresses,
essays, lectures. I. Heim, Kathleen M.
Z668.S75 1982   020'.23   82-7887
ISBN 0-918212-62-6   AACR2

To Sister Mary Field, O.P., former Director of the Rebecca Crown Library at Rosary College, who demonstrated the importance of a strong woman administrator in the functioning of a model college library and provided me with much good advice and guidance when beginning my library career; and to Kathleen Weibel, whose manifesto "Towards a Feminist Profession" continues to be a daily source of inspiration and hope.

ACKNOWLEDGMENTS

Marsha Kraus Fulton, my research associate at the Graduate School of Library and Information Science (GSLIS) of the University of Illinois at Urbana-Champaign during the first year this book was underway (1980-81), was of great help with correspondence, organization, and preparation of the biographical notes on contributors. The merging of the copious footnotes of the authors into a single bibliography, to avoid duplication in documentation, was greatly facilitated by the work of John Olsgaard, Abdus Sattar, Saw Keok Ch'ng, and Irene Hoffman, all advanced students at the GSLIS. Julia Hansen Koehler, my research associate during 1981-1982, was indefatigable in her verification of citations, correspondence with archival curators, and general restructuring of supplementary materials. Katharine Phenix and Mary Mallory, feminist librarians at the University of Illinois Library, provided all-night assistance at the eleventh hour to assimilate changes in the manuscript. I am especially grateful to the support staff at the GSLIS: Donna Bigler, Sally Eakin, Janet Fredrick, Kathryn Painter, Donna Stanczyk, Kathleen Stango, and Thressa Todd, who not only helped me type the manuscript but remained patient throughout the project. The editorial staff at Neal-Schuman is also due thanks for their professional development of the book, especially Maureen Crowley, Felice Swados, and Sheldon Winicour.

CONTENTS

Foreword MARIANNE A. FERBER	vii
Introduction KATHLEEN M. HEIM	1
Revision versus Reality: Women in the History of the Public Library Movement, 1876-1920 SUZANNE HILDENBRAND	7
Sex-Typing in Education for Librarianship: 1870-1920 BARBARA ELIZABETH BRAND	29
The Recruitment of Men into Librarianship, Following World War II NANCY PATRICIA O'BRIEN	51
Undergraduate Women as Potential Recruits to the Library Profession PATRICIA REELING	67
Assertiveness Training for Library-School Students ADELAIDE WEIR SUKIENNIK	99
Biographical Research on Women Librarians: Its Paucity, Perils, and Pleasures LAUREL A. GROTZINGER	139
Profiles of the Careers of Selected Black Female Librarians LELIA GASTON RHODES	191
The Woman Academic-Library Administrator: A Career Profile JANICE C. FENNELL	207
Salary and Position Levels of Females and Males in Academic Libraries JEAN K. MARTIN	243
Women in Academic-Library, Higher-Education, and Corporate Management: A Research Review BETTY JO IRVINE	287
Mobility and Professional Involvement in Librarianship: A Study of the "Class of '55" MARION R. TAYLOR	321
Geographic Mobility and Career Advancement of Male and Female Librarians JUDITH SCHIEK ROBINSON	345
An Analysis of the Study, "Career Paths of Male and Female Librarians in Canada" ELIZABETH FUTAS	393

The Reentry Professional Librarian
   KATHERINE MURPHY DICKSON   425

Biographical Notes   MARSHA KRAUS FULTON   437

Bibliography   443

Index   475

FOREWORD

THE 1970 CENSUS lists twenty-one categories of professional and technical workers. Among these, six have a substantial majority of women, while all the others have a considerably smaller percentage of women than the labor force as a whole. The professions with a female majority rank among the lowest seven in terms of earnings. (Only one predominantly male occupation—religious workers—falls into this low group. It may well be that they primarily expect rewards other than monetary.) Education alone does not account for this poor showing, for only two of the six female-dominated occupations rank among the lowest in this respect, while the other four rank as high as ninth to twelfth. Neither does number of weeks worked per year, for only workers in one of the six occupations—teachers other than college and university—worked significantly fewer than the standard fifty or more weeks.

Librarians are a particularly striking case of low pay combined with a high proportion of women, high educational qualifications, and not significantly fewer weeks worked per year. They rank third highest in proportion of women in the occupation, ninth in years of education, and work forty-eight weeks per year on the average, but they rank seventeenth in earnings.

Thus one important question is why women are most heavily represented in the lowest paid professions or, conversely, why professions with the largest proportion of women are the lowest paid. But that addresses only part of the problem. The other question is why women are invariably paid less than men in the same occupation.

Using data from the 1970 Census shown in the appended table, we find that men in the professions are, on the average, paid $11,640, while women are paid only $6,140 or 53 percent as much. If women had the same occupational distribution as men, but received the same wages in each occupation as at present, they would earn $6,700, or 58 percent as much as men. If they had their present occupational distribution, but were paid as much as men in each occupation, they would earn $8,780, or 76 percent as much as men. These data show that both occupational segregation and low wages within occupations contribute to the earnings gap between professional men and women, but that the contribution of the latter is considerably greater.

Social scientists have done a great deal of research in recent years to determine what causes women to enter particular occupations. The occupation of mothers, early childhood training, and occupational counselling in high school and college have all been found to have some effect. Economists have especially emphasized the importance of the greater likelihood of women, who tend to drop out of the labor force, at least for a time, in choosing occupations where such discontinuity is not severely penalized. Similarly, many factors have been cited as contributing to women's lower earnings within occupations. Among these are lower levels of education and training, shorter work weeks, fewer weeks per year worked, less continuous on-the-job experience, and less likelihood that a woman will be willing to move to get the job best suited to her skills.

It is important to note, however, that none of the models devised succeed in fully explaining occupational segregation, or the earnings gap. This failure is frequently and plausibly interpreted to show that discrimination continues to play a part in keeping women out of nontraditional occupations, keeps them from moving up the ladder, and keeps their wages low. Furthermore, there is good reason to believe that such discrimination tends to reinforce the behavior of women, for which they are then further penalized. A woman who expects to be excluded from jobs that have upward mobility and high earnings is less likely to acquire many years of education and training, to want to work long hours, to continue working throughout her life, or to move to further her career.

The conclusion is therefore inescapable that discrimination does play a part in keeping women's earnings low, and for that matter, keeping earnings low in women's occupations for all its members. For this reason it was often assumed that one way to upgrade a woman's profession was to attract more men to join it. Librarians were somewhat successful in accomplishing this purpose. In 1950 only about 10 percent were men, by 1970 the percentage had increased to slightly over 20 percent. But it is not at all clear that women librarians benefitted by this change. For, as is generally the case, men tended to move into the best and highest positions, ensuring the continuation of the earnings gap within the occupation, and, as we have seen, librarians continue to fare poorly in relation to other professions.

This book is written to show the historical development and present status of women librarians. How they are faring is of considerable interest to women in general, for librarians are the most highly educated of the "female" professions, and because the varied and independent nature of their work provides a solid basis for their claiming to be not merely paraprofessional. What can be done to improve their depressed condition so convincingly documented in this volume?

One obvious solution to low earnings in female occupations is for fewer women to enter them. Restricting the supply of workers is a tried and true way of increasing the wages of those who remain, and in this case, the women who enter nontraditional occupations are also likely to gain. But, given traditional attitudes, this approach will work only

Foreword ix

slowly. Furthermore, radically changing the occupational structure, and possibly depriving people of the opportunity to do the work that is most satisfying to them, is a high price to pay for reducing the earnings gap. An alternative is to expand current legislation requiring equal pay for equal work to cover equal pay for work of comparable worth. Though it poses the problem of determining the relative worth of different kinds of work, equal pay for comparable worth appears to be well on the way to becoming the major economic women's rights issue of the 1980s. Coupled with greater opportunity for upward mobility, these changes would be expected to encourage women to continue their increasing professional commitment and help them to approach equality in status and in pay.

MARIANNE A. FERBER

Data from 1970 Census

	Total Number	% Female	Median Earnings	Median Earnings of Men	Median Earnings of Women	Earnings as % of Male Earnings	Years of Education	Years of Education of Men	Years of Education of Women
Accountants	720,617	25.5	9.4	10.7	5.8	54.3	16.1	16.1	16.1
Architects	57,081	3.7	13.0	13.2	7.0	53.0	16.8	17.0	12.8
Computer Specialists	263,622	19.5	10.3	11.0	7.8	70.7	15.7	15.4	17.0
Engineers	1,256,935	1.7	13.1	13.2	9.6	73.4	16.2	16.2	16.2
Farm Management Specialists	8,282	13.1	10.3	10.8	6.8	63.1	16.8	16.9	16.4
Foresters and Conservation Workers	42,433	4.1	7.8	8.0	3.2	40.1	13.6	13.7	12.1
Home Management Advisors	5,657	97.3	5.5*	18.9	7.1	—	16.5*	—	16.5
Lawyers and Judges	277,695	4.8	18.4	18.9	9.0	47.6	17+	17+	17+
Librarians, Archivists & Curators	130,154	78.7	6.5	7.7	6.2	80.5	16.6	16.9	16.5
Mathematical Specialists	36,712	35.1	10.3	12.0	7.1	59.5	16.1	16.7	15.1
Life & Physical Scientists	208,857	13.2	11.4	12.0	7.5	62.5	16.8	16.9	16.5
Operations & Systems Researchers & Analysts	80,770	9.7	11.1	11.5	8.5	74.0	14.5	14.6	14.0
Personnel & Labor Relations Workers	297,202	31.5	9.9	11.4	6.7	58.4	14.6	15.4	12.9
Physicians, Dentists & Related Practitioners	541,453	8.3	18.3	19.3	7.8	40.5	17+	17+	17+
Registered Nurses, Dieticians and Therapists	966,585	94.5	5.6	7.4	5.5	74.8	13.5	14.5	13.4
Health Technical Workers and Technicians	265,281	69.9	5.9	7.4	5.2	70.3	13.9	14.7	13.6
Religious Workers	258,428	10.1	5.8	6.2	2.6	41.8	17+**	17+	14.4
Social Scientists	111,274	18.6	12.3	13.3	7.7	57.9	17+	17+	17+
Social & Recreation Workers	276,010	58.8	6.9	7.9	6.2	77.7	16.3	16.4	16.3
Teachers, College & University	496,412	28.6	9.8	11.2	6.2	55.3	17+	17+	17+
Teachers, Other than College & University	2,785,783	70.6	7.1	8.7	6.4	73.1	16.7	17.0	16.6

*Only data for women.
**17+ counted as 17.5.
Source: Census of Population: 1970, Subject Reports, Occupational Characteristics, Final Report PC(2)7A, Washington, D.C.: G.P.O., 1973.

The Status of Women in Librarianship

Introduction

KATHLEEN M. HEIM

LIBRARIANSHIP IS A PROFESSION of particular interest to labor-force analysts, sociologists, and economists, because of its demographic peculiarities. In the aggregate it exhibits classic characteristics of occupational segregation, in that the majority of practitioners are of one sex: female. In its component parts, however the obverse is true—the field is stratified, in that positions of greater power and prestige are predominantly held by males. Thus the field is at once occupationally segregated among the spectrum of occupations and intraoccupationally segregated by positions and specialties.

The intraoccupational segregation of librarianship is evident in the inclination of men and women to differentiate themselves by type of library work. While over 95 percent of those librarians who work with children are female, close to 40 percent of those in academic libraries are male. For a field that is, by most statistical calculations, 80-85 percent female and 15-20 percent male, these ratios should hold across types of library specialization. Since they do not, we may infer that the field is occupationally segregated by specialty. The fact that certain areas attract men and certain areas attract women indicates that there are some types of library work in which men feel more comfortable and which they perhaps perceive to be more prestigious. In addition to male/female differentiation by type of library work, the field is stratified by position. Most large academic and public libraries are directed by men. The power, the prestige, and the largest salaries within the field go to the minority of practitioners, who are male.

Sociologists have often discussed library work in the context of the "marginal professions" or "semiprofessions," such as teaching or nursing. While this comparison appears to be appropriate, owing to the numerical dominance of women in these fields, it is a comparison that does not hold if one examines the structure of the three occupations. Comparisons to teachers are inadequate, for, generally speaking, there are only two types of duties in education: classroom teaching and administration. Although it has been noted frequently that women work as teachers, while men hold the majority of administrative posts in schools, the analogy with libraries falls short. Library work is quite different from teaching. It is quite possible for a practicing librarian to move vertically and horizontally within a single library institution and thus gain a variety of different experiences and perform a diverse array of duties. In the more bureaucratic library setting there is far more opportunity for the librarian, male or female, to gain quasi-administrative experience at the middle-management level than there is in the teaching profession, where it is the norm to be either a teacher or an administrator.

Comparisons of nursing and librarianship are also inadequate for purposes of generalization. Rigidity about credentials in the medical professions effectively blocks the rise within the institutional hierarchy of the working nursing professional without extensive additional training and degrees. In library work, theoretically, most practitioners begin from the same starting line and have the same opportunity, given inclination and ambition, to rise to the administrative ranks. That is, the master's of library science should enable any talented and motivated individual to be equal to any other in the competition for top posts.

Since there are many opportunities to gain administrative experience and since additional credentials are not needed for advancement, the predominance of men in the top echelons of the profession is even more troubling than it is in teaching or medicine. Since we cannot lay the blame on the fact that administrative experience can only be gained by a few (as in teaching), or that more degrees are needed (as in medicine), we must explore the supposition that it is outright discrimination that prevents the disadvantaged majority of women librarians from reaching top positions within the field.

This volume presents the results of research by fourteen women into reasons for women's depressed status in librarianship. Social, historical, and educational patterns are analyzed, in order to begin to gain a better understanding of the different roles of men and women within the field. While much rhetoric has been heard over the last decade in describing inequities that exist, those in power have eschewed polemical discussions and contended that there is insufficient research to prove that real discrimination against women exists. In fact, a substantial body of research into the problems that face women in the library profession has begun to be assembled. It is the purpose of this volume to present a portion of this research, much of it for the first time, in order to chip away at the reasons for differential male/female advancement within the field.

The first two essays provide historical perspective on women's place in librarianship. Suzanne Hildenbrand brings up some controversial issues for historians who address the role of women in the library field.

Her analysis of the work of Dee Garrison brings research in the history of women in libraries to a much-needed second stage of development and interpretation. To date, the role of women in the field has been subjected to only limited historical scrutiny. So little has been done that it has been difficult to challenge any work that has gone on. Hildenbrand's analysis of Garrison's work helps us to question and reinterpret truisms about women's place in the field. Hildenbrand's is a strongly polemical essay, which brings up hard issues and should engender much debate among library historians. Barbara Elizabeth Brand examines the foundations of library education, in order to support Epstein's (1975) assertion that women's occupational achievement is restricted by their exclusion from channels for professional recruitment and advancement. Brand places the entry of women into the library profession within the context of occupational alternatives available to educated middle-class women in the late nineteenth and early twentieth centuries, focusing on Dewey's admission of women to the first school of library economy, Katharine Sharp and the first university library school, and specialization within the field. She details the desire to slow the feminization of the profession, reported on in the Williamson Report (1971) and notes the need for research into relative access, recruitment, and socialization to the profession for men and women.

Nancy Patricia O'Brien carries on the work suggested by Brand, in her discussion of the aggressive recruitment of men into librarianship, following World War II. Through use of materials in the ALA Archives she illuminates some of the behind-the-scenes maneuvering intended to make the profession more attractive to men. The ease with which men could move to higher-paying administrative posts was used as a selling point to men who might be otherwise discouraged by the low starting salaries.

Patricia Reeling is also concerned with recruitment, but her focus is the ability to predict what characteristics typify undergraduate women as potential recruits; she identifies factors influencing the decision to enter the library profession and evaluates the effectiveness of recruiting techniques. Reeling's study is also concerned with the poor image of librarianship—held by the nonlibrarian. Presumably, if the profession could be presented in a more positive light, it would have a more broad-based population from which to draw librarians.

Adelaide Weir Sukiennik also examines the personality of the librarian, as well as professionalism, in order to argue that only basic social change that fundamentally alters the role of women will change the role of the librarian. Since the revolutionary/evolutionary process needed for such change can best begin to be implemented in professional schools, she posits that curricular and extracurricular programs could be models for helping women to identify inappropriate attitudes and behaviors that are a result of their sex-role socialization and could provide them with appropriate alternatives. She presents the results of her study in which assertive training for women library-school students was used to change their attitudes toward feminism, librarianship as a career, and the assertiveness of their personalities. Though the program she describes has yet to be implemented in library schools, Sukiennik provides library educators with a challenge that should not be ignored.

Laurel A. Grotzinger's state-of-the-art essay on biographical research on women librarians is treated specially within this set of essays, for it is the only one not documented in the collective bibliography contained at the end of the volume. Since most of Grotzinger's citations are unique, and so intricately bound up with her discussion, it seemed most useful to employ a standard footnote style in her chapter. Grotzinger, the biographer of Katharine Sharp and one of the leading biographical scholars on women librarians, has developed a bibliographical essay which explores the paucity of biographical detail on the thousands of women who have labored in the library profession, evaluates types of studies (nonscholarly tributes, theses and dissertations, and collective scholarly biographies), and illuminates the lives of a variety of library women. Grotzinger's chapter is a watershed piece in the development of biographical research on women librarians. Future scholars will find this essay an important starting point, not only for its richness of bibliographical detail, but for the serious concerns she raises about the quality of biographical research.

Lelia Gaston Rhodes also uses the biographical approach to discuss a central issue for women in librarianship. Through oral-historical techniques she has profiled the lives of fifteen prominent black women librarians, in order to understand their success and how that success might inspire other young minority women to achieve success in the library profession.

Janice C. Fennell has developed a profile of women directors of the largest academic libraries in the United States, which includes personal characteristics, factors influencing career achievement, and advice for other women wishing to attain administrative positions. Fennell focuses on the fact that there is a scarcity of women in these positions, and notes that if the number of women in the upper echelons of library administration is to increase, basic questions about qualities needed to attain such positions should be examined, in order to encourage other women to aspire to these posts.

Jean K. Martin uses several test instruments to focus on a number of variables that may account for differential status among librarians employed in ARL libraries. These include measurements related to task orientation, perseverence, fear of failure, social acceptance, reaction to success/failure, orientation toward the future, competitiveness, independence, and rigidity, as well as indicators of attitudes toward sex roles in management. These measurements, coupled with demographic information, provide Martin with a rich body of data from which to discuss various factors affecting the achievement and success of the librarian employed in a large academic institution.

Betty Jo Irvine's research review identifies major studies in three institutional structures—academic libraries, higher education, and corporate management—in order to delineate career aspirations. Her goal, like Rhodes's and Fennell's, is to provide guidance for women seeking to develop career paths to the executive suite.

Mobility is often cited as a major factor in differential achievement of male and female librarians. Marion R. Taylor asks whether or not mobility, or lack thereof, contributes to the semiprofessional status of librarianship. Her paper is intended to gain insight into the relationship between professional activity and mobility, by an examination of career patterns, mobility characteristics, and evidence of professional involvement. She focuses on a group of librarians who entered professional life in 1955, chosen from *Who's Who in Library Service* (1966). Her analysis of this cohort provides an interesting comparison between librarians who have changed positions and those who have remained immobile, and although no significant difference is found in the mobility of men versus women, there are identifiable differences in the supervisory responsibility granted those with greater mobility.

Judith Schiek Robinson also explores mobility as a factor in the variable career advancement of men and women. She focuses on geographic mobility as well as propensity to move among male and female academic librarians in the South. Surprisingly, she finds that the depressed status of women cannot be attributed to differences in the frequency of job moves. Since this variable is most often used to explain away the difference in male and female status, we are edged closer to the unavoidable conclusion that simple discrimination may be the cause.

This observation is strongly supported by the findings of a group of Canadian researchers who found that such often-used reasons to explain male/female differential as lower education qualifications, lower positions held, lower motivation, or little career planning (at least in regard to salaries) could not be proven when measured in a tightly controlled research model. The Canadian study is described and analyzed by Elizabeth Futas, who not only discusses the full intent of the study for the first time, but also evaluates the possibility of using its research methodology as the basis of further studies.

The volume concludes with a call by Katherine Murphy Dickson for further research into a hitherto-unexplored area of concern for women in libraries: the plight of the reentry librarian. Dickson delineates the problems that arise for the librarian seeking to reenter the field after a career interruption and suggests means by which the profession as a whole might help alleviate the difficulties that face the librarian seeking to reenter the work force.

There are many topics that have not been explored in this volume. One notable omission is the failure to identify a researcher to examine the role of the Catholic sister in the development of American library service. This is a fascinating chapter in American library history, which remains to be written. There are many issues, both historical and causal, that may be examined in the future as we seek to understand the continuing tendency of the field to reward its male practitioners out of proportion to their numbers in the work force. This volume is a beginning step, for it marshals the major pieces of research that have been executed and helps to organize the attendant literature for further inquiry.

Revision versus Reality: Women in the History of the Public Library Movement, 1876-1920

SUZANNE HILDENBRAND

REVISIONISM AND CONTEMPORARY HISTORICAL WRITING

Social historian Dee Garrison recently published a history of the American public library movement, entitled *Apostles of Culture: The Public Librarian and American Society, 1876-1920* (1979). Garrison's book is a piece of "revisionist" history. Revisionist historians, who are much in fashion lately, review familiar historical facts and reinterpret them to fit a new political context: they reenvision and they revise. Their reinterpretations may be either left- or right-leaning, politically, but in either case they write "thesis" history: they postulate new explanations of familiar problems; they don't just retell familiar stories.

Revisionist historians in recent years have utilized approaches increasingly common in general social history. They have drawn heavily on social-science concepts, employed systematic techniques of quantification, and taken an ambitiously theoretical approach. They have often drawn on Marxism. Successful revisionists have made a strong political case, regardless of the tools utilized, and generally they have been skeptics: they have understood politics as a question of "who gets what, and how," as well as the "art of the possible."

This is in line with the fact that much revisionist historical writing in recent years has reflected the crisis of authority in the United States and in the Western world generally. Thus, older historical writing on the Cold War reflected faith in the United States government's accounts of U.S.-Soviet relations in the immediate postwar period, but those explanations lost credibility as cynicism about U.S. government politics spread; and in the revisionist view of the Cold War, Soviet treachery was no longer seen as its principal cause. Similarly, institutions that previously seemed to have a benevolent origin and purpose came to be seen in a much less positive light. Schools, for example, were frequently presented by revisionists as agencies of social control.

Revisionist historians of education have changed the character of the history of education dramatically; they may indeed have banished the old, self-congratulatory style for all time. The history of education has been brought into the mainstream of U.S. history, by those who are historians first and educators second. Such works as Bernard Bailyn's *Education in the Forming of American Society* (1960), which assesses the role of education in colonial society, and Lawrence Cremin's *The Transformation of the School* (1961), which links progressive education to the progressive movement in American politics, are acknowledged classics. More recently revisionist historians of education have challenged the rhetoric and practice of the profession itself. Works such as Michael Katz's *The Irony of Early School Reform* (1968) and *Class, Bureaucracy and School* (1971) challenge the ideal of ever-expanding educational opportunity trumpeted by educators, by arguing that extensions of schooling have served mainly to extend social control over the lower classes. Clarence Karier (1973) and Joel Spring (1976) have challenged testing and tracking, and shown the racial bias of the early testers. Such challenges to practices still widely followed enrich contemporary professional debate, with the "provocative questions" that even their harshest critic (Ravitch, 1970) has acknowledged the revisionists ask.

This revisionist history of education is of particular interest to librarians. Most librarians work either in libraries affiliated with educational institutions or public libraries, which are—typically, at least—loosely linked to state departments of education. Moreover, traditional library histories and traditional histories of education have been similar in many ways. Both have been descriptive rather than interpretive; both have generally been written by insiders, writers who are outside the mainstream of historical writing. They have both tended to be narrow in focus and to isolate professional developments from general social and economic currents. They have tended toward the laudatory history of institutions and the uncritical biography of individuals. Professional rhetoric has abounded: phrases such as "people's university," used to describe public libraries, have been accepted without challenge. In short, like histories of education, traditional library histories have often been little more than self-serving recitals of the triumphs of an American profession by its own boosters.[1]

The appearance of a revisionist history of librarianship promises similar benefits. Such an approach promises to challenge traditional rhetoric about the role and function of librarianship, and thus to raise the level of professional practice and debate. Furthermore, the establishment of a link between the history of librarianship and general U.S. history would do much to offset the intellectual and cultural isolation that is a major professional hazard in the field.

GARRISON'S REVISIONIST THESIS

It is with considerable interest, then, that the librarian turns to Garrison's revisionist history of public libraries. Unfortunately, readers expecting a stimulating new vision will be disappointed. They may even find themselves regretting that Garrison was not content to write a piece of traditional history.

Garrison's thesis is that the public library movement, far from being the benevolent and democratic one described by library boosters, was a conservative strategy aimed at extending the social control of the upper classes and maintaining the status quo. Potentially troublesome segments of the population—the working classes, women, children, and youth—were to be pacified, as it were, especially in those urban areas where immigrant populations and industrialization were likely to present significant challenges to traditional structures. In support of this view Garrison demonstrates the ready acceptance among librarians of the role of the library in promoting the traditional social structure and traditional roles for all. Abundant quotations attest to a widespread allegiance to the status quo.

Yet, despite the evident willingness of librarians to play this role, librarianship failed in its social-control mission. This failure Garrison attributes to the large numbers of women in library work, for it was women who willingly played the traditional feminine role who shaped the occupation, Garrison (1973) believes, but playing this "tender" role prevented them from acquiring the firm knowledge base and personal authority required of true professionals. It was their numerical predominance that led to the rather limited and highly practical training developed for librarianship by Melvil Dewey. Worst of all, in establishing a library atmosphere that suited their own "true nature," women effectively excluded those very working-class males who should have been a major target of controlling efforts, although Garrison concedes that long hours and low literacy and reading levels may have contributed to the lack of worker interest in the public libraries.

A CRITIQUE OF GARRISON

Garrison's thesis is highly political, inasmuch as she is concerned with the ability of the modern state to enlist the willing compliance of the mass of its citizens in arrangements that are not necessarily in their own best interests and that may indeed be detrimental to them. The vital role of cultural institutions in maintaining the "hegemony" of the ruling class has been a crucial area of concern for revisionist social scientists and historians, both in and out of the Marxist tradition. But having chosen a highly political thesis, Garrison largely avoids political analysis. Furthermore, she reveals serious lapses from traditional historical standards in the selection and evaluation of evidence. And the primary reason for these faults is her view of women.

Women have generally been treated in three separate ways in historical and social-science writing. First, they have been written out of accounts by those who wrote, as if describing the male experience summed up the human experience. Second (and more common recently), they have been recognized as having a different experience, in particular as having less chance to participate in public life than men have, either because of discrimination against them or because of their own peculiar characteristics.[2] These characteristics, of course, might be either biological or cultural in origin. Probably most contemporary American historians and social scientists who have written about women have treated them in the second way, and thus tended to recommend laws or rules against discrimination, or special training, for example in assertiveness, to help women overcome characteristics that keep them from full participation.

The third view, insisted upon by a small minority, is that full participation is denied women by the very structure of the system—or of the major institutions of the system. It would appear that Garrison's thesis, with its emphasis on "social control" and "class origins,"[3] would be most compatible with this viewpoint. She proceeds, however, mainly under the influence of the second model. She recognizes discrimination but emphasizes the peculiar characteristics of women library workers. And most important, her account of these characteristics is flawed at almost every point, by a firmly rooted, although perhaps unconscious, prejudice against women.[4] This prejudice manifests itself in the application of a kind of double standard to the selection and evaluation of evidence and the use of social science concepts: that which supports a negative view of women is accepted uncritically, while others are weighed more carefully. This prejudice prevents her from developing a realistic account of the interaction between the history of the library movement and the history of larger institutions and movements. Her women are passive victims, evidently slaves to the traditional rhetoric of sex roles. Yet, more than merely blaming the victim for low wages, long hours, and dead-end work, Garrison holds her responsible for exerting a baneful influence over an otherwise promising institution and stifling it. And this despite the fact that the evidence can equally well support the opposite view: that the very marginality of the public library is responsible for the large number of women workers in public libraries, not the reverse.

In *The Nature of Prejudice*, Gordon Allport (1954) described how the minds of the prejudiced were influenced in the "selection, accentuation and interpretation" of materials relating to the object of their prejudice. A brief examination of Garrison's treatment of sex role and professional rhetoric and of two social-science concepts, "professionalism" and "obsessive compulsive," serve to illustrate the extent of her prejudice and the degree to which it has impaired her historical judgments.

Traditional language is often used to make departures form tradition more palatable—its rhetorical function is to mask the reality of frightening change. Yet Garrison (1979) overvalues much of the traditional language she finds in the written record;[5] she *accentuates* it to confirm her thesis about the harmful influence of women. Thus she gives the reader numerous glimpses—quotation after quotation—of male library leaders and women library workers emphasizing the suitability of library work, and particularly cataloging and children's work, to the feminine nature. Yet she herself gives the reader a glimpse of the consequences of deviation from this line: "even if some women librarians did not subscribe to the concept of women's sphere...they had to appear to do so in order to not offend the many who did. Not to surrender to the Victorian mystique was to run the terrible risk of being deviants in their society, or being judged abnormal because of a challenge to well-established values" (p. 185). Yet despite this, only a few pages later she once again deplores the fact that "the first timid ventures of middle-class women into the public arena" were unaccompanied by "feminine demands for radical social change," and that they represented their new public roles as an extension of their traditional role as moral guardian and protector of children (p. 196).

The use of this "woman's-place" rhetoric has not been confined to librarians, or to the progressive period. It is the job of the historian to get beyond the rhetoric, to reality. The period 1880-1920 brought a 236-percent increase in the number of professional women. (They were recruited, not surprisingly, primarily from the middle class.) Garrison (1979) minimizes this, by stressing that these women "merely left the home, not the women's sphere" (p. 168). Yet there is a wealth of literature in the various social sciences on the impact—good or bad—of women's expanding role in the work force.[6] In fact, Garrison herself appears to think that work outside the home influenced women's consciousness: "Women's increased economic activity after World War II was a necessary precondition for the rebirth of feminist conciousness" (p. 239).

Garrison takes the rhetoric of early profession-building librarians as uncritically as she does that of woman's place when it too can serve her thesis. Several prominent librarians have written about the need to have scholars direct public libraries. Garrison writes: "There is no intrinsic reason why the public library...could not have evolved with an educated scholar-librarian in charge of the distribution of books to the public...the foremost barrier was the overwhelming presence of women in librarianship" (p. 167). Yet Garrison surely doesn't think that American public-library boards would seriously consider recruiting scholar-librarians, or that American communities want scholars to direct their library services. Indeed, as she reminds us, Andrew Carnegie withdrew his offer of funds for library construction in 1917 because of lack of response. Nor does a look at the schools, colleges, universities, and churches of these same communities suggest strong support for scholarship, scholarly libraries, or scholar librarians. (Hofstadter, 1963). In short, Garrison has *selected* a bit of inconsequential professional rhetoric, *accentuated* it out of all proportion, and *interpreted* it to show the unfortunate effects women have had on public libraries.

The operation of a double standard is obvious when one examines the far more critical treatment Garrison (1979) gives the extravagant claims made for children's services by the female founders of these services. She finds that the emphasis on the child was "overdone," women librarians "waxed ecstatic" in the first years of service to children, and it wasn't until the first World War that "library service to children had boiled down to more normal and more modern proportions" (p. 216). What was "normal" was that extending public-library services to children gave the public library a huge constituency. The development of children's service came to account for more than half the circulation of materials from public libraries (Leigh, 1950, p. 99). Minerva Saunders and other founders of children's services may well have provided the public library with its major justification for existence in many communities. Not surprisingly, Garrison emphasizes the connection between the development of children's services and the female role. She all but ignores the general progressive interest in the child.

With the concepts of the social sciences, as with sex role and professional rhetoric, Garrison exhibits a pattern of prejudice. This is particularly true regarding her use of the concept "professionalism." She traces American librarianship from its earlier Boston Brahmin, gentleman-amateur beginnings to its attempted rationalization and professionalization by Melvil Dewey. But surprisingly—for a revisionist—she relies heavily on the older sociological views of professionalism, and, accordingly emphasizes a theoretical knowledge base, lengthy training, and service orientation. Newer views tend to stress the politics of professionalism and the key issue of autonomy.[7] She cites, for example, the work of Peter Rossi (1962), a sociologist who wrote about librarianship from the earlier perspective and who argued, in a passage Garrison (1979) quotes: "Women depress the status of an occupation because theirs is a depressed status in society..." (p. 187). Rossi suggested that for librarianship, the route to true professionalization lay in...its even greater sex stratification.[8] Surely it is striking that Garrison chose to select such an approach when there are others to choose from, and did not even indicate why this view is superior to others. When a concept confirms Garrison's view of women, she does not even seem to recognize the availability of others.

Among others, for example, is James Grimm (1978), a sociologist who has specialized in the study of female-intensive occupations. Grimm writes that "the mere presence of large numbers of women in these fields cannot explain why female-dominated professions are less powerful than male-dominated professions" (p. 294). He also states that professionalization means a process whereby an occupation claims and receives "legal autonomy to exercise a monopoly over the delivery of an important service" (p. 294). And Christopher Jencks and David Riesman (1977), who have found many male-intensive occupations as well as female-intensive ones to be "semiprofessions," have stressed that the hallmark of the true professional is the state-granted power to judge the work of colleagues. And by these terms, sex ratio has no bearing at all on the professional status of librarians, since public librarians have lacked even the power to insist that all librarian positions in public libraries go to librarians.[9] Ultimately, it seems that no occupation that began—or continues—primarily in the public sector has achieved any significant degree of "professional" autonomy.[10]

If Garrison used a view of the social-science concept of professionalism that placed responsibility for the low status of librarianship on women, she used another social science concept, "obsessive compulsive," to largely remove Dewey from personal responsibility.[11] For, turning from the sociological view to the psychological, Garrison finds Dewey to be "obsessive-compulsive."[12] And this despite the fact that one of her best and most convincing sections is a group portrait of the early library elite, which stresses their common social origins and viewpoints. Her psychologizing about Dewey removes him almost totally from the context of progressive America and does not add to an understanding of his role in the library movement. It is never clear just how his mental condition related to the public library as an agency of social control, or to the feminization of public librarianship. In particular, it makes Dewey's exploitation of women library workers—economic, emotional, and, evidently, sexual—the work of an isolated, aberrant individual. This treatment of Dewey's life is particularly unfortunate; since much of the material appears in print for the first time, this may well be a case of premature revision. In choosing this approach to Dewey, Garrison does recognize that she is making a choice—in marked contrast to her treatment of professionalism—and explains her decision in a lengthy footnote. The double standard again.

To recapitulate, Garrison has chosen a political thesis but sidesteps a political analysis and substitutes for it a case against women. This reduction of professional failings to female failings, this explanation of professional problems[13] by gender, cannot stimulate useful professional debate, nor can it illuminate professional practice. Indeed, it doesn't even make sense on her own terms. Garrison (1979) tells us that before feminization, "the popular concept of the librarian was that of a preoccupied man in black—a collector and preserver who was never so happy as when all the volumes were safely on the shelf. He was thought to be ineffectual, grim and 'bookish'" (p. 194). It is unlikely that this fellow could have attained a significant role in terms of social control or true professional status—or been able to recruit men who would have. How, then, did his replacement by a woman make any difference? Only—it seems—in the area of children's services, which might not have developed without "feminization."

AN ALTERNATE MODEL: ABORTED AMBITION, OR WOMEN AND THE PROFESSIONS, 1876-1920: THE CASE OF THE PUBLIC LIBRARIAN

A history of the same developments Garrison presents, making use of the same facts, could be written to illustrate an entirely different thesis: namely, that the marginality of public libraries accounts for the presence of women in large numbers in library work. What follows is an outline of such a history, based on familiar histories of progressive America and of women, relevant contemporary social-science research, and Garrison's book itself. This alternate model is based on three major elements: the emergence of reformism as a career in progressive America, the pioneer roles for women fostered by this emergence, and the evident failure of the public library to function adequately as an institutional vehicle for the major reformist ideology. The life and career of Melvil Dewey provides a summary illustration of these elements.

Reformism as a Career: The New Middle Class and Bureaucratization

As Robert Wiebe (1967) has shown, the breakup of the old "island communities," in which individuals derived their identify from a complex and visible network of relationships, fostered the emergence of a "new middle class." This new class was national in outlook—though it was actually centered in the large northeastern cities—and it based its claim to status on a new set of skills, which could solve the new social problems created by this same breakup or actually improve the new society. The professionalization of the progressive period, then, was rooted in "doing good."

This movement was sponsored and supported by both the state and that community of interests that can loosely be termed the ruling class. It had these powerful allies because it helped to sustain the view that the promise of America was individual opportunity, not welfare or security—these were individual matters. These allies also supported the new professionalism because it helped to depoliticize many issues, turning them into administrative or technical matters to be settled by experts.[14]

Members of this new middle class were largely motivated by the "earnest desire to remake the world upon their private models" (Wiebe, p. 113). University training helped them establish a community of interests, gave them access to validation by "scientific research," and gave them a common style. Thus they may have feared immigrants, but tended to express this fear, not with outright hatred or contempt, but in terms of "social problems." For example, Southern Italian peasants may have been seen as undesirable, but the reason advanced for their exclusion was likely to be that they compounded public-health problems.

Although, looking back, it is easy to see the political role played by this group as one of "social" control, the experience of the individuals in the groups was an exhilarating one—they were advancing their own position by doing good. Wiebe tells us that they were "enthusiastic" and "self-conscious pioneers." Revisionist historical analysis may tell us that public-health services were meager and really only served to deflect attention from low wages, which were the basic cause of poor health. But the pioneering public-health nurses and doctors who treated sick babies on a day-to-day basis may have had a different feeling about their lives and their function. Their clients, too, may have had different—and varied—views. The energy and optimism of these pioneers are an important part of the historical record.

Women Pioneering New Roles

The pioneer women of progressive American participated in these reform-oriented careers, and faced the issue of reconciling that participation with the traditional views of women. Of course men from the old, "island communities" had traditions to divest themselves of as well, but the transition for the women was probably more dramatic. Encouraged to think of themselves as fragile or "tender" and used to a more subjective mode of life, among familiar faces, where their status and security were dependent upon being known as one man's daughter or another's sister, these pioneer women now had to discipline themselves to partake in a public role that required working among strangers and accommodation to bureaucratic—that is, objective and impersonal—procedures, in situations in which their family status was no direct help. Probably the mothers of most of these young women had not worked outside the home, either before or after marriage.

It is difficult to know the socioeconomic status of these early careerist-reformers, and to know how it varied from career to career. But Garrison (1979) tells us about the "Wellesley half dozen," Dewey's first assistants at the Columbia College, in the 1880s. Dewey's bride, Annie, was the daughter of a wealthy man, had attended Vassar, and was working as an assistant at the Wellesley College library when she met her future husband, in 1876. Garrison tells us that early children's librarians tended to look down on schoolteachers, to whom they felt socially superior. How different were the young Wellesley women from their classmates who entered other careers—medicine, social work, and so on? It seems clear that by the end of the period, librarianship would be chosen primarily by women of a humbler background. Downward mobility may have characterized a significant number of them. Garrison tells us that women were more competent than men available for the same wages. She says that they suffered far less than men from what are generally thought of as imaginary illnesses, and this suggests that they had better morale and a greater zest for what they were doing, though it might mean merely that the men were dissatisfied with their lot.

Whatever social characteristics separated the women who chose librarianship from those who made other choices, it is not difficult to see what the attractions of library work were. It was a new profession, and thus one that might have had special appeal for a pioneering generation. And because it was a previously male activity, it may have seemed more important or challenging than, say, teaching school. Many women may have believed Dewey to be a true champion of women's rights. Indeed, he sounded like one, at least in comparison with the minister who, upon learning of plans to admit women to Columbia, warned of "the destruction of womanhood" (Garrison, 1979, p. 133). Women who knew of his support for a women's college at Columbia as well as for training women in librarianship must have seen him as a man who sincerely sought to widen educational horizons for women. Within library work, children's work must have had a special appeal, not only because almost everyone believed that women had special talents for working with children, but because of the general progressive emphasis on children. (This was, after all, the dawning of *The Century of the Child* [Key, 1909]). And children's librarians could compare themselves favorably with schoolteachers, for while the latter merely forced reluctant children through their lessons, librarians opened the worlds of great art and literature to willing ones. Entry into library work, as into all occupations, was supported by traditional rhetoric about women's nature, which, among other things, may have helped to reassure men who felt threatened (Wiebe, 1967, p. 113).

It is clear today that these pioneer women—so full of energy and zest—were establishing a pattern that persists to this day. Even talented and energetic women would be trapped in low-paying jobs in women's occupations and in the backwaters of the more prestigious male professions (Cain, 1976). Many women would find themselves in work so bureaucratized that it would stifle them, and this would encourage in them a less flexible orientation toward social issues and perhaps make them less sensitive to their own plight (Miller, Schooler, Kohn, and Miller, 1979). Public libraries, along with other large bureaucracies, came to reward conformity and passivity disproportionately. But what were the options available to these women? Toward the end of this period many women left public libraries for better salaries in offices—and even less autonomy (Garrison, 1979, p. 231).

Ideological Failure of the Public Library

Unlike the public schools, and more like the zoos, parks, and museums maintained by public authority, the public libraries have not been firmly identified with a successful ideology. Public schools, particularly since the progressive period, have been identified with opportunity. They became a kind of frontier of opportunity after the closing of the geographical frontier, and this is particularly true for the children of immigrants in the large urban centers of the East. In fact, concern over the disappearance of the frontier helped fuel progressive concern with social control. By contributing to a highly individualized view of opportunity, the schools helped to discourage support for class-based movements for improvement. The schools also helped to legitimize and to perpetuate social stratification patterns in American life, by encouraging the elevation of educational requirements for all types of work. And since children of the middle and upper classes received the most education and acquired the greatest number of diplomas and degrees, this served (and serves) to keep the poor trapped in their poverty.[15]

In short, for those seeking evidence of social control via cultural institutions, education has seemed to provide the classic model, decked out, as it has been, in the guise of unlimited opportunity and, on the whole, quite popular.[16] The public libraries have tried to identify themselves with this opportunity model over the years, but with limited success. It has been difficult for the library to gain recognition for its opportunity-fostering role, when it has lacked the power to grant the passport to mobility—the diploma or degree. The idea of the "people's university" failed precisely because, unlike the elite university, it offered no degree. Library literature, however, at least since the days of the big Americanization programs, has stressed helping immigrants learn English and helping adults prepare for civil-service exams and so on. Works such as Mary Antin's *The Promised Land* (1911), Betty Smith's *A Tree Grows in Brooklyn* (1943), and the charming children's book by Sydney Taylor, *All-Of-A-Kind Family* (1951), attest to the importance of the public library in the lives of the urban poor at the turn of the century. But in recent years, the most successful libraries, in terms of continuing support, have come to be those serving constituencies in which readers have not needed to acquire credentials through the library, because of their ready access to high schools, colleges, and universities. These readers have primarily sought entertainment in the public library, not opportunity. They have been willing to pay taxes simply to supply themselves and their children with materials for recreational reading.[17]

Melvil Dewey: Making Good by Doing Good

C. Wright Mills celebrated the sociological imagination for its ability to illuminate the intersection of history and biography, where individual lives are lived. Looked at from this sociological perspective, Dewey's personal story—with all its colorful episodes—illuminates the history of the public-library movement. Thus this "alternate-model" account of Dewey focuses on the intimate association between personal mobility and reform in his life,[18] his effort to find an ideological role for public libraries, and his relations with pioneering women librarians.

Dewey's penny-pinching, dour, Baptist mother urged her son to make his fortune and to do good at the same time,[19] and many of Dewey's personal traits can be traced to his early years in her household: in particular, loneliness and an obsession with the passage of time—this latter typical of the upwardly striving lower-middle-class youth anxious to make good use of every minute.

"Efficiency equalled morality" for Dewey (Garrison, 1979, p. 163), and this common progressive attitude must have been reinforced in a home where inefficiency—or waste—was so deplored. Dewey was an active member of the Efficiency Society of New York, an organization devoted to extending the principles of scientific management to all walks of life, and his paternalistic attitude toward labor, in the typical progressive fashion, was "scientific": he believed laborers would refuse to unionize if they understood the underlying rules of economics governing wages. Dewey was so convinced that what advanced his fortunes was good for society—and vice versa—that he could not understand the ire of the partners whose money he lost. His best-known private entrepreneurial venture was the Lake Placid Club, which was intended to be a "university in the woods," providing numerous uplifting activities in a healthful atmosphere. He forbade all drinking, and smoking by women—because the more sensitive, female nervous system was likely to be damaged by tobacco. The resort made money for the Deweys and in 1922 he established the Lake Placid Education Foundation, to promote "public welfare through education." There can be little doubt that Dewey built his life on the faith, held by progressives, that he would make good by doing good; and, according to his views, he did just that.

Dewey's labors to establish what we see as an ideological role (to him these labors were simply efforts to gain political support commensurate with the importance of the public library) were long and arduous. As New York State Librarian and Secretary to the New York State Board of Regents, he urged that public libraries be empowered to grant the whole range of academic credentials, from elementary-school diplomas to doctorates, by aiding adult learners to prepare for special New York State Regents Examinations that would qualify them. Representatives of public education successfully fought back this incursion on their turf (Garrison, 1979, p. 139). In a speech before a convocation of New York State educators, he placed the library beside the school and the church as a guide and supervisor of the restless, uneducated masses—a characteristic progressive effort to link the public libraries to social control. And in that progressive, professionalizing spirit, Dewey opened the first university school of "library economy," in 1887, at Columbia—against the wishes, it appears, of the Columbia faculty and trustees. Yet in just a few years Dewey would be advising librarians to think of their work as a kind of "high-grade business" activity (Garrison, 1979, p. 96), one in which their job was to organize materials efficiently, so that patrons could make their own selections. Clearly, Dewey, who had never adhered to the old cultural ideals of the earlier library elite, had not been able to find a credible substitute for them.

Dewey's relationship with his female colleagues in pioneering professional librarianship defies easy characterization. The old phrase "pedagogical pasha," with its suggestions of arbitrary power and sexual access, seems apt. (Perhaps research in the 1980s on sexual harassment will help to explain these relationships.[20]) Yet from the standpoint of the history of the public library and the role of women in it, the whole pattern of his public career is more illuminating than his private adventures. Librarianship was the pioneering professional path that took Dewey from Adams Corner, New York, to Columbia University, to the state government at Albany, and to the ownership of the Lake Placid Club. Dewey's interest in libraries had dated from his student days at Amherst, when, appalled at the inefficient arrangement of the books, he developed the Decimal Classification scheme. From there he launched a private library-supply company and a library publishing venture and gained a prominent position in the American Library Association. But he effectively abandoned library work in 1889, at age 39, when he took up his post in Albany as State Librarian and Secretary to the New York State Regents; that is, he left the details of the running of the state library, and the library school that came with him to Albany from Columbia to a group of trusted female lieutenants. As for himself, he devoted his best efforts to educational reform and the Lake Placid Club, at which, of course, the routine work was handled by his wife, Annie, his most trusted female lieutenant. Those energetic and talented Wellesley women wound up their days entrapped in routine, highly bureaucratized work, with little possibility of mobility.

The career of Melvil Dewey illustrates how one member of the new middle class combined personal advancement and social uplift. When he recognized that the benefits and opportunities available to librarians were limited, he exercised an option more available to male members of the profession and went on to newer, more promising areas. He left behind an army of able women whose similar personal and social ambitions—were doomed to frustration.

NEEDED: A NEW HISTORY OF LIBRARIANSHIP

Garrison's book is an important contribution to the history of librarianship, if only because it shows there is a need for further research and gives some indication of the direction that research should take. Other histories of the public library have ignored the social function, class roots, and role of women, and much new insight is needed before the political reality of the early public library emerges and the history of librarianship is integrated into general American history. Attention must be paid to political realities: concepts in the social sciences should be used when they illuminate those realities and eschewed when they do not. Two perspectives of particular interest would be the "woman's-sphere" view and the Marxist view. The former, based on a study of the women's personal records, examines "women's discovery and creation of psychic and social resources in their given situations" (Cott, 1977, p. 148). A Marxist interpretation, with a focus on hegemony and the dialectical relations between the ruling class and the major cultural institutions, would also be of interest. As a more mature historiography of librarianship develops, other valuable interpretations will emerge.

In the following list, some topics are sorely in need of being further researched, for the available information is meager. Other topics require a fresh attempt to make them comprehensible within their, and our, political context.

1. The progressives and public culture. Comparison of public libraries, zoos, and museums. Social and political support, and sources of funding. The progressive esthetic: fiction, art, and music.
2. History of the origins of children's services in public libraries in the progressive period, from the woman's-sphere point of view.
3. The world of women library workers, drawing on their papers for an illumination of that world. The hopes and ambitions of, and opportunities for, these women.
4. The constituency of the public library in historical perspective: social profile of registrants and borrowers.
5. Comparison of women library workers with women in a) other female-intensive professions and b) male-intensive professions. Social origins, education, marriage rates, and so on.
6. Males in female-intensive occupations: same social profile as above.
7. Origins of the organization and structure of library work: government regulations, influence of the business model.
8. Historical perspective on unionization: impact on women in education and librarianship.
9. Historical perspective on censorship/selection controversies.
10. Historical study of an individual public-library system from a more critical/political position. Progressive politics, municipal government, and the library.

GARRISON'S BOOK AND LIBRARIANSHIP TODAY

Garrison's description of an earlier library world offers useful background to the contemporary library scene, even if her explanations of that world are rejected. She provides historical background, for example, on the tendency to equate masculinization with upgrading, and the concomitant role of academic credentials. She also describes the acceleration of masculinization during the Depression (without any noticeable increase in status or earnings for the profession). Garrison (1979) tells us, for example, that in 1902 the library school at Albany began requiring a college degree for admission. This school had the highest percentage of male students of any library school, and Williamson (1923), in his hallmark study of library education, equated the degree requirement with male attendance. Graduates of this school, who were more likely to be male than graduates of other schools, went out to assume leadership positions in the library world (p. 77). (Dewey also established the American Library Institute to represent the library elite, including the ex-presidents of the ALA; the group was almost exclusively male.) The Depression "exaggerated the already debased status of women librarians," and by 1938, Garrison (1979, p. 233) found, men were openly favored over women, with laws passed prohibiting the employment of married women.

While it seems unlikely that such laws will reappear, it is important to note that female-intensive professions are being masculinized. Economists who have studied labor markets, such as Blau and Hendricks (1979), and who agree that there has been and will be little change in the sex ratios of most occupations, note that "while males moved into the typically female professions (for example, elementary school teacher, librarian, nurse, social worker) the movement of women into male cateories was concentrated in sales and clerical jobs" (p. 206). As Garrison showed us for the earlier period, which she studied, the only place for the most women to go was down. There is tendency today to require or prefer additional academic credentials when filling library positions. Recalling the result of the degree requirement at Albany, all involved should be concerned that these further degrees relate to the tasks to be performed, and do not serve merely as a sorting device. For whenever further degrees are required, the pool of eligible applicants becomes more masculine, white (and Anglo), and middle class.

If we reject the attempt to upgrade librarianship by masculinization, what, then, can be done to alleviate the plight of the public library and the public librarian? There are two paths of action, the first of which is to push for equal pay for comparable work, or pay equity.[21] This should be supported by all librarians, for it promises to bring the salaries of all persons—male and female—in the female-intensive professions in line with the training, responsibilities, and social worth of their work. In this struggle librarians have powerful allies in the blue-collar world and in the unions. There have already been some interesting court cases, including one clear victory. At least one major state system of higher education has agreed in principle to the need to upgrade librarians' pay under this doctrine.

The second path of action is to struggle for greater autonomy and opportunity. Librarians have been much concerned with the issue of professionalism, perhaps too much so. Professionalism may fade as a major issue as a higher percentage of the population receives a college education and joins the white-collar or service sector of the economy. Simultaneously, a growing percentage of the "true professionals"—lawyers and doctors—will become salaried, perhaps public, employees. More attention should be paid to the issue of career structures and bureaucratic settings. Librarians need to inform themselves about the impact of work structures on behavior and self-esteem, and apply these findings to their own situation. Sociologist Rosabeth Moss Kanter has found that those "stuck" in jobs with little hope of advancement are likely to display many undesireable traits, such as passivity and overattention to detail. This finding holds true for men as well as women—and one can recall many cruel portraits in literature of fussy male clerks or petty bureaucrats, for example. The female-intensive professions, with their short career ladders, and with many people working for years at the same level, have an enormous potential for promoting the negative qualities that go with being stuck. A thorough reexamination of library careers is needed to determine how greater flexibility, more opportunity to advance—for example, as administrators or information officers in other agencies—and more autonomy can be developed.

In the struggle for equal pay for comparable work, and for career reform, librarians can be aided by the existence of convincing new evidence provided by sociologist Barbara Heyns (1978) that the public library does indeed contribute to the equalization of opportunity for inner-city ghetto children. The product of careful social research, this new evidence is uncontaminated by either testimony of friends or professional rhetoric. Heyns surveyed Atlanta school children to identify the summertime activities that contributed to their retention of school learning.[22] She found that the summertime acitivity that most helped children retain school-acquired learning, thus reducing social inequalities, was reading. She argues that the public library directly influences children's reading, and therefore greatly helps to reduce inequality. "More than any other institution, including the schools, the public library contributed to the intellectual growth of children during the summer" (p. 177). Poor black children gained more from the use of public libraries than did their white counterparts. Heyns argues that budget cutters who think they are merely depriving the middle class of entertainment when they cut library funds are in reality inflicting a far greater loss on the children of the poor, who have no other access to reading materials. It is important for librarians to know about this research and to make their constituencies aware of it.

Ironically, then, in the light of Garrison's thesis, the best-documented service performed by the public library in support of the political structure—library services to children—was founded by women during the period of most rapid feminization. Political realities, not fanciful revision, must govern our view of ourselves and our past.

NOTES

1. Michael Harris (1973), librarian and professor of library science, has produced pioneering revisionist sketches of library history. Unfortunately, he as not developed any of these into a full-length study.
2. It is important not to fall into the trap of thinking that "discrimination" is the liberal position and "peculiar characteristics" the conservative one, even though this may be the case for racial and ethnic minorities. Only women menstruate, become pregnant and bear children, and it is by no means obvious how to put their biology into a realistic—and feminist—perspective.
3. It no longer seems adequate for a historian to expose the fact that public-library boards—or any other boards controlling cultural, civic, or economic institutions—were dominated by middle- or upper-class white men. It would be hard to find anything that wasn't.
4. It is beyond the scope of this analysis to speculate on the sources of this prejudice, but the reader is referred to Helen Mayer Hacker's oft-cited "Women as a Minority Group" (1951), in which she describes the "race relations cycle" and its various phases, the last of which is assimilation.

    A more recent article (Freedman, 1979) warns of the dangers of "individualist integration of the kind that undermined feminism after the first wave of political and educational progress." For although the suffrage amendment was passed, women failed to achieve advancement through the ballot, and although some token women were integrated into male power structures, the female presence in these power structures eventually diminished or disappeared. The author attributes this to the failure of a female community with political clout to develop.
5. Nancy Cott (1977) has shown that women's history based on sources describing woman's proper role tends to portray women as victims. Garrison's work, relying heavily on such sources, can be seen as an example of this kind of women's history.
6. These women, of course, were employed primarily in female-intensive occupations. This term, borrowed from feminist economists Beatrice and Edwin Reubens, seems more accurate than "female-dominated." In fact, there is no female-dominated occupation, for domination suggests power, and there is no occupation in which budgetary and policy-making decisions are in the hands of a mostly female group. Numbers have little to do with the issue, and no one, for example, writes of the dominance of the enlisted personnel over the military apparatus. "Female-intensive" also matches the familiar economic term "labor-intensive." See Beatrice and Edwin Reubens (1979).
7. Part of the politics of professionalism is the evolution of a professional culture, shaped by both practitioner and client. Garrison is sure that women librarians kept males out of the public libraries. How does she know that women librarians were not merely responding to the feminine clientele by providing the kind of atmosphere it wanted? Doctors' offices, not lawyers', have waiting rooms stocked with "women's magazines," for

women patronize doctors far more than men do; lawyers' clients are far more likely to be men. Meager data indicate that reading and library use may be more feminine than masculine activities.
8. Rossi, of course, was writing before the revival of feminism and before the publication of William Ryan's *Blaming the Victim* (1971).
9. Consider, for example, the appointment of Harvard University professor Kevin Starr to the position of director of the San Francisco Public Library. Vigorous protests by librarians' organizations went ignored, and Starr served until he resigned, to pursue a career in journalism. Not exactly what those early library boosters had in mind in calling for scholar-librarians in the public libraries, Starr seems to relish the world of politics and journalism. His negative feelings about public librarianship are apparent in his fictionalized account of his years at the SFPL in Kevin Starr, *Land's End* (1979).
10. One final observation of Garrison's views of professionalism is required, even though it has little direct bearing on women and libraries. It does serve to illustrate the limits of depoliticization of professionalism. Garrison believes that as a profession becomes more firmly rooted in the scientific and technical, and relies less on the personal status of its practitioners for its authority, its tendency to moralize diminishes. But the history of medicine does not seem to support this. Doctors from Edward Clarke, in 1873, to Edgar Berman, in 1970, have warned against the evil effects of a wider participation of women in society, without much scientific evidence. See Edward H. Clarke (1873) and Christopher Lydon (1970). One might speculate that professionals repay that state for the autonomy they receive, with extensive moralizing in support of the status quo. Or one might argue that the constituents or patrons of doctors expect doctors to provide scientific support for views shared by doctors and their constituents. Hence the medical attacks, until recently, on homosexuality, with very little scientific basis.
11. A critique of depoliticized social history has warned that it quickly dissolves into neoantiquarianism. (Elizabeth Fox-Genovese and Eugene Genovese, 1976). In Garrison's treatment of Dewey, however, there is something closer to gossip: private details, unrelated to a public or political reality.
12. It is difficult to reconcile the facts of Dewey's life with the obsessive-compulsive's craving for order. Dewey was a shady businessman, and several times during his life his irate partners lost their investments and demanded satisfaction of him. His involvements with young female librarians—their exact nature unknown, because of the delicacy of the language of the day—also produced scenes of hysteria and, in his seventy-ninth year, a lawsuit. The notorious anti-Semitic policies of the Lake Placid Club, which he and Mrs. Dewey owned and directed, caused him to be ousted from his post on the New York State Board of Regents, and earlier he had been ousted from Columbia University for "insubordination."
13. It seems clear that Garrison is on the public-demand side of the book-selection/book-censorship question. That is, she seems to believe that the public should indeed have access to women's fiction and the Elsie Dinsmore and Horatio Alger books in the public library. Yet she faults female public

librarians for not asserting guidance, for merely following the wishes of the public. And although she makes it clear that it is the female presence that has kept public librarianship from developing a sound knowledge base, she does not provide much direction on what that knowledge base might consist of. Just as, formerly, professors of literature and history (among others) preempted the area of knowledge about the books, now computer scientists have preempted the area of access.

14. This is the period when the city-manager plan of government emerged, in an attempt to take the politics out of municipal government, which had been notoriously corrupt. It was often said that there was no "Republican or Democratic way to collect garbage." This may only show the irrelevance of the parties to politics, however, since several mayors have discovered that access to such important resources as the city's snow-removal and garbage-removal equipment is a highly political issue.

15. For a description of the relationship—or lack thereof—between education and job requirements, see Gregory Squires (1979).

16. Those who attribute the fact that the public school has been more successful than the public library to the lack of compulsory attendance at the latter miss the point about ideologies. It is faith, not force, that has given the schools their strength. In recent years, as faith in the public schools has plummeted, attendance has fallen alarmingly. High-school divisions of some large urban districts report attendance rates of only about 50 percent. Can such districts really afford to force those absentees to attend?

17. Whether one traces the roots of our society to the progressive or the puritan tradition, it is a work-oriented one. Accordingly, there is a great distaste in it for maintaining at public expense institutions perceived primarily as sources of entertainment, and viewing paintings or animals, or reading novels, are only reluctantly supported by the general public. Hence the heavy use of volunteer labor, and the practice of charging admission fees and soliciting gifts.

18. Although best known for his library work, Dewey was also active in helping to establish Barnard College, founding the American Home Economics Association, bringing the winter Olympics to Lake Placid in 1932, and promoting spelling and metric reform, educational standardization, professional licensure, prohibition, shorthand, the use of abbreviations, and scientific management.

19. Far from placing him in a "double bind," as Garrison (1979, p. 108) suggests, this advice seems to have fitted him admirably for his world. Dewey's mother was certainly not a member of the new middle class. In fact, this sort of advice is deeply rooted in the American tradition.

20. Explanations of his preference for female associates will have to be left to armchair psychoanalysts. While it is easy to assume that he feared competition from younger male associates, his interest in these women was considerably more than professional. His chief assistants boarded with the Dewey family—indeed, they seem to have formed a kind of extended family. And while this was still the day of the young teacher-boarder, the picture of a group of women working with him daily, who lived with his

family, and participated in his family's activities, does seem strange.
21. For an overview of the movement for equal pay for comparable work, see Grune (1980). For a discussion of the impact of this issue on librarians, see Heim (1979b). For the experience of librarians in the California State University system, see Reynolds and Whitlach (1978).
22. The larger purpose of Heyns's (1978) study was to challenge academic and popular critics who, by the mid-seventies, had written off the influence of schools on the life outcomes of children. And in fact she found that, although family socioeconomic status had a profound influence on pupils' scholastic achievement, "education reduces socioeconomic inequality when compared to that which would exist in the absence of schooling" (p. 11).

Sex-Typing in Education for Librarianship: 1870-1920

BARBARA ELIZABETH BRAND

STUDIES ON THE STATUS OF WOMEN in the professions have demonstrated the low status of "women's" professions, the lower prestige and marginal positions of women in "men's" professions, and the lower prestige and income of women even in predominantly female professions such as librarianship, when a significant proportion of men are present in the field (Morlock, 1973; Patterson, 1973; Schiller, 1974). A number of theoretical models have been used to explain both the association of gender and professional occupations and the status of women within professions. McClelland (1967), a social psychologist, concluded that women are found in such occupations as nursing, social work, teaching, and office work because of fundamental sex differences, detected in psychological experiments. These include differences in mathematical ability, perception of spatial relations, field independence, aggressiveness, tendency to be nurturant, and receptivity to social stimulation. Men are better suited to such occupations as selling, law, the military, and engineering, according to this interpretation.

Maccoby and Jacklin (1974), as well as other psychologists, have challenged McClelland's conclusions on a number of grounds. Relatively few psychological sex differences have been established conclusively. Where sex differences have been found, men's and women's distributions overlap substantially, failing to explain the extreme sex segregation of occupations. Most importantly, however, the psychological argument fails to explain differences in status and income between men's and women's occupations.

Functionalist sociologists, most notably Simpson and Simpson (1969), attempted to explain the association of female gender and professional occupation as a function of women's primary social role in American life, that of homemaker. As homemakers primarily, women's occupational roles are distinctly secondary. Possessing little ambition, women characteristically support cultural norms yielding leadership positions to men and are content to settle for bureaucratic rather than autonomous professional positions. More generally, functionalists contend that women prefer diffuse, expressive interchange rather than the ideal-typical professional-client relationship characterized by Parsons and Bales (1956) as functionally specific, instrumental, affectively neutral, and universalistic. Women, therefore, are appropriately found in semiprofessions such as librarianship, social work, and teaching. Although women's socialization to expressive rather than instrumental roles limits their occupational achievement, it contributes to social stability, by preventing disruptive competition within the family. The major theoretical explanation of the status of women in early librarianship, that of Dee Garrison (1979), relies heavily on Parson's functionalism. According to her account, women failed to assume leadership positions, and librarianship itself failed to become fully professional, because women were socialized to perform expressive rather than instrumental roles. The women who became librarians were content to be nineteenth-century "true women"; self-sacrificing, willingly subordinate, and interested in being hostesses rather than experts. Rossi (1967) and others have criticized this school of functionalism as conservative and overconcerned with social stability while paying little attention to conflicts of interest among groups. Where status differences exist, a "blaming-the-victim" approach justifies the existing hierarchy.

McClelland and the Simpsons agree that, while sex segregation exists in professional occupations and women are not represented in positions of occupational power, no injustice is done, because this is women's appropriate place. Epstein (1975) has questioned this assumption. She asserts that, regardless of their aspirations or ability, women are kept down by societal limitations on their occupational achievement. Focusing on structures and processes limiting women in contemporary predominantly male professions, Epstein has found the restriction of women's professional achievement to be due to their exclusion from channels of professional recruitment and advancement. Occupational sex-typing and status-set typing operate as mechanisms for the social control of women (Epstein, 1975, p. 753).

This chapter reports evidence supporting Epstein's explanation in the field of librarianship, where women have long formed the majority of the work force but a minority of the leadership. It focuses on the development of educational programs for librarianship during the period from 1870 to 1920, when the profession was established in the United States. As the "core of the professionalization project,"[1] education plays a major role in all occupations aspiring to professional status. Since higher education is an important means of access and recruitment, the following questions are considered. Was either sex particularly recruited to the field? If women were recruited, why? Was access limited for either sex by discriminatory quotas or other means? Higher education also transmits and develops the knowledge base on which the occupation's claim to be a profession rests. Did the curricula during the period studied emphasize qualities considered masculine or feminine at the time? Was a systematic body of knowledge developed, or was the field simply left technical? In addition, higher education socializes students to professional norms. What behaviors did the educational programs encourage? Were these defined as particularly appropriate for one sex? What responsibilities were students expected to assume when the completed their education? Did leading educational institutions offer women as role models and mentors? Finally, what factors encouraged or discouraged women's achievements?

OPTIONS AND LIMITS IN TRADITIONAL LEARNED PROFESSIONS

What occupational alternatives were available to educated middle-class women in the late nineteenth and early twentieth centuries? Although piety was an approved and even prescribed element in the composition of the idealized nineteenth-century "true woman," pastoral leadership was a male career in most religious denominations in the United States. The U.S. Commissioner of Education, A.E. Miller (1896), suggested in his 1893-94 report that the few women who enrolled in schools of theology either sought new fields to conquer, had a general interest in temperance and reform, or were missionaries "who needed theological studies for a full measure of success" (pp. 976-77). Law also engaged only a small number of women. Its competitive, argumentative aspects as well as its association with politics and government at a time when most women could not even vote conflicted sharply with contemporary conceptions of the feminine role.

The right of women to receive medical education and become physicians was the most publicized and hard fought of the nineteenth-century campaigns for women's entry into professions. However, the increase in the number of women physicians during the late nineteenth century was a short-lived phenomenon. The major factors that reduced the number of women physicians by the early twentieth century were the demise of sectarian medical schools, which had been particularly hospitable to women, the closing of most women's medical colleges, restrictions on the number of women enrolled in regular medical schools, and the advent of internship training, to which women were rarely admitted (Walsh, 1977).

Few women obtained appointments to college and university faculties, outside of women's colleges and normal schools. Christine Ladd Franklin (1904) reported to the Association of Collegiate Alumnae in 1904 that 255 Ph.D. degrees had been awarded to American women between 1880 and 1902. She concluded, "For most [women], as far as consequences are concerned the certificate of their doctorate is but an empty honor" (p. 54). William Rainey Harper (1903), the pioneering president of the University of Chicago, chided his colleagues for the small number of women on the faculties of coeducational colleges and universities. He asserted that discrimination, not a scarcity of well-prepared and able women, was responsible for their absence. "If opportunity were offered...women would show that they possess the qualifications demanded. The fact is that to women there do not come the opportunities to show their strength which come to men" (pp.661-62). Even at the University of Chicago, however, if a woman was appointed to the faculty, it was likely to be in a recognized woman's field, regardless of her background. For example, Sophonisba Breckinridge, appointed instructor in household administration in 1904, held both a Ph.D. in political science and a J.D. (Lasch, 1971).

Common school-teaching was widely recognized as women's "great profession" by the late nineteenth century, even though many women realized that their hearty welcome in that field was due, primarily, to the fact that they accepted low salaries. Many educators, however, recognized that a single profession in which women were welcome was not sufficient. The abundance of women in teaching tended to keep their salaries and status down. Varied abilities and interests among women also called for wider professional opportunities. Some women's abilities were wasted in teaching, and some women not suited for or interested in teaching entered the field because of the lack of alternatives (Bancroft, 1885, p. 590; Lange, 1916, p. 482). Women were more readily accepted in the developing professions of social work, public health, and librarianship than in the entrenched, traditional professions. While these developing professions did not rival teaching in terms of numbers, they provided important alternatives for educated women.[2]

EARLY EDUCATION FOR LIBRARIANSHIP

Before the advent of formal training programs, women entered library work. The report issued by the U.S. Dept. of the Interior Bureau of Education (1876) on public libraries listed 306 women out of a total of 1,612 public librarians. Few of these, however, depended on library work for their livelihood (Wells, 1967, p. 3). A number of early library leaders did recruit women for full-time positions. William Poole of the Boston Atheneum, in particular, hired and trained a number of women who later assumed leadership positions. Poole recommended that directors searching for librarians inquire "at some of the large libraries where young persons of both sexes have been regularly trained. (U.S., Department of the Interior, Bureau of Education, 1876, p. 489) A year later at the Conference of Librarians held in London, Poole spoke favorably about the number of women employed in libraries in the United States. Justin Winsor, librarian of the Boston Public Library, added that well-educated women not only were available for and suited to library work; they would accept lower salaries than men (Conference of Librarians, London, 1878, p. 177).

Although both Poole and Winsor—highly influential men in librarianship—supported women's entry into the field, neither believed that academic training in library work was necessary. A thorough literary education, if possible at the college level, followed by a period of apprenticeship in a well-run large library was sufficient preparation. Melvil Dewey was the first to develop specialized library education.

Dewey was appointed Librarian in Chief at Columbia in 1883, to develop a library that would support instructional reforms. Traditional college methods of instruction—the textbook, recitation, and daily drill—were being replaced by methods adopted from German higher education—the lecture, the seminar, and research in original sources. These newer methods depended on a library as a vital center of scholarly activity. Dewey had been interested in library education for several years, attending meetings at which the subject was discussed, and publishing an article proposing a more formal version of the current apprentice training in large libraries. His position at Columbia offered an opportunity to initiate some kind of educational program. His plan to make the school coeducational was a point in its favor with President Barnard. Barnard, one of the major proponents of coeducation in higher education, had attempted for years to persuade the trustees not only to admit women to the College but also to undertake teacher education, which would have brought many women to Columbia. In 1884 Barnard succeeded in getting the trustees' approval for a School of Library Economy, which would begin instruction in 1886 or as soon thereafter as practicable. The question of the admission of women was not addressed.

Leading librarians, however, offered little support for the establishment of the school. The American Library Association endorsed Dewey's proposal only to the extent of hoping "that the experiment may be tried." The Association did, however, organize a Committee on the Proposed School of Library Economy. While the Committee justifiably criticized Dewey's plans as vague, few models existed for modern professional education. The Johns Hopkins Medical School, which served as the model for the reform of medical education and later as a model for professional education in other fields, did not open until 1893. Dewey rejected existing European plans for library education (none of which was put into effect) as "too antiquarian." The Committee also objected to Dewey's emphasis on college education and library administration rather than mechanical and bibliographical work (Report of the Committee, 1885).

Dewey clarified his position in a conciliatory way in the 1886-87 "Circular of Information" (Columbia University, 1886). While he regarded a college degree as highly desirable preparation for library work, it would not be a prerequisite for admission. In addition, the School would prepare students for a variety of library jobs, not just administrative positions:

The plans all contemplate special facilities and inducements for catalogers, and asssistants who do not expect or desire the first place. Special attention will be given to the training of assistants, catalogers and indexers, without diminishing in any degree the efforts for chief librarians and those who expect to become such (Columbia University, 1886, pp 36-42).

Dewey did not indicate, however, that he expected to prepare women for subordinate and men for superior positions.

The circular also outlined the final plans for curriculum and methods of instruction. A variety of topics relating to practice in a variety of library types were to be covered. Methods of instruction were a combination of methods derived from the German university—lectures, independent reading, seminars, and comparative study—with technical methods—visiting libraries and publishing houses, solving practice problems, and actually working in a library. Members of the library staff were to give instruction in library economy, while professors in the College were to give instruction in bibliography. Specialists in book-related fields—such as binders, printers, publishers, and book-sellers, as well as leading librarians, would give special lectures. Dewey considered the length of the three-month program to be less than ideal, but the most feasible plan at the time.

The School, which opened in January 1887, faced immediate difficulties. No classroom space was allocated. Whether this was because the majority of the student body was women or for other reasons is unclear. Nevertheless, Dewey was able to arrange extemporized facilities in a storeroom, and the work proceeded generally as he had outlined. In addition to the basic instruction in library economy, he was successful in securing as unpaid lecturers such important librarians as John Shaw Billings, then head of the Army Medical

Library; Ainsworth Spofford, Librarian of Congress; and Caroline Hewins, a pioneer in the development of children's services. He also brought in former Commissioner of Education Henry Barnard, publisher G. Haven Putnam, and book importer Gustav Stechert as specialists in book-related fields. A number of Columbia professors—including Nicholas Murray Butler and Edwin R.A. Seligman—also lectured on the bibliography of their respective fields (Columbia University, 1887, p. 8). The number of leaders in many fields whom Dewey enlisted indicates that he did not plan to prepare the predominantly female student body merely for routine technical tasks.

The following year Dewey pressed for a longer school term, better facilities, and formal recognition for completion of the program. He was successful only in lengthening the term. The trustees, obviously unfavorably disposed to the School, rejected his request for money to remodel quarters and buy furnishings as well as his request that the name of the program be changed from the School of Library Economy to to the School of Library Science, a change that Dewey believed would signify instruction beyond the technical level. They also refused to implement the recommendations in Barnard's annual report in 1887 that classrooms and lecture rooms be set aside for the School and that a diploma or certificate bearing the seal of the College be awarded for successful completion of the course (Trautman, 1954, p. 16).

Dewey's difficulties with the Trustees had several causes, but the admission of women to the School was the major one. The question of admission of women to the College did not involve the School of Library Economy alone. Nicholas Murray Butler and President Barnard were struggling at this time to bring about a merger of Teachers College and Columbia. The trustees were adamant in their refusal to accept such a combination, since it would bring a large number of women to the College. In May 1887, after women had enrolled in the first class in the library school, the trustees clarified their position on the admission of women by adding to the Statutes of Columbia College a statement that "no woman shall be admitted as a student in any department of the College, other than the Collegiate Course for Women, except by special order of the Trustees." (Trautman, 1954, p. 19). The Collegiate Course for Women was, in fact, not a course but merely permission for women to prepare themselves to take Columbia examinations.

Dewey, however, with Barnard's backing, continued admitting women to the second class. After Barnard's resignation for reasons of ill health, both Dewey and the School came under increasing attack. Resolutions pertaining to Dewey's suspension and dismissal were considered at the trustees' meeting on November 5, 1888, and the School was authorized to continue for the third year only because students had already arrived. Just what couse the trustees intended to pursue is uncertain, because no resolutions were printed. Nevertheless, they accepted Dewey's resignation promptly when he offered it, on January 7, 1889, to become secretary, treasurer, and chief executive officer of the Board of Regents of the University of the State of New York as well as state librarian and director of the New York State Library School, to be established in Albany. A month later the trustees agreed to the transfer of the School of Library Economy to the State Library in Albany. The College returned, at least temporarily, to being a masculine preserve.

The New York State Library School

The transfer to Albany, in April of 1889, was unfortunate for the development of library education, yet it could not have been avoided. The School no longer had the resources of a large metropolitan community or an academic institution. The move away from an institution of higher education tended to freeze training at a technical level rather than expand it, as Dewey had hoped to do at Columbia. While the School continued under a more definite grant of authority and could award degrees, it received no funding from the State. In addition, Dewey's interest in the School waned. Other duties and interests, first as secretary of the Board of Regents and later as developer of the Lake Placid Club, took precedence, and no comparable leader emerged to take his place.

Dewey and Women in Librarianship

Dewey's attitudes toward and relations with women were complex and often contradictory. He asserted that men appropriately received higher salaries than women because women had poorer health, lacked business and executive training, and often did not plan to work permanently. Even if an individual woman did not possess these disabilities, she would have to accept lower pay "because of the consideration which she exacts and deserves on account of her sex" (Dewey, 1886, pp. 20-21). On the other hand, he showed unusual empathy for ambitious middle-class women who wished to establish a career, and unusual acceptance of women in leadership positions in an occupation in which he himself was engaged. He recruited many able women to librarianship and promoted their careers. Many of his contemporaries considered Dewey's unconventional familiarity with women scandalous. Epstein (1975, p. 757) has pointed out that suspicions of sexual relations almost always surround male-mentor/female-protegee relationships and are a major reason that they are so uncommon. Whether there was substance to the gossip is still unclear, although Dewey did encourage a kind of emotional dependence that limited his protegees (Garrison, 1979, pp. 153-56).

Katharine Sharp and the first University School

A number of Dewey's protegees organized library schools elsewhere. Given the technical emphasis of the program that Dewey transferred from Columbia to Albany, technical institutes such as Pratt, Drexel, and Armour were the academic institutions most suitable for similar programs. Two of these new institute schools, Pratt and Drexel, disavowed any purpose beyond technical training for librarians of small libraries or assistants in larger ones. The Pratt Institute Catalog for 1894-95, for example, contained the following statement:

The work of this school of training must not be confounded with that of the Library School at Albany, which is the official school of the American Library Association [sic]. It is planned to meet a different demand, its aim being to prepare young men and women for the charge of small libraries, or to fit them for competent assistants in large ones (University of Illinois Library, 1892-1912).

From the time of her appointment in 1893, however, Katharine Sharp, of the Armour Institute School, was more ambitious (Grotzinger, 1966).[3] Although as part of a technical institute the Department of Library Science was to prepare high-school graduates, via a short technical course, to become library assistants, she was eager to go beyond this in requiring more education for admission, lengthening the course of study, and preparing students for more demanding positions. This was opposed to the very nature of technical education, which first developed in European countries, where class divisions were strong. Short-term, specialized schooling in accepted vocational techniques enabled students to assume a place in the nation's work force. Such education was not designed to educate social or intellectual leaders (White, 1976, p. 34).

Nevertheless, despite a series of letters and telegrams from Dewey discouraging her plans, Katharine Sharp persisted. She succeeded in adding a second year of advanced work in 1895-96 and in raising admission standards by recommending, though not requiring, two years of study beyond high school and preparation in history, literature, and languages (Armour Institute, n.d.).

In spite of the favorable aspects of location in Chicago, the lack of funds and equipment at Armour and its nature as a technical institute limited the possibilities for future expansion. This was the major reason that Sharp decided to leave and to transfer the School to the University of Illinois in 1897. The new location offered a number of advantages—academic status for the staff, two years of college preparation required before entrance, and a B.L.S. degree to be awarded after two years in the library school.

President Draper's selection of Sharp as librarian indicated unusual acceptance of a woman for an important university position, and his enthusiastic announcement to the press of the transfer seemed to indicate strong support for the new educational program as well. One article, headed "University of Illinois absorbs a Library School; The Only One in the West," continued:

President Draper informs the *News* today that the University of Illinois after sharp rivalry has secured the library school conncected with the Armour Institute in Chicago....With this school will come Miss Katherine [sic] Sharp, one of the foremost librarians of this country (Times Herald, 1897).

Sharp hoped that both men and women would enroll. In a recruiting article published in *The Illini* she used the masculine pronoun in referring to librarians and paraphrased Dewey's comments about the preferability of college-bred women for the field. "We greatly prefer," she asserted, "college-bred men and women in selecting new librarians." (Librarianship as a Profession, 1897, pp. 1041-43). The predominance of women students, however, did not disturb her. While she welcomed able students of either sex, ability rather than sex was the important factor.

Sharp also expected that her new location would provide an opportunity to go beyond existing forms of library education. In a report to the American Library Association in 1898 she presented five advantages that none of the other existing schools possessed:

It is one of the recognized schools of a state university, accepted on equal terms.

Its director is a full professor in the university, and other members of the staff occupy corresponding positions.

It has the advantages of assistance from a large university faculty.

It has the environment of university life.

Its tuition is free at present (Sharp, 1898, p. 66).

Nevertheless, Sharp faced the problem of lack of support from the outset. She was not given the number of assistants she had been promised, and when she protested, Draper declined to press the matter with the Board of Trustees. Draper also failed to support Sharp's request for a recognized place for the Library School within the university structure. The statement that she had made to the ALA implied the School had a status comparable to other University professional schools, which the Library School did not have. Its place in the University organization was unclear, despite Sharp's attempts to have it recognized as a college comparable to the College of Law.

In the fall of 1901 Sharp (1902a) presented a paper at the Association of Collegiate Alumnae meeting in Buffalo, entitled "Library Schools on a Graduate Basis." She urged in this paper "that the library schools connected with universities require a degree for entrance and accept no substitute" (p.28). The University of Illinois Council did not act on her proposal to require an undergraduate degree, although her initiative influenced the New York State School to institute such a requirement.

The following year she presented another proposal, this time suggesting a requirement of three years of university work, rather than a full degree, for admission. In her proposal she restated her belief that Illinois should be preparing leaders for the profession:

We believe that it is the province of this School to fit for the highest positions if it has to choose its line of work. Each library school has its specialty. Ours should be university work and this cannot be creditably given if students are insufficiently or unevenly prepared. Those who are satisfied with subordinate positions can doubtless fill them after our first year of work. If they cannot meet the requirements for that work, they can find opportunities for instruction upon competitive examination at Pratt or Drexel Institute or in the numerous summer schools and apprentice classes. We should scatter our energies if we tried to provide for all grades of positions with our present equipment. (Sharp to Draper, 1902b)

Although this proposal was accepted, Sharp was still unable to expand her program, because of the poor financial situation of the Library School. Two of her most able instructors, Margaret Mann and Isadore Mudge, left in 1903 for better-paying positions. At the salaries she could offer, Sharp had to resort to her own recent graduates for faculty.

Sharp resigned her positions at the University of Illinois and left librarianship entirely in 1907. A major reason was the lack of support within the University for the Library School. From her arrival, time and resources for the School had to be squeezed from appropriations for the library. Would the School have received more support from the presidents of the University if most of the students and faculty had not been women? Any answer to this is, of course, speculative. President Draper dismissed the one woman on the University faculty at the time of his arrival, apparently because she was too outspoken. The pressure applied by a wealthy and influential woman trustee, rather than Draper's initiative, was responsible for most of the improvements in women's status at the University during his administration (Filbey, [n.d.], pp. 7-12). President James, a German-trained scholar, was interested in research and in the development of the library but showed little interest in women's education or in the Library School. Both presidents were willing to tolerate the school, whose students and faculty also operated the library, but had little interest in its development or expansion.

Garrison (1979, p. 192) has asserted that the failure of early library education to rise above the technical level is explained by the acceptance by women librarians of their socialized feminine role. They accepted and expected administrative controls, low autonomy, and subordination to clerical, routine tasks. Sharp, however, did not hold this view of the librarian's role. She believed that the University of Illinois Library School should recruit people temperamentally and intellectually prepared to become library leaders and educate them for the highest positions. The Library School should be a graduate program, and its curriculum should include important areas of specialization. She was hindered in accomplishing this, not by any view of women's proper role, but by the limited resources available to her.

EMERGING SPECIALIZATIONS

Most graduates of the Columbia-Albany and University of Illinois as well as other library schools found employment in public libraries, which were increasing rapidly in number and size (White, 1976, p. 88). A number of other library specialties developed almost simultaneously. The most important in the period before 1920 were academic and research librarianship, legislative reference service, and children's services.

Academic and Research Librarianship

Daniel Coit Gilman, former librarian at Yale and president of John Hopkins University, expressed his belief in the importance of the librarian to higher education and advocated training for the position. "The librarian's office," he contended, "should rank with that of professor.... The profession of librarian should be distinctly recognized. Men and women should be encouraged to enter it, should be trained to discharge its duties, and should be rewarded, promoted and honored in proportion to the services they render (Gilman, 1898, p. 255).

Formal library training, however, was rarely required for important positions in academic or research libraries during this period (Downs, 1976). Although articles appeared occasionally in the library literature about the need for specialized education for such positions, no program was developed. Library schools and such auxiliary training agencies as summer schools and library training classes supplied graduates, mostly women, to manage small public libraries and serve as assistants in larger ones. A more informal mentor-protege system served to prepare those persons, mostly men, who occupied administrative positions in large libraries and positions in research libraries. Preparation for positions at the New York Public Library provides a particularly good example of these two types of training, since it included both an endowed research library and a public circulating library system.

Although John Shaw Billings had played a key role in the reform of medical education before coming to the New York Public Library, he showed no particular interest in the development of professional education for librarians. To fill responsible positions in the research library, he contacted academic and library colleagues for the names of suitable young men. Harry Miller Lydenberg and Charles C. Williamson were both recruited in this way and prepared by Billings and the assistant director, E. A. Anderson, to assume important positions. Lydenberg became chief reference librarian and Williamson head of the department of economics (Dain, 1972, p. 110; Metcalf, 1976, p. 342; Vann, 1971, pp. 179-192).

To prepare those who would assume more routine duties, Anderson suggested to Billings that the Library establish a school. He pointed out that the Library could not compete for the "best products" of the existing library schools. However, a school of its own "in proper hands," could attract "college women (and why not some men?)" who wanted to live in New York and would therefore be willing to work at the salaries the library could afford to pay (Dain, 1972, p. 332). Billings agreed to the plan, and Anderson organized the school, which opened in 1911. The students, as Anderson had anticipated, were almost all women. Until the School merged with the former Albany School at Columbia, in 1926, it continued to serve the purpose announced by Billings in his 1911 report: [The school] exists primarily to provide the library with trained assistants and incidentally to fit for library positions elsewhere suitable candidates who do not care to reside in New York." (Dain, 1972, p. 332).

Legislative Reference Service

Legislative reference emerged in association with the progressive movement. Beginning in 1901, Charles McCarthy provided information services to Wisconsin state legislators to counteract the influence of information provided by special-interest groups. These services included gathering reports, bills, and laws from around the country related to proposed legislation, preparing abstracts of important documents, writing or wiring for expert opinion on a topic, and bill drafting. The Wisconsin Legislative Reference Library has been called the forerunner of the special library (Bailey, 1930, pp. 7-9).

To augment his own staff and to prepare legislative reference librarians for other states, McCarthy recruited male graduate students educated in political science, economics, and law to assist him. He gave them responsibility and close personal supervision in exchange for their work. Many of his proteges moved on to organize similar services elsewhere. Charles C. Williamson was recruited by McCarthy and was offered a graduate fellowship in economics at Columbia (Vann, 1971, p. 191).

Although McCarthy called himself a librarian, he was associated with progressive political groups, rather than library professional groups. He therefore did not borrow from contemporary ideas on library education, and his ideas had little impact on library education in general. His biographer suggests that he identified himself as a librarian to appear as innocuous as possible and so deflect criticism that his bill-drafting service exerted undue influence on legislators (Fitzpatrick, 1944, p. 65).

Children's Services

In contrast to academic and research librarianship and legislative reference, children's work was an emerging specialty in which women predominated. Although many influential male librarians supported library work with schools and children's services in public libraries, working directly with children was assumed without question to be appropriate only for women. No attempt was made to recruit men directly for library positions or for places in the educational programs developing for work with children.

Between 1895 and 1910, many large urban public libraries created specialized positions for work with children and appointed women as superintendents to oversee these services in the central and branch libraries. These women established principles and set standards for the specialty; they also acted as mentors for new children's librarians. A number of them also organized training programs. Children's librarianship was unusual among contemporary library specialties in creating a knowledge base beyond the techniques of the work.

Anne Carroll Moore (1898) who organized the first formal education for children's services at Pratt, in 1898, emphasized comprehensive knowledge of children's literature as well as development of standards of literary and artistic judgment. In 1906 Moore took charge of children's work in the New York Public Library, where she hoped to develop a staff that would surpass any in the country. In order to prepare existing staff as well as new children's librarians, she organized a six-month program of supervised experience and training, known as the qualification test for the children's librarian grade. Those selected by Moore worked in branches of varying size as well as in her office and participated in discussions based on assigned reading, to develop critical ability and independent judgment.

While preparation for the qualification test resembled a training class, since students were employed by the library during their training, the program had far more than local significance. Moore prepared her students for leadership in the specialty. Members of her staff went on to other libraries to organize work with children or to become editors or writers of children's books. She served as a mentor to many talented women. One wrote:

...the gift of her friendship, the lasting lifelong strength of her support, the eagerness with which she brought people to a realization of latent abilities of which they themselves were unaware—these were incomparable, outweighing all else. Pages could be filled with the names of those whom she discovered in their chrysalis state, to whom she gave encouragement and in whose subsequent triumphs she rejoiced (Sayers, 1972, p. 130).

Moore herself played a key role in the production of good children's books. She brought authors and artists together, encouraged publishers to establish departments for children's books, and became a nationally known critic.

Frances Jenkins Olcott, supervisor of children's work at the Carnegie Library in Pittsburgh, developed another educational program, with a different focus. Moore's emphasis was aesthetic, while Olcott's was sociological. Moore developed associations with writers, artists, and the book world of Manhattan and London, while Olcott developed associations with pioneers in social work. She urged that work with children be based on studying the social conditions of the people who would use the library:

Nationality, religion, occupations, and living conditions should be considered, books selected and methods adjusted according to actual needs. This requires, on the part of the children's librarian, a wide knowledge of books and some experience in working with different classes of people (Olcott, 1905, p. 75).

Olcott was well acquainted with the Pittsburgh Survey, a model comprehensive study financed by the Russell Sage Foundation and published in 1908, which involved many of the prominent social workers of the period. In a library map of Pittsburgh published in *Survey*, a social-work journal named after the study, Olcott related social data to library use. She concluded:

> Fourteen years of library experiments among the wage earners and immigrants of Pittsburgh show that the solution of the reading problem so far as the librarian can effect it lies largely in the work with children. Let the library establish the reading habit in a child, teach him to choose good books and to think independently and he is likely to continue reading for the rest of his life (Olcott, 1910, p. 854).

Students in the Training School for Children's Librarians, in Pittsburgh, studied "social conditions and betterment" and attended civic meetings and special lectures offered by social workers (Olcott, 1905, p. 75; Smith, 1921, p. 792).

The developing scholarly field of child psychology was given less attention than might have been expected in programs to prepare children's librarians. Yet frequent references to G. Stanley Hall, the foremost scholar in the field, show that many children's librarians were aware of its potential contributions. The difficulty of incorporating the insights of child psychology into the knowledge base of children's librarianship may have stemmed from Hall's biases. He believed strongly in natural psychological differences between the sexes and exalted women's child-bearing function, which he warned would be undermined by intellectual development. He was highly critical of women's higher education "based upon the assumption, implied and often expressed, if not universally acknowledged, that girls should primarily be trained to independence and self-support." He recommended instead a "pre-maternal" curriculum organized around the "Sabbath" of the menstrual period (Hall, 1907, p. 639). This could hardly have been acceptable to women, most of them single, who were attempting to organize a profession. Hall addressed a library organization on children's reading in 1908. According to his theory child development recapitulated the development of civilization but major differences always existed between the sexes, boys showing originality and energy and girls conformity and quiet domesticity. These differences were reflected in reading preferences. Because of the tremendous sex differences he concluded that women librarians could not understand or recommend books for boys (Hall, 1908, pp. 123-28).

Clara Whitehill Hunt, Supervisor of Children's Work at Brooklyn Public Library and head of a training class, took issue with Hall's view. Children's librarians, she asserted, need not accept the criticism of men concerned about the feminization of the library who declared that "no woman, certainly no spinster, can possibly understand the nature of the boy." The youthful movement could be proud of its achievements. She continued:

Another notion that dies hard is one assuming that since the children's librarian is a woman, prone to turn white about the gills at the sight of blood—or a mouse—she can not possibly enter into the feelings of the ancestral barbarian surviving in the young human breast, but must try to hasten the child's development to twentieth century civilization by eliminating the elemental and savage from his story books (Hunt, p. 140).

Hunt concluded that children's librarians sought to understand and meet a variety of interests and stages of development in the books they recommended. They were not the stereotyped creatures Hall portrayed. In the period before 1920, children's librarians made a promising start toward developing a professional specialty and education for it.

If the argument that women's socialization prevented them from contributing to professional development is correct, one should expect the most feminized specialty, children's librarianship, to be the weakest. In fact, this specialty, which offered women an alternative frame of reference for the development of values and self-esteem as well as providing opportunities for leadership, showed remarkable internal strength, although this was not reflected in high status in the profession. A specialty in which children were clients and women all the professionals did not receive adequate recognition.

THE WILLIAMSON REPORT

A state of affairs in which men could attain important library positions without specialized preparation and in which poorly-funded technical programs constituted most of what passed for professional education was not likely to gain librarianship recognition as a profession. Yet few library leaders were disturbed by the state of library education in 1920. Movement for educational reform came from outside.

The Carnegie Corporation, concerned about poor service in libraries housed in Carnegie buildings, sponsored a study of existing programs of library education. Charles C. Williamson, an economist who had worked in libraries, was appointed in 1919 to conduct the study. During the following year he visited all 15 of the existing library schools.

In his confidential report, submitted to the Corporation in 1921, Williamson recommended in particular that "consideration...be given to the need of checking the feminization of library work as a profession. Men as well as women should be in training not only for administrative positions, but for the kinds of library work which require special mastery of techniques and extensive book knowledge" (Williamson, 1971, pp. 230-31).

Feminization could be checked in two ways, he suggested. Professional library work, which he described as work "requiring extensive and accurate book knowledge, advice and direction in the use of books, skill in organization and administration, and expert technical knowledge in many special lines" (Williamson, 1971 p. 15), was not uniquely feminine. Clerical and routine work, on the other hand, was clearly "women's work" in his mind. If professional and clerical library work were disentangled, many women could be moved outside professional boundaries. A side benefit was that clerks could be offered still lower wages, thus releasing money to increase professional salaries.

Feminization could also be checked by organizing programs that would attract men. Graduate schools associated with major universities would be most likely to appeal to male students, Williamson believed. While the existing poorly funded technical programs were sufficient to educate women, improvements were necessary for programs that would educate men.

Dewey and Sharp would have endorsed all of Williamson's specific recommendations for improving library education. These included the requirement of a college degree for admission, association with a university, greater financial resources, division of responsibility for providing education for specialized fields, fellowships and scholarships, and availability of correspondence instruction. Neither Dewey nor Sharp feared feminization, however, since they believed that women could provide the necessary leadership.

Williamson's recommendations were supported by Carnegie Corporation funds. Williamson himself was appointed director of a new Columbia University School of Library Service, incorporating the New York State Library School and the New York Public Library School. The Corporation assured Columbia of $25,000 per year for 10 years for the school's support. A still larger amount, over a million dollars, was allocated to the University of Chicago for the establishment of a graduate library school. Women were not excluded from either school, although only further research will show whether able women were recruited and their careers encouraged on an equal basis with men.

CONCLUSION

I return now to the questions posed in the introduction relating to access and recruitment to the field, transmission and development of professional knowledge, and early socialization into the profession.

Access and Recruitment

Dewey recruited women to the program that he established, primarily because well-educated women were available. A number of subsequent schools, such as the one organized at the New York Public Library, recruited women not only because they were educated but because they would accept subordinate positions and low pay. Sharp recruited able students of both sexes. She was not disturbed that a majority of women enrolled, because women as well as men could fill leadership positions. An alternative to education for professional recruitment and access existed in the form of informal contacts between heads of large libraries (predominantly male), who recommended promising candidates to one another for training in informal mentor-protege relationships for leadership positions. Women were excluded, for the most part, from these channels.

Knowledge Base

Although clerical work was not considered exclusively feminine in the 1880s and 90s, by 1920 Williamson regarded it as "women's work." The more routine aspects of library work were judged to appeal particularly to the "housewifely instinct." While library education before 1920 was predominantly technical, as Dewey's experience at Columbia and Sharp's at the University of Illinois showed, programs that aspired to develop beyond technical education and that for the most part enrolled women had serious difficulties in attracting resources and support. No adequately supported programs existed until the Carnegie Corporation provided funds for library schools at major universities in the 1920s particulary to attract men. The single-sex specialties, legislative reference and children's librarianship, were more successful in developing a knowledge base, perhaps because they did not have to deal with questions of sex superiority or subordination. While the legislative reference program organized by McCarthy had no formal curriculum, he recruited young men with advanced preparation in economics, political science, and law, to apply their knowledge to gathering information and drafting legislation. Because he was oriented primarily toward progressive reform rather than libraries, his program had little influence on library education. Programs to educate children's librarians also went beyond techniques to develop standards for judging children's services. Outside the specialty, however, children's librarianship did not enjoy high prestige and had little influence on library education for other fields.

SOCIALIZATION

Most library educators seem to have assumed that students would not be aggressive and ambitious, but would be orderly and cooperative. Educational programs for librarianship prepared students for positions in a bureaucracy. Students were not expected to become autonomous professionals, like many physicians and lawyers. Programs differed, however, in their expectation for the eventual advancement of women to supervisory or administrative positions. Educators in library schools in technological institutes and the New York Public Library School expected students to remain in subordinate positions. Dewey and Sharp asserted that women graduates, after some experience, could assume important administrative positions. However, library education was rarely required for important positions.

A number of women educators, including Sharp and Moore, did serve as mentors for able women, guiding and encouraging their careers. The close personal-professional relationships Dewey formed with many women, however, show the difficulty of male-mentor/female-protegee associations. The existence of sexual as well as occupational interests created confusion and ambiguity. Most male library leaders avoided this dilemma by selecting men as proteges.

In librarianship before 1920, women did experience specific limitations on their occupational achievement. Socialization to expressive roles is insufficient to explain their exclusion from channels of recruitment and advancement to important positions. Even in a predominantly female occupation, sex-typing served as a mechanism for their social control.

Since sex-typing still exists and women are still excluded from channels of recruitment and advancement in librarianship, what implications does this research have for contemporary librarianship? To redress past discrimination, affirmative recruitment of able women and provision for their support in library school is desirable. In addition, institutionalized mentor-protegee relationships between women who have achieved success and promising women should be established, perhaps on the model of Council for Library Resources internships. Since problems faced by women librarians are common to other predominantly female occupational groups, representatives of these occupational groups should work together. Compensation on the basis of comparable worth is one goal toward which these groups might work.

NOTES

1. Larson (1977) describes professionalization as a project undertaken by those interested in establishing monopolistic control over a market for particular services. Legitimation of a professional monopoly depends on societal recognition of the existence of a body of knowledge required for competence, and belief that this knowledge can be obtained only through systematic education approved by the occupational organization. Thus development of educational programs is central to the campaign to win

professional status (pp. 14-18; 49-52).
2. For information on women and the development of early educational programs in social work and public health as well as librarianship, see Brand, 1978.
3. I am indebted to Grotzinger's (1966) portrayal of Sharp for much of the following section.

The Recruitment of Men into Librarianship, Following World War II

NANCY PATRICIA O'BRIEN

FROM HELEN SEYMOUR FARRINGTON'S (1948, p. 1162) PLEA in 1948 to get rid of the old-maid image, to Margaret Bennet's (1965) forceful injunction against accepting misfits, there has been great concern over the image librarianship conveys to society at large. The lack of women at the top levels of administration is in part responsible for this image problem. While men have been actively recruited into the profession with promises of administrative positions, women have remained in the lower ranks. The end result is a disproportionately large number of male administrators in a profession dominated by women. This chapter documents the aggressive recruitment of men into the library profession since 1940 and the effect of this recruitment on the number of male library administrators, following World War II.

Because of the shortage of trained librarians occasioned by World War II, the years following were concerned with recruitment and training (Holly, 1976, p. 194), and a campaign was mounted to encourage more young men and women to enter the field. In particular, young men were encouraged to apply to library schools throughout the nation, since, with the influx of returning veterans, it was thought that a more equitable balance of men and women in the library field might be maintained. The techniques employed, as well as the incentives offered men in the process of recruiting, help to explain the presence of men in so many top-level positions.

As has been observed in other fields typically considered the domain of women, such as social work and teaching, a man, particularly an ambitious man, receives greater respect from his peers than does a women (Simpson and Simpson, 1969, pp. 226-7). Both Schiller (1974) and Etzioni (1969) have discussed the sometimes-detrimental effects of having a greater number of women than men in a given profession.

Because nearly all occupations in which women participate show a preference on the part of governing boards for men in administrative positions (Bryan, 1952, p. 30), it is not surprising to discover that librarianship could be attractive to an ambitious man. The greater prestige, benefits, and larger salaries that male librarians frequently received in comparison to their female counterparts were inducements used to attract men to the library field after World War II. Because librarianship today is still affected by that campaign, it is important to study the methods used to recruit both women and men.

PRE-1940

As the following table indicates, the occupations heavily dominated by women during the last quarter of the nineteenth century and first half of the twentieth were not professional for the most part. It is little wonder that women librarians were anxious to be able to advance in a professional capacity and resented the fact that often inexperienced men were quickly promoted and given administrative power.

TABLE 1
Percentage of Women in Work Force, 1870-1940

	%
Housekeeper for family	99.2
Dressmaker and seamstress (not in factory)	98.2
Laundress for family	98.2
Trained nurse	97.9
Practical nurse	95.7
Attendant in physician's or dentist's office	95.3
Telephone operator	94.6
Milliner (not in factory)	94.2
Stenographer, typist, secretary	93.5
Servant for family	91.5
Librarian	89.5
Office machine operator	86.1
Dancer, chorus line	80.6
Teacher	75.7
Religious worker	74.6

source: Hooks (1947).

As early as 1938, an editorial in *Library Journal* expressed the concern of several readers that an undue emphasis had been placed on the recruitment of young men for college and public libraries ("The Weaker Sex," 1938). Ruth Savord (1938), Librarian, Council of Foreign Relations, stated her concern that the effects of the first World War on the library field were still being felt 20 years later. She argued that many capable women librarians were not being considered when administrative positions fell vacant. Savord felt that young men recently graduated from library school who had possibly failed in another field were being given positions that rightfully belonged to experienced women librarians. Because few men had entered the library profession during the First World War, there was a lack of male librarians with sufficient experience for administrative positions. There were a number of capable women with the requisite experience and expertise, available for those vacancies. Nonetheless, qualified women were overlooked in favor of inexperienced male librarians.

In response to Savord's observation that there was not an equitable distribution of administrative posts among men and women in the library field, Lightfoot (1938) wrote that proportional representation by gender would be unsatisfactory. He feared that such a situation would drive men from librarianship and keep out more of the best minds than did the present system. His failure to indicate why the present system was more effective or exactly what the "present system" involved, rendered his case inconclusive. Lightfoot's argument did suggest that "the best minds" were connected to a male physique, however.

Summarizing the debate over the 1938 editorial in *Library Journal*, Banning (1938) stated her belief that competency rather than sex or marital status should determine how library positions were filled. Although she decried a "militant feminist attitude" regarding the situation, she personally preferred to have more men in the profession, with women in the top administrative positions.

The note of compromise on which the debate ended typified the reception of such a volatile topic as the recruitment of additional young men. Although initial reactions were generally strong, a soothing, idealistic solution appeared on paper and the furor died down. Unfortunately, the problem remained.

In the attempt to attract candidates "of the type that make good lawyers or doctors, possessed of vigor and personality" (Herbert, 1939, p. 50), a major recruiting program was initiated. The campaign to find career-oriented recruits with professional attitudes was mapped out in Clara Herbert's *Personnel Administration in Public Libraries* (1939). Herbert considered men to be the only ones capable of professionalism, and specifically recommended that married women or women with young children not be appointed to library positions.

There was concern over recruiting practices in the years preceding the Second World War. Sexual discrimination in hiring and promotion practices have already been mentioned in conjunction with the shortage of librarians precipitated by the First World War. In the following years a pattern of recruitment procedures to attract more men to librarianship emerges.

1941-1950

The decade of the 1940s saw numerous articles similar to "Let's Start Recruiting," which encouraged the profession to "make every effort to attract young men who are strong, vigorous and progressive" (Alvarez, 1941, p. 367). In 1940 Rena Cowper ironically observed, in an article titled "Not in our Stars," that men received the administrative posts in librarianship. In a vocational text, it was stated that "it is true that many librarians are women, but in general, the most important jobs in the profession are now held by men" (Kitson, 1942, p. 236).

Some concerns of the library world regarding the recruitment of men were that women would be displaced or disregarded when filling top administrative posts, that men were given preferential treatment, that men who had failed in other fields were readily accepted into librarianship, because of sex rather than ability, and that higher salaries would be given to men rather than women.

The ALA Board of Education for Librarianship (BEL) was very actively engaged in addressing these issues. In 1942, letters to directors of library schools expressed the need, as seen by the BEL, for the library school to take an active part in both the recruiting of qualified students and the elimination of undesirable applicants.

All conditions reported by libraries make it clear that recruiting capable young people for librarianship is now a critical major problem. Upon the librarians who receive professional education in the next two or three years will depend in large part the maintenance and development of library service in the post-war period. Several of the library schools have recently issued new leaflets to place librarianship before college students as a desirable profession for their consideration.

The suggestion has come to A.L.A. Headquarters that fellowships be established for men as a means of preventing after this war the same dearth of men librarians which marked the period following the last war (Hostetter, 1942).

In a second letter, the need to maintain or raise high standards in recruiting rather than enrolling large numbers of students was emphasized. Because other fields could offer attractive salaries, it was stressed that librarianship should be interpreted to potential librarians in terms of its intellectual challenge. Because some library-school directors feared that more librarians than could be employed might be trained or that unsuitable individuals might apply for training, the Secretary of the BEL encouraged recruiting with the goal of avoiding the period of unemployment and low salaries that followed the First World War (Hostetter, 1942).

Low salaries in comparison to other service professions was a major concern in attempting to recruit for librarianship. In an article entitled "Eighteen Thousand Librarians Wanted," Alice G. Higgins (1945) cited low salaries, lack of job descriptions and expectations, and a poor image as the primary problems in trying to recruit for the profession. She recommended more consistency in professional goals and a system of principles for the profession.

Higgins, like many others, observed that there was a need for higher salaries, but offered little advice for remedying the problem. According to a summary of facts and opinions assembled by executive-committee members of the Association of American Library Schools, inadequate salaries as well as a lack of suitable recruiting literature were stumbling blocks to successful recruiting. Again, no solution was offered.

It may have been the unsuitability of the recruiting literature citing the salary ranges for librarians that proved the stumbling block. Many of the pamphlets and literature of the era were quite honest in describing the salary to be expected as a librarian. *"Books and People: A Career in Library Service"* (1947) described salaries as low, but added that one could expect raises. This particular pamphlet, published by ALA was aimed at both men and women and predicted a shortage of 18,000 librarians in the six years following the war.

In another, undated recruitment brochure, published by the New York Library Association, salaries were mentioned as "known to be low," but moving upward (Are You Interested...). The range given was from $1200 to $10,000 with the higher figure commanded by head librarians. Interestingly enough, the pamphlet went on to state that women as well as men had the opportunity to advance to the top levels. The fact that it was felt necessary to include this information in a brochure dating from the period 1947-1956 indicates that there was some concern that the profession was viewed as preferring men in top positions.

In a 1944 informational bulletin from Army headquarters to personnel and soldiers about to be discharged, librarianship was described as "unusual in the variety of positions that it offers and in the sense of public service that it gives. Financial rewards are equivalent to those in other social professions" (U.S. Army Service Forces, 1944).

A 1945 occupational brief gave a factual presentation of librarianship as a service occupation with little or no glorification. These occupational briefs were prepared for use in the educational programs of the armed services by a division of the War Manpower Commission. Salaries were cited in a straightforward manner as being low but providing security (The Job of the Librarian, 1945).

As can be seen in the foregoing brief description of recruiting pamphlets, the returning GI was not promised a hefty salary and early promotion, at least in black and white, but was offered a chance to have a reasonable income, security, and community respect. However, the information was provided by the armed services. The literature from library associations was somewhat different.

Although both the armed services and library associations stressed the service aspect of librarianship as its attractive feature, neither denied the fact that salaries were low. Instead, comparisons were made to other service occupations whose salary ranges were similar. Library associations cannily pointed out that administrators received better pay. At times, this fact was coupled with the information that men usually held the top positions. In other instances it was perhaps hoped that the preference for men as administrators would be obvious in a scrutiny of librarianship. In an interview, published in the *New York Times*, Ralph A. Ulveling, president of the American Library Association, indicated: "The Association foresees an especially strong demand for administrators, particularly men..." (Ulveling, 1945, p. 457).

In 1945, however, the Association of American Library Schools found that literature appropriate for recruiting young men was unavailable. The pamphlets designed to reassure the recruit that a librarian was a normal human being of either sex, capable of earning a decent salary, were yet to be written. Owing to the shortage of librarians, recruiting literature came under careful scrutiny and was found wanting. An article in *Library Journal*, "Recruiting for Librarianship Literature Sadly Inadequate" (Leonard, 1947, p. 1181), was only one of numerous complaints about the quality and timeliness of the literature.

While the recruiting literature was being examined, the debate over the roles of men and women in the library continued to rage. In 1946, Duff predicted that the influx of veterans into colleges would result in an increased demand for library services. Although he saw a need for both men and women in the field, Duff believed the expansion of services and facilities offered an opportunity to recruit "men of superior natural qualities" for librarianship. As he pointed out, the library dominated by women was at a disadvantage in a world dominated by men (p. 1182).

A text on vocational research published the following year reinforced Duff's statement regarding the positon of men and women in librarianship. In listing the appealing aspects of librarianship, the text stated that "there are good opportunities for administrative positions for men in both the school and college library field," and conversely that one of the unattractive features was that "many of the administrative positions in the college field go to men, making this an undesirable feature for women" (Institute for Research, 1947, n.p.).

The observation that men were given preference in when administrative posts were filled, was made by a research institute independent of libraries. Unfortunately, librarians paid little heed to this unbiased statement made by a research organization. Concern was still focused on the shortage of librarians rather than on the ratio of men to women at the administrative level.

In 1947, a form letter to a few librarians was sent out by the executive secretary of ALA, Carl H. Milam (1947). In brief, the letter requested criticism and comments on an enclosed statement regarding employment trends and outlook for librarians that had been prepared for the U.S. Bureau of Labor Statistics. The estimate for librarians needed for the period 1947-60 (see Table 2) was projected from a study done in 1944 (see Table 3). Given the emphasis placed on the number of librarians required to fill postwar vacancies, it was not unexpected that returning veterans were initially targeted for recruitment. As Munn (1949) was to point out, benefits from the G.I. Bill allowed many men to attend college who otherwise might not have considered it.

In 1949 Ralph Munn's provocatively titled article "It is a Mistake to Recruit Men" triggered a series of responses. In essence, his argument was that librarianship needed to reassess the traditional belief that more men were needed in the profession. He called for both men and women of superior abilities but disagreed with the recruitment of additional average men in an effort to increase the proportion of men. Munn feared that the trend of appointing men to top positions would be extended if there were more men to appoint to such posts. Those appointments would result in a refusal by superior women to enter a field that reserved most of the rewards for men.

Responses to Munn's position did not deny that most of the rewards were reserved for men. That issue was either skirted or ignored. Bannister (1950) and McCann (1949) both felt that superior men and women should be encouraged to enter librarianship. McCann's request for a more balanced enrollment in library schools was based on the fear that "any working group in which a man is outnumbered 250 to 1 is not going to permit him to make a proper adjustment to the task in hand. He will be coddled, and shielded, his blunders and bad manners excused away (p. 1802). McCann speculated that it may have been the uncertainty of the public regarding the librarian's function, that encouraged the placement of men in top-level positions. Reasoning that

TABLE 2
Estimated Needs for Additional Professional Librarians 1947-60
Projected from 1944 Estimates

Present shortage		4,900
Normal replacements		22,760
Additional librarians needed for planned expansion and the improvement of substandard libraries		36,500
Public libraries	15,000	
College and university libraries	6,000	
School libraries	12,000	
Special and other libraries	3,500	
Additional librarians required		64,160
Librarians in the armed forces, military libraries, etc., who will probably return to civilian libraries		2,000
Librarians to be recruited 1947-60		62,160

The American Library Directory 1945 lists 11,380 libraries in the United States. These libraries are classified as follows:

Public	7,995	Federal	223
Higher Education	1,178	Medical	204
Special	558	Hospital	187
Junior College	435	State	157
Law	312	Institutional	131

The total figure omits the number of school libraries in elementary and secondary schools that are administered by full-time school librarians.

In January 1944, *Post-War Library Personnel: A Report from the American Library Association on Post-War Educational Opportunities for Service Personnel* was issued. Estimates of needs for the six-year period following the war were made after consulting administrators of libraries of various types and sizes about the expansion essential for postwar library service. It is believed that the 1944 study still presents a realistic rather than an optimistic picture of the needs of the library profession. The figures in the present estimates were projected from the 1944 report and submitted to library schools and selected libraries for criticism. A special study could not be made because of lack of time. It should be pointed out that if a substantial program of federal aid to libraries is provided, these predictions may prove to be conservative.

source: Library of Education, Board of Education for Librarianship Subject File, 1914-1956; 1947, University of Illinois Archives.

TABLE 3
Summary of Postwar Personnel Estimates
Additional Librarians Required for Postwar Library Service

Present shortage		3,500
Librarians in armed forces	1,300	
Librarians in military libraries and temporary government positions	1,200	
Shortage of library-school graduates	1,000	
Normal replacements (for six years after end of war)		6,500
Additional librarians for planned expansion (for six years after end of war)		10,000
In: Public libraries	3,500	
College and university libraries	1,500	
School libraries	4,000	
Special libraries	1,000	
Additional librarians required for postwar library service		20,000
Librarians now in armed forces, military libraries, etc., who will probably return to civilian libraries		2,000
Librarians to be recruited		18,000
January 29, 1944		

source: Library of Education, Board of Education for Librarianship Subject File, 1914-1956; Record Series 28/50/6, Box 3, Folder: Personnel—Postwar Library Personnel, 1947, University of Illinois Archives.

society might view some duties as being beyond the capabilities of women, the placement of men at the administrative level was one way of assuring the public that libraries were being governed properly.

In speaking to Munn's argument, Bannister maintained that the recruitment of men with outgoing personalities was necessary because men were serious in pursuing their careers. Women frequently entered librarianship to fill time before their marriages or to assist their families financially, according to Bannister (1950, pp. 141-2). If this argument were elaborated, it would be clear that women were not only uninterested in matters outside family life, but were incapable of handling a prolonged position of responsibility in a job.

Oboler (1950) felt that Munn should not be concerned about the balance between men and women in librarianship. The fact that top library positions had been given to nonlibrary-trained administrators and educators because of the lack of trained, qualified men was of great concern to Oboler. He hastened to add: "Men for various psychological, physiological, and historical reasons, too numerous and lengthy to enumerate here, usually do happen to make better administrators than women." (p. 98). However, Oboler introduced a concern in the debate over men versus women that had not formerly been addressed in any depth. The ALA had already acknowledged, two years previously, the problem of nonlibrarians being appointed to directorships of large libraries, in its outline of a recruiting program designed to meet the librarian shortage (Opportunities for Constructive Giving," 1945, p. 3).

The fact that men were preferred as administrators was acknowledged both within and outside the library profession during the 1940s. A tremendous shortage of trained librarians drew attention to the problem of inadequate salaries. In addition, at the close of the decade it was beginning to be recognized that the image of the librarian was an obstacle to recruiting.

1951-1960

As Ernest Reece (1949) pointed out in *The Task and Training of Librarians*, one aspect of librarianship that seriously deters potential recruits from entering the field is "the conspicuous position of mechanical routines in libraries" (p. 67). He felt that the lack of opportunity to function at a level in keeping with the professional training required of librarians discouraged potential candidates. Nor was he alone in his thinking. In her study of methods used for recruiting librarians, Dorothy Scott Jones (1951) concluded:

Over almost two hundred years public opinion had crystallized into the conviction that library work was dull, menial, and uninteresting, and that librarians led dull, secluded lives guarding books. Unfortunately this impression of librarians and librarianship has not changed very much in the seventy-six years that the American Library Association has been in existence. It has even been fostered by the fact that most of the work which the public sees in a library is of a routine and clerical nature (p. 5).

Jones suggested that the problem of an unattractive image could be rectified. Her recommendations included educating the public about librarianship by employing a public-relations firm, subsidizing writers to improve the image of librarians, encouraging a worthwhile comic strip to be produced, improving the recruitment literature, individual recruiting by librarians, and providing scholarships. There was little doubt that the recruitment literature needed improvement. In a review of library recruitment propaganda by vocational education specialists, a list of unfavorable characteristics had been cited (Woerdehoff, 1953).

In 1953, Martha Baldwin Cox compared recruiting literature and techniques in librarianship, nursing, and teaching. Among the recommendations made by Cox for a successful recruiting campaign was the suggestion that the image needed to be improved, as did the recruiting literature. She felt that the successful programs undertaken by the nursing and teaching professions should be duplicated by the library profession. Specifically she recommended that the National Advertising Council be contacted for assistance, community service be stressed as an inducement in recruiting, a clearinghouse for recruiting materials be established, guidance counselors be kept informed, and library schools made more responsible for screening undesirable applicants (Cox, 1953).

Each of those recommendations echoes endless articles in the library literature citing the need for recruits and the reasons individuals are not attracted to the library profession. However, Cox was among the first to point out the parallels with other women's professions and the possible use of similar programs to upgrade the profession and hence attract a wider, more vigorous pool of recruits.

Alice Bryan (1952) found that little had been done to improve women's positions in librarianship. She observed that there was a greater proportion of men than women in the administrative groups of public librarians surveyed. In addition, top male administrators were five years younger than their female counterparts, on the average. Bryan concluded that men not only had a better chance of reaching the top, but they would get there faster (p. 33).

Bryan's findings confirmed the fact that men were indeed given the top positions. This gave an incentive to the male librarian or recruit to strive for an administrative post. For women librarians and recruits, Bryan's findings signaled that the scope of their careers should remain within the lower ranks.

The popular literature used to enhance the profession for young women recruits differed greatly from the recruiting literature directed toward men. One item used to attract young women was *Miss Library Lady*, described by one librarian as "the richly rewarding story about a girl who loved books and travel and who, through library work, found romance and an exciting, happy life in Hawaii" (quoted in Kemp, 1954, p.50). Although it is not within the scope of this paper to examine the rewards offered to male and female recruits, it is easy to gauge which group would bear the greatest brunt of disillusionment, given such examples as those cited here. Men offered security undoubtedly would achieve it more frequently than would the women offered travel and romance.

In the mid-1950s the tone of recruitment literature and programs began to change. Women were assured that "there are no barriers to women who qualify for administrative positons..." and that librarianship is a profession women can return to after they are married ("Careers Ahead..." 1955, p. 3). In part, the estimated need for librarians in the years following World War II had a direct influence on the change in incentives offered female recruits. The shortage was so severe that both women and men were courted in the recruiting process.

It was beginning to be recognized that the image of librarianship was in large part responsible for the shortage of desirable recruits. As has been pointed out, there has not been a single positive image of the librarian. The images presented have ranged from an educated individual anxious to help the patron locate the needed information, to the morally conservative spinster (Leigh and Sewny, 1960, p. 2090). Regardless, the effect of the image on potential recruits was decidedly negative. Agnes Lytton Reagan (1957) concluded: "As a group, college students hold an unflattering stereotype of the librarian, and they comment with disfavor on the personalities of librarians (pp. 49-50). She also pointed out that college students felt that the existence of community respect for the librarian was questionable. However, the major factor in rejecting librarianship as a career was the impression of library work held by college students, who felt it was dull and routine (Reagan, 1957).

Despite Reagan's findings, an increase in recruits was observed during the 1950s. Men were beginning to enter the field in greater numbers, according to the U.S. Department of Labor. The influx was viewed by the government as an effect of increased salaries and opportunities for advancement to administrative positions (U.S. Department of Labor, Bureau of Labor Statistics, 1959, p. 201). As librarians observed at that time, the quality of work, poor image, and inequities at administrative levels were deterrents to recruiting. However, owing to the phenomenal shortage of librarians, some of these problems were being examined and solutions proposed.

1961-1970

The 1960s saw an increasing concern with the image of librarianship and how that image was portrayed in recruiting materials. The proportion of men and women also received a good deal of attention. Drafts of a recruitment brochure authorized by the ALA indicate how the effect of men's entering the profession in increased numbers was officially viewed. In an initial draft, a marketing consultant suggested that a pamphlet to be entitled "The Librarian-Merchant of Ideas" contain the following: "The best evidence of increased advantages and financial opportunities in the library field is indicated by the number of men entering it." The final draft of that brochure included a quote from Myrl Ricking, then Director of the ALA Office of Recruitment: "More and more men are becoming librarians, which in itself is evidence of the rising pay scale" ("The Librarian—Idea Consultant"). The brochure had been retitled to fit in with the trend toward professional nomenclature. (Demco Production File, ALA Archives, n.d.)

That equal opportunity for advancement did not exist was pointed out to a mass audience in the April 1964 issue of *Esquire*. The reader was advised: "Most of the top jobs in the profession want male librarians to fill them" ("Young Man, Be a Librarian").

As the shortage continued, the need for extensive recruiting of both men and women was acknowledged by the production of pamphlets that pointed out the predominance of men in top library positions, while maintaining that women were also eligible for such positions (Indiana State Library, n.d.).

The Special Libraries Association (SLA) (1956) published recruitment literature encouraging men to enter the profession. Admitting that women were predominant because of prior possession, the SLA described the ratio as decreasing. Men, according to one pamphlet, were active especially in the areas of administration, science and technology, and computer-information systems (Special Libraries Association, Recruitment Committee, 1962).

At first glance, the pamphlets described above may appear contradictory. Upon closer scrutiny, however, each states that women comprise the majority of librarians, that men are entering in increasing numbers, and that men hold the top positions, although both men and women qualify as administrators. The status quo remained intact.

A female recruit examining recruitment brochures would find that the literature attempted to attract more men by offering them security and quick advancement, yet reassured women that they still had the opportunity to rise to the top ranks. By inference, it could be seen that the top ranks of women existed mainly in smaller, notably public, libraries. As one writer observed in 1968, the directors of the 50 largest academic libraries in the United States were all men, while 86 percent of the 50 largest public-library directors were male (Lowenthal, 1971, p. 2599). Therefore, a recruit examining the profession in its entirety would assume that a man might become a director of one of the major libraries in the nation, but it was unlikely that a woman could achieve the same. By setting an example, one of the recruiting techniques heavily emphasized in the literature ("Report on Recruiting", 1948, p. 113), success was equated with being male.

In criticizing recruitment materials, Gummere (1967, p. 810) found the literature, addressed to women, was apologetic for the low salaries and poor image of librarianship. Kemp (1954) and Comeau (1967) provided guides and analyses of recruitment literature for different time periods, but both found the efficacy of the recruitment materials doubtful. The problems in producing a successful brochure were the problems inherent in librarianship. The primary deterrents were the image, including the notion that librarians perform many clerical tasks and the pay scale. Although the question of the physical format of a recruitment brochure was raised (notably by Cox, 1953, p. 39), it is unlikely that this would be considered a major problem. The matters of size, color, illustrations, and amount of information to be included are secondary to the preconceived notion an individual has about a profession. As Jesse Shera (1962, p. 4487) pointed out, little girls *don't* play librarian, and for very good reason. The image of the librarian is not conducive to imitation. In addition, the basic science of librarianship has not been visible to the public. (Goode, 1969, p. 286). Unconvinced that librarians have professional goals and activities, the public remains unaware of their numerous and varied responsibilities.

Library literature contains numerous articles on recruitment and image. Besides the articles based on research or successful recruiting experiences, many are opinion pieces, which are frequently contradictory (Willey, 1965, p. 50). It is not the intent here to pursue the efficacy or failure of any of the various recruiting programs aimed at men and women. It is enough to agree with Virginia Speider's (1961) finding that the "over-all view of librarianship is not one calculated to encourage young people to enter the profession" (p. 38).

As Margaret Bennet stated in 1965, there has been great concern over the image of librarianship in society.

In the public mind, librarianship seems to have become a kind of American Foreign Legion, the officially recommended "way out" for doctoral candidates who can't screw their courage to the sticking place to take their prelims, for battered teachers who want to escape the classroom, for people in business who buckle under the stress of competition, and for all those college graduates who have never quite figured out what to do with themselves. We want people to become librarians for positive reasons—because they have a consuming interest in ideas and knowledge and because they have strong public-service feelings, rather than because they happen to have asthma or a cosmetic difficulty or a hormonal imbalance; or a touch of schizophrenia.

Following World War II, the inducements used to recruit men into librarianship described the misfits Margaret Bennet warned against accepting. As Munn pointed out in 1949, library schools received applications from men who had little or no interest in libraries but had read or been told by a vocational counselor that a shortage of librarians existed. Applicants were interested in a "depression-proof job" that offered security and could be obtained utilizing the benefits of the G.I. Bill to attend college. As Bryan (1952) observed in her study of public librarians, over two-fifths had worked at least a year in other occupations before starting a library career. It is apparent that many librarians felt that standards were lowered in the process of recruiting more men into librarianship.

1971-1980

In the 30 years following World War II, the impact of the sudden surge of men into librarianship intensified the existing trend of placing men in top administrative posts. Between 1940 and 1950, the number of men in the profession nearly doubled, and did so again between 1950 and 1960, as Table 4 indicates.

TABLE 4
Number of Librarians Employed

Year	Female	Male
1940	32,546	3,891
1950	49,027	6,303
1960	72,431	12,248
1970	101,000	22,286

source: U.S. Department of Commerce, Bureau of the Census, *United States Census of Population:* 1940, 1950, 1960, and 1970.

Although the number of women in librarianship remains considerably higher, the percentage of increase is not as dramatic as it is for men (e.g., from 1950 to 1960, the number of women increased by 46.0 percent while that of men increased by 90.7 percent). The recruiting campaign to attract men into librarianship was somewhat successful, as the figures in Table 4 show. The success of that campaign was due to many different factors.

Heim (1979a), in her comparison of professional education, noted that those fields dominated by women often termed semiprofessions have had varying degrees of success in legitimizing their status. As librarianship moves toward acceptance as a full-fledged profession, it is imperative that the effects of professional status on the public and on potential recruits be recognized.

The public is not convinced that there is a basic science of librarianship: the skill is thought to be only clerical or administrative...Moreover, there has been little research and thus little accumulation of knowledge relative to the central professional task of librarianship, the organization and codification of library materials and the development of principles concerning the retrieval of that information (Goode, 1969, p. 286).

CONCLUSION

It is undeniable that an inequity between men and women at the administrative level of librarianship exists. That an increase of men in librarianship occurred following World War II is also irrefutable (see Table 4). It seems that there is a correlation between the two. The sudden surge of men into librarianship, encouraged by various recruiting methods, provided a wider selection of candidates for top-level positions. That men would be primary candidates for such positions has been shown in the preceding text. The influx of men and the appointments made 25 years ago are still affecting the library world today. If an average of 30-40 years are spent in a library career by those appointed to administrative posts, a change of administrative structure should be visible in the next 15 years. It is to be hoped that in the future, appointments will be made on the basis of competency, not sex. As men enter librarianship in ever-increasing numbers, governing authorities will have an embarrassment of riches from which to select candidates. Men and women both will be able to offer their unique skills to the library world. By understanding the manner in which men were recruited following World War II, and the incentives offered, it should be possible to avoid having a structure top-heavy with male administrators, similar to the one that exists today. At the same time, it may be possible to sympathize with the administrators suddenly caught in a situation in which new recruits advance on the basis of merit and are consequently resentful of predecessors who may have achieved their status on the basis of sex or by default. Recruitment for librarianship must continue on an ever-increasing scale of selectiveness. By understanding past policies and examining methods already proved unsatisfactory, it should be possible to attract candidates interested in intellectual challenge and capable of defining the basic science of librarianship by their professional attitudes.

Undergraduate Women as Potential Recruits to the Library Profession

PATRICIA REELING

ATTRACTING QUALIFIED RECRUITS to librarianship has been a major concern of the profession since World War II. Earlier research (Reagan, 1958a; Reagan, 1958b; Forsyth and Harvey, 1965) showed that undergraduate women attending liberal-arts colleges—especially liberal-arts colleges for women—represented a fruitful source of potential librarians. Therefore, a study (Reeling, 1969) was initiated in 1965 with the premise that it would be possible to identify traits typifying undergraduate liberal-arts-college women who might be potential recruits to the profession. It should be noted that even though there was an acute shortage of librarians in the early 1960s, the investigator was concerned not just with the recruitment of large numbers of individuals, but especially with the recruitment of those undergraduate women who would show some potential for professional leadership.

The purpose of the study was threefold: (1) to determine to what extent it might be possible to isolate and define certain measurable characteristics that typify undergraduate women who are potential recruits to the library profession; (2) to identify those factors that have influenced undergraduate women to consider or reject a possible career in librarianship; and (3) to evaluate the relative effectiveness of selected library recruitment activities in stimulating undergraduate women to consider or reject a career in librarianship.

PRIOR STUDIES

The investigator was unable to locate any studies that attempted to identify characteristics common to potential librarians at the time they were enrolled at the undergraduate college level. Therefore, this survey of related research concentrates upon those studies concerned with: (1) personality traits and other characteristics of women who were already professional librarians or who were students enrolled in a library-science program; (2) factors influencing the selection of librarianship as a career; (3) and attitudes of students toward librarians and librarianship. Only those research studies having direct impact upon the design of this study are cited here.

One of the first studies concerned with characteristics of library-school students was conducted by Eugene Wilson (1937). After examining records of 808 library-science students who had completed 30-31 semester hours at the University of Illinois between 1926-27 and 1935-36, Wilson was able to describe the "typical" library-school student as a female unmarried college graduate, twenty-six years of age, with a middle-class social, economic, and cultural background, and somewhat better-than-average undergraduate grades.

By far the most comprehensive effort in providing a representative profile of public librarians was Alice Bryan's (1952) study, conducted as part of the Public Library Inquiry. Part II of her book deals with the personal and economic characteristics of some 3,000 public librarians, their educational status, and their attitudes toward librarianship as a career. As part of her research, Bryan utilized a personality test known as the Guilford-Martin Inventory of Factors (GAMIN), from which she was able to construct the following personality profile.

> The typical female librarian has a personality profile that is remarkably similar to that of her male colleague. As compared with the average woman university student, she is submissive in social situations, lacks self-confidence, feels inferior, has an average amount of drive for overt activity, and feels a normal degree of nervous tension and irritability. She is normally feminine in her attitudes and interests. Like the typical male librarian, she seems reasonably well adjusted (p. 43).

Two other national surveys yielding considerable data describing social and economic characteristics of librarians should be noted here. The first, prepared by Henry Drennan and Richard Darling (1966), derived its data from the 1960 U.S. population census and was concerned only with public and school librarians. The second, conducted by Anita Schiller (1969a), surveyed 2300 college and university librarians associated with approximately 600 institutions. In both studies, the majority of the librarians were female, and they had similar preprofessional backgrounds.

Robert Douglass (1957) was concerned primarily with the librarian's personality. His population consisted of 400 women and 125 men enrolled in 17 accredited library schools in 1947-48. Almost 80 percent of his subjects had attended a liberal-arts college or university, and nearly 40 percent reported literature as their major field of undergraduate study. Five personality inventories were used by Douglass to obtain data. (One of them—the Allport-Vernon Study of Values—was also selected by this investigator for the study under discussion.) Douglass concluded that in terms of personality structure, the library profession does exercise a selective influence in recruiting its members. In comparison with the average nonlibrarian, Douglass found the average librarian to be more orderly, conscientious, conservative, responsible, undominating, interested in people but not merely gregarious, and less inclined toward anxiety and neuroticism.

Rainwater's (1962) master's thesis used the Edwards Personal Preference Schedule to measure personality traits, an instrument also utilized in the present research study. Rainwater analyzed scores obtained on the Edwards Personal Preference Schedule by 94 students enrolled in the University of Texas Graduate School of Library Science in 1957-60. She concluded that in comparison with nonlibrarians, the library-school student was more driven to achieve, was more deferent, orderly, and had greater endurance. Conversely, the library-school student was significantly less exhibitive, affiliative, dominant, heterosexual, and aggressive.

Several years later, the Edwards Personal Preference Schedule was utilized in this researcher's preliminary investigation of personality traits of prospective librarians, comparing 128 Indiana University undergraduate students indicating an interest in librarianship with 133 students rejecting librarianship as a possible career choice (Reeling, 1965). Results of this study definitely tended to corroborate Rainwater's findings. For example, students contemplating a graduate major in library science obtained higher mean scores for the manifest needs of "achievement," "deference," and "nurturance," and lower mean scores for the manifest needs of "exhibition" and "aggression."

Perhaps the most significant study to be reported in the literature concerning factors influencing the selection of librarianship as a career was that conducted by Agnes Reagan (1958b). After examining the educational background of some 8500 library-school graduates and students enrolled in accredited library schools during the period 1948-55, Reagan was able to identify 51 liberal-arts colleges, teachers' colleges, and universities that had been attended by relatively large numbers of these individuals. To determine what in these institutions of higher education had influenced students in their decision to become librarians, Reagan sent questionnaires to 1479 librarians who had attended them. As a result, she concluded that five factors were especially important: (1) individuals—most often librarians; (2) publicity—primarily printed recruitment literature; (3) use of libraries—especially in colleges where academic programs encouraged heavy use of library materials; (4) work experience in libraries—principally in institutions where student library assistants associated closely with the professional librarians; and (5) library education—in those colleges where undergraduate library-science courses could serve as an introduction to the field.

A survey sponsored by the Association of American Library Schools (1952) of 1200 students representing the 36 library schools accredited at that time yielded results similar to those found by Reagan. Of these students, 38 percent attributed their choice of a career to the influence of a particular librarian, 19 percent to their experience of working in libraries, 10 percent to their use or observation of libraries, and 10 percent to the influence of printed recruitment literature. Forty-nine percent of these students had decided to become librarians by the time they had completed college, and 32 percent made this career choice sometime during their college years.

Presumably, the choice or rejection of librarianship as a career is also related to the concept or image young people have of librarians. William Form (1946), a sociologist, asked students at Kent State University to write their frank impressions to the question, "What kind of people are librarians, in your estimation?" The dominant stereotype to emerge was one of an intelligent, single woman who appears quiet and poised, yet underneath is inhibited, slightly neurotic, and conservative in her social relations. Form was interested chiefly in the personality and social character of the individual librarian and made no effort to learn what people thought of library work or a possible career in librarianship.

Dorothy Jones (1951) asked 180 Upsala College sophomores and 265 seniors attending East Orange High School, in New Jersey, if they would like to make librarianship their career. Only four high school students and one college student indicated an interest in librarianship. The majority of the students seemed to feel that library work would be boring. Additional reasons given for rejecting library work included the following themes: "Librarianship is woman's work," "Not enough young people," "Low pay," "Lack of opportunity for advancement," etc. Several students criticized librarians as having disagreeable personalities.

Since Agnes Reagan and Dorothy Jones adequately traced the literature pertaining to the history and development of library-recruitment activities, no attempt will be made here to review that literature. This writer concluded, however, after making her own survey of related research dealing with library-recruitment activities, that although library literature seemed to abound with articles giving suggestions on how to recruit librarians, very little scientific evaluation regarding the effectiveness of the recruitment programs was taking place. No one could say with authority which recruitment methods worked best, for what type of audience, and why. Thus, the present study is the first to attempt to evaluate the effectiveness of various library-recruitment activities and to establish criteria for identifying potential recruits at the undergraduate level.

HYPOTHESES

To be as precise as possible and identify specific objectives, the following hypotheses—stated in null form—were tested during the conduct of this study.

1. Undergraduate women will not choose or reject a possible graduate major in library science to a significantly greater or lesser degree than they would choose or reject a possible graduate major in any other area of specialization.
2. Undergraduate women who have been exposed to some specific form of library-recruitment activity (such as a library-recruitment talk) will not differ significantly—in terms of their attitude toward a possible career in librarianship—from undergraduate women who have not been exposed to that same form of library recruitment activity.
3. Undergraduate women choosing a possible graduate major in library science will not differ significantly from undergraduate women rejecting a possible graduate major in library science in terms of:
   a) Intelligence
   b) Personality traits
   c) Years of college completed
   d) Major subject area
   e) Scholastic record (grade-point average)
   f) Participation in extracurricular activities
   g) Reading habits and use of library
   h) Work experience
   i) Family educational and occupational background
4. The development of interest in, or rejection of, librarianship as a possible career choice by undergraduate women is not related significantly to such factors as their:
   a) Perceived future goals and needs
   b) Concept of libraries and librarians, as previously influenced by:
      i. Individuals
      ii. Library recruitment publicity
      iii. Association with libraries.

SUBJECTS

The women serving as subjects for this study were 658 full-time students attending Edgecliff College in Cincinnati, Ohio, a private undergraduate liberal-arts college for women, during the 1965-66 academic year. The large majority of these students were drawn from the greater Cincinnati area, with a median age of 19 years. It should be noted that 650 (or 98.5 percent) of these students provided both pre- and posttest data for the study.

The students at this college were chosen as subjects after it was determined that Edgecliff College was representative of a number of generally-accepted criteria of undergraduate liberal-arts colleges for women: (1) level of instruction, (2) accrediting agency, (3) geographical location, (4) control, (5) type of program offered, (6) full-time student enrollment, and (7) size of library.[1]

In addition, since the college administration allowed the investigator unlimited access to the students (and their records), it was decided to use the entire universe[2] of eligible subjects rather than attempt to draw a representative sample of undergraduate female liberal-arts-college students from a sample of other comparable institutions. To have chosen the latter alternative might have produced a more heterogeneous, but not necessarily more representative, group of students. Also, it probably would not have afforded the investigator an opportunity for adequate testing of the second hypothesis by the conduct of a controlled experiment. However, because any college has unique qualities, one should be aware that if this study had been conducted at another institution of higher education, it is altogether possible that different results would be forthcoming.

DATA—GATHERING INSTRUMENTS AND SOURCES

Data needed for this study were obtained from four primary sources: (1) student responses to a questionnaire and rating scale, (2) student performance on standardized tests, (3) official high-school and college records, and (4) personal interviews.

The questionnaire and rating scale were constructed by the investigator to elicit information pertaining to the subjects' personal and family backgrounds, and their choice of possible graduate majors. Two souces of information proved helpful in designing the instrument. The scale for rating graduate majors was developed with the aid of a standard list of graduate fields of study utilized by the U.S. Office of Education (U.S. Dept. of Health, Education, and Welfare, 1965a) in classifying its data for earned degrees conferred in higher education. In addition, a questionnaire prepared by the Bureau of Social Science Research, Inc. (National Science Foundation, 1963) for its survey of the work and further study activities of a cross section of college graduates was used—with some adaptations—as a model in developing the questionnaire for this study. The resulting questionnaire/rating scale was pretested on a group of students at Caldwell College for Women, in Caldwell, New Jersey.

Three standardized tests were utilized: (1) Edwards Personal

Preference Schedule (EPPS); (2) Allport, Vernon, Lindzey Study of Values; and (3) College Entrance Examination Board Scholastic Aptitude Test (SAT). These tests were selected primarily because of the personality and intellectual traits they purported to measure. However, ease of administration was another prime factor taken into consideration when selecting the personality tests. Also, the EPPS and Study of Values had been used in prior research dealing with library-school students.

Official college records were another source of data used to describe the subjects in this study and verify the accuracy of the data obtained by means of the questionnaire.

The final source of information was an interview schedule developed by the researcher, to be used in conducting semistructured interviews with selected students. An attempt was made to learn about the subjects' future career plans and their views of librarianship. Another purpose of the interviews was to determine the rationale for student change of opinion concerning librarianship after being exposed to one or another of the experimental recruitment factors in this study.

PROCEDURES FOR OBTAINING AND ANALYZING DATA

Figure 1, a diagrammatic flow chart, may be used as a guide for the following discussion of methodology.

Hypothesis 1

To test the first hypothesis, the questionnaire and rating scale were administered to the available student body on October 6, 1965. After a second administration during a scheduled make-up period, a total of 650 students (out of 658 eligible to participate in the study) had completed this instrument. From responses indicated by these students on the scale for rating graduate majors, it was possible to determine—by means of the nonparametric chi square test—whether they would choose or reject a possible graduate major in library science to a significantly greater or lesser degree than they would choose or reject a possible graduate major in any other area of specialization.

Hypothesis 2

The 650 students who completed the initial (pretest) administration of the questionnaire and rating scale also served as subjects in testing the second hypothesis, concerning the effectiveness of various recruitment techniques. The total group of subjects was divided by a process of

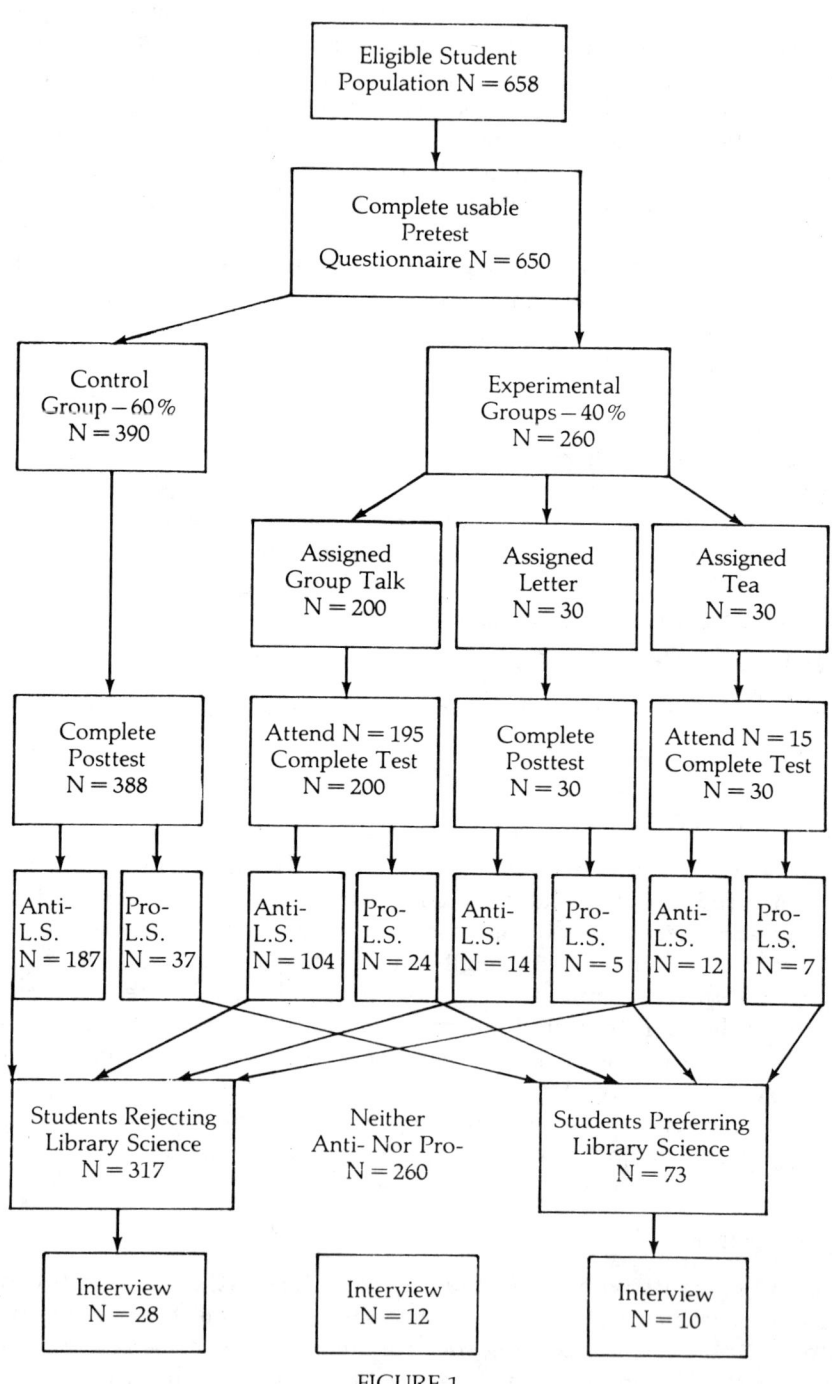

FIGURE 1.
Flow chart of major research activities.

representative random sampling into one control group (390 students) and three experimental groups.

In all cases, it was determined that $p > .95$ concerning the hypothesis that the experimental and control groups were representative of the total population for the factors of: (1) attitude toward library science as a possible graduate major; (2) class standing; and (3) undergraduate major. (Refer to Table 1 for a description of the three experimental groups.)

The three recruitment activities to which the experimental groups were exposed follows:

1. A recruitment talk was given by the researcher to a small group of students during an informal reception held in the college library. The subjects exposed to this experimental activity were invited by the librarians of Edgecliff College to attend a "tea" honoring the researcher, a recent alumna of the college. Of the 30 students invited, 15 students actually attended. At this time the researcher met informally with the students and chatted with them concerning career opportunities in librarianship, and scholarships and fellowships available for graduate study. Each of the students attending the tea was given two recruitment pamphlets, a reprint from *Changing Times* entitled "The Crying Need for Librarians" (1964) and "Future Unlimited; What You Need to Be a Librarian," a booklet prepared by the Office for Recruitment of the American Library Association (American Library Association, n.d.). The students also were encouraged to examine a display of library-science recruitment materials and to take any additional pamphlets of interest to them.

2. Essentially the same recruitment talk, in terms of content, was given by the researcher to a large group of students; however, this time there was no opportunity for interaction with the speaker through questions or discussion. Of the 200 students assigned to attend this session, 195 actually attended. Although recruitment materials were on display in the auditorium at the time of the large-group talk, most of the students did not take time at the conclusion of the assembly to examine these materials. Instead, most of the students saw only the same two pamphlets that had been given students at the informal reception and were distributed prior to the speaker's entrance at the large assembly.

3. A personal letter was sent to 30 students accompanied by recruitment literature chosen to appeal directly to each student's major area of subject interest. In addition to this individualized recruitment literature, each student received the same two general pamphlets distributed to all the subjects participating in the experimental groups.

All students assigned to the experimental groups were told that the

TABLE 1
Comparability of Experimental Groups and Total Population
with Regard to Three Primary Differentiating Factors

	Percent of subjects in				
	Experimental groups				Total population (N=650)
Differentiating factor	Talk (N=200)	Tea (N=30)	Letter (N=30)	Total (N=260)	
LIBRARY SCIENCE AS POSSIBLE GRADUATE MAJOR					
Definitely prefer	1.0	3.3	3.3	1.5	0.7
Might consider	5.5	6.7	6.7	5.8	6.0
Undecided (Neutral)	11.5	13.3	6.7	11.2	11.5
Probably reject	14.5	13.3	10.0	13.8	14.0
Definitely reject	67.5	63.3	73.3	67.7	67.8
CLASS STANDING					
Senior	9.5	10.0	6.7	9.2	9.5
Junior	15.5	16.7	20.0	16.2	16.0
Sophomore	25.5	26.7	23.3	25.4	25.4
Freshman	49.5	46.7	50.0	49.2	49.1
UNDERGRADUATE MAJOR					
Education	31.5	26.7	30.0	30.6	31.2
Home economics	9.0	3.3	6.7	8.0	8.5
Art	7.5	6.7	6.7	7.3	7.2
English	7.5	10.0	6.7	7.7	7.2
Psychology	7.0	6.7	10.0	7.3	7.2
Sociology	7.0	6.7	10.0	7.3	7.1
Mathematics	4.5	6.7	6.7	5.0	5.0
History	4.5	6.7	6.7	5.0	4.9
Biology	4.0	6.7	6.7	4.6	4.6
French	3.0	3.3	3.3	3.1	2.8
Speech	2.0	3.3	. .	1.9	2.0
Chemistry	1.5	3.3	3.3	1.9	1.7
Medical technology	1.5	. .	. .	1.2	1.5
Spanish	1.0	3.3	. .	1.2	1.2
Music	1.0	. .	3.3	1.2	1.1
Political science	1.0	3.3	. .	1.2	0.9
Foods	1.0	. .	. .	0.8	0.7
Philosophy	0.5	. .	. .	0.4	0.3
Miscellaneous	1.5	. .	. .	1.2	1.7
No major indicated	3.5	3.3	. .	3.4	3.2

researcher would be available on campus to meet personally with any students desiring more information about librarianship. At that time, the researcher had available bulletins from all of the accredited library schools plus additional information concerning library careers, and scholarships and fellowships available for graduate study.

After the experimental recruitment activities had been conducted, the rating scale of graduate majors and one section of the questionnaire, "Future Educational and Occupational Aspirations," were administered a second time, to the entire group of subjects. After make-ups were completed, 648 students completed this posttest. It was then possible to compare the pre- and posttest responses and to determine—by utilization, again, of the nonparametric chi square test—to what extent the control group and the experimental groups differed significantly (each one from the others) in terms of the dependent variable; i.e., the subjects' change in attitude toward library science as a possible graduate major.

Hypothesis 3

To test the third hypothesis, the subjects were categorized as either: (1) preferring, or (2) rejecting, a possible graduate major in library science. The 73 potential library recruits—i.e., the "students preferring library science"—included those subjects who rated library science on the posttest as a graduate field of study they would either: (1) "definitely prefer" or (2) "might consider." Conversely, the group of 317 "students rejecting library science" included those subjects who, on both the pre- and posttest administration of the rating scale, indicated that library science was a field of graduate specialization they would "definitely reject."

These two groups of subjects then were compared on the following variables:

1. Responses listed on the questionnaire pertaining to their backgrounds.
2. Information obtained from official college records.
3. Scores obtained on three standardized tests.

In comparing the group of students preferring library science with the group rejecting library science, with respect to the foregoing traits and characteristics, both parametric and nonparametric statistical techniques were employed.

The critical ratio (or t-test) was used to compare the difference between the means of the two groups for those test data that were normally distributed. The nonparametric median test was used to determine the difference between the medians of the two groups for the data that were not distributed in a normal manner. Finally, concerning data resulting from the subjects' response to different categories of answers on the questionnaire, the chi square test was utilized to determine if there was any difference between the manner in which the two groups of students responded to these various questions.

It was possible, then, to construct a "profile" of the potential library recruit that would differentiate students in this group from those students definitely not interested in a library career.

Hypothesis 4

To gather the necessary data to test the fourth hypothesis, semi-structured interviews with some representative random students were conducted for the purpose of obtaining information not likely to be elicited in questionnaire responses. Interviews were scheduled with fifty students who were chosen on a representative random basis. The stratification included the following factors: (1) attitude toward library science as a possible graduate major, (2) class standing, (3) undergraduate subject major and (4) degree of change of attitude, either positive or negative, toward library science after experimental library-recruitment activities. The extent to which the interview sample was representative of the total population with regard to the first three factors just noted is illustrated in Figure 2.

Each student selected to be interviewed was contacted individually by the researcher. Forty-eight agreed to meet with the researcher and complete the 15-minute interview.

HOW UNDERGRADUATE WOMEN RATED LIBRARIANSHIP AS A FUTURE CAREER CHOICE

Using data derived from the administration of the pretest rating scale listing 19 graduate fields of study, it was possible to ascertain student attitudes toward library science as a possible graduate major. As can be seen in Table 2, these undergraduate women did not look favorably upon library science as a possible graduate major. Only five students ($p<.001$) indicated they would "definitely prefer" a graduate major in library science. As might be expected, the graduate fields with the greatest number of "definitely prefer" responses were education (N = 260) and the social sciences (N = 107).

Essentially the same pattern prevailed with regard to the responses for the "definitely reject" category. Only engineering, architecture, and law—considered to be male professions at the time this research was conducted—were in more disfavor with the female subjects than was

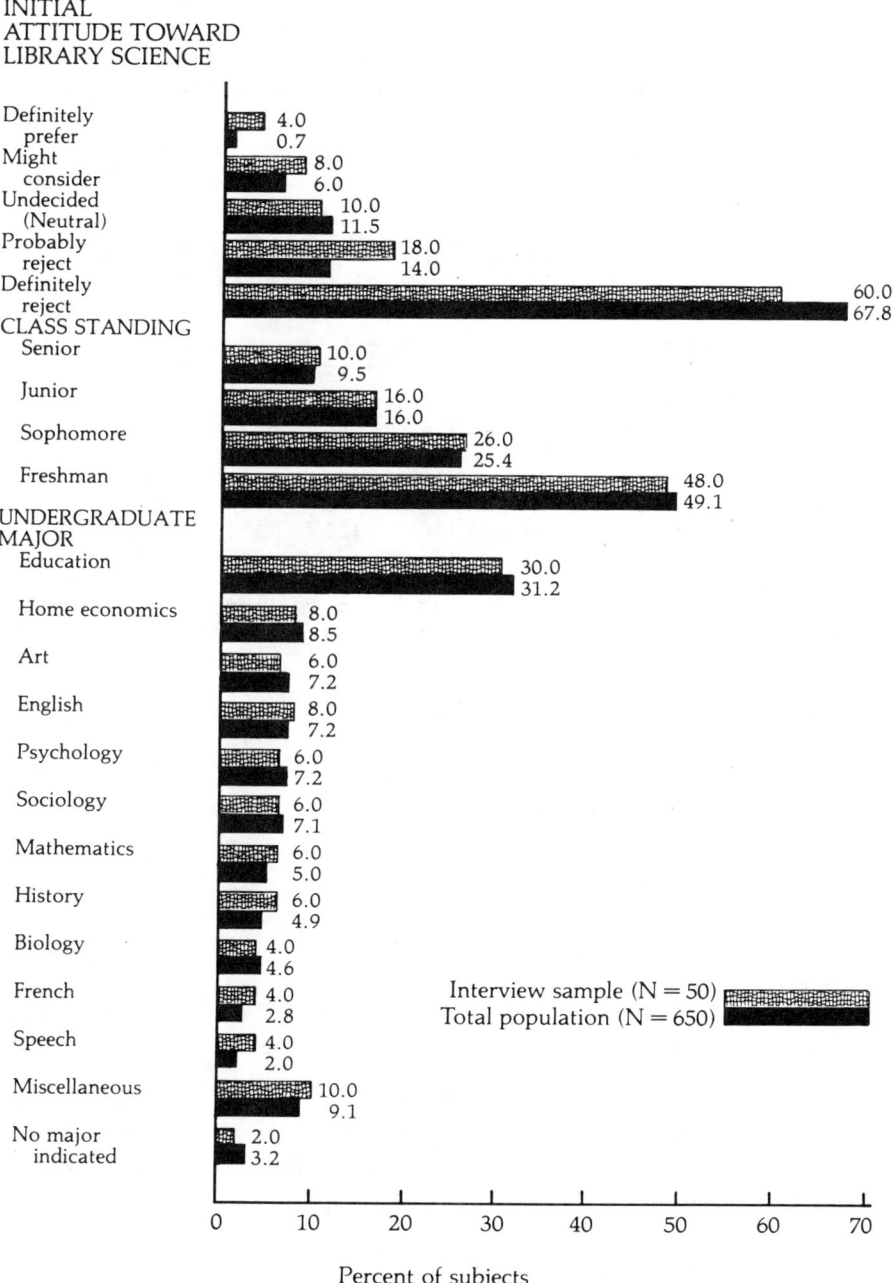

FIGURE 2.
Comparability of interview sample and total population with regard to three primary differentiating factors.

TABLE 2
Attitudes of 650 Undergraduate Female Students Toward
Various Fields of Study as Possible Graduate Majors
Prior to Librarianship-Recruitment Activities

Field of Study	Number of students checking each category					
	Definitely prefer (1)	Might consider (2)	Undecided (Neutral) (3)	Probably reject (4)	Definitely reject (5)	No response
Architecture	10	38	37	85	476	4
Biological sciences	48	87	64	124	324	3
Business & commerce	13	83	98	134	318	4
Education	260	194	69	57	67	3
Engineering	4	10	16	48	568	4
English & journalism	71	157	80	127	209	6
Fine & applied arts	96	138	120	124	167	5
Foreign language	71	176	106	111	181	5
Geography	18	82	84	156	306	4
Health professions	34	97	94	125	294	6
Home economics	81	130	105	100	231	3
Law	13	44	34	86	469	4
Library science	5	39	75	91	440	..
Mathematical subjects	46	66	60	78	398	2
Philosophy	19	119	115	118	273	6
Physical sciences	17	84	83	108	348	10
Psychology	99	245	123	61	119	3
Religion	19	95	154	129	248	5
Social sciences	107	173	95	95	177	3
Totals						
Number	1031	2057	1612	1957	5613	80
Percent	8.4	16.6	13.1	15.8	45.5	0.6

the graduate field of library science (p <.01). This finding was not unexpected, in light of the fact that prior research also had shown that library science was not a graduate field of specialization likely to appeal to undergraduate students.

EFFECTIVENESS OF RECRUITMENT ACTIVITIES UPON LIBRARIANSHIP AS A CAREER CHOICE

Would the overwhelmingly negative attitudes expressed by these students toward library science be changed as a result of their exposure to the experimental recruitment activities? To answer this question, approximately three weeks after the recruitment activities took place, the entire student body was again asked to complete the same rating scale of graduate majors. The result of this posttest administration can be seen in Table 3 (648 of the 650 students who completed a usable pretest administration of the rating scale also completed a usable posttest administration). This time, 13 students— as compared with 5 on the pretest—indicated that they would "definitely prefer" a graduate major in library science.

TABLE 3
Attitudes of 648 Undergraduate Female Students Toward
Various Fields of Study as Possible Graduate Majors
after Librarianship-Recruitment Activities

	Number of students checking each category					
Field of study	Definitely prefer (1)	Might consider (2)	Undecided (Neutral) (3)	Probably reject (4)	Definitely reject (5)	No response
Architecture	9	54	60	120	404	1
Biological sciences	58	115	84	141	247	3
Business & commerce	17	95	129	154	251	2
Education	290	182	60	56	58	2
Engineering	5	17	25	80	520	1
English & journalism	83	176	96	134	154	5
Fine & applied arts	114	161	128	118	126	1
Foreign language	75	201	104	109	158	1
Geography	24	91	144	150	237	2
Health professions	41	123	108	147	228	1
Home economics	98	149	119	110	172	.
Law	15	50	73	109	400	1
Library science	13	60	83	136	356	.
Mathematical subjects	52	64	58	100	371	3
Philosophy	21	95	133	150	248	1
Physical sciences	25	92	89	145	293	4
Psychology	117	243	116	82	88	2
Religion	21	97	151	153	223	3
Social sciences	134	174	114	98	128	.
Totals						
Number	1212	2239	1874	2292	4662	33
Percent	9.8	18.2	15.2	18.6	37.9	0.3

To ascertain the relative quantitative improvement for library science's position as a possible graduate major, the responses to Question 37 (indicate preferred graduate fields) on the questionnaire also were utilized. As may be noted in Figure 3, the degree to which students chose library science as a possible graduate major on the posttest administration of the questionnaire, compared to the prettest administration, was dramatically greater than for any other listed field of study.

With regard to the three experimental recruitment activities, it was found that they differed significantly in terms of their effectiveness. The informal small-group talk proved to be the most effective means of

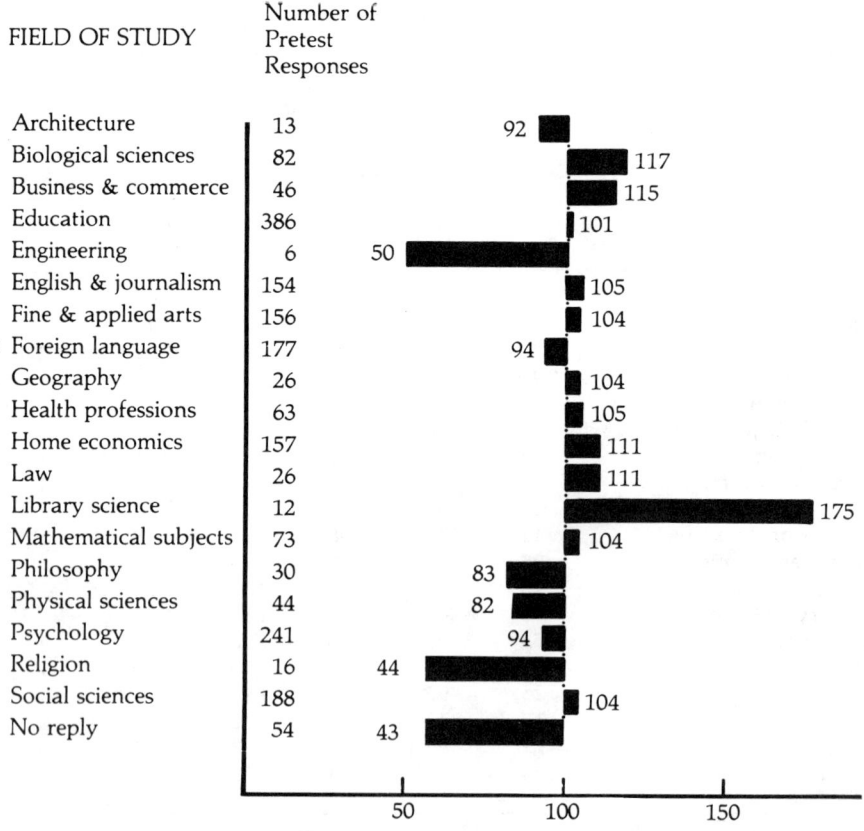

FIGURE 3.
Relative change in choice of graduate majors before and after librarianship recruitment activities.

instilling positive attitudes toward library science in the undergraduate-women subjects. The change in attitude among the 15 students attending the tea was not only quite dramatic, but highly significant statistically (p<.001). Thus, while only 3 students of the 30 invited to the tea had indicated on the pretest administration of the rating scale that they either "definitely preferred" or "might consider" a graduate major in library science, 7 of the 15 students who attended the tea selected one of these responses as representing their attitude on the posttest administration of the same scale for rating graduate majors (see Figure 4). Even taking into account the entire group of 30 students, including those 15 students not attending the tea, the change of attitude toward library science for the total group assigned to the tea resulted in a p<.05. To what extent these changes might or might not be sustained over a longer time span was beyond the scope of this study.

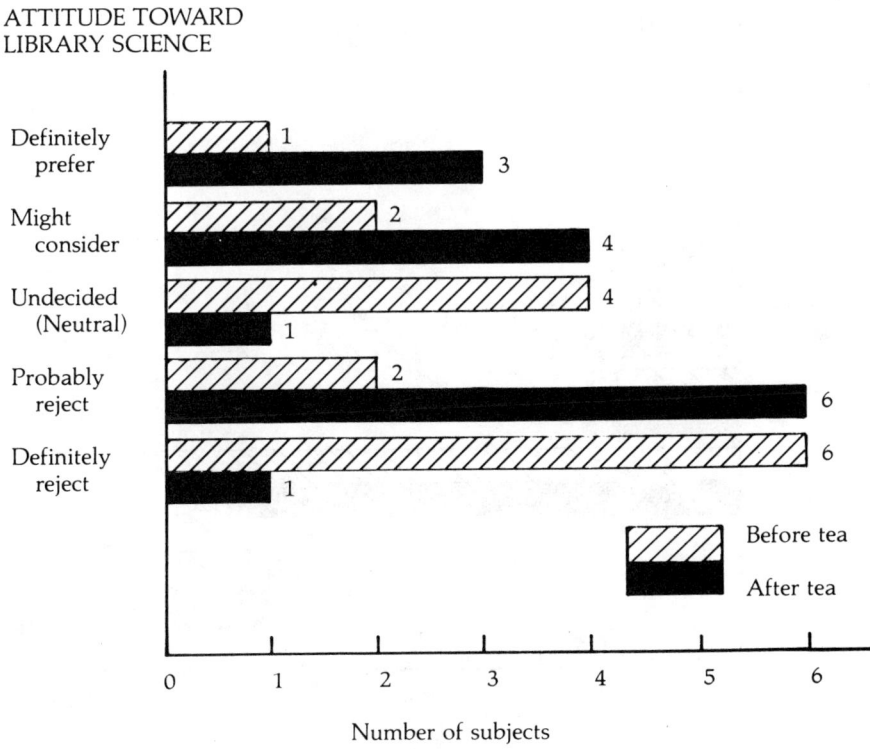

FIGURE 4.
Change in attitude of 15 subjects toward library science as a possible graduate major, after attending a library recruitment tea.

84 WOMEN IN LIBRARIANSHIP

With regard to the other two experimental recruitment activities, the personal letter accompanied by individually selected recruitment literature that was sent to another group of 30 students appeared to be a more effective means of favorably changing attitudes toward library science than was the large-group talk, attended by 195 students (see figures 5 and 6). However, the changes in attitude that followed these two experimental recruitment activities were in neither case statistically significant.

THE POTENTIAL LIBRARY RECRUIT—A PROFILE

In order to develop a profile of the potential library recruit, it was necessary first to determine statistically those traits common to the "average" potential recruit. Then this group of potential library recruits (N=73) was compared with a similar group of subjects rejecting a

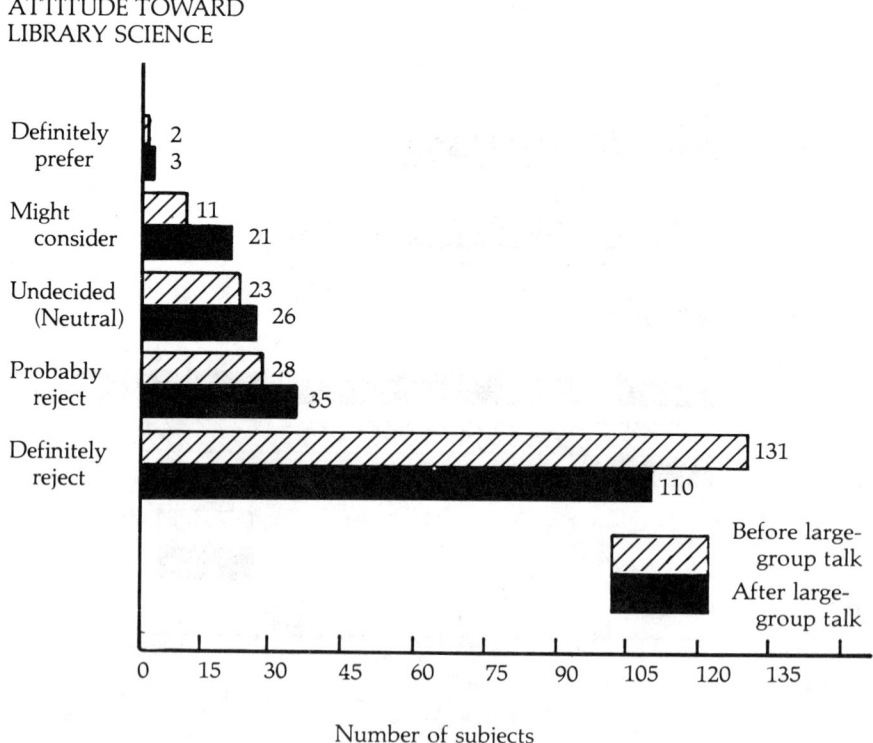

FIGURE 5.
Change in attitude of 195 subjects toward library science as a possible graduate major, after attending a large-group recruitment talk.

graduate major in library science (N=317). As a result, it is clear that the two groups could be differentiated on a number of variables, as indicated below.

Intelligence

Potential library recruits achieved significantly higher mean scores on both the verbal and mathematics sections of the College Entrance Examination Board Scholastic Aptitude Test. (In both cases, $p<.05$; see Figure 7.)

Personality traits

Administration of the Edwards Personal Preference Schedule revealed statistically significant differences between the mean scores of the undergraduate women preferring a graduate major in library science as

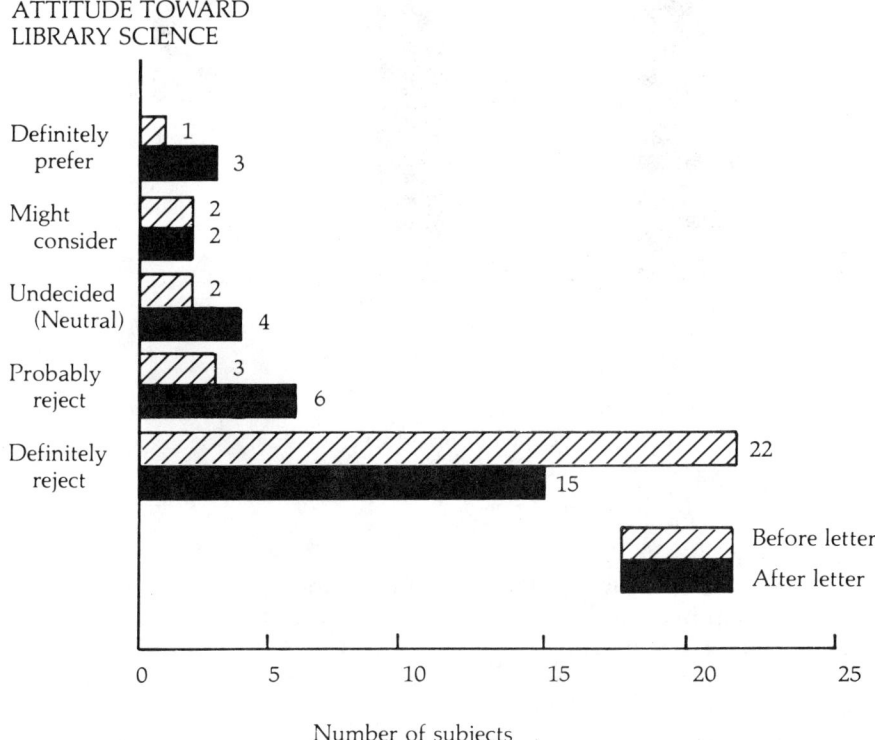

FIGURE 6.
Change in attitude of 30 subjects toward library science as a possible graduate major, after receiving a library-recruitment letter.

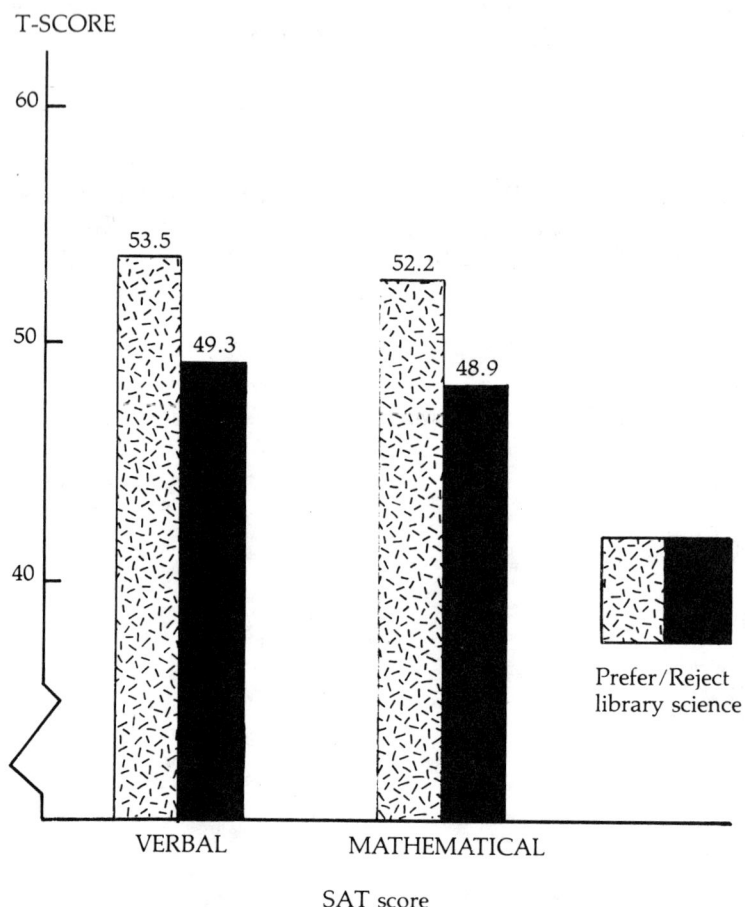

FIGURE 7.
SAT T-scores for subjects either preferring or rejecting library science.

compared with those students rejecting library science because of certain "manifest needs." The potential library recruits attained a higher mean score ($p < .05$) for the manifest need of "order," and lower mean scores ($p < .05$) for the manifest needs of "autonomy" and "heterosexuality" (see Table 4).

These findings indicated that the undergraduate women preferring a graduate major in library science would be more likely than those rejecting such a major (according to the definitions given in the EPPS Manual [Edwards, 1959, p. 11]) to be persons who would have written work neat and organized, make plans before starting on a difficult task, have things organized, keep things neat and orderly, make advance plans when taking a trip, organize details of work, have things arranged so that they run smoothly without change (Order).

On the other hand, they would be less likely to be persons who would

be able to come and go as desired, say what [they] think about things, be independent of others in making decisions, criticize those in positions of authority, and avoid responsibilities and obligations (Autonomy);

go out with members of the oppostite sex, be in love with someone of the opposite sex, be regarded as physically attractive by those of the opposite sex, read books and plays involving sex, listen to or tell jokes involving sex, become sexually excited (Heterosexuality).

On the Allport, Vernon, and Lindzey Study of Values, the group of potential library recruits attained a higher mean score for the value of "aesthetic" ($p<.01$), and lower mean scores for the "economic" ($p<.05$) and "political" ($p<.01$) values (see Figure 8).

TABLE 4
Percentile Equivalents for Mean Scores Obtained on the
Edwards Personal Preference Schedule
by Undergraduate Female Students

	Percentile Rank		
Manifest need	Total college population	Students preferring graduate major in library science	Students rejecting graduate major in library science
Achievement	48	54	44
Deference	42	48	39
Order	51	63	46
Exhibition	63	61	65
Autonomy	61	51	65
Affiliation	50	47	51
Intraception	46	40	46
Succorance	63	71	63
Dominance	40	36	41
Abasement	66	69	70
Nurturance	60	62	60
Change	57	53	57
Endurance	50	56	48
Heterosexuality	50	40	51
Aggression	65	64	67
Consistency	55	49	53

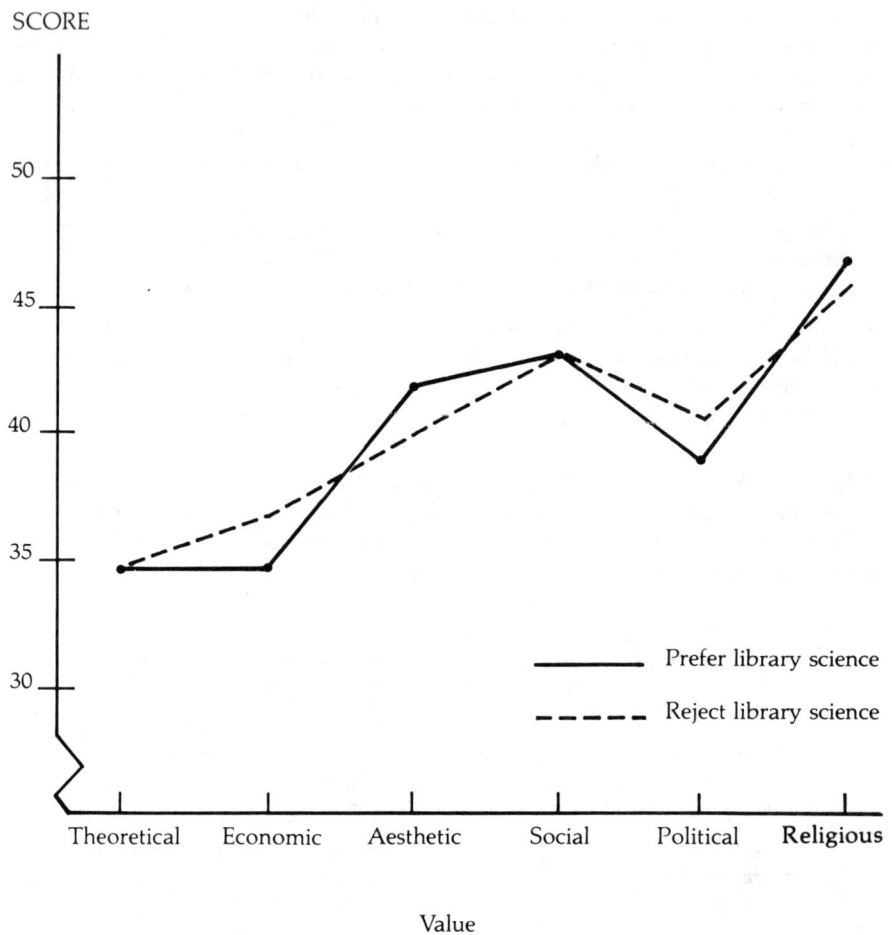

FIGURE 8.
Mean scores obtained by undergraduate female students on the Allport, Vernon, Lindzey Study of Values.

Thus, utilizing the descriptions given by the authors of the *Study of Values* (Allport, et al., 1960, pp. 4-5), the undergraduate students preferring a graduate major in library science would more likely be persons who would

see their highest value in form and harmony. Regard life as a procession of events; each single impression is enjoyed for its own sake. Each single experience is judged from the standpoint of grace, symmetry, or fitness (Aesthetic).

On the other hand, they would be less likely to be persons who would characteristically be interested in what is useful. Based originally upon the satisfaction of bodily needs (self-preservation), the interest in utilities develops to embrace the practical affairs of the business world—the production, marketing, and consumption of goods, the elaboration of credit, and the accumulation of tangible wealth. This type is thoroughly "practical" and conforms well to the prevailing stereotype of the average American businessman (Economic).

be interested primarily in power. Their activities are not necessarily within the narrow field of politics. Leaders in any field generally have high power value. Since competition and struggle play a large part in all life, many philosophers have seen power as the most universal and most fundamental of motives. There are, however, certain personalities in whom the desire for a direct expression of this motive is uppermost, who above all else for personal power, influence, and renown (Political).

Years of college completed

No reliable difference was found between the two groups of students, with respect to class standing. Seniors seemed more inclined than other class groups to prefer library science, while the sophomores tended more to reject library science. Neither difference, however, was statistically significant.

Major subject area

Potential library recruits were more likely to major in education ($p < .05$) at the undergraduate level and less likely to choose home economics ($p < .05$) as an undergraduate major than were students not interested in a library career.

Scholastic record

Not only did the potential library recruits obtain higher mean scores on the SAT taken in their senior year in high school, but they also graduated from high school with a higher academic rank ($p < .05$). Their ability and motivation to earn good grades evidently carried over into the college years, for they achieved higher grade-point averages than the other group of students during all four years of college. These differences were statistically significant at the freshman level ($p < .05$), as well as at the sophomore level ($p < .001$). In addition, the potential library recruits achieved a higher overall undergraduate grade-point average ($p < .05$) than did those students rejecting library science as a possible graduate major.

Participation in extracurricular activities

Although approximately the same proportion of students from both groups participated in college-sponsored activities and held membership in some civic, religious, or social organization, the potential library recruits were less likely to hold office in any club or organization. However, this difference did not meet the required level of statistical significance.

The two groups of students, however, did differ significantly with respect to their favorite recreational activities. As might be expected, the potential library recruits listed "reading" as their favorite recreational activity ($p<.001$), while the students rejecting library science preferred an "outdoor sport or game" ($p<.05$).

Reading habits and use of the library

As reading was found to be the favorite recreational activity of the potential library recruits, it came as no surprise to discover that these students had read more books, both fiction ($p<.05$) and nonfiction ($p<.05$), during a designated five-week period than had the students rejecting library science. The potential library recruits also reported more frequent use of libraries. Thus, while attending high school, they used their public library or school library more often than the other group, both for school assignments ($p<.01$) and for personal reading enjoyment ($p<.05$). While attending college, they continued to use both public libraries as well as their college library more frequently than the students rejecting library science for their own reading enjoyment ($p<.01$).

Work experience

Although the most frequently reported part-time job held by both groups of students was babysitting, significant differences were found with respect to two other types of part-time work. More students rejecting library science had held part-time jobs as salesgirls ($p<.05$), while more potential library recruits had been library assistants ($p<.01$).

Family educational and occupational background

A factor that significantly differentiated undergraduate students preferring, from those rejecting, library science as a possible graduate major was the educational achievement of their parents. A lower level of terminal education characterized both the fathers ($p<.001$) and the mothers (p<.05) of the potential library recruits. With regard to parental occupations, on the other hand, no statistically significant difference was found between either the fathers or the mothers of these two groups of students, although fewer of the fathers of the potential library recruits were engaged in clerical or sales work.

Two additional findings resulted from testing the third hypothesis. Potential library recruits as a group were much more likely to complete a library-science course at the undergraduate level (p<.001), and a much greater proportion of this group also was considering teaching as a future career (p<.01).

FACTORS ASSOCIATED WITH CHOICE OR REJECTION OF LIBRARIANSHIP

The primary purpose of the interviews was to ascertain what factors influence undergraduate women to choose or reject a possible career in librarianship. Specific factors investigated included: (1) the subjects' perceived future goals and needs; (2) their concept of libraries and librarians, as previously influenced by individuals; (3) the effectiveness of library-recruitment publicity; and (4) their association with libraries. Although 50 students had been selected to be interviewed, 2 students were ill at the time the interviews took place. Data resulting from these 48 interviews did not lend themselves in all respects to analysis by inferential statistics, but the findings presented below appeared to the interviewer to be warranted.

Perceived Future Goals and Needs

The potential library recruits, as compared with the undergraduate women not interested in library science, were more career-oriented and much more willing to consider a career requiring a professional or graduate degree. In addition, a primary job requirement for these potential library recruits was "financial security," whereas the "opportunity to exercise leadership ability" was relatively unimportant (see Table 5).

The desire to work with people and to be helpful was mentioned in one way or another by practically all of the students. Of course, it should be realized that these interviews were conducted at a time when many of the students were vitally interested in serving in the Peace Corps or in the local poverty programs. Whenever the interviewer mentioned library service in poverty areas, she usually struck a responsive note. Indeed, several students from the control group were enthusiastic about this concept of library service when the idea was first presented to them, at the time of the interview.

Table 5
Requirements Undergraduate Female Students Felt Were Necessary in the "Ideal" Job or Profession

Requirements for "ideal" job or profession	Number of undergraduate female students							
	Professing an interest in library science (N = 10)				Not indicating an interest in library science (N = 38)			
	Choice				Choice			
	1st	2nd	3rd	Total	1st	2nd	3rd	Total
Financial security	2	2	1	5	3	2	4	9
Opportunity to earn quite a lot of money	—	1	—	1	—	—	1	1
Social status and prestige in the community	—	—	1	1	—	—	2	2
Opportunity to exercise leadership ability	—	—	—	—	1	4	—	5
Opportunity to use my special abilities or aptitudes	3	1	—	4	9	3	6	18
Opportunity to be creative and original	1	—	2	3	6	2	5	13
Opportunity to be helpful to others	2	2	1	5	6	10	6	22
Opportunity to work with people rather than things	—	2	1	3	7	8	5	20
Opportunity for adventure	—	—	3	3	1	1	3	5
Opportunity for intellectual growth	2	2	1	5	5	8	6	19

Many of the students thought that library work would be boring, routine, clerical in nature, and also physically confining. As one sophomore said, "Librarians are individuals who like clerical work... accuracy and precision. And that's not me!" Another student who was considering a career in journalism said: "Librarians don't lead a very adventurous life. They get their kicks out of reading rather than doing things." She also stated that she was not interested in "labeling books" for a living. A junior history major felt she was sure she would "feel out of touch with life" if she worked in a library.

Another student did not think career opportunities for women in the library field were good, "since the heads of departments and libraries are usually men." She noted that "some women at the Cincinnati Public Library have held the same position for the last 30 years."

Five of the ten potential library recruits indicated during the interview sessions that they probably would have to become teachers after graduation, not librarians. Without exception, these students felt a financial obligation to accept employment immediately after receiving their baccalaureate degree. Thus, they favored completion of part-time graduate work in the field of education, rather than enrolling in a full-time program in library science. Moreover, as several of them noted, there were no universities offering graduate library-science programs within the commuting distance of Cincinnati. Two of the students also mentioned that their parents definitely would not approve of their going away to graduate school, since they were "girls."

The remaining five potential library recruits who were interviewed gave these reasons for wishing to become librarians: (1) "I like medicine and want to work in a related area" (future medical librarian); (2) "I want to use my subject major" (future reference librarian); (3) "I want to help people love books"; (4) "I want to work with children" (future children's or school librarian); and (5) "Intellectual growth is important to me."

Concept of Libraries and Librarians as Influenced by Individuals

The individuals discussed in this section will be categorized as either nonlibrarians or librarians. With regard to nonlibrarians, the researcher was unable to identify during the course of the interviews even one high-school counselor or teacher or any college professor who had suggested librarianship as a possible career choice to any one of the 48 interviewees. In contrast, the students frequently mentioned high-school counselors, teachers, parents, family, and friends as having had a considerable influence upon their choice of other careers, especially teaching.

Only one student could recall her mother's suggesting that she consider librarianship, and this student "definitely rejected" a library career. Indeed, the few comments made by nonlibrarians concerning librarianship as a future career choice appeared to have had a definite negative effect. For example, one of the subjects commented that her brother frequently teased her about becoming an old-maid librarian, and another student was certain her neighbor's suggestion that she become a librarian was not meant to be flattering. Indeed, one of the potential library recruits mentioned that her friends' unfavorable comments upset her so much when she announced her decision to become a librarian that she had some misgivings concerning this career choice.

With regard to the effectiveness of librarians as recruiting agents for the profession, those librarians with whom the interviewees came into contact rarely seemed to have motivated them to consider future library careers. Even more revealing was the fact that a number of the librarians mentioned by the students actually seemed to have had a negative influence and caused the students to reject even the possibility of future attendance at a graduate library school. These "unfriendly" librarians, as characterized by the interviewees, seemed to be more concerned with the clerical aspects of running their libraries than with helping the students to use and enjoy them.

As might be expected, the potential library recruits had experienced a greater degree of positive association with individual librarians than had those students not indicating an interest in library science. The difference between the two groups is statistically significant ($p < .001$) for the response to the question: "Did any librarian ever suggest librarianship to you as a possible career choice?" The students professing an interest in library science tended more often to answer "yes" to this question. Even so, only six potential library recruits and one student not indicating an interest in library science could recall any librarians ever having suggested that they consider library careers, and in two of these cases the librarian referred to was the researcher herself. Other librarians mentioned by the interviewees as influencing them to consider librarianship included the librarians of Edgecliff College, two high-school librarians, and two public librarians, one of whom was a relative.

For the most part, the librarians cited by the students as having been a positive influence tended to recruit actively only after they were aware of a girl's interest in librarianship. For example, one of the potential library recruits recalled:

After I started working part-time in the public library and became interested in becoming a librarian, I happened to meet my old high-school librarian at an alumnae meeting. When I told her I was thinking about becoming a librarian, she gave me a whole lot of material about library jobs and salaries and information about library schools. Ever since, she's gone out of her way to be friendly, but why didn't she do this before?

With one exception, not even the librarians who were personal friends and relatives of the subjects were active recruiters. Several of the students mentioned that their friends seemed to enjoy their work very much, but they could not recall their ever having tried to brief them on the advantages of becoming a librarian.

Library-recruitment Publicity

The most significant factor with regard to library-recruitment publicity was its almost total absence. Most of the subjects interviewed could not recall ever having read about library careers—prior to the experimental recruitment activities, that is—or having seen any library recruitment films, posters, advertisements, etc., although scholarship information was posted on bulletin boards.

While the potential library recruits usually read some vocational material concerning library careers after they became interested in the profession ($p < .05$), the interviewees—as a group—were for the most part uninformed about librarianship and its opportunities, and most were unaware of the existence of graduate library-education programs. Thus, the researcher would have to agree with a statement made by Agnes Reagan (1958b): "Where students were influenced by printed materials, it was quite often evident that they were already thinking about the possibility of library work. The interest or the inclination was there, and the materials consulted tended to solidify, rather than to originate, interest in the profession" (p. 61).

Informal publicity, such as a book talk given by a librarian on TV, seemed to have had a positive influence in several cases, but the unattractive image of the librarian, as portrayed occasionally in books, magazines, films, and so on, served to deter students from choosing a library career. For example, in giving her impression of a librarian, one student mentioned a TV dandruff commercial utilizing a "real old, frail lady librarian."

In attempting to stimulate interest in librarianship, the interviewer found that these students were especially curious about the work of special librarians, with whom they had not previously come into contact, and whose responsibilities seemed more glamorous to them than those of public or school librarians. They also enjoyed hearing about the "library of the future" and the role computers can play in improving library service.

All of the interviewees who had attended the tea had favorable comments about this experimental recruitment activity. Such was not the case in regard to the large-group talk. The forced-attendance atmosphere of this experimental recruitment activity seemingly caused many of the students to feel resentful. Consequently they "tuned out," and the researcher was, for the most part, unsuccessful in capturing their attention.

As for the interviewees who were sent letters and recruitment literature in the mail, in a few cases the recruitment material immediately sparked their interest in a library career; in other cases the interviewees admitted tossing out the material without looking at it.

Association with Libraries

Figure 9 shows the response of the interviewees to questions pertaining to their access to and use of libraries. As the data in the figure indicate, there is no discernible difference between the two groups of students concerning their use of or access to libraries.

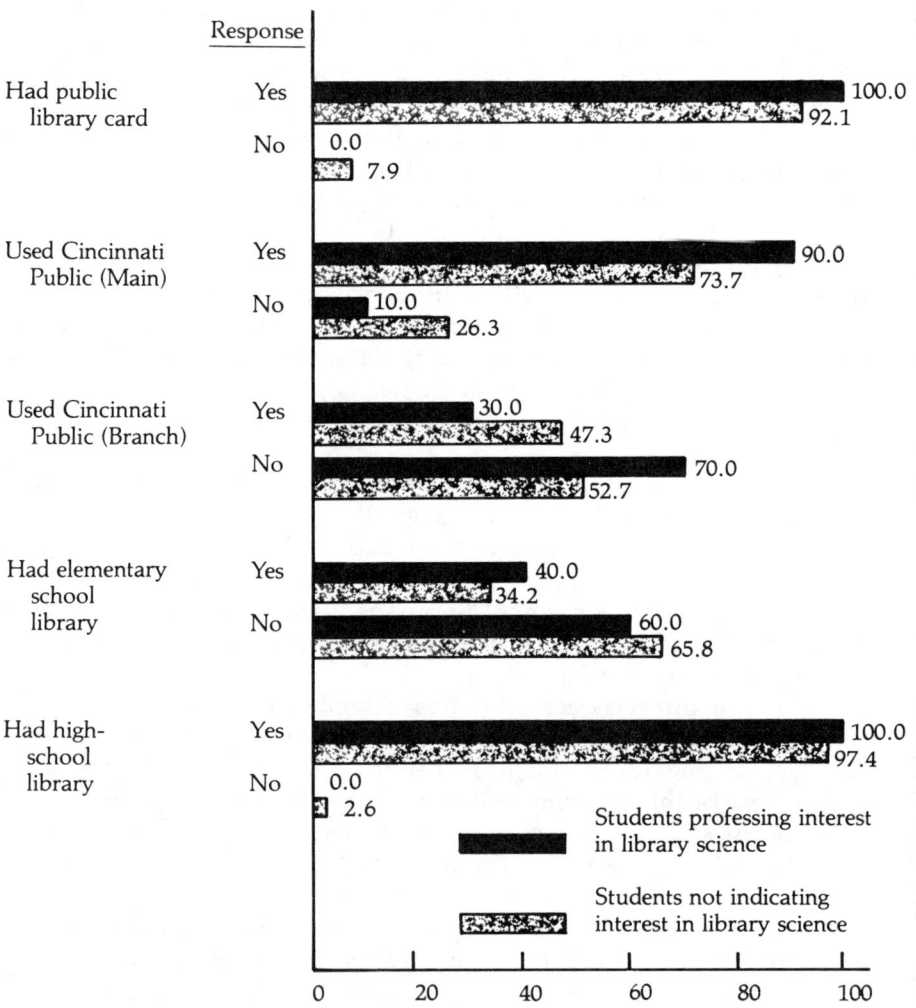

FIGURE 9.
Access to and use of libraries by undergraduate female students.

As already reported, a greater proportion of potential library recruits had completed some part-time work in libraries. Of those students who had done so, more of the potential library recruits had been assigned some challenging tasks, while most of the students rejecting library science had been given only what they considered to be menial and distasteful jobs, such as shelving books and filing catalog cards.

PROFILE OF A POTENTIAL LIBRARY RECRUIT— A SUMMARY

In summarizing the findings of this study, especially with regard to the testing of the third and fourth hypotheses, it was possible to draw a profile of an undergraduate woman who can be characterized as a potential recruit to the library profession. The characteristics and traits that comprise this profile were determined by comparing potential library recruits with those undergraduate women rejecting a graduate major in library science.

Thus, the potential library recruit comes from a family in which both father and mother have achieved a relatively low educational level. Neither parent is likely to have attended college. The recruit herself, however, has a high intellectual aptitude, both verbal and quantitative. She received good grades in high school and will continue to achieve a high-grade point average in college.

The potential library recruit enjoys the "aesthetic" values of life and especially likes to read. Outdoor games and sports, on the other hand, do not hold as much appeal for her as for the average college student.

As reading is her favorite recreational activity, the potential library recruit generally makes frequent use of libraries and comes to know, and is known by, librarians. Both in high school and in college, she regularly uses her school library, as well as the public library, not only to complete school assignments but also for her own reading enjoyment. As a rule, the potential library recruit will make an effort to learn how to use the resources of a large research library, rather than to rely upon an easier-to-use and more conveniently located branch library. While in college, the potential library recruit is likely to enroll in an introductory course in library science. In addition, she usually has some library-work experience, which she has found challenging and rewarding, even if it were only volunteer assistance in a high-school library.

With respect to personality traits, the potential library recruit may be characterized as an "orderly" person; i.e., one who likes her work to be neat and well organized. She is not interested in being a leader, as evidenced by her low test score in "autonomy" and her low interest in "political" values. Moreover, she does not express a desire to have the "opportunity to exercise leadership ability," nor is she likely to hold office in any of the clubs or organizations to which she belongs. The fact that both she and her father tend to avoid sales work indicates that she will be unlikely to seek a job that involves continuous interaction with other people.

The potential library recruit is career-oriented and is willing to consider graduate study. She is not likely to be planning marriage immediately after college graduation and may well anticipate the likelihood of an unmarried life (a possibility substantiated by her low score on the "heterosexuality" portion of the EPPS). Perhaps because she faces the prospect of earning her own living, the potential library recruit is interested in "financial security," although she does not express a desire "to earn quite a lot of money"; nor does she have high "economic" values.

Finally, the potential library recruit will have much the same career goals as the education major and will herself frequently choose to major in education at the undergraduate level. However, at the time she decides to make teaching her future career, she is likely to be unaware of the opportunities the library profession could offer her.

If one impression was made preponderantly clear to the investigator during the conduct of this study, it was that the best stimulus the library profession could offer, with regard to attracting top-quality undergraduate women with the potential for professional leadership, would be to improve the image of the "librarian." A great many of the students interviewed described librarians in most unflattering terms. Many students also believed that library work is primarily clerical in nature and thus would be boring and unchallenging. Most students used the word "librarian" in reference to all library personnel and were unable to distinguish clearly between professional librarians and clerical and subprofessional library employees.

NOTES

1. Data were derived from three sources: Cartter (1964), Parker (1965), and U.S. Dept. of Health, Education, and Welfare (1965b).
2. Not included in the group of 658 subjects were 126 nuns and 110 nurses enrolled at Edgecliff College at the time the study was being conducted.

Assertiveness Training for Library-School Students

ADELAIDE WEIR SUKIENNIK

THE FEMINIST MOVEMENT, which began in the eighteenth century (Schneir, 1972) and at the present time continues to be a major social issue, is of central importance to any profession that includes a large number of women, because the social role of women, in essence, defines the role of such professions. Whether one believes that women are discriminated against economically, politically, and legally, and are socialized from infancy to become passive, dependent individuals whose true spirits and natures are repressed, or whether one adheres to the traditional beliefs regarding woman's nature and social role, the fact remains that women are active in large numbers on all levels of the work force in the United States today and that these women are in a demonstrably disadvantaged position in comparison with men workers, regarding both position and salary. The differential between men's and women's salaries actually has increased since 1955, due primarily to overrepresentation of women in low-skilled, low-paying jobs. Salary comparisons for professionals, however, also show differentials by sex (U.S. Department of Labor, 1970). Quite logically, women earn the most money in jobs requiring above-average educational preparation. The fact that women also earn more in fields that employ smaller numbers of women is of less-evident logic, until one examines the situation of women in fields that are predominantly female and at the same time analyzes the situation of these occupations and professions vis-a-vis those that are predominantly male.

Three characteristics are evident in all fields that are predominantly female:

1. Within the hierarchy of all occupations/professions, they are low in status, prestige, and income.
2. Administrative positions are usually held by men.
3. Men earn more than women who are at equal levels of occupational/professional development (Simpson and Simpson, 1969).

This situation is evident in librarianship, as well as in the other "women's" professions of teaching, social work, and nursing. Despite the major significance of this problem, however, it has not been taken seriously, or even identified as a problem. Little attention has been paid to it in education for librarianship, and only a limited amount of research has dealt with any of its aspects. Research touching, in some way, on women librarians, may be divided into three categories: (1) research dealing specifically with women librarians, (2) research concerning the personality of the librarian, and (3) research on the career of the librarian. Only selected works from the body of research will be reviewed here. Other essays in this volume elaborate on the rest.

WOMEN LIBRARIANS

Holt (1957) examined women graduates of one library school for a 19-year period, to determine what trends could be observed. While this research is not concerned with the status of women per se, it includes some relevant findings:

1. The average interim between undergraduate school and library school for women tended to be decreasing.
2. An increasing number of women were entering academic, special, and armed-forces libraries.
3. Over half of the women either had remained in one position or had changed jobs only once. No detailed analysis was made of how many women left the profession for marriage and/or the rearing of children, but the comment was made that "several" left the field to become full-time homemakers, while still others, after an interim of a few years, return to to the profession when home responsibility lessens. Of the 592 women who responded to the questionnaire, 6 never entered library work, and 10 did so but later went into other areas of employment (p. 15).

Parrott (1962) described the women librarians listed in *Who's Who of American Women, 1958-1959*. Ward (1966) studied the problem of the employment of married women librarians in Great Britain. The population surveyed was a group of qualified women who had left the profession after marriage. Factors they cited that prevented their return included problems such as inconvenient and inflexible hours, lack of part-time positions, difficulty in finding child care, and the problem of obtaining domestic help. Other reasons mentioned were prejudice against the employment of married women, lack of refresher courses, and lack of encouragement to return.

PERSONALITY OF THE LIBRARIAN

Coker's (1958) study involved a content analysis of library literature from 1927 to 1958, in search of a list of personality traits deemed desirable for librarians. From this list Coker developed a checklist to be used by library-school faculty for the evaluation of students, both at entry and at graduation. No real sex-related orientation can be discerned in the checklist, nor can any clear-cut picture be drawn of the ideal librarian, according to the literature surveyed. The final list of traits is a variegated one, beginning with courtesy, emotional stability, friendliness, and appearance, and ending with health, attitude toward work, productivity, alertness, and approachability for the library's public. These qualities seem desirable for persons in any occupation. Apparently, the librarians who wrote during the years studied could define no unique set of traits related to a specific task orientation; i.e., desirable personality traits related to aspects of job performance.

Bryan (1952), Douglass (1957), Rainwater (1962), and McMahon (1967) studied varying populations of librarians from 1952 through 1967, by gathering demographic data from questionnaires and administering personality instruments. All four studies showed the "average" librarian to be more deferential than the general population and to possess to a greater degree a set of qualities that can be summarized by the term "endurance." They also showed the librarian less likely to be affiliative, less dominant, less heterosexual in interests, and less aggressive than the normative populations. All the studies agreed that the same variables applied to both males and females within the total population of librarians.

Rainwater (1962), using the Edwards Personal Preference Schedules on a group of 94 University of Texas Graduate School of Library Science students, found the experimental group rated significantly higher than established norms, when tested for achievement, deference, and order, and lower in exhibition, heterosexuality, and aggression. There was no significant difference in the other six variables (autonomy, intraception, succorance, abasement, nurturance, and change). The men in the group rated significantly higher than the male norm in achievement, deference, and order, and lower in exhibition, heterosexuality, and aggression. The women's scores were higher than the female norm in deference, order, and endurance, and lower in exhibition, affiliation, dominance, and aggression. Within the experimental group, there was no significant difference between the scores of the men and the scores of the women. The women in the group were older than the men, and were 12 years older, on the average, than the women in the normative group.

Bryan's (1952) work utilized the Guilford-Martin personality inventory as part of a study of the public librarian published in 1952. This instrument measures the following traits: (1) pressure for overt activity, (2) leadership and ascendency in social situations, as opposed to submissiveness, (3) masculinity/femininity of attitudes and interests, (4) self-confidence, and (5) lack of irritability and nervous tension. In general, male librarians were more submissive socially than, and did not exhibit leadership tendencies as strong as, the normative group (university students). Their attitudes and interests fell within the "normal" range of masculinity, as defined by this test. A lack of self-confidence, accompanied by feelings of inferiority, was revealed, but not excessive nervous tension or irritability. The female librarian revealed a strikingly similar personality profile.

Douglass's (1957) study is the most detailed. The results, like Bryan's, must be evaluated in terms of their historical context. From the literature and from a rating by library-school students, Douglass formulated a character not unlike the stereotype of the librarian—meticulous, compulsive, conservative, conformist, introspective, non-social, passive, submissive, mild, irritable, and inhibited, and tending to be a follower rather than a leader. From these qualities, he formulated eight hypotheses, which he tested on a population of 525 men and women enrolled in 17 accredited library schools in 1947-48 and on 20 men enrolled from 1955 to 1957 at the library school of the University of Texas. Using five different tests, he accumulated an impressive array of findings concerning the personality of the librarian. In general, he arrived at a picture not so extreme as the stereotype that emerged from his literature survey and student ratings, but akin to them in many ways. His most significant finding was that those librarians tested lacked ascendency, drive, leadership qualities, and motivation. One often-misinterpreted finding of this study is that, according to the test used in determining femininity/masculinity, the men are markedly more feminine than the normative group. Most tests used to determine femininity/masculinity are sexist by present standards, including the one Douglass employed. They equate femininity with interests in the literary, aesthetic, and cultural aspects of life. The term "feminine" to describe persons with such interests is an unfortunate misnomer. Yet much has been made of the "femininity" of male librarians as determined by this and other similar tests. Douglass's conclusions, on the whole, are negative. He states that the small group of librarians *not* conforming to the norms indicated by his study may possibly provide "the leadership, the scholarship, and the research required for progress in the profession" (p. 125), but he saw little hope if the majority prevailed.

McMahon's (1967) study was conducted on a group of 30 Australian librarians working in public, university, and special libraries. She used two of the same instruments as Douglass, the Minnesota Multiphasic Personality Inventory and the Allport-Vernon Study of Values, plus two others and an information sheet. The population was extremely small, and representative of a comparatively isolated part of the world. Therefore, one might expect the results to be somewhat different from the others already cited, but they were essentially the same. One positive conclusion was that the subjects seemed to have a "mildly favorable" attitude toward librarianship.

CAREER OF THE LIBRARIAN

Reeling (1969) studied 396 undergraduate female students, of whom 73 indicated a preference for library science, while 317 definitely rejected the field (see chapter 4 of this volume, by Reeling). The potential library recruits, in comparison with the others, possessed the following traits: (1) parents with a lower terminal-educational level; (2) higher scores on the Scholastic Aptitude Test; (3) higher scores for "manifest need of order," and lower for "autonomy" and "heterosexuality" on the Edwards Personal Preference Schedule; (4) higher scores for aesthetic values, and lower scores for economic and political values on the Allport-Vernon-Lindzey Study of Values; (5) higher grades in high school and college; and (6) they were readers, users of libraries, and often part-time workers in libraries. Interviews revealed that the potential recruits to librarianship were career-oriented, concerned about supporting themselves, and willing to consider a profession requiring a graduate degree, whereas the nonrecruits were less oriented to these concerns and more interested in getting married. Students said they were deterred from librarianship by the negative image of the librarian, whom they often confused with a clerical worker. Only one out of ten potential library recruits who were interviewed indicated they were not interested in working outside the home after marriage. Reeling's study suggested a highly motivated female.

Two major career studies have been done, by Morrison (1969) and by Schiller (1969). Morrison set out to study "the social origins, educational attainments, vocational experience, and personality characteristics of a group of American academic librarians (p. 17). He studied two groups: (1) major executives who were heads of libraries, reporting statistics to the Association of College and Research Libraries in 1956-57, and who earned more than $6000 a year; and (2) a control group of 476 librarians, selected from the 1955 edition of *Who's Who in Library Service*.

Morrison's findings and conclusions with regard to women in the profession were very definite and explicit. He stated that women in major executive positions and those earning high salaries were more likely to have graduated from large institutions than were comparable men, because "apparently a man does not need the advantage of graduation from a large school...to the extent a woman does...A woman may use the fact of graduation from a large school...to offset the inherent disadvantage of being a female in American society" (p. 17).

In discussing the implications of his findings, Morrison mentioned the complaints, written by women on their questionnaires, about isolation and being in a dead-end job. The academic community, he concluded, is predominantly masculine, and it is easier for a man to communicate with other specialists than for a woman, who traditionally may not relate to a man as a colleague. As a result, academic librarianship has become masculinized, despite the fact that the qualifications possessed by the women are as good as, or better than, those of the men. No respondents to the questionnaire suggested how this situation could be improved. Morrison commented that women could become engaged in more scholarly and professional activities; this is his only specific suggestion for women.

Schiller's (1969a) study was based on data collected in 1966-67 for a U.S. Office of Education-sponsored research project. The survey covered one out of five positions in more than 2000 college and university libraries in both public and private institutions in the United States. All figures were broken down by sex, so that many findings pertinent to women librarians were made. For example, the median salary for men was $1500 higher than for women, and the difference between the mean salaries was even wider, about $1850. In the salary ranges studied, 27 percent of the men and only 11 percent of the women earned from $10,000 to $13,999, and 10 percent of the men but only one percent of the women earned $14,000 or more.

A survey of academic librarians' salaries done 10 years after Schiller's study reveals little progress for women (Talbot and von der Lippe, 1976). A problem clearly still exists, a multifaceted, complex problem rooted in a basic social institution that a workshop of the American Economic Association identified as "occupational segregation...an interlocking set of institutions with sociological, psychological, and economic aspects and with deep historical roots (Blaxall and Reagan, 1976, p. ix). Change, then, will be a slow process and will have to be planned and effected over the broad area of activities in all occupations, especially those in which women are segregated.

SEMIPROFESSIONS

Professions that are predominantly female are sometimes called "semiprofessions" and are characterized by a comparatively short preparation time accompanied by a weaker claim to a unique knowledge base. Professionals in such fields have relatively little autonomy. They work within a bureaucratic structure, and rising to an administrative position within that structure constitutes professional and economic advancement (Goode, 1969). The contention is made that, because such professions require less dedication in terms of learning and keeping up with the knowledges and skills required to practice them, and because the work involved entails little independent action or decision-making of the life-or-death variety, women are well suited to them. The reasons advanced are that women have discontinuous work histories and low motivation to work outside the home, and that even when they do work, they are less interested in a career than in a job, considering their prime career commitment to be that of wife, mother, and housekeeper. Furthermore, societal norms dictate that women should not, unless of a very high social class, be in a position of authority over men (Caplow, 1964). Societal norms also cause women to be passive and submissive to authority in general, and to male authority in particular.

Continuing with this rationale, educated women gravitate toward the semiprofessions, where the tasks of lower-level positions are suitable for them. Within these fields, an elite and predominantly male managerial class develops, but this situation does not constitute discrimination, or if it does, it is readily justifiable.

It is easy to demonstrate that men get more than their proportionate share of the best jobs in the semi-professional fields, as in other occupations, and it is plain that individual women are often the victims of discrimination in hiring and promotion. But a case can be made that women's lack of occupational success is not always due to discrimination, and that when discrimination does occur, there may be valid grounds for it from the organization's standpoint (Simpson and Simpson, 1969, p. 222).

Plate (1970) used Simpson and Simpson to justify the denial that discrimination against women exists in libraries and to claim that studies of the librarian's career, such as Schiller's (1969a; 1970a), which show inequities, reveal "more about women in librarianship than about discrimination in libraries" (Plate, 1970; p. 644). Schiller's response (1970b) to Plate was to express her concern that equality between men and women librarians is a professional goal that "is not only desirable but essential and attainable" (p. 644).

The unequal status quo, so aptly illustrated by the interchange between Schiller and Plate, has been ingnored by most. Although many articles, especially since the mid-sixties, have discussed the problems found by women in the field, few have linked these with the prestige, image, and status of librarianship, despite the obvious cause-effect relationship. Rossi (1962) expressed surprise that the profession did not make "some comment on the major reason why librarians find it difficult to achieve a substantial spot in the array of professions." The major reason, Rossi says, is because a majority of librarians are women, who always "depress the status of an occupation because theirs is a depressed status in the society as a whole." Further, such professions develop a "division of labor and accompanying status along sex lines," and "much could be done to raise the status of the entire field [of librarianship] by making the division of labor as radical as that accomplished by medicine, where nursing is the female occupation and doctoring the male" (p. 82).

The structure that Rossi describes has been developing since women entered the field, although a radical and complete division of labor has never been accomplished. As recently as 1971, when the impact of the feminist movement and also of laws that attempt to assure women equal employment opportunity had been felt, an organization that published the *Index of Opportunity in the Library and Information Sciences* (1971) as part of its Career Series made the following statement, in a section entitled "Personal Requirements": About 80% are women, with men more frequently employed in technical libraries and in executive and administrative positions in large libraries" (p. 4). The veracity of the statement as an indicator of the status quo cannot be questioned, but it also carries the implication that one's sex constitutes a personal requirement for certain positions. This publication was distributed free, in large quantities, to library schools, which then passed it on to their students as an aid in job-hunting. Hundreds of women students that year were sent a clear message about their "place" in the career for which they were preparing.

According to the research cited here on their personality and characteristics (which will be discussed later in this chapter), women librarians have the ability to achieve leadership in the profession, and even allowing for both the subtle and overt attitudes that facilitate the careers of men and inhibit those of women, one might assume that the sheer number of women in the field would give them a great advantage in attempting to rectify their status. Yet it has not. Social mores have traditionally dictated that women must defer to men and must not be placed in a position of authority over them. This belief has paved the way for male leadership in the predominantly female professions.

Norms about women's roles are tightly integrated into our culture. They are vividly acted out in the books that children read (Key, 1971, U'Ren, 1976), in the programs and commercials that they view on television, and most of all, in the verbal and nonverbal communication that they receive from adults (Gornick, 1971; Komarovsky, 1972; Bem and Bem, 1973). By the time persons have matured, they have formed set concepts about sex roles; the process of socialization makes this concept formation inevitable. Thus, women librarians, who perceive themselves in the traditional feminine role, are often unable to behave in ways that would end their secondary position in the profession. These beliefs are so deeply ingrained in their cognitive and affective patterns of thought and behavior, that they behave accordingly. Society reinforces this behavior and at the same time uses it against them as the reason for "justifiable discrimination."

Librarians are, of course, in an acceptable "woman's field," where few overt struggles because of their sex arise and where role conflict is minimal, so long as they accept the norm of male leadership. When the women members of the profession, however, aspire to high achievement, particularly in administration, they cease to be Traditional Women, women who select occupations composed largely of female members. Instead, they become Role Innovators, women who venture into fields traditionally reserved for men (Tangri, 1969). In these situations, role conflict is maximized, and it is under such conditions that women exhibit Horner's (1968) much-studied and controversial Motive to Avoid Success. Since, by the previously cited definition, no women who enter librarianship are Role Innovators, it is not surprising that so few have been willing to cross over into administration, education, and other leadership roles, nor is it surprising that the lot of those who do, is not an easy one, because of the need for changes in attitudes and behaviors—changes that are not reinforced by peer attitudes or by what the woman has learned during her education for librarianship.

To understand more fully this situation within the profession, one must examine the theory regarding the nature and identity of professions in our society. Sociological studies of occupational roles generally recognize law, medicine, the ministry, and university teaching, the "four great *person* professions (Goode, 1969, p. 267), as the traditional areas to which society has accorded the highest status and which can unquestionably be labeled professions. Over the years, other occupations have risen to the status of professions, according to general social consensus, and many more aspire to it, usually claiming professional identity as part of their ideology, even though the society as a whole does not in fact concur with this assessment. Sociologists have described various sets of definite actions that an occupation takes to transform itself into a profession. Caplow (1964) suggests four steps.

1. A professional association is established, with definite membership criteria which eliminate the unqualified.
2. The name of the occupation is changed to reduce identification with its

previous status, to assert a "technological monopoly," and to provide "a title which can be monopolized," as opposed to the former one, which is in general use.
3. A code of ethics is developed which states the profession's social usefulness and its relationship to the public welfare and which sets rules that help further to eliminate those who are unqualified or who refuse to live up to these rules. Such a code, although it often has hypocritical aspects, "imposes a real and permanent limitation on internal competition."
4. A lengthy period of political agitation is undertaken, designed to obtain official legal support for the occupational requirements that have been established. The first state of this process is usually the granting of a title to persons who have passed a specific examination (professional engineer, certified public accountant). It may ultimately be carried to the extent that a person who acts in the capacity of a given profession without holding the necessry credentials is commiting a crime (medicine) (pp. 139-40).

Concurrent with these four steps, which may be extended over a very long period of time, are other activities.

1. The development of schools controlled in some way by the professional association, particularly regarding entrance and exit requirements.
2. The establishment of privileges of confidence, with legal action necessary to set precedence.
3. Elaboration of the rules of the code of ethics.
4. Conflict with related professional groups, followed by the establishment of a working relationship with them.

Caplow asserts that this process may be observed at work today in all manner of occupations, including some that are entirely commercial, some that have never been independent, and some far removed from the economic arena. He hypothesizes that the "professional society may eventually be counted among the major social institutions" (p. 140).

Caplow's eight criteria have been fulfilled to some extent in the case of librarianship. The professional association, however, does not have membership criteria that eliminate the unqualified. The code of ethics is not central to the practice of librarianship (Petros, 1971). Steps taken regarding certification have been directed toward setting up minimal requirements for the nonprofessionals, who often staff smaller public libraries, more than toward certification on a professional level. (The term "professional" is used here to mean a person who holds the master's degree in library science.) Similarly, efforts to change the name have been directed toward calling nonprofessionals by a variety of titles such as library assistant or library associate, while retaining the title "librarian" as the professional one, despite the fact that the public often confuses nonprofessional employees with librarians.

Wilensky (1964b) offers another version of the steps toward

professionalization: (1) full-time acitivity at the task; (2) the establishment of university training; (3) the establishment of a national professional association; (4) the assignment of certain more menial duties to subordinates, via a redefinition of the core task; (5) conflict between older members of the group and new members who are seeking to upgrade its status; (6) competition between the emerging profession and related ones; (7) political agitation and the subsequent establishment of legal requirements for members of the new profession; and (8) acceptance of a code of ethics (p. 145).

Librarianship has worked through the first six points that Wilensky lists but has not entirely fulfilled the latter two, which like Caplow's, deal with a code of ethics and legal certification. One might surmise from the foregoing descriptions that in the eyes of scholars who specialize in the sociology of work, librarianship is very close to reaching full professional status. Goode (1969, p. 276) however, points out that such itemizations neglect the "core, or generating traits" as well as those that are "a predictable outcome" of these basic characteristics. He defines the central, generating characteristics of a profession as: (1) a foundation of theoretical, abstract knowledge unique to that field and not derivative from other fields; and (2) the service ideal.

This foundation of knowledge, and the skills deriving from it, must be organized into a codified body of principles that are applicable to the problems of life, and able, according to the belief system of the society, to solve the problems. Society must also accept the propriety of handing over this specific set of problems to the given profession, because it alone possesses the knowledge and skill to solve them. The profession, further, creates, organizes, and transmits the knowledge; it alone can decide on the validity of a solution to any given problem within its realm. Finally, "the amount of knowledge and skills and the difficulty of acquiring them should be great enough that the members of the society view the profession as possessing a kind of mystery that it is not given to the ordinary man to acquire, by his own efforts or even with help" (Goode, 1969, p. 278).

The basis of the service ideal, also called a collectivity orientation, is that it is the norm for the professional to arrive at solutions based on the client's needs (as opposed to self-interest or societal needs), and that the professional's decision cannot be changed by the client or another person. Further, the professional has to make sacrifices both while preparing for this career and from time to time during the course of it. Social visibility occurs when society accepts this mystique of professional commitment and service, and the profession itself sets up a reward-and-punishment system based on the fulfillment of these standards. These two core elements produce the recognized traits of the established professions; e.g., high income and prestige, autonomy with regard to practice, control of certification or licensing boards, a strong degree of commitment to the profession, and a close identity with the reference group comprised of other professional colleagues (Goode, 1969, pp. 278-279).

Goode (1962) predicts that librarianship will not achieve professional status within the next generation. He attributes this fact to society's doubt that there is a basic science of librarianship; the skill is thought to be only clerical or administrative and to the sparsity of research and, hence, the little accumulation of knowledge concerning the central professional task of librarianship, the organization and codification of library materials, and the development of principles concerning the retrieval of that information. He thus echoes the usual doubt expressed in most discussions of librarianship concerning the existence of a unique body of knowledge that librarians create, organize, and transmit. Parsons (1959) also points out a concrete application of the effect of the questioned knowledge base, that of role conflict and the resulting role strain. In the analysis of a study of censorship in school and public libraries, Parsons sees the cases described as

an almost classic instance of *anomie*. The term is borrowed from the Greek and means simply "normalness." It refers to a state of relative "disorganization" of a system of social relationships where people are disoriented and disturbed because of a lack of adequately clear-cut definitions of expectations of behavior at the level of the relatively generalized norms which apply differentially to their functions as distinguished from other functions in the system...Groups exposed to *anomie* situations in this sense are faced not only with a cognitive problem of knowing what is expected of them but with a problem of knowing emotional adjustment; not knowing involves not only cognitive bafflement, but also anxiety and tends to lead to various types of reaction which, in the psychological sense, are "defensive" (pp. 77-78).

Librarians, in effect, have sometimes become censors, because of a "nonrational disturbance of relations between values and behavior" (p. 81). Parsons sees this irrational disturbance as being caused by the difficulties inherent, on one hand, in separating the clerical from the truly technical areas of library competence, and on the other hand, in separating the knowledge the librarian has from the knowledge the subject specialist has. In addition, the librarian, who "facilitates access rather than prescribing," generally assumes a passive, neutral role, "fair to all the interests involved" (p. 91). Yet the mores of librarianship call for a dominant role in educating the client to better standards, in setting standards of excellence, and in making knowledge active and functional to the society. These two sets of factors combine to create a role strain that often results in highly fearful, defensive behavior. The clerical versus the scholarly aspects of the role and the facilitative versus the educative aspects have never been resolved. Hence, the *anomie*, with its resulting defensiveness and its passive acquiescence to a correct, inoffensive, helpful, but nonassertive role. This defensive behavior and uncertain role identity manifests itself in aspects other than the censorship battle; for example, the strenuous efforts of academic librarians to attain full faculty rank and status, and the tendency of many librarians to demean degrees from their own professional schools (including the basic M.L.S.) and to idealize "subject-area" degrees.

Most significant, however, is the connection that Parsons makes between these behavior patterns and the fact that librarianship is dominated by women. Parsons (1959) comments that

> this general predisposition has probably been reinforced by tendencies to selective recruitment. The most tangible index of this is in the sex composition of the profession. Generally speaking, there is a tendency for women to gravitate into "supportive" types of occupational roles where functions of "helpfulness" to the incumbent of more assertive and ultimately, in the social function sense, more responsible roles is a major keynote...Sex composition should therefore be considered both a symptom and a partial determinant of the pattern with which we are concerned (p. 94-95).

He thus links the sex role of the majority of librarians to the core of the problem of professionalism. This essay, in fact, is one of the few pieces in library literature to do so, including the current spate of articles about discrimination against women in the professions. The question is not so much one of discrimination as it if of sex role. In other words, one cannot begin to remove the discrimination without making a dramatic change in the concept of the role of women in society. Nor can one change librarianship till the role of women changes. As women's role has been defined by society, so the role of librarianship has followed the same path. The chief publication that supports these statements is a collection of studies on predominantly female professions (Etzioni, 1969), from which work by Goode and by the Simpsons, cited earlier, have been taken. The premises and conclusions of the Simpsons' (1969) work are worth a more detailed examination at this point, because of their many apparent applications within librarianship.

The Simpsons state that the prevalence of women in the semi-professions is a major reason for the bureaucratic pattern of control in such organizations as nursing services, schools, libraries, and social-work agencies, as opposed to the control by autonomous collegial groups found in a law firm, a medical association, or the university.

Semiprofessionals are accountable to their superiors, and the organization itself is accountable to an outside lay board. Duties are differentiated by the level of the hierarchical rank, and those duties that deal directly with the occupational goal are carried out at the lower levels. Toward the top of the hierarchy, these primary tasks have been replaced by administrative duties. Primary tasks thus lack prestige, whereas supervisory and administrative ones are rewarded. Such a system is a self-renewing one, which lessens any tendency toward autonomy.

Professionals resist any such control with the weapon of knowledge. The Simpsons maintain that semiprofessionals lack specialized knowledge as well as strong colleague-reference-group identification, with its internal controls over standards of work. Bureaucratic surveillance is thus not only possible, but necessary. Further, they say, semiprofessionals do not demand autonomy or fight bureaucratic control. Lacking a prestige system built around performance of tasks, they defer to administrative superiors, because of their official position and the prestige that it carries within the semiprofessions.

All these forces working toward bureaucratic control are strengthened by the predominance of females in the semiprofessions. The reasons given are descriptive statements of the condition of society that carry implications of some of its inequities toward women:

1. The public is more willing to grant autonomy to men than to women.
2. The family role is woman's primary attachment. She therefore is less committed to work and to the maintenance of a high level of knowledge.
3. The work motives of women are utilitarian rather than task-oriented, as are the men's, "so they may require more control" (Simpson and Simpson, 1969, p.199).
4. Women are less likely to develop identity with colleague reference groups, because of their attachment either to their family or to their clients (or to both).
5. Women frequently accept the cultural norm that they should defer to men, and therefore they are more willing than men to accept bureaucratic controls.

The Simpsons have examined the literature about semiprofessional women, their work orientation, and the resulting effect of their work organization. They present the following composite figure of the woman teacher, nurse, social worker, and librarian. (1) The majority are upwardly mobile, having come from family origins below their present status. (2) They have chosen their occupations as an easy way up. (3) Many have made their career choice late in college, or even after college, especially in the case of librarianship (which is reported as "less socially visible," having a "less clear public image," and not requiring "a library degree to become a librarian" [p. 202]). (4) They are attracted to their respective fields not because of the intellectual content but because they "want to work with people and to be of service," values to which women are conditioned from infancy. (5) Their academic performance is often average or below average, and they often feel inadequate, and thus unlikely to succeed in other fields. (6) They also have low occupational commitment. (7) Their career aspirations most likely decreased during the course of their undergraduate education. (8) Their family role, around which woman's self-image is built, competes with their work role, particularly because of household tasks. (9) Often their career is interrupted or permanently ended by childbearing and -rearing. (The turnover rate among men is also high, but for reasons of professional advancement.) (10) The women who remain in the field do so out of economic need or to maintain a higher standard of living for their families.

Ironically, in these professions so closely identified with women, discrimination against them is the norm. The Simpsons discuss this discrimination at length, citing society's norms that women should not be in positions of authority over men or share a collegial relationship with men in an equivalent position. They mention that large libraries tend to bar top positions to women for the foregoing reasons, as well as because they would have to represent the library in the local political arena, a fact that Garceau (1951) also discussed many years ago. Regarding discrimination, the Simpsons conclude that "the low motivation and discontinuous work histories of women raise questions about the prevailing assumption that women are discriminated against in occupations where they compete with men" (p. 222). They then advance the argument, cited in the beginning of this chapter, that while women are often discriminated against, their lack of occupational success is not always caused by discrimination; and that furthermore, organizations often have valid grounds for the discrimination that does occur.

The statement and conclusions in this work must be reckoned with as a reflection of society's view of women. By extension, society sees the professional librarian in exactly the same way. All the mores, the customs, the beliefs, the traditions, the myths that comprise the social stereotype of the female are extended to the librarian. The problems of professional identity, image, and status cannot be addressed accurately without also addressing the social role of women.

NEED FOR BASIC SOCIAL CHANGE THROUGH ASSERTIVE TRAINING

This analysis indicates that only basic social change that fundamentally alters the role of women will change the role of the librarian. Social change is a long, slow process, combining periods of revolution and evolution. Librarianship can participate in this revolutionary/evolutionary process, because it does have professional schools, all attached to universities, which provide basic and continuing professional education to librarians. Since the majority of library-school students are women, it follows logically that certain curricular and extracurricular programs could be developed to assist these women:

1. In identifying inappropriate attitudes and behaviors that are a result of their sex-role socialization and learning more appropriate alternatives.
2. In identifying inappropriate attitudes and behaviors exhibited toward them by others in their working situation and indicate discriminatory practices and/or reflect traditional thinking about women's roles, and learning appropriate and productive ways to deal with them.

In searching the literature for existing programs and/or techniques being used to help women achieve competency in the two areas just cited, two sources were found: a short preliminary report of research, entitled, "Teaching Women Not to Discriminate Against Themselves" (Butler, 1973) and a full-length study reporting on initiation and influence activities of women in mixed-sex groups working on a job-related task (Hall, 1972). The former study indicates that assertive training is an important technique, which can help women to stop behaving in self-discriminating ways; while the latter indicates that most women in mixed-sex groups, even if the groups are predominantly female in composition, display notably unassertive behavior, and that those who do behave assertively feel uncomfortable about their behavior. This researcher was unable to identify other education or training models that would accomplish both of the purposes listed above. The major training model now being used for women is traditional management training, which has a somewhat different focus and is not concerned with female sex-role socialization processes and their consequences. Assertive training is especially suited to the problems of women, because a lack of assertiveness is synonymous with many of the stereotyped traits of "normal" femininity, which characterize women as dependent, passive, noncompetitive, timid, subjective, and minimally intelligent, whereas the "normal" male stereotype includes exactly the opposite characteristics (Bardwick, 1971). Longitudinal studies show that the traits of passivity-dependence and aggression in males and females change or remain the same over the life span, according to whether the person's inclination to these traits conforms with the cultural ideals of masculinity and femininity (Kagan and Moss, 1962). Women are expected to have personality traits less dominant or aggressive than those of men. By the late teenage years, when pressure to conform to this pattern becomes very strong, the majority of young women adapt themselves accordingly (Komarovsky, 1972). The "masculine" traits, however, have come to be identified as those necessary for success in the working world of business and the professions, and in many other social interactions as well. In fact, they have become the norm to such an extent that they are also equated with the mentally healthy personality, whereas the stereotyped "feminine" traits are identified as symptomatic of varying degrees of emotional maladjustment (Bardwick, 1972).

Assertive training is designed to help individuals free themselves of inadequate ways of dealing with anxiety-producing situations, which may be defined as events so distressing to an individual that she or he responds with behavior characterized by fear, defensiveness, hostility, or passivity. These inadequate ways of behaving are linked with many of the stereotyped "feminine" traits, such as timidity, submissiveness, dependence, and passivity. The method was originated in the field of behavior therapy by Wolpe (1958), based on the work of Salter (1949), who applied the use of assertive responses to a wide range of situations. Wolpe uses them "only for overcoming unadaptive anxieties aroused in the patient by other people during direct interchanges with them" (Wolpe, 1969, p. 61). He defines "assertive" as applying "to the outward expression of practically all feelings other than anxiety. Experience has shown that such expressions tend to inhibit anxiety" (Wolpe, p. 61). Assertiveness usually involves behavior that is aggressive to some degree, but it may also express friendly, affectionate, and other nonanxious feelings (Wolpe, 1969). Wolpe and Lazarus (1966) specify that expressions of anger or resentment are the most common type of assertive response in the therapeutic situation, but they list other examples of assertive behavior, including

1. Polite refusal to accede to an unreasonable request.
2. A genuine expression of praise, endearment, appreciation, or respect.
3. An exclamation of joy, irritation, adulation, or disgust.
4. All socially acceptable expressions of personal rights and feelings.

In a later publication, Lazarus (1971) defines assertive behavior in terms of acquiring habits of emotional freedom. He cites the importance of the difference between assertion and aggression, since "outbursts of hostility, rage, or resentment usually denote pent-up or accumulated anger rather than the spontaneous expression of healthy emotion" (p. 79). He dislikes the term "assertiveness," which Wolpe has applied to emotional freedom, because assertive training has become associated with "oneupmanship, and other deceptive games and ploys which Wolpe includes under this heading and which have no place in the forthright and honest expression of one's basic feelings" (p. 80). He uses the term "assertive behavior" to "denote only that aspect of emotional freedom that concerns standing up for one's rights because it cannot convey all the nuances of emotional freedom... Training in emotional freedom implies the recognition of each and every affective state" (p. 82).

Wolpe (1969) suggests two major techniques for assertive training: (1) simple, direct instruction; and (2) behavior rehearsal, a kind of behavioristic psychodrama in which the therapist takes the role of a person who produces a neurotic anxiety reaction in the patient and instructs the patient in the expression of the true feelings toward that person, which are usually inhibited. Lazarus (1971) employs these methods also, and adds, for particularly difficult cases, the technique of rehearsal desensitization, or behavior rehearsal within a desensitized framework. Nonthreatening role-playing situations are employed, followed by the enactment of more specific anxiety-producing situations, arranged in a hierarchy of increasing difficulty. Initially the therapist models the appropriate behavior for the client (role reversal), who then enacts the role when he or she feels capable of doing so.

During the decade following Wolpe's original publication on assertive training, the method was used by behavior therapists within the context of their practice, scholarly interest in it was limited, and popular interest nonexistent. Beginning in the late 1960s, however, an increasing interest occurred both on the scholarly/professional and the more popular level. Publications reporting the results of experimental studies increased, such as articles by Boordem and Flowers (1972)); Eisler, Hersen, and Miller (1973); McFall and Lilessian (1971); McFall and Marston (1970); McFall and Twentyman (1973); and Rathas (1972). General scholarly articles on the various aspects of assertive training also increased, such as those by Hersen, Eisler, and Miller (1973); Fensterheim (1972); Gambril (1973); Neuman (1967); and Lomont, Gilmer, Spector, and Skinner (1969). From 1968 to 1974, 20 dissertations can be identified that deal with assertive training or assertive responses; and, finally, assertive training has become popularized by such books as Fensterheim and Bauer (1975); Smith (1975); and Alberti and Emmons (1975), the latter based on their earlier work (1974), directed toward a professional audience.

The application of assertive training to the problems of women began receiving attention in the early 1970s. Butler (1973) and her colleagues conducted voluntary, mixed-sex assertive-training groups, three of which were administered as an assertive instrument. The male group score showed a significant difference in the level of assertiveness (i.e., significantly more assertive). When specified items on the inventory were categorized and the responses to these subgroups analyzed, differences by sex in areas of assertiveness problems were apparent. More women than men had difficulty in expressing negative feelings (anger or disagreement), and in setting limits, and were being overly apologetic about their competence, power, or authority. Men reported the greatest difficulty in expressing positive feelings. In group situations, women practiced negative self-labeling by describing their assertive behavior as impolite, bossy, or parental, thus minimizing their power and competency and discriminating against themselves.

Hall's (1972) study is one of the most relevant for librarians, because it investigates secondary-school teachers to determine assertive behavior of men and women in mixed-sex groups that have been assigned a job-related task. After reviewing the literature on behaviors in mixed-sex groups, she arrived at three generalizations:

1. The average man initiates more verbal acts than does the average woman.
2. Men are more influential; i.e., women are less likely to yield to another woman's opinion than to the opinion of a man.
3. When one categorizes the behavior of men and women in groups, more men initiate acts in an "attempted answers" category, while more women initiate acts in the "social-emotional positive" category. Men spend more time making suggestions and giving opinions and/or orientation to the group, while women devote more time to agreeing with or praising others.

Hall formulated hypotheses from these generalizations and tested them on mixed-sex groups of prospective teachers working on simulated team-teaching problem situations. All three of the hypotheses were supported at the .05 level of statistical significance. In cases where women were the top initiators of group activity, there was no indication of negative responses to them, of their suggestions being ignored, or of a lack of group cordiality. These top-initiator women, however, rated themselves low on cordiality, indicating that they were nervous about or uncomfortable with their assertiveness, even though other group members did not react negatively toward it. Hall suggests two alternatives for changing the pattern of male dominance observed in these groups: (1) expectation training, which is designed to raise the expectations of others (male teachers) about the competence of a given subgroup (female teachers), by giving that subgroup special knowledges or skills, which they then teach or demonstrate to the entire group; or (2) specific training in group-management skills. Hall prefers the latter, however, because of the practical problems involved in applying expectation training outside a highly controlled experimental setting. She also lists seven suggestions designed to increase assertiveness, which could be given to working women who are receiving training in group-discussion skills, but does not specifically suggest assertive training as a possibility.

Both Manderino (1974) and Winship (1974) have reported favorable results in experimental assertive-training programs with groups of women. The former worked with 35 undergraduate women who viewed themselves as nonassertive, and the latter studied 25 university nursing students who had scored below the mean on an assertiveness inventory and who volunteered to participate in the experimental group. At the time this research was undertaken, nothing specific had been published regarding assertive-training procedures for women. Both of these dissertations contain helpful formats. Other studies include Jakubowski-Spector (1973a; 1973b); Bloom, Coburn, and Pearlman (1975); Osborne and Harris (1975); Phelps and Austin (1975); and Butler (1976); all deal with assertive training for women.

As this record of publication indicates, assertiveness training began to attain prominence as one of the major vehicles for teaching women social skills appropriate to all types of situations, both personal and professional. As such, it provides a highly desirable method to teach women librarians an array of behavioral skills that will maximize their potential for professional development and at the same time sensitize them to the problems of women in the feminized professions. The more recent research on the career and personality of the librarian, cited earlier, indicates that women librarians as a group are talented, skilled, career-oriented people, contrary to the earlier research, which the Simpsons reviewed in their study and upon which their rather negative picture of the woman librarian, as well as of other women in the feminized professions, is based. A need for such training is strongly indicated by the fact that women librarians, in spite of their demonstrated capabilities, continue to lag behind men in salary and professional status. Since they represent such a large numerical majority in the profession, self-discrimination, as well as social discrimination, must be one of the major factors responsible for their continuing disadvantaged position.

STUDY PURPOSE

A program was designed, based on assertiveness training and focusing specifically on the situation of women librarians, both historically and in the present, and tested on a group of women library-school students, to ascertain whether this methodology would be productive and could be used as a model for the further development of such training and could be incorporated into library education. The training sessions included the reading and discussion of handouts on the role and status of women in librarianship, the viewing and discussion of a film on the women's movement, and three assertiveness-training sessions, which utilized role playing, largely of work-related situations. Responses of the students to the training were measured by administering three pre- and posttests, the first measuring assertiveness, the second measuring attitudes toward feminism, and the third measuring attitudes toward librarianship.

The study was conducted under the following assumptions, based on the literature previously discussed:

1. Women librarians are Traditional Women, the group comprised of women who select the usual female occupations. They are not Role Innovators, women who venture into fields usually reserved for men. Advancement to high levels in librarianship really requires that a woman be a Role Innovator.
2. As a group, their positions and salaries are lower than those of their male peers.
3. This disadvantaged position is partly the result of discrimination against them and partly the result of their own attitudes and behavior patterns.
4. Because they fit into the group defined as Traditional Women, they are relatively unaware of their disadvantaged professional position, or if they do perceive it to any degree, they are reluctant and/or unable to take corrective measures.
5. Because of the values that women librarians, in common with all women have internalized concerning careers, they often display ambivalence, experience role conflict, and have diffused or unfocused career goals.
6. Because of the values they have internalized regarding appropriate patterns of female behavior, they lack assertiveness, particularly in dealing with male peers in task-oriented situations, thus limiting their contributions to the profession as well as their own career advancement.
7. Women librarians represent a reservoir of untapped talent available to the library profession. They have abilities in many areas; e.g., leadership, decision making, scholarship, and writing.
8. A special training course, based on assertive training, would help to facilitate their personal and professional growth.

Based on these assumptions, the following research hypothesis was formulated:

Women library-school students who participate in a special program based on assertive training will show a statistically significant increase in their scores on tests that measure their assertiveness, their attitudes toward feminism, and their attitudes toward librarianship as a career.

The methodology selected to test the research hypothesis was the experimental-group/control-group format. The following research questions were developed to guide this methodology.

1. Will participation in a short-term assertive-training group (experimental group) increase the mean score of female library-school students on the Lawrence Assertive Inventory (hereafter referred to as LAI) at a statistically significant level (0.05)?
2. Will participation in the training group (experimental group), which includes, in addition to assertive training, the reading and discussion of materials about the problems of the library profession, of women librarians, and of women workers in general, increase the mean score of female library-school students on the Women's Liberation Scale (hereafter referred to as WLS) at a statistically significant level (0.05)?
3. Will the methodology as described above for the experimental group also result in an increase in the mean score on the Thornton Scale to Measure Librarians' Attitudes Toward Librarianship (hereafter referred to as the Thornton Scale) at a statistically significant level (0.05)?
4. Will a group of women library-school students who do not participate in the training group (control group) show no increase in scores on the above-cited tests at a statistically significant level (0.05)?

INSTRUMENTATION

The instrument used to measure assertive responses in the population selected for study was the Lawrence Assertive Inventory (Lawrence, 1970). Based on the Wolpe-Lazarus Assertive Inventory (Wolpe and Lazarus, 1966), for which no hard data had been compiled, this test consists of a series of hypothetical situations to which the subjects indicate the manner in which they would be most likely to respond. Lawrence developed the test, using a population of 54 female college students, and then employed it to compare three methods of modifying assertive behavior and to evaluate the concept of assertion as a general personality trait. He points out that few controlled studies of assertive therapy had been performed up to the time of his work, and that no instrument existed for the measurement of assertive behavior, except informal ones of a questionnaire type, none of which had ever been systematically studied on a specified population by subjecting the results to statistical analysis. Manderino (1974) also employed this instrument, to measure the results of her study of the effects of a group assertive-training procedure on a group of 35 undergraduate women. This instrument, therefore, was selected for use on the population to be studied in the experiment, as the only one at that time for which any type of comparative statistical data were available.

Two additional instruments, one to measure librarians' attitudes toward librarianship, and one to measure attitudes toward feminism, were used. The Women's Liberation Scale developed by Gruzen (1970), as tested by O'Keefe (1971), was selected to research feminist attitudes. It consists of 30 questions that measure stereotyped concepts of female and male roles, set up on a seven-point Likert scale, and is mixed with a larger scale.

The third instrument was the Thornton Scale to Measure Librarians' Attitudes Toward Librarianship, developed by Thornton (1963) and also utilized by McMahon (1967). Thornton tested this scale on a group of 111 Georgia librarians; McMahon's population consisted of 46 Tasmanian librarians. The scale is comprised of 46 statements designed to measure attitudes toward librarianship, set up on a five-point Likert scale.

SAMPLE

The merits of a probability sample instead of a structured sample were given serious consideration. Ideally, a random sample is, of course, the most appropriate procedure. The original plan was to select participants from a random sample of all women students enrolled in the master's-degree program, on the assumption that enough people from the sample would agree to participate to make up an experimental and a control group. This effort failed, because regulations concerning the protection of human subjects made it impossible to obtain enough information to contact all of these individuals. Even the provision of the basic list of names, with no accompanying data, was deemed questionable. Therefore, because of this current emphasis on protecting the privacy of human subjects, the population was recruited from a required course at the Graduate School of Library and Information Sciences, University of Pittsburgh.

Both methods of selection possessed an inherent weakness, however In either case, participation in the experimental group was purely voluntary, thus creating the potential of a self-selected group whose members were already interested in and biased positively toward women's issues. In the case of assertiveness training, however, it is customary to seek group members who feel that they have problems in this area, so the voluntary aspect is not crucial to this part of the training. For this reason, and also because the only other alternative was to abandon the project entirely, it was decided to pursue the method described. A "captive audience" of library-school students or librarians simply was not available.

The population, therefore, consisted of female students enrolled in a master's-degree program at the Graduate School of Library and Information Sciences, University of Pittsburgh, in January 1976. The sample group of all-female students enrolled in the two sections of a required course. The three tests were administered at an orientation session, with no explanation except for the appropriate instructions and the statement that they were for research purposes. The tests were labeled "Instrument I, Instrument II, and Instrument II," and were not further identified in any way.

At the next session, the students were told about the nature of the research, and those women who expressed an interest in participating were given a handout that explained the purpose of the training sessions in more detail. Seventeen women elected to participate in the training group. The experimental group was retested at the conclusion of the training sessions. All remaining members of the sample group agreed to serve as a control group and to be retested at the end of the term.

The following objectives guided the design of the training program:

1. To teach ways of developing behavioral skills that will help women to overcome the elements of female sex-role conditioning that are detrimental to effective, competent, professional performance.
2. To present information on the historical role and current status of women in librarianship and its relation to the role and status of the profession.
3. To create a heightened consciousness of the feminist movement and the feminist analysis of women's roles.

In designing the assertiveness-training component of the sessions, to fulfill the first objective, both methods used for individuals and groups and for the general population as well as for women specifically were reviewed. Basic components of assertive training include

1. Giving information to the person or group that rationally explains ways of dealing with situations in an assertive manner.
2. Discussing specific instances where the client(s) did not behave assertively and how those instances could have been handled effectively (often, together with the first point, referred to as "cognitive restructuring").
3. Assigning tasks to the client(s) that she is to practice in her life situation (often referred to as behavior homework or behavior assignments).
4. Practicing behavior in simulated situations—a kind of role-playing referred to as "behavioral psychodrama" or, more commonly, as "behavior rehearsal," and usually accompanied by "modeling," which consists of a demonstration by the group trainer of assertive behavior appropriate to the behavior-rehearsal situation (Wolpe and Lazarus, 1966, pp. 38-53).

A fifth item often added to this basic list is the practice of setting up hierarchies of anxiety-provoking stimuli, which are then used as a basis of discussion, task assignments, and behavior rehearsal. This technique is adapted from another method of behavior therapy, relaxation therapy, in which the hierarchy is used as a framework for systematic desensitization to increasing amounts of anxiety-producing stimuli (Wolpe, 1958, pp. 139-40).

These basic components, developed and used by behavior therapists for individual counseling in clinical settings, are also employed in group assertive-training situations. Various models have been constructed from them. All the recent works geared toward procedures for women's groups, reviewed earlier, contain fruitful training models and concrete suggestions for their implementation.

The model employed in designing the assertive-training sessions given to the experimental group in this study was based on the components set forth by Osborne and Harris (1975).

1. Coaching—the provision of descriptions of appropriate performing responses.
2. Behavior Rehearsals—accompanied by modeling of appropriate behavior.
3. Assigning "homework" to be done between sessions—specific behavioral patterns that each participant is to observe in herself and attempt to change.
4. Basing the foregoing activities on a hierarchy of anxiety-producing situations (pp. 49-71).

The group met three times, for a total of 12 hours. The training focused primarily on increasing the members' assertive responses in the work situation, by the use of explanation and discussion (the logical-directive approach) and of modeling and behavior rehearsal. Evaluative criteria used in discussion of the modeling and behavior rehearsals were as follows:

1. How anxious or relaxed were you, based on the following elements:
    (a) Relaxed posture, appropriate body position
    (b) Consistent eye control
    (c) Absence of nervous laughter or excessive, repetitious hand, foot, or body movements
2. What did you say?
    (a) Concise, definite, firm comments, addressed to the point
    (b) Appropriate assertiveness for the situation
    (c) Factual reasons, without overly long explanation
    (d) Absence of excuses or apologies
3. How did you say it?
    (a) Absence of overly long silences or of interruptions of the other person
    (b) Appropriate and even tone and loudness of voice
    (c) Even flow of voice—absence of hesitancy, stammering, or stuttering or of overly-rapid speech
4. How do you feel about your performance? (Osborne and Harris, 1975, pp. 57-58).

The hierarchy of anxiety-producing situations formulated by Osborne and Harris was written on the blackboard as an example. The group elected to use it as structure, with the addition of the eleventh point at the suggestion of several group members. Groups of a longer duration usually construct their own hierarchy as part of the group process. The higher the number, the greater amount of anxiety the situation produces:

1. Calling attention to unfair behavior.
2. Discussion of job aspects with boss
3. Asking favor or help
4. Embarrassment for others and self
5. Finishing thoughts or sentences
6. Speaking up in discussion
7. Initiating conversation
8. Maintaining eye contact, being loud, close, etc.
9. Taking clear position, taking disagreeing position
10. Expressing feelings of resentment, fear, etc.; negative feelings
11. Making mistakes; self-expectation of perfection (p. 54)

The second and third objectives of this training program concern the presentation of information on the role and status of women in librarianship, in relationship to the role and status of the profession and the creation of a greater awareness of the feminist analysis of women's roles. It was hypothesized that the incorporation of these elements into an assertive-training program might result in positive changes in attitudes toward librarianship and toward feminism. No other research that ties these elements together could be identified. Furthermore, research on attitudinal change has produced the often-replicated finding that attitudes resist change, that they change slowly, over a long period of time, if at all, and that, in fact, attempts to change them often result in the reinforcement of existing attitudes (Oppenheimer, 1966; Fishbein, 1967; Davis, 1965). Nevertheless, it was decided to test for any possible shifts in attitudes, since attitudinal factors are such an important part of the argument concerning the compatibility or incompatibility of "the normative principles and cultural values of professionalism, organizations, and female employment (Etzioni, 1969, v-vi). That this attempt to change attitudes over a short period of time and to change them within the context of assertive training constituted a limiting factor in the research was recognized.

In an effort to effect attitudinal change, the following components were incorporated into the training sessions:

1. Two papers, summarizing the historical and current status of women in librarianship and analyzing librarianship within the theoretical construct of the semiprofession, were given to the group to read as homework and were then discussed at the next session.
2. A film, *The Emerging Women,* reviewing and summarizing the history of the Women's Movement in Great Britain and the United States, was shown and discussed briefly at the end of the first session.
3. Emphasis was placed on the following elements in the assertive-training program: (1) how the group felt about the role and image of the librarian; (2) how they dealt with male peers in professional situations, particularly where potential discriminatory situations existed; (3) how they could handle specific problem situations for women librarians, presented to them in the form of written case studies.

The emphasis of the training sessions was on assertive training; the amount of time and the degree of treatment on the two attitude components was minimal and largely indirect.

These elements of the training program were incorporated into three sessions, each one four hours long. A professional group trainer conducted the sessions, in order to eliminate the possiblity of experimenter bias and also to provide greater expertise than was possessed by the investigator. However, the researcher did prepare program and presentation methods based on the purpose and scope of the study.

A brief outline of each session follows. The sequence and techniques were adapted from Osborne and Harris (1975, pp. 101-140).

FIRST SESSION
1. Discussion of group expectations.
2. Discussion of librarians' role(s), image, and self-concept as viewed by the group.
3. Introductory comments on women in librarianship, accompanied by the distribution of the two papers on this topic.
4. Behavior rehearsal and modeling of professional behavior in anxiety-producing situations, as defined by group members.
5. Showing a film, *The Emerging Woman,* a history of the Women's Movement, past and present.

SECOND SESSION
1. Assertiveness exercise, "Boundaries" (moving into someone else's space and/or defending one's own space).
2. Behavior rehearsal and modeling of job interviews with a male interviewer, who purposely behaved in a discriminatory manner.
3. Introduction exercise, based on cards that participants were asked to fill out.
4. Assignment: Participants were asked to observe how they agreed and disagreed with other people, for the purpose of behavior rehearsals of anxiety-producing situations at the next session.

THIRD SESSION
1. Discussion of the history and status of women in librarianship.
2. Rehearsals of appropriate behaviors in hierarchy of anxiety-producing situations.
3. Discussion of group process and evaluation of session.
4. Posttest.

Both the experimental group and the control group were retested, respectively, at the conclusion of the training sessions and at the conclusion of the term. It was hypothesized that those who participated in the training would show an increase in the mean score on all three tests, significant at the 0.05 level, whereas there would be no significant difference in the pretest and posttest scores of the control group. The instruments were scored in the following manner to collect the data:

Lawrence Assertive Inventory

This consists of descriptions of situations, each one followed by five different ways of reacting to it. Only one of these five is considered to be appropriate assertive behavior. One point is scored for each assertive response that is selected. Comparative means and standard deviations are listed in Table 1.

Women's Liberation Scale

This consists of 30 statements designed to measure stereotyped concepts of male and female roles. The responses are set up on a seven-point Likert scale, ranging from a low of (1)—strongly disagree to a high of (7)—strongly agree. The score consists of the sum of the points on the scale selected by the respondent. Certain specified questions are scored in the reverse direction. This scale is buried in a larger scale, consisting of 39 items from 2 other scales, which are not scored. Comparative means are listed in Table 1. Standard deviations were not reported in the research.

Thornton Scale to Measure Librarians' Attitudes Toward Librarianship

This consists of 46 statements designed to measure the respondent's attitudes toward librarianship. The responses are set up on a five-point Likert scale, which was scored from a low of (1)—strongly agree—to a high of (5)—strongly disagree. (Thornton scored in the opposite direction from a low of (1)—strongly agree—to a high of (5)—strongly disagree.) The scoring was changed in this study to agree with the

TABLE 1
Comparative Means and Standard Deviations

LAWRENCE ASSERTIVE INVENTORY
(FEMALE FORM ONLY)

	Lawrence*		Manderino				Sukiennik			
			Pretest		Posttest		Pretest		Posttest	
	Experimental		Experimental	Control	Experimental	Control	Experimental	Control	Experimental	Control
Mean	36.67		35.29	41.16	52.33 / 52.88	N.A.	42.94	39.17	50.56	41.47
S.D.	10.49		6.87	11.60	9.30 / 11.62	N.A.	10.01	9.81	8.73	10.03

*Reported from a preliminary trial of the test on 60 female subjects.

WOMEN'S LIBERATION SCALE

	Gruzen		O'Keefe				Sukiennik			
			Pretest		Posttest		Pretest		Posttest	
	Experimental	Control	Experimental	Control	Experimental	Control	Experimental	Control	Experimental	Control
Mean	145.19				130.37		159.75	154.10	166.37	155.41
S.D.	N.A.				18.42		16.29	14.62	13.87	15.10

SCALE TO MEASURE LIBRARIANS'
ATTITUDES TOWARD LIBRARIANSHIP

	Thornton		McMahon				Sukiennik			
			Pretest		Posttest		Pretest		Posttest	
	Experimental	Control	Experimental	Control	Experimental	Control	Experimental	Control	Experimental	Control
Mean	N.A.				191.58		172.65	181.75	173.39	170.94
S.D.	N.A.				18.55		16.41	17.31	15.47	19.50

method used on the Lawrence Assertive Inventory and thus avoid the possibility of confusion during the administration of the two tests. Thornton does not give sufficient statistical data to compute an adjusted mean for purposes of comparison; McMahon utilized this test scoring it from a low of (0)—strongly disagree—to a high of (4)—strongly agree and did not supply sufficient data for the purposes of computing a comparable mean, which is given in Table 1. This table displays all available information on comparative means and standard deviations for each test.

Following standard formulas, the mean for each test was calculated as a summation of all the scores divided by the number of scores, and the standard deviation for each test was calculated as the square root of the summation of the squared differences between each score and the mean divided by the number of scores minus 1.

These procedures were followed for both the pretest and the posttest. Utilizing these means and standard deviations on both the pre-and posttest scores of the experimental and control groups, the standard t test was performed in order to determine whether changes in the mean significant at the 0.05 level of statistical significance had ocurred. The t test of significance was chosen because it is the most suitable for relatively small samples of population.

The data from the results of these calculations will be presented as follows: (1) statement of the null hypothesis (2) presentation of the findings in a statistical table, and (3) a discussion of the results.

HO1 There will be no significant difference between the means of the pretest and posttest scores on the LAI, administered to the experimental group.

HO2 There will be no significant difference between the means of the pretest and posttest scores of the LAI, administered to the control group.

The results, summarized in Table 2, revealed a difference significant at the 0.05 level between the pretest and the posttest scores of the experimental group. The null hypothesis (HO1), therefore, was rejected. The actual level of significance was close to the 0.02 level. The difference between the pretest and posttest scores of the control group was not found to be significant at the 0.05 level, although there was a slight increase in the mean score (41.47 >39.17). The null hypothesis (HO2), therefore, was rejected.

HO3 There will be no significant difference between the means of the pretest and posttest scores on the WLS, administered to the experimental group.

HO4 There will be no significant difference between the means of the pretest and posttest scores of the WLS, administered to the control group.

TABLE 2
Lawrence Assertive Inventory

FREQUENCY DISTRIBUTION

Class Intervals	Experimental Group		Control Group	
	Pretest	Posttest	Pretest	Posttest
65-68	0	0	0	0
61-64	0	2	0	0
57-60	1	3	0	1
53-56	2	2	2	2
49-52	2	3	4	2
45-48	2	2	4	2
41-44	2	2	5	3
37-40	2	1	2	1
33-36	2	0	4	2
29-32	2	1	2	1
25-28	0	0	4	3
21-24	1	0	1	0
17-20	0	0	1	0
13-16	0	0	0	0

t=Test of Significance at the 0.05 Level

Evaluated Statistical Data	Experimental Group		Control Group	
	Pretest	Posttest	Pretest	Posttest
Mean ($\bar{X}$)	42.94	50.56	39.17	41.47
Variance (σ^2)	100.31	76.25	96.21	100.72
S.D. (σ)	10.01	8.73	9.81	10.03
N	16	16	29	17
2α	0.05		0.05	
ν	30		44	
t	2.29		0.76	
$t_{\alpha,\nu}$	1.96		1.96	

Final Conclusions	2.29 > 1.96	0.76 < 1.96
	There is a significant difference at the 0.05 level.	There is a significant difference at the 0.05 level.

The results, summarized in Table 3, indicate no difference significant at the 0.05 level in the pretest and posttest scores of either the experimental group or the control group. The mean score of the experimental group did show an increase (159.75 < 166.37), and that increase was greater than the slight one shown by the control group (154.10 < 155.41), but the increase was insufficient to be statistically significant. Both null hypotheses, HO[3] and HO[4], therefore, were accepted.

HO5 There will be no significant difference between the means of the pretest and posttest scores on the Thornton Scale, administered to the experimental group.

HO6 There will be no significant difference between the means of the pretest and posttest scores on the Thornton Scale, administered to the control group.

The results are analyzed in Table 4. They show no difference significant at the 0.05 level in the pretest and posttest scores of either the experimental or the control groups. The mean score of the experimental group did increase by nine points, from 172.65 to 181.75, while the mean score of the control group dropped slightly, from 173.39 to 170.94, but neither change is significant at the 0.05 level. The null hypotheses, HO[5] and HO[6], therefore, were accepted.

Tables 2, 3, and 4 are arranged in the same format. The first part of the table displays the groupings of the test scores. For example, in Table 4, six persons in the experimental group had scores on the pretest of the Thornton Scale of 168 to 175 points. For this particular test, groupings of seven points (class intervals) were used.

The second part of the table displays the statistical data derived for that test from the standard formulas and from a standard statistical table. The t-test of significance analyzes the differences between the means of the experimental and the control groups on both pre- and posttests. It utilizes the bell-shaped normal curve of distribution with a statistical formula that applies to small samples (less than 30). The mean is the average score and is derived from the standard formula. Variance is used to indicate how far the other scores fall on either side with respect to the average score. S.D. (Standard Deviation) is the distance on both sides of the mean, which contains approximately 68 percent of the scores in each test group: N is the symbol for the number of scores in each test group. Two alpha (2α) represents the level of significance selected. Nu (ν) represents the number of scores in the group. The symbol t represents the results of the computation of the standard formula, and this particular symbol is used to emphasize that

TABLE 3
Women's Liberation Scale

FREQUENCY DISTRIBUTION

Class Intervals	Experimental Group		Control Group	
	Pretest	Posttest	Pretest	Posttest
188-193	0	0	0	0
182-187	0	0	0	0
176-181	3	2	1	2
170-175	4	3	3	1
164-169	0	2	2	1
158-163	3	2	7	4
152-157	0	1	5	3
146-151	4	1	3	3
134-139	1	0	3	1
128-133	0	0	1	0
122-127	1	0	1	0
116-121	0	0	0	1
110-115	0	0	0	0

t=Test of Significance at the 0.05 Level

Evaluated Statistical Data	Experimental Group		Control Group	
	Pretest	Posttest	Pretest	Posttest
Mean ($\bar{X}$)	159.75	166.37	154.10	155.41
Variance (σ^2)	265.31	213.86	192.37	227.42
S.D. (σ)	16.29	14.62	13.87	15.10
N	16	16	29	17
2α	0.05		0.05	
ν	30		44	
t	1.21		0.07	
$t_{\alpha,\nu}$	1.96		1.96	
Final Conclusions	1.21 1.96 There is no significant difference at the 0.05 level.		0.07 1.96 There is no significant difference at the 0.05 level.	

TABLE 4
Thornton Scale to Measure Librarians'
Attitudes Toward Librarianship

	FREQUENCY DISTRIBUTION			
	Experimental Group		Control Group	
Class Intervals	Pretest	Posttest	Pretest	Posttest
216-223	0	0	0	0
208-215	0	1	0	0
200-207	0	1	2	0
192-199	0	5	2	1
184-191	3	0	1	2
176-183	3	4	7	5
168-175	6	1	6	4
160-167	2	1	8	2
152-159	1	1	0	1
144-151	0	2	1	1
136-143	0	0	0	0
128-135	0	0	1	0
120-127	1	0	0	0
112-119	0	0	0	0

t=Test of Significance at the 0.05 Level

Evaluated Statistical Data	Experimental Group		Control Group	
	Pretest	Posttest	Pretest	Posttest
Mean ($\overline{X}$)	172.65	181.75	173.39	170.94
Variance (σ^2)	269.29	299.81	239.45	379.70
S.D. (σ)	16.41	17.31	15.47	19.50
N	17	16	28	17
2α	0.05		0.05	
ν	31		43	
t	1.55		-0.47	
$t_{\alpha,\nu}$	1.96		1.96	
Final Conclusions	1.55 1.96 There is no significant difference at the 0.05 level.		-0.47 1.96 There is no significant difference at the 0.05 level.	

this is the t-test or t-distribution. The values of $t_{\alpha,\nu}$ are derived from a standard statistical table, which can be used for samples up to 30. "Final Conclusions" summarizes the findings of the t test regarding the level of significance selected, which is based on probability theory. An 0.05 level of significance indicates a 95 percent probability that the results did not occur by chance but are the effect of the experiment and that there is only a 5 percent chance that they occurred by accident.

The null hypothesis was rejected in the case of the Lawrence Assertive Inventory, thus upholding the hypothesis that a statistically significant difference would occur between the pretest and the posttest scores of the experimental group but not of the control group. The training sessions did increase significantly the level of assertive responses. On both the Women's Liberation Scale and the Thornton Scale, however, the null hypothesis was accepted. The hypothesis that significant differences between the attitudes of the experimental group, but not of the control group, would occur, was not supported. No significant level of change was reported in either group's attitudes toward women's liberation or toward librarianship.

In summary, results of the analysis of data, as described above, revealed that

1. There was a difference significant at the 0.05 level between the pretest and posttest scores of the experimental group on the Lawrence Assertive Inventory (LAI), but there was no significant difference between the pretest and posttest scores of the control group.
2. There was no difference significant at the 0.05 level between the pretest and the posttest scores of either the experimental or the control groups on the Women's Liberation Scale (WLS).
3. There was no difference significant at the 0.05 level between the pretest and the posttest scores of either the experimental or the control group on the Thornton Scale to Measure Librarians' Attitudes Toward Librarianship.

The analysis of data, therefore, upheld only the part of the hypotheses dealing with an increase in the level of assertiveness measured in the experimental group as opposed to no significant change in the control group. In the case of the other two scales, no significant difference appeared in either the scores of the experimental group or the control group with regard to their attitudes toward feminist thinking and toward librarianship as a career.

Various factors that may account for this lack of consistency in results will now be examined. Most of the time in the sessions was spent on assertive training. Attitudes toward work, women's roles, and librarianship were dealt with largely within the context of the assertive training. They were considered directly only during the viewing of a short film about the feminist movement and during the discussion of two papers on women and librarianship, which the group was first asked to read.

Some participants may not have read the papers, and even if every one of them did, these papers are not equivalent to a careful, considered reading of the works on which they are based, followed by unhurried group discussion, preferably spread over a longer time span. Time and emphasis thus were possibly detrimental to the results and inadequate to facilitate any significant attitudinal changes.

Three other factors also need to be considered here with regard to the finding of no significant difference on the attitude test. One is the often-replicated finding, mentioned earlier, that attitudes resist change, that they change slowly, over a long period of time, if at all, and that, in fact, attempts to change attitudes often result in the reinforcement of existing ones.

The second factor pertains to the Women's Liberation Scale. O'Keefe (1971), working with an undergraduate sample, obtained a mean, on this scale, of 121.16 for men and 130.37 for women. The means scored in this study by the experimental group and the control group (female graduate library-science students) were 159.75 and 154.10 on the pretest, 166.37 and 155.41 on the posttest. Assuming that the women library-school students did not have an exceptionally strong feminist orientation and that the undergraduate women tested in 1970 did not have an unusually strong antifeminist bias, one might conclude that women's attitudes toward feminism have changed sufficiently in the intervening six years to invalidate the results and make the test itself questionable, so that to test for additional attitudinal change on the basis of this instrument is fruitless. A related problem with this test involves the emphasis of the test versus the emphasis of the training sessions, where women's roles, the Women's Liberation Movement, feminism, and the like, were dealt with in the context of career matters such as interviews, attitudes of male supervisors and coworkers, ways of dealing with discrimination, and ways of behaving assertively in all of these situations. The test does not deal with this specific area of content, with the exception of a few questions. Rather, it covers the broad perspective of women's roles in all sociocultural aspects.

The third factor pertains to the Thornton Scale. The investigator may have erred in the assumption concerning the elements that would create a more positive attitude toward librarianship as a career. The notion was that the combination of assertive training and exposure to the intertwined problems of women's roles and the role of the library profession would generate a more positive attitude among women toward librarianship as a career, as well as a greater consciousness of feminist thinking. This seemed to be a logical assumption at the time, but it may have been erroneous. The possibility was also considered that such knowledge could actually create a more negative attitude, so that one way or the other, there would be a change. In the opinion of this researcher, however, the most plausible explanation as to why the experimental group showed no significant change on either attitude instrument lies with the basic difficulty of changing attitudes, particularly within a limited framework of time. The time problem appears to have been the major factor. An additional review of the tapes of the sessions revealed that the trainer repeatedly emphasized the cause-effect relationship between self-image and overt behavior. Responses by the group indicated that they clearly perceived this point. The trainer often extended this concept to show a similar relationship between self-image and professional identity, but this never really seemed to register with the group. Considerably more time would have been required to develop it adequately, and it is possible that a greater change in attitudes toward librarianship might have then resulted.

The positive findings on the LAI are very strong. Actual degree of statistical significance measures near the 0.02 level. The greatest emphasis in the experimental sessions was the assertive training, set within the framework of an examination of attitudes toward women's roles and toward librarianship, how nonassertive behavior develops from traditional notions of appropriate "feminine" behavior, and how such behavior is detrimental both to effective functioning in job situations and in one's life in general.

In summary, the expected increase in assertive behavior was achieved, but the expectation that this change would also facilitate change in the other two areas proved to be false. The results actually agree with the other pretest/posttest experimental design research on assertive responses, which consistently shows a change significant at the 0.01 to the 0.05 level of significance. The results of the two attitude tests are also consistent with other research on attitudes, which shows that it is difficult to obtain statistically significant changes. As pointed out in the summary of the statistical results, increases in the means of both tests did occur for the experimental group, but they were not great enough to be statistically significant. Therefore, no definite conclusions can be drawn as to the relationship between assertiveness and attitudes toward feminism and toward librarianship. The increase in the means, however, indicates that further research would be profitable.

In addition to the limitations of this study, just discussed, several others should also be mentioned.

1. One cannot, on the basis of this study, predict whether the increase in assertiveness would endure permanently after the training. Manderino (1974) also points this out as a limitation of her study, and it appears to be a

general limitation of all the hard-data studies on assertive responses. Although therapists such as Wolpe and Lazarus do report long-term gains, in follow-up studies of former patients who have received assertive training, none of these studies has been put into any type of formal research design and/or quantified in any way.
2. The size of the sample is relatively small, as is the case with most of the research reported on assertive training.
3. The number of students who completed the posttest in the control group dropped by approximately 10 persons.
4. Participation in the experimental group was basically voluntary. It is therefore possible that those women who volunteered constitute a biased sample. The experimental group's pretest means on the LAI and WLS were somewhat higher than those of the control group (LAI—42.94 > 39.17; WLS—159.75 > 154.10), while the control group scored just slightly higher than the experimental group on the Thornton Scale (172.65 < 173.39). However, at the first session, when asked for their reasons for participating, only a few expressed an awareness of the problems of women in librarianship. The trainer states that in her opinion the group was not highly motivated to change. She perceived only a negative motivation, i.e., it was as easy to do a class assignment and/or a more interesting activity than the alternative assignment. The students were not, she said, goal-oriented in terms of the experimenter's stated purposes for the group.

RECOMMENDATIONS

Based on the results of this study, three groups of recommendations have been developed, concerning (1) use of a similar format in library education; (2) further research of a similar nature; and (3) additional related research on librarians. The need for attention to the problems of women in librarianship and the effect of these problems on the profession has been extensively documented. In the past five years assertive training has come to the forefront as the major tool that women can use, and are using, to achieve desired changes in their behavior. It is easy to set up, positive results can be achieved in a short time, and trained group facilitators are readily available. In the time between the proposal of this study and its execution, several excellent guides to assertive training for women have been published, as reviewed earlier. Using these guides and the information from this experiment, assertive training could easily be incorporated into library-education programs, either as part of a formal curricular offering or as an informal acitivity. A trained facilitator is essential to the success of the sessions, in order to insure the desired results and also to deal with the high levels of anxiety and anger that inevitably surface.

I would also suggest, in addition, the development of a formal course dealing with librarianship as a career and emphasizing two components of this study: the role and status of women in the profession and its close relationship to the place of librarianship within the hierarchy of the professions. The literature concerning this content area was read by this investigator over a relatively long period of time. A real understanding of the problem, its history, and its complexity requires such an approach. There is a solid, extensive content area to be dealt with here that cannot be absorbed and comprehended by reading a summary of the literature, as the experimental group did for the purposes of this experiment. A serious examination of content, which requires concentrated cognitive activity, cannot be handled within the context of an assertive-training group, where learning occurs primarily within the affective domain. These statements represent the author's opinion, based on experience with the subject area, observations of the group sessions, and the analysis of the test results.

Although this experiment utilized only a female sample, no inference should be drawn that these recommendations apply only to women students. All future librarians would profit from the formal course that is recommended. The benefits of assertive training depend on the personality of the individual, male or female. Since lack of assertion has traditionally been classified as a desirable "female" trait, and women have been socialized accordingly, women students are more likely to benefit from assertive training, but this does not exclude the possibility that some male students would find it helpful. In fact, mixed-sex groups would add an additional dimension to the training, since lack of appropriate assertive responses in women is most likely to occur in their interactions with men (Hall, 1972).

Replication of research similar to that done in this study would provide a more solid factual basis about present and future librarians, and would, ultimately, build sufficient hard data to allow some generalizations that cannot yet be made, even using the research on the personality of the librarian, most of which notes traits corresponding to nonassertion. The following would be desirable:

1. Additional studies on the assertiveness and the attitudes toward librarianship and toward feminism of library-school students, both male and female.
2. Similar studies of in-service librarians.
3. Comparative studies of assertiveness, attitudes toward feminism and career attitudes of women in other traditionally "female" professions and women in the nontraditional fields, along the lines of the studies done by Tangri (1969), Horner (1968), and others, and well reviewed in *Women and Achievement* (Mednick, Tangri, and Hoffman, 1975).

In such studies, it is recommended that consideration be given to the following factors:

1. Utilization of additional and/or different instruments, i.e., (a) use of a personality instrument; (b) use of an additional assertive measurement specifically designed for women, such as the one developed by Harris and

Osborne (1975), as well as continued use of Lawrence; (c) further refinement of the Thornton Scale and the development of a uniform scoring system; (d) use of another instrument to measure attitudes towards women's roles, preferably the Bem Scale, which identifies feminine, masculine, and androgynous traits (Bem, 1974).

2. Use of a mixed-sex population and the incorporation of some of the components of Hall's (1972) research design set within a training group.
3. Concentration on assertive behavior in job situations and no formal attempt to deal with feminist history and thought, or with the situation of librarianship, except by a short introductory explanation at the beginning of the first session, accompanied by a brief handout, similar to those given to the experimental group in this study, but in a more condensed format.
4. Continued use of attitude and personality instruments, but for the purposes of data collections, which will eventually amass a more accurate picture of the personality and attitudes of librarians and how they change, or remain the same, as a group over a period of years, not for the purposes of measuring attitude change within a given experiment.

This researcher's opinion, initially formed a number of years ago, after reading Simpson and Simpson's (1969) essay stating that not enough current data are available about librarians, has not changed. Many of the studies on the personality and career of the librarian, from which major conclusions were drawn in the Simpsons' work, are old, and even then, the total number, both new and old, is low. The following types of studies would be useful:

1. A large survey of women librarians, using a personality instrument and a questionnaire based on the Simpsons' composite picture of the "typical semi-professional woman" and designed to measure the degree to which women librarians match this picture.
2. Studies of the personality and career of the librarian, such as those done by Schiller (1969a) and by Morrison (1969) on academic librarians, but covering all types of libraries in addition to updating their data on academic librarians.
3. A general study of the history of women in librarianship from 1923 to the present, continuing where the Wells's (1967) study ended, and a publication of both Wells and the new study, so that this information is more readily available (e.g., for use by classes).
4. Additional studies of the history of women in librarianship, dealing with selected specific aspects as identified by researchers.

Biographical Research on Women Librarians: Its Paucity, Perils, and Pleasures

LAUREL A. GROTZINGER

IN CATHERINE DRINKER BOWEN'S delightful work, *Biography: The Craft and the Calling*,[1] there is a chapter describing biographical research in terms of its perils and pleasures. Among the other topics noted in the text, Bowen briefly refers to the concept of credibility or internal criticism as a key issue. She addresses the eternal question of determining "what is fact?" or, as more specifically defined, the problem of establishing the meaning and value of the data that are examined in order to recreate the historical perspective. Bowen also touches on the biographer's obvious anxiety related to the humiliation of being found in error as well as the need to risk that disgrace in order to achieve the ultimate goal of the biography. As Shera characterized it, the biographer's mission is to create "an active understanding that can draw from this reconstruction of the past a synthesis, a series of generalizations, that not only will give the past a living reality, but will make of it a medium for the better understanding of the present."[2]

Bowen's concerns are legitimate, and Shera's definition precisely focuses on the ultimate goal of collective biography when it can utilize the specific instance; that is, find the study that brings to life the essence of the individual as placed within the framework of a society, a profession, and a universe at a point in time. However, it is important that we in librarianship, especially in examining the role of women in librarianship, do not concern ourselves so much with the errors that we may commit, or even with the ultimate quality of our methods, as with the commitment we must make to researching those who have built our heritage. Women in librarianship, through their own priorities, as well as by the nature of what is acceptable or publishable, have helped to contribute to the problem. We are close to losing our feminine historical perspective, our "herstory," our "roots," through the not-too-subtle dangers of ignorance, disinterest, and stupidity. In approaching the material that serves as a foundation for this chapter—i.e., the question of the types and methods of biographical research on women librarians—the investigation quickly revealed a preliminary problem. Biographical research on women is almost nonexistent, or if it exists, the average investigator will find it difficult to obtain the research without considerable expense and delay. Here, the researcher becomes aware of the dearth of resources, the insufficiency of retrieval mechanisms, and, to a degree, the paucity of that which should be available. Once these limited resources are obtained, it is then possible to consider the serious question of the quality of the research, the methods employed, and the results. Therein lie the perils of historical criticism. This issue is addressed in the second section of the chapter. Finally, in conclusion, is addressed the general character of the research as it portrays unique women, uniquely employed. There, of course, even with reservations, lies the lost pleasure of knowing women as librarians who lived, worked, and, in so doing, changed our profession.

PAUCITY

It is hard to underestimate the problem that occurs when investigating biographical research on women librarians, since it is clear that the problem of biographical research on librarians in general is unresolved. Noted library historian Edward Holley echoes the sentiments of many who have pointed out that in our "neglect of the greats," we have left "many of our pioneer librarians...untouched by biographical hands."[3] Michael Harris, in his valuable survey of materials on American library history,[4] reinforces Holley's comments when he concludes that "the need is still great for in-depth scholarly studies of many important American librarians."[5]

The exacerbation of this problem with respect to women can be seen in several different ways. One example is illustrated in the Harris and Davis volume, *American Library History: A Bibliography.*[6] That indispensible tool, published in 1978, will obviously, as Wayne Wiegand noted, "quickly become a first source for library historians to consult before commencing research projects."[7] A particularly relevant section, "Biographies of Librarians and Library Benefactors," has a brief introduction, which concisely reviews the evolution of the literature of American library biography and highlights the stages reflected in that evolution as: (1) brief tributes on occasion of death or retirement; (2) the American Library Association's attempt to produce a series of monographs on pioneers;[8] (3) autobiographies; (4) documented, scholarly monographs often developed as dissertation projects and, with some regularity, formally published; (5) numerous, less thorough, and usually unpublished masters'-degree papers; (6) miscellaneous portrayals included as a part of commemorative works or found in publications that interpret an institution, an idea, an event, or even an era; (7) special series, such as the Heritage of Librarianship publications currently sponsored by Libraries Unlimited, Inc.;[9] and (8) retrospective collective biographies found in dictionary or directory format.

The problem of the paucity of such research relating to women, or possibly an implicit criticism of "what exists," is demonstrated by the fact that of the 34 librarians who are cited as examples within the eight categories identified by Harris and Davis, only 3 are women. Indeed, in examining some of the most authoritative articles that survey library history, as published in the last four years, the personal references become curiously redundant and clearly nonfemale. In the eighth volume of *Advances in Librarianship*, published in 1978,[10] David Kaser reviews current issues relevant to American library history, surveys recent research, and makes some general observations. Naturally, examples are included to give an indication of the "best" of that which exists. However, of the 81 citations found at the end of the article, only 1[11] specifically refers to a woman librarian, although certain other titles suggest that there would be feminine biographical data incorporated.[12] Furthermore, in the special issue, July 1976, of *Library Trends*, entitled, *American Library History: 1876-1976*, of the two articles that are logically keyed to citing relevant sources, Colson[13] and Holley,[14] the first is critical of the methodology used in researching a woman,[15] and the second, while noting that "women became prominent in the library profession quite early,"[16] then goes on to demonstrate that those same prominent women did little to assume leadership roles, a thesis advocated by historian Dee Garrison in her work on the feminization of libraries.[17] The essay by Holley concludes with the citation of only one major published study of a women,[18] although he does emphasize the current concern about the role of women in libraries, gives special emphasis to Mary Wright Plummer, and cites several significant articles.

Still another example, as related to academic librarianship, is found in Downs's article, "The Role of the Academic Librarian."[19] His bicentennial comments on

> those who rose to "prominent posts" note a Windsor, but not a Katharine Sharp, a Williamson, but not an Isadore Mudge; cite as notable contributors to the library literature a Billings, but not an Adelaide Hasse, a Bishop, but not a Margaret Mann; or find reason to mention a Charles Smith but not a Flora Belle Ludington or a Genevieve Walton.[20]

Unfortunately, Downs, Harris, and other contemporary writers are well reinforced by several decades' of collective biography. For example, a review of women librarians included in the distinguished *Dictionary of American Biography*[21] reveals only 6 women classified as librarians, while 74 men were recognized for their contributions to the field. Similarly, the less exclusive *The National Cyclopedia of American Biography*[22] cites only 13 women, in contrast to 125 men, associated with libraries. Although slightly more statistically encouraging, it is not especially reflective of the actual role of women when, on occasion of the 75th anniversary of the American Library Association, in 1951, an article in *Library Journal* noted 13 women and 27 men.[23] Moreover, even when turning to biographical tools that emphasize women, librarians have not been selected for investigation. A 1925 work, *The Biographical Cyclopaedia of American Women*,[24] identified only three women for their work in libraries. Another tool, *American Women*, which covered nineteenth-century women, cited two "librarians."[25] The scholarly and historically oriented reference work, *Notable American Women, 1607-1950*,[26] includes only 18 librarians in its 1359 biographies. The 1980 supplement[27] does little to change that picture when it adds four additional biographies—although there is a total of 442 in the volume.

One recently published volume, which is a collective biographical and bibiliographical study, has a slightly improved approach to identifying women librarians. *Librarian Authors: A Bibliography* by Rudolf Engelbarts[28] is a survey of "108 [sic 109] men and women who were outstanding as librarians and who in addition were authors. Most of these persons were Americans"[29] Engelbarts makes no claim to inclusiveness; in fact, he asserts that "hundreds and hundreds more librarians who were authors could be listed"[30] However, Engelbart's listing does include 23 notable women librarians along with this author's count of 86 males. In some instances, it could be argued that the women "authors" who are included are more notable for their other achievements, as opposed to their contributions to the literature of either library science or any other field. For example, both Margaret Mann and Adelaide Hasse are not mentioned, and both have published over 30 articles and books, yet Mary Frances Isom is included. Isom, who was notable for her service during World War I in France, as well as for her major contribution to the libraries of Oregon, did not publish widely. Similarly, Katharine Lucinda Sharp, a unique woman who made many contributions to the field, published relatively little—a dozen articles and a survey of Illinois libraries. However, she is included, while Flora Belle Ludington, who wrote and published widely about a variety of subjects, is not. Regardless, Engelbarts deserves commendation for approaching his subject with obvious attention to women as well as men, even though the final ratio is still unbalanced.

The paucity of a reasonable number of studies devoted to women can be documented in other ways as well. Although women dominated the profession numerically in the late nineteenth century, selection for biographical study is usually determined by the contributions of the individual. If women did little to assume roles as library leaders, then the failure to give them biographical recognition might be based on a lack of professional substance or merit. However, even this somewhat tenuous argument cannot be effectively demonstrated. When Brugh and Beede reviewed the question of discrimination against women in librarianship, they pointed out:

Within the past few years, several efforts have been made to examine the early years of the American library profession to determine how sexist preconceptions took root. The development of children's librarianship in the late nineteenth and early twentieth centuries reflects some of the problems faced by women. It was a woman's field from the beginning. As Margo Sasse pointed out, "American women...originated what has been called America's most valuable contribution to the library world—library service to children." Yet the status of children's librarians was and is low in relation to other groups of librarians. Sasse showed that children's librarians, who should be regarded as pioneers, have been excluded in the main from major biographical sources such as *Notable American Women, 1607-1950*. Sasse concluded that "a necessary reordering of priorities should both provide tribute to the women founders of children's service and a realignment of the status of those currently providing children's services.[31]

Although Sasse is directing her attention specifically to "Invisible Women: The Children's Librarian in America,"[32] her analysis of three important biographical tools is a documented criticism of that which should exist but does not. The specialization of librarians who work with children is an essential, if not *the* essential, component of our library system. Every major advocate in the profession for the past several decades would be seriously challenged if he or she were to ignore that fact. Yet, the librarians who pioneered in this work have been ignored in many areas of study. It is possible, as Sasse notes, that such women have not left sufficient records for adequate analysis and evaluation, but this is a poor excuse when the situation is examined in more detail. Sasse's analysis of three of the biographical tools noted earlier raises many questions. One identifiable children's librarian, Mary Wright Plummer, is found in the prestigious *Dictionary of American Biography* (DAB). However, she was also director of two library schools, president of the American Library Association, and a recognized author of literary works. It is not possible to conclude that her specialized work with children was the major reason for inclusion in the *DAB*. As Sasse notes, at least four other women of renown in the area of children's services are not in the *DAB*. Minerva Amanda Sanders, Caroline Maria

Hewins, Sarah Bogle, and Theresa West Elmendorf are not included among those who have "made some significant contribution to American life in its manifold aspects."[33] Furthermore, Sasse points out that *The National Cyclopedia of American Biography*, while more comprehensive in that Hewins, Bogle, Elmendorf, and Plummer are included, still omits Sanders as well as other significant women who pioneered in work with children, notably Mary Hall, Anne Carroll Moore, and Lutie Stearns. Finally, in appraising the valuable publication, *Notable American Women, 1607-1950*, Sasse closes her indictment by noting that the volumes have biographies of only four children's specialists among the 1359 entries. Moreover, only token recognition is given to the profession as a whole as it related to women. A section titled, "The Progressive Era: 1890-1920" is found in the introduction. One brief paragraph summarizes the role of librarians.

Though library work, which officially became a profession in 1876, was never entirely a woman's field, women from the beginning made up a majority of librarians. In certain kinds of work they took a leading part, founding and heading some of the most important library schools, and pioneering in work with children, and in the development of readers' advisory services.[34]

Given the brevity of this statement, it is not too difficult to comprehend why only 18 of the entries can be associated with libraries and librarianship. It is also not hard to understand Sasse's concern when she points out that of the 18, only Bogle, Hewins, Plummer, and Stearns were selected for inclusion, but other uniquely qualified children's librarians were not—for example, Sanders, Effie Power. As mentioned earlier, a supplementary volume to the original set has been issued. The update, *Notable American Women: The Modern Period*,[35] contains biographies of significant women who died between 1950 and 1975. If it could be argued that the late emergence of librarianship meant that many notable women librarians were still alive when the selection was made for the original collection and had since died, then the supplement might well include a higher ratio of librarians, especially children's librarians. However, it is a continuing indication of the nonrecognition of the profession and its women that only 4 of the 442 entries in the 1980 volume are librarians. One outstanding children's librarian, Anne Carroll Moore, is included. The other three are Linda Eastman, Helen Haines, and Isadore Mudge—notable, indeed, but hardly representative of a period that saw several women serve as ALA presidents, leaders in library education, and in many other phases of library work. That fact is emphasized in the introduction to the supplement, which ignores library work, in its comments about trends toward professionalization even in traditional "women's" fields. Home economics, nursing, and social work are identified; librarianship is not.

The paucity of research on women in librarianship can be demonstrated, finally, by examining five categories of information that attempt to provide a relatively comprehensive overview of existing biographical data on either women librarians or librarians in general. They are: (1) the bibliography prepared by Harris, *A Guide to Research in American Library History*,[36] and the bibliography prepared by Harris and Davis, *American Library History: A Bibliography*;[37] (2) the informal but useful compilation made by Cynthia S. Cummings, in 1976, at the University of Wisconsin, *A Biographical-Bibliographical Directory of Women Librarians*;[38] (3) the publications of the American Library Association, specifically its series on American Library Pioneers,[39] and the *World Encyclopedia*;[40] (4) the *Encyclopedia of Library and Information Science*;[41] and (5) the first major, scholarly compilation of biographies of American librarians, the *Dictionary of American Library Biography (DALB)*[42].

The bibliographies that library historian Michael Harris has helped to compile constitute a valuable look at the existence of writings about women in the field. The first edition of Harris's *A Guide to Research in American Library History* was published in 1968. Revised in 1974, the volume served, until the publication of the Harris and Davis bibliography, in 1978, as the major "annotated list of works which deal with the increasingly voluminous published literature on American library history."[43] Chapter 10, "Biographies of Librarians and Library Benefactors," is a list of theses and dissertations devoted, with one exception, to the study of a single librarian. The earliest work cited is a biography of Alexandre Vattemare, completed as a thesis at Columbia in 1934;[44] this was followed by a thesis on Ainsworth Spofford, George Washington University, in 1938,[45] and a University of Virginia dissertation on Thomas Jefferson completed in 1942.[46] No other studies on individuals associated with librarianship were identified until 1950, when the first thesis on a woman was cited—a study of Effie Louise Power.[47] It ought to be noted that this bibliography does not preclude the existence of other acceptable theses, but Harris did not locate them in his review of the literature. In fact, a second thesis on a woman, Margaret Mann,[48] *was* completed in the same year, 1950, but omitted in the Harris list, although he does include the Mann biography in his 1978 bibliography. Regardless, the first and second editions of *A Guide to Research* once again provide evidence of the failure of the profession to compile studies on women. The chapter noted earlier contains 65 entries, arranged alphabetically by the name of the biographee. Only one study, #611, a thesis on Ohio librarians,[49] cannot be placed within a male/female framework. Of the remaining 64 studies, 41 are devoted to men, and 15 of those studies are identified as dissertations. Only 23 studies, in the entire time-frame, deal with women; moreover, only 1 study is a dissertation. Supporting earlier conclusions, an examination of the dates indicates that the 1950s and 1960s were the prime periods for the study of individuals by students preparing library-school theses. Those devoted to women will be considered later in this chapter, with respect to their quality as historical studies. However, the relatively small number of studies does little to support the conclusion that women did play a significant role in the development of libraries and library services—at least if selection for investigation is a criterion.

The 1978 publication by Harris and Davis, *American Library History: A Bibliography*, is a more extensive, although unannotated, expansion of the earlier *Guide*. The focus of the two editions of *A Guide to Research* was on theses and dissertations. The 1978 volume is an attempt "to reflect a comprehensive picture of what has been written about American libraries and related areas."[50] One section, as noted earlier, deals with "Biographies of Librarians and Library Benefactors" and contains 434 items, in contrast to the 65 noted in the *Guide*. It is not a simple matter to analyze those entries without reexamining the material to determine its actual nature, but one fact can be quickly assessed. Of the 434 cited works, which are organized by the name of the subject, only 90, or 21 percent, are related to women. In actual number of male/female subjects, 66 (29 percent) are women, while 162 (71 percent) are men. The bibliography does contain citations of theses, dissertations, books, festschriften, articles, bibliographies, parts of books, and so on. When categorizing by type of publication, material relating to men is cited at an even higher ratio; i.e., 83 percent of the citations are found in books or parts of books, with the remaining 17 percent devoted to women. It is coincidental, but also indicative, that the same ratio is found when examining the journal articles; 83 percent are either about men or are autobiographical; 17 percent are about women or are autobiographical. The only surprising aspect of the work is that the pattern of theses and dissertations is not a continuation of the earlier *Guide* by Harris. Sixty-three titles are cited and identified as theses or dissertations; however, 41 percent of those titles are about women, with the remaining 59 percent about men. This is somewhat surprising when recalling that the earlier publication, which included 65 entries, had 41 (63 percent) devoted to the study of males, while only 23 (35 percent) were devoted to women. This discrepancy is explained, however, when examining the names of the subjects. No woman noted in the *Guide* is omitted in the 1978 bibliography, although one dissertation was published and is listed as a book. In reality, there are two new theses and one dissertation. However, the titles on men which were included in the *Guide* have been reduced in number, owing to the fact that some of the men cited earlier had tangential involvement in librarianship and have been omitted. In addition, several of the dissertations on men have been published. It is clear that the study of women has not expanded significantly. Moreover, the number of doctoral studies, as opposed to master's papers, indicates that the more definitive work is still related to males, as opposed to females. In the period covered, only two dissertations on women are noted. Again, notable omissions in the compilation can be found; for example, the excellent dissertation on Isadore Mudge.[51] However, it can still be concluded that the preponderance of biographical and autobiographical material, as compiled by Harris and Davis, focuses on the male librarian.

Probably few individuals have seen the Cummings publication, since it is an inexpensive booklet, reproduced from typed copy, which was supported by the Women's Group of the University of Wisconsin-Madison Library School. Cummings comments in her preface that she "was interested in finding out what type of women have made significant contributions to our profession,"[52] and she chose to limit her selections to those who had completed their careers, retired, or, if still active, were members of the American Library Institute or mentioned in a publication of the School of Library Science at the University of Michigan. This last item, titled *Women in the Library Profession*,[53] was the result of papers presented by five distinguished women alumni who dealt with the general theme, "Women in the Library Profession." Cummings used the papers and their numerous references as a source of additional references. She also surveyed standard sources such as *DAB, Notable American Women, Who's Who in America, Who's Who in Library Service,* and *Who's Who of American Women*. The publication is admittedly limited, but must be recognized as one of the few attempts to review women librarians in such a way as to give a glimpse of their value. There are 81 entries; each entry gives a brief biological sketch and cites selected publications from which the data were taken. Some entries are so brief as to do little more than identify the person and places where she worked; others are relatively complete and include half a dozen or more citations. There many errors and omissions, especially in the citations, but the major points to be noted are that Cummings was able to focus and collect data on numerous women who had made contributions, and she is able to identify women who have been omitted, for whatever reasons, from other, more sophisticated titles. For example, this is the only publication, of those cited in this section, that gives a biographical sketch of Tessa Kelso, the controversial librarian who shaped the foundations of the Los Angeles Public Library in the 1890s.[54]

When examining the literature of librarianship with respect to the other possible sources of studies on women, certain established works were noted earlier. For instance, the American Library Association made a concerted effort during the 1920s to produce a series of significant textbooks for library schools, and also to sponsor a series of volumes that would highlight "leaders [who] had left a strong imprint on the profession of librarianship and the development of American libraries."[55] The American Library Pioneers Series began in 1924 with the famous Lydenberg assessment of John Shaw Billings, and was followed by six studies highlighting Samuel Green, Cutter, William Howard Brett, Dana, Dewey, and Jewett—obviously not a single woman among the first seven. However, the Pioneer Series changed its approach in volume eight, which was identified as *Pioneering Leaders in Librarianship, First Series* [56] Published in 1953, it readily admitted that some of the inclusions were not strictly library pioneers or even librarians—18 individuals were included. For once, women dominated in number; 10 of the entries were biographies of women, and 11 of the authors were women. That the series was edited by Emily Miller Danton may have been significant in determining this ratio, but it is also striking that this slim volume is the source of biographical material not found in any other noteworthy title devoted to librarianship, including the *Dictionary of American Library Biography.* Unfortunately, this "First Series" was the last series issued by the Association, and women continue to be ignored in other key reference works.

It is difficult to consider the study of women in the field without examining the still-in-progress publication, the *Encyclopedia of Library and Information Science.* At the time of the preparation of this chapter, 30 volumes had been published. Since no index yet exists, the only means to identify the entries is to read the contributors' names and "pull out" the obviously female biographies that are included. Although this method has its faults, since biographical material is included in articles that discuss such topics as, for example, the "Margaret Mann Citation in Cataloging," the fact is that the *Encyclopedia* is apparently one of the most uniquely sexist set of volumes in existence. Not a single woman is given a separate biographical article until volume 10, when Adelaide R. Hasse and Helen E. Haines are covered. In the preceding nine volumes, at least 37 biographies of men had been selected for articles. From volume 10 through volume 30, two other women were uncovered as main entries,[57] Lucile M. Morsch and Isadore Mudge. Yet the editors claim that the "biographies of many prominent figures...are included."[58] However, this author finds it difficult to justify an entry on the Melvil Dui Marching and Chowder Association when Anne Carroll Moore, Minnie Sears, and Theresa Elmendorf are either neglected completely or given short shrift.

Finally, it is important to consider two of the most recent and thorough publications of the field: the *ALA World Encyclopedia of Library and Information Services* and the *Dictionary of American Library Biography.*

The *ALA World Encyclopedia* was initiated in 1976; when published in 1980 it contained 452 articles written by 364 contributors from 145 countries. It is not difficult to assess the biographical coverage with respect to nationality or focus of emphasis, since there is a classified "Outline of Contents," which has a biographies subdivision. As a result, the user can observe that 4 male biographies were included in the section on the ancient world; 4 male biographies were included in the period covering the Middle Ages through the Renaissance, and in the modern-world category, males and females can be located in biographies associated with continents. The final totals indicate that there are 35 women in the volume, including 2 from Africa, 1 from Asia, 4 from Central America, 2 from Europe, 2 from South America, and 24 from North America. This is in contrast to 124 men in the modern-world classification, including 72 from North America. Once again, the basis for selection tends to elude the historian. A number of the individuals included are living, which creates an even greater concern as to the criteria for selection. The question must be asked as to the reasons why Edward Gailon Holley is found there, but not Peggy Sullivan or Elizabeth Stone. If considering those who have died, it is not easy to perceive a clear distinction between the contributions of Mary Peacock Douglas, who is not included, and Minnie Sears, who is. Regardless, the final number of entries devoted to women still must be questioned, especially in light of the fact that the *Encyclopedia* might have focused more heavily on prominent living librarians, since the *Dictionary of American Library Biography (DALB)* is limited to deceased contributors to the profession.

Although there is little doubt that the *Dictionary of American Library Biography* must be considered valuable, timely, and a much-needed reference work in the profession, an element of the problem of the paucity of research on women continues to be evident. An excellent review of the work is found in the Fall 1978 issue of *The Journal of Library History*.[59] J. Perriam Danton has analyzed the 301 biographies of men and women who have made contributions of significance to library history. Of the 301 entries, 214 are men; 87 are women. It may well be possible to justify those women—e.g., Tessa Kelso or Genevieve Walton—who were excluded because of the carefully stated criteria that national influence or scholarly contributions were essential for selection. However, the history of women in librarianship indicates that essential roles were played at a regional level by women who, for a variety of personal and societal reasons, continued to function at that level. The end result of the use of this selection process means, once again, that it is difficult to locate a relatively complete body of scholarly, thoroughly researched data on women librarians of the past century.

To summarize the preceding pages is to present a major problem and challenge to those involved in capturing the essence of the historical role of women in librarianship. Although research exists, it does not exist to the degree that might be expected in a field that was numerically feminine by the turn of the century. However, as precisely described in the introduction to *The Role of Women in Librarianship 1876-1976: The Entry, Advancement, and Struggle for Equalization in One Profession*,[60] numerical dominance is not the issue.

The profession's predominance by women has until recently been largely ignored in the monographic and journal literature dealing with the development of librarianship, libraries, and library associations.... The reemergence of the women's movement, its impact on librarianship, and the development of an interdisciplinary approach to the study of women have resulted in increasing attention to the analysis of the role and status of women in American librarianship. Yet, this attention is not reflected in recent general historical studies of the profession in either the United States or Great Britain. Women in librarianship have been mainly treated by women scholars...and as anthologized pieces or conference papers. Rarely have women been integrated into a history of the profession.[61]

Although the data regarding biographical studies of women librarians address only one aspect of the implications of this quotation, they are striking in and of themselves, since few women librarians have been the subject of serious research. According to the latest compilation of dissertations prepared in the field of library science,[62] there have been only four biographical studies of women in the period from 1930 to 1980: Katharine Lucinda Sharp, 1964;[63] Isadore G. Mudge, 1973;[64] Mary Josephine Booth, 1975;[65] and Mildred L. Batchelder, 1977.[66] This fact is matched by the minimal attention given to women librarians in several key reference sources, as described earlier. The journal and book literature reflects the same lack of recognition and/or interest in portraying outstanding women librarians.

One further note ought to be added in terms of a review of biographical studies. In addition to the fact that few libraries own extensive back-runs of library periodicals or have a collection of library-science monographs, it is extremely difficult to obtain the theses and dissertations at a reasonable cost. The four doctoral dissertations just noted are presumably available from University Microfilms International; hard copies currently cost $18.00 in the U.S. However, when this author attempted to order the 1977 publication on Batchelder, it was not available. So even UMI is not completely reliable. The master's theses are not normally available on microfilm; costs of photocopying, when available, tend to make the development of a good collection prohibitive. A literature that is geographically scattered, is indexed in few sources, and is not readily accessible is, for all practical purposes, nonexistent. That is the final and most frustrating conclusion on the paucity of the literature that this reviewer discovered.

PERILS

The approach to evaluating methodology found in biographical studies of women associated with libraries and librarianship can take several different forms—no one of which is completely exact or perfectly objective. This factor is complicated by the fact that the nature of biographical study is a topic of considerable controversy. In one respect, it is a unique form of history in and of itself:

The biographer's art is a curious one, combining history, psychology, and other diverse fields. By focusing upon one individual, the biographer's lens necessarily distorts figures tangential to the main narrative, contemporary events in which the principal figure was involved and subsequent occurences that fall outside of the tiny slice of time which the biographer has chosen to chronicle.

It is this perception that has produced numerous volumes on the style and substance of writing biographies, as, for example, the work by Catherine Drinker Bowen cited in the first paragraph of this chapter.[68] Barzun, in his classic text, *The Modern Researcher*, states that "biographies almost always raise special problems because their subjects, so to speak, force the biographer's hand. The writer must follow where they lead. But to this guidance the author must add his own imagination. The subject of a biography has to be resurrected, and this requires the creation of a distinctive pattern."[69]

However, Barzun devotes only a few short paragraphs in his text to the nature of biography, therein following a pattern articulated clearly in the renowned guide to historical method written by Louis Gottschalk.[70] His *Understanding History*, first published in 1950, clearly deserves its subtitle, *A Primer of Historical Method*. In examining the contents of the work, it is easy to observe that none of the chapters (11 in number) nor any of their subdivisions—over 160—suggests that particular attention should be given to a "biographical method" as opposed to the historical method in general. Therefore, a critique of existing biographical studies of women in the field of librarianship could use an approach that emphasizes the biographical problems, or could place biographical studies within the overall historical framework. Obviously, either approach has its limitations, since the authors' personal philosophies are largely unknown unless addressed in an opening section of their works.

Unfortunately, the problem of evaluation does not end with the fact that these two critical approaches exist. As noted in the first section of this chapter, an eight-part classification or set of categories is provided in the introduction to the Harris and Davis bibliography that deals with the biographies of librarians and library benefactors. In that chapter, the compilers argue that "the literature of American library biography follows a pattern familiar to students of American history, though successive stages appear to have come much later in library history."[71] Harris and Davis conclude that the evolution of library biography has moved from unsophisticated, nonmethodological tributes to individuals assessed in full, well-documented studies to the contemporary production of scholarly, retrospective reference compilations. These phases of biographical development were reviewed in the first section of this chapter with respect to their coverage of women. Although the dearth of material that is available on women is documented in *that* section, *this* section of the chapter, in an attempt to evaluate the existing studies, must inevitably deal with several forms of biographical products. To make a complex matter more difficult, it must also be noted that it is not possible to review all of the existing studies on women librarians. Often they were not obtainable through obvious sources and, in some instances, were simply too costly to pursue, in terms of time and geography. Therefore, the following pages focus on a sample of studies taken from (1) journals and books; (2) theses and dissertations; and (3) biographies found in collective reference works.

Nonscholarly Tributes

In examining the biographer's skill with respect to "tributes" to women whose contributions and personalities should not be forgotten, a "reasonable" wealth of subjective material is identifiable. The tendency, if not the total goal, of the authors, is to write, as Powell described it, "of those who were truly great."[72] Powell further documents his assumption by quoting from an article by Stanley Pargellis that sets the style of such articles and books: "Librarians can take inspiration from the lives and achievements of the great librarians of the past and from their concepts of the purposes of libraries.... [There must be] a sense of the significance of the profession which does not change as it is handed down from generation to generation...."[73] The weakness of such works—whether by men or women—was accurately critiqued by Kraus when he commented that "after re-reading these biographical sketches one has the uneasy feeling that he has somehow wandered into a world of unassailable virtue of Butler's *Lives of the Saints.*"[74] Certainly there is nothing in the studies of women that contradicts that assertion. Indeed, the "history" that is involved is that which Barzun describes as the "story" and not the "*fashioning* of written history. This, he knows, requires method."[75] For instance, Gratia Countryman, a notable woman librarian herself, is unabashedly writing "A Tribute" to Clara F. Baldwin in her 1951 article published in *Minnesota Libraries* on the occasion of Baldwin's death.[76] Countryman was, admittedly, a close friend, and as she writes of Baldwin's accomplishments, she cannot help but be subjective in her interpretation. As is true of the vast majority of articles, there are no footnotes, no references, no citations of a corroborative authority—not even a sequence of activities.

Somewhat more informative, in the historical sense, is a commentary on Janet Doe, medical librarian, which makes textual reference to several of her publications, concludes with a "Bibliography of Janet Doe," and provides a reasonably clear chronological framework to her life.[77] At the same time, no footnotes are attached to identify the quotations, no author is identified with the article, and the conclusion states that "this account does not pretend to cool objectivity. That we leave to some future library student poring over Miss Doe's writings for a learned thesis. Here we can paint only the picture seen by friends and colleagues, an affectionate tribute to a friend, a colleague, and a mentor."[78]

In the same vein, the books published in this format, while few in number, reflect the noncritical stance that is found in the oft-criticized biography of Dewey whose title reflects its bias: *Melvil Dewey: Seer, Inspirer, Doer, 1851-1931.*[79] One striking example of this affectionate approach is *Fervent and Full of Gifts*,[80] the "life" of Althea Warren as written by her friend, Martha Boaz. The problem created by Boaz for Boaz is articulated in her introduction:

I remember the kindness of Althea Warren....I remember her exuberance and her affection....I remember her as a generous-minded woman whose high intelligence and great spirit have left a profound mark in the lives of those who knew her. It is to try to recall these qualities and to record them for others to read that I write this book.[81]

Here is the historian at her worst, irretrievably set on a particular road, a self-fulfilling hypothesis at work. Moreover, Boaz, who, of course, knows the nature of the historical method, chooses not to provide citations to her data so that a future, more objective historian has references to consult.

The examples of this form of history are not as numerous as they ought to be, regardless of their lack of methodology or critical perception. Perhaps, and this is more of a sexist notion than an actual reality, the only difference between these female "tributes" and the "male" tributes is that the majority were written by women praising women and there is a sense of "feminine" approbation, the necessity to be supportive of that which has not been adequately documented, or, if the researcher searches for psychological motivation, the belief that in the study of women *by women* there is a recognition that there is a "growing sisterhood of non-submissive, life-affirming women who are commited to action programs in democratically run libraries."[82]

Regardless, in examining some of the known titles that are "herstories," the historian must take methodological exception to the approach and outcome. As noted earlier, there are few published monographs related to significant women librarians. Among those which exist is a volume entitled *Caroline M. Hewins: Her Book; Containing a Mid-Century Child and Her Books*[83]—an essay by Hewins that constitutes the bulk of the slim Horn Book volume. It is followed by a biographical sketch of Hewins written by Jennie D. Lindquist. The later section, to which we must direct our attention, comprises some 20 pages of the total volume. There are no footnotes, no approach to historical methodology, no structure in the sense of historical biography as advocated by Bestor, who suggested, in a publication directed to librarians, that "genuine verifiable knowledge in any field...must be based upon something in the here and now that can be examined or at least observed not only by the person who professes to make a contribution to knowledge, but also by those who wish to certify his results."[84] On the other hand, two nationally published studies, one titled *Etta Josselyn Giffin, Pioneer Librarian for the Blind*[85] and the other, *Ina Coolbrith: Librarian and Laureate of California,*[86] serve as qualified models for biographical studies that, in the words of one biographer, give "the reader a vivid sense of the reality of the past, enables him [sic] to relive in imagination the life of another and, in most cases, a more important person than himself [sic]."[87] Although these words do not suggest a scientific approach, the same author goes on to describe the values of external criticism—i.e., the authenticity of documentation—and internal criticism—i.e., the credibility of analysis. Therein lies the value of the two studies cited: each is carefully constructed with appropriate citations, adequate "historiography"—i.e., the *writing* of history—and the methodological structure that allows a critic to review the reliability and validity of the conclusions. However, the number of titles that exist in this category—that is, formally published monographs on women librarians—constitutes such a small sample that it is difficult to draw any conclusion of significance. If one uses the Harris and Davis bibliography as an authoritative source, the biographies just cited plus four others appear.[88] Only one, the published biography of Katharine Sharp, falls into the area of formally published historical biography on women.[89] Beyond these few titles, published monographs either do not exist or were not examined or identified for this evaluation.

Theses and Dissertations

The second major area of biographical study of women lies in the area of theses and dissertations. As noted earlier, the number of these studies does not match the number of men who have been evaluated in the past half century. In preparation for this analysis, the author obtained twenty-plus theses and dissertations for review. It is important to note, as pointed out earlier, that no single library is apt to have collected these titles, if they are master's papers, since many are available only through personal photocopy, and, furthermore, those titles approved as dissertations are not necessarily obtainable through University Microfilms International.

The range of the titles is formidable in terms of detailed assessment. The best means of surveying the subjects, although not complete, is to review the Harris listing in *A Guide to Research in Library History*.[90] The following outstanding/unique/deserving-of-interest women librarians have been studied:

Julia Brown Asplund
  New Mexico librarian and library advocate[91]
Susan Dart Butler
  Pioneer library service to Southern blacks[92]
Linda Anne Eastman
  Public librarian in Cleveland[93]
Louise Franklin
  Public librarian in Houston; library educator[94]
Bessie Graham
  Author of *The Bookman's Manual*; library educator[95]
Julia Grothaus
  Public librarian in San Antonio[96]
Lillian Gunter
  Public librarian in rural Texas[97]
Alice S. Harrison
  School librarian in Austin[98]
Caroline Maria Hewins
  Pioneer children's librarian[99]
Julia Bedford Ideson
  Public librarian in Houston[100]
Anne Carroll Moore
  Children's librarian in New York[101]
Minnie Sweet Monti
  Public librarian in Cleveland[102]
Cornelia Marvin Pierce
  Library educator, pioneer state librarian in Oregon[103]

Effie Louise Power
   Children's librarian in Cleveland[104]
Octavia F. Rogan
   State librarian in Texas, Houston public librarian[105]
Jennie Scott Scheubar
   Public librarian in Fort Worth[106]
Katharine Sharp
   Library educator in Illinois[107]
Lois F. Shortess
   School librarian in Louisiana[108]
Alice Sarah Tyler
   Library educator in Iowa, Ohio[109]
Rose L. Vormelker
   Special business librarian in Cleveland Public Library[110]
Elizabeth Howard West
   Special librarian in Texas, services to blind[111]

In addition to these women, identified by Harris in 1974, other theses and dissertations have focused on:

Mildred Batchelder
   Texas children's librarian[112]
Mary Josephine Booth
   Illinois academic librarian[113]
Gratia Alta Countryman
   Minnesota public librarian[114]
Margaret Mann
   Cataloger, classifier, library educator[115]
Mary P. Martin
   Canton, Ohio, public librarian[116]
Isadore G. Mudge
   Reference librarian, library educator[117]

Of the 27 librarians just cited, the theses and dissertations of Asplund, Booth, Butler, Countryman, Eastman (2), Franklin, Graham, Grothaus, Gunter, Harrison, Hewins, Ideson, Mann, Moore (2), Monti, Mudge, Pierce (a published article based on her thesis was examined), Power, Rogan, Scheuber, Sharp, Tyler, Vormelker, and West were examined. Three studies were not available or obtained for review: Batchelder, Martin, and Shortess.

Conclusions regarding the examination of these titles must logically, for the majority of the works, be divided between master's theses and dissertations. The dissertation, one assumes, would demand a great deal of methodological sophistication; the master's thesis, on the other hand, is not usually required to meet the rigors of doctoral examination with respect to sources, methodology, and generalizability. For this essay, only three dissertations of women librarians were able to be examined out of four that were located. One is the author's; it is not included in the analysis, although reviews of the published work can be obtained through a search of *Library Literature* during the 1966-68 period. Of the remaining two that were examined, i.e., Booth and Mudge, there is little to fault in either with respect to the quality of biographical study. The analysis of Mudge, for those who know of her contributions in general, provides a comprehensive dissection of her activities built on a broad base of library history. It is surprising that Harris and/or Davis have never cited the biography in their volumes. This omission, in the best bibliographies available, is indicative of the problem that confronts the researcher who attempts to locate studies on women.

The Mudge volume, in many respects, is a model biography. John Waddell was able to meet the three major criteria of a key historical study. He gained accessibility to the documents; the nature of the period and a perspective on it were available to him in terms of interpretation; and he had the ability to place the work within a historical framework of reference service, a factor that made Isadore Mudge unique in American librarianship. Although the structure of the work might seem to be a simple chronology of events, Waddell described Mudge in such a way as to recreate her personality and contributions; she became "not merely the best-known as well as the most important and the most influential figure in the field for a long period of years."[118] In documenting those facts, Waddell addressed two significant questions: what were the causal factors that brought about her ability to do what she did; and could her success be demonstrated through historical fact? The 300-plus pages of his dissertation are a powerful answer to those questions. They achieve the basic goals that illustrate effective historical methodology. The who, where, when, what, and why of Isadore Mudge are effectively explored and explained.

The Mudge dissertation stands and speaks for itself, but, as noted earlier, few have apparently examined its contents. The best "quick" assessment of the quality of this dissertation—which is not accessible to many—is found in the entry in the *Encyclopedia of Library and Information Science*. In that article, which is less than five pages long, Waddell is able to communicate the sense of "the most distinguished and the most successful figure in the annals of American reference librarianship...."[119] In the larger study, his dissertation, he gives the full "life and times" of that unique woman, Isadore Mudge.

The second dissertation which was examined in detail is that of Mary Josephine Booth. The table of contents discloses a reasonably scientific approach to the problem. There is a brief introduction that interprets the "problem;" there is a review of related literature; there is a description of the procedures for collection and analyzing data; and then, on page 38 of a work encompassing 185 pages, the data relative to M.J. Booth are begun. Not surprisingly, given the nature of historiography, the reader of that biography can locate such headings as the "Time and the Period," "Appraisal," "The Challenge of Growth," "The Individual," "Philosophy Toward Work," "Weaknesses and Strengths," and finally, "Summary, Findings, and Recommendations." As expected, there are additional appendices, reproducing selected original sources, data gathering-instruments, and so on, and a detailed bibliography. Although Ms. Booth, because her major impact was regional, was not included in *DALB*, Lawson's summary comment still is clear: "Her love of books and dedication to librarianship as a profession, and a strong desire to be of service to others also carried her influence beyond the borders of the State of Illinois to the battlefields of France and Germany and to a stumbling library in Louisiana."[120] Despite the fact that a perfect or at least semiaccurate assessment of any historical study would involve the reexamination of the sources used by its author it is important for the researcher to note that Lawson's bibliography, in and of itself, is *selected*. Yet it includes papers and manuscripts, official reports and publications, books and monographs, articles, and unpublished material. The Mudge biography, organized in a different fashion begins with 30 citations of unpublished materials, followed by a list of published books and pamphlets, and concludes with periodical articles and serials. Waddel then proceeds to identify Mudge's own publications and his interviews with individuals who were knowledgeable about her work. In this respect, both Waddell and Lawson have attempted to reach/examine/analyze the basic resources available to them. They have reviewed original and primary sources, considered secondary and tertiary material, attempted to locate quantitative "cliometric" data, and, when available, looked to nonprint, oral, and folk history as well as surviving forms of historical "record."

When the researcher of women's biographical studies turns to the theses—i.e., master's-level products—the lack of similar sophistication of methodology is obvious. Although the several theses published since 1950 do contribute to our knowledge of women in the field, the historical method leaves much to be desired. In brief, the following paragraphs assess the thesis approach to the women librarians listed earlier.

Julia Brown Asplund's life is described in a thesis prepared at the University of Texas; the study attempts to assess the work of an individual whose real work was as a "public servant" as opposed to a practicing librarian. The thesis, 58 pages long, notes that Asplund "destroyed her personal files of letters and other materials which might have been of interest...."[121] The four-page bibliography is evidence of that observation as well as being indicative of the fact that secondary materials were not heavily consulted. The table of contents reflects a typical chronological approach—1875-1955. The five-page summary and conclusions reflect the depth of the study and the materials available. Asplund is not included in *DALB*, presumably because of her regional involvement, in New Mexico, as opposed to national significance.

The second thesis examined was that on Susan Dart Butler, 1888-1959; she is found in *DALB*. Her efforts to establish public library service for blacks drew attention in 1959 when her biography was prepared at Atlanta University. A marginal 31 pages attempt to recreate a life; it is also the only source cited by Virginia Lacy Jones in the article she prepared for *DALB*. Ethel Bolden, the author of the thesis, outlined her methodology in the thesis; she had examined the library literature, interviewed Mrs. Butler, interviewed librarians who had worked with her and after her at the Charleston Free Library, and had gathered selected primary resources. However, her bibliography cited only 18 items—both primary and secondary. Although it would be hard to fault the need to document Butler, the analysis presented is, at best, superficial, and, at worst, colored by personal devotion to the individual and not the history. (In the following paragraphs analyzing theses, footnotes have been omitted except in cases of direct quotation. Refer to footnotes 91-117 for complete bibliographical data.)

Turning to another library school, the University of Minnesota, it is possible to examine a 136-page thesis on Gratia Alta Countryman. Although it would be hard to argue that she was other than a "regional" librarian, she did win election to the presidency of ALA—reason for automatic inclusion in *DALB*. Her biographer, Mena C. Dyste, in 1965 reviewed materials available in Minnesota. She did have access to several books of clippings, as well as published material including articles prepared by Countryman, and she solicited primary material from surviving colleagues. There is also some evidence that secondary material was reviewed. The organization of the work is, again, familiar, in that it proceeds from "The Beginnings" to "Finale." It is all too obvious that the tone of the work is reverential and not critical; the hypothesis was accepted before it was tested; i.e., Countryman was "an outstanding librarian."[122]

When, in a world of limited study, not one but two theses on an individual have been prepared, it is unfortunate to conclude that the methodology is wanting, but a cursory examination of the theses on Linda Eastman does little to document otherwise. One was prepared in 1952 at Kent State University; the other was prepared in 1953 at Western Reserve. The first, numbering 79 pages, includes a five-page bibliography. Both were, of course, written while Ms. Eastman was still alive; she died in 1963. Once again, if measured against the criteria of *DALB*, she was, indeed, a regional if not a municipal librarian—her inclusion in *DALB* was due to her presidency of ALA. The thesis prepared in 1953 by Alice Wright is even briefer in terms of documentation than the first mentioned. Cecil Phillips, with only a single page of formal sources, has fallen into or has chosen the biographer's trap; he is devoted and not evaluative. The same can be said of Wright, but she, admittedly, does not attempt to measure Eastman's impact and does provide a summary chapter which, while noncritical, is more evaluative than that of Phillips. In this respect, when classifying historical study, Phillips is clearly descriptive, while Wright, although her primary purpose is "to present" Miss Eastman, attempts to discuss her work.

As this discussion of theses continues, a number of studies, written while the subject is still alive, will be described. Given the fact that these are women who have often had a major impact on the community in which the biographer is working, the outcomes invariably are less than critical. At the same time, selected studies emerge as more constructive analyses of the examined life. One such is the thesis by Claudie Pettigrew which, while undeniably reverent, looks thoroughly at the contributions of Louise Franklin, a Houston public librarian who established and maintained a superb reference department for some 40 years. The thesis also looks with care at the "cornerstone" of her education, the Department of Library Science at the University of Texas. Moreover, in the preface, the author notes her own inadequacy as a historian and biographer—her words are useful to any beginner in the field: she "followed some false trails assiduously...she spent far more time and effort in research [on the library school] than its relationship to the total work should have justified; consequently she had too little time to spend on more important facets of the study."[123] The biographer also provides a checklist of the available resources—material often not covered in theses. The bibliography, five pages in length, contains many original sources, a number of unpublished documents, and identifies 10 key individuals who were interviewed—including Franklin herself. There are copious footnotes, which provide reasonable evidence to support the statements found in the seven "chapters," which move logically from Franklin's preprofessional library years to her full-blown career in the Houston Public Library. The final section, an assessment, is built almost completely on data obtained from personal interviews. It is laudatory, but there is also a deep sense of reality when Pettigrew concludes that "the range of her experience compared to that of pioneer library leaders in Texas, i.e. other biographies, was narrow, and, unlike many of them, she was not a dynamic personality nor a trail blazer."[124]

Turning from the study of Franklin to that of Bessie Graham, a thesis prepared in 1953, there is, once again, a return to a study based more on admiration than attention to the biographer's critical acumen. Bessie Graham, at the time of the research, was a highly respected living legend, and Campbell's bias is seen on page two, when she proposes "to present an intimate picture of the vibrant personality, the keen sense of humor, and the human qualities which Miss Graham possesses....As one who has enriched librarianship and whose personality has influenced librarians both *in posse* and *in esse*...Miss Bessie Graham is worthy of being more widely known."[125] Campbell does outline her sources of information, but an examination of the extensive bibliography discloses several pages of references to Graham's own publications, and less than two dozen citations to articles or material relevant to her. Manuscript sources were either nonexistent, unavailable, or not located. At the same time, Campbell must be given credit for her thorough analysis of Graham's written contributions, especially *The Bookman's Manual*; there is, in the study, a comprehensive evaluation of the subject's personal philosophy as demonstrated in her publications. Moreover, Campbell herself writes with a sense of style and authority; her text is liberally but effectively spiced with quotations thoughtfully directed to the point of the discussion. As a result, despite a perfect example of the self-fulfilling hypothesis, the thesis provides a good basis for a more critical work—yet to be authored.

Another librarian eulogized while still alive is Julia Grothaus, whose biographer, Donald Drummond, takes a solid approach to the "great person" theory of history. He poses a tentative interrogative hypothesis when he indicates that "the identification of...various influences in her career is a primary concern."[126] As a secondary goal, he also proposes to determine her accomplishments and influence as a librarian during her 40-year career as the major public librarian in San Antonio, Texas. Drummond then outlines his sources of information: interviews with Grothaus and her associates, Texas library journals, the archives of the Texas Library Association and the Southwestern Library Association, minutes of the San Antonio Public Library, assorted miscellaneous manuscripts, and any secondary material that appeared relevant. His bibliography reflects the use of several secondary monographs, approximately 30 articles, 8 newspapers, assorted primary sources mainly drawn from educational institutions, archival records, and a few select items such as unpublished speeches of Grothaus. Drummond also makes note of the limitations of his sources, a problem well known to most library historians, since library archival records are not only incomplete, but often nonexistent, in many institutions.

The paper follows a common descriptive pattern, with a chronological approach dictating most of the organization. A final section, "Summary and Observations," is unabashedly laudatory. Still, there is a unique value in the work, as in the regional studies noted earlier, since no other source has produced any record of significance. The material found in these papers is irreplaceable even though flawed in the use of internal criticism by the amateur; that is, the credibility of much of the data has not been established and is corroborated only to a minor degree.

As illustrated in the following paragraphs, studies of Texas women librarians dominate the geographical distribution. This coverage is due, of course, to the strong influence of library historians in the library school at the University of Texas, Austin. In addition to the two women already discussed, Franklin and Grothaus, six other theses are devoted to Texas pioneers. One dissertation, on Mildred Batchelder, could not be obtained for examination.

The six women who were also subjects of research at a thesis level are Lillian Gunter, Alice S. Harrison, Julia Ideson, Octavia Rogan, Jennie Scheubar, and Elizabeth West.

Two of the biographees, Ideson, and especially Rogan, provided considerable personal data for their researchers. Gunter, who excelled in county library development, left a major primary source, "The Gunter Diary," and papers deposited in the State Historical Museum, North Texas State University, Denton. Harrison was not known personally by her biographer, but there were archival material, secondary sources, and friends and relatives as well as professional colleagues to interview. The work on Jennie Scott Scheubar, by Robert N. Taylor, contains a unique introduction with a frank admission that much of the material that might have been examined was not. Yet, of all the thesis studies consulted for this essay, this work maintained the most critical attitude; weaknesses as well as strengths were noted. Moreover, the bibliography, while not unusual in terms of the number of citations, included more original sources than most of the others that were examined. As a result, the methodology is open to far less criticism than, for instance, the glowing conclusion of the biography of Alice Harrison, pioneer school librarian, or the "evaluation," some 40 lines, which characterizes Elizabeth West's work.

The work on Harrison has one unique attribute: she alone has been treated, because of her role as a *school* librarian, as a subject for research. Other examples are clearly directed to the public librarian, including the children's librarian; such women have received, even in a limited universe, more emphasis than all other specializations in librarianship. The single other documented historical commonality lies in the fact that the majority of the subjects were involved, at some point in their productive careers, in one or more of the library schools that were emerging during the first half of the century. Some were closely associated with library education; e.g., Katharine Sharp and Alice Tyler. Others were called to teach because they had special knowledge; e.g., Vormelker and Harrison.

One point to be noted with respect to the Harrison thesis is basic to the production of an acceptable piece of research—the professional expertise of the author. Herring had obtained a B.S. in elementary education, had taught, and was pursuing a career in elementary-school libraries. Therefore, she brought an "expert" opinion to her interpretation of Harrison's role in planning and directing the development of "school libraries as an integral part of the public school program in Austin."[127] The thesis, while undeniably noncritical, did draw heavily from published and unpublished resources, including family papers. Yet, Herring still includes a disclaimer regarding the paucity of source material. One section of her introduction merits quoting:

> As soon as Miss Harrison was chosen as biographee, a search for information about her was started. Published sources were first searched. Then official files, scrapbooks of clippings and archives were examined and useful items noted for later study, and interviews were begun. Records were later studied with care and full notes taken. When the search for information seemed to have reached a dead end, the Brooks-Harrison Estate Family Papers became available and only they made possible the completion of the project. The search was concluded with correspondence (to verify dates and confirm unsubstantiated "facts"), and with some final interviews (in a last search for missing details).
> Information was then organized and assimilated and the plan followed in presenting the thesis was drafted.[128]

In reviewing the University of Texas studies on women, one eventually reaches the thesis prepared by Goldia Hester on Elizabeth H. West. West made major contributions to Texas librarianship in several areas, from state librarian to academic librarian to work with school and public libraries. She was an author of both professional and literary works, and active in several professional organizations. The thesis prepared by Hester is as reverent of its subject as any examined, but it is solidly based on the resources that were available to her. Unfortunately, two key areas of West's service were 8 years in the state library and 17 years at Texas Technological College. As Hester regretfully notes, she encountered a problem not uncommon to any library historian: "Unfortunately the State Library has preserved very little of Miss West's correspondence, and three biennial reports were not published during Miss West's years at the State Library."[129]

Despite the lack of a critical approach to West's contributions—that is, the work is another example of the self-fulfilling hypothesis on greatness—there is much to be praised in the thorough analysis of the material that was available. Many interviews were conducted, all known manuscripts were consulted, and numerous secondary resources were examined. The major weakness, which some might consider a strength, lies in the fact that the work was one in a series of theses relating to Texas librarians as such. That approach is not inappropriate, for it did produce a series of studies that would otherwise never have been written, on key figures in Texas library history. However, it is also true that there is a commonality among the works that begins to appear *pro forma*; in each there is an introductory preface that states the worthiness of the subject, outlines the sources, and may speak to the procedure. This is then followed by several descriptive chapters, which reproduce the activities of the individual in detail. Most are footnoted carefully, make heavy use of quotations, and conclude with a bibliography. They cover secondary and primary materials to the degree that they were located. Moreover, when examining these pioneer women as a group, there were special interrelationships among them that were reflected in their accomplishments. There was, albeit untitled, a strong "old-girl network" operating in Texas through the first half of the twentieth century.

At the same time, the use of secondary background resources is demonstrably inadequate. The larger historical backdrop in these studies is neglected in order to provide the details of a library's operations and growth. For example, a readable, well-footnoted study on Julia Bedford Ideson was purposely focused on one woman's professional achievements in Houston, Texas. Although the bibliography is substantial, the reader who is unaware of the larger framework of library evolution does not relate Ideson to the history of librarianship in general. Here was a woman who lived and worked during unusual times, 1903-45, yet there is a sense of regional isolation as if the Texas library world existed of and for itself. In the same vein, a study of Octavia Rogan, based heavily on hours of interviews with Rogan, establishes the details of a life that apparently existed in a single state. The final comment by her biographer indicates the particular failure to move beyond the specifics of a life in order to write evaluative or explanatory biographical history. As Banks commented, Rogan "was capable; she was well-educated; and she performed outstandingly as a Texas librarian."[130] Once again, it needs to be emphasized that these are not failures as research papers. Rather, they fall into the questionable category of "sentimental chronicles and [are] anything but critical in approach."[131]

The theses not yet mentioned were prepared at several different institutions, although Western Reserve also produced at least four studies considered here. The work on Caroline Hewins, pioneer children's librarian, was submitted in 1959 to the New Haven State Teachers College, now Southern Connecticut State College. As mentioned earlier, one published volume, *Caroline M. Hewins: Her Book*,[132] contains a short biographical study by Jennie D. Lindquist; it is a perfect example of the collegial "tribute." Unfortunately, the thesis that was reviewed, while adding certain professional facts to the published biography, must also be judged as another uncritical account of her life: "That girl was Caroline Maria Hewins who for fifty years was the beloved librarian of Hartford, Connecticut, a dynamic pioneer in the American public library movement, and an inspiring early leader in the field of library science."[133] The thesis is short and notably lacking in footnotes based on primary documentation other than Hewins's own works. Even in the preparation of the two key sections, an assessment of Hewins's "contribution to the professional organizations" and Hewins "as author, bibliographer, and compiler," there is a failure to cite manuscript sources. This is further illustrated in the bibliography, which contains no citations to primary sources other than Hewins's writings. It is hard to challenge Hewins's special service to the field, but the biography of librarians needs to be more interpretive and not an exercise in description.

Two theses that attempt to explicate the life and contributions of Anne Carroll Moore were also examined. Moore is one of two women librarians who have merited more than one study; the other was Linda Eastman, discussed earlier. The first study of Moore was prepared in 1951 at Pratt; the second, in 1966, at Southern Connecticut State. In examining the 1951 paper, there is evidence of the use of significant resources.

Source material, so scattered, has proved plentiful and the data garnered, when sorted and organized, proved more than sufficient. The journals of the library profession and periodicals devoted to literary matters contain a large amount of information. Such magazines as the *Horn Book, Publisher's Weekly*, the *Library Journal*, the *ALA Bulletin* and the *Wilson Bulletin* were most helpful, for they provided necessary facts, dates, and inspirational material, contributed by Miss Moore and by her admirers and co-workers. Books written by Miss Moore, *My Roads to Childhood, Nicholas, Nicholas and the Golden Goose*, and *Three Owls* were helpful for facts, for insights into her personality, and for a clear statement of her standards for children's literature. I have depended heavily, too, on the annual reports of the New York Public Library and the Pratt Institute Free Library for the years of her service in each institution.

An interview with Miss Moore was helpful, not so much for data, but because the personal contact, however brief, increased my respect for her and helped me to visualize the impact of her personality on her work. I have received similar impressions from association with persons who have known her.[134]

Although Akers did not have access to a set of archival records, she did much with the sources available in preparing a firmer biographical study than some of those just noted. Certainly, there is recognition of Moore's tremendous personal impact on children's work; it is also evident that Akers did have a sense of writing style. The thesis is relatively short—40-plus pages—but the significance of Moore's contributions is easy to grasp in the phrasing of Akers's introduction when she notes that Moore's "intangible contributions...with which she endowed her field do not always lend themselves to mere dates. Love of beauty, honesty, and tradition, a feeling for childhood, and an aspiration to genuineness in all things, and above all, her own strength of character and her insistence on strength and substance in children's literature are innate...."[135] Fifteen years later, the second thesis, by Anne Poor, is easily the more comprehensive study, but undoubtedly profited from the first, which it cites. This study has a valuable table of contents, which abstracts each chapter in terms of its coverage, and includes an introduction to the "Introduction" that identifies, in 10 lines, the purpose, problem, and methods of the research:

purpose: that the study of one who became a proven example of fine librarianship will be of value to others in the field of library science.

problem: to show through the evidence of her background, her profession and her personal attributes that she had significant influence in the growth of children's books.

methods: readings covered in general, reports of her work, writings about ACM, and her own writings. Other investigations took the forms of correspondence and interviews with former associates, artists and illustrators, publishers and editors.[136]

Poor's study is considerably longer than Akers's, and also has a sense of historiography. In one brief commentary, "Some Uses of Biography,"[137] the author asks the question, "So how does one judge a biography?" His answer is demonstrated, to a degree, in the Poor thesis: "The biography must recreate its central character so as to give the reader a sense of rounded reality showing how this person discharged his obligations to himself, to his family, to his community, and to the human race."[138] Poor's bibliography and footnotes indicate extensive use of available resources; the organization of the material treats first the basic biographical data, and then examines, in seven chapters, Moore's contributions as a professional librarian and her influence on the creation of children's books. There are, finally, two brief chapters on achievements and significance of her work and some limited "conclusions and recommendations." One recommendation, in particular, ought to be noted: "It is hereby recommended that students of library science be given greater opportunity to study such aspects of librarianship by reading or research into the lives and work of many other notable librarians."[139]

Moore, obviously, was an individual worthy to be studied and, without any doubt, an ideal topic for a study. Others are neither so recognizable nor as well handled. A second institution that produced a number of biographical studies is Western Reserve, now Case Western. The studies done there on Alice Tyler, Rose Vormelker, Minnie Monti, and Effie Power provide a quasi-spectrum of biographical quality. The work on Monti, written while she was alive and heavily influenced by her conversations, is a mixed compendium. Its author, Frederick Earnshaw Hershey, devotes a minimum of commentary to his subject and, even then, interrelates her professional competencies to her skill as a homemaker! Moreover, the first fourth of the thesis focuses heavily on accomplishments of Monti's librarian mother and the close relationship of mother and daughter to the Italian community in Cleveland. The concluding pages then deal with her work as a librarian, with numerous references to her husband, sons, and general interests. Monti, needless to say, is not included in *DALB*; her contributions to the collection department of the Cleveland Public Library and to the people who knew her were important in a limited framework. The thesis, at best, chronicles material that would otherwise be lost. At worse, it is a casual assessment of an individual; as Hershey notes, "in no sense is this an introspective or intimate biography."[140]

The other theses prepared at Western Reserve, which were examined, aspire to a more conscientious approach. The first one, prepared in 1950, deals with Effie Louise Power, another librarian who pioneered in work with children. It benefits from the fact that its author, Margaret Becker, carefully framed Power's contributions within the context of the overall development of the field. The study avoids the usual chronicle of Power's life, and provides, instead, an opening chapter, "Library Service to Children before 1900," following that with the specific movement in Cleveland that first caught up Power in the children's movement. This chapter is marked by its heavy use of annual report material that documents the public library as much as it sets the stage for biography. Then the biographer turns to the development of work with children as perceived in the reports of the annual meetings of the American Library Association from 1889 to 1906. Here, for the first time we see the individual emerging in the larger context of the library community. It can be criticized, as many contemporary critics of library history note, that this perspective is still not enough, that such developments must be set in the larger social perspective,[141] but, as already pointed out, few theses approach their subjects with any sense of the library, much less the nation, as a whole.

Finally, in Chapter IV of the work, the thesis turns directly to Power as a supervisor of children's work at the St. Louis Public Library, at the Carnegie Library, Pittsburgh, and returns, to conclude her career, to the Cleveland Public Library from 1920 to 1937. The sources cited are heavily dependent on Power's own annual and official reports to the libraries, her published articles, and a few reminiscences of colleagues. Becker ends with a brief summary of her accomplishments; it does not speak to her weaknesses. At the same time, this biography does give a sense of what was achieved. As a result, it serves one biographical role, in that "we do not have to start our own lives from the ground, but from the shoulders of the people whose lives we read."[142]

The thesis on Alice Tyler, prepared by Cora Richardson in 1951, is related, in general, to her work in Cleveland and at Western Resrve, although Tyler, of course, was nationally renowned. It is, admittedly, in the same mold as many of the previously identified papers; Richardson has "not attempted to dramatize her life, but rather to gather and recount the details of her career to the end that what she worked for and what she achieved may not be forgotten."[143] There is evidence of considerable conversation with friends and associates as well as the use of manuscript material. One weakness of any thesis prepared within the environs of the geographical location in which the subject spent most of her life is that those sections that relate to service elsewhere usually lack primary documentation. As a result, in the Tyler thesis, discussion of her work in Iowa is largely based on secondary sources, as opposed to the material found in Cleveland by a student of an institution located there. When Tyler returned to become director and dean of the library school, the sources are more direct and primary. The major weakness of this section is the lack of any opinion suggesting that Tyler had human or professional faults. As a biographer of an individual who founded the library school in which this author studied, it must be noted that the tendency is to avoid criticism. However, it is possible to note weaknesses of human nature without destroying a professional reputation. For this failure, the Richardson thesis must be particularly noted. Tyler was a major force in American librarianship, but she is not seen in other than her superhuman role. Indeed, it must be noted again, "Nothing distinguishes critical history from popular history more clearly and decisively than the former's insistence...that every narrative contained in a primary source is to be described and treated simply as a piece of evidence, never as an "authority."[144]

The final paper examined that was prepared at Western Reserve was completed by Magner in 1957 and dealt with Rose Vormelker, the famous founder of the special business-service area of the Cleveland Public Library. Vormelker "pioneered, developed and organized this bureau [the Business Information Bureau (BIB) of the Library] into one of the country's most highly regarded sources of business information."¹⁴⁵ The introduction to the thesis proposes not only to give the biographical essence of its subject but to describe her method for establishing the BIB. As might be expected, the student worked with and interviewed Vormelker several times and had access to considerable manuscript material as well as to surviving friends and associates. The problem with heavy dependence on Vormelker as a source has already been noted with respect to several other papers; it exists here as well. Magner does not choose to footnote regularly the "facts" as based on personal conversations; she opens the first chapter with a footnote that simply says: "Any statements or anecdotes related by Miss Vormelker in a series of four interviews will not be footnoted unless the situation described or the information contained therein is of exceptional interest to the reader."¹⁴⁶ It should be noted, however, that many references are to those same personal interviews. As a result, there is a strong sensitivity to the individual through her own interpretation of past events. The thesis is a unique testimonial to an unusual woman; it is not, of course, critical history.

One thesis, by Shaw on Margaret Mann, is the last to be discussed. It was one of the first studies of women to be prepared at a library school; it was written at Drexel in 1950. It is not an intensive study—Mann is reviewed in 26 pages. However, the author was able to interview many professional colleagues, and she also devoted the bulk of her writing to an evaluation of Mann's philosophy as a cataloger, classifier, educator, and author. Once again, this is basically a noncritical study, which serves mainly to provide a historical record of an individual of note.

Although the thesis by Melissa Ann Brisley on Cornelia Marvin Pierce was not examined, her work on the woman who played a key role in Oregon library affairs was published, in summary form, in *The Library Quarterly*.¹⁴⁷ It is evident from that article that Brisley was well versed in the historical tradition that involved effective use of historical methodology. The footnotes reflect availability of primary sources as well as the use of valuable secondary resources. Moreover, there is a sense of the larger national perspective within which Pierce functioned as a state librarian. Although other theses were occasionally able to project this discerning approach, Brisley was especially able to meet the criteria of one commentator on biography who stated: "The hallmark of a good biographer is not passion but good sense. He has to weed out the irrelevant and seek what is strong, novel and interesting. He needs a profound knowledge of human nature, wide sympathies, and an impersonal standpoint.¹⁴⁸

In concluding this section relating to theses and dissertations, it is unnecessary to belabor the number of the critical flaws found in existing biography of women in librarianship. The flaws are not unique to biographies of women; they do reflect the fact that little work was done in the fifties and sixties that reflected effective historical methodology. As Wiegand notes, in *The Journal of Library History*'s latest review of the literature of American library history, "the profession needs more biographies, more monographs, and more articles based on meticulous research into primary source materials, each of which should relate its subject matter to the development of American libraries and librarianship within larger environments."[149]

Collective Scholarly Biographies

The final section related to the "perils" of preparing studies on women addresses the most recent phenomenon of the field: the publication of articles on women in collective biographical reference works. Although other collected works exist, as noted in the first section of this chapter, the following comments will relate specifically to *Notable American Women*, the *ALA World Encyclopedia*, and *Dictionary of American Library Biography (DALB)*. The one source, of the three just cited, that does not specifically address itself to the library world is *Notable American Women*; however, it is obviously relevant to the historical study of women. As noted in the first section of this chapter, it cannot be evaluated as unique in its coverage of women in the field of librarianship. In fact, its attention to those women is cursory; only 18 "librarians" were included in the original three-volume set.

In evaluating the authority of the articles, the authors of the articles can usually be identified as well-known librarians, although most are not especially renowned as library historians. For example, the article on Mary Eileen Ahern,[150] whose major fame is associated with her editorship of *Public Libraries*, is written by Harriet D. MacPherson, who was best known as a library educator in the field of cataloging and classification. The article on Jennie Maas Flexner,[151] who was involved closely with collection development and reader services, is prepared by Sigrid A. Edge; Jennie Lindquist,[152] devoted friend, appears as author of the Caroline Hewins article; and Katherine Coffey[153] has prepared an assessment of Beatrice Winser. It is true that historian/biographer Sarah Vann shows up in association with Sarah Bogle,[154] and Phyllis Dain,[155] in the first supplement to the set, *The Modern Period*, writes about Isadore Mudge, but the authors were not, to this author's eye, selected because of their general historical knowledge of the librarian in society.

When the resources for the articles are examined, the pattern that can be seen in other collective biographies—whether related to men or women—is evident. The sketch on Sarah Askew,[156] well-known New Jersey librarian, is apparently based largely on a nonscholarly article found in *Pioneering Leaders in Librarianship*,[157] a few published references, and some limited manuscript data. On the other hand, the study of Belle da Costa Greene[158] has a more detailed reference list, which includes published and unpublished correspondence and secondary resources. Similarly, the article on Helen Haines,[159] found in the supplemental volume, is replete with references to her papers and other related publications. Although it is clear, as it is when examining *DALB*, that some individuals are known through a minimal amount of primary data, it cannot be concluded that the articles on librarians in *Notable American Women* display any greater methodological weakness than those on entertainers, social workers, or scientists. A well-known brochure advocating the need for libraries to acquire research on the history of women catches the problem precisely in its headline: "So much has been written about women...but so little has shown up in the libraries."[160] Therefore, any library researcher faces the special problem of locating personal papers, records, and even secondary publications, owing to the inadequacy of existing indexing systems as well as collection development directed to different objectives.

The situation, however, has taken a turn in the past five years that recognizes, on occasion, the need to describe accurately the nature of the discipline as well as its major contributors. Although the *ALA World Encyclopedia of Library and Information Services* is not a source that provides special coverage of the neglected female species of librarian, it does include biographies for "172 [sic: only 167 are indexed] individuals, both living and deceased, who have served as librarians or library educators or have contributed substantially to library development."[161] In examining the articles relating to well-known women librarians, the careful selection of qualified biographers is evident: Mary Eileen Ahern is studied by Elaine Fain; Sarah Bogle by Doris Dale; Theresa Elmendorf by Dennis Thomison; Caroline Hewins by Budd Gambee; Elizabeth H. Morton by Samuel Rothstein and Marion Gilroy; and Mary Wright Plummer by Donald G. Davis, Jr.[162] Although other biographers in this work are not as well known as those just cited, there is a significant number of library historians among the contributors. On the other hand, the documentation varies from none at all, on occasion, to a selected number of major sources. This is, of course, a weakness of the volume. Betty Milum, commenting in 1978 on certain challenges posed by Haynes McMullen,[163] puts that factor within its true framework when she flatly says, "Far more damaging to historiography than the issue of interpretation, in fact, is the failure to cite sources. Interpretation even at its worst always allows for reexamination. Withholding the sources eliminates all possibility of fair play, both to the author and to the reader, and overlooks a fundamental rule of scholarship."[164]

The final tool examined in this section relating to the perils of biographical history is the well-received *Dictionary of American Library Biography (DALB)*, published in 1978 by Libraries Unlimited, Inc. As already noted, the selection criteria emphasize

contributions of national significance to library development; writings that influenced library trends and activities; positions of national importance (presidents of the American Library Association and Librarians of Congress were automatically included); major achievements in special fields of librarianship; significant scholarly, philanthropic, legislative, or governmental support or activity that affected American libraries.[165]

These criteria eliminate many of the women described in the section on theses and dissertations, especially those whose contributions were geographically limited to their region or their community. However, the overall strength of the work must be considered. The volume includes 301 sketches of deceased librarians; each contributor was specifically instructed to prepare a "critical" biography. As in *Notable American Women* and the *ALA World Encyclopedia*, there are characterizations of less quality than others, but, proportionately, it would be difficult to say that those of women are less adequate than those of men.

One conclusion might be drawn from an examination of the entries: those devoted to women seemed to average less space than many devoted to men. Part of this is due to editorial decisions, as noted in the preface.

The original letters inviting contributors specified lengths of sketches (ranging) from 1,000 to 6,000 words), but such assignments of space were necessarily estimates based on limited initial knowledge of the bigraphee. Upon receipt of all the sketches in the Libraries Unlimited editorial office, each sketch was evaluated as to the length of its narrative and the relative importance of the biographee vis-a-vis the established giants in the profession (Dewey, Cutter, Poole, etc.)[166]

As a result, it might be concluded that women did not receive as thorough analysis as did men. However, it should be noted that the problem of documentation was as prevalent here as critiqued earlier; in some cases additional data to support a longer narrative were unavailable.

Danton's review of the work shows that there were 87 women and 214 men included.[167] He also categorized major areas of contribution and concluded that, as noted earlier when examining theses, the largest number of women librarians were associated with public librarianship, 34.5 percent, with library-school faculty members falling into the second largest work category, 19.0 percent. Additional categories show that women in areas such as architecture, philanthropy, foundation management, and statesmen/politicians were either nonexistent or not identified. However, one surprising conclusion of the Danton analysis is that no single "college" woman librarian is among the entries although 4.5 percent of the women included were involved in university librarianship.

It has already been suggested that the length of the article was normally established by the editors' assessment of the contributions of the woman under study. Of the 87 women who were included, 31 generated articles that were two pages long or more. The individual who received the most "space" consideration was Mary Wright Plummer. Others who received significant coverage (more than two pages) were: Sarah Bogle, Mary Salome Fairchild, Jennie Flexner, Marilla Waite Freeman, Helen Haines, Adelaide Hasse, Caroline Hewins, Alice Kroeger, Hannah Logasa, Flora Belle Ludington, Margaret Mann, Allie Beth Martin, Anne Carroll Moore, Lucile Morsch, Isadore Mudge, Cornelia Marvin Pierce, Evelyn Seymour, Katharine Sharp, and Alice Tyler.[168] Certainly, all are deserving of more than average coverage. However, it must be noted that certain other individuals were given short shrift for one reason or another; e.g., Edith Coulter, Bessie Graham, Mary Evelyn Hall, and Minnie Sears.[169]

The authors of the articles on women are largely women: 63 of the 87 biographical sketches are either authored by a woman or have a woman as part of a team of contributors. The contributors in general are well known; as Danton comments, there is a greater degree of specialization in *DALB* than in the uniquely distinguished *DAB*. "Clearly, a good biography does not require of the biographer expert knowledge of the biographee's field of activity, but clearly, also, such knowledge is an advantage. It appears likely that the *DALB* scores better in this regard."[170] Among the authors of the sketches on women are recognizable librarian-historians Doris Dale, Lawrence Powell, Donald Davis, Jr., Jesse Shera, Budd Gambee, Haynes McMullen, Ed Holley, Melissa Brisley Mickey, John Colson, and Martha Boaz. Several of the studies are authored by individuals who prepared larger works; e.g., John Waddell on Mudge, Grotzinger on Sharp, and Raymund Wood on Ina Coolbrith.

The editors also stressed that careful documentation must be provided sketches that includes personal reminiscences and quotations but concentrates on "biographical listing and obituaries, books and articles about the biographee, and primary sources and archives, if known."[171] The end result, for women as well as men, is a reference source of special attributes. Danton's lengthy analysis of the volume, published in *The Journal of Library History*, can find little to fault in the work as a whole. Regardless of the selection of the subjects or the qualifications of the biographers, he concludes, "the *DALB* is a splendid piece of work. It will be used for years to come, and it can be used with confidence."[172]

Summary Thoughts

In approaching this section, the scene was set by noting that any biographer faces the special problem of accurately portraying the life of his or her subject. When that subject is a woman, it is even more difficult, since few resources exist to supply material relevant to the biographical study of women—much less women librarians. Barbara Turman, in "Women's Studies and Library History," written in 1980, reviewed three titles that "contain a wide range of feminist scholarship designed to support women's studies curriculums [sic] with undergraduate enrollments."[173] At the same time, she notes their value as sources for "biographies, autobiographies, letters, diaries, journals, memoirs, and microfilms collections...."[174] She concludes that two of the titles, *Women's Studies*[175] and *Women in America*,[176] "are more concerned with contemporary sources that deal with the historical and sociological status of women in librarianship."[177] The third title, *Women's History Sources*,[178] provides "over 200 references to archival materials in the area of librarianship."[179] Moreover, Turman notes that "the records and papers of 104 librarians are also in this volume."[180] She specifically cites the works of Constance Winchell and Jacqueline Noel as examples of resources whose historiographer has yet to emerge. Therefore, the hope for future sources of value to researchers is strong and growing. At the same time, much of the criticism directed to the earlier papers would not have existed if, first of all, the authors had assumed a responsible role as historians and as writers. An article in the *Chicago Book World* that reviewed *Telling Lives: The Biographer's Art* points out that "personages can freely record dialog and events long after they occur, but a biographer must be much more cautious. If he uses dialog and depicts sensational episodes without sufficient evidence, he may be accused of masquerading as a novelist producing fiction."[181] Similarly, a *Time* essay entitled, "Biography Comes of Age" notes that "biography has always been a demanding discipline....A good biographer should combine the skills of the novelist and the detective, and add to them the patience and compassion of the priest."[182] That same essay notes the second major flaw of biographies of women librarians, the failure to provide adequate evidence, as opposed to anecdote: "Very often the erroneous stories see print, properly buttressed by improper footnotes and references."[183] Finally, there is a significant difference between the citing of facts and the interpretation of a life. If done well, the reader "has a life to examine: someone was here before him, suffered and was happy, did foolish and wise things, endured."[184] If those three factors existed in the studies just cited, then the study of women in librarianship by men and women would be far superior than this commentary has suggested. The ultimate problem, however, is precisely noted by library historian Holley, who pointed out:

> No one wants to do injustice to the personalities which inhabit our professional past or claim more than the evidence warrants, but how do you know? Sometimes you don't, but you have to make an educated guess based on the best evidence at hand, always recognizing the tentativeness of your conclusions and being careful not to say more than the evidence warrants.[185]

PLEASURES

The second and major section of this chapter was an attempt to grapple with a difficult problem; that is, the dangers of writing library biography with respect to a definition of significant, scholarly, and well-researched studies. It was quickly evident that much of what is available does not meet minimal criteria if the basic requirements of historical methodology are used as an evaluation instrument. In concluding that section, a brief quotation was taken from an article by Ed Holley, a premier biographer of librarians. However, the article from which the quotation was taken does much more than note the difficulties of library biography; it sets the stage for this concluding section, which intends to look at some of the material that exists on women and to enjoy them, their personalities, and their world. Holley recounts, in his closing pages, that when submitting a manuscript, "ALA at 100,"[186] he sent it to Allie Beth Martin for review. He felt that the article did not have "personality," as he described it. Martin responded that "librarians have not been a very sparkling group which is not your fault and you have provided warmth and human interest throughout."[187] Holley appreciated her comments but goes on to raise a key question:

> Was she right that librarians weren't "a very sparkling group?" Some of them were; most were not; but many were interesting people and one doesn't find it difficult to identify with some of their opportunities and problems, even if they weren't of world-shaking importance. Moreover, one finds them repeatedly described as having a sense of humor which alleviated the difficult problems they faced.[188]

Holley does not conclude that librarians are uniquely interesting, but this author, in reviewing the many articles, theses, dissertations, books, and reference biographies that served as a basis for the essay, did sense the quality and *humanity* that emerged even in the Victorian world of the late nineteenth and early twentieth centuries. Therefore, the following excerpts are taken from a variety of the materials reviewed. They were selected, in most instances, randomly; hundreds of other examples might have been used, for there *were women who helped to mold a profession.*

Florence Woodworth

One of Dewey's devoted coterie who taught with unique dedication at the Albany school, Woodworth was also one of the special "six" whom he brought to Columbia to reorganize its libraries and, in so doing, began the "feminization" of the field. She was, according to him, the first student to enter the first class of the first library school in the world.

She always kept herself in the background, but those of us behind the scenes knew to whose long hours (often of night work at home) and to whose skillful attention to minute details we wer indeted for so much of the best of our planning and executing. Her little body held a great soul and the pair was always redy for efficient service. In the 38 years since she first came to our Columbia University school, I never knew her to dodge a responsibility or shirk a duty. Her chief fault was that she wud always do more than her share.[89]

Alice S. Harrison

Unfortunately, few biographies of school librarians have been written—even in unscholarly format—but Alice Harrison was one of the Texas women who received attention through the historical emphasis directed by Esther Stallman at the Uhiversity of Texas.

She was gifted with an alert, inquisitive mind and with the ability to communicate her ideas persuasively. Although she was more skilled as a practitioner than as a scholar, she exhibited respect and admiration for scholarship insofar as it contributed to the enrichment of human life....She had a quiet, subtle sense of humor and a capacity to see the beautiful in the commonplace.[190]

Mabel Ray Gillis

Gillis's career spanned almost 47 years of service to the California State Library, where she followed in the footsteps of a famous father, James Gillis, and also pioneered in developing the Books for the Blind Division. Her accomplishments are seen in an article written in 1968 by Peter T. Conmy, who quoted from a letter written by a friend:

...she was a quiet person with considerable reticence and shyness counterbalancing her terrific drive for accomplishment. So you'll find that she did not tend to get herself into pictures and articles written about herself, but wanted the article to be written to help accomplish the goals she'd set for herself in the library world.[191]

Tessa Kelso

Little has been written about Kelso, a fact reflected in the brief article prepared for an ALA Centennial Vignette in 1975. Kelso was an "Unfinished Hero of Library Herstory"; her career at the Los Angeles Public Library encompassed only six years, when she lost her position because of political problems related to censorship. Yet in those brief years, she left a mark in terms of her innovative approach to a discipline barely emerging. Evelyn Geller describes what is generally known, and then compellingly notes that

there is something pathetic in seeing that compassionate, perhaps tactless, idealism so suddenly silenced. She is with Baker and Taylor for awhile, then works for Scribner's, then drops out of sight. Reading her few lines, we sigh at paths the profession never followed. Had she survived as a leader, we might have been able to boast of our own Jane Addams.[192]

Mollie Huston Lee

Mollie Lee was the first Afro-American to receive a scholarship to study at Columbia, an investment that more than repaid the profession. Again her major service was to the public library, one that served blacks in Raleigh, North Carolina.

It was no easy task to be black and make a contribution in the 1930s. Yet this was a period in which blacks produced some of their most memorable works in the arts and humanities. Only a determined, qualified black could hope to break away from a stigmatized subordinate status and reach to the heights in a profession. Mollie Huston Lee, challenged by the need to expand cultural awakenings for the Negro, did just this and distinguised herself by making a worthy contribution to public libraries.[193]

Fannie Elizabeth Ratchford

Few probably recognize the name of this librarian, who is internationally known for her rare-book work at the University of Texas. However, she was also a writer and lecturer who gained fame as a literary detective; in fact, she received a Guggenheim award in 1939 to pursue her special research on nineteenth-century forgeries. Her personality was captured, in 1951, in a few words by Autrey Wiley: "When she has a hunch—and she is never lacking the like—she gives relentless pursuit. Insatiable curiosity urges her on, whetting her uncanny ability to hunt out facts. Her thinking is lightning fast, straight as an arrow. The pursued is trapped the minute she pursues it."[194]

Electra Collins Doren

Electra Doren was a community librarian who singlehandedly, it seemed, built a public library, and built it forcefully, in Dayton, Ohio. She also, of course, served as the first director of the Western Reserve School of Library Science. Her biographer paints a familiar but valuable picture.

> She was a disciplinarian. Always her staff had the feeling that library affairs were administered by a firm hand. For the reference and circulation staffs the dictum was "absolute decorum when before the public." Personal conversation between assistants was forbidden. "The library must present a dignified front at all times." Concentration and absence of irrelevant conservation was expected also behind the scenes. This discipline hurt none of us.[195]

Katharine Lucinda Sharp

Katharine Sharp was a product of Dewey's philosophy and the Albany school, a library educator who established its focal point in the Midwest, at the University of Illinois. She was an individual of tremendous strength, who was held in awe by her many pioneer peers. In the summer of 1897, she attended the Second International Library Conference in London. Dewey recounted one story of her personality, in his own inimitable style:

At the Queen's Jubilee, wher she was a delegat from the Univ of Illinois, she resievd a wholly unpremeditated compliment, greater becauz it had sprung instantly from the hart of a man who had abundant opportunity and ability to juj. Several prominent Englishmen, including some members of Parliament, gave a group of official delegates a dinner. Sir John Lubbock in his speech spoke of his admiration for the ability with which our American women delegates had taken ther parts in the international discussions, and exprest surprise that they wer not married. Instantly F M Crunden, my predecessor as the senior ex-president of the A L A voiced the admiration felt by American librarians who knew by saying "I shud like to see a man who tho't he was good enuf to marry Katherin Sharp."[196]

Helen E. Haines

In 1950, a special dinner was given for Helen Haines by the Alumni Association of USC's School of Library Science. Her speech, "Through Time's Bifocals," highlighted others as well as herself.

Here were Tessa Kelso, Harriet Wadleigh, Mary L. Jones and Althea Warren—all librarians of the Los Angeles Public Library, all sowing seeds that germinated and brought increase of strength and fruitfulness to librarianship. Here was Katherine Wells Smith, for so many years on the library Board of Commissioners, through all these years a friend of books and of the library staff, whose affection carries its tangible evidence into today and tomorrow and whose catholicity of book love years could never stale.[197]

Mary Frances Isom

A product of the Pratt class of 1901, Mary Isom immediately moved to the Northwest, where she, along with Cornelia Marvin Pierce, promoted libraries vigorously throughout the region. She was first employed by the Library Association of Portland to catalog a special collection. The librarian, however, departed abruptly. Without hesitation, the board named the new young assistant as librarian, and "Mary Frances Isom found herself at 37, in the first year of her first employment in charge of a public library just perilously launched, financially shaky, unorganized, and expected to do the impossible. She calmly set about doing it."[198]

Alice Bertha Kroeger

As still another among those who profited from Dewey's special influence at the Albany school, Kroeger spent her life in library education and produced the original work[199] from which the Mudge, Winchell and Sheehy volumes were to evolve. When she died, at a young 45, one student wrote anonymously to *Library Journal*.

It is with the feeling that I am giving expression to what is true, not alone for myself but for many girls scattered throughout the country, that I say: to the splendid, systematic training which we received at Drexel, a training which Miss Kroeger directed and in which she took part; to the enthusiasm in the work we were undertaking—enthusiasm awakened in us by her whose heart and soul were in the work, who saw and made us see its opportunities and its many phases of interest and benefit to us....[200]

Jennie Scott Scheubar

One of several who made a special contribution to Texas librarianship, Jennie Scheubar devoted her life to the Fort Worth Public Library in particular but also to Texas public libraries in general. She was, in many respects, a prototype woman librarian of her period, the late 1890s through the 1940s.

Jennie Scott Scheubar was of relatively short stature and had a tendency toward plumpness. While her face was not conventionally atractive, she had good posture and carried herself with natural dignity and poise. She made a striking appearance because of her bright eyes and unwavering gaze, and when, in her later years, her hair turned white she was a distinguished-looking woman, even if her soft features were belied to an extent by a still-determined jaw.[201]

Ida Angeline Kidder

Another remarkable woman who made a key contribution in the West, Ida Kidder was associated with the Oregon State Agricultural College from 1908 to 1920 and then served as a hospital librarian in World War I.

Mrs. Kidder was definitely a feminist as far as the library profession was concerned. Writing to her good friend, Miss M. E. Ahearn [sic], editor of *Public Libraries*, she said, "...so far as I have come in contact with library workers of the country, the women have seemed to me much more alive, broadminded, and progressive. I have certainly received my inspiration from them rather than the men, with two or three exceptions."[202]

Josephine Adams Rathbone

Rathbone, whose influence at Pratt matched that of Sharp at Illinois or Kroeger at Drexel, is quickly brought to life in a recollection by Fenneman.

She looked up from some papers as I entered, flicked off her pince-nez with a movement of her nose which sent them flying to the limits of the black cord she wore about her neck...and scrutinized me frankly. After a brief exchange she asked me where I was staying....Mis Rathbone was not pleased. She scented danger, and she acted with characteristic promptitude to dispatch it. "You had better move to Brooklyn," she said. I recognized command—and I did![203]

The "pleasures" of reading the biographies of women librarians—and of writing them—do go far beyond the few examples just compiled. It is, in these recollections, that all of the methodological criticism that justifiably has been directed toward that which exists, tends to take a back seat to the sheer enjoyment of rediscovering so much of the lost "herstory." Writing recently in *Wilson Library Bulletin*, Hillary Hart interviews well-known biographer Justin Kaplan about the nature and role of biography.[204] Kaplan makes a clear distinction between "two basically very different kinds of biography;"[205] the first, the scholarly studies, have been the basis for criticism used in terms of biography of women librarians. Kaplan himself, and many of the individuals who have just been quoted or use direct quotations from their subjects, are strongly committed, instead, to the individuals they depict, with respect to their personalities and their "rich lives." As Kaplan describes his studies of Mark Twain and Walt Whitman, "I happen to have been passionately interested in these people, and as a *writer* I have very powerful feelings about what biography is all about and how it works. If you take that stance, you can come up with an entirely different kind of book than the scholarly biography."[206]

In identifying that sensitivity, the belief in what he calls a form of storytelling, Kaplan expresses the pleasure shared by many of the biographers just reviewed. There was a joy in their recreation of special people, special women librarians who made unique contributions under unusual conditions. Perhaps the final comments is best stated in the words of one of those women, Lydia Margaret Barrette. In *There Is No End,* her biography of a "library," she, of course, writes her autobiography as well. Her dedicated life, 35 years' worth, was spent in Mason City, Iowa, where she dreamed an American dream of libraries, books, and their users. When she retired, she described that leaving, and in that description the reader could relive her essential nature:

My own hands were as cold as the keys I was about to lay down. Suddenly I realized that it was getting dark. I had no need to turn on the lights. It was all so familiar. This was the awful moment—the moment of symbolic abdication. Later there would be public acclaim of the sort a small prairie town can give, an acclaim accompanied by cake and coffee with gentle non-controversial speeches in which everybody says the expected things and nobody challenges anybody's prejudices or pet peeves. And there would be a white orchid, symbol of the dream itself.[207]

And that essential nature, in deed and in fact, is the unadulterated pleasure of the biography of women who were also librarians.

NOTES

1. Catherine Drinker Bowen, *Biography: The Craft and the Calling* (Boston: Little, Brown and Co., 1969).
2. Jesse H. Shera, "On the Value of Library History," in *Knowing Books and Men; Knowing Computers, Too* (Littleton, CO: Libraries Unlimited, Inc., 1973), p. 177. (Originally published in *The Library Quarterly* 22 (July 1952): 240-51.)

3. Edward G. Holley, "Neglect of the 'Greats': Some Observations on the Problems of Writing the Biographies of American Librarians." *Library Journal* 88 (October 1, 1963): 3551.
4. Michael H. Harris, *A Guide to Research in American Library History*, 2nd ed. (Metuchen, N.J.: The Scarecrow Press, Inc., 1974).
5. Ibid., p. 8.
6. Michael H. Harris and Donald G. Davis, Jr., *American Library History: A Bibliography* (Austin: University of Texas Press, 1978).
7. Wayne A. Wiegand, "The Literature of American Library History, 1977-1978. "*The Journal of Library History* 14 (Summer 1979): 320.
8. Arthur E. Bostwick, ed. *American Library Pioneers*, Volumes 1-7 (Chicago: American Library Association, 1924-1951.) The first seven biographies were of John Shaw Billings, Samuel Swett Green, Charles Ammi Cutter, William Howard Brett, John Cotton Dana, Melvil Dewey, and Charles Jewett. In 1942 Emily Danton Miller became editor of the "First Series" of *Pioneering Leaders in Librarianship*, which was published in 1953, as the eighth volume of the original series; no other volumes were published. See Lawrence Clark Powell, "On the Grindstone," *Library Journal* 87 (October 1, 1962): 3404, 3418.
9. Michael H. Harris, gen. ed., *The Heritage of Librarianship Series*, Vols. 1- , 1975- (Littleton, CO: Libraries Unlimited, Inc.). At the present time, four volumes have been published; the subjects are Charles Coffin Jewett, Ainsworth Rand Spofford, Charles Ammi Cutter, and Melvil Dewey.)
10. ——, ed., *Advances in Librarianship*, Vol. 8 (New York: Academic Press, 1978).
11. L.A. Grotzinger, *The Power and the Dignity: Librarianship and Katherine [sic] Sharp* (Metuchen, N.J.: The Scarecrow Press, 1966). Cited in *Advances in Librarianship*, Vol. 8, Kaser, David, "Advances in American Library History," p. 197.
12. See David Kaser, "Advances in American Library History," in *Advances in Librarianship*, Vol. 8, 1978, citations of L.A.K. Evaraiff, D. Garrison, D.J. Lehnus, and E.F. McCauley.
13. John Calvin Colson, "The Writing of American Library History, 1876-1976," *Library Trends* 25 (July 1976): 7-22.
14. Edward G. Holley, "Librarians, 1876-1976." *Library Trends* 25 (July 1976): 177-208.
15. Colson, "Library History," p. 12.
16. Holley, "Librarians, 1876-1976," p. 183.
17. Dee Garrison, "The Tender Technicians: The Feminization of Public Librarianship," *Journal of Social History* 6 (Winter 1976): 131-59.
18. Holley, "Librarians, 1876-1976," p. 206, Note 97.
19. Robert B. Downs, "The Role of the Academic Librarian, 1876-1976." *College & Research Libraries* 37 (November 1976): 491-502.
20. Laurel A. Grotzinger, "Women Who 'Spoke for Themselves.'" *College & Research Libraries* 39 (May 1978): 175.
21. *Dictionary of American Biography*. Under the auspices of the American Council of Learned Societies, ed. by Allen Johnson and Dumas Malone, 20 vols. and index (New York: Charles Scribner & Sons, 1928-1937). The 6 supplements cite at least 17 male librarians but only 2 additional women.

22. *The National Cyclopaedia of American Biography*, Vol. 1- (New York: White, 1892-).
23. "A Library Hall of Fame," *Library Journal* 76 (March 15, 1951): 466-72.
24. *The Biographical Cyclopaedia of American Women*, 2 vols. (New York: The Halvord Pubg. Co., 1924; The Franklin W. Lee Pubg. Corp., 1925). (The "librarians" cited are Hannah Johnson Claxton, Frances Elizabeth Earhart, and Caroline Margaret McIlvaine.)
25. *American Women* [A Revised Edition of *Women of the Century*]. *A Comprehensive Encyclopedia of the Lives and Achievements of American Women During the Nineteenth Century* (New York: Mast, Crowell, and Kirkpatrick, 1897; Detroit: Gale, 1973). (The "librarians" cited are Rosa Lee Tucker and Mrs. E. H. Stevens.)
26. *Notable American Women, 1607-1950: A Biographical Dictionary*, 3 vols. (Cambridge: Harvard University Press, 1971).
27. *Notable American Women: The Modern Period.* Ed. By Barbara Sicherman and Carol Hurd Green (Cambridge: Harvard University Press, 1980).
28. Rudolf Engelbarts, *Librarian Authors: A Bibliography* (Jefferson, N.C.: McFarland, 1981).
29. Ibid, p. iii.
30. Ibid.
31. Anne E. Brugh and Benjamin R. Beede, "American Librarianship," in *Library Lit. 7- The Best of 1976*, ed. by Bill Katz (Metuchen, N.J.: The Scarecrow Press, Inc., 1977), p. 25.
32. Margo Sasse, "The Children's Librarian in America," [School] *Library Journal*, [19] 98 (January 15, 1973): [21-5] 213-17.
33. "Introduction," *Dictionary of American Biography*, vol. 1 (New York: Charles Scribner's Sons, 1928), p. vii.
34. *Notable American Women*, "Introduction," p. xli.
35. *Notable American Women*, loc. cit.
36. Harris, *A Guide to Research in American Library History*, 2d ed., 1974.
37. Harris and Davis, *American Library History: A Bibliography*.
38. Cynthia S. Cummings, comp., "A Biographical-Bibliographical Directory of Women Librarians" (Madison: Library School Women's Group, University of Wisconsin, 1976).
39. See note 8.
40. *ALA World Encyclopedia of Library and Information Services.* Ed. by Robert Wedgeworth (Chicago: American Library Association, 1980).
41. *Encyclopedia of Library and Information Science.* Ed. by Allen Kent and Harold Lancour (New York: Marcel Dekker, Inc., 1968-).
42. *Dictionary of American Library Biography.* Ed. by Bohdan S. Wynar (Littleton, CO: Libraries Unlimited, Inc., 1978).
43. Harris, *A Guide to Research*, p. v.
44. Elizabeth M. Richards, "Alexander Vattemare and His System of International Exchanges" (Master's thesis, Columbia University, 1934).
45. Charles H. Miller, "Ainsworth Rand Spofford, 1825-1908" (Master's thesis, George Washington University, 1938).
46. William H. Peden, "Thomas Jefferson: Book Collector" (Ph.D. dissertation, University of Virginia, 1942).

47. Margaret B. Becker, "Effie Louise Power: Pioneer in the Development of Library Services for Children" (Master's thesis, Western Reserve University, School of Library Science, 1950).
48. Dorothy B. Shaw, "The Life and Work of Margaret Mann" (Master's thesis, The Drexel Institute of Technology, School of Library Science, 1950).
49. Sidney Cohen, "Biographical Data on the Librarians of the Ohio State Library, 1817-1960" (Master's thesis, Kent State University, 1961).
50. Harris, A Guide to Research, p. [ix].
51. John N. Waddell, "The Career of Isadore G. Mudge: A Chapter in the History of Reference Librarianship" (D.L.S. dissertation, Columbia University, School of Library Service, 1973).
52. Cummings, "Women Librarians."
53. "Women in the Library Profession: Leadership roles and Contributions" (Ann Arbor: University of Michigan, School of Library Science Alumnus in Residence, 1971).
54. Evelyn Geller, "Tessa Kelso: Unfinished Hero of Library Herstory," American Libraries 6 (June 1975): 347.
55. Emily Danton Miller, ed., *Pioneering Leaders in Librarianship*. First Series (Chicago: American Library Association, 1953), p. [i].
56. Ibid.
57. Volume 11 was not available for examination.
58. Allen Kent and Harold Lancour, "Preface," *Encyclopedia of Library and Information Science*, Vol. 1 (New York: Marcell Dekker, Inc., 1968), p. [xii].
59. J. Perriam Danton, "The Essence of Innumerable Biographies: A review essay on the *Dictionary of American Library Biography*." *The Journal of Library History* 13 (Fall 1978): 451-63.
60. Kathleen Weibel and Kathleen M. Heim, with assistance from Dianne J. Ellsworth, *The Role of Women in Librarianship 1876-1976: The Entry, Advancement, and Struggle for Equalization in One Profession* (Phoenix: The Oryx Press, 1979).
61. Weibel and Heim, "Introduction," Women in Librarianship, p. xv.
62. Charles H. Davis, Comp., *Library Science: A Dissertation Bibliography* (Ann Arbor: University Microfilms International, 1980).
63. Laurel A. Grotzinger, "The Power and the Dignity: Librarianship and Katharine Sharp" (Ph.D. dissertation, University of Illinois, 1964).
64. John N. Waddell, "The Career of Isadore G. Mudge: A Chapter in the History of Reference Librarianship" (D.L.S. dissertation, Columbia University, 1973).
65. Richard W. Lawson, "Mary Josephine Booth: A Lifetime of Service, 1904-1945" (Ph.D. dissertation, Indiana University, 1975).
66. Dorothy J. Anderson, "Mildred L. Batchelder" (Ph.D. dissertation, Texas Woman's University, 1977).
67. Andrew Reed, "Re-wording History," *The Common Reader* (November/December 1980): 1.
68. Bowen, *Biography*.

69. Jacques Barzun and Henry F. Graff, *The Modern Researcher*, 3rd ed. (New York: Harcourt Brace Jovanovich, Inc., 1977), p. 293.
70. Louis Gottschalk, *Understanding History: A Primer of Historical Method* (New York: Alfred A. Knopf, 1950).
71. Harris and Davis, *American Library History*, p. 184.
72. Lawrence Clark Powell, "On the Grindstone," *Library Journal* 87 (October 1 1, 1962): 3404.
73. Stanley Pargellis, quoted in Powell, "On the Grindstone," p. 3404.
74. Joe W. Kraus, quoted in Powell, "On the Grindstone," p. 3404.
75. Barzun and Graff, *Modern Researcher*, p. 40.
76. Gratia Countryman, "Clara F. Baldwin: A Tribute," *Minnesota Libraries* 16 (1951): 291-2.
77. "Janet Doe," *Medical Library Association Bulletin* 45 (1957): 281-4.
78. Ibid., p. 283.
79. Grosvenor Dawe, *Melvil Dewey: Seer, Inspirer, Doer, 1851-1931* (Essex County, N.Y.: Lake Placid Club, 1932).
80. Martha Boaz, *Fervent and Full of Gifts: The Life of Althea Warren* (New York: The Scarecrow Press, Inc., 1961).
81. Ibid., p. v.
82. Weibel and Heim, *Women in Librarianship*, p. 287.
83. Bertha Mahoney Miller, ed., *Caroline M. Hewins: Her Book; Containing a Mid-Century Child and Her Books* (Boston: Horn Book, 1954).
84. Arthur Bestor, "History as Verifiable Knowledge: The Logic of Historical Inquiry and Explanation," in *Research Methods in Librarianship: Historical and Bibliographical Methods in Library Research*, ed. by R.E. Stevens (Urbana: University of Illinois Graduate School of Library Science, 1971), p. 107.
85. Victoria Faber Stevenson, *Etta Josselyn Giffin: Pioneer Librarian for the Blind* (Washington, D.C.: National Library for the Blind, 1959).
86. Josephine DeWitt Rhodehamel and Raymund Francis Wood, *Ina Coolbrith: Librarian and Laureate of California* (Provo, Utah: Brigham Young University Press, 1973.
87. Richard N. Current, "Biographical Research: Some Personal Observations," in Stevens, *Research Methods*, p. 63.
88. Lydia Margaret Barrette, *There is No End* (New York: Scarecrow Press, 1961); Lawrence Clark Powell, *The Example of Miss Edith M. Coulter* (Sacramento: California Library Association, 1969); Laurel A. Grotzinger, *The Power and the Dignity: Librarianship and Katharine Sharp* (Metuchen, N.J.: Scarecrow Press, 1966); and Margaret B. Stillwell, *Librarians Are Human: Memories In and Out of the Rare Book World* (Boston: 1973).
89. Grotzinger, *Power and Dignity*.
90. Harris, *A Guide to Research*, ad ed.
91. Ann B. Honea, "Julia Brown Asplund: New Mexico Librarian, 1875-1958" (Master's thesis, University of Texas, 1967).
92. Ethel E.M. Bolden, "Susan Dart Butler—Pioneer Librarian" (Master's thesis, Atlanta University, 1959).
93. C.O. Phillips, "Linda Anne Eastman: Librarian" (Master's thesis, Western Reserve University, 1953); Alice E. Wright, "Linda A. Eastman: Pioneer in Librarianship" (Master's thesis, Kent State University, 1952).

94. Claudie L. Pettigrew, "Louise Franklin: The Education of a Texas Librarian" (Master's thesis, University of Texas, 1967).
95. Mildred M. Campbell, "Bessie Graham, Bibliophile" (Master's thesis, Texas State College for Women, 1953).
96. Donald R. Drummond, "Julia Grothaus, San Antonio Librarian" (Master's thesis, University of Texas, 1964).
97. Margaret I. Nichols, "Lillian Gunter: Pioneer Texas County Librarian, 1970-1926" (Master's thesis, University of Texas, 1958).
98. Billie Grace U. Herring, "Alice S. Harrison: Pioneer School Librarian, 1882-1967" (Master's thesis, University of Texas, 1968).
99. Alma Dekenis, "Caroline Maria Hewins: Pioneer in the Development of Library Service for Children" (Master's thesis, Southern Connecticut State College, 1959).
100. Mary B. McSwain, "Julia Bedford Ideson, Houston Librarian, 1880-1945" (Master's thesis, University of Texas, 1966).
101. Nancy M. Akers, "Anne Carroll Moore: A Study of Her Work with Children's Libraries and Literature (Master's thesis, Pratt Institute, 1951); Anne M. Poor, "Anne Carroll Moore: The Velvet Glove of Librarianship" (Master's thesis, Southern Connecticut State College, 1966).
102. Frederick E. Hershey, "Minnie Sweet Monti: Her Life and Influence" (Master's thesis, Western Reserve University, 1957).
103. Melissa A. Brisley, "Cornelia Marvin Pierce: Pioneer in Library Extension" (Master's thesis, University of Chicago, 1967). Summary in *The Library Quarterly* 38 (1968): 125-53.
104. Margaret B. Becker, "Effie Louise Power: Pioneer in the Development of Library Services for Children" (Master's thesis, Western Reserve University, 1950.)
105. Kalani Banks, "Octavia F. Rogan, Texas Librarian" (Master's thesis, University of Texas, 1963).
106. Robert N. Taylor, "Jennie Scott Scheuber: An Approach to Librarianship" (Master's thesis, University of Texas, 1968).
107. Laurel A. Grotzinger, "The Power and the Dignity: Librarianship and Katharine Sharp" (Ph.D. dissertation, University of Illinois, 1964).
108. Bernice C. Theriot, "A Study of the Contributions of Lois F. Shortess to Louisiana's Public School Library Development" (Master's thesis, University of Southwestern Louisiana, 1968).
109. Cora E. Richardson, "Alice Sarah Tyler: A Biographical Study" (Master's thesis, Western Reserve University, 1957).
110. Mary Jo Magner, "The Businessman's Librarian—Rose L. Vormelker" (Master's thesis, Western Reserve University, 1957).
111. Goldia Ann Hester, "Elizabeth Howard West, Texas Librarian" (Master's thesis, University of Texas, 1965).
112. Dorothy J. Anderson, "Mildred L. Batchelder" (Ph.D. dissertation, Texas Woman's University, 1977).
113. Richard W. Lawson, "Mary Josephine Booth: A Lifetime of Service, 1904-1945" (Ph.D. dissertation, Indiana University, 1975).
114. Mena C. Dyste, "Gratia Alta Countryman, Librarian" (Master's thesis, University of Minnesota, 1965).

115. Dorothy R. Shaw, "Life and Work of Margaret Mann" (Master's thesis, Drexel Institute of Technology, 1950).
116. N.P. Wetzel, "Mary P. Martin and the Canton Public Library, 1884-1928: A Study in Library Leadership" (Master's thesis, Kent State University, 1969).
117. John N. Waddell, "The Career of Isadore G. Mudge: A Chapter in the History of Reference Librarianship" (D.L.S. dissertation, Columbia University, 1973).
118. Waddell, "Isadore G. Mudge," p. 3.
119. John Neal Waddell, "Mudge, Isadore Gilbert," in *Encyclopedia of Library and Information Science*, Vol. 18 (New York: Marcel Dekker, 1976), pp. 287-291; quotation is from Waddell, "Isadore G. Mudge," p. 1.
120. Lawson, "Mary Josephine Booth," p. 147.
121. Honea, "Julia Brown Asplund," p. v.
122. Dyste, "Gratia Alta Countryman," p. 3.
123. Pettigrew, "Louise Franklin," p. v.
124. Ibid., p. 114.
125. Campbell, "Bessie Graham," p. 2.
126. Drummond, "Julia Grothaus," p. iv.
127. Herring, "Alice S. Harrison," p. iii.
128. Ibid., p. vi.
129. Hester, "Elizabeth Howard West," p. iv.
130. Banks, "Octavia F. Rogan," p. 117.
131. Harris, *A Guide to Research*, p. 8.
132. Miller, *Caroline M. Hewins*.
133. Dekenis, "Caroline Maria Hewins," p. 1.
134. Akers, "Anne Carroll Moore," pp. 2-3.
135. Ibid., p. 1.
136. Poor, "Velvet Glove," p. ii.
137. "Some Uses of Biography," *The Royal Bank of Canada Monthly Letter* 54 (August 1973): 2.
138. Ibid.
139. Poor, "Velvet Glove," p. 109.
140. Hershey, "Minnie Sweet Monti," p. v.
141. Wayne A. Wiegand, "The Literature of American Library History, 1977-1978" *The Journal of Library History* 14 (Summer 1980): 319-20.
142. "Some Uses of Biography," p. 4.
143. Richardson, "Alice Sarah Tyler," p. i.
144. Bestor, "History as Verifiable Knowledge" p. 109.
145. Magner, "Businessman's Librarian," p. i.
146. Ibid., p. 1.
147. Brisley, "Cornelia Marvin Pierce."
148. "Some Uses of Biography," p. 3.
149. Wiegand, "Library History," p. 340.
150. Harriet D. MacPherson, "Ahern, Mary Eileen," in *Notable American Women, 1607-1950: A Biographical Dictionary (NAW)*, Vol. I. ed. by Edward T. James, Janet Wilson James, and Paul S. Boyer. (Cambridge: Harvard University Press, 1971), pp. 25-26.

151. Sigrid A. Edge, "Flexner, Jennie Maas," in *NAW*, Vol. 1, pp. 633-634.
152. Jennie D. Lindquist, "Hewins, Caroline Maria," in *NAW*, Vol. 2, pp. 189-191.
153. Katherine Coffey, "Winser, Beatrice," in *NAW*, Vol. 3, pp. 630-632.
154 Sarah K. Vann, "Bogle, Sarah Comly Norris," in *NAW*, Vol. 1, pp. 187-188.
155. Phyllis Dain, "Mudge, Isadore Gilbert," in *Notable American Women: The Modern Period*. Ed. by Barbara Sicherman and Carol Hurd Green. Cambridge: Harvard University Press, 1980, pp. 503-504.
156. Mabel Johnson Niemeyer, "Askew, Sarah Byrd," in *NAW*, Vol. 1, pp. 61-62.
157. Emily Danton Miller, ed. *Pioneering Leaders in Librarianship*, First Series (Chicago: American Library Association, 1942).
158. Dorothy Miner and Anne Lyon Haight, "Greene, Belle da Costa," in *NAW*, Vol. 2, pp. 83-85.
159. Anne C. Edmonds, "Haines, Helen Elizabeth," in *Notable American Women: The Modern Period*. Cambridge: Harvard University Press, 1980, pp. 298-299.
160. Advertising brochure published by Research Publications, Inc., 12 Lunar Drive, Woodbridge, CT 06525. Distributor for Women's Herstory Research Center Microfilms: Herstory, Law, Health/Mental Health.
161. Kenneth G. Peterson, "Review of the ALA World Encyclopedia," *College & Research Libraries* 41 (September 1980): 453.
162. Elaine Fain, "Ahern, Mary Eileen (1860-1938)," pp. 29-30; Doris Cruger Dale, "Bogle, Sarah Comly Norris (1870-1932)," pp. 92-93; Dennis Thomison, "Elmendorf, Theresa Hubbell (West) (1855-1932)," pp. 189-191; Budd L. Gambee, "Hewins, Caroline Maria (1846-1926)," pp. 237-238; Samuel Rothstein and Marion Gilroy, "Morton, Elizabeth Homer (1903-1977)," p. 382; Donald G. Davis, Jr., "Plummer, Mary Wright (1856-1916)," pp. 432-433 in *ALA World Encyclopedia of Library and Information Services*. ed. by Robert Wedgeworth (Chicago: American Library Association, 1980).
tion, 1980).
163. Haynes McMullen, "The State of the Art of Writing Library History," *The Jounal of Library History* 13 (Fall 1978): 432-440.
164. Betty Milum, "Comment," *The Journal of Library History* 13 (Fall 1978): 442.
165. *Dictionary of American Library Biography*, ed. by Bohdan S. Wynar. (Littleton, Colorado: Libraries Unlimited, Inc., 1978), p. xxxi.
166. Ibid., p. xxxv.
167. Danton, "Innumerable Biographies," p. 454.
168. Robert A. Karlowich and Nasser Sharify, "Plummer, Mary Wright (1856-1916)," pp. 399-402; Peggy A. Sullivan, "Bogle, Sarah Comly Norris (1870-1932)," pp. 41-43; Budd L. Gambee, "Fairchild, Mary Salome Cutler (1855-1921)," pp. 167-170; Margaret E. Monroe, "Flexner, Jennie Maas (1882-1944)," pp. 179-182; Rose L. Vormelker, "Feeman, Marilla Waite (1871-1961)," pp. 188-191; Robert D. Harlan, "Haines, Helen Elizabeth (1872-1961)," pp. 223-226; Budd L. Gambee, "Hewins, Caroline Maria (1846-1926)," pp. 240-243; Laurel A. Grotzinger, "Kroeger, Alice Bertha (1864-1909)," pp. 295-298; Irene P. Norrell, "Logasa, Hannah (1879-

1967)," pp. 319-322; Anne C. Edmonds, Ludington, Flora Belle (1898-1967)," pp. 322-324; Laurel A. Grotzinger, "Mann, Margaret (1973-1960)," pp. 339-342; Frances Kennedy, "Martin, Allie Beth Dent (1914-1976)," pp. 345-347; Adele M. Fasick, "Moore, Anne Carroll (1871-1961)," pp. 368-371; Phyllis A. Richmond, "Morsch, Lucile M. (1906-1972)," pp. 373-377; John N. Waddell and Laurel A. Grotzinger, "Mudge, Isadore Gilbert (1875-1957)," pp. 377-379; Melissa Brisley Mickey, "Pierce, Cornelia Marvin (1873-1957)," pp. 395-398; Sarah K. Vann, "Seymour, Evelyn May (1857-1921)," pp. 468-470; Laurel A. Grotzinger, "Sharp, Katharine Lucinda (1865-1914)," pp. 470-473; Helen M. Focke, "Tyler, Alice Sarah (1859-1944)," pp. 522-524 in *Dictionary of American Library Biography*.

169. Lawrence Clark Powell, "Coulter, Edith Margaret (1880-1963)," pp. 97-98; Mary Jane Platou, "Graham, Bessie (1881-1966)," pp. 210-211; Patricia B. Pond, "Hall, Mary Evelyn (1874-1956,)" pp. 226-227; Harry E. Whitmore, "Sears, Minnie Earl (1873-1933)," pp. 467-468 in *Dictionary of American Library Biography*.
170. Danton, "Innumerable Biographies," p. 460.
171. *Dictionary of American Library Biography*, p. xxx.
172. Danton, "Innumerable Biographies," p. 463.
173. Barbara Turman, "Women's Studies and Library History: A Review Essay," *The Journal of Library History* 15 (Fall 1980): 467.
174. Ibid.
175. Esther Stineman, *Women's Studies: A Recommended Core Bibliography*. Littleton, CO: Libraries Unlimited, 1979.
176. Virginia R. Terris, ed. *Women in America: A Guide to Information Sources*. American Studies Information Guide Series, vol 7 (Detroit: Gale Research, 1980).
177. Turman, "Women's Studies," p. 469.
178. *Women's History Sources: A Guide to Archives and Manuscript Collections in the United States*, 2 vols. Vol. 1 ed. by Andrea Hinding; Vol. 2 ed. by Suzanna Moody (New York: Bowker, 1979).
179. Turman, "Women's Studies," p. 469.
180. Ibid.
181. Harvey Einbinder, "The Quest for Heroes, Villains," *Chicago Tribune Book World* (June 10, 1979).
182. Gerald Clarke, "Biography Comes of Age," *Time* (July 2, 1979): 83.
183. Ibid., pp. 83-84.
184. Ibid., p. 84.
185. Edward G. Holley, "The Past as Prologue: The Work of the Library Historian," *The Journal of Library History* 12 (Spring 1979): 115.
186. Edward G. Holley, "ALA at 100," in *The ALA Yearbook*, 1976 Centennial Edition, ed. by Robert Wedgeworth (Chicago: American Library Association, 1976), pp. 1-32.
187. Allie Beth Martin to Edward G. Holley, quoted in "The Past as Prologue," p. 123.
188. Holley, "The Past as Prologue," p. 123.
189. Melvil Dewey, "As It Was in the Beginning," *Public Libraries* 30 (November 1925): 482.

190. Billie Grace U. Herring, "Alice S. Harrison: Pioneer School Librarian, 1882-1967" (Master's thesis, University of Texas, 1968), p. 95.
191. Grace Murray to Peter T. Conmy, quoted in "Mabel Ray Gillis, California State Librarian...The Fulfillment of the Destiny of Inheritence," *News Notes of California Libraries* 63 (Spring 1968): 292.
192. Evelyn Geller, "Tessa Kelso: Unfinished Hero of Library Herstory," *American Libraries* 6 (1975): 347.
193. Ray Nichols Moore, "Mollie Huston Lee: A Profile," *Wilson Library Bulletin* 49 (1975): 433.
194. Autrey Nell Wiley, "Fannie Elizabeth Ratchford," *Texas Library Journal* 29 (1951): 15.
195. Virginia Hollingsworth, "A Dedicated Life: Memories of a Great Librarian—Electra Collins Doren," *Wilson Library Bulletin* 28 (1954): 785.
196. Letter from Melvil Dewey to Frances Simpson, March 21, 1922, Katharine L. Sharp Papers, Memorial Correspondence, University of Illinois Archives, Urbana, Illinois.
197. Helen E. Haines, "Through Time's Bifocals," *California Librarian* 12 (1950): 85.
198. Bernard Van Horne, "Mary Frances Isom: Creative Pioneer in Library Work in the Northwest," *Wilson Library Bulletin* 33 (February 1959): 410.
199. Alice Bertha Kroeger, *Guide to the Study and Use of Reference Books: A Manual for Librarians, Teachers and Students,* ALA Annotated Lists (Boston: American Library Association, 1904).
200. A Member of Miss Kroeger's Class of 1909, "Tribute to Alice Bertha Kroeger," *Library Journal* 34 (December 1909): 551.
201. Robert N. Taylor, "Jennie Scott Scheuber: An Approach to Librarianship" (Master's thesis, University of Texas, 1968), p. 72.
202. William H. Carlson, "Ida Angeline Kidder: Pioneer Western Land-Grant Librarian," *College & Research Libraries* 29 (1968): 220.
203. Nordica Fenneman, "Recollections of Josepine Adams Rathbone," *Wilson Library Bulletin* 23 (June 1949): 774.
204. Hillary Hart, "Working in Biography: An Interview with Justin Kaplin," *Wilson Library Bulletin* 55 (April 1981): 589-92.
205. Quoted in Hart, "Working in Biography," p. 592.
206. Ibid.
207. Lydia Margaret Barrette, *There Is No End* (New York: The Scarecrow Press, 1961), p. 165.

Profiles of the Careers of Selected Black Female Librarians

LELIA GASTON RHODES

SOCIAL, POLITICAL AND ECONOMIC PRESSURES, along with the advent of technological advances, have had their impact on the field of librarianship. The opportunity of providing useful library service to its populace is one which librarians have accepted as a rewarding responsibility.

REASONS FOR THE STUDY

As educational opportunities for blacks have become geographically more diffuse, campaigns to integrate predominantly white institutions have intensified, and innovations for the improvement of blacks' education outside the black college have gained attention. Nevertheless, investigations are needed concerning the period when black students did not have as many options available to them regarding their college and postgraduate education as they do at present. A study was undertaken concerning the career backgrounds of selected black female librarians, age 45 and over, who had achieved "success" in their profession during this difficult period (Rhodes, 1975).

Out of the segregated pattern of education for blacks in the United States, there did emerge a group of remarkable women, associated with library science, who possessed a desire for fulfillment and a desire to disprove the notion that blacks are inferior and cannot achieve. Emerging as a group of pioneers in the profession, these women stood tall and ready to be counted.

During an era when much has been written about the women's movement, it becomes increasingly apparent to the investigator that there have been few research studies focusing on the black woman. More specifically, studies do not exist on the black female librarians who have made significant contributions to their field during a period when they often labored under the double burden of the struggle for the emancipation of their race as a whole as well as their rights as women—black women in particular.

During the second half of the 1960s black librarians for the first time "emerged from isolation," to satisfy the queries of their white counterparts for scholarly materials relevant to black culture. Black librarians were in the forefront of the development of materials for programs of black studies, by virtue of both their cultural background and their professional expertise. But in a larger sense, black librarians have contributed to the progress of libraries of all types, and although black female librarians have played an active role in advancing the field of librarianship, many of their contributions have gone unnoticed.

Their emergence in the field began in 1905, in the Louisville Free Public Library. An apprentice class is the first registered attempt in the South to provide training for prospective Negro librarians. "That it served a need of the time is evidenced by the fact that other cities, such as Houston and Memphis, sent their Negro branch librarian to Louisville for their professional education" (Gleason, 1941). No other library school was established for training blacks, until the opening of Hampton Library School, founded through a Carnegie grant in 1925.

Hampton, the first and only black library school to issue a bachelor's degree, closed its doors June 1939, because of lack of funds ("Hampton to Close," 1939, p. 339). It had graduated 183 librarians during its 14 years of existence (Gleason, 1942, p. 506), and had been accredited by the Board of Education for Librarianship as a Junior Undergraduate Library School. In September 1934, it was rated as a Type II library school, which gave it graduate status ("Accredited Library School Histories," 1937, p. 27).

More than a year elapsed between the closing of Hampton and the founding of the Atlanta University School of Library Service, in 1941. In 1975 it was still the only predominantly black school accredited by the American Library Association that awarded the master's degree in library science. Throughout its entire history, of over 30 years, there have been only two deans serving the school. Both are black women who earned doctorates from the University of Chicago Graduate Library School, and both are included in the present investigation.

At the time of this investigation (Rhodes, 1975), limited data were available about black female librarians who were attracted to the field of librarianship. Many questions come to mind about these women. Why did they select librarianship as a career? From what kinds of home backgrounds did they emerge? What educational and professional training did they have?

This investigation was an attempt to seek answers to these questions and to

1. identify physical and psychological roadblocks encountered in the career route;

2. identify factors that influenced them to choose librarianship as a career;
3. ascertain the beliefs of the respondents concerning librarianship; and
4. determine similarities and differences in educational backgrounds and career experiences.

The purpose of this study was to determine the socioeconomic backgrounds of 15 black female librarians, to identify the factors that influenced them to choose librarianship as a career, to determine their educational and professional preparation, and to identify their satisfactions and dissatisfactions with librarianship. The intention was to investigate possible cause-and-effect relationships by observing their current situation and searching back through personal, educational, and professional histories for plausible causal factors, in contrast to the experimental method, which collects data under controlled conditions in the present.

The investigator proposed to analyze the factors that ultimately led to these women's success. "Critical analysis" as used here denotes a detailed examination of factors in order to understand causes and effects. It was expected that patterns of motivation, educational background, and racial obstacles would emerge. Being black and being women, what psychological and physical barriers were encountered? What routes were taken to attain present positions?

The investigator attempted to ascertain similarities and differences in education and training, size of institution attended, rank of institutions, governance of institution or type of institution, location of institution, major subjects of undergraduate education, minor subjects, and opinions about undergraduate education. Information regarding graduate education was obtained regarding advanced subject degrees, highest degrees earned, and institutions awarding them.

Of particular significance was professional education for librarianship—type of library school attended, reputation, and the types of advanced degrees earned there. Additionally, what roadblocks did black women librarians encounter? Why did they choose the route that ultimately led to the position held now or at the time of their retirement?

The study did not test a hypothesis. Investigation was directed to an analysis of the responses to questions that served to reveal pertinent data regarding factors that contributed to the successful careers of these black women.

Although not primarily an oral-history project, this investigation employed some oral-history techniques. The data collected represent information that could not be gleaned otherwise—spontaneous reactions, the interviewees' attitudes, emotions, and personalities—all of which adds a dimension that the printed page cannot reveal.

Elwood Maunder characterized oral history as "a means of communicating how we remember our times, our part in those times, our notion of how our story relates to the mainstream of history of which we are a part, and how it in time has been molded" (Colman, 1968, p. 137).

The data include taped interviews, which show the usual shortcomings of oral history: (1) respondents' tendency to exaggerate; (2) incomplete recall of events and dates; and (3) the forgetting of certain facts. The interviewer must accept these limitations in this type of approach and balance them against the riches of personal introspection. To supplement the interviews, a thorough search of all available facets of the lives of the women in the study was made, in an effort to minimize questionable information.

One of the specific objectives that prompted this study was the lack of an organized body of information concerning the achievements of black female librarians. The writer does not propose a definitive study of black female librarians in the United States. The concern here is not with a statistical analysis of the careers of the population, but to make an attempt to reveal the basic beliefs that have guided the respondents in their careers.

SIGNIFICANCE OF THE STUDY

Inasmuch as a study in this area utilizing the oral-history approach had not been undertaken, data collected and analyzed provided significant insight regarding the achievement and contributions of these librarians. Despite the limitations inherent in selecting only 15 subjects, the study is relevant to ongoing research projects in library womanpower and will form a nucleus for a more comprehensive study. From the early 1930s through the mid-1960s, many black students were denied entrance to library schools, because they had poor academic records, low GRE scores, and financial problems. The study provided a comprehensive look into the circumstances confronted by a select group of successful black women with some insight into their motivation.

Five of the women included in the study have earned doctorates and have served or are serving as deans of library schools. In their study, the Carpenters (1970) found the motivating factors common to librarians who had received deanship appointments were the reputations of the institution, opportunity for research, and salary offered. It is both interesting to know and important to determine what role was taken by the black female librarians to achieve similar status.

Because blacks are in such a minority in librarianship, it is important to review a few of the most significant studies of two critical areas:

socioeconomic background of black librarians, and the reasons black students decide to become librarians.

SELECTED RELATED LITERATURE

Socioeconomic Background

Ralph F. Berdie (1943) observed that family relations have long been recognized as basic factors in determining personality and vocational interests.

The cultural level of the home is determined by the socioeconomic status, the ability, and the occupation of the parents. These factors are, in turn, all related to the father's occupation.... Family expectations are often determined by the level of the father's occupation, and the prestige and attraction various occupations have varied with the types of home from which they come. As the occupation of the mother is seldom important to her or to her family, we need not be surprised at the little relationship this bears to vocational interests. Family income is related to father's occupation and determines to some extent the range and type of experiences to which the children are exposed (pp. 260-61).

As the head of the family and bread winner, the black male has not been always viewed in the same manner as the white male. Joyce A. Ladner (1971) asserts: "Black women play highly functional, sometimes autonomous, roles within the family and society because the same economic and social conditions which allowed for the emergence of a female-dominated society during slavery still perpetuates this type of family structure" (pp. 27-8).

These observations provide a portion of the background from which the investigation approached an analysis of the careers of 15 black female librarians. Also important was the literature on the reasons for choosing librarianship as a career.

Decision to Become a Librarian

Several studies have indicated that librarians decide relatively late on librarianship as a career. Mary Jane Ryan (1967, pp. 101-102) in *Librarians' Perceptions of Librarianship,* reported that more than 57 percent of her respondents did not make their career choices until after college, 30 percent decided during college, and the remainder made the decision in high school. With respect to library administrators, Bundy and Wasserman (1972a) found that a large number—36 percent of academic, and 22 percent of public, librarians—made their career-choice decision after they had completed their college careers.

Cohn's (1970) doctoral dissertation focused on an analysis of the factors which influenced library directors of nine institutions in the Florida system of higher education to enter the field of librarianship that ultimately culminated in directorships. Included in this study were eight men and one woman, including one black man. Cohn examined what had motivated academic library directors to make the career decisions that have shaped their professional lives. Data were obtained through taped interviews and questionnaires. Two types of information were gathered for analysis, statements of the factors that were influential in career decisions, and statements of opinions concerning career decisions and related topics. The areas in which decisions were made, included reasons for (1) entering the field; (2) choosing a particular library school; (3) choosing a branch of librarianship; (4) choosing and rejecting specific positions; (5) choosing to enter into library administration and choosing one's current position. Briefly stated, Cohn's findings revealed that all nine directors agreed that they had chosen the proper field and that they would choose it again. A number of common factors were found in their backgrounds and reasons for entering the profession: all but one had worked as student assistants in a college library; some had also worked in a high-school library. This gave them the initial impetus or reinforced their earlier decision to enter the field.

Perry D. Morrison (1969), concerned with the total academic-library professional staff, was primarily interested in the social origins and personality traits of his sample group, but also included educational attainments outside of librarianship. Morrison found that academic librarians tended to have chosen the career of librarianship relatively late in their college education, which he attributes to lack of exposure to the field at an early stage (pp. 43-47).

Studies of Black Librarians

Frances M. Pollard (1964) did a survey of the characteristics of chief librarians of Negro colleges, comparing selected characteristics of two groups of chief librarians. This study involved 143 white and 57 black librarians from four-year degree-granting institutions accredited by the Southern Association of Colleges and Schools with enrollments of less than 5000 during the academic year 1960-61. Some significant differences were found.

Black chief librarians were younger than the whites. The demand in the South for professionally educated Negro college librarians is such that they do not have to wait as long as the whites before becoming chief librarian. The segregated system influences the comparatively rapid environment of the Negro college librarian (p. 282).

With respect to academic promotion, the black librarian had placed more emphasis on obtaining the master's degree in library science, whereas whites had placed more emphasis on obtaining a master's degree in a subject discipline. Some of the black librarians had, or were in the process of pursuing, advanced degrees (Pollard, 1964, p. 283).

Negroes entered the field of librarianship later than whites, and although Negro college library development lagged behind that of college libraries in general, there have been persistent efforts, especially since 1925, to develop a body of professionally educated Negroes for the occupation of librarianship (Pollard, 1964, p. 284).

The findings of Shockley (1967, pp. 423-26) were similar.

E.J. Josey (1970) edited a compilation of essays written by black librarians, titled *The Black Librarian in America*. Several librarians have contributed to this document, five of whom are included in the study being discussed here.

SELECTION OF SAMPLE

Fifteen black women in top-level administrative positions were chosen for this study. "Top-level" posts were defined as those held by deans and former deans of library schools, directors of libraries, coordinators, curators, supervisors of special collections, and state librarians.

In the Oral History Association's Guidelines (1968) for interviewing, it is suggested:

In order to obtain a tape of maximum worth as a historical document, it is encumbent upon the interviewer to be thoroughly grounded in the background and experiences of the person being interviewed, and, where appropriate and if at all feasible, to review papers of the interviewee before conducting the interview. In conducting the interview, an effort should be made to assist his recall. It is important that all interviews be conducted in a spirit of objectivity and scholarly integrity and in accordance with stipulation agreed upon (p. 2).

With the application of the oral-history technique, the writer's primary concern was to capture firsthand the reflections of these black female librarians, all but two of whom witnessed and participated in more than five decades of segregation, coupled with the stigma of oppression. Despite this, or because of it, each woman in her own right rose to a position of dignity. Her struggles in the past and achievements in the present are thus documented for posterity.

Some of the women have written brief essays about their careers; but at this writing, a document does not exist in which has been captured the reminiscences and interpretations of these 15 women, knowledgable about the eras in which they have lived and the subjects that they expounded.

Sixteen letters of inquiry were mailed to individuals, regarding their willingness to participate in a tape-recorded interview. They included:

1. Augusta Baker: Retired (May 1974). Coordinatior of Children's Services, New York Public Library.
2. Dorothy W. Collings: Dr. Collings has been in the service of the United Nations family of organizations since 1948. From 1948 to 1953, she was with UNESCO at its headquarters in Paris, in the Department of Education. For the next three years, she worked in Egypt with UNESCO's Technical Assistance Programme as Chief of the Regional Clearing House at the Arab States Fundamental Education Centre (ASFEC). In 1956 she joined the staff of the United Nations as Chief, Education Liason Section, Office of Public Education, United Nations Headquarters, New York. In 1971, with UNESCO's assistance, she organized the library school at the University of the West Indies, Kingston, Jamaica, and served as its director until 1974.
3. Eliza Atkins Gleason: First dean of the Atlanta University School of Library Service, Atlanta, Georgia. First black to get a Ph.D. in library science; Phi Beta Kappa (Graduate of University of Chicago); professor, Northern Illinois University, DeKalb, Illinois.
4. Vivian Davidson Hewitt: Special Librarian, Carnegie Endowment for International Peace, Nominee for President of Special Library Association.
5. Jean Blackwell Hutson: Chief of the Schomburg Center for Research and Black Culture, New York Public Library, New York City.
6. Alma S. Jacobs: State Librarian, Helena, Montana.
7. Clara Stanton Jones: Director, Detroit Public Library, Detroit, Michigan.
8. Virginia Lacy Jones: Dean, School of Library Service for 30 years, Atlanta University, Atlanta, Georgia.
9. Ernestine Anthony Lipscomb: Former reference librarian, Schomburg Center, New York. Director of Jackson State University Library, Jackson, Mississippi.
10. Effie Lee Morris: Coordinator of Children's Services, San Francisco Public Library, San Francisco, California.
11. Annette Lewis Phinazee: Dean, School of Library Science, North Carolina Central University, Durham, North Carolina.
12. Dorothy Burnett Porter: Curator of the Moorland-Spingarn Collection, Scholarly Black Collection, Howard University, Washington, D.C.; Phi Beta Kappa.
13. Carrie Coleman Robinson: Retired State Supervisor of Libraries, State Department of Education, Alabama; Associate Professor, Auburn University.
14. Ann Allen Shockley: Associate Librarian, Special Collections, Fisk University Library, Nashville, Tennessee.
15. Jessie Carney Smith: University Librarian, Fisk University Library.
16. Charlemae Rollins: Did not respond to letters. It was later learned that her silence was due to illness.

SUMMARY OF RESULTS

The data were collected by tape-recorded interviews for thirteen of the respondents. Forty hours' of interviewing and hundreds of pages of transcript support the analysis. Two of the librarians in the study consented to respond to a questionnaire. Inclement weather in Helena, Montana, during the months of January and February 1975, prohibited travel to interview one of the respondents. One respondent would not consent to a tape-recorded interview but did respond to a questionnaire.

Factors influencing the educational background included strong motivation from family, which was indicated as important by all the respondents. A number of the parents were educated, had teaching positions, and were a strong influence in the communities.

The respondents, for the most part, attended segregated schools in the South, both before and during their college career. All of the respondents stated that going to college was the natural course of events, something that each one was expected to do.

Educational Background of Parents

Seven of the librarians responded that one or both parents had attended college for more than two years and/or graduated, while two indicated that their parents had earned a master's degree. One noted that her father had earned a medical degree, in 1905. Three responded that their parents were not educated. Two did not give the specific educational-attainment level of their parents. It can be generalized that most of the respondents came from middle-class backgrounds, of educated parents. One respondents mother was educated in the British West Indies at a private school and in Paris. The majority of the respondents grew up in the South, in segregated neighborhoods (Table 1). They emerged from middle-class and upper-class black families.

From an analysis of the respondents' testimony relating to the family's economic conditions, there was very little difference. One family stood out as representing the upper class. The occupation of the librarians' parents most frequently represented was teaching. A father of one of the respondents was a college president. Two respondents' parents taught on the college level. The majority of the fathers had a high level of schooling. Joyce Ladner (1971), in *Tomorrow's Tomorrow: The Black Woman*, states:

> Today's black women play highly functional and sometimes autonomous roles within the family and society because the same economic and social conditions which allowed for the emergence of a female dominated society during slavery still perpetuate this type of family structure (pp. 27-28).

Table 1
Birthplace and Date of Birth Reported by Respondents

Name	Birthplace	Date	Age at Time of Study
Baker, Augusta	Baltimore, MD	Apr. 1, 1911	65
Collings, Dorothy	New Haven, CT	Sept. 22, 1911	65
Gleason, Eliza	Winston-Salem, NC	Dec. 15, 1909	67
Hewitt, Vivian	New Castle, PA	—	—
Hutson, Jean	Summerfield, FL	Sept. 7, 1914	61
Jacobs, Alma	Lewistown, MT	Nov. 21, 1916	59
Jones, Clara	St. Louis, MO	May 14, 1913	62
Jones, Virginia	Cincinnati, OH	June 25, 1912	63
Lipscomb, Ernestine	Atlanta, GA	June 10, 1912	63
Morris, Effie	Richmond, VA	—	—
Phinazee, Annette	Orangeburg, SC	July 25, 1920	55
Porter, Dorothy	Warrenton, VA	May 25, 1905	70
Robinson, Carrie	Jackson, MS	Apr. 21, 1912	63
Shockley, Ann	Louisville, KY	June 21, 1927	48
Smith, Jessie	Greensboro, NC	Sept. 25, 1930	45

The median reported age of the respondents is 64; the youngest respondent is 45, and the oldest is 70. Nine (60%) are over 60; two (13%) are over 40 but less than 50; two (13%) are over 50 but less than 60; two did not report their ages.

The families of the women studied believed that through the pursuit of an education, one's economic condition could improve. Contrary to Ladner's observations, the fathers of most of the respondents were the strong motivating forces in the families. However, three respondents felt that the mother was the stronger influence in their early lives.

Respondents' Education and Decision to Enter Librarianship

Because of segregation in housing accommodations at the University of Michigan, one respondent, while pursuing the undergraduate degree, brought suit against the university. The lack of confidence on the part of some black university administrators to involve women at the decision-making level afforded little opportunity for advancement. There was the constant fight of proving that women were capable of performing the job at a high level of competency. All but two respondents graduated from a private college, with a liberal-arts or social science-background (Table 2).

Table 2
Universities and Colleges Attended By Respondents as Undergraduates

Name	College	Location	Major	Minor	Degree	Year
Baker, Augusta	Albany State	Albany, NY	English	Educ.	BA	1933
Collings, Dorothy	Hunter College	New York, NY	English/Poli. Sci.	—	BA	1932
Gleason, Eliza	Fisk	Nashville, TN	English/Social Anthropology	—	BA	1930
Hewitt, Vivian	Geneva	Beaver Falls, PA	French/Psychology	—	BA	1943
Hutson, Jean	Barnard	New York, NY	English	—	BA	1935
Jacobs, Alma	Talladega	Talladega, AL	Sociology	—	BA	1938
Jones, Clara	Spelman	Atlanta, GA	English/History	—	BA	1934
Jones, Virginia	Hampton	Hampton, VA	Social Studies	—	BS	1936
Lipscomb, Ernestine	Spelman	Atlanta, GA	History	—	BA	1932
Morris, Effie	Flora Stone Mather	Cleveland, OH	Social Science	—	BA	1945
Phinazee, Annette	Fisk	Nashville, TN	Modern Foreign Languages	—	BA	1939
Porter, Dorothy	Howard	Washington, D.C.	History	—	BA	1928
Robinson, Carrie C.	Tougaloo	Tougaloo, MS	English	—	BA	1933
Shockley, Ann	Fisk	Nashville, TN	History	—	BA	1948
Smith, Jessie	North Carolina A&T	Greensboro, NC	Home Economics	—	BS	1950

Ten (or 60 percent) of the respondents reported having been graduated from college during the 1930s. The youngest respondent reported having been graduated from college in 1950.

Librarianship was not first career choice for the majority of the respondents. Teaching was most frequently mentioned as their first choice, because that was one of the few jobs open to Negroes and because their parents expected them to follow in their footsteps.

Some of the librarians had not met a Negro librarian during their college career. They had had contact with the "library lady" while they were in high school, who was in charge of the black-neighborhood branch library, located in a poorly-furnished, run-down building. This "library lady" was untrained and usually very "unfriendly." The respondents were turned off, and frequently, for them, the library was only a place in which to locate a book they might choose to read. In many instances, there were no libraries in the high schools they attended.

Five of the respondents had engaged in library work on a full-time basis before pursuing the professional degree in library science. Often the library course they had taken, coupled with their work in a library during the time they were in college, prompted the principal to assign them library work along with their teaching duties. Two of the respondents had worked in public-library systems to earn money to return to college; in this way they developed the desire to pursue librarianship as a career.

Common factors in the repondents' decisions to choose librarianship included

1. Wanting an opportunity to serve people.
2. Wanting an opportunity to help change the status of the Negro in the educational arena; they felt they could be more involved in helping to change the stereotyped image of Negroes as inferior.
3. An attraction to the position because of its prestige.
4. Financial attractions.
5. Fulfillment of a dream to be one of the best in whatever position was chosen.
6. A disapproval of the status quo.
7. Wanting an opportunity to prove that one can be black and competent too.
8. A desire to prove that being a black woman does not necessarily mean one's performance will be mediocre.
9. Wanting to prove one's capacity to move into the mainstream of American life.
10. The presence of high motivation and willingness to begin at the bottom, while maintaining a high degree of confidence in one's self.
11. Wanting to prove one can overcome the handicap of segregation if given the opportunity.

The respondents attended the top library schools in the nation at that time (Table 3). Five respondents earned the doctorate in library science,

Table 3
Library Schools Attended, Degrees Awarded By Year
As Reported By Respondents

Name	Library Schools	Location	BLS	Year	MLS	Year	PhD	Year	DLS	Year
Baker, Augusta	Albany State U.	Albany, NY	X	1934	—	—	—	—	—	—
Collings, Dorothy	Simmons College	Boston, MA	X	—	—	—	—	—	—	—
	Columbia U.	New York, NY	—	—	X	1936	—	—	—	—
	U. of Chicago	Chicago, IL	—	—	—	—	X	1947	—	—
Gleason, Eliza	U. of Illinois	Urbana, IL	X	1931	—	—	—	—	—	—
	U. of California	Berkeley, CA	—	—	X	1936	—	—	—	—
	U. of Chicago	Chicago, IL	—	—	—	—	X	1940	—	—
Hewitt, Vivian	Carnegie Institute of Technology	Pittsburgh, PA	X	1944	—	—	—	—	—	—
Hutson, Jean	Columbia U.	New York, NY	X	1936	—	—	—	—	—	—
Jacobs, Alma	Columbia U.	New York, NY	X	1942	—	—	—	—	—	—
Jones, Clara	U. of Michigan	Ann Arbor, MI	X	1938	—	—	—	—	—	—
Jones, Virginia	Hampton Institute	Hampton, VA	X	1933	—	—	—	—	—	—
	U. of Illinois	Urbana, IL	—	—	X	1938	—	—	—	—
	U. of Chicago	Chicago, IL	—	—	—	—	X	1945	—	—
Lipscomb, Ernestine	Columbia U.	New York, NY	X	1939	—	—	—	—	—	—
Morris, Effie	Western Reserve U.	Cleveland, OH	X	1946	—	—	—	—	—	—
	Western Reserve U.	Cleveland, OH	—	—	X	1945	—	—	—	—
Phinazee, Annette	U. of Illinois	Urbana, IL	X	1941	—	—	—	—	—	—
	U. of Illinois	Urbana, IL	—	—	X	1948	—	—	—	—
	Columbia U.	New York, NY	—	—	—	—	—	—	X	1968
Porter, Dorothy	Columbia U.	New York, NY	X	1931	—	—	—	—	—	—
	Columbia U.	New York, NY	—	—	X	1932	—	—	—	—
Robinson, Carrie	Hampton Institute	Hampton, VA	X	1932	—	—	—	—	—	—
	U. of Illinois	Urbana, IL	—	—	X	1949	—	—	—	—
Shockley, Ann	Western Reserve U.	Cleveland, OH	—	—	X	1959	—	—	—	—
Smith, Jessie	Peabody	Nashville, TN	—	—	X	1957	—	—	—	—
	U. of Illinois	Urbana, IL	—	—	—	—	X	1964	—	—

three in the 1940s. A majority of the respondents reported that they experienced prejudice while pursuing their degrees.

Careers of Respondents

Most of the respondents were employed in academic libraries, and a majority of the institutions they worked in were black. The public library ranked second for respondents' employment. Six of the respondents had worked at Atlanta University Library School. Each respondent has been involved with library education at some point in her career, by teaching library-science courses, directing library-science workshops, or serving as a guest lecturer in library schools. One of the respondents, who has served in public libraries, academic libraries, and library education had spent most of her work life in predominantly white academic libraries.

It can be generalized that these black women rose to their positions through the ranks, and before 1965 a small percentage were employed in administrative positions in integrated settings.

Librarianship was found not to be the first choice of a large majority of respondents, but they have enjoyed the work and feel that they have achieved a modicum of success. Collectively, they are not prolific writers, although individual respondents have made great contributions to librarianship, in professional journals.

A large majority of the respondents encountered roadblocks in their careers but were able to surmount the obstacles.

Respondents attribute their success in attaining positions to the following: (1) knowing themselves; (2) believing in themselves and what they say; (3) not being afraid of responsibility—accepting it as a challenge; (4) working hard and being able to adapt—having vision; (5) accepting criticism—those who do nothing are never criticized; (6) being sensitive to the needs of others—being happy with oneself; (7) having had a good, broad educational background at the best schools in the country and attaining high grades; (8) getting reinforcement from parents that they were as good as anyone else and could achieve anything they wanted if they worked hard enough at it; (9) motivation, dedication, and determination; (10) the belief that if one is competent, others will see it and recommend one regardless of color and sex; (11) having a level head—using logic rather than emotions; (12) being black and being a woman's giving one the motivation to work hard to help negate the stigmatism of "inferiority"; and (13) not limiting one's goals because one is black and a woman.

Advice from these successful women to new librarians includes: (1) be prepared academically; (2) be competitive; (3) know who you are and be willing to work at it regardless of the obstacles and/or roadblocks—have inner determination; (4) get a broad educational background, but subject background is also important; (5) get into a position where you can be creative and grow personally and professionally; (6) set standards of excellence for yourself, because nothing else will do; (7) if blacks want to get the "book message" and the "material message" over to black people, seek public-library work for service to those out in the "boondocks." Far too many students go into college- and university-library work; more trained blacks are needed in public-library work.

RECOMMENDATIONS

Research studies on minority librarians, and more specifically on black librarians, are missing from the literature. It is hoped that findings in this study will provide data for a more extensive, definitive study on black librarians in the United States, male and female.

The writer recommends that a comparative study of black and white library administrators be undertaken. A study should be made of black female and male librarians, who hold the doctorate degree, to determine the role they are playing in library education and administration. Additionally, studies should be conducted to determine the factors that prevented some of the librarians from achieving their goals in librarianship. The writer recommends that a study be done of white female librarians with equal educational training, to determine what type of positions they have attained. These data can serve as a basis for bringing bright young recruits to the field, and may serve as guidelines in assisting library educators in evaluating applicants.

The Woman Academic-Library Administrator: A Career Profile

JANICE C. FENNELL

BACKGROUND

IN 1877 JUSTIN WINSOR EXPLAINED that women were wanted in the library field because "they soften our atmosphere, they lighten our labour, they are equal to our work, and for the money they cost...they are infinitely better than equivalent salaries will produce by the other sex" (Schiller, 1974, p. 117). In the 1880s, when the main professions open to women were teaching and nursing, Melvil Dewey gave a lecture entitled, "Librarianship as a Profession for College-Bred Women" (Dewey, 1886). Prior to that lecture, librarianship was chiefly a masculine preserve. However with Dewey's and Winsor's encouragement, the influx of women began. Women came into the profession in such great numbers that by 1920, 90 percent of all librarians were female, and secure career opportunities were possible. Women held many of the top administrative positions in college libraries. Since that time, many things have changed in library service.

With the passage of the GI Bill in 1944, men began reentering the field, and women's career opportunities diminished. While educational and professional requirements continue to be the same for men and women in the library profession, the rewards are not equal, once beyond the lower levels of employment.

A 1930 survey of 74 large college and university libraries showed that 19 head librarians were women and 55 were men. In 1969, in the same institutions, there were 3 women and 71 men directors; also in the same year, not one of the 50 largest academic libraries in the United States was headed by a woman (Schiller, 1969b, p. 1098). In 1966-67 not one of the 74 Association of Research Libraries was directed by a woman. By 1973 the number of ARL institutions had increased to 84, yet only 4 women held the position of director (Gaver, 1973, p. 1820). And with 104 current institutions, in 1976 the number of women directors remained 4 (Association of Research Libraries, 1976, pp. 103-7). Now there is only "tokenism at the top" (Holden, 1965, p. 647).

Librarianship as a profession is 84 percent female, yet "the majority exercise neither the influence, control, or power which dominance implies" (Little, 1972, p. 10). Such terms as "disadvantaged majority" (Schiller, 1970a, p. 345) and "the 4/5 minority" (Smart, 1975, p. 14) are often used to describe women librarians. Increasing concern is shown over the lack of representation of women in certain positions. Although women predominate in number and have proven themselves capable and qualified, their rise to influential positions within the power and leadership structure of librarianship—namely, in top-level administrative positions—has been slow. For the past century, statistics consistently document the fact that, particularly in the largest influential academic institutions, women in libraries make up a majority of the professional personnel, yet the number of women in policy-making positions has declined. Men currently hold 15 percent of the professional positions but dominate the administrative ranks. Ninety percent of library administrators are men. Linda Phelps (1974) stated that several factors caused this domination by the minority.

Many employees claim that women are passive and less keenly professional. Male egotism often causes males to ask for and be granted higher salaries than advertised. The more dynamic leadership of men is causing increasing numbers of men to enter the profession, thus allowing males to hire males. The lack of vacancies in the more creative posts leaves the housekeeping chores of serials, acquisitions, and cataloging to females. Women's traditional reduced commitment to work, lower motivation, and career work patterns are other factors (p. 10).

During the past few decades, women have received much support from the Federal Government in the form of legislation. Even with the Civil Rights Act of 1964, amended by the Equal Employment Opportunity Act of 1972; the Fair Standards Act of 1938, as amended by the Equal Pay Act of 1963 and Education Amendments of 1972; and Executive Order 11246, as amended by two additional executive orders pertaining to Affirmative Action, the library profession has seen little real change.

At a 1975 conference, Women in Library Administration, attended by 80 librarians, women were encouraged to school themselves in budgetary matters and to prepare themselves (both emotionally and vocationally) to push into male echelons. While acknowledging that "American women face difficulties in achieving, preparing for, and carrying out the duties of administrative positions" (Women in Administration, 1975, p. 718), it was noted that success is by no means impossible.

In 1904 Salome Cutler Fairchild (1904, p. 161) asked "whether women will ever hold the highest administrative positions in libraries." That question currently remains open. The most important positions of leadership and administration in the academic-library profession are reserved for men, or, at best, include only a small proportion of women. Yet, who are these women? Little effort has been made to learn about women directors of the largest academic libraries in the United States, and an analysis of their backgrounds and factors influencing their career achievement need investigation. Furthermore, their insight is needed in helping other women attain administrative positions in the profession.

This study developed a composite picture or career profile of the women directors of the largest academic libraries in the United States. Many aspects of the women's lives were examined. Information was gathered relating to the personal characteristics of the administrators, their family background, education, training, work history, and current status. Factors influencing their career achievement were investigated, and each woman was asked to give suggestions or make recommendations that might assist other women in attaining administrative positions.

The largest institutions were chosen because of the scarcity of female head librarians in larger libraries; in small libraries, women administrators are found in greater proportions. A 1970 survey conducted by the American Association of University Women found that greater opportunities for women in library administration existed in women's colleges and in schools with enrollemnts of under 1000, while women were less likely to be head librarians in schools with enrollments above 1000 (Oltman, 1970, p. 14). Fewer women will be found as directors of all types of libraries as the size of the library increases (Schiller, 1974, pp. 112-16). It is logical, then, to assume that those women who presently hold directorships in the largest academic libraries are a select group and comprise a population from which much can be learned.

If the number of women in academic-library administrative positions is to increase, not only must institutional barriers, myths, and fallacies be eliminated, but women must also be prepared to assume these roles. The answers to some of the following basic questions can assist in preparing women for administrative roles, in gaining their acceptance by institutions, and in encouraging other women to aspire to administrative positions in academic librarianship.

1. What kind of personal background is conducive to women who gain directorship positions?
2. What is the influence of early environment on women's career achievement?
3. What personal characteristics do women administrators of academic libraries possess?
4. What type of experience, both educational and work, have women academic library directors found to be helpful in their positions?
5. Do women academic-library directors have a strong sense of career commitment and identification?
6. Are they productive by academic standards?
7. What professional responsibilities do they have?
8. How involved are they in the profession?
9. What job characteristics are important to them?
10. Have they had any influential role models in their career?
11. How do they feel about their roles?
12. What influences affected their career choice?
13. What effect has being female had on their career?

Questions such as these can be answered only by the female academic library directors themselves.

METHOD

This study focuses upon women who are currently directors of the largest academic libraries in the United States. Determination of the size of a library is based upon three factors: (1) number of volumes, (2) total operating expenditures, and (3) number of regular library staff in full-time equivalents. Of the 164 libraries within the scope of this study, 17 were determined to have female directors. Of these 17, 11 agreed to participate in the study.

Data were collected by personal, tape-recorded interviews with eight of the respondents. The investigator was unable to interview three of the women personally. These three were sent blank cassette tapes and the list of questions to be anwered. All three returned their responses to the investigator.

The interviews were semistructured, in that a basic outline was followed by the investigator; however, the participants were permitted and encouraged to depart from the outline in their responses.

THE FINDINGS

In the development of a career profile, it is necessary to understand the background from which a person comes. Personal, educational, experiential, and professional backgrounds are often interrelated and often have similar influences. Described below are demographic variables of the respondents under the following categories: age, birthplace and geographical location in which reared, family information, marital status and information about the husbands of those who are currently married, the number of children, education and training, and career information. Factors that were perceived by the respondents as being influential in their career achievement are discussed within each category.

PERSONAL BACKGROUND

The women in this study range from 40 to 64 years of age, with a median of 53 years of age. Seven are between 50 and 60 years of age. Three are between 40 and 48 years of age, and one is 64 years of age. None is younger than 40, with 48 the average age.

All 11 of the respondents were born in different states. Birthplaces were Massachusetts, New York, Michigan, Washington, Pennsylvania, New Jersey, Ohio, South Dakota, Colorado, Maryland, and Texas.

Four respondents grew up in the Northeast; two each in the Northwest, Southeast, and Midwest; and one in the Southwest. Four moved with their families from the place of their birth to other locations.

Two respondents relocated often with their families as youngsters, such moves necessitated by their father's work. When asked if moving had any effect, one replied: "It makes you a loner, but I don't know whether it's a disadvantage. You just learn not to care too much what the rest of the world thinks of you, because you're always a little bit on the outside." The other stated: "A lot of people say they feel uprooted, but I was always interested in seeing new places and new people, and I don't think it adversely affected me." Both later implied that these moves may have given them the flexibility that is needed by a library administrator.

Alan Bayer (1973), in a study of teaching faculty in academe, found that the modal educational level of the fathers of faculty members was eighth grade or less; the modal level of mothers was completion of high school.

The modal educational level of the mothers of the respondents in this study is identical: high-school graduate. However, two of the fathers had a graduate or professional degree, two had attended college but were not graduates, two were high-school graduates, and two had less than a high-school education.

Three of the fathers were owner-operators of farms, although one also owned a grocery store. Two others were grocers. Other occupations of the respondents' fathers were engineering, both mining and chemical; university teaching; head of an office-supply company; painting contractor; and a civilian employee of the military.

Nine mothers of the respondents were housewives, and two were teachers. One teacher worked periodically during the Depression, and the other teacher worked part-time from the time her daughter was "age 3 until about age 8" and then again when she was about 11 to 15. Four of the housewives held jobs for brief periods of time. One helped in the family store, one was a secretary during World War II, another was a restaurant manager during the Depression, and one worked in a dry-cleaning establishment. For those who worked either full-time or part-time, a typical response was, "basically she was a housewife, and mother of the family."

The number of children in a family greatly influences the opportunities afforded to an individual child, both in attention to personal aspirations and the distribution of financial resources toward those aspirations. Helen Astin (1969, p. 25) found that women doctorates came from small families. Forty-seven percent had just one sibling or none, and only 9 percent had six or more. One woman in this study was an only child, but five had just one sibling. One respondent came from a family of five children.

Studies have shown that firstborn children tend to be high achievers in both educational and career pursuits and that birth order can be a powerful predictor of achievement. Hennig and Franklin (1977, p. 76), in a study of women enrolled in the M.B.A. program at Harvard Business School in 1963-64, found that 80 percent of their population were either eldest or only children. The remaining 20 percent, while not firstborn, had experiences similar to those of firstborn children. Hennig and Jardim (1977, p. 77), in another study, of 25 women administrators, found that all were firstborn children. Each was an only child or the eldest in an all-girl family of no more than three children.

In the current study, five of the women were firstborn or only children; two were second-born; and the remaining four were third-born or later. Of the six who were not firstborn or only children, half of them had childhood experiences similar to those of firstborn children.

Some comments relative to childhood experiences similar to those of only children are as follows:

She [sister] was older. Mother always said she had two only children.

There was enough of an age difference... that I was very well aware of being an only child and being the center of attention.

I am the firstborn. She came along as number two, but there is a fifteen-year age gap between us.... I think she associated me more as a third parent rather than as a sister, until she got into her teens.

Positive parental attitudes toward and support of educational pursuits were seen by the respondents as being an important influence in their decisions to attend college and to have a career. The following comments indicate the parental support of and belief in education for the respondents:

I came from a long line of college-educated people; it never occurred to me that there was anything else to do but go to college.

My father was an educator but he didn't think that girls needed a college education. And this was a bone of real contention between him and my mother. Mother always said that...we could do whatever we wanted to do after we went to college.

She [mother] had great career aspirations for all her children. My parents were very encouraging toward all of us—wanting us to move ahead and achieve greater educational goals than they did. It became apparent that I would pursue a college education, when I was in grade school....My parents not only encouraged but influenced the careers of every one of the children.

I kid about it, but it's almost true that I didn't realize that one had a choice about going to college, until I got there. It was absolutely assumed that I had to go to college, and I assumed everybody heard that at home.

I just took it for granted, as a very young child, that I would go to college. It was something that I dreamed about, and in my high-school years my family was even willing to mortgage their home so that I could attain a college education.

When the question regarding parental attitude toward a higher education was asked, 8 of the 11 women prefaced their statements with comments regarding the family's financial situation. Although all of the respondents came from middle- to upper-middle-class backgrounds, finances were an important consideration. Four mentioned the fact that they were growing up and attending school during the Depression years. Those who did not grow up during that period also mentioned finances as being an influence in their lives. Regarding finances, typical responses included:

The assumption was always that there wouldn't be any money for it [college].

I was raised during the Depression; we didn't have money at all...

he [father] couldn't afford to put me through graduate school, since my sister was coming along, and on his salary, the best he could manage was to get us both through college.

there wasn't very much money in the family...

The educated woman faces a number of important decisions that clearly affect her career pattern. Perhaps one of the most influential is whether to get married or to remain single. According to the 1970 Census Report, an average of 8.7 percent of the female population between 25 and 65 are single, 75.1 percent married (with spouse present), 5.5 percent widowed, and 4.8 percent divorced (U.S. Department of Commerce, 1972). Helen Astin (1969, p. 26), in her study of women doctorates, found that 55 percent were or had been married. Ginzberg (1966, p. 25) found that 60 percent of the women he studied were married. Five of the women administrators in this study are currently married, three are single, one is a widow, and two are divorced.

Educated people, in general, tend to marry somewhat later than less-educated ones. Astin (1969, p. 26) found that 5 percent of women doctorates had married before college and 70 percent at some time during their college training, indicating that about three-fourths of her sample had successfully combined the roles of wife and student. One-third of the group of women doctorates had married during graduate school.

Perhaps it was the period during which the administrators in this study were growing up, but those who are or had been married, emphatically stated that "nobody got married in those days during college." Another statement indicative of a similar feeling is: "That was the day when you didn't get married until you could support yourselves." Consequently all of the eight women who are or had been married did so after obtaining the bachelor's degree. Of those, four married after the master's program and one after the doctoral program.

Education places greater restrictions on the woman's choice of a spouse than it does on the man's. "In our society a man is more likely to marry a person of lower social status than is a woman" (Simon, Clark, and Galway, 1972, p. 83). The respondents in the present study seemed to marry men with similar educational backgrounds: four of the five husbands of those married at the time of the study had at least a master's degree, and two of those had the doctorate. One had not received a college degree.

The husbands' occupations were consistent with their level of education attainment: three are university faculty members, one is an administrator in a research institute, and one was a stone contractor and is currently a realtor.

In view of the high level of occupational achievement of this group of women, their earning power within the family was explored. Eight of the 11 respondents considered themselves the principal wage earner of the family. Of these eight, five were married at the time of the study; however, three said that they were "equal wage earners" with their husband, and not the principal wage earner.

One of the major concerns about women in professional positions is the time that will be taken from their families. Fertility rates of educated women are lower than those of women in the general population between ages 25 and 65. According to the 1970 Census, 11 percent of married women have no children (U.S. Department of Commerce, 1972). Eli Ginzberg (1966, p. 25), in his study of educated women, found about 18 percent of those married had no children. Astin (1969, p. 29), in her study of married women doctorates, found the proportion of that population who were childless was more than twice as large as the proportion of women in general; 28 percent of the women doctorates had no children.

The administrators in this study exercised their options to attend college, determine when and if they wanted to marry, and whether or not they wanted to have children. Of those who had been married at any time, only two had children. One had three, and the other had two, children. One of the respondents had her family long before she attended graduate school. Her youngest child was the only one at home at that time, and she was in high school. This respondent commented that she got much support from her children.

The other respondent had two children and worked part-time but over twenty hours per week, prior to and after the birth of both children. At no time was she out of work because of her children for longer than six months. She did not begin working full-time until her children were of school age.

What influence did husbands and children exert on these women? Were all influences of a positive nature? One respondent indicated that a very influential factor regarding her career and ultimate attainment of an administrative job was the fact that she had gotten a divorce. In regards to a career she stated that "I would not have one if I were still married." She expressed doubt that she would have quit the profession; however, she seemed certain that she would have remained a "working wife," as opposed to a "career person," and would have remained in a regular nine-to-five job. Her husband did not want her to be involved with a career and would not allow her to attend meetings other than during regular working hours. Thus this respondent received no support whatsoever from her husband, and she felt that her divorce was the best thing that could have happened to her career.

Another respondent, when asked about her husband's feelings toward her graduate education (obtained after they were married) and her subsequent career, exclaimed, "He lets me do anything I want. He is extremely supportive and has always been very thoughtful of whatever it was I wanted to do...he has always encouraged and sort of pushed me on and been very helpful." For the past two and a half years, this respondent and her husband have held positions in different parts of the country and commuted on weekends. They have missed "no more than half a dozen weekends," and she finds the three-hour plane trips a time to do "catch-up" work.

The separation necessitated by positions in two areas of the country apparently was a partial cause of the break-up of the marriage of one of the respondents. After she had been commuting cross-country for eighteen months, her marriage ended. Even though her husband had been supportive during her graduate education and subsequent career and, in fact, had been supportive of the move to an administrative job in a library across the country, she found that the supportive structure was not as strong as she had hoped.

While most husbands were seen as being "supportive," some still held conservative ideas regarding the place of a wife. One, although proud of his wife's position and considered supportive, "is still enough of a product of his generation that I am director of libraries from 8 till 5," but "he expects me to devote a good deal of the nonscheduled time to our lives rather than to the career." Another supportive husband is described thus:

If anything, he was as chauvinistic as any male except that he realized for our joint happiness that it was better for me to be working in a library. As long as everything went on at home and his clean shirts were there and his dinner was there, he was never loath to give a hand. He wouldn't mind, on the weekend, doing the grocery shopping or throwing the clothes in the washing machine if that was going to make it possible for us to have guests for dinner or anything else. It was a good marriage, that's one thing.

Being a "faculty wife" was seen by one repondent as a decided advantage in learning about administration. She stated that the fate of university libraries is in the hands of the faculty. If one can't talk to the faculty, can't understand faculty research, and can't know the committees and their responsibilities, then there is no way to be an administrator. These aspects of a university she learned from her husband.

Three respondents thought that being unmarried was a disadvantage. Fitting into the social life of a university is seen as being more difficult if one is unattached. Similar comments were made by these in relation to their single status. One stated that the "disadvantage that women have is that a man has a wife and what a woman needs is a wife," while another remarked that "it was an obstacle not to have a wife. If I were a male and married in this job there are a lot of things I wouldn't have to worry about that I have to take care of now." Still another saw her single status as being a drawback. She stated that "it is hard to mix socially, because couples are still couples. Wives resent women with whom their husbands work, and men tend to be a little bit embarrassed about their female colleagues when they have wives with them. Now that may have changed to a greater degree than I think it has."

EDUCATION AND TRAINING

Education and training are two of the most important predictors of occupational achievement. In attempting to ascertain the influence of formal and informal study and training and related experiences on the career achievement of women academic-library directors, the following factors are explored: highest degree earned, fields of study, graduate courses taken not leading to a degree, financial aid during any educational period, career counseling, the importance of education and experience in developing administrative skills, and the influence of certain related education and training factors.

A recent study by the American Council on Education reported that of the 53,034 respondents in their study of teaching faculty in academe, almost half had master's degrees and one third had either a Ph.D. or an Ed.D. In the group, 61.6 percent of the faculty women reported the master's degree as their highest degree, and 19.9 percent of the women indicated that they held a doctoral degree of some type (Bayer, 1973, p. 15).

Three of the women directors reported their highest degree as being the doctorate; only one is currently working on her Ph.D. For seven, a master's degree in some field is the highest degree held; and one holds the fifth-year Bachelor of Science in Library Science. Nine hold the master's in library science, three hold the doctorate in library science, two hold the Bachelor of Science in Library Science (B.S.L.S.), and two hold a master's in a field other than library science. The highest number of degrees held by one person is four, these being a B.A., an M.A., an M.A. in Library Science, and a Ph. D. in Library Science. Three of the respondents hold three degrees each; and the remaining seven hold two degrees.

All respondents except one had completed their master's and doctoral degrees in library science. The other, although not having a master's in library science, had received a master's in English and a certificate in library science. At the baccalaureate level, the women tended to major in a broad spectrum of subjects: English, geography/geology, German, history, music, philosophy, and political science.

Continuing education was important to several of the respondents. Six of the 11 have taken at least one nondegree-related course. Of those taking formal courses, graduate courses in management were mentioned most often. Several of the respondents indicated that they had participated in workshops, seminars, weekend sessions, continuing-education classes, "dribs and drabs here and there," and "odds and ends" in courses. Most of the nondegree work was unstructured.

One of the most frequently cited barriers to women's study at the graduate level has been lack of financial assistance; however, the literature disclosed little evidence of discrimination in the awarding of fellowships and assistantships. Patricia Cross (1974, p. 43) stated:

> Among all graduate students, men are a little more likely to derive primary support from fellowships or assistantships, but the differences are not large, especially considering the high level of student assistance available in the sciences (where few women are enrolled)

Considering the financial backgrounds of the respondents and their families, it is natural to assume that financial assistance for educational pursuits would be a very influential factor in determining their future. When asked about financial support of their education, either undergraduate or graduate, 9 of the 11 women indicated that they had received financial assistance. Examples of the types of aid that the respondents received were a fellowship to work in the library, a scholarship covering the cost of tuition, a full scholarship, governmental research grants, internships, scholarships based on financial need, and, most significantly, a Higher Education Act Title IIB fellowship, which provided for all of one of the respondent's support during her three years of work on the doctorate. Several also responded that they worked during summers as well as during the school year to cover expenses.

Career counseling often has a decided effect upon the career one chooses. Six of the directors, however, received no career counseling, either in high school or college. Five recalled taking some kind of vocational tests. Those five were encouraged in diverse ways.

One respondent remembers, based on the inventory of vocational skills, that she was advised not to be a librarian, but to go into sales and stop retiring behind desks. Two others had evaluations made of their aptitudes and skills, during their freshman year in college. One recalled: "I took a whole battery of aptitude tests, and they all showed up essentially the same thing. My skills lay in the areas having to do with language and communications; therefore, I could be a librarian, a jounalist, an interpreter, or I could teach languages." The other remembers taking a "battery of tests" including aptitude tests. However, to her recollection, "we never got the results of those....I can't for the life of me remember anyone saying to me that I would be better at thus and so...." So even though five respondents did take tests, presumably with the idea of having career counseling, only one woman remembers that librarianship was identified as a career for which she was suited.

When asked questions about original career plans, the choice of librarianship as a career, and subsequent education, various responses were given. Librarianship as a career was the first choice of seven of the respondents. The only other choices mentioned were philosophy teacher, veterinarian, geologist, and musicologist.

The decision to pursue a library-science education (master's or fifth-year degree) was not a conscious decision by three of the respondents; it was "just always known." One respondent did not make a decision to pursue the master's degree in library science until twenty-five years after getting her bachelor's degree. She was working in a public library as a clerk at the time and decided that library work provided a satisfying work experience. Four others made the decision to enter librarianship either while they were employed in libraries or after they had served as an apprentice in a library. One respondent decided in high school that she would not teach but, because she liked to read, would become a librarian (she admitted this "is probably the worst reason for choosing a career"); one couldn't see herself as a "teacher of anything," and her husband-to-be was in the city where she attended graduate school. And the last shamefully confessed:

I probably wouldn't admit this to most career people. I looked around to see what I could finish in a year...There were two things I could finish in the time that he [husband] had left. One was speech pathology, and the other was librarianship. And I knew that I couldn't stand being a speech pathologist. So I went to library school.

EXPERIENTIAL AND PROFESSIONAL BACKGROUND

The work pattern of administrators is important to investigation. Data were gathered regarding the administrators' nonlibrary work experiences, full-time professional job experiences, length of employment, and career interruptions.

Since the majority of the respondents had made their career choice early in life, over half of them had no nonlibrary-work experiences since graduation from college. Six had no nonlibrary work experience. This is not to say that during their high school and college years, they didn't work elsewhere. In fact, several of them held a variety of jobs, such as telephone operator, soda jerk ("I can make the best Malted milk you ever had"), babysitter, department-store clerk, cook, and eyeglass lens shaper.

However, five of the respondents held nonlibrary-related jobs after graduation from college. Again there were a variety of job experiences. One respondent, whose father had been a grocer, was employed by the Kroger Grocery Store chain immediately following her completion of the bachelor's degree. As she stated during the interview, "[They] chose to offer me an administrative position, a manager of one of their stores, and I chose not to accept it." A secretarial position with an oil company provided one of the respondents with many opportunities to learn and develop administrative skills.

Another respondent described her first position upon graduation from college as being a "pencil pusher—SP something" for the Bureau of Standards. She worked in the Length and Measurement Section and "learned a lot about geodetic survey tapes." One woman worked for a year in a music store, selling records, while her husband was a graduate student; the second year, she worked in a Sears catalog department. She responded that she "could find stuff in that catalog faster than anybody." She utilized this ability later as a reference librarian. The only other person who had nonlibrary experience worked as a technical editor for an electrical company. It was this company which, because she was "bookish," promoted her to the position of librarian and later financed her graduate library education. Virtually none of these positions was administrative in nature.

Ginzberg (1966, p. 89) found that he could classify educated women according to four career patterns; straight (in which job experiences remained closely related to one field), broad (in which they expanded within the same general area), changed (marked by a more or less radical job shift at some time), and variant (with little direction or progression from one job to another).

The administrators in this study could be classified as having straight or broad patterns. All of their routes to administration were via previous library experience. Although some of the women had changed their initial career aspirations, these transfers were within the field of librarianship. This is a concept of career "development" which, according to Ginzberg (1966), carries with it a "sense of purposefulness, direction, and progression" (p. 91).

To investigate the routes the administrators took in their careers, their two previous library positions were examined. All of the administrators entered their current positions directly from other administrative or supervisory positions. Prior to their previous positions, 9 of the 11 respondents had held supervisory positions. Six had been directors or heads of either small college libraries, special libraries, or departmental libraries—e.g., graduate library, graduate school of business library, campus library—two had served in the administrative realm of the library at which they were employed; two had served as department heads; and one was an associate librarian. The entire spectrum of librarianship, circulation, reference, public services, cataloging, serials, music and science, special, and research, was covered in the nonsupervisory positions that had been held by the respondents.

The number of years of professional employment since receiving the master's degree or equivalent, ranged from 16 to 36 years, with the mean being 24.9 years and the median, 26 years. In addition to the total number of years of professional employment, the women directors were queried as to length of service at present institution and length of service in present administrative position. The shortest length of time any one person had been at the employing institution was 2 years, while one respondent had been employed by the same institution for 31 years. The mean length of employment at the present institution was 11.8 years, and the median was 9 years. Five of the respondents had been working in their present institution for 5 years or less; two had been employed between 11 and 15 years, and two between 16 and 20 years.

Not one respondent had held her present position longer than 10 years. Seven had been directors at their present institution for less than 6 years. The average length of time the respondent had served as director at the present institution was 4.8 years, with the median being 4 years.

Of the combined total of more than 270 years' of service to the library profession, the respondents represent employment at 37 employing institutions. Twenty-eight of that number were academic institutions, five were public libraries, and four were special libraries. Only the University of Michigan had employed more than one of the respondents.

Ginzberg (1966), in his study of educated women, described three types of work histories: continuous (full-time jobs throughout the adult life, with only minor interruptions); intermittent (three or more periods away from work or working part-time only); and periodic (dropping out of the labor market one or more times, each time for three years or more). He found that a continuous work history was almost a prerequisite for high occupational achievement (p. 78). According to him, "a woman cannot reach the top of her field unless she is willing to devote a major portion of her life to work (p. 102).

The administrators in this study primarily followed the pattern of "continuous" employment, with one having an intermittent work history. This respondent did state, however, that she was careful to work just over twenty hours per week, because that number was the figure by which the state computed length of employment. If one worked over twenty hours, it was considered full-time. The only other respondent who had a career interruption of over two years was unemployed for close to three years, while she worked on her doctorate degree. One respondent took off one year to attend graduate school, and two others mentioned interruptions—one for a month between jobs, when "literally I was unemployed" and the other when "I left one job and took a trip and applied for another one. Usually I had at least six months between jobs." As a group these women exhibited a continuous work pattern.

Each respondent was asked questions about the influence of others who might have encouraged or discouraged them during their work experiences. They were also asked about their perceptions of the attitudes of others toward women in general and women in administration in particular. Questions concerning any barriers that had been encountered by them were asked.

The attitudes of employers not only affect the entry level in an organization but also each subsequent step up the organizational ladder for an employee. According to Cynthia Epstein (1970a, p. 966), another factor also determines access to the higher levels of most professions—that of sponsorship, or a protege relationship.

On-the-job encouragement by others was reported by many of the respondents. The following comments are examples that are indicative of the kinds of supportive and encouraging people with whom the women have had contact.

The librarian...had asked for me to come...with the intent of grooming me to take over as director. She wanted very much to have another woman follow her in that position. There's never been a male librarian [director].

I think my boss lent the most. He was the one who suggested that I should take on this, and he sort of pushed me screaming at each step.

I had heard about librarianship from two very wonderful bosses that I had in college.

One of the people that probably had the most influence on me was the man who was my boss for a number of years, and in two different capacities....He was extremely good, patient, understanding, helpful. When I needed help and guidance, he was there.

It's really one person....He became my boss. We worked well together, and I admired a great many of his ideas. I liked his training, and I learned a huge amount from him. I've learned all I know about automation from him. He's as close as I've had to a mentor.

I've had pretty good bosses throughout my career....[One] was very patient and provided enough flexibility but still enough direction...[another] was always very supportive, but if he saw something that he didn't agree with, he would always tell me.

One respondent spoke highly of an encouraging coworker outside the library field. She tells it this way: "There was...a very excellent lab man who had a lot of integrity. He was very smart, and he encouraged me to continue my career, to go back to college and get a library degree." Although several of the women spoke highly of administrative-internship programs as excellent vehicles for developing appropriate skills, none had served as interns.

Support from the employing institutions and the top-level administrators has been another influential factor in some of the respondents' careers. Each person was asked what the attitudes of previous, as well as current, employers had been toward hiring women and how they felt about women in administration. With one exception, all of the respondents had succeeded a male director. Therefore the investigator thought that academic administrators' attitudes toward these women directors might not be positive. This, however, did not prove to be the case. Comments made by the respondents reflected the idea that the attitudes of their administration had been positive, tolerant, supportive, receptive, easy, or open and wholesome. Indicative of such attitudes are the following comments:

We have an easy relationship. He [immediate superior] has a good deal of confidence in me, and I know how he's going to react to most things.

My institution is currently receptive toward the notion of women in administration...he [provost] is tolerant toward women in administration.

[Their] attitude toward women in administration is quite positive. In the first place, they hired me.

[H]iring women was no particular problem, because librarianship was primarily a woman's field; therefore, there wasn't a lot of choice. The top administrative positions always went to men, without any question. And this, I think, was assumed by pretty much everybody....One of my bosses at one time said to me, "You have to work twice as hard and be twice as good, because you are a woman."

I guess it is very positive, but we don't have as many women on the faculty as we should have...the attitude is very supportive.

Two of the women made comments suggestive of the fact that, owing to affirmative action, their administrations might have been "forced" to look more favorably upon women. The two comments were: "We were in the middle of the whole affirmative-action bit and they were quite anxious to have a minority or a woman, as so many campuses are these days," and

Because it was about 1970-71 that affirmative action was coming in, universities were beginning to be pushed on this. Our university had one woman dean and was interested in having another woman administrator. I was there: I was asked to be a candidate for the job and thought this was kind of laughable, knowing past history.

As a further indicator of institutional attitudes toward women, the investigator asked if personal questions were asked during job interviews, and if so, what kind. Two respondents gave indications that personal questions, relating to marriage, had been asked but gave no specific examples. One woman had been asked if her husband was moving with her, although she did not view this question with negativism. Only one respondent gave a definite example of this as a problem. She related that the director of libraries at the time was the "prototype of the male-chauvinist pig" and that "he hired me after I had to assure him that I wasn't going to get pregnant again." None of the other interviewees had ever had questions of this nature asked of them.

When asked if there were specific sexual barriers encountered during the pursuit of a career, four of the respondents replied negatively. One declared that she was "not one of those who thinks I have to campaign for woman's lib." Another remarked that "sometimes people create sexual barriers for themselves."

The opposing viewpoint was expressed by the seven other respondents. Some gave specific examples:

When I finished my degree, I was not made head librarian, because the president wanted a man.

One day the director wrote me a letter saying that maybe I ought to look to my professorial wifely duties.

A lot of the middle management of the college are men, and it's one of those kind of male-type clubs....It's like the locker room at the golf club....There really isn't any way to break into it very satisfactorily.

Another respondent added that "males were hired for the most part. I don't think that they [administration] made any concerted effort toward hiring women in administration." She further observed that she thought she was being "groomed" for the job as head of a department. However, the director of libraries had other ideas at that time. There was a "bright young male law student" without experience or library degree who was hired for the position. At that point the respondent decided to look elsewhere for a job. Reflecting upon this experience she related now that she's unsure as to whether the young man received the position because he was a male or because the director was more interested in seeing the career of the young man advance than he was in seeing hers progress. At the time this incident happened, the respondent thought that it was "absolutely the worst thing that could have happened to me. But as it turned out, it kicked me out of the nest, so to speak. There's no question in my mind that it was a significant turning point. It maybe was the best thing that could have happened at that point in time."

A turning point in career decision was reached by another respondent when she met what she feels was "discrimination by sex." Before reaching the decision to become a librarian, this person had been encouraged to look into the possibility of becoming a patent agent. She studied the patent laws for approximately six months and made the necessary application. One week before she was to take the examination, she received a letter from the commissioner of patents, who disqualified her from taking the exams. No reason for the decison was given. Later she was told by friends that there were no women employed as patent agents, and the patent office might have taken that into account when denying her the position. She decided to "play the game" and pursue a career in which women were accepted as top administrators. That career happened to be in academic librarianship.

One respondent summarized both the positive and negative feelings of the group of women directors, with her remarks:

Sure, there are barriers; there are an awful lot of the men that are still essentially of the opinion that women are second-class citizens as a group. And yet I have, as a rule, never felt that I was terribly impeded by them.

Because two of the respondents expressed the opinion that affirmative action had definitely played a significant role in assisting them in getting a director's position, the investigator queried them regarding affirmative-action programs for women. Listed below are some comments that reflect the dichotomy of the respondents' feelings.

I'm all for them; however, I think sometimes they're circumvented.

I'm much more interested in the case of minorities....When they have told us that the next three people that we hire must be women, I'm annoyed with them.

Generally speaking, I am thoroughly disgusted with affirmative action, because I think it's an artificial, time-consuming, and costly procedure that can do us more harm than good.

I support the affirmative action program a hundred percent. I don't think we need it just for women.

It [affirmative action] has opened up things tremendously [for women], because we have been educated and we have been training ourselves for these positions, whereas minorities haven't had that kind of control over their destiny.

My feeling about affirmative-action programs in the case of women is very positive...such programs have made institutions aware of the fact that they should make a conscious effort to seek out and employ qualified women for their vacancies...

I certainly do believe that affirmative-action programs are essential if women are to have any type of upward mobility.

I think it's too bad that we have to legislate this. But...in the absence of better attitudes among people, I think the affirmative-action programs are a good thing.

All of the respondents worked with subordinates of both sexes. When asked if there were any differences in the attitudes of men and women toward them or if a negative feeling had ever persisted on the part of any subordinates, all of the respondents replied in a similar manner. No difficulties had been perceived, few problems were present, and no troubles were had with any of them. As one respondent remarked, "attitudes vary, and they vary from day to day."

The difference in working with males and females was not seen as a sexual problem—it is a people problem. In response to the question, "What are your feelings about working for women, as opposed to men?" a typical reply was, "I think it depends on the individual, and I have worked for men and women. I resent it when someone makes a remark like that." None of the respondents objected to working for a woman; yet none objected to working for a man either.

The administrators were asked to provide information about any obstacles encountered that had influenced their careers. The major obstacle mentioned was the period during which the women were making career decisions or beginning their careers. One did not pursue her first career choice, because "at that time people hooted and hollered at the idea of a female being a veterinarian." Another did not aspire to an administrative position because of the "climate of the time." When she began her professional career, women were not encouraged to aim for administrative positions.

ROLE OF WORK

Each woman was asked her reason for working, the professional activities in which she is presently involved, and reasons for her involvement. The satisfactions and rewards of each person's present job were investigated as were the dissatisfactions. Most women were asked to compare a career in librarianship with any other career. Lastly, all were asked about future goals and ultimate career objectives.

For the most part, when the respondents were asked their reasons for working, most replied that they "enjoyed" it. For several it was economically necessary for them to work during some period of their lives. Some never realized that they worked out of necessity rather than for enjoyment. An example of this is the statement one respondent made: "It didn't occur to me until I was unhappy at one location, that I had to work to support myself. That was the first time in my life that I ever realized that was the case, but of course, that is a factor." Two other comments indicative of the economic necessity for work are: "I've had to work to support myself," and, "It certainly was economically necessary for me to be employed prior to my marriage."

Although three respondents mentioned money as being a reason for working, two others had diverse viewpoints about salaries in the field of librarianship. One person stated, "I like the money," and yet another, differing with her, said, "I must not have wanted money, because I never got it."

While finances were mentioned by some of the respondents, a sense of satisfaction, of productivity, and of making a contribution were listed more frequently than any other reasons for working. None of the respondents could be classified as lazy; in fact, several mentioned that they were "workaholics" or could not imagine themselves "just sitting around all day or pushing a broom." The following comments typify this feeling.

I work because I want to realize myself. It's an ego matter, pure and simple. I want to do something; I want to make a contribution; I want to be recognized.

I like it. I really do. I work for my own personal satisfaction: I need something that is stimulating, challenging, rewarding in some kind of way. It's the need for the stimulation...

I like the feeling of satisfaction of knowing that I've done a job well. The fact that you can see something progressing and developing. Perhaps more, that you can see people progressing and developing... I couldn't get those kinds of satisfactions if I stayed home.

I want to contribute somehow to the betterment of the institutions of higher education and through my efforts in libraries to help students achieve their educational goals. Another reason is to help people achieve something; "people" being the staffs of the libraries. Also, another reason is to achieve some feeling of service... I think that the feeling of contributing is probably most important... I want some feeling of accomplishment.

I want three things out of work. I want and need intellectual stimulation; I need a sense of achieving something—achievement for myself, not necessarily for the outside world; and I want the satisfaction in knowing that I've achieved something and done it well.

One respondent summarizes the feelings of the group by philosophizing, "It's rather a cyclical thing. You feel some sense of accomplishment in your work and then you want to work so that you can achieve some sense of accomplishment."

Job characteristics and reasons for working were sometimes interrelated. Some of the respondents had a difficult time separating the two when they were being asked questions. The majority of the respondents gave "challenging work" as the most important characteristic of librarianship. One respondent wanted an "action-oriented-type job"; therefore, she chose librarianship rather than teaching. Another important characteristic mentioned by the respondents was environment. In using the term "environment", most women were referring to the intellectual environment rather than anything else. Security/pay/-

benefits and recognition/advancement were seldom mentioned. Attitudes of the respondents toward work and their careers ranged from "it's there" to "mostly positive" to "I would not survive without work.... I like it very much" to "I really liked it even though sometimes I groaned and spit and swore."

A source of great satisfaction and also dissatisfaction is contact with people: staff, other librarians, administration, and users of libraries. At least nine of the respondents, when asked about this particular aspect of librarianship, referred to people. They saw the satisfactory aspects of involvement with people:

[having] opportunities to talk to beginning librarians and to give them my perception of the future of librarianship.

Certainly one of the greatest satisfactions and the greatest rewards is helping young people get a start and get them off on the right track, give them opportunity and watch them grow and develop.

developing staff and watching them grow and get better positions.

the association with a campus as a community, and committee work with people across the campus.

I enjoy working with people and really enjoy the relationship with them and getting them to develop.

Some comments revealed the dissatisfactions associated with working with people.

you're working with an enormous number of people, and so many of them seem to have blinders on...

I guess every library is, shall we say, blessed with a few people that you wish were not there.

I think one of the most pressing problems of an administrator are the personnel problems. When you have a number of staff of one kind or another, you get problems.

Not being able to get everybody on the staff to do what they need to do. I've never solved that problem, and I don't think we're ever going to solve it.

Other rewards and frustrations were voiced by the directors in this study. None, however, was so pronounced as the ones concerning people. Two of the respondents felt that their involvement in associations at the state level was most rewarding. Both mentioned the developing cooperative efforts or networks. One mentioned "power and influence"; one mentioned watching "the library, within the university, grow." In relation to this comment, another enjoys "being able to see the whole picture." Two others described their rewards idealistically. One received a "good feeling" because she is doing the best she can do to "contribute to society's well-being." The other received great satisfaction from the capacity to dream up a plan and see it come to fruition without someone stopping it.

The second most often-mentioned dissatisfaction was of a budgetary or financial nature. At least five respondents mentioned being restricted or restrained by budgetary limitations. Such lack of financial support was thought to be the "most pronounced problem we have." One person summed up the situation at many of the respondents' institutions by saying, "It [the university] was adding new schools; our budget wasn't increasing to do this; there was increasing pressure on my staff to try to perform more and more work."

Additional frustrations voiced by individual respondents were "not enough hours in the day and everything can't be done at once"; "it's really a lot of work"; the "isolation" of being an administrator; the realization that "the buck does indeed stop there"; the "intense and conflicting demands"; "the necessity for outside reports"; and, lastly, "one of the greatest frustrations is to have to make pragmatic decisions that you really don't believe in, but something has to be done right now. So you have to make a decision that is short of the ultimate one you'd like to make, and that's frustrating.

Three indicators of professional commitment to one's chosen career are membership in professional organizations, research and publications, and special awards or recognitions received for professional achievement. Each woman was asked questions regarding each of these aspects of her career. Additionally, all were asked about the importance of these in relation to the attainment of a top-level administrative position.

All 11 of the respondents are members of the American Library Association and most of them have served as officers or councilors. All 11 are also quite active in their individual state and various regional associations. Other library-related organizations that the respondents belong to are the Special Libraries Association and the American Society for Information Science. Membership and active involvement in professional organizations was viewed by the respondents as important.

The major reasons stated by the respondents for holding membership in, and attending meetings of, professional organizations were to continue their education, to make a contribution to the profession, or to fulfill a commitment to one's self. Several of the women mentioned that active participation in professional associations was one way to continue their education, by learning more, keeping aware, and growing professionally. Some of the respondents felt it was their duty to contribute to the profession. One responded that people who are administrators and have the resources should be the ones to make such contributions. She mentioned the importance of the individual and said that a "broader experience and awareness" of the library field was gained through professional involvement. Another respondent felt that she gained knowledge from the members and that in turn she was able to contribute to the profession. She stated:

> I get a lot out of... the people that you see, the people that you get to know. And learning what's going on in other libraries. I also feel that I have something to contribute from what I know. One of my strengths as an administrator, I think, is the fact that I'm very good in nurturing or helping other people to develop. It's very rewarding to go into an association and serve on a committee and take somebody who is new and relatively shy, help them along and help them to develop. That can be a very rewarding experience. That's basically what I get out of associations.

When the administrators were asked about what research they had done and what, if anything, they had published, the answers ranged from "very specifically, zero" to "I have published several books and written somewhat extensively." Two respondents have written nothing and done no research. Of the remaining nine women all except one admitted that their writings were "minimal" or "fairly lightweight." Several also admitted that they wouldn't call their publications "research oriented"; one stated that she had done "precious little of what I call research." Thus, the respondents collectively were not prolific writers.

Six of the respondents did feel that it is increasingly a necessity in academic circles to have done some research and had some publications. One commented that it is one of the ways by which an administration will judge a library director. Another advantage to being published is that it makes one's name known in the field.

Two respondents, however, expressed a disparate view. One commented, "I've always thought that there was really too much of this publish-or-perish bit...now we're reaping the deleterious effects because costs of all publications are going up and here we are with all this stuff that needn't really be published." The other was even more emphatic: "I think that most of the stuff that people write to be published is nonsense. I know damn well that too many people are writing who have nothing to say and it gets published....I think a professional attitude and a willingness to learn and experiment with all those things is more important than writing a lot of stuff that's been said before."

As a group the respondents have received few special awards or recognitions. Those mentioned were Phi Beta Kappa, a Higher Education Act Title II B fellowship for doctoral study, an honorary doctorate, the Scarecrow Press Award for Library Literature, and the University of Michigan Alumni-in-Residence Award. Two respondents mentioned that they felt it was an honor to be chosen to serve as an officer of a national organization or to be assigned national committee work. One respondent humorously stated that the special honor that she received for professional achievement was "getting a job."

Comments made regarding special awards or recognition indicate that these things are "all part of your record" and that they "can't do any harm" and they "probably do a lot of good." One person added that whether or not they are helpful in regard to a career, they are definitely helpful to the individual as a person and as a librarian.

In determining the value that each respondent placed upon her career, each administrator was asked to compare her career in the library field with other careers with which she was familiar. She was also asked whether, if she could choose her career again, she would still choose library administration. Lastly, each woman was asked a question regarding her desired goal in employment and if she had in fact reached her ultimate career objectives.

One respondent was not sure she would choose librarianship again, because so many more options were now open to women. Ten respondents were quite sure they would choose librarianship as a career a second time. One of those expressed doubt that she would choose administration because it "lacks the satisfaction that the practical day-to-day librarian has on the job"; however, she liked the "broad program of librarianship." One would choose the same career; she would do things differently in training. This particular respondent had received a B.S. in Library Science, and an M.A. in library science. Another respondent stated that she would "probably fall into the same groove." Thus, the majority of the respondents like their present careers enough to choose the same one again.

When asked to compare librarianship with another career, most respondents made positive statements. One responded, "Any career is going to be satisfying if somebody is interested in it. The secret is to be interested in it.... One of the interesting things about librarianship is that it is sort of a job in which every little odd piece of information sooner or later find its niche. Librarianship doesn't stay out of anything." Another administrator gave a parallel view of her feelings about librarianship: "Librarianship provides a marvelous opportunity for service, for continually being where new ideas are being developed....of being on the floor plan of what's going on, even if it's vicarious, through contact with the faculty members. I think it's a great place to be."

ROLE MODELS

Psychologists have found that having role models to imitate influences to a great extent one's ability to successfully perform a certain role. Role models can be male or female. There is little mention of role models in studies of librarians. It may be that women library administrators do not encounter role models whom they wish to emulate. Questions asked of the respondents sought to determine if any person or persons had served as a role model. Were there key persons who had influenced these women? Had any one person been more influential than any other in the direction their career had taken?

Although many of the women mentioned helpful and supportive persons in their lives, only three mentioned a particular person in answer to the question regarding role models. One respondent described the librarian at the small county library when she was in high school. The respondent was excused from school and allowed to act as "librarian" for a period of three weeks when the librarian was sick. "She made it interesting and a challenge, and I could see it would be a good field into which to go."

Another respondent mentioned the former director of her college library, who "valued her career so greatly." The other woman who mentioned a specific person described a great-aunt, who began the practice of medicine in an era when women were not accepted as professional people. Consequently her life had a great impact on the interviewee.

One respondent suggested a reason for the lack of role models: "[librarianship is] probably an eclectic business, if it's anything." Another one suggested that "men, as a rule, have mentors, and the way in which they rise...is by latching themselves on to somebody who is known and experienced and learning at their feet, if you will, and then being pushed and promoted by those individuals—the good-old-boy syndrome." She insinuated that women generally are not privy to this type of relationship.

Other respondents mentioned specific people, male and female, who had been influential in their lives and careers. But these people were not really role models because as one respondent stated, "I'm not an administrator like either of them.... I'm very different but I learned an awful lot from both of them."

The librarians who were influential in the lives of the respondents had held many positions and lent support and encouragement in various ways. Most of the administrators who were influenced by another librarian claimed that they do not have the same administrative style, but picked up such attributes as attitude, willingness to listen, the importance of knowing one's staff personally, and the ability to pick good people with whom to surround oneself.

It appears that although all of the respondents had experiences with influential persons during their lives, a person identified as a role model was present in only three of the respondents' lives.

SUPPORT MECHANISMS

Each respondent gave her perceptions of the career paths open to women in librarianship; the qualities that women have to offer to administrative positions; the skills, knowledge, attitudes, and competencies necessary for library administrators; and the qualities that are most needed by women who wish to become successful administrators. Each woman was asked to make suitable recommendations for anyone who aspires to an administrative position in an academic library.

The majority of the respondents, while seeing education and career as being of great value to women, did not feel that the career paths leading to administration were as open to women as they were to men. Two respondents stated that they had always felt that they had to work twice as hard and be twice as good as anyone else, because they were women. Two respondents mentioned career interruptions as being possible causes for inequality of opportunity. One commented that "women, being women, have a lot of restraints. Often a woman goes into a career, not for a lifetime, but as a stop-gap." Another responded that it was difficult to have a break in a career, for children or any other reason, and then "to regain the momentum." She suggested that women not get too ambitious before they have their families. And still another felt that "women must continue to work, because if they take the other option...they'll close themselves out." Another woman summed up these feelings by saying, "For a woman to marry, have children, have a happy marriage, or at least a lasting marriage, and become an administrator is difficult. I think you have to make [the choice that] is most important to you."

Another frequently-noted deterrent for men and women in the library field was the "old-boy system" of identifying people. The lack of an organized network for identifying competent and qualified people is a definite liability of the profession. Seven of the respondents felt that "who you know" or "the good-old-boy syndrome" is still very important. One is hopeful that it will not continue much longer. She believes that "as more women get into that level [upper administration] ...more women will get the same benefits of that system as men do." Comments by the respondents that were indicative of their feelings about the "old-boy system" are as follows:

[W]ho you know is an important aspect of it, and more males are somehow in this network of knowing one another. There is a good-old-boy system at work...possibly the beginning of a good-old-girl system.

I do feel that males receive administrative positions because of who they know. I believe that the old-boy system is at work and always will be at work. I have not yet experienced a new-girl network. I certainly think that one is needed.

I'd like to see it a people system.

[W]ho you know is not limited to men. I think it has been that way, but I don't think it's going to continue....In fact, women will get the same benefits of that ["old-boy"] system as men do.

The lack of any system for identifying qualified people capable of serving as top administrators was mentioned by several of the respondents. When asked about how qualified people are or can be identified, one respondent stated that some of the internship programs have helped. Although she knew very few of the people chosen to participate in internship programs, she felt that such programs give individuals some exposure to the profession on a national basis and that "such programs also give people an opportunity to do something a little different from what they have been doing."

Other respondents suggested that more career guidance was needed, that the six-year programs offered by some library schools could be used to help identify prospective administrators, and that the sponsorship by ALA of a session on women administrators was a "step in the right direction."

QUALITIES OF WOMEN

When asked whether women have distinctive qualities to offer as administrators, the respondents were fairly evenly divided in their replies. Five replied yes; four were uncertain or found it "hard to tell"; and two replied with a definite no. One of these stated that a woman had nothing in the way of administrative qualities that any good administrator didn't have.

What do these women who are directors of the largest academic libraries in the United States feel are the unique qualities women have to offer as administrators? A variety of attributes were listed and discussed.

They have a little more, maybe, compassion, they are apt to have more empathy than a male...they're a little more apt to see extenuating circumstances.

The women in my experience have...had a little bit firmer grip on integrity than the men...

A lot more patience, as a rule, and a willingness to deal with detail....[M]en often are more idea-oriented; they haven't got the interest, the patience, or the kind of mind to enable them to follow through and bring an idea into fruition. You know they say, 'Behind every man there's a good woman.'

Possibly, a little more humanity than men in dealing with people as subordinates; we're more apt to treat them with a little more consideration and I'm sure there are exceptions in all cases.

[T]hey have a lot of insight and they're goal-oriented, not necessarily for their own egos but for the welfare of the institution....[T]hey're often willing to listen to people.

Thus the particular characteristics listed by the women respondents are compassion, empathy, patience, idea orientation, goal orientation, consideration, insight, and willingness to listen. Several of the women did indicate, however, that they may have been overgeneralizing or making "sweeping generalizations" but from their experience this was true.

Several of the respondents expressed concern over the "approaching crisis in academic library management" because of the number of vacancies and the fact that there were fewer women than men available for the directorships of the larger ARL libraries. Another concern was that even though many institutions would probably like to hire women, there were few qualified candidates. One respondent felt that women have not come up through the ranks fast enough and there are still too many women tied to a geographical location. She emphasized that that will have to change before more women will be seen in academic administrative posts.

Each person was asked to name the special skills and knowledge, attitudes, personality, and abilities fundamental to successful administrators. The respondents maintained that knowledge and skills can be learned or innate. The learning can come from formal classroom situation or can be learned on the job, from others or in a variety of ways. Knowledge of business administration practices including budgeting, supervision, personnel, public relations, and marketing were the areas most frequently cited as being needed. At least five of the respondents stated that a knowledge of the political context in which an academic library is placed is necessary. This involves not only an awareness of law in general and the laws of the jurisdictions in which one works but also adeptness in working with the political process. Two respondents emphasized an understanding of the "administrative structure under which one works" or the "power structure from the presidency on down." In connection with this another respondent claimed that at times one needed to "be an organization person." When asked to expand on that topic she replied that there are many times in the working world where one has to put the organization first and forget their personal life.

Knowledge in the field of library science was something else that was mentioned quite freqently by the respondents. Intelligence and a good academic record were also seen as being important. Communication skills or "people skills", a basic knowledge of statistics, and tact are all necessary skills.

The attitude most often suggested by the respondents as necessary for women hopeful of going into administration was one of "professionalism" or a "commitment to the profession." One respondent suggested that such commitment could be measured by such qualities as membership in ALA or by "learning things that have nothing to do with their jobs but learning things because they're needed or because a person in this century should know them."

Another aspect of the desire to work in administration was seen by several of the respondents as the need to be ambitious, motivated, and/or receive enjoyment from one's work. One should "like to work." In fact, as one respondent stated, one should have "a lot of drive" or "the willingness to work [give] 150-percent effort at perhaps 75 percent of the salary."

Two of the directors made the following comments about ambition. One said, "she [shouldn't] wait until somebody comes and taps her on the shoulder." The other made a similar comment: She should have "the sense to seize an opportunity when it shimmers on the horizon rather than wait for something to fall into one's lap."

Other terms used by the respondents to describe attitudes necessary for those going into administration were "open-mindedness," "sensitivity" but "not touchiness," having "the grit and courage of one's convictions," and having a "sense of fair play."

What personality type would the respondents encourage to go into library administration? Mixed feelings were expressed on this point. The repondents were evenly divided on whether one could truly change, would desire to change, or would find it necessary to change one's personality.

An "extrovert, outgoing, somewhat gregarious person," one who is a "social creature and enjoys being with people" might do best in this field, stated several respondents. However, this statement was disputed with the comment, "If the people are meek and hesitant but still are brainy and have a basic strength, they may be able to be trained out of some of that hesitancy, with enough positive reinforcement." One respondent claimed that "it may very well be that administration, at least 60 percent of it, is personality."

In describing the personalities of women whom the respondents thought would be good directors, they used such terms as "aggressive, almost brash," "having a great deal of common sense"; a "sense of humor"; "no phoneyness"; "flexible" without being a "chameleon"; "self-confident"; and having a certain amount of "gutsiness."

This "gutsiness" or "toughness" was the second most often-mentioned personality trait. The respondents described a person who was strong, tough, and courageous as being likely to succeed. One respondent, explaining why this was so, said that often one is the only woman in a group and courage is frequently needed to speak up. There are times when one must say something, and often one is gambling on the possibility that one will make a mistake; yet this woman recommended that one should let oneself be heard.

Many of the abilities mentioned by the respondents fell within the category of knowledge and/or skills. Mentioned most frequently once again was the ability to work with people, both as individuals and on committees. To communicate with the administration, the faculty, and the staff, and "being able to translate library talk into academic talk (it's one jargon to another) is still necessary," claimed one administrator. Other abilities cited by the respondents were the ability to be organized and to have an organized mind, "to look ahead without getting embroiled in the day-to-day activities," to be persuasive, and to be decisive.

In summary, the respondents were asked if there was a particular type of person who should be discouraged from entering academic library administration. Given without any hesitation, the reply was the "closed-minded person" and the "lily-livered, shrinking-violet types, male or female."

RECOMMENDATIONS FOR WOMEN WITH ADMINISTRATIVE ASPIRATIONS

Since the administrators in this study have been successful in mobilizing and utilizing individual and environmental resources and in reducing obstacles in their paths to career achievement, they were asked to offer guidelines, suggestions, and recommendations to others with administrative aspirations in academic librarianship.

The following quotations from the women are representative of their interest in assisting others and the variety of recommendations they offered.

You've got to be lucky. I don't care how good anybody is...you have to be in a position to take advantage of an opportunity, which means you have to know about it, and you have to strike somebody just so at a certain time....

[T]here are two routes you can take. One is harder than the other. One is to go to work with a good librarian; see what his or her style is, see how he or she is effective, see their strengths and weaknesses. The other way...is to go do it on your own...it's lonely. You don't always have the opportunity to work through and bounce ideas off peers or people who have had more experience than you have had.

Get broad experience in more than one area, as broad as you can but without seeming to flit from one job to another. Work hard; don't be afraid to do more than is expected of you. If you don't you'll never be all you can be. Don't worry about being taken advantage of. If somebody keeps piling on these special projects... because they know you are a doer and you'll get them done, go ahead and do them. The rewards in the long run will more than compensate for that extra effort. Don't lose your sense of humor. Put yourself in the other's position as much as you can. But at the same time don't be afraid to make the hard decisions.

Choose your job very carefully... choose as much your supervisor as you choose your job. And don't be so concerned about money that it becomes the most important guiding factor in the job you take. In the long run, if you really want to move up, try to find a job that you think will be helpful in terms of moving up. And perhaps in a library where you will have the opportunity to get to know a lot of people that are known on a national basis.

[There is] one thing that I think is going to be more and more important, and that is the doctorate.... You have to be ambitious and you have to want to move forward, and that means planning your career... You start out by being competent and choosing your positions for advancement. Be mobile. Don't expect, because you are a woman, that you should get things without your doing the things that need to be done. And that does mean pretty much being ready to take the next opportunity where it is.

I would say that it's very important for a person to get an advanced degree. You really shouldn't take yourself too seriously.... you have to kind of be objective and cool about things or you're going to lend a personal slant on things.... don't have a closed mind about things... try to remember that other people can be right as well... Mobility is very important. And I think just doing well in every position that you hold as you move along is an important attribute.

[O]ne of the most important things for women administrators is to realize that it's a lot of hard work and you have to like to work.

Welcome additional responsibility that's thrust upon you. Now, you may then discover that you've got more than you can handle, but that'll give you an opportunity to do some delegating—which is good experience, too.

A young person needs mobility. Too often I've seen people locked into a situation and stay there because they enjoy the community. The community, the job, the pleasantness of work is not important. If a professional wants to climb ahead, one has to job-hop. One ought to have impeccable credentials. If one seeks an administrative position, one should have tucked under one's belt a modicum of management courses, short seminars, anything that would show the person doing the hiring that the person is interested in administration.

One ought to have done well in library school... A young woman must view her profession as something that is going to excite her the rest of her life... At each step of the way in library administration one needs clearly defined goals, and one has to work out for oneself a career pattern, for the next five to ten years, that one hopes to achieve.

The formula for success can be summarized as: get an advanced degree, work hard, be mobile, and choose your job because of the person with whom you will be working rather than for any other reason.

The respondents focused on the developmental process necessary to produce quality administrators of the future, rather than on how to break down institutional barriers. They showed a strong commitment to identifying, encouraging, and recognizing young women with administrative aspirations. This may have been because of the lack of role models in their careers and the influence that men, as opposed to women, had in their careers. Although (and perhaps because) these women had gained their administrative skills primarily through on-the-job experience, they expressed the great need for formal education and training in administration and management. Also, great emphasis was placed upon internships and the importance of these programs in tapping bright young women for administrative positions.

The emphasis on encouraging young women with leadership ability may have been greatly influenced by the average age of the administrators. Several of the group indicated that there will be crisis in the profession in the future, because of the increasing number of academic library directorships and the lack of qualified applicants.

CAREER PROFILE

The investigator constructed a career profile, using findings from the analysis of these data (Figure 1). The profile is constructed from data about backgrounds and perceptions of the majority of the women participating in this study. While the profile may not be generalizable to any other women, it is felt that any woman aspiring to a top-level administrative position could profit from understanding it.

The female director of a large academic library shows the following career pattern. She was born in the northern United States and raised in the northeast. She is 48 years old. Her parents are well educated in comparison to the general population, her mother having at least a high-school diploma and her father some high-school education. She is from a middle-class background. She is from a small family, of no more than two children. Both received parental support for higher education. She has married once but has no children.

The highest degree she possesses is the master's degree; however, she is interested in both formal and informal continuing education. She sees the most important types of continuing education to be workshops, seminars, and noncredit classes. She has received some type of financial assistance, in the forms of scholarships, fellowships, assistantships, and grants-in-aid for the pursuit of her education. Her career

FIGURE 1
Career Profile of a Woman Director of a Large Academic U.S. Library

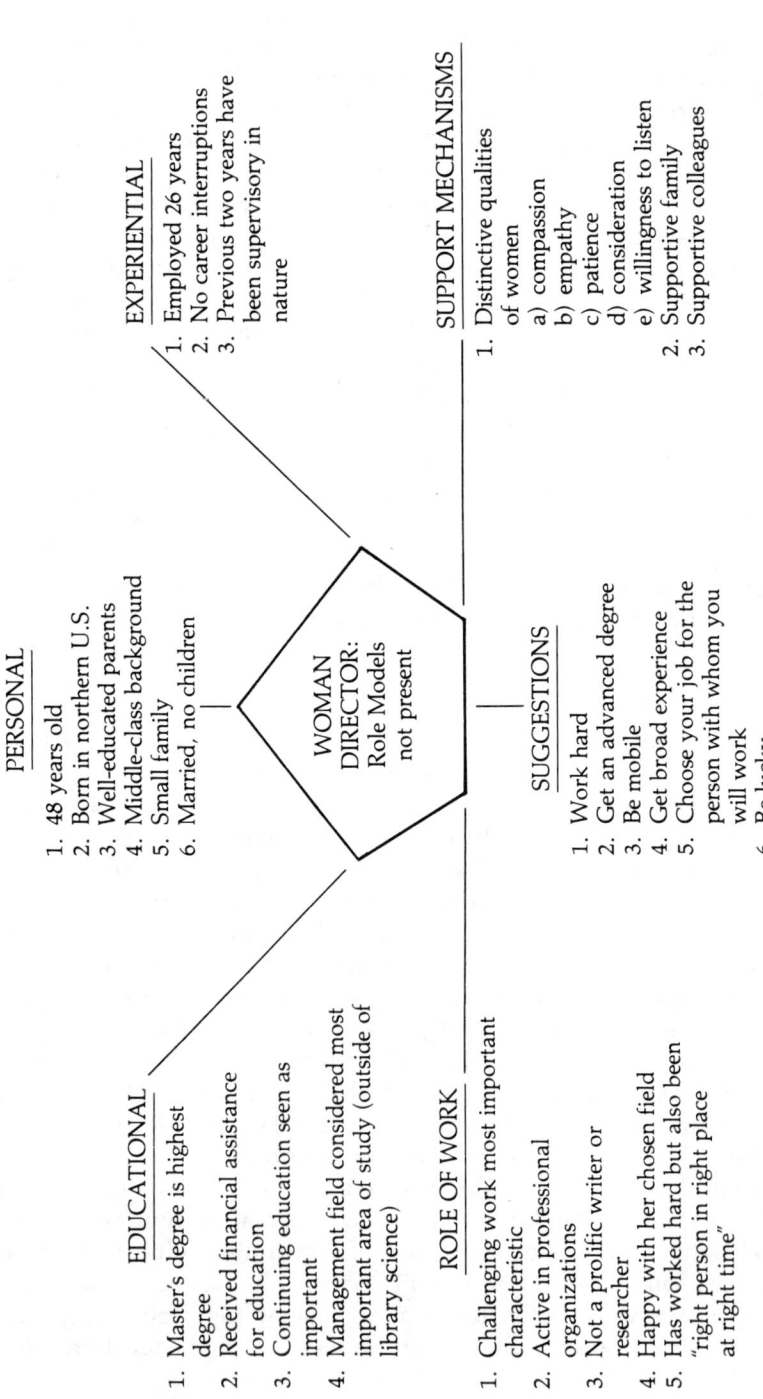

choice was made early in life, and she has had only library-work experience since graduation from college.

She entered her current position, which she has held for less than 10 years, directly from another administrative position; likewise, she held a supervisory position prior to her previous one. She has been gainfully employed for 26 years and has had no career interruptions. A variety of persons, parents, employers, and coworkers, have lent her support and encouragement; although role models have not played an important part in her achievements.

She works in order to gain a sense of satisfaction and of being productive and to make a contribution. An important job characteristic for her is challenge. She is "people-oriented," seeing relationships with others as a source of satisfaction.

She is an active member of national and state professional associations. She is not a prolific researcher or writer but is aware that being so is increasingly important for those who would like to obtain an administrative position. She has received few, if any, commendations, awards, or recognitions for her professional achievement but is happy with her chosen profession. Although she has worked hard to attain a position of leadership in academic librarianship, she attributes her attainment of her present directorship to "being the right person at the right time in the right place."

She identifies the following traits and qualities as most important for women who aspire to top administrative positions: (1) mobility; (2) intelligence and a good academic record; (3) ability to work with people; (4) ambition; (5) outgoing personality; (6) a sense of humor; (7) toughness; (8) an attitude of professionalism; (9) a knowledge of business administration practices; and (10) knowledge of state and institutional politics.

Such a woman did not consciously plan her career. She recognizes, however, that haphazard planning is not conducive to acquiring her ultimate career objective. A woman whose objective is a career in adminstrative librarianship must increasingly be cognizant that her advancement will be secured through the demonstration of the qualifications and abilities discussed in this essay. While luck may be one element in achieving success, careful career planning is a necessity.

Salary and Position Levels of Females and Males in Academic Libraries

JEAN K. MARTIN

BACKGROUND OF STUDY

WITHIN THE LAST DECADE there has been a growing awareness in librarianship of the disproportionate ratio of male to female library managers, as compared with the total population of professional librarians. This awareness has perhaps partially been brought about by the social change referred to as the "feminist movement" and by the enactment of legislation that provides protection against discrimination in employment for women and minorities.

The abundance of literature on women in management written during the past 10 years points to a need for further data collection and analysis to ascertain some of the variables that may relate to the disproportionate representation of women in management, as well as their lower salary levels. This study seeks to meet that need.

Previous Research

Position and Salary Differentials
In the United States, about 80 percent of all librarians are female; however, women are disproportionately underrepresented in managerial positions. It has become apparent during recent decades that the trend has been toward an even more disproportionate share of managerial positions going to men. For instance, whereas in 1930, 64 percent of deans of library schools were men, the figure had jumped to 79 percent by 1970. Between 1960 and 1970, the proportion of men who headed state library agencies almost doubled (Kronus and Grimm, 1971). In 1930, 74 percent of chief librarianships in 74 randomly-selected large academic institutions were filled by men. By 1969, men occupied 95 percent of those positions (Schiller, 1969b).

The amount of inequity differs according to type of library. For instance, Schiller reported data from the late 1960s indicating that women held only 39 percent of the top administrative positions in large public libraries, 37 percent of similar positions in large special libraries and information centers, and only 8 percent in the larger academic libraries (Schiller, 1975).

The Association of College and Research Libraries (ACRL) conducted a salary study in 1975-76 of over 13,000 academic librarians in 1308 institutions in the United States. The ACRL data provide statistics on proportionate representation in various positions as well as salary data. Results show the pattern of underrepresentation of women continues. For example, in the 224 university libraries surveyed, women occupied 62.3 percent of all positions but only 15.9 percent of directorships. Further statistical data reveal that whereas 16.7 percent of all men occupy upper managerial positions (director or assistant or associate director), only 3.4 percent of women university librarians occupy similar positions.

Not only are female librarians underrepresented in these managerial positions, but their salaries are lower than those of males holding similar positions. The ACRL study provides combined data for all types of institutions, which reveal that for all levels of positions, men have higher salaries than women—ranging, for example, from a 4.7 percent difference in pay of male and female cataloging-department heads to a 23.3 percent difference in directorships. For lower-level managers and nonsupervisors, figures are provided by number of years of experience. The discrepancy between sexes ranges from 3.2 percent for less than five years' experience to 10.7 percent for over 15 years' experience (Talbot and von der Lippe, 1976).

After surveying over 2000 academic librarians in 1966-67, Schiller (1969a) stated that although there is a "direct relationship between experience and salary, this relationship is stronger for the men than for the women"(p. 85). At all levels of experience, men have higher median salaries than women, even when level of education is held constant; in fact, the gap widens as experience increases. The same inverse relation holds true for age, with salary gaps between women and men widening with increasing age (Schiller, p. 85). In addition, men who were not heads of libraries earned more than women who were (Schiller, 1970a). When level of education varied, salary also varied with increasing education; however, women's salaries at every level of education were less than men's salaries (Schiller, 1969a).

There is much speculation as to the reasons for such discrepancies in salaries between the sexes. Lynch (1977) suggest that lower salary levels for women may be partially attributable to their not having the same level of skills, commitment, and education as men. However,

Cooper (1976) believes that most of the differences are probably attributable to sex discrimination in promotion and hiring.

In order to determine what other factors might account for the underrepresentation of women in managerial ranks as well as their lower salary levels, this researcher further reviewed the literature for variables that may be related to career fields.

Effects of Career-Development Variables
The career-development variables discussed in the following sections include experience, education, age, marital status and children, mobility, work continuity, attitudes toward sex roles, professional development, career commitment, and personal-achievement motivation.

WORK EXPERIENCE IN LIBRARIES   Morrison speculates the length of service as a professional does not seem to be as important for either sex as in the past, and suggests that such variables as education and variety of experience may be important.

Men typically enter the profession later than women, notes Schiller, but they attain higher positions at a younger age than women. Schiller (1969a) further states that women tend to have held the same position for longer periods than men. Based on her 1966-67 survey of over 2000 academic librarians, she reports that "nearly one-fifth of the women (but only one-tenth of the men) have held the same position for eleven years or more" (p. 46).

Tarr (1973) presents data from a 1971 study of librarians at UCLA that supports this view. A chart showing number of years from date of hire to present rank indicates that in each of the five ranks, men averaged less time than did women, varying from .4 years difference between the first and second levels to a difference of 13.1 years from date of hire to the highest rank. Similarly, number of years for promotion from one rank to the next showed that women had a longer waiting period "in rank" at all levels except the highest, in which women remained in rank only 3 years, compared to 5.7 years for men.

Thus it appears that generally men tend to move more quickly through the ranks, either through promotion within the same library or by moving to another library.

EDUCATION   Academic librarians tend to have at least a master's degree, generally in library or information science. In Schiller's (1969a) survey, five-sixths of the academic librarians had at least a master's degree in library science.

Studies of educational backgrounds of librarians reveal that men tend to have more education, especially more advanced nonlibrary degrees, than do women. Nonlibrary master's degrees were held by 30 percent of the men and 18.3 percent of the women in academic libraries studied by Schiller (1969a, p. 38); nonlibrary doctorates were held by 6 percent of the males and 1.2 percent of the females.

Morrison's (1969) study also revealed that about twice as many men as women (58 versus 26 percent) held a master's degree in a nonlibrary subject field. Morrison found that even lower-level males had a higher proportion of advanced degrees than did female executives. The discrepancy between number of men and women holding doctorate degrees in library science is even greater than for subject advanced degrees, with 1.7 percent of men and only .3 percent of women holding the doctorate, according to Schiller's (1969a) survey.

Lynch (1977) is concerned that women may be achieving lower salary levels and rates of promotion because of not having skills levels (i.e., higher-level degrees) that men have. For example, she notes that in 1973-74, only 36 percent of the 47 librarians who were awarded the Ph.D. degrees were women.

Heinen and his colleagues (1975), McCord (1971), and many others have emphasized the importance of formal business training, as well as specialized programs, for women who want to attain managerial positions in business.

On the basis of the data presented here, one might conclude that women are less likely to seek advanced degrees than men. There are not enough data on participation in noncredit courses, particularly library-science courses, to make a generalization about the proportion of each sex who do participate.

AGE   Survey data for the variable of age likewise reveal an interesting comparison between the sexes. Men librarians tend to be younger, with academic-library males having a median age of 41.3, and females, 48, in Schiller's (1969a) study. Even so, males reached higher positions at a younger age than did women.

The college librarians in Harvey's (1961) survey assumed their first professional positions at an average age of 27. However, those in Schiller's (1969a) study, about 10 years later, tended to be older, with 50 percent of the males and 46 percent of females being 30 or older. Only 11.1 percent of men and 26.8 percent of women were under 25 when they received their library-science degrees.

MARITAL STATUS AND/OR CHILDREN   Whereas being married seems to have a positive effect on men's careers, it may work negatively for women. Harvey's (1961) study of academic-library directors revealed that 92 percent of those in the largest libraries were males and the same percentage (in libraries of all sizes) were married. He also found that married males advanced more quickly than either females or unmarried males.

Many authors have noted the difficulties a woman experiences in trying to combine marriage and family with a career (De Fichy, 1973; Freedman, 1970). Whereas managers expect male employees to give their jobs top priority when conflicts develop between job and family, they expect women will sacrifice their careers for family responsibilities (Basil, 1972; Buzenberg, 1975; Chapman and Luthans, 1975). One of the most subtle barriers is society's equation of masculinity with superiority. This problem causes many women to forego promotions in order to play a subordinate role to their husbands, states Buzenberg (1975). If a husband is not understanding, it is difficult for a woman even to have a career (Hackamack and Solid, 1972).

An additional problem for a married woman is that with today's typical family's isolation from other relatives, the burden of household tasks often falls on the wife (Buzenberg, 1975). Family responsibilities create difficulties in finding adequate child-care facilities and problems of obtaining household help (Buzenberg, 1975; De Fichy, 1973).

Women may experience role conflict, on the one hand believing that home and family are primarily women's duties, and on the other, desiring a career. Pressures from family, relevant others, and their own self-concepts may force women to sacrifice professional careers for family responsiblilities (Terborg, 1977). De Fichy (1975) believes that family-oriented responsibilities are one of the reasons women have difficultly attaining managerial positions.

Schiller's (1969a) study found that 68 percent of men and 40 percent of women academic librarians were married. Interestingly, more women than men were either single, divorced, separated, or widowed.

Lynch (1977) believes that women's wanting either not to work or to work only part-time when their children are small results in some obsolescence in skills. She believes that such choices as women make concerning their participation in the labor force hamper their chances for promotion and limit their salary increases, since rewards are made by administrators upon comparing levels of skills. Lynch further believes that the desire for part-time work creates an oversupply of highly skilled professionals, and the salaries for them drops below that for full-time professionals.

Women who attempt to combine a career with marriage and/or children evidently do experience very real problems in creating a balance between them. In addition, no matter how much in control a woman may be concerning the responsibilities of running a home, her coworkers and supervisors are likely to assume she will not be able to be as effective in her career as those who do not have such obligations.

Marital status and children also affect a woman's mobility and work continuity, as will be noted.

MOBILITY The characteristic of geographic mobility is very important to professional advancement, since often a promotion depends on being able to move to another location to accept a better position. Presthus (1970) notes that the position of head of an academic library is seldom filled from within the organization.

In Schiller's (1969a) study of academic librarians, it was found that over one-fourth of the women, but only one-sixth of the men, had had eleven or more years' professional experience at the same institution. She notes further that those librarians who can and do move, earn considerably more than those who do not. Thus, women who do not have the necessary mobility are at a disadvantage.

Mobility may present a dual problem for married women, as noted by Carey (1971). To maximize one's opportunities, one must be able to move to the right place at the right time. If a husband is settled in a position and is not able to move with his wife, her career may be jeopardized by having to decline an offer of a promising position and settle for a more limited number of possible positions in a small geographic area. Conversely, if the female librarian is on a good promotion track in her own organization, and her husband is offered a position in a geographic location that does not offer her good opportunities for advancement, she is faced with another dilemma.

Women's lack of mobility is a problem cited by business managers, in Basil's (1972) survey. Baron (1977) emphasizes that steps taken by men or women executives for development in business must be the same, including relocating to allow for a wider variety of experiences.

WORK CONTINUITY Various studies lend support to the belief that men have better records of work continuity than do women. In Schiller's (1969a) study of academic librarians, 17.3 percent of all men and 28.1 percent of women surveyed had left library work for six months or more. The most common reason was to marry or have a family (given by 53 percent of the women who left). The second most frequent reason, to obtain additional education, was given by 28 percent of the women and 44 percent of men who had taken leave.

In another paper, Schiller (1969b) discusses the critical nature of the "timing" of such leave, stating: "When women leave their library jobs to marry or deal with family responsibilities, they are likely to do so at just that point when their careers are becoming established. When they return to work, they are likely to find that they have been overtaken by others who have continued their careers" (p. 1100).

Schwartz's (1971) study of male executives in large and small businesses revealed that the men felt women were not as stable in terms of employment patterns (that is, longevity or continuity) as men, and thus, women would not provide as much return on a company's investment in terms of education and training. The same beliefs were expressed by managers in Basil's (1972) study.

ATTITUDES TOWARDS SEX ROLES   If one expects an occupational category, or a role within that category, to be more appropriate to one sex than the other, one's attitude will reflect that bias. Several authors have expressed the opinion that the traditional attitudes of both men and women toward masculine and feminine roles is a big obstacle preventing women from attaining managerial positions (Chapman and Luthans, 1975; Hackamack and Solid, 1972; Heinen et al., 1975).

Some authors state that women are expected, and often content, to play a supportive role (Morrison, 1969; Schiller, 1975; Sherif, 1975). In order to dispel negative expectations, women will have to make adjustments in their own thinking. Tarr (1973) states that "attitudes about women are not going to change until women change their attitudes about themselves" (p. 31). This will be a first step toward solving the inequities that currently exist.

Women have internalized norms that are formidable obstacles to their entering the managerial ranks. For instance, Hooyman and Kaplan (1977) comment:

Women are socialized to perform a "stroking function" which disqualifies them from competitive, challenging jobs and deflects them from their highest potential achievement.... Socialized to meet others' needs, women generally are not taught intellectual aggression or problem-solving abilities. Women grow up thinking of a career as a contingency plan; until recently, many women entered a profession idiosyncratically rather than as a result of deliberate planning (p. 109).

Thus, when women are promoted to high-level administrative positions they often experience inner conflict and ambivalence. They may resolve the conflict by relinquishing their position or by trying to become a "superwoman" and accomplish both the roles of wife and administrator in a manner one would not expect of either a full-time housewife or a male administrator (Hooyman and Kaplan, 1977).

Sex-role stereotypes tend to influence choice of career for many women. Terborg (1977) notes, for example, that "female college students with traditional sex role attitudes scored high on conventional sex-typed occupations, whereas those with more liberal attitudes had little in common with such occupations" (p. 648). One may speculate whether perhaps female librarians who are attracted to the profession in fact have traditional sex-role attitudes, and, if so, whether this factor contributes to the problem of inequity in managerial positions filled by women.

Schein's (1975) survey of male and female middle managers confirmed her hypothesis that "successful middle managers are perceived to possess those characteristics, attitudes and temperaments more commonly ascribed to men in general than to women in general" (p. 343).

Other studies indicate that males are seen as being more oriented toward prestige, power, and initiative, and women as being more sympathetic, maternal, compassionate, nonaggressive, dependent on others, and concerned for their welfare (Rosen and Jerdee, 1974, Heinen et al., 1975).

Kronus and Grimm (1971) state that often men are selected as candidates for promotion in preference to women for two primary reasons. First, a leader must be acceptable to those being supervised; second, the person selected must be looked upon as an appropriate leader-type by the "public." Therefore, since women in general have not been looked upon favorably as leadership types, they may be rejected for promotion.

The somewhat pessimistic views expressed by Kronus and Grimm may help explain some of the important factors that seem to be preventing women in academic libraries from attaining their proportionate share of upper-level management positions. At least two other authors seem to share this view. Morrison (1969) and Tarr (1973) note that in academic environments, where males predominate on faculties and in administrative positions, it is felt by many that male library managers fit in better, since they would be more readily accepted as leaders than females.

Osmond and Martin (1975) examined sex-role attitudes of university juniors and seniors. The authors conceptualized a sex-role continuum in which individuals with more traditional viewpoints on sex differentiation and typing would be at one end and individuals with a more modern or flexible and dynamic view that transcends sex-role constraints would be at the opposite end. Male respondents who were characterized as traditional in orientation differed from traditional females in that males felt men are more capable leaders than women, would not like working for a woman supervisor, and believe women are not as able as men to make a career commitment. Traditional women expressed such views as that women like to be dependent on men, and women who have preschool children should not work. Even the men who were near the "modern" end of the continuum in rejecting female stereotypes felt, as did traditional men, that men would make better leaders and they would feel uncomfortable working under the supervision of a woman.

Rosen and Jerdee (1973) conducted a study to determine whether societal expectations regarding behavior of males and females would influence occupational role expectations for supervisors in formal organizations. Their subjects consisted of 98 banking supervisors and 158 undergraduate business students, who were asked to read a supervisory problem and decide on the appropriateness of four alternative solutions. The sex of the supervisors and the subordinates was sometimes stated as being male and sometimes female to determine whether there would be differences in judgments of appropriateness of behavior for the two sexes. Contrary to expectations, men were not judged to be more effective leaders than women. The data did not support the stereotypical expectations of males being perceived as more aggressive, and females as more compassionate and helping. There were no significant differences between the sexes or occupational roles of the subjects who made the ratings. Therefore, Rosen and Jerdee (1973) concluded that the similarities in ratings seem to show that "men and women share common perceptions and expectations regarding what constitutes appropriate behavior for males and females in supervisory positions" (p. 47).

Terborg and his colleagues were also interested in sex-role stereotypes, particularly attitudes toward women as managers and how such attitudes may influence behavior. A study by Terborg and Ilgen (1975) showed that attitudes seemed to be related to subsequent behavior only when subjects were provided little information about the female. As more information about the women was obtained, the effect of sex-role stereotype was diminished.

Terborg, Peters, Ilgen, and Smith (1977) found that women had more favorable attitudes toward women as managers than did men, and that members of both sexes whose mothers were employed outside the home were more favorable to women as managers than those whose mothers did not work. In addition, there was a positive relation between degree of commitment to a career by women and their favorable attitudes toward women as managers; also, women with higher levels of education and high salaries had the most favorable attitudes.

PROFESSIONAL DEVELOPMENT In Stone's (1969) study, interesting differences were found between men and women, when questioned about professional activities they considered more important, with males emphasizing such areas as research and nonlibrary professional associations, and female librarians having more interest in formal course work for personal enrichment, teaching library-science courses, and speaking to community groups.

A "professional index" was developed by Stone (1969) to identify attitudes of librarians toward "occupational attributes, knowledge, characteristics, and responsibilities" (p. 64) as well as degree of participation in professional-development activities. Those who generally had higher scores tended to have a greater number of publications, more professional-association memberships, produced more research, and read more books in their area of specialization than low scorers.

Morrison's (1969) data showed a strong correlation between the number of publications produced and the level of position and salary, with a higher correlation for males than for females. Stone's (1969) survey revealed similar findings among the 1961 library-science graduates. There were significant relationships between librarian's salaries (higher levels and larger increases) and larger numbers of books read and published, nonprofessional-association memberships, offices held in professional associations, and quantity of research.

Morrison's (1969) data on participation in professional-association activities indicated that the major executives participated far more than did the minor executives or the control group, with the latter ranking lowest of all. Although Morrison's data do not distinguish between males and females, he indicates that men have a better record for participation in professional and scholarly activities, and suggests: "Among the things that women themselves might do more frequently if they wish to improve their lot in the profession is to participate in scholarly and professional activities, i.e., work in professional organizations, engage in research, and publish the results" (p. 116).

Schiller's (1969a) sample of academic librarians showed that about the same percentage of males and females held membership in national, state, or regional library associations, with two-thirds of all respondents reporting memberships, one-half of whom belonged to only one association.

Lynch (1977) points out that generally women who enter librarianship are not particularly concerned about publication or research, but since academic institutions place high priority on these activities, those who do engage in them will be given preference.

CAREER COMMITMENT   Some observers have commented that women are less committed to a career in librarianship than men (Carpenter and Shearer, 1974; Wood, 1971), who have better records than women in the area of professional development, because of "the higher economic and status motivation of the man, for whom librarianship is virtually always a primary and permanent career activity, whereas for women it may be a temporary one, pending marriage, or a supplemental one to the career of a husband" (Morrison, 1969, p. 116).

Lynch (1977) is also concerned that women tend to lack a career orientation. She states: "The interest of women in the field has been an immediate and practical interest. Being a trained librarian has meant getting a good job. For many women, it has been the job and not the career that they have sought" (p. 125).

Studies in the field of management reveal that differences in career orientation are also perceived between the sexes.

In surveying managers from large and small businesses, Schwartz (1971) found two prevalent attitudes among male managers regarding career commitment of females: women are less likely to become as totally committed to a management career as men, and women do not take any deep interest in a career; rather, they see their work as just a job.

Recent research seems to indicate there is a very real difference between the sexes, regarding career orientation. Hennig and Jardim (1977) conducted in-depth interviews with over 100 women managers, finding that their views of a career were very differenct from those held by men. While men relate their jobs to their career, women separate the two. Hennig and Jardim further found that men see their careers as integral parts of their lives and find it difficult to separate career goals from personal goals, resorting to trade-offs when the two conflict. However, women tend to try to separate their personal from their career goals.

Veiga (1977) compared responses of 500 male and 500 female managers in business and industry who had attended career-development workshops, to determine their attitudes and opinions about careers and advancement. He found two distinctly different perspectives. The majority of males seemed to have a "plan-ahead strategy"—focusing not only on career goals, but also on how to attain those goals. However, women more often emphasized the importance of "proving one's ability by doing a good job" (p. 32), which Veiga likened to a Horatio Alger philosophy. He strongly urges women to begin to recognize their ability to influence their future and take responsibility for what happens, rather than accept what life offers.

PERSONAL-ACHIEVEMENT MOTIVATION Achievement motivation is described by Bardwick (1971, p. 168) as a "motive to be competent in a situation in which there are standards of excellence." Achievement involves a question of motive—does one achieve primarily to receive praise from others (external motivation) or because one has an internal standard of excellence? Some authors suggest that the achievement motive is prompted by internal standards of excellence for boys, but by external ones for girls.

Stein and Bailey (1973) reject the notion that women are motivated by a need for external social approval or affiliation rather than an internalized desire for excellence, as a number of writers have speculated. Rather, they interpret various research findings to mean that "attainment of excellence is often a goal of females' achievement efforts, but the areas in which such attainment is sought are frequently social skills and other areas perceived as feminine" (p. 362).

It has been suggested that achievement motivation in women merely becomes channeled in ways that are socially acceptable (Heinen et al., 1975). Bardwick (1971) feels that although the achievement motivation in males may be internalized and independent of other motives, in women there may be a fusing of the motives of affiliation and achievement.

Bardwick's views are consistent with those expressed by Stein and Bailey (1973) who state that achievement needs of women may be satisfied, while at the same time reducing sex-role conflicts, by entering a "feminine" occupation or by remaining in a low-status position in another occupation of their choosing.

Evaluation and Conclusions About Literature Discussed

Reliable data have been gathered in support of the argument that women librarians are disproportionately represented at the managerial levels, and further, that the level of pay for females is less than that for males. However, salary surveys tend to give only gross figures, without trying to determine whether other factors, such as level of education or years of experience, may have an effect on the discrepancies. Other variables, such as commitment to librarianship as a career, amount of involvement in professional-development activities, and personal achievement motivation, also would seem to bear a relation to the issues of managerial level and salary. A further limitation on some of the studies cited is that they did not tabulate data separately for each of the sexes, on some of the variables of interest.

The present study considers all relevant variables and relates them to the sexes at various levels of position, when appropriate, in order to attempt to explain reasons for the underrepresentation of women in managerial positions.

METHODOLOGY

In order to study the topic of representation of women in library management more effectively, it was felt that a survey should be conducted among librarians to ascertain the ratio of males to females at all levels (from nonmanagement to upper management). The study should not only determine managerial and salary levels, but also be concerned with other variables, named in the preceding discussions, which would help explain any discrepancies between the sexes at various levels. In the following pages, how the study was designed and carried out is discussed.

Scope of the Study

Data collection was restricted to a sample of university librarians in the United States employed by the 105 members of the Association of Research Libraries (ARL). The institutions from which librarians were to be selected had to be fairly well structured, with several levels of administrative hierarchy. Furthermore, a population easily accessible to the researcher was needed. Finally, it was felt that the type of institution should be one in which the disproportionate underrepresentation of women in managerial positions was strongly evident.

Statement of Hypotheses

In view of previous researchers' findings, several hypotheses were formulated and tested. The research generally led to the conclusions that men are more highly motivated, more committed to a library career, have greater professional involvement, a better record of work continuity, greater mobility, and have taken more advanced courses and gotten more advanced degrees than women. In addition, previous surveys reveal that men tend to have higher salaries and be clustered in the upper managerial ranks. Therefore, the following hypotheses were formulated within the framework that men are better qualified than women for management positions:

H1 Male librarians will have higher scores on personal-achievement motivation than female librarians.
H2 Men will have higher salaries than women in comparable levels of position.
H3 A higher percentage of men than women will express a commitment to librarianship as a career.
H4 Men will show more involvement than women in professional-development activities, such as continuing-education courses, professional-association membership and office-holding, reading professional publications, publication, and presentation of professional papers at conferences.
H5 Men will have a stronger record of work continuity than women.
H6 Men will have been more mobile than women during their careers as librarians.
H7 Men will have taken more courses for credit than women.
H8 A higher percentage of men than women will have completed advanced degrees in a subject field, and a higher percentage will have completed doctoral degrees in library or information science.

Research Methodology

Subjects
The sample consisted of professional librarians employed in university libraries in the United States that are members of the ARL. Using a rank-order table of professional staff published in *ARL Statistics, 1976-77*, a systematic random sample was drawn from among the 88 academic libraries in the United States (Frankie, 1977, p. 29). Fourteen libraries were selected, with a total of 832 professional librarians on their staffs (see Appendix A).

Test Instrument
The questionnaire used in the survey includes short-answer and multiple-choice questions, and consists of two parts (see Appendix B). The first section contains 41 statements requiring respondents to indicate relative agreement or disagreement, according to a forced-choice Likert-type format, with four response alternatives. The second portion consists of 27 short-answer or multiple-choice questions or statements that provide personal data.

Among the first 41 questions are 35 concerning achievement motivation, which are drawn from a test instrument developed by Ory and Poggio (1976). This instrument was based on items that a review of achievement-motivation literature indicated discriminated among subjects with high or low achievement motivation. The 35 items selected were taken from Ory and Poggio's 106 items, which factored into 15 categories. Reliability coefficients from the Ory and Poggio instrument ranged from .36 to .75 (Cronbach's α). The 35 statements are from 9 factors, labeled by Ory and Poggio as follows: task orientation, perseverance, fear of failure, social acceptance, reaction to success/failure, future orientation, competitiveness, independence, and rigidity. The pretest included 4 items from an additional factor, parental affection; however, several subjects in the pretest commented that the statements were either objectionable in content or seemed highly unrelated to other portions of the questionnaire. Therefore, the "parental" items were deleted from the final questionnaire.

For purposes of this research, items were assigned a value from one to four, according to the directionality established by the research of Ory and Poggio. Rather than attempting to factor the items on the librarian's questionnaire, scale scores were found by summing response values from the factors identified by Ory and Poggio. Appendix C lists statements from the questionnaire that are pertinent to each of the factors.

A group of 6 statements from the first 41 were included as an indicator of attitudes toward sex roles in managerial positions. No hypotheses were formulated concerning attitudes toward women as managers, since it was felt that any results would be very tenuous, based on only a 6-item scale. However, as discussed in the literature review, many researchers believe that attitudes toward sex roles is an important variable in helping to explain why men are often perceived as leaders and women as followers. Thus it was decided to include the 6 items, which it was felt might give a tentative indication of the importance of the variable as one to be considered for future research.

The 6 items were selected from a 21-item "Women as Managers Scale" (WAMS), developed by Terborg et al. (1977). Though the original scale was in a Likert format with 7 response alternatives, the number of responses was reduced to 4, and the 6 questions were intermixed with the 39 achievement-motivation statements. Appendix D relates the items on the WAMS to the factors identified by Terborg et al. (1977).

The remaining 27 items were designed to gather personal data from respondents, which would permit testing of the hypotheses on such variables as salary, career commitment, professional development, work continuity, mobility, formal course work, and advanced degrees, as well as other general information such as experience, age, and marital status. When feasible, the questions are generally open-ended, to provide for a greater range of variability in response.

A pretest of the questionnaire was conducted, using a sample of 15 librarians, whose comments resulted in omission of 4 items from an achievement-motivation instrument, plus a few minor changes in wording.

Procedures

Addresses and telephone numbers of libraries were obtained from the *American Library Directory, 1976-1977* (1976). Names of current library directors were verified, and a letter of inquiry and sample questionnaire sent to each director, requesting permission to survey the library professional staff.

About a week after the letters were anticipated to have been received by the directors, the researcher telephoned each director to ascertain the director's willingness to permit the survey. As positive responses were received, the appropriate number of questionnaires, covering letters, and self-addressed, postage-paid return envelopes were mailed to directors, who were asked to distribute the materials to each professional librarian on the staff (defined as one who holds a master's degree in library science). It was requested that the survey be returned by a specified date—about two weeks after estimated time of receipt. Shortly after the requested due date for each library, follow-up letters extending the deadline were sent to all librarians, through their library directors.

RESEARCH FINDINGS

Introduction

Complete, usable questionnaires were returned by 420 respondents. The analysis is based on 266 responses from females (63.3 percent) and 154 responses from males (36.7 percent).

Inasmuch as this research focuses on comparisons between female and male librarians in various levels of position within the library, Table 1 shows the distribution by rank of each sex. "Upper manager" was defined for respondents as holding the position of director, or associate or assistant director; "middle manager" refers to the next lower level, such as head of a department, section, or branch library; "lower manager" or "first-line supervisor" refers to an individual who supervises one or more employees at the lowest level of management; and "nonmanager" or "nonsupervisor" is self-explanatory. Only 403 responses were coded by both sex and rank—255 females (63.3 percent) and 148 males (36.7 percent); however, the proportions remain the same as for the entire sample. For both sexes, the larger proportion of respondents are at the middle managerial level, followed by nonmanagers.

TABLE 1
Comparison of Females and Males by Position Level

Position Level	Females		Males	
	n	Percent	n	Percent
Upper management	14	5.5	16	10.8
Middle management	96	37.6	50	33.8
Lower management	70	27.5	36	24.3
Nonmanagement	75	29.4	46	31.1
Total	255	100.0	148	100.0

Table 2 shows the proportion of each position held by males and by females.

If each position level were proportionately distributed between each sex, there would be about 63.3 percent females and 36.7 percent males at each level. Table 2 shows that females have slightly more than their proportionate share of lower-and-middle-management-level positions, but less at the upper management level. A two-way chi-square statistic was used to compare the sexes by position level. However, results

TABLE 2
Proportion of Positions Occupied by Each Sex

Position Level	Total n Occupying Position	Percent Female	Percent Male
Upper management	30	46.7	53.3
Middle management	146	65.8	34.2
Lower management	106	66.0	34.0
Nonmanagement	121	62.0	38.0

indicated that differences between the sexes were not significant at any of the levels (chi-square = 4.38, df = 3, $p < .22$).

Results of Hypothesis Testing

Hypothesis 1 stated that male librarians will have higher scores on personal-achievement motivation than will females. Scores on the 35-item achievement-motivation scale were summed for each respondent, and mean scores obtained for males and for females. The highest possible achievement score would have been 140. The mean score for women respondents was 92.73, and for men, 91.96. A t-test compared mean score for the sexes, resulting in a t-value of .69 ($p < .48$). Thus the hypothesis that men would have higher scores on achievement motivation was not supported.

Hypothesis 2 predicted that men would have higher salaries than women in comparable positions. A Pearson correlation coefficient of .21 was obtained when comparing salary by sex. This was significant at $p < .001$.

T-tests were then performed to compare mean salary levels for both sexes, controlling for position. Results are reported in Table 3. For purposes of reporting the salary means in the table, one column for each sex reports the means by salary level, according to the codes assigned to the nine salary levels on the questionnaire. The t-values and probabilities are calculated from means of the nine assigned values, and estimated salaries were calculated.

Table 3 shows that among male and female nonmanagers, there was not a statistically significant difference between salary levels. However, among the other three levels, there were statistically significant differences between the sexes. Hypothesis 2 is supported at the three managerial levels but not at the nonmanagerial level.

Hypothesis 3 predicted that a higher percentage of men than women would express a commitment to librarianship as a career. To test this hypothesis, the chi-square statistic was used to compare frequency of men and women who indicated they plan to continue a career as a

TABLE 3
Salary Means for Females and Males by Position Level

	Salary Means				n			
	Females		Males					
Position Level	By Salary Level	Estimated	By Salary Level	Estimated	Females	Males	t	Probability (1-tail)
Nonmanagers	2.81	$12,400	3.06	$13,250	75	46	1.28	.102
Lower managers	2.87	12,625	3.27	13,750	70	36	1.95	.028*
Middle managers	3.77	15,250	4.30	16,750	96	50	2.84	.003**
Upper managers	6.21	22,600	7.25	25,600	14	16	1.67	.054*

*Significant at $p < .05$
**Significant at $p < .005$

librarian in the foreseeable future. Answers were in the predicted direction, with 96.7 percent of men versus 94.0 percent of women expressing a career commitment. However, the results were not statistically significant (chi-square = 1.033, $p<.30$). Therefore, hypothesis 3 is not supported.

A further comparison was made between men and women who expressed a desire to continue a career in librarianship. Respondents were asked to indicate the level of position they wanted to reach by the end of their career. The chi-square statistic compared the sexes by position level; however, the results did not approach statistical significance (chi-square = 3.34, $p < .50$).

Hypothesis 4 concerned involvement in professional-development activities, such as continuing education, professional-association membership and office holding, reading professional publications, publication, and presentation of papers at professional meetings. The hypothesis stated that men would show more involvement in these activities than women. Analyses treated each of the variables separately.

The chi-square statistic was used to compare the sexes in terms of whether or not they had taken any work-related workshops or continuing-education short (noncredit) courses during the last three years. Contrary to expectations, a significantly greater proportion of women than men reported taking continuing-education courses (chi-square = 4.51, $p.<.03$).

Other variables considered in this section as part of professional development are based on self-report data of number of times or instances of participation. Therefore, the t-test was used to compare mean scores between the sexes. Table 4 provides a comparison of all professional-development activities.

Results of the t-test revealed that the number of continuing-

TABLE 4
Professional Development Activities Reported

	Females (n = 266)			Males (n = 154)			
Variable [a]	Mean	S.D.	n	Mean	S.D.	n	t [b]
1. Continuing education	4.31	3.20	210	3.39	3.21	104	2.39 [c]
2. Current association memberships	2.26	1.10	241	2.40	1.31	128	-1.04
3. Meeting attendance per year	2.52	2.11	235	2.48	1.83	121	.16
4. Offices held	2.67	3.29	1.29	2.71	2.95	68	-.09
5. Periodicals read regularly	4.78	4.30	254	4.82	3.82	137	-.08
6. Books read in last yr.	4.62	7.55	151	5.40	6.53	99	-.88
7. Books published	6.33	20.91	18	3.00	4.84	20	.66
8. Articles published	2.41	2.62	71	3.81	3.79	70	-2.56 [d]
9. Books reviewed	9.07	16.46	46	5.71	10.15	42	1.16
10. Manuscripts critiqued	9.27	19.44	15	3.77	3.66	26	1.08
11. Publications edited	2.90	5.19	38	2.05	1.99	22	.90
12. Papers presented	1.53	.95	57	2.09	1.41	46	-2.31 [e]

[a] Variables 1, 4 and 12 refer to activities engaged in within the last 3 years; variables 7-11, within last 5 years.
Negative t-value indicates results are in predicted direction; probabilities are one-tailed.
[b] $p<.009$
[c] $p<.006$
[d] $p<.012$
[e] $p<.012$

education courses taken by women exceeded those taken by men, to a statistically significant extent, with a mean for women of 4.31, and for men 3.39 (t = 2.39, p <.009). Men had significantly higher means than women on two variables—presenting papers at meetings and having published articles. For the latter, males had a mean of 3.81, compared with 2.41 for females (t = 2.56, p<.006). On the variable "papers presented" the mean for males was 2.09, and for females, 1.53 (t = -2.31, p<.012). There were no significant differences between the sexes on any of the other variables.

Thus, significant differences were found on only three variables—number of continuing-education courses attended, number of articles published, and number of papers presented. The continuing-education variable was not in the predicted direction.

It was felt that there might be differences between males and females at the nonmanagerial level; therefore, additional t-tests were conducted on the three variables that had shown statistical significance for the total sample. None of the variables reached statistical significance, however.

Hypothesis 4 is supported on only two variables—number of articles published and number of papers presented.

Hypothesis 5 stated that men would have a stronger record of work continuity than women. Two questions explored this subject—one asking whether the respondent had ever worked as a librarian on a part-time basis, for a period of a year or more, and the other questioning whether the repondent had taken leave for six months or more at any time during the library career.

Regarding part-time work, 23.8 percent of women and only 14.2 percent of men responded that they had worked part-time for a year or more. The computed value of chi-square is 4.80, which is significant ($p < .03$). A similar pattern existed regarding leave time, with 19.8 percent of women but only 10.1 percent of men reporting having taken leave (chi-square = 5.68, $p < .02$). Thus, hypothesis 5 was clearly supported.

Hypothesis 6 predicts that men will have been more mobile than women during their careers as librarians. This hypothesis was tested using data from two questions—one asking how many years the respondent had worked in his or her present library, and the other asking in how many libraries the respondent had worked as a librarian. T-test were performed on the data for males and females on each of the two variables. Women respondents (n = 243) reported working in their present library an average of 7.76 years, while men (n = 143) reported an average of 6.98 years (t = 1.25, $p<.10$). Women (n = 263) had worked in an average of 2.39 libraries, and men (n = 152), 2.19 libraries (t = 1.25, $p < .08$). Thus results of the t-test indicated that there were no significant differences between the sexes on either variable; the data failed to support the hypothesis.

Hypothesis 7 states that men will have taken more formal courses for academic credit than women. The sexes were compared both for percentage of individuals who said that they had taken courses for academic credit and for the number of courses they reported having taken.

A chi-square statistic compared females and males on whether or not they stated they had taken formal courses. Contrary to what was expected, there were more women than men who stated they had taken one or more courses (36.0 percent of the women and 25.3 percent of men). Results indicated there was a significant difference between the sexes on this variable (chi-square = 4.60, $p<.032$). A t-test was used to compare means representing number of courses respondents reported having taken. Results indicated the mean for men was 7.15, and for women, 4.26). The differences were significant at $p < .013$ (t = 2.30).

Thus, the hypothesis is partially supported. Although a larger percentage of women took courses, they averaged fewer courses than men.

Hypothesis 8 states that a higher percentage of men than women will have completed advanced degrees in a subject field, and a higher percentage will have completed doctoral degrees in library or information science. The chi-square statistic was used to compare males and females concerning the highest degree they indicated they held in library or information science, as well as the highest degree they held in a subject field.

Table 5 reports the findings in library/information science. Although there was only a small difference between the sexes at the master's level, men held far more Ph.D. degrees, and a larger percent of women held only bachelor's degrees, with results significant at $p<.001$.

TABLE 5
Comparison of the Sexes by Highest Degree
Held in Library Science *

Highest Degree Held	Percentage of Each Sex	
	Females	Males
Bachelor's	7.0	.7
Master's	92.6	95.9
Doctorate	.4	3.4
	100.0	100.0

*Chi-square = 13.78, $p \leq .001$

The discrepancy between males and females is even greater when one considers the highest subject degree held (see Table 6), with men having far more master's and Ph.D degrees than women (significant at $p < .0001$).

The data reporting degrees held in subject fields, as well as in library science, clearly support hypothesis 8.

Table 6
Comparison of the Sexes by Highest Degree
Held in Subject Field *

Highest Degree Held	Percentage of Each Sex	
	Females	Males
Bachelor's	71.5	41.4
Master's	26.5	42.8
Doctorate	1.9	15.8

* Chi-square = 48.34, $p < .0001$

Analysis of Related Data

The preceding discussion concerned results of research to test several hypotheses. Additional analysis will now be provided to augment this research on women and men in library management.

One of the more interesting findings pertains to the six questions in the first section of the questionnaire that were taken from the Women As Managers Scale (WAMS). Developed by Terborg et al. (1977) and discussed in the methodology section, the WAMS measures attitudes toward women as managers. The responses from the survey were scored from 1 to 4, according to the directionality provided by Terborg et al. with the higher numbers indicating more favorable attitudes. Scores of respondents were cumulated, and the t-test was used to differentiate between the mean scores of males and females on the WAMS items. Among the 266 female respondents, the mean score was 20.40 S.D. = 2.94), and among males, the mean was 17.96 (S.D. = 3.35), indicating women had much more favorable attitudes than men, toward women in the role of managers. The resulting t-value was 7.52, which had a significance greater than $p < .0001$ (two-tailed).

The variable "children" appears to be related to work continuity, as dealt with in the section on hypothesis 5. In order to determine whether children affected a person's having taken leave or worked part-time, the sexes were compared, using the chi-square statistic. Women showed significantly more part-time work and leave-taking when they reported having children; results were not significant for individuals who reported no children. Table 7 compares the sexes regarding leave and part-time work, as affected by children.

TABLE 7
Part-time Work and Leave as Affected by Children

Variables	Children			No Children		
	Females %	Males %	X^2	Females %	Males %	X^2
Worked part-time	37.7	14.3	11.32*	12.1	14.9	.11
Took leave	25.4	10.4	5.74**	14.6	10.4	.36

* $p < .0008$
** $p < .017$

As is indicated in Table 7, the difference between females and males, when children are considered, is significant at $p < .0008$ for part-time work and $p < .017$ for taking leave. However, for those who did not have children, the percentages for men and women were very close, and not significant.

Two additional demographic variables were analyzed—age and marital status. Responses from the open-ended question asking for age were grouped into five intervals (under 29, 30-39, 40-49, 50-59, and 60 or over). The sexes were compared, using the chi-square statistic, to determine whether there were significant differences between the sexes in proportion within each age bracket. Results were not significant (chi-square = 3.97, p < .41).

In comparing males and females to determine proportion that were married, the chi-square statistic was used. The data indicated that 50.9 percent of women and 62.1 percent of men were married; results were significant (chi-square = 4.43, p < .035).

Two additional measures of professional experience, not discussed previously, are number of years in present position and number of years as a professional. In examining the variable for number of years in present position, data were grouped into approximate 10-year intervals, except for the categories 21 years and over, and under 5 years, which the researcher wanted to consider separately for comparison with other studies. Again the chi-square was used, to compare the sexes on the years-in-position variable; results were not statistically significant (chi-square = 6.78, p < .08).

The final variable concerning professional experience is number of years as a professional. Data were grouped into 5-year intervals, except for 20 years and over being one interval. The chi-square statistic revealed no significant differences between the sexes (chi-square = 2.88, p<.58).

In view of the preceding data, it would seem useful to explore more explicitly the relations of the major variables to the variables, position level, and salary. With this in mind, a stepwise multiple regression was performed, using 25 variables that would seem to be related to the criterion variables of salary and position. Two separate analyses were performed for each sex—one using salary as the criterion variable and the other using positon level. Table 8 presents the stepwise regression summary for the criterion variable "salary" for each sex.

For females, R^2 = .466, indicating that 46.7 percent of the variation in salary is explained by the 9 variables operating jointly. The value of R^2 = .559 for males, meaning that 55.9 percent of salary variation is accounted for by the joint operation of the 13 variables listed.

The most powerful predictor variables for salary, for females, are number of years as a professional librarian, number of papers presented, and number of manuscripts critiqued. For males, the most powerful predictor variables for salary are number of years as a professional, number of articles published, number of papers presented,

TABLE 8
Comparison of Females and Males on Salary Using Stepwise Multiple Regression

Rank Order	Variables Related to Salary for Females	Beta Weight	Variables Related to Salary for Males	Beta Weight
1	# Yrs. as a Professional	.49	# Yrs. as a Professional	.41
2	# Papers Presented	.24	# Articles Published	-.27
3	# Manuscripts Critiqued	.23	# Papers Presented	.26
4	Position level to which aspire	.16	# Memberships in associations	.24
5	# Memberships in Associations	.14	Achievement Motivation	-.18
6	Achievement Motivation	-.12	Have a Degree in Subject Field	.16
7	# Periodicals Read	.10	Have Children	-.14
8	# Articles Published	.09	# Manuscripts Critiqued	.12
9	# Libraries in Which Worked	-.09	Have a Library Degree	.12
10			Married (Yes)	-.10
11			# Books Reviewed	.10
12			# Publications Edited	.10
13			# Courses for Credit	-.09

and number of memberships in professional associations.

As noted by comparing the rank orders of the two sets of variables, only the first variable, number of years as a professional, has the same rank for each sex. Additionally, it has by far the most powerful beta weight of any variable for either sex (.49 for females and .41 for males). Five other variables appear on the summary tables for both sexes—number of papers presented, articles published, manuscripts critiqued, memberships in professional associations, and achievement motivation.

A second stepwise multiple regression was performed, using the same 25 variables as for salary. The second regression used position level as the criterion variable, and again separate analyses were obtained for males and for females. Table 9 presents the stepwise regression summary for the criterion variable, position level, for each sex.

The value of R^2 = .384 for females, indicating that 38.4 percent of the variation in position level is explained by the eight variables operating jointly. For males, R^2 = .403, meaning that 40.3 percent of the variation in position level is accounted for by the joint operation of the eight variables listed.

The most powerful predictor variables for position level, for females, are age and position level to which they aspire. For males, the most powerful predictor variables are not having worked part-time and number of meetings attended per year.

In contrast to the stepwise multiple regression for salary, there seem to be few of the same variables operating for both sexes. The only three that are important for both sexes are age, number of libraries in which worked, and number of publications edited.

DISCUSSION

Based on previous work that found disparity between male and female librarians in both position and salary, the purpose of this research was to study variables that would relate to promotion and salary for librarians. First, differences between male and female librarians on these variables were examined, and then the relationships between these variables and promotion and salary were studied.

Discussion will focus first on findings related to position, then on salary variables, and finally on differences between male and female librarians on some of the variables under study. The variables that have been considered in this study seem to be easily categorized into three meaningful groupings--library experience, professional and educational accomplishments, and personal and family influences. Research findings in relation to the three categories, to facilitate understanding of their interrelationships, will be discussed.

Variables Relating to Position

A comparison of females and males was made to determine whether there were significant differences between the sexes at the four position levels (nonmanager and lower, middle and upper manager). Results of the analysis showed that there were no significant differences at any level.

The following discussion focuses on the results of the stepwise multiple-regression analyses that related variables in the study to position level (as presented in Table 9). It is important to remember that these analyses do not necessarily indicate variables that are related to promotion decisions. Rather, many of these analyses probably identify variables that differentiate librarians in higher- and lower-level positions in terms of activity patterns. For example, "publications edited" is negatively related to position level for women. This is most clearly interpreted as indicating that lower-level female librarians, on the rise in their careers, are more active in this area than are older, established librarians. This information can be important for gaining insight into the future balance between male and female librarians.

Library Experience

Variables of library experience that relate to position level for women are: not having taken leave for six months or more and number of libraries in which they have worked. Variables important for men are: not having worked part-time during their library careers and number of libraries in which they have worked. Thus it seems that, in general, continuity of work and job mobility are positively related to position level for both males and females. It will be recalled from the preceding section that there were no significant differences between the sexes in terms of job mobility. However, there were significant differences between males and females in that males took less leave from their career field and had less part-time work.

Professional and Educational Accomplishments

Variables important for women in this area are number of papers presented, number of memberships in professional associations, and number of publications edited. For male librarians, the following variables operate: number of meetings attended per year, number of manuscripts critiqued, publications edited, and books published. Thus, there seems to be only one variable in common for both sexes among these accomplishments—number of publications edited. It was one of the variables on which the data revealed there were no significant differences between the sexes. However, it is noted in Table 9 that the beta weight is negative for women and positive for men, indicating that

TABLE 9
Comparison of Females and Males on Position,
Using Stepwise Multiple Regression

Rank Order	Variables Related to Position for Females	Beta Weight	Variables Related to Position for Males	Beta Weight
1	Age	.34	Part-time work not taken	.30
2	Position level to which aspire	.33	# Meetings attended/year	.26
3	Leave not taken	.17	# Libraries in which worked	.15
4	# Papers presented	.15	# Manuscripts critiqued	.15
5	# Memberships in associations	.14	Have children	-.14
6	Married (yes)	-.11	# Publications edited	.13
7	# Libraries in which worked	.11	Age	.13
8	# Publications edited	-.07	# Books published	-.11

women in higher positions tend to edit fewer publications than those at lower levels; the reverse is true for men.

Both sexes report activities concerning professional associations. The data from the survey reflect the fact that males were significantly different from females, in having presented more papers at meetings of professional associations; however, there were no significant differences between the sexes in holding memberships in associations or attending meetings. The remaining variables concerning professional and educational accomplishments are number of manuscripts and number of books published. There were no significant differences between the sexes on these variables. It is observed that the variable "number of books published" does have a negative beta weight, however, signifying that book publishing is being done by men in lower-level positions.

Personal and Family Influences
Variables of consequence for females are age, level of position to which they aspire (a measure of career commitment), and being married. There are two variables in this category that seem important for men, age and having children, the former being also noted for women. It will be recalled that there were no significant differences in age groupings between the sexes.

The variable "position level to which one aspires" reflects the fact that women in lower-level positions tended to have lower aspirations, and those in higher positions had higher aspirations. The sexes did not differ significantly on this variable. A significantly higher proportion of men than women were married. The negative beta weight indicates that women in higher-level positions tend to be married. The last variable, whether or not one had children, was not analyzed to determine whether there were statistically significant differences between the sexes. However, having children is evidently related to a man's attaining a higher-level position.

Summary
Since the study did not show statistically significant differences between the sexes on the variable "position" and since the stepwise multiple regression for position for each of the sexes seems to show few similarities, it is more difficult to generalize as to the implications for the sexes. However, there are relationships between the findings that appear to be of consequence. As is reflected by the beta weight in Table 9, it seems important to work in a larger number of libraries, have greater work continuity in one's career (i.e., no disruptions by taking a leave or doing part-time work), to be active in professional associations (including holding memberships, attending meetings, and presenting papers), to be productive in publication activities (such as

editing, publishing books, and critiquing manuscripts), to aspire to a higher position, to be generally older, married (more important for women), and to have children (more important for men).

These findings suggest that librarians, both male and female, in higher-level positions have a greater tendency toward work continuity and are more professionally active than those in lower-level jobs. Both sexes seem involved in professional association activities. The number of papers presented at conferences is an important variable for females in predicting position level but is not listed for males. This can be explained by the fact that the data show men, as a group, present more papers than women. Therefore, men at all levels must be presenting papers; thus, it is not a good predictive indicator of position level for males. Evidently, younger men are engaged more in book publishing than older ones; likewise, younger women are more heavily involved in editing publications than are older women. It may be that as males and females move into higher-level positions, they find less time for such activities. One could suggest that in the future, if the librarians of both sexes at the lower levels continue to publish, actively participate in professional associations (including attending meetings and presenting papers at them), be geographically mobile, and maintain work continuity, they will advance to higher-level positions in similar proportions.

Variables Relating to Salary

The second major focus of the study was salary. A brief summary will be given of the findings comparing males and females. Then the variables that seem to predict salary, as revealed by the stepwise multiple regression reported previously, will be considered.

When salary levels for the sexes at each position level were analyzed, it was found that males had significantly higher salaries than females, for all three managerial levels, providing support for the second hypothesis. However, among nonmanagers, there were no significant differences between the sexes.

In order to provide a better understanding of the salary variable, the discussion will refer to the stepwise multiple regression in Table 8. The summary table provides a rank-order listing of variables for each of the sexes that are predictors of salary level. As in the section Variables Relating to Position, this discussion will group the variables according to the three basic categories and be followed by a brief summary.

Library Experience

There are two variables important for females—number of years as a professional and number of libraries in which one has worked. For males, number of years as a professional is the only variable in this category. Analyses discussed previously revealed that there were no significant differences between the sexes for this variable or for number of libraries in which one has worked.

Professional and Educational Accomplishments
There are four variables that are salient for both sexes—number of papers presented, manuscripts critiqued, memberships in professional associations, and articles published. An additional variable for females is number of periodicals read; for males there were an additional five variables of importance in this category—having an advanced degree in a subject field, as well as one in library science, number of books reviewed, publications edited, and courses taken for credit.

Statistical analyses reported in Research Findings showed that on five of the variables in this section, men differed significantly from women in having presented a larger number of papers, published more articles, and taken more courses for academic credit; additionally, they had higher levels of degrees in library science as well as in subject fields. It is observed in Table 8 that one of the variables held in common by both sexes, number of articles published, has a negative beta weight, indicating that at the lower salary levels, there is a higher publication rate. A negative beta weight is also given for the variable "number of courses for credit" (taken by males), which again is an indication of a higher level of activity among the lower-salaried males. There were no statistically significant differences between the sexes on the other variables—number of periodicals read, books reviewed, publications edited, manuscripts critiqued, and memberships held in professional organizations.

Personal and Family Influences
Only one variable is important to both sexes—achievement motivation. The other variable for females is position level to which they aspire (reflecting career commitment); variables of consequence for males are having children and being married.

Statistical analyses revealed that there were no significant differences between the sexes on the variable "achievement motivation." The variable has a negative beta weight for both sexes, indicating a higher level of achievement motivation is evident in lower-salaried librarians than in those at higher salary levels. Regarding position level to which one aspires, as was noted in the discussion of variables relating to position, there were no statistically significant differences between the sexes. The last two variables, having children and being married, were also discussed in the last section. Differences of statistical significance were noted between the sexes concerning marital status.

As noted earlier, the variable "children" was not analyzed for statistical differences between the sexes. Both the variables "married" and "children" have negative beta weights, indicating that men with higher salaries tend to be married and have children, which is not unexpected, in view of the fact that they are probably older than unmarried men without children.

Summary

Since men in this survey generally have higher salary levels than women, it may be useful to examine variables that are listed as predictor variables on the multiple-regression table for males, since the data reveal that men have significantly more variables in their favor. Comparison of these variables with results of previous data analysis indicates that on 5 of the 13 variables predictive of salary for males, men have higher levels of attainment on the following: number of articles published, papers presented, and courses taken for credit; they also have higher levels of degrees in library science and subject fields. The first 2 are predictor variables for women's salaries also. Two of the 5—number of articles published and papers presented—rank second and third in importance. As discussed earlier, the strongest variable for both sexes is number of years as a professional. Other variables of importance to both sexes are number of manuscripts critiqued, memberships in associations, and achievement motivation.

In view of the importance of these predictor variables and the fact that the research findings indicate men report significantly larger amounts of activity in the areas termed "Professional and Educational Accomplishments," it is not surprising that there are salary differentials between males and females. It would seem reasonable to assume that many of the newer male and female professionals in the field are among the nonsupervisors, and they have not yet had sufficient time in which to build a record of accomplishments in publishing, association activities, or academic work. Thus, they would have relatively similar salaries (as verified by data in the present study), assuming they entered the field with similar backgrounds. However, individuals who are highly motivated to achieve will soon seek ways to attain recognition and rewards. (It is therefore not surprising to see that the variable, "achievement motivation," has a negative beta weight on the multiple-regression table, indicating the lower-salaried librarians tend to be more highly motivated than those at higher salary levels.) It would appear that at a point fairly early in their careers, men are given salary increases on the basis of their accomplishments and move ahead of women. It is not clear, from the data in the present survey, whether men do tend to work toward accomplishments in these areas in much greater proportions than women; however, this would be a reasonable assumption. A possible explanation could be that in the early years of their careers, many women are beginning families and are not so motivated toward professional accomplishment that they are willing to take time from their families to engage in the necessary activities. A common complaint among female librarians is that they are not permitted time during their normal work week to work on professional-development activities, such as research. For men, this may be less of a problem, because they can more readily engage in professional development outside library hours, since their home environment may make fewer demands on their time.

These findings would seem to weaken the case that discrimination against women accounts for salary differences, since higher salaries for males can probably be attributable to higher levels of education and greater number of publications and papers presented, which are important indicators of competence, particulary in an academic environment.

Other Variables

Other variables that this study indicates were statistically significant will be briefly presented. Since none of them appeared on the stepwise multiple regression for position or salary, it is assumed that they have a lesser relationship to position and salary.

In the category of Professional and Educational Accomplishments, there is only one variable of statistical significance, which was not discussed in the preceding sections. A significantly larger number of women than men reported having taken courses for credit. It will be remembered that men had significantly higher means for number of courses taken. Perhaps the discrepancy between the two findings reflects a more goal-directed orientation of some men—that of working toward an academic degree, and in the process, accumulating academic credits. However, perhaps women take credit courses merely to fill in an occasional gap in knowledge or simply for enjoyment, rather than because they are committed to working toward a degree.

Another interesting variable is that of attitudes toward women as managers. Results of the present study revealed that women had more favorable attitudes than did males, and results were statistically significant. It is not known what effect, if any, this variable may have on the promotion of women into managerial positions. One might speculate that men, who have typically held the larger ratio of managerial positions, may have tended to be prejudiced against women and thus not hired or promoted many into managerial positions. However, additional studies would have to be conducted to explore this possibility.

Three variables, discussed previously, seem worthy of mention here because of their interrelationship and their possible negative effect on the careers of women. Data were presented that showed that having children significantly related to disruptions in work continuity for women. It was shown that women who reported having children took leave and had worked part-time to a significantly greater extent than either women without children or men (whether or not men had children). As was discussed in Variables Relating to Position, work continuity is one of the more important variables pertaining to library experience. Therefore, women who have children and have experienced work discontinuity may be at a disadvantage concerning promotion.

SUMMARY AND CONCLUSIONS

This section summarizes the major research findings and relates them to those of previous researchers. Conclusions and implications for librarians will be made.

One of the major findings of this research that contrasts with findings of previous research concerns level of position. The present study revealed that there were no statistically significant differences between the sexes at any level. Previous studies had shown that males dominate the managerial ranks (particularly upper managerial level). For instance, the ACRL study revealed that university women held only 25.5 percent of upper managerial positions (Talbot and von der Lippe, 1976, p. 13); in the present study, the comparable figure was 46.7. One may assume either that the present sample was biased in favor of women or that great strides in promotion of women have been made during the past two years. Since the ACRL study consisted of a total population of 224 university libraries, and the current one, a sample of 14, it is more likely that the present sample was not truly representative of the population of university librarians. However, no definite statement can be made.

The other major criterion variable, salary, reaffirmed the results of previous studies that indicated that men are paid more than women at each level of position for managers. However, in contrast with previous studies, there were no significant salary differences between the sexes at the nonmanagerial level. In comparing the data of the present survey with that provided in the ACRL study, one is led to believe that there is a narrowing of the salary discrepancies between the sexes at all levels below $22,000. Of course, one must be cautious in assuming any trend is underway, because of the relatively small size of the present sample.

Another finding of statistical significance that tends to provide support for findings of previous researchers is that males have more advanced degrees in subject fields as well as in library science, and that leave time is taken by a larger proportion of women than men.

There were several findings in which there were no statistically significant differences between the sexes, in contrast to findings of previous researchers. These include length of time spent in present position and present library, number of libraries in which employed, total number of years as a professional, age, and achievement motivation.

In view of the findings of the present study, there seems to be no evidence that females and males are being treated differently, so far as promotion and salary are concerned. Librarians of both sexes seem to be promoted based on similar criteria—those of publication and association activity, as well as experience. Regarding the salary variable, there are significant differences between the sexes at all managerial levels. Since men are receiving higher salaries, a closer look was taken at the variables that the stepwise multiple regression listed as being important for them. Results clearly showed that such variables as having advanced academic degrees, presenting papers, and other publication activities were important predictors for males. As discussed previously, women are less active in these areas, to a statistically significant extent, which must account for their not having received salary increases comparable to those for men. Those who do have higher salaries evidently have been more active in some of these areas (though not in degrees received), as would seem reasonable from interpretation of the multiple-regression table. As in the case with promotion criteria, salary increases seem to be made on the basis of accepted criteria in academic institutions.

The findings of this research point to a number of variables that could be important predictors for position and salary level. Therefore, it seems that if librarians (male and female) desire better salary increases and promotion opportunities, they will need to assure themselves that they are planning their careers to maximize their opportunities. This would include having geographic mobility to enable them to work in more libraries and minimizing or eliminating disruptions in their careers (bearing in mind that longevity is important for salary increases, and age for position advancement). Also, they should become actively involved in professional associations—holding memberships, attending meetings, and presenting papers. They should develop skills in writing and publishing, particularly in areas such as publishing articles and books, editing, and critiquing manuscripts. Another important concern is higher education; more emphasis should be placed on taking courses for academic credit and working toward advanced degrees in subject fields, as well as Ph.D. degrees in library science. Being married seems to be an asset for both sexes, and while having children seems to aid men, it tends to be a handicap for women if work continuity is interrupted.

APPENDIX A
Academic Libraries Included in Survey

Case Western Reserve University, Cleveland, Ohio
Colorado State University, Fort Collins, Colorado
Johns Hopkins University, Baltimore, Maryland
Ohio State University, Columbus, Ohio
Princeton University, Princeton, New Jersey
Rice University, Houston, Texas
Stanford University, Stanford, California
State University of New York at Stony Brook, Stony Brook, New York
University of Alabama, University, Alabama
University of Chicago, Chicago, Illinois
University of Cincinnati, Cincinnati, Ohio
University of Massachusetts, Amherst, Massachusetts
University of Texas at Austin, Austin, Texas
Virginia Polytechnic Institute and State University, Blacksburg, Virginia

APPENDIX B
Survey of Professional Academic Librarians

We want to know how you feel about the following statements. It is realized that some of the statements are dependent on the situation, but we want your choice to be the one which best reflects your opinion in general. Please mark an "X" in the applicable space to the right of each statement to indicate relative agreement or disagreement. There are no right or wrong answers. Please answer all statements.

	Strongly Agree	Agree	Disagree	Strongly Disagree
1. I am highly motivated when I know that a task is difficult.	( )	( )	( )	( )
2. It is important to finish something once it is started.	( )	( )	( )	( )
3. I am usually realistic about my goals and aspirations.	( )	( )	( )	( )
4. Social acceptance is more important than personal success.	( )	( )	( )	( )
5. Challenging work is more important to men than it is to women.	( )	( )	( )	( )
6. I generally aim my activities toward a future goal.	( )	( )	( )	( )
7. I enjoy competing against the clock.	( )	( )	( )	( )
8. I prefer to work on difficult projects with someone, rather than trying them alone.	( )	( )	( )	( )
9. A true challenge is one that is practically impossible to accomplish.	( )	( )	( )	( )
10. Women have the objectivity required to evaluate library situations properly.	( )	( )	( )	( )
11. I often choose moderately difficult tasks rather than very difficult ones.	( )	( )	( )	( )
12. I like to live by the saying, "Never give up."	( )	( )	( )	( )
13. Other people influence my opinions more than I would like them to.	( )	( )	( )	( )
14. Women cannot be aggressive in managerial situations that demand it.	( )	( )	( )	( )

15. I will work longer on problems I believe I can solve, than on those I consider close to impossible. ( ) ( ) ( ) ( )
16. I freqently find myself doing something now, in preparation for the future. ( ) ( ) ( ) ( )
17. Tasks are performed best through group efforts rather than through individual effort. ( ) ( ) ( ) ( )
18. I would rather have my supervisor set the deadlines than set them myself. ( ) ( ) ( ) ( )
19. I feel as though I can take a short break after successfully completing each stage of a large project. ( ) ( ) ( ) ( )
20. Very difficult problems are more motivating than moderately difficult ones. ( ) ( ) ( ) ( )
21. I become frustrated easily. ( ) ( ) ( ) ( )
22. One cannot be truly successful if he/she is not also popular. ( ) ( ) ( ) ( )
23. It is less desirable for women than men to have a job that requires responsibility. ( ) ( ) ( ) ( )
24. After successfully completing a task, I like to relax for a short period before attempting something new. ( ) ( ) ( ) ( )
25. I am not as much concerned about the present as I am about the future. ( ) ( ) ( ) ( )
26. I can accomplish simple manual tasks faster than most people. ( ) ( ) ( ) ( )
27. Unfinished tasks bother me until I get a chance to finish them. ( ) ( ) ( ) ( )
28. I seldom ask for someone's help while I am working on a problem. ( ) ( ) ( ) ( )
29. It is more important to have friendly co-workers than flexibility in the job. ( ) ( ) ( ) ( )
30. Women are not ambitious enough to be successful in managerial positions. ( ) ( ) ( ) ( )
31. I enjoy completing many easy tasks rather than just a few difficult ones. ( ) ( ) ( ) ( )
32. I often feel at peace with myself. ( ) ( ) ( ) ( )
33. Social recognition is the primary goal of any undertaking. ( ) ( ) ( ) ( )

34. I dislike giving up on a task. ( ) ( ) ( ) ( )
35. Monetary rewards are the best way to motivate me to do my best. ( ) ( ) ( ) ( )
36. I enjoy being in groups with people of equal ability. ( ) ( ) ( ) ( )
37. I consider myself very conscious of time. ( ) ( ) ( ) ( )
38. I would rather work for a library that pays well, than work for a library that pays less but affords job flexibility. ( ) ( ) ( ) ( )
39. I prefer to work alone. ( ) ( ) ( ) ( )
40. Women would no more allow their emotions to influence their managerial behavior than would men. ( ) ( ) ( ) ( )
41. I would rather change my opinion than disagree with the consensus of the group. ( ) ( ) ( ) ( )

Please answer the following questions in the space provided.

42. Indicate which of the following most closely corresponds to the position you currently hold:
    (a) __ Non-supervisory
    (b) __ First-line supervisor (supervise 1 or more employees)
    (c) __ Middle manager (e.g., head of department, section or branch library)
    (d) __ Upper manager (e.g., director, or associate or assistant director)
43. If you checked (b), (c), or (d) above, please indicate how long you were a professional librarian before assuming your first management/supervisory position. _____ years
44. How many years have you held your present position? ___ years
45. How many years have you worked in your present library? ___ years
46. How many years have you worked as a professional librarian? ___ years
47. Have you ever worked as a librarian on a part-time basis, for a period of a year or more? Yes ____ No ____
48. After beginning your professional employment, did you ever leave library work for a period of six months or more? Yes ____ No ____
49. What is your age? _____
50. In how many libraries have you worked as a librarian? _____
51. Are you a female? _____ male? _____
52. Are you married? _____ unmarried? _____
53. Do you have one or more children? Yes _____ No _____

54. Do you plan to continue a career as a librarian in the foreseeable future?
    Yes _____ No _____

55. If your answer to 54 is yes, what level of position do you want to reach by the end of your career? (a) First-line supervisor _____
    (b) Middle manager _____ (c) Upper manager _____ (d) Not applicable _____

56. In your career as librarian, have you ever been offered a promotion which you rejected?
    Yes _____ No _____ If your answer is yes, why?

57. Please check the range in which your present annual salary in full-time equivalent falls:
    Less than $10,000 _____ $16,000-$18,999 _____ $25,000-$27,999 _____
    $10,000-$12,999 _____ $19,000-$21,999 _____ $28,000-$30,999 _____
    $13,000-$15,999 _____ $22,000-$24,999 _____ $31,000 or over _____

58. (a) Have you attended any work-related workshops or continuing education short courses (not for credit) during the last 3 years?
    Yes _____ No _____ (b) If (a) is yes, how many? _____

59. Have you taken any formal courses for academic credit during the last 3 years (exclude courses taken toward M.L.S. degree)? Yes _____ No _____
    (b) If (a) is yes, how many? _____

60. What is the highest level of degree you hold in library or information science?
    Bachelor's _____ Master's _____ Ph.D _____

61. What is the highest level of degree you hold in a subject field?
    Bachelor's _____ Master's _____ Ph.D. _____ Name of Field _____

62. In how many national, state, or regional library or information science associations are you a member? _____

63. How often do you attend meetings of national, state, or regional library or information science associations? _____ per year

64. (a) Have you held office or committee appointments in a library or information science association within the last 3 years?
    Yes _____ No _____ (b) If (a) if yes, how many? _____

65. How many library science periodicals do you regularly read? _____

66. How many books in the library/information science field have you read within the last year? _____

67. Please indicate your publication activities during the last 5 years:
    (a) Number of books published _____ (d) Number of publications edited _____
    (b) Number of articles published_____
    (c) Number of book reviews _____ (e) Number of manuscripts of articles or books critiqued for editors _____

68. How many papers have you presented before library or information science professional groups during the last 3 years? _____

> Thank you very much for your assistance. Please return this questionnaire to the University of Georgia College of Business Administration in the attached postage-paid envelope.

APPENDIX C
Achievement Motivation

Below are the achievement-motivation items as given on the questionnaire, and their relation to the factors noted by Ory and Poggio (1975).

Question
No.

Factor 1. Task Orientation

1. I am highly motivated when I know that a task is difficult.
11. I often choose moderately difficult tasks rather than very difficult ones.
20. Very difficult problems are more motivating than moderately difficult ones.
31. I enjoy completing many easy tasks rather than just a few difficult ones.

Factor 2. Perseverance

2. It is important to finish something once it is started.
12. I like to live by the saying, "Never give up."
27. Unfinished tasks bother me until I get a chance to finish them.
34. I dislike giving up on a task.

Factor 4. Fear of Failure

3. I am usually realistic about my goals and aspirations.
13. Other people influence my opinions more than I would like them to.
21. I become frustrated easily.
32. I often feel at peace with myself.

Factor 5. Social Acceptance

4. Social acceptance is more important than personal success.
22. One cannot be truly successful if he/she is not also popular.
33. Social recognition is the primary goal of any undertaking.
35. Monetary rewards are the best way to motivate me to do my best.

Factor 6. Reaction to Success/Failure

15. I will work longer on problems I believe I can solve, than on those I consider close to impossible.

Question
No.

19. I feel as though I can take a short break after successfully completing each stage of a large project.
24. After successfully completing a task, I like to relax for a short period before attempting something new.
36. I enjoy being in groups with people of equal ability.

Factor 7. Future Orientation

6. I generally aim my activities toward a future goal.
16. I frequently find myself doing something now, in preparation for the future.
25. I am not as much concerned about the present as I am about the future.
37. I consider myself very conscious of time.

Factor 11. Competitiveness

7. I enjoy competing against the clock.
26. I can accomplish simple manual tasks faster than most people.
38. I would rather work for a library that pays well, than work for a library that pays less but affords job flexibility.

Factor 12. Independence

8. I prefer to work on difficult projects with someone rather than trying them alone.
17. Tasks are performed best through group efforts rather than through individual effort.
28. I seldom ask for someone's help while I am working on a problem.
39. I prefer to work alone.

Factor 13. Rigidity

9. A true challenge is one that is practically impossible to accomplish.
18. I would rather have my supervisor set the deadlines than set them myself.
29. It is more important to have friendly co-workers than flexibility in the job.
41. I would rather change my opinion than disagree with the consensus of the group.

APPENDIX D
Women as Managers Scale

Following is a list of three factors developed by Terborg et al. (1977) and the questions to which they relate:

Question
No.

Factor I. Acceptance of women into managerial positions

5. Challenging work is more important to men than it is to women.
23. It is less desirable for women than men to have a job that requires responsibility.
10. Women have the objectivity required to evaluate library situations properly.

Factor II. Female-specific barriers (biological-cultural stereotypes)

40. Women would no more allow their emotions to influence their managerial behavior than would men.

Factor III. Traits necessary for managerial success

14. Women cannot be aggressive in managerial situations that demand it.
30. Women are not ambitious enough to be successful in managerial positions.

Women in Academic-Library, Higher-Education, and Corporate Management: A Research Review

BETTY JO IRVINE

FEW WOMEN REACH THE TOP of the administrative career ladder. Whether a profession or institution is male- or female-dominated, a woman in the executive suite is not a common phenomenon. When studies focus on women administrators in academic libraries, in higher education, or in corporate institutions, the findings are similar—women are a scarcely utilized resource. In its study *Opportunities for Women in Higher Education* (1973) the Carnegie Commission on Higher Education reported that women are "so rarely represented in top administrative positions as to be practically nonexistent in the upper echelons"(p. 123). While women are not "nonexistent" in top administrative positions in academic libraries, they are not represented in proportion to their percentage of the academic-library population. Studies of organizational patterns in libraries document an internal division of labor in which men lead and women support—a pattern that parallels men and women's domestic roles. Over the past 50 years, research on library, higher education, and business leaders has documented the demographic and career characteristics of a generally male population. Concomitant with the increasing concern about women's issues in the 1960s, significant research investigations on the status of women in academic libraries, in higher education, and in the corporate sector have been conducted and published in recent years. As the organizational context of women workers has been examined, comparative analyses of the differences and similarities between female and male careers have been possible. This review will identify major studies in three institutional structures—academic libraries, higher education, and the corporate sector—in order to delineate those factors that commonly define and inhibit women's administrative career aspirations, and to provide guidance for women seeking to develop career paths to the executive suite.

ACADEMIC LIBRARIES

According to the U.S. Department of Labor, Bureau of Labor Statistics' library manpower study (1975), women constituted 66 percent of the librarians employed in academic libraries in 1970 (p. 14). In the same year, the U.S. Office of Education funded research that was conducted at the University of Maryland School of Library and Information Services on administrative manpower in libraries. The Maryland study (Bundy and Wasserman, 1972a,b,c,d) encompassed academic-, public-, school-, and special library administrators and found that chief administrators in large academic libraries,[1] were 92 percent male. In 1976-77, the Association of Research Libraries (Frankie, 1977), began collecting data on the sex composition of administrators in its member institutions. Within this group of major research libraries in the U.S. and Canada, men held 89 percent of the directorships, and 70 percent of the associate- and assistant-director positions, although women made up 62 percent of the professional staff (p. 33).

The percentages for men and women administrators in 1977-78 (Frankie, 1978) were similar. By 1978-79, men held 88 percent of the directorships and 63 percent of the associate- and assistant-director posts, thereby increasing their representation at this administrative level from the 1976-77 level of 32 percent. The entrance of more women at the assistant-director level than has previously occurred should contribute to the development of a larger pool of qualified women to apply for executive posts in academic research libraries.

In its report, *Salary Structures of Librarians in Higher Education for the Academic Year 1975-76* (Talbot and von der Lippe, 1976), the Association of College and Research Libraries (ACRL) compiled data from over 1000 accredited universities, 5-year institutions, and 4-year and 2-year colleges. Although primarily concerned with salaries, the ACRL study can be used to document the following career and institutional patterns: (1) the small percentage of women in administration relative to their total academic-library population; (2) how women consistently occupy the lower ranks of administrative posts (associate and assistant directorships); and (3) the increase in the number of women in administrative posts as the size and scope of the degree programs of an institution decrease. Table 1 summarizes the ACRL data. Women represented 61.5 percent of the total professional staff of the colleges and universities in the ACRL survey. With the exception of the associate- and assistant-director positions in four-year and two-year colleges, women consistently occupied fewer than 50 percent of the

TABLE 1
Percentage Distribution of Women Administrators in College
and University Libraries by Type of Institution, 1975-76

Position A	Universities n = 224	5-Year Institutions n = 319	4-Year Colleges n = 309	2-Year Colleges n = 356	Total n = 1208
Director	16	26	44	49	36
Associate Director	24	48	67	50	39
Assistant Director	33	45	65	68	45

A For directors, n = 1153; for associate directors, n = 297; and for assistant directors, n = 577.
Source: Talbot and von der Lippe (1976), Tables 1 and 2.

administrative posts, with this percentage declining sharply among the universities surveyed.

During the same academic year in which ACRL conducted its survey of salary structures, the College and University Personnel Association (CUPA) was collecting data from over 1000 coeducational, women's, men's, and minority institutions in the U.S. (Van Alstyne, 1977). The CUPA study was the "first comprehensive analysis of higher education administration.... to compare the employment patterns and salary levels of women and minorities with those of white men"(p. 13). Fifty-two positions were classified into five major categories: (1) chief executive officers (e.g., president/chancellor); (2) administrative-affairs officers (e.g., chief planning officer); (3) academic-affairs officers; (4) student-affairs officers; and (5) external-affairs officers (e.g., director, community services). Each position was reviewed by sex, minority representation, and by salary differentials. Among the 18,035 individuals who held these positions across the country, 79 percent were white men, 14 percent were white women, 5 percent were minority men, and under 2 percent were minority women (p. 2). At the chief executive level, men held 96 percent of the positions in coeducational (predominantly white) and minority institutions, 69 percent in white women's colleges, and 100 percent at white men's colleges (p. 2).

Library directors were identified as "head librarians" in the academic-affairs-officers' category. In coeducational public institutions, white men comprised 69 percent of the head librarians, white women 27 percent, and minority men and women 3 percent; in coeducational private institutions, the percentages were resepectively, 60 percent, 38 percent, and 2 percent (minority men only) (p. 27).

HIGHER EDUCATION

In 1975, the Office of Women in Higher Education of the American Council on Education (ACE) began collecting data on the number of women chief executives in higher education institutions. Of over 2500 accredited institutions, 148 (6 percent) were identified as having a woman chief executive ("Up 2%," p. 2). By 1978, 177 women occupied these positions, representing an increase of 20 percent but an overall percentage of only 7. According to the ACE data, women were more heavily concentrated in women's and church-related colleges in 1975, and by 1978, there was more diverse representation of women in coeducational institutions. The greatest increase in women executives was in four-year private institutions from 1975 to 1978. The numerical and percentage increase of women executives in private four-year colleges was 16 percent from 1975 to 1978. In four-year public colleges, there were 5 women executives in 1975, and 9 in 1978 (p. 2).

The National Association of State Universities and Land-Grant Colleges (NASULGC) report, *Women in Administration* (1979), identified women in administrative ranks of its member institutions, i.e., from the office of the president or chancellor through associate or assistant to chief officers of academic, research, or administrative units. At the chief executive level in 106 state and land-grant colleges and universities, only 1.6 percent of the presidents or chancellors were women (p. 1). Women held the highest percentage of administrative positions in the following two categories: (1) assistant to presidents or to chancellors (30.6 percent), and (2) associate or assistant to chief officers of academic, research, or administrative units (27.6 percent). As noted by NASULGC, "women administrators tended to be more prevalent in the lower rather than the upper administrative ranks. Overall the number of women administrators had increased 30.5 percent for the 70 institutions providing comparative data for both 1975 and 1978" (p. 20).

A report on the status of women in academia sponsored by the American Association of University Women (AAUW) (Howard, 1978) noted that about 25 percent of the faculties of colleges and universities are women. The AAUW study also indicated a decline in women's representation in some leadership areas in higher education, using the following illustration: "For example, more men were serving as chief librarians in the 1973-76 period than in the 1967-70 period" (p. 20). Although the overall percentages reflect a positive trend in the representation of women in administration in higher education, the actual placement of women in the organizational hierarchy of colleges and universities tends to be in staff rather than line positions.

CORPORATE SECTOR

In the corporate sector, very few women have achieved promotion to executive-level positions. Calculations of the number of women in such positions are primarily derived from the data issued by the U.S. Bureau of the Census on occupational-earnings levels. Based upon the Bureau's occupational category of "managers and administrators, except farm," women represented 3 percent of this population earning $15,000 or more in 1969 (U.S. Dept. of Commerce, 1973, pp. 16, 19). For managers and administrators having four years or more of college, women again constituted only 3 percent of the population (pp. 110, 112). A subcategory of "managers and administrators" is "school administrators, college." In this subgroup, women occupied 7 percent of the total positions paying $15,000 or more annuallly but only 2 percent of these positions at an earnings level of $25,000 to $29,999 in 1969 (pp. 16, 19). Although comparable data are not yet available from the 1980 census, the overall percentage of women as "managers and administrators" has increased 67 percent from 1972 to 1978 (civilian noninstitutional population 16 years and over), from 21 women per 100 men to 30 women per 100 men (U.S. Dept. of Commerce, Bureau of the Census 1980, p. 60). However, significant increases in the numbers of women at higher salary and position levels is unlikely. In 1977, women managers and administrators had a median income of $9,799, compared to $18,086 for men, i.e., women earned 54 percent of men's median income (p. 76). Commonly, women have held few administrative posts, and when they do, they are typically lower-level, lower-salaried ones.

RESEARCH STUDIES

The following review encompasses three major areas of research studies: (1) men and women in academic-library administration, (2) women in higher-education administration, and (3) women in corporate management. Within these categories, emphasis has been placed on studies that identify demographic and career characteristics of individuals holding top administrative positions. Research on attitudes toward women in management, achievement motivation, and job satisfaction, and studies yielding personality inventories of men and women in librarianship and in mangagement were excluded unless such research included substantive references to demographic and career characteristics. The general absence of women in executive-level posts is pervasive throughout the public and private sector; consequently, research on women in library administration, in higher education, and corporate management exhibited a number of common demographic and career patterns.

Studies in Library Science

By the beginning of the 1930s, a pattern had emerged regarding the characteristics of academic-library administrators. This pattern was succinctly described in Randall's (1932) study[2] of the college library, financed by the Carnegie Corporation of New York.

The ratio of women to men as head librarians in this group of colleges is about three to one. Although the women are much more numerous, the men excel them in salary, academic training, and experience. The women have more professional training.... The larger libraries are under the control of men, and the smaller under the control of women. The fact that the men excel in academic training, and the women in professional training, is further evidence that the college administrator puts considerable emphasis on the former in choosing librarians (pp. 63-64).

At the end of the decade, a change was beginning to occur in the ratio of women to men as heads of college libraries. Alvarez (1938) offered the following explanation for this change:

Recent appointments in the college field have been more numerous, and admittedly have gone more often to young men. There are, however, several reasons why men have been chosen for these positions. In the first place, their predecessors have been men. Then again, the masculine character of a college faculty seems to call for a male librarian. But more important than these reasons is the fact that the college presidents were looking for persons with a Ph.D degree, and more men than women have this degree (p. 178).

Among the chief executives of university libraries, references to the differences in qualifications between men and women were largely irrelevant, because women rarely held positions at this administrative level in major research institutions (Kraus, 1950; McGowan, 1972). Kraus's report on the qualifications of university librarians in 1933 and in 1948 identified one woman out of a group of 31 librarians administering collections of over 380,000 volumes (p.17). This group of libraries represented the major research institutions at that time that were members of the Association of American Universities (AAU). The libraries of the AAU represented the core group that formed the Association of Research Libraries (ARL) in 1932 (McGowan, 1972, p. 4). When the ARL was founded only two of the 37 member university libraries were headed by women, and these served in an acting capacity (pp. 61, 242).

By mid-century, the tremendous growth of American universities since 1900 was beginning to have an impact on how the administration of the library was viewed by the head librarian (Wilson and Tauber,

1945). In 1942, McDiarmid, Director of the University of Minnesota Libraries, stated:

There are three important factors in the development of library leaders: (1) personal qualities and characteristics; (2) proper education, both academic and professional; and (3) adequate experience.... The old, one-man type of library administration should be dispensed with, and in its stead should arise a new type of administration where, although the chief executive retains final authority, more discretionary responsibility is placed upon subordinates and department heads (pp. 614, 619).

During the 1940s, academic libraries did not commonly have positions such as assistant or associate librarian, and administrative assistants; consequently, McDiarmid continues:

In the past, the librarian has come to his position largely because of an outstanding reputation in some library operation: a cataloger, a rare-book man, or an expert reference librarian. The number of librarians who have gone to the top position after broad administrative experience is still relatively small (pp. 618, 620).

The relative absence of auxiliary administrative positions meant that both men and women had limited access to the apprenticeship mode of upward mobility. Throughout his paper, McDiarmid emphasized the need for appropriate library experience prior to assuming a position of leadership. Appropriate experience was defined as a combination of beginning training in various library functions, and administrative experience "in management matters which affect the institution as a whole and in which the individual must make decisions affecting others, relying largely upon his own judgment (p. 616). Both McDiarmid and Williamson (1939) stressed the need to give men and women an opportunity to gain experience that would provide the appropriate background for administrative work. However, the prospects for women achieving varied library experience appeared to be rather limited, as Munn (1949) observed in *Library Journal*:

Women have had to become reconciled to the preference of library boards for men as top administrators... men now direct the public libraries in 71 of the country's 92 cities of more than 100,000 inhabitants. Men are now appearing in much larger numbers as administrators in smaller cities. The universities and major colleges display a strong preference for men, not only as chief librarians but as department heads (p. 1640).

Alice Bryan (1952) surveyed over 3000 public librarians in the late 1940s as part of the Public Library Inquiry, with the results of her research culminating in the first major study of librarians in the U.S. Although her study did not include academic librarians, she did document personal and career characteristics of her population that were later reflected in research on college and university librarians (Schick, 1950; Harvey, 1958, 1961; Bradley, 1968). For example, Bryan found that women tended to be unmarried; were less likely than men to have academic degrees; less likely to hold administrative positions, and when they did, were concentrated in smaller libraries; earned less; and were, on the average, five years older than men occupying comparable positions (pp. 35, 57; 83-87, 35). Of particular significance was Bryan's identification of a "dual career structure for public librarians differentiated on the bases of sex—an accelerated library career for the minority, composed of men, and a basic library career established within considerably lower limits for the majority, who are women" (p. 86).

Although the number of administrative officers began to increase substantially in academic libraries during the 1950s and 1960s, the chief executive continued to be the primary focus of published studies. During these two decades, however, a number of research reports did include references to women occupying executive-level positions in college and university libraries. In a study of 155 chief librarians of the largest college and university libraries in the U.S., Schick (1950) reported that men constituted 84 percent of the directors and that "not a single woman is in charge of a library in a school with more than 10,000 students. Three-fourths of the women work in the smallest size schools surveyed (2450 to 4999 students) (p. 1019). He also observed:

Women apparently have more difficulty in reaching the top position through recruitment from other libraries. Slightly more than half of them were promoted from positions in the same library compared to only 28% of the men. Even within the same library their chances for advancement seem less good, as their tenures are considerably longer than those of the male librarians. Two-thirds of them have served in their present position for over 10 years (p. 1019).

Tenure for male librarians ranged from 5 to 10 years, with almost 50 percent serving fewer than 5 years in their present position (Schick, pp. 1018, 1019). Seeking to explain the difference in the representation of men and women as chief administrators, Schick pointed out that 20 percent of the women lacked academic degrees or only had a B.A., compared to 5 percent of the men, and that only one woman had a doctorate, while about one-third of the men held this degree (p. 1019).[3]

Harvey's (1958; 1961) study of the chief librarian's career included college, public, and university librarians listed in *Who's Who in Library Service* in the 1950s. Among the 629 college and university librarians he identified, 61 percent (384) were women. Over 90 percent of the large college and university libraries were administered by men, while women comprised about 70 percent of the chief librarians of small college libraries. Marital status was also a distinguishing characteristic of these administrators. Fifteen percent of the women and 74 percent of the men were married (Harvey, 1961, pp. 144-45). For women librarians, positions of leadership were commonly held by unmarried women in colleges, universities, and in public libraries (Korb, 1946; Labb, 1950; Bryan, 1952). In addition, chief librarians in the larger libraries were older (average age, 61) than those in small libraries (40), and they averaged more years of professional library experience (31 years) than their colleagues (11) in smaller libraries (Harvey, 1961, p. 145). Harvey (1958) also observed that

those with a variety of experience always included a significantly higher percentage of men than of women.... Therefore, in this sense, there is no question but that men were better prepared by their experience for administration and for top-level positions than were women, no matter how capable they were, nor how much innate ability they may have had (p. 109).

Thus, it also followed that "the most mobile were to be thought of as married males and the least mobile as single females (p. 109). Another aspect of Harvey's (1961) research included a comparative analysis of "Fast, Slow, and No Advancers" (p. 146). He defined "Fast Advancers" as those who achieved high-level positions at a relatively young age, and "No Advancers" as those who spent their careers at the same low level. He concluded: "Fast Advancers were males to an even greater extent than expected, and No Advancers were female to even greater extent then expected (p. 146). Married males composed the majority of the "Fast Advancers" group, and single females dominated "No Advancers".

Morrison's (1969) classic study of the career of the academic librarian surveyed over 700 librarians from three groups: (1) major executives (chief librarians of colleges and universities earning $6000 or more annually); (2) minor executives (middle managers; i.e., department and branch heads); and (3) others (librarians without extensive supervisory responsibility). Categories (2) and (3) were Morrison's control groups. In examining the demographic and career characteristics of these groups, Morrison analyzed selected data on the basis of differences between female and male respondents. Of particular relevance are those characteristics summarized in Table 2. Among major executives, men represented 73 percent, and women 27 percent. As in Randall's (1932) findings, men were still more likely than women to have academic training, but by 1960, such training was usually in addition to the professional degree. Although men commonly dominated executive-level positions, they tended to enter librarianship at a later

TABLE 2
Comparison of Characteristics Between Men and Women
Major Executives and Control-Group Librarians

	Men		Women	
	Major Executives	Control Group	Major Executives	Control Group
Possession of a Subject Master's Degree (%)				
	n = 169	n = 113	n = 62	n = 352
Have	50	44	37	24
Age at Entering Librarianship				
	n = 166	n = 112	n = 62	n = 352
Mean Age at entry	27.1	28.5	24.3	26.25
Mobility: Number of Libraries in Which Full-time Positions Were Held (%)				
	n = 161	n = 106	n = 60	n = 339
4 or more	54	32	50	36
Number of Publications (%)				
	n = 169	n = 113	n = 62	n = 252
9 or less	63	44	33	18
10 or more	36	17	10	6

Source: Morrison (1969), pp. 25, 46, 57, 64.

age than women. For career mobility, Morrison compared his data with Harvey's (1958) research on college librarians to determine that there was a trend among chief executives to work in a greater number of libraries in the late 1950s than previously; however, in opposition to Harvey's finding that women were less mobile than men, Morrison found that the variety of experience was not significantly greater between the two groups: "...there are virtually as many women as men in the control group with experience in several libraries, but despite this, we are very safe in assuming that a greater number of men will become chief librarians" (p. 58). As Morrison also observed, neither his nor Harvey's research confirmed "that women are unwilling to move in order to achieve positions of leadership" and that "no matter how willing a person may be to move to another enriching experience, he (or in this case, she) must have the opportunity to do so" (p. 57).

"Frequency of publishing" is a commonly utilized criterion to gauge an academic librarian's level of professional activity. Morrison's data revealed a significant difference in the number of publications by men and women; men in both major-executive and control groups published more than women at comparable levels (p. 64).

Several other studies conducted during the mid-1960s confirmed the continuing trend toward the executive domination of large academic libraries by men. In Bradley's (1968) thesis on the characteristics, qualifications, and succession patterns of 100 large U.S. academic and public libraries, he identified 50 men who were heading academic libraries, and 43 men administering public libraries. Among the administrators who had preceded this group, there had been 4 women academic library directors and 12 women public library directors (pp. 10, 24, 18, 30). All of these academic libraries ranked as ARL libraries. Because of the small number of women in Bradley's two groups, he did not attempt any comparison between men and women.

Simultaneously, Blankenship (1967) examined the sex composition of over 400 college-library heads. Focusing on colleges ranging in enrollment from about 500 to 5000, Blankenship found that although women represented 51 percent of the head librarians, they were concentrated in smaller colleges (enrollments less than 1500) and in privately supported institutions (pp. 42-3). Blankenship observed that women demonstrated lower mobility rates than men; i.e., 32 percent of the men and 53 percent of the women had occupied their present administrative position more than 10 years (p. 43). Men also became heads of college libraries at an earlier age than women; i.e., 32 percent of the men and 9 percent of the women were less than 30 years old. Thirty percent of the men and 56 percent of the women were 50 years or older (p. 44). Thus, women achieved executive-level positions at an older age than men, and tended to stay in the same position longer than men.

Schiller's (1969a) major study, *Characteristics of Professional Personnel in College and University Libraries*, included over 2200 academic librarians selected from a representative sample of 551 colleges and universities. Although 26 percent of Schiller's respondents held administrative positions either as chief, associate, or assistant librarians, her data analysis was primarily limited to differences between men and women throughout the library organizational hierarchy rather than to one specific group (p. 45).

Despite the relatively small size of many of the institutions that she studied, she still found that among all of the women (1448), 11.8 percent were chief librarians and 9.7 percent were associate or assistant directors, while the percentages, respectively, for men (831) were 21.6 percent and 11.4 percent (p. 45). The same percentage of the men and women (36 percent) were working at the department- or division-head level, but men were still more likely than women to supervise larger staffs. "One-fourth of the men as opposed to one-tenth of the women supervise more than ten people (pp. 45, 49). Schiller also observed the marked trend since the 1930s to hire men rather than women as chief librarians, and noted that of the 50 largest academic libraries in the U.S., not one was administered by a woman (p. 46).

Of particular relevance are the following characteristics, which are summarized from Schiller's report (Table 3).

TABLE 3
Comparison of Characteristics Between Men and Women College and University Librarians [A]

	Men (%)	Women (%)
Possession of Nonlibrary Advanced Degrees		
Master's Degree	30	18.3
Doctorate	6	1.2
Enrolled in Doctoral Program		
Library Science	15	2.1
Other doctorate	21.1	9.9
Number of Years in Present Position		
Less than 5 years	69.7	60.5
5-10 years	20.2	20.4
Over 11 years	10.1	19.1
Number of Years of Professional Experience in Present Institution		
Less than 5 years	60.2	50.5
5-10 years	23.3	21.8
Over 11 years	16.4	27.6

[A] For men, n = 828, and for women, n = 1439.
Source; Schiller (1969a), pp. 38, 41, 46, 47.

Although the median age of men (41.3) was younger than that for women (48), men were more likely to have nonlibrary advanced degrees and to be enrolled in a doctoral program (p. 24). Men were also more likely to be married (68 percent) than women (40 percent) (p. 24). Women tended to stay in the same position and in the same institution for longer time periods than men.

A number of studies on academic library administrators were published in the 1970s. A hallmark paper by McAnally and Downs (1973) reflected concern for the status of the university library director who could expect to change jobs every three years (50 percent) and averaged from five to six years at any single institution (p. 103). At this time, the turnover rate for directors was also greater at larger ARL libraries (60 percent) than at smaller ARL libraries (45 percent) (p. 104). Although later studies would indicate that job tenure ranging from 3 to 6 years for ARL directors represented an exceptional rather than a standard pattern.[4] McAnally and Downs alerted the academic library community to the pressures, both internal and external, facing and displacing directors, and to the need for a "new type of leadership within the library," which required an individual to be a "leader" and "not merely an authority" (p. 123).

The second greatest pressure on the director, identified by McAnally and Downs, was that exerted by the library staff, particularly regarding the staff's role in the mangement of the library. By the end of the 1960s the movement toward participative management was being increasingly experienced by chief librarians (Marchant, 1976). With participative management came the opportunity for greater numbers of the staff throughout the library's hierarchy to gain experience in reviewing management concerns and to become a visible force in recommending change. Sharing the management experience would be of particular relevance to women in the academic library, as they had not, historically, played a visible role in the executive suite. Moreover, as studies had and would continue to indicate, variety of experience was becoming an increasingly sought-after characteristic of the potential library administrator (Taylor, 1973; Parsons, 1976; Fennell, 1978; Martin, 1978). In this context, variety of experience includes both a varied work history—involving the attainment of positions of increasing responsibility—and professional activity—e.g., articles, papers presented, and organizational commitments. Parsons (1976) reviewed the characteristics of ARL directors, based upon 1973 data, which he gathered from published sources. Nearly 80 percent of the directors were married, and their average age was 53, with a mean of 25 years of professional and 9 years of administrative experience. Over one-third had previously been library directors, and the majority had been recruited from other institutions (pp. 613, 616, 617). Parsons also compared his 1973 group of directors with those holding positions in 1958, finding that there had been a general trend toward greater turnover and external recruitment of the later group (p. 617).[5] Nearly 60 percent of the directors had received their library degrees from four schools: Columbia University, the Universities of Chicago, Illinois, and Michigan. Seeking to explain the small number of library programs that dominated this group's educational preparation, Parsons observed that they were generally recognized for their "preeminence in librarianship," and " second, that an "old boy" system of recruitment of ARL directors prevails in the field, and that contacts formed at these library schools go a long way toward establishing reputations in the research library world" (p. 615).

The value of a system of relationships based upon educational, social or career contacts has been generally recognized as a critical aspect of achievement among aspiring managers (Hennig and Jardim, 1978; Kanter, 1978; Orth and Jacobs, 1971). Kanter (1977) has provided the following explanation of the significance of the "old boy system":

The informal social network that pervades organizations can be very important...In a large complex system, it is almost a necessity for power to come from social connections, especially those outside of the immediate work group. Such connections need to be long-term and stable and include "sponsors" (mentors and advocates upward in the organization), peers, and subordinates...Sponsors have been found to be important in the careers of managers and professionals in many settings. In the corporation, "sponsored mobility" (controlled selection by elites) seems to determine who gets the most desirable jobs, rather than "contest mobility" (an open game)...If sponsors are important for the sucess of men in organizations, they seem absolutely essential for women (pp. 181-3).

While each of its member libraries represents a large research institution, ARL itself can also be viewed as "a large complex system." In McGowan's (1972) history (1932-1962) of the ARL, 156 individuals who were identified were associated with its activities, including both directors and those who were "drafted to serve on committees". Of those 156, 4 were women, three of whom were *acting* directors. Those drafted to serve on committees were usually either associate or assistant directors in ARL libraries. Male librarians consistently have served as "sponsors" or mentors for their male colleagues and as role models for aspiring library managers (pp. 225-242).

During the 1970s, several studies were completed that addressed topics of relevance to women in academic-library management. Although his research did not include ARL libraries, Metz's (1978) study of over 200 college library directors yielded data on administrative succession that may have implications for large research libraries. Of the 200 directors, 70 percent were men, and their average age was 47.5 years. Women were three times as likely as men to be found in private institutions of higher education, and more likely to be hired from within an institution, which reflects Schiller's (1969a) and Massman's (1972) finding that women tend to stay in the same academic library longer than men. Fifty-four percent of the women were internal successors, as compared with 17.1 percent of the men (Metz, 1978, p. 362). As an explanation for this phenomenon, Metz posited:

It may be that an external female successor is regarded as especially threatening or disruptive. The data indicate that neither women nor insiders are preferred for directorships. This hypothesis suggests an interaction between the variables of sex and external succession such that the "wrong" combination of the two, for whatever reason, is considered especially unacceptable.

...Clearly, further research which includes data on marital status and other variables not measured here, will be required before the relationship between sex and administrative succession can be fully understood. The serious underrepresentation of women in administrative positions justifies the necessity for such research (p. 363).[6]

Metz also contended that limited geographic mobility of women may contribute to their likely selection as internal successors. However, several studies have provided documentation indicating that there is not a statistically significant difference in the mobility rates of men and women in academic libraries (Morrison, 1969; Taylor, 1973; Schlacter and Thomison, 1974; Martin, 1978; Braunagel, 1979). Earlier studies (Blankenship, 1967; Massman, 1972; Schiller, 1969a) had based their conclusions regarding women's mobility on the length of time individuals had worked at their present institution, while research by Braunagel (1979) and Martin (1978) has analyzed mobility rates based on the number of institutions in which a librarian has worked during his/her entire professional career.

Martin's (1978) study of factors affecting women in academic library management in 14 ARL libraries found that there was not a statistically significant difference in the number of years of professional experience of men and women and in their mobility rates.[7]

Planning for administrative careers in academic libraries includes a number of variables, ranging from educational credentials to professional activities, that seem to be potent factors in climbing the library ladder to the top. General research on academic librarians would support the tendency of women to be less active than men in promoting their own careers through the attainment of the appropriate accoutrements of success; however, documentation on women who have achieved executive-level positions needs to be obtained to determine the extent to which women library directors' demographic and career characteristics differ from or reflect those of men in comparable positions. Only one research project has focused on women academic library directors. Fennell (1978) utilized interview mythodology to secure information on 11 women directors, 7 of whom were at ARL libraries.[8]

Salary studies have shown a consistently significant difference between men and women at all management levels, whether in academic, public, or special libraries in the U.S. and in Canada (Talbot and von der Lippe, 1976; Heim and Kacena, 1979; Cheda, Fisher, Wasylycia-Coe, and Yaffe, 1978; "SLA Salary Survey," 1976). Schiller (1969a) and Martin (1978) also confirmed the pattern of differential compensation for men and women librarians. Moreover, as a librarian proceeds up the administrative career ladder in academic libraries, the salary differences exhibit increasing disparity between the sexes. For example, in the 1975-76 study of salaries of men and women librarians in Canada (Cheda et al., 1978), at the beginning levels, the average salary for men was $388 higher than that for women, and at the executive level, men earned $4554 more than women.[9] ACRL's 1975-76 salary survey (Talbot and von der Lippe, 1976) included over 1000 universities, five-year institutions, and four-year and two-year colleges in the U.S. At the director's level, men earned, on the average, $5180 more than women, and among professionals with under five years' experience, $372 more than women. ARL's 1978-79 salary survey indicated a similar pattern. At the director's level, men earned $460 more than women, and with under five years' experience, $385 more than women. Given the specificity of the ARL salary breakdown, another aspect of salary differentials between men and women is illustrated. For the assistant director's position, the salary difference is $2310, and for the associate director's position, it is $719 (Fretwell, 1980a). The average difference for all three levels in $1163. Apparently, women assume administrative posts at substantially lower salaries than men, and the difference decreases as women occupy the higher-level positions.

Studies in Higher Education

Jessie Bernard's (1964) research constituted the first comprehensive examination of the demographic characteristics and career patterns of academic women. Although her primary focus was on women as members of the teaching faculty, she concluded that "the administrative channel for upward mobility is not one in which academic women have been preeminent.... they are likely to be in such staff positions as personnel and counseling rather than in line positions" (179-180). According to Bernard, in the 1950s, there were some 120 women college presidents, and 20 of these were in coeducational institutions (p. 180). Academic women were also more likely to be unmarried, and, when married, to have fewer children than their male counterparts. Helen Astin's (1969) research on women doctorates showed similar marital and family patterns. Ginzberg's (1966) work on the life styles of educated women stressed that a continuous and full-time work history was critical to a woman's ability to hold an administrative position, and that the number of children a woman had, negatively affected her ability to exhibit an uninterrupted career pattern.

Another factor affecting women's attainment of administrative positions, according to Ginzberg, has been the prevalence of men in these positions, who prefer to appoint and to promote their own sex (pp. 95-96). Caplow and McGee's (1977) analysis of recruitment in the academic marketplace determined that the most common pattern for hiring was "He knew someone here," or the "bestowal of patronage by reason of relationship rather than merit"(p. 110). They provided the following explanation regarding women in the recruitment process:

The major universities may seek men from abroad before they will seek them from the minor league at home. Failing to discover a candidate to their taste in a foreign land, they may decide not to hire at all; or they may even hire a woman, who being outside the prestige system, cannot hurt them (p. 112).

Although Caplow and McGee conducted their research on the academic profession in the late 1950s, their placement of women "outside the prestige system" continues to reflect women's status in academic institutions. Generally, the more prestige associated with an institution, the fewer the number of women on the faculty or in administrative positions (Astin and Bayer, 1973; Howard, 1978). In its report on the status of women in academia, the AAUW observed:

What was true in 1967-70 is true in 1976—women rarely occupy the highest administrative posts of president, chief academic officer, or business officer. Women are less likely to be top-level administrators in large, coeducational schools and in public institutions than in private schools or schools with enrollments fewer than 1000. However, even here, women are more concentrated in the lower echelons of the university hierarchy of administrators (Howard, 1978, p. 6).

The value of association with a prestige system relates to the previously cited studies of the "social network" or "system of relationships" based upon educational, social, or career contacts, which can influence an individual's career prospects for climbing up the career ladder in an organization (Hennig and Jardim, 1978; Kanter 1977; Orth and Jacobs, 1971).

In academia, careers can be pursued within the professorial ranks or by holding teaching or research positions at institutions of progressively increasing prestige, or by holding administrative positions. However, women are not as likely as men to attain an academic rank that may result in promotion to an administrative post. The National Project on Women in Education (U.S. Dept. of Health, Education and Welfare, 1978) reported:

The number of women who attain full professorships is not in proportion to the increase in the number of doctoral degrees conferred on women.... women faculty are forced to wait 2 to 10 years longer for promotion than their male colleagues. Thus, one of the problems in higher education is that women do not rise to the ranks from which they can be promoted to administrative positions (p. 55).

According to 1979 data from the National Center for Education Statistics (NCES), 28 percent of the male faculty and 58 percent of the female faculty occupy the instructor and assistant-instructor ranks in universities (U.S. Dept. of Health, Education and Welfare, 1979, p. 103). Among male faculty, 41 percent hold full professorships, while 12 percent of the women are at this level. At the same time, men are three times as likely as women to hold doctorates in universities; i.e., 45 percent of the men and 16 percent of the women faculty have a Ph.D. Although the difference in rank may be attributed to not having a doctorate, Astin and Bayer concluded: "When a woman attains the doctorate from a prestigious institution and demonstrates great scholarly productivity, she still cannot expect promotion to a high rank as quickly as her male counterpart"(p. 348). Commonly, the prevalence of women holding administrative positions in higher education also relates to the financial support structure of a given institution. NCES data (U.S. Dept. of Health, Education and Welfare, 1979) indicate that in publicly controlled institutions, men hold 78 percent of the executive, administrative, and managerial posts, and in privately controlled institutions, 68 percent (p. 101). Metz (1978) documented a similar pattern of women holding more library-director positions in private than in public colleges.

Personal characteristics of women faculty also appear to influence their upward mobility in higher education. Astin and Bayer (1973) found that remaining single, and, for those married, having fewer children than men, positively correlates with a woman's ability to reach a higher faculty rank. Ferber and Loeb (1973) also confirmed a positive correlation between being a single woman and having a higher rank on the faculty. Studies of women in higher-education administration indicate that they are usually first-born (or the youngest), married, and have no, or one to two, children (Douglas, 1976; Niebor, 1975; Pfiffner, 1975; Tessler, 1976; Vance, 1978; Walsh, 1975). Productivity (number of publications) has also been related to marital status. Astin and Bayer (1973) concluded that women publish less frequently than men, but research by Ferber and Loeb (1973) and Simon, Clark, and Galway (1967) indicated that "although married and single women are about as productive as men, both lag behind men in salary and rank; and...single women are closer to men in salary and rank than are married women (Ferber and Loeb, 1973, p. 999). Notwithstanding the authors' statement, Simon, Clark and Galway refined their conclusions by noting that "married women publish as much or more than men, and unmarried women publish slightly less than men" (Simon, Clark, and Galway, 1967, p. 231). Clark (1977), however, concluded that "unmarried female faculty's publication rates surpass the rates of their married female counterparts" (p. 108). Apparently, the differences in productivity between men and women faculty are not as clearly delineated as those between men and women librarians.

A number of salient career characteristics are commonly associated with women administrators in college and universities. They are likely to have continuous work histories of full-time employment (Douglas, 1976; Fecher, 1972; Gasser, 1975; Walsh, 1975), and there is a tendency for them to have been promoted internally rather than recruited from another institution (Douglas, 1976; Fecher, 1972; Stevenson, 1973;

Vance, 1978). In addition, women administrators are concentrated in the lower administrative ranks and receive lower salaries than men in comparable positions (*Women in Administration*, 1979; Howard, 1978; U.S. Dept. of Health, Education and Welfare, 1979). A common assumption is that women are less mobile than men; however, Curby (1980) found that "women administrators demonstrate a propensity toward geographic mobility...are generally willing to make geographic changes to accept jobs for economic reasons, such as higher salary, as well as upward mobility," and give priority to such changes based on "job-related" rather than "personal or social preferences" (p. 23).

Although Stevenson's (1973) research on women administrators in the "Big Ten" universities indicated a general absence of sponsorship for women, other studies on college and university administrators have positively identified the influence of a mentor on career development for women (Niebor, 1975; Pfiffner, 1975; Vance, 1978). As previously noted, entrance to upper-level positions can be affected by sponsorship, with a resulting negative effect for those individuals outside such a system. Cynthia Epstein (1970a) provided the following explanation of women's difficulty in securing a mentor in academia:

The sponsor-protege...relationship may inhibit feminine advancement. The sponsor is apt to be a man and will tend to have mixed feelings about accepting a woman as protege. Although the professional man might not object to a female assistant—and might even prefer her—he cannot easily identify her (as he might a male assistant) as someone who will eventually be his successor.
...If the sponsor wants to minimize his risks in adopting recruits, the collegial group will not favor an unsuitable member likely to weaken its intimacy and solidarity and it may exert pressure on the sponsor to pick the protege with whom it will be comfortable...For a sponsor, a protege (1) eases the transition to retirement...(2) gives him a sense of continuity in his work, and (3) gives some assurance that his intellectual offspring will build on his work. It is considered unwise to depend on a woman for these (p. 969).

Thus, women's academic careers may be inhibited by their gender even when the highest levels of achievement and potential growth are exhibited.

In concluding its report on affirmative action (*Opportunities for Women in Higher Education*; 1973), the Carnegie Commission on Higher Education made the following recommendation regarding academic women's careers, which is equally applicable to women in academic libraries and in the corporate sector:

Colleges and universities should take especially vigorous steps to overcome a pervasive problem of absence of women in top administrative positions. Women should be given opportunities by their departments to serve as departmental chairmen, because academic administrators are usually selected from among persons who have served ably as department chairmen. Most important is an administrative stance that is highly positive toward providing opportunities for women to rise in the administrative hierarchy. Also very important is the provision of management training opportunities for both men and women who have potential administrative ability but do not hold administrative positions (p. 151).

Although a barely perceptible percentage of women do make it to the top of the academic hierarchy, the woman who aspires to be a university president faces multifarious obstacles related to her personal and family lives, her education and training, her academic and professional career development, and her systems of peer and sponsor relationships.

Women in higher-education administration exhibit a number of similarities associated with female library managers. Both are likely to be married, have no, or one to two children, and have a continuous, full-time work history. They are both more likely to be holding administrative posts in private institutions than their male counterparts, and to have been internally recruited. Female faculty members and librarians are less likely to have doctorates and are likely to earn lower salaries than male colleagues in comparable positions. Although women are commonly stereotyped as less geographically mobile than their male colleagues, research on women administrators in higher education and on women academic librarians has indicated a pattern of mobility that is either not significantly different from that of men or, if different, is not a reflection of a lack of willingness on the part of women to move if desirable career opportunities arise.

Studies in Management

In 1978, 41 percent of the labor force was composed of women, and 66 percent of the women with four years or more of college were employed; however, 83 percent of all employed women were concentrated in four major occupation groups: (1) clerical (35 percent); (2) service workers, including food and health services (21 percent); (3) professional, technical, and kindred workers, with the majority in elementary and secondary education, nursing, dietetics, and therapy (16 percent); and (4) operatives (11 percent) with the majority working as assemblers, sewers and stitchers (U.S. Dept. of Commerce, 1980, pp. 42, 59, 64). Women having four years or more of college were more likely than men to be professional, technical, and kindred workers (66 percent of the women and 53 percent of the men), and although 52 percent of all white-collar workers in 1978 were women, they were still less likely than men to hold managerial and administrative positions. In 1972, women represented 18 percent of all managers[10] and by 1978, 23 percent—an increase of 28 percent (U.S. Dept. of Commerce, 1980, pp. 60, 63). Although the absolute number of women managers has increased substantially since 1950, their proportion to male executives has remained relatively small (Bowman, Worthy, and Greyser 1965, p. 22). Whether a woman has had one to three years, or four or more years, of college, the likelihood of her being a manager has been about the same, in contrast to the experience of a comparably educated man (see Table 4).

TABLE 4
Comparison of Men and Women Managers and Administrators with One or More Years of College

	1 to 3 Years of College (in %)	4 or More Years of College (in %)	Percent of Difference
Men	22.6	25.3	2.7
Women	9.3	9.1	.2

Source: U.S. Department of Commerce (1980), p. 65.

Given the paucity of women in management positions, studies on corporate managers have generally reflected what Acker and Van Houten (1974) term "the male bias in organizational research": "Organizational theory and research has been heavily weighted toward the study of male society. Studies of top level managerial and professional workers usually focus on men, since men are usually in positions of power and leadership" (p. 152).

Warner's (1962) classic study on the careers of American business and government executives was complemented by a comparative study of academic presidents by Ferrari (1970). Warner's research was based on data collected from over 8000 business and 13,000 government leaders, and the subjects of Ferrari's analysis included 760 college and university presidents. Although Warner did not provide figures on the percentage of women business executives, he found only 1 percent of the federal executives were women, while Ferrari found 11 percent of academic presidents were women (10 percent in Catholic liberal arts colleges for women; 1 percent in private liberal arts colleges for women). Generally, the results of these studies represent demographic and career patterns of a "male society" and provide a framework against which female careers can be examined.

From a demographic perspective, the occupational origins of academic, business, and federal executives as described by Ferrari, were relatively similar. Within each of these categories of male executives, over 75 percent of their fathers' occupations were concentrated in four areas: (1) executive and business owner, (2) professional man, (3) farmer, and (4) skilled laborer. Over 60 percent of the business leaders' fathers had been either executives or professionals. Both academic presidents and federal executives were more likely than business leaders to have had fathers who had been skilled laborers or Farmers. Ferrari (1970) concluded that, "when compared with the general population, most fathers of business, government, and academic leaders have tended to come in disproportionately high numbers from the business-executive or business-owner levels or from professional fields"(p. 28). Among academic presidents, the professional groups most frequently represented by their fathers included clergymen and elementary-/secondary-school teachers, while the fathers of business leaders were more likely to be lawyers or clergymen, and the federal executives' fathers, lawyers and college professors.

The value of higher education was consistently underscored by the backgrounds of academic, federal, and business leaders:

About 57 percent of business leaders and 81 percent of federal executives were college graduates... all the academic presidents are college graduates, and nearly three-fourths have earned academic doctorates.... Six universities—Yale, Harvard, Michigan, New York, California at Berkeley, and Chicago—were among the top ten universities for business leaders, for federal executives, and for academic presidents (p. 30).

As noted earlier, Parson's (1976) study of academic library directors identified 4 universities from which 60 percent of the directors had received degrees—Columbia, Illinois, Michigan, and Chicago. All 4 of these institutions were also among the top 10 universities from which academic presidents had earned degrees (Ferrari, 1970, p. 30). Illinois and Columbia were listed, respectively, among the top 10 universities for business and for federal executives. Warner (1962) underlined the value of higher education:

Higher education, which gives a broader view of the world around the person so trained, fits closely with the needs and the broad scope of large business enterprise. As such, it is also the instrument by which the ambitious born to low position can equip themselves to compete for top positions in government and business (p. 122).

Cohen and March's (1974) study of the American college president was prepared for the Carnegie Commission on Higher Education. They analyzed presidential careers, addressed leadership problems facing academic presidents, and included the following summary of the demographic characteristics of college and university presidents:

American college presidents today and in the recent past are most commonly middle-aged, married, male, white, Protestant academics from a relatively well-educated, middle-class, professional-managerial, native-born, small-town family background (pp. 7-8).

Their data included and reflected Ferrari's findings, and they also confirmed that women presidents are primarily located in women's colleges (p. 12). According to Cohen and March, institutional filters insure that academic presidents exhibit relatively homogeneous backgrounds:

> Future presidents move horizontally and vertically through a family of similar administrative organizations located relatively "close" to one another. They arrive in office at the end of a fairly long series of filters. At each promotion or transfer, people with the appropriate background have a slightly higher probability of moving closer to a presidency....
>
> The result of this process is the selection of presidents who are likely, insofar as one can judge from social backgrounds, to be acceptable to the main internal and external groups concerned with the college....on the whole, presidents embody the educational, racial, ethnic, sex, class, and local attributes that are recognized as appropriate (p. 24).

Although they admit that there may be exceptions to their delineation of the prototypal academic president, Cohen and March also stressed that certain demographic characteristics have not been viewed as positive attributes of leaders: "Traditionally in American society, men have been acceptable to women as leaders of women and whites have been acceptable to blacks as leaders of blacks, but the converse has generally not been true"(p. 24).

Warner (1962) and Ferrari (1970) also examined career paterns for academic, business, and federal leaders. Business executives experienced the most rapid entry into executive-level positions, by comparison with federal and academic leaders. Although business executives usually began as white-collar workers (clerical worker, salesman, laborer, or, in the professions, engineer and lawyer), 15 years after their first occupation over 80 percent of them were in executive-level posts. Federal executives had similar work origins—white-collar and professional—and after 15 years, nearly 50 percent were in executive posts. Ninety percent of the academic presidents began their careers in the education profession, and at the end of 15 years, 30 percent were presidents; by the end of 20 years, over 60 percent were presidents (Ferrari, 1970, p. 31). Ferrari noted the following career pattern for academic presidents: "In the majority of cases, there was a steady movement up the higher educational hierarchy from college teacher to department head to college dean or academic vice president (provost) to president (p. 31). The average age of business, federal and academic leaders when they assumed their positions was 45 (p. 31). By comparison, Parson's (1976) study of ARL library directors recorded an average age of 53, and Metz's (1978) study of 200 college and university directors, an average age of 47.5. The fact that men tend to enter the library profession in their late twenties may contribute to the age difference between library directors and academic, business, and federal executives (Morrison, 1969, p. 46).

In 1965, in concert with the equal employment impact of Title VII of the Civil Rights Act, the *Harvard Business Review* (*HBR*) published its survey of women in management, provocatively titled, "Are Women Executives People?" (Bowman, Worthy, and Greyser, 1965). Although the equality of women under law was not disputed, the *HBR* report did document various demographic and career differences between men and women executives.[11] Among women, 30 percent were unmarried, by comparison with only 5 percent of the men. Eleven percent of the women and 1 percent of the men had been divorced. Women were older than men—58 percent of the women, and 41 percent of the men, were over 45 years of age. Men were better educated than women—26 percent of the women, and 37 percent of the men, had college degrees. Only 9 percent of the women had advanced degrees, compared to 44 percent of the men. Women were also more concentrated in smaller companies than men. Among the conclusions of the *HBR* survey were the following: "Both men and women executives believe that women have moderate but not equal opportunity in business in general...[and] both...strongly agree that a woman has to be exceptional, indeed overqualified, to succeed in management today" (p. 15). Based upon the academic qualifications of the *HBR* respondents, factors other than college training apparently contributed to women's achievement of executive positions in business. Livingston's (1971) research, reported in the "Myth of the Well-educated Manager," might have implications for women, as they have tended to assume management positions after having had more years' of experience than men:

Managers are not taught in formal education programs what they most need to know to build successful careers in management. Unless they acquire through their own experience the knowledge and skills that are vital to their effectiveness, they are not likely to advance far up the organizational ladder.

...Until managerial aspirants are taught to learn from their own firsthand experience, formal management education will remain secondhanded (pp. 79, 88).

Related to an aspiring manager's "firsthand experience" is the availability of appropriate role models who have built "successful careers in management" and mentors who assist in the informal acquisition of "knowledge and skills" to complement the formal training that an organization provides its executive pool.

The most extensive study of women in top management was conducted by Margaret Hennig (1971) for her Harvard Business School doctoral dissertation, entitled "Career Development for Women Executives"[12]. Later, Hennig and Anne Jardim (1978) coauthored *The Managerial Woman*, which includes Hennig's original dissertation results and expanded research data on women executives, with comparative information on those women who had not achieved positions higher than the middle-management level. Since Hennig's dissertation, several research monographs on women in management have been published, of which the most notable are Loring and Wells' (1972) *Breakthrough: Women into Management*, and Kanter's (1977) *Men and Women of the Corporation*. In addition, books of collected essays and research reports, including both original and reprinted papers, have been edited by Ginzberg and Yohalem (1973), Gordon and Strober (1975), Jewell (1977), and Stead (1978). A recurrent theme in the literature is the sex-role stereotyping of the managerial position, and the accompanying sex-structuring of organizations.[13] This theme is exemplifed by the monographs cited, and by the papers of Bartol (1978), O'Leary (1974), Osborn and Vicars (1976), Rosen and Jerdee (1974), Schein (1973, 1978), and Terborg (1977). O'Leary (1974) summarized this concept in the following statement:

American society values success and the model upon which the definition of success is based as essentially a male sex role appropriate one. For example, it is the male, not the female, sex role stereotype which coincides with the managerial model (p. 811).

The sex-structuring of organizations is correlated with the male managerial model, because this model tends to perpetuate an organizational hierarchy in which women are stopped, at critical transition points, from ascending the management ladder to the executive suite. Bartol (1978) has related Edgar Schein's research on career stages to the sex-structuring of organizations:

Schein argued that from the point of view of individual career progress, the organization can be conceptualized as a multidirectional filtering system which allows or obstructs movement of individuals horizontally across functional lines, vertically up the hierarchical levels, or radially to inclusion or membership in "inside" groups. The movement through these boundaries takes place over basic career stages and involves crucial transitional points. At the transitional or decision points, the organization is permeable and allows the individual to pass through or becomes impassable, blocking the individual from important career moves (p. 809).

Although numerous studies have documented that there are not significant differences between men and women's ability to perform as managers, the demographic factor of sex has tended to filter women out of the management pool (Jacklin and Maccoby, 1975; Kanter, 1977; Loring and Wells, 1972; Osborn and Vicars, 1976; Reif, Newstrom, and

Monczka, 1975; Schein, 1978; Terborg, 1977; Terborg et al., 1977). Even in a female-dominated environment such as the library or the social services organization, bias against the woman manager has been identified (Grimm and Stern, 1974; Petty and Miles, 1976; Simpson and Simpson, 1969).

Prior to facing the sex-structuring component of organizational life, the woman may be socialized, via family life, to limit her occupational aspirations to female-stereotyped roles. While librarianship is stereotyped as a female occupation, managerial positions are commonly associated with males (Panek, Rush, and Greenawalt, 1977). Loring and Wells (1972) analyzed the conflict between demographic and career variables that affect men and women, by defining the primary role patterns to which each sex tend to conform:

> Inextricably intertwined are at least three major role patterns that affect the relationships between men and women and create difficulties for women in the process of becoming managers.
> ...First are *sex-roles*: which underlie the pattern of male "superiority" and "female inferiority." Second are *marital-roles* of husband and wife where power, intelligence and responsibility traditionally rest with the husband while the wife is perceived as helpmate "living through" her husband and children. Third are *work-roles* where men are in the leadership and decision-making roles and women are in the housekeeping and nurturing tasks of industry, government, education and services (pp. 98-99).

"Sex-roles" act as inhibitors to women's management aspirations, by defining their status as secondary rather than equal to that of men's. Traditional "marital-roles" have demanded that the married woman's primary responsibility is to her family, rather than to a career or to a combination thereof. "Work-roles" have contributed to the stereotyping of male and female occupations and to the common placement of the woman behind a typing table rather than an executive desk.[14] The limited role patterns attributed to women contributed to a dearth of nontraditional role models. O'Leary (1974) provided the following explanation of the significance of role models:

> The essential quality of the role model is that he (or she) possesses skills and displays techniques which the actor lacks (or thinks she lacks) and from which, by observation and comparison with his or her own performance, the actor can learn. Hence, in order for achievement to occur, the actor needs a role model to emulate (p. 818).

With regard to female role models, O'Leary contended that

> mere imitation of the male managerial model cannot necessarily be expected to result in a viable model to be emulated by other women. The absence of female role models functioning successfully in a masculine sex role appropriate position may be considered a barrier to the occupational aspirations and achievement directed behaviors of women in the labor force (p. 819).

Although there have been relatively few women in management in proportion to men during the 1970s, the trend has been toward an increase in the absolute numbers of women managers, so that more individuals are coming in contact with a female managerial mode. Identified as a significant finding of the *HBR* survey (Bowman, Worthy, and Greyser, 1965) was the fact that over 80 percent of the men and over 90 percent of the women respondents "reported individual and/or company experience with women executives" (p. 26). Based on her research on career and professional women, Epstein (1974) concluded: "It is essential to create a critical mass in management, a large enough proportion of women to make their presence a matter of course rather than a phenomenon (pp. 13-14). This "critical mass" will provide women with an appropriate peer group and enable aspiring women managers to identify with female managerial models. The importance of a peer group is related to the development of the "informal social network" discussed in the section, "Studies in Library Science." In a review of research on women in management, Terborg (1977) cited the utility of the "formation of group bonds" as being an important aspect of career development, in that,

if the newcomer is different from the group on sex or race, the newcomer will be viewed as a "solo" or "token" by the group. This serves to exclude the token newcomer from formal and informal work contacts, and elicits extreme evaluations, in either direction, from group members (p. 652).

How women learn to associate with and work with men can affect their ability to succeed in a male-dominated culture. Hennig and Jardim's (1978) research on managerial women documented close relationships between these women and their fathers, especially in the pursuit of a range of masculine activities:

They believed that they had been given unusually strong support by their families in following their own interests regardless of the sex-role attributes of those interests. Finally, they thought that they had developed a very early preference for the company of men rather than of women (pp. 99-100).

They noted another factor reinforcing the close relationship between father and daughter: these women were the firstborn children "or the eldest in all-girl family of no more than three children" (p. 100). Crawford's (1977) research on women in middle-management positions also indicated a tendency toward firstborn women's occupying positions at this level (p. 111). Additional studies documenting the incidence of the firstborn or eldest-child phenomenon among women who have achieved positions of stature are cited in the section, "Studies in Higher Education."

In Hennig and Jardim's (1978) study, the majority of the fathers were in management positions, with the remaining in college administration.

Born into upwardly aspiring middle-class families between 1910 and 1915, these women executives had mothers whose work was primarily confined to domestic activities; however, their mothers' educational levels were equivalent, and in over 50 percent of the cases, superior to that of the fathers'. Recent research by Broverman, Vogel, Broverman, Clarkson, and Rosenkrantz (1975), Crawford (1978), Rosenfeld (1978) and Tangri (1975) has cited the importance of a working mother and her educational level, as far as career aspirations of the daughter are concerned. As Rosenfeld (1978) noted, if the mother works outside the home, then her career influences the daughter's but if she does not work, then the father's career "has a stronger relationship with daughter's occupation" (p. 44). This thesis is consistent with Hennig and Jardim's (1978) findings on women executives who chose their fathers as their role models, attended coeducational universities, majored in professionally oriented rather than liberal-arts programs, and selected a career related to their fathers'. Comparatively, however, the mother is more likely than the father to become the primary role model for the daughter if certain variables are present. Klemmack and Edwards (1973) indicated:

When father's career and education are held constant, a positive and significant correlation exists between the mother's education and the ambition level of the offspring, especially that of females—ambitions which, of course, may be partly fulfilled through occupational attainment (p. 512).

If the working mother is also an educated woman with a bachelor's or advanced degree, there is an even greater degree of correlation between it and her daughter's occupational choice than would occur among less-educated working mothers, according to Tangri (1975): "More educated working mothers, particularly those who are themselves in male dominated occupations, are taken as role models by such daughters" (p. 270). Epstein (1974) has observed: "Successful women tend more than men to come from higher-income families and to have mothers who have been professional workers (p. 15). Having a working mother who successfully combines a career with family life tends to produce female offspring with a similar orientation (O'Leary, 1974, p. 818).

The woman executive is less likely to be married than her male counterpart (Basil, 1972; Bowman, Worthy, and Greyser, 1965); however, this trend may be changing. In Hennig and Jardim's (1978) study, all the women executives were married, but had not until they were about 35 years old, and they did not have children. The general higher incidence of married women in the labor force since the 1950s—including those with preschool children—has been documented by Oppenheimer (1973) and may tend to influence future studies on the marital status of career women. Epstein (1970) identified an increase in the number of professional women who were married and an increase in married women who have attained positions of prestige in their professions. Women's careers may also be related to the career patterns of their spouses. Within the major occupation groups, there are often similarities between the husband's and wife's occupations. For example, if the husband is a professional or technical worker, 41 percent of the wives are in the same occupational category. Among male managers and administrators, the greatest percentage of their wives were clerical workers (41 percent). At the same time, however, women who were married to managers were also more likely to be a manager themselves (12 percent) than women married to men in any other occupational group (U.S. Dept. of Commerce, 1980, p. 66).

The professional or executive woman is less likely to have children than women in other occupation groups (Bailyn, 1974; Crawford, 1977; Robinson, 1974). However, given a 1978 average of 1.6 children per woman, small families have become a standard rather than exceptional pattern (U.S. Dept. of Commerce, 1980, p. 42), although women with young children are still more likely to experience career interruptions than women in general. Consequently, although less of a deterrent to careers than in the past, the presence or prospect of children may affect a woman's career aspirations more than a man's. However, according to Loring and Wells (1972), most women have their last child at 26, and "at that age, they are rarely under consideration for a management position"; yet "no other single factor discriminates against women's employment so totally as motherhood" (p. 147). In addition, when women are considered for comparable-level positions, they are generally older than men (p. 147). By the time women experience what Loring and Wells refer to as "women's 10-year lag in promotions, compared to men" (p. 34), they are usually past their childbearing years.

When age and type of job are held constant, turnover rates for men and women are approximately the same. Given the difference in age for men and women at comparable career levels, Strober (1975) noted that "the turnover rate for an older woman is likely to be lower than that for a young man" (p. 84). Although women may begin career planning later than most men, for family or other reasons, once on a specific career path, they tend to exhibit an uninterrupted work pattern, or, at minimum, a work history that exhibits no more turnover than that of men (Robinson, 1974).

While men may begin career planning in college, women typically begin this process in their early thirties. Without career commitment and directed effort, women may not experience what Hennig and Jardim (1978) describe as the "normal" career path:

The typical management career path moves individuals from an initial experience in a technical or specialist's role to the more general role of a middle manager. From that point career paths lead upward to new levels of specialization which demand a broader and more conceptual approach to decision-making and problem-solving (p. 55).

A significant difference between women who stay at the specialist or middle-management level and those who advance to the executive level is the ability to plan their careers to achieve optimal technical skills while focusing on career advancement as a primary objective, rather than on the immediate job as an end in itself. According to Hennig and Jardim, the major variables that career-development theorists attribute to career choice by men are "irrelevant to the great majority of women":

The theorists assume that the individual brings with him knowledge and skill as well as talent and intelligence; that socio-economic pressures have combined to develop aspirations and expectations, a positive disposition toward acquiring an objectively measurable, demonstrable competence, a recognition of the importance of the environment and some definition of what he wants to do and where he wants to go (pp. 142-143).

A man's reading of his environment is based upon both the formal organization and the informal network of sponsors and peer groups at each organizational level who can either expedite or impede his progress through various career stages. In Buchanan's (1974) research on organizational commitment, he confirmed that the following factors are important to the "socialization of managers in work organizations": "years of organizational service, social interaction with organizational peers and superiors, job achievement, and hierarchical advancement... (p. 544-545).

Among women workers, Kanter (1977) stated, "There is evidence that in general the jobs held by most women seem to have shorter chains of opportunity associated with them and contain fewer advancement prospects" and that women are less likely than men to expect job promotions to management positions (pp. 159, 160). Thus, women tend to have limited access to the variables that contribute to career planning and commitment. Another factor indicative of career achievement is salary level. The salary differential between men and women remained about the same between 1970 and 1977, with women earning 59 percent of that of men in comparable positions (U.S. Dept. of Commerce, 1980, p. 2). Among managers and administrators, women's earnings in 1977 were 54 percent of those of men in comparable jobs, and 55 percent of men's in 1970 (U.S. Dept. of Commerce, 1980, p. 76). Even though coverage under the Equal Pay Act was extended in 1972 to include executive, administrative, and professional employees, women are still receiving considerably lower salaries than men in comparable occupations (Meacham, 1975, p. 63).

Although more women are entering management positions, an organization's executive levels are still not seen as equally permeable by both men and women; consequently, women are still less likely than men to prepare for management careers. The number of women majoring in business and management has increased in recent years, but men still predominate as recipients of undergraduate and graduate degrees (U.S. Dept. of Health, Education and Welfare, 1979, p. 117).

A number of salient demographic and career characteristics have been delineated in the preceding review. Female corporate executives are likely to be firstborn children and to have had fathers and/or mothers with college degrees. The parent having the highest level of education and/or career commitment and involvement is the one most likely to have influenced the daughter's occupational choice. A woman executive is less likely to be married than a man, and if she does marry, she will probably not have any children. She will also have assumed an administrative position at an older age than her male counterpart. In general, her career has not demonstrated the preparatory rituals that her male colleagues have performed. She is less likely than a man to have had academic training in management, and she will have had limited access to informal peer networks and to the sponsor-protege system. While women have not readily related to and emulated the male managerial model, they should be able to establish their own managerial models, based on a feminine rather than a masculine prototype, with both prototypes capable of effective coexistence.

Summary

Among the three categories of executive women discussed here (library administrators, higher-education administrators, and managers), a number of demographic and career similarities have been indicated by the research reviewed. Each is more likely than comparable male executives to be married, and to have childless families. Once initiated, their careers exhibit continuous, full-time work histories. Women in academic library and higher-education administration are likely to be in small, private institutions and to have been internally recruited. Their corporate female colleagues are more likely to be in large than small companies, but they have probably been internally recruited. Women leaders in each group are also less likely than men in comparable positions to have advanced degrees and to earn equivalent salaries.

Although professional women with advanced academic credentials do not predominate in higher education, they still do not occupy a proportional share—small though it may be—of administrative posts. While women do predominate in the library profession and among white-collar workers, the probability of their becoming administrators is still substantially less likely than it is for a man.

The general absence of administrative role models for women faculty, librarians, and corporate employees has not been conducive to an environment that encourages women to aspire to executive-level positions. In addition, the absence of role models in these professions has resulted in women's dependence upon men as sponsors of their administrative career development. Although some male administrators have provided such support, research indicates that there are significant variables that still reduce the probability that a woman will share the leadership ranks with men in academic libraries, higher education, and the corporate sector.

FUTURE RESEARCH

Notwithstanding the scope of this review, our knowledge about women administrators is still quite limited. Those studies that have focused on the chief administrative officer of libraries, and academic and corporate institutions, have been devoted primarily to men, with the few notable exceptions cited. With the aid of diverse research studies, a sketch of the female executive has been drawn; however, a full-length, definitive portrait has yet to be developed. Of particular concern to this author is the need for a comparative analysis of the demographic and career characteristics of men and women holding comparable administrative positions in one type of institution. Pursuant to this objective, the author is engaged in dissertation research on men and women in academic-library administration, with emphasis on a determination of those factors that have mitigated against proportional representation of women at the executive level in ARL libraries. ARL libraries have been selected because they represent over 100 major research collections in the U.S. and Canada that have benefitted from the presence of numerous regional, national, and international library leaders as their administrators. The demographic characteristics and career patterns of these directors at the executive, associate, and assistant levels could provide guidance to those aspiring to positions of leadership in academic libraries.

The absence of women library administrators is a subject suffering from a dearth of information, and requires in-depth examination and research in order to determine the factors contributing to women's scarce utilization. Based upon their analysis of internal labor market structures in female-dominated professions, Grimm and Stern (1974) reinforced the need for extensive research in the following statements:

A significant contribution to our understanding of why men *do* dominate the higher echelons of the semi-professions will come when systematic empirical studies are conducted to determine how available administrative positions in these fields are filled....

Knowledge of what the patterns of growth, hiring, and promotion in the administrative sectors of the semi-professions *are* will help to explain rather than merely describe the limits to women working in these fields (pp. 703-704).

It is hoped that future research will complement previously published studies on academic-library administration and provide new documentation on the men and women who are and will be the potential leaders of academic libraries up to the end of this century.

NOTES

1. Libraries in institutions with enrollments of 3000 or more.
2. Randall studied 205 college libraries with collections averaging 35,000 volumes serving four-year liberal arts institutions in the U.S.
   Zimmerman's (1932) thesis on the education of 260 college and university head librarians cited the same differences in the academic and professional training of men and women and also concurred with Randall's conclusion that men rather than women controlled large university libraries (pp. 78-79).
3. The one-year master's degree in library science was not awarded until 1947. Until the late 1950s, however, the two-year master's degree was the primary degree granted for advanced study of library science, and the fourth- and fifth-year bachelor's degrees in library science were the commonly held professional degrees for librarians (Carroll, 1970, pp. 61-64).
4. Parsons (1976) found that ARL directors averaged less than 8 years per institution, and Metz (1978), in an analysis of academic libraries having 500,000 or more volumes, determined an average tenure of 10.9 years.
5. Cohn's (1976) study of 1973 ARL directors indicated that the four women serving as directors had all been internally recruited, with two appointed after the age of 60 years ("the only two incumbents past sixty at appointment") (pp. 142-43).
6. Helmich and Brown's (1972) research in the corporate sector supported the hypothesis that organizations experiencing inside succession "exhibit less organizational change" in the executive suite than those who recruit externally.
7. Chapter 9, by Martin in this volume.
8. Chapter 8, by Fennell, in this volume.
9. See Chapter 13, by Futas, in this volume.
10. Civilian noninstitutional population 16 years and over.
11. HBR respondents totaled 2000 executives, half men and half women.
12. Margaret Cussler's (1958) research for *The Woman Executive* was based primarily on women in middle management. However, her treatment of topics such as career entry, sponsors and proteges, marital status, and "working with men" are generally reflective of current research on women

in management. In this review, emphasis has been placed on research conducted since 1960.
13. Sex-role stereotyping of an occupation occurs when a large majority of its members are of one sex and when "there is an associated normative expectation that this is as it should be," according to Robert K. Merton (Epstein, 1970b, p. 152).
14. In 1978, over 98 percent of all secretaries, stenographers, and typists were women, and 80 percent of all clerical and kindred workers were women (U.S. Dept. of Commerce, 1980, p. 63).

Mobility and Professional Involvement in Librarianship: A Study of the "Class of '55"

MARION R. TAYLOR

NEW PRACTITIONERS in most professional fields stand at the threshold of their profession after completing a prescribed educational program and receiving a professional certificate or degree. Within the restrictions inherent in the field and those imposed by personal inclinations, the neophyte professional faces a number of career choices, both initially and in years to come. If career goals are strong, career choices are probably directed toward achieving "success" in the profession. The word "success" does not necessarily imply assumption of a leadership role, but, with rare exceptions, it tends to be equated with attainment of a high level in the professional structure. On the other hand, if career motivation is weak, career choices might be dictated by nonprofessionally-oriented factors, such as location in a congenial environment or loyalty to a particular institution. In such cases the individual may fail to take advantage of opportunities for self-advancement through changes in position.

These two types of career orientation have been characterized as the purposive-rational and the short-run hedonistic modes by Beshurs and Nishiura (1961). Although these authors see the professional career as cast in the purposive-rational mode, this may not hold true for some occupations, such as librarianship, which are sometimes termed semi-professions (Etzioni, 1969, p. v). Hughes (1958), speaking of professions in transition, which includes librarianship, delineates two groups, the *homeguard* and the *itinerant*:

Even among those who qualify as professionals, some will be swept more completely than others into the main stream of change and professionalization. Some will have drifted into the occupation, and will not want to leave home to take new jobs. Others, more fully committed and more alert to the new developments, will move from place to place seeking ever more interesting, prestigeful and perhaps, more profitable positions. The latter become itinerants, interchangeable parts in a larger system of things, at home in any given place not because of personal attachments but because of the work to be done and the conditions of doing it. Those who stay in one place, whether because they have no opportunity to move, or because they have attachments, build even more attachments, become less moveable and perhaps more resistant to changes the latter propose and promote (pp. 135-6).

It may be inferred, then, that the rate of mobility and the kinds of career patterns that are characteristic of an occupation bear a relationship to the professionalism exhibited by its practitioners. This does not mean that in each instance the mobility exhibited by an individual is a valid measure of that person's professionalism. Rather, taken in the aggregate, the extent of mobility and the kinds of career patterns that are characteristic of a given field would be an indication of the professional orientation of the group as a whole (Form and Miller, 1947; Reiss, 1955; Ladinsky, 1967b).

There are two salient characteristics of the discipline and practice of librarianship that tend to adulterate the professional commitment of its practitioners in terms of identification with the profession as life-work and the desire to achieve "success" in the profession. The first characteristic is the deprecatory attitude of the public toward librarians, based largely on the belief that librarianship is primarily a woman's occupation. Sociologists who have studied the field appear unanimous on this point. In a 1946 report on public opinion about librarians, for example, Form (1946) presented the dominant stereotype of librarians as "a group of intelligent, educated, single women who appear quiet and self-possessed. Underneath they are inhibited, slightly neurotic, and conservative in their personal and social relations" (p. 853).

Much the same view was reflected some twenty years later by Goode (1961) and reiterated by Ginzberg and Brown (1967, pp. 12-14), though the latter stress the increasing predominance of married women in the field. In view of the negative public image of the librarian, it is possible that some people, including some men, may be attracted to library work because of the seemingly less demanding nature of librarianship when compared to other professional work.

A second characteristic is the comparatively easy entry into librarianship. In the United States, technical and professional knowledge is usually concentrated in a one-year program superimposed on a general liberal-arts background. Librarianship is, then, attractive to those seeking a career change and to those who are latecomers to employment ranks (e.g., women who begin a "career" after raising a family), because of its minimal educational requirements. Furthermore, the beginning librarian need not expend capital for equipment or waste time building up a clientele. It is also undeniable that some librarians view library work as an opportunity to achieve security in white-collar employment with a nominal expenditure of time and money. It is certainly true as well that some librarians do have a deep sense of dedication, but that dedication may sometimes be to a particular institution or may be devotion to scholarship in a special subject.

These characteristics and others, which might reflect a weak career commitment of the professional work force in librarianship, do not (with the exception of insititutional loyalty) pose constraints to mobility. The question then arises, is mobility, or the lack of it, a characteristic that contributes to the semiprofessional status of librarianship? If Hughes's depiction of conflict between "homeguard" and "itinerant" is accurate, the issue of mobility may be central to the development of professionalism in librarianship.

MOBILITY IN LIBRARIANSHIP

Before the 1970s, there was little concern with the measurement of mobility in librarianship, and virtually none with the relationship between mobility and professionalism. Some studies did consider mobility tangentially or in relation to specific groups within the profession; these suggest that as a group, librarians are not mobile, even at the administrative level (Harvey, 1957; Bolino, 1969; Morrison, 1969; Bundy and Wasserman, 1972a,b,c,d).

Although it was common practice in such studies to make an assessment of the involvement of librarians in professional activities, none attempted to compare professional activity and mobility. Moreover, the investigations were concerned primarily with library administrators. The mobility of the profession at large and the relationship of that mobility to professionalism remained obscure. It was the aim of the investigation at hand to gain insight into this relationship by examining career patterns, mobility characteristics, and evidence of professional involvement of graduate professional librarians at all levels. In view of criticism directed toward the predominance of women as a major reason for the failure of librarianship to achieve true professional status, the investigation was also designed to scrutinize differences in the behavior of men and women with respect to mobility and involvement.

Two factors that colored the investigation and its findings should be noted. In the first place, the study was exploratory in nature, since the methodology of earlier works that treated the mobility of librarians was inadequate in approach to the measurements of mobility.[1] For this investigation, it was necessary to develop techniques used in general mobility studies (Davidson and Anderson, 1937; Lipset and Bendix, 1952; Lipset and Bendix, 1967). The second factor concerns the time frame of the study. The career period under study covered the years 1955-69. If the study has been extended into the next decade, its results would undoubtedly have been affected by the diminishing job market and, if extended far enough, the influence of affirmative action and the growing acceptance of the woman administrator in librarianship.

At the inception of the investigation, a number of decisions conditioned the conduct of the research. First, it was decided that the investigation should cover the full range of library practice at the professional level and be limited to those holding fifth-year degrees from United States' library schools accredited by the American Library Association, but no restriction would be made as to type of work, library affiliation, or status in the profession. Second, the decision was made to confine the study to a group of librarians entering professional life at the same time: 1955. Such a selection would minimize the effect on mobility of disparate economic and sociological factors and also simplify analysis, since each "career" would be of the same duration, from 1955 to 1969.

The biographical directory *Who's Who in Library Service* (1966) was chosen as a source from which to identify the "Class of '55" in librarianship. In all, 355 names were located that fit the criteria for the study: graduates of accredited library schools in the United States who completed the fifth year of study in 1955 and who were active in library work in 1965.[2] The designation "Who's Who" does not, in this case, connote prominence in the field; instead, the directory endeavored to include all active professionals.

One problem in using *Who's Who in Library Service* as a source came to light as biographies were scanned to identify those who had received a library master's degree in 1955. It was immediately apparent that the selected group contained an unexpectedly high proportion of men. Perhaps women responded less readily to the publishers' request for information. Yet, when considered in another light, the proportion of men appears a less extreme factor, as shown by Hoage's (1950) study of library-school graduates of 1937, which reported that the drop-out rate for women (after 12 years) was 39 percent, as compared to 18 percent for men (p. 39). If the percentage of women leaving the profession is double that of men, the proportion of "active" males among graduates of any given year would be expected to increase with each passing year.

THE SURVEY

In order to secure as complete information as possible about the group isolated through *Who's Who*, a questionnaire was mailed to these individuals, constructed to secure information about employment, professional interests, and such background characteristics as age, sex, marital status, education and "lifetime" geographic mobility.

Of the 355 questionnaires mailed, 216 completed forms were returned, a response rate of 60 percent. Some of the returned questionnaires had to be eliminated from the study: three responses did not meet the criteria—they graduated from library school and entered the profession in 1955. Employment records of others (mostly married women) contained extensive gaps in employment, which necessitated rejection for reasons of statistical analysis. The remaining 194 responses formed the data base for the investigation. In other words, the group under study contained 194 librarians who graduated from accredited library schools in the United States in 1955, who had been continuously engaged in library-related work through 1969, and who completed the *Who's Who* questionnaire. The designation *Study Group* is used hereafter to refer to these 194 individuals.

BACKGROUND CHARACTERISTICS OF THE STUDY GROUP

The Study Group was 56 percent women (108) and 44 percent men (86). Fewer than half of the women and a third of the men were single. About a fourth of the women were separated, divorced, or widowed (SDW), while the number of men in this category was negligible. The mean age of the SDW women (54 years) was considerably higher than the mean age (about 44-46) of all other sex/marital status categories.

Women in the Study Group were associated more with the South than with any other region of the country. More than a third of the women were born, raised, and attended library school in the southern states; almost two-fifths were employed in southern libraries in 1969. In contrast, only a fifth of the men had southern origins and only a fifth were employed in the South in 1969.

Few of the Study Group librarians has pursued academic majors in the sciences. Undergraduate study was generally in the humanities or social sciences, with women favoring education and English, and men, English and history. About 18 percent of the group had additional library science study beyond the master's. The males had more formal education than the females: 10 men and no women held doctoral degrees, although 4 women reported working toward a higher degree and one had received a sixth-year (library) credential. Twenty-nine men had master's degrees in fields other than librarianship, as compared to 18 women with a second master's. Most of these degrees were earned prior to library-school enrollment.

An examination of educational patterns displayed by members of the Study Group was pertinent to the investigation, since late choice of librarianship as a profession, evidenced by delay in undertaking professional study, could affect the kind of commitment the individual has toward the library career. Twenty-six percent of the men completed the total educational process (undergraduate study plus the library master's program) in 8 years or less, following graduation from high school. Almost half took from 9 to 15 years, and one-fourth did not receive the professional master's until 16 years had passed. Slightly more women (29 percent) received the library science master's within 8 years of high school graduation, but almost half (46 percent) took 16 or more years in the process. The additional time for women is accounted for almost entirely by SDW; this segment of the group had a mean of 22.8 years, as compared to 13 years for single and married women.

Most delay in the process occurred between college graduation and entrance into library school. An interval of two or more years separated college and library school for 70 percent of the group. For 44 percent of the women and 26 percent of the men, the interval lasted for six or more years. Wartime conditions and the draft made military service an inevitable part of the preprofessional life of many of the males, and three women also indicated prior military-service work. The other major causes of delay, graduate study in another field and employment (other than military service), would seem to indicated that librarianship was a second career choice for some respondents.

A majority of the Study Group (82 percent of the women and 84 percent of the men) had full-time employment experience before entering library school, with teaching and library work the most frequent preprofessional occupations. While the teaching activities of men were generally at the college level, all teaching by women was in primary or secondary schools. Women had more years of preprofessional work experience than men; the average for women was 8.5 years; for men, 6.0. Prelibrary-school work experience in libraries (including part-time work) was characteristic of 60 percent of the women and 38 percent of the men. A fifth of the women held "professional" positions as school librarians or heads of small special libraries. More women (49 percent) than men (20 percent) held full-time jobs while attending library school, in part, perhaps, a reflection of the GI educational benefits available to some of the men.

CAREER MOBILITY

In sociological studies, mobility is broadly defined as movement or capacity to move. Mobility within the framework of a single occupation—librarianship—must be considered in terms of movement within the institutional structure of library practice; that is, in terms of changes in position or function within a single library unit or change from one institution to another.

The term *external mobility* denotes movement by an individual from one employing institution to another, as distinct from *internal mobility* denoting change in position within an institution or system. The concept of external movement is narrowly interpreted in this study. A shift from one library unit to another distinct unit remains an internal move so long as both units are under control of a single agency. For example, a shift from one school library to another in the same school system, or movement from the main library of a university to the law school of that university, or even to a teaching position in that institution, constitutes internal movement. External mobility was the focus of the investigation; other aspects of mobility were treated as collateral to this major emphasis.

Data collected from the Study Group covered a 14-year "career" period, beginning with the receipt of the professional library degree (1955) and ending with the time of the survey (fall 1969). In this period, the "career-job sequence" of each individual consisted of all full-time employment of at least six months duration. Any period of full-time study was considered equivalent to a "job." In a few cases (for married or SDW women), lapses in employment lasting no longer than two years were treated as part of the job sequence.

Since each "career" was of the same length, external mobility was an easily measured variable. An external mobility rating (EMR) could be established for each member of the group by counting the number of changes in employer. The only complication encountered in this measurement arose from cases in which the subject took leave to assume a temporary assignment.[3] In these cases, the intervening job was counted as a change in employer but the return to the former position was not counted.

More than one-fourth of the Study Group did not change employers during the 14-year period, while two individuals made seven changes, giving a range from 0 to 7 in EMR for the group. In order to simplify presentation of the findings, descriptive phrases were assigned to specific levels of external mobility exhibited by the Study group members, as follows:

Immobile—respondents with 0 EMR
Mobile—those with EMR of 1 or above
Less mobile—those with EMR of 2 or less
More mobile—those with EMR of 3 or more
Low mobility—those with EMR of 0 or 1
Moderate mobility—those with EMR of 2 or 3
High mobility or highly mobile—those with EMR of 4 or more[4]

Men appeared to be slightly more mobile than women, but the difference in EMR by sex was not statistically significant. Thus, a null hypothesis that there is no difference in mobility rates of men and women could not be rejected. On the basis of these data, a relationship between mobility and sex could be neither proved nor discounted.

When married status was added as a variable, it was found that 50 percent of the SDW women were immobile; only one woman in this category made as many as four job changes. In comparison with all other SDW women, the difference in proportion of immobile women was significant. It would appear, therefore, that this difference resulted from an association between immobility and the SDW condition, with the possible implication that this group had greater constraints to movement than other women. Since, however, the SDW were, as a group, somewhat older than other women in the Study Group, there is a strong possibility that it was the age variable rather than marital status—or a combination of the two—that was operational here.

While for other women, differences in EMR were not found to be significant, the data are worth noting. Single women also seemed somewhat reluctant to move. Thirty percent of all single women were immobile; half as many (15 percent) were highly mobile. Although marriage is frequently cited as a barrier to the mobility of women, only 20 percent of the immobile females were married. The proportion of all married women who were immobile (19 percent) differs little from the proportion who were highly mobile (22 percent). Apparently, among this selected group of librarians, marriage did not constrain movement and, in fact, may have induced movement, since the wife, professional or not, is frequently forced to change jobs if her husband relocates.[5]

As expected, age and mobility were found to be associated. The younger librarians moved more frequently than their older colleagues. The association between age and mobility was most apparent in the case of women. The difference in mobility of younger and older male librarians cannnot be asserted with confidence. Interestingly, the average age of immobile males was lower than that of males who had made one or two changes.

Analysis of the relationship between mobility, sex, and age showed that, while the difference in mobility of males and females in the younger age range (34-44 years) was not significant, among older librarians (45 years and over), there was an association between sex and mobility; older males moved more readily than older females.

GEOGRAPHIC MOBILITY

Change in employer does not always involve change in geographic location. Indeed, for librarians with the armed forces, geographic movement may occur without change in employer. In order to make a comparison between external and geographic movement during the professional career period, each respondent was given a Geographical Mobility Rating, or GMR, by counting the number of moves across state (or foreign country) boundaries. The GMR of the Study Group ranged from 0 to 6. A majority of the women and more than a third of the men spent their professional lives within one state. Less than a tenth of the whole group made as many as four moves from one state to another. Fifty-four percent (47 percent of the women and 75 percent of the men) were both externally and geographically mobile. For every 10 changes in employer, there were about 6 geographic changes. In other words, three-fifths of the job changes involved migration to another location. Eighteen percent changed jobs one or more times during the 14-year period but remained within the same state.

The SDW women were conspicuously immobile geographically, but, as in the case of external mobility, the possibility that age was the major factor here cannot be disregarded. The age difference also modifies conclusions based on findings with respect to differences in geographic mobility of men and women. Even though a significantly higher proportion for females had a GMR of 0, it cannot be stated unequivocally that there was a difference in the geographical mobility of the sexes. Examination of the distances involved in relocations indicated that female librarians may be more venturesome than males. Of the 51 females and 54 males who moved from one state to another, 88 percent of the women moved to another division of the United States, as compared to 83 percent of the men, and 25 percent of the women worked overseas at some time, as compared to 11 percent of the men.

For women, the association between age and GMR was strong. A significantly greater proportion of the younger women were out-of-state migrants, and the probability that this difference was the result of chance is small. For men, age was associated with the upper ranges of geographic mobility, with a greater proportion of younger males making three or more geographic moves.

FUNCTIONAL MOBILITY

Like geographic changes, change in function does not necessarily coincide with external movement. Frequently change in function occurs internally and a move can be made from one library to another without change in the kind of work performed. While no attempt was made to investigate functional change fully, attention was given to this aspect of mobility in order to observe its relationship to external mobility.

Among the various facets of library practice that can be considered to constitute a change in "function," the most readily discernible relates to the type of employing institution, basically the type of library. Although the lines of demarcation by function are not always precise, it is generally conceived that there are four basic types of libraries: academic, public, school, and special. In general, these four types have distinctive purposes, so a change from one type to another can be considered a change in function. A fifth "type" category was used, to embrace library-related employment (library-school teaching, work with publishers, and so on). Of the 139 respondents who moved one or more times, 29 percent worked in one type of library, 48 percent worked in two types, and 22 percent in three or more.

The academic library was favored by Study Group members over all other library types in 1955 and remained the most popular in 1969, particularly for males. Half of the women and almost three-fourths of the men worked in academic libraries at some point in the career period. A third of the men and almost one-fifth of the women never worked in any other type of library.

The other types of libraries were favored almost equally by women. Throughout the career period, somewhat more than a third of the women worked in public and school libraries, and a little less than a third, in special libraries. In 1969, as compared to 1955, the number of women employed in special libraries showed a slight increase, while the number in public and school libraries declined. The public library ranked second for men consistently—in 1955, 1969, and throughout the career; only 12 percent of the males remained in public library work for the whole 14 years. The small number of male school librarians were inclined to remain in that field. Although more males worked in special libraries than in school-library positions, only one man worked only in special libraries over the entire period.

For 6 women and 2 men, the initial position was in library-related work, including work with library associations and full-time study. In 1969, 10 women and 9 men were in such "other" positions—generally, at that time, as library-school teachers.

Changes in the type of work performed are not as easily categorized as changes in type of library. Meticulous detail would be required to distinguish specific jobs from among the intermixture of traditional library functions and specializations in subject and form. Moreover, the administrative role characteristic of many library positions adds to the complexity of accounting for changes in work.

Although the distinction of function was rendered difficult by lack of standardized terminology and the ambiguity of some responses, it was fairly easy to make a distinction on the basis of "specialization." Three categories of special work were discerned: service to children and young adults (including school-library work), work with special forms of material (serials, films, maps, and so on), and work relating to specific subjects or disciplines. When respondents engaged in these specializations were isolated from those performing "general" library work, it was found that women were more inclined to specialize than men. Over the whole career period, all but 15 percent of the women and 27 percent of the men had done some special work.

In terms of conventional library functions, public-service work was initially attractive to both men and women. Over half of the men and over a third of the women began work in public-service posts, but by 1969, only a quarter of the respondents held public-service positions. The proportion of the group engaged in technical services was approximately the same in both 1955 and 1969 (about 19 percent). Records for the whole career period, however, showed that, while 40 percent of the respondents had worked in technical services at some time, just 6 percent of the women and 3 percent of the men worked exclusively as technical-service librarians. As would be expected, there was a shift to administrative positions, with over half of the total group in this category in 1969. The shift was more notable in regard to males, since a substantial number of women (40 percent) began as "administrators" (including all of the school librarians and many who were heads of small special libraries).

The two areas with the greatest change in "type-of-work" function were public services (those pertaining to the interface between librarian and patron) and technical services (those relating to the acquisition and organization of materials). When investigation was limited to these areas, it was feasible to consider the extent of change in each career. From the standpoint of individual behavior, over two-thirds of those in the Study Group were functionally mobile in regard to type of work. Only 8 percent (15) worked exclusively in public-service positions, and only 5 percent (10) exclusively in technical-service positions. Thirty-four (18 percent), serving generally as administrators of small libraries, reported no specific public- or technical-service assignments.

In testing the association between external mobility and functional change, emphasis was placed on exclusivity. In other words, respondents who worked exclusively in one type of library throughout the career period were regarded as having "stable" professional experience, while those who switched from one type to another had "varied" experience. Likewise, the librarian who worked in both public- and technical-service positions was considered as having "varied" experience, while the experience of all others was designated "stable." In making a distinction between "stable" and "varied" experience by type of library, library-related work was disregarded. The bulk of the work not in libraries consisted of library-school teaching and full-time study, which could usually be assumed to be related to work done as a library practitioner. The immobile librarians were also omitted, in order not to overweight the "stable" category. Using the dichotomization stable/varied, it was demonstrated that librarians in the Study Group who had varied work experiences were more mobile than those who remained in one type of library or line of work. In both cases, the association between external mobility and functional mobility was statistically significant.

VERTICAL MOBILITY AND CAREER PATTERN

Vertical mobility refers to change in status, usually upward, within the overall library hierarchy in relation to either external or internal movement. The term career pattern refers to a depiction of successive moves in professional employment. It is not restricted here to depicting an orderly upward progression but is used to describe any work sequence of these librarians, whether upward, downward, or lateral, orderly or haphazard. In a restricted sense, "A career, viewed structurally, is a succession of related jobs, arranged in a hierarchy of prestige, through which persons move in an ordered, predictable sequence" (Wilensky, 1964a, p. 314). While it was not possible to examine career sequences in detail or to test how well they met this criterion, sufficient attention was given to this aspect to warrant the observation that the career paths of few of these librarians followed "an ordered, predictable sequence." Viewed as a whole, much of the movement over the 14-year period appeared haphazard. Shifts were frequently made from one type of library to another and from one kind of work to another. Yet considered from the standpoint of vertical mobility, there can be no doubt that the general trend of movement was upward. Career advancement for the Study Group as a whole was demonstrated by comparison of positions held in 1955 and 1969 according to administrative level and library size. By 1969, the number holding positions as head librarian increased substantially—though most of these were in libraries staffed by fewer than 10 professionals. Greatest gain was seen in the number serving in administrative posts at the middle management level, as head of sections, divisions, branches, and departmental libraries.

Although advancement occurred in the careers of most respondents, it would be difficult to establish valid measures of vertical mobility on the basis of the data, not only because of the lack of precision in reported job descriptions but because of the need to reconcile, or equate, position levels in libraries of varying types and sizes. It was observed that some upward movement was as common to the immobile as to the mobile. For example, one male librarian now heads the library in which he began work as a page. For women, the greatest advances were made by those who remained with the armed-forces library services. Yet the general impression is that those who moved readily made greater advances than those who have been less mobile. If library size is used a criterion, postulating that larger libraries offer greater opportunities for advancement, findings support this impression. A significantly greater proportion of those working in 1969 in libraries employing 50 or more professionals had moved at least twice, even though there was, on the whole, a slight drift from larger systems to smaller institutions.

Other elements characterizing the final position in the career sequence might have been used as evidence of achievement in the profession over the 14-year period. However, since salary scales are subject to regional and other differences and some upper-echelon positions in librarianship are nonsupervisory, data covering these elements could not, within the limited scope of the study, be used to establish definitive measures. Nevertheless, examination of supervisory role and salary pertaining to the final (1969) position of Study Group members was useful in the overall determination of the relationship between mobility and professional involvement.

There is an assumption that in librarianship the professional quickly moves into an administrative post, supervising the work of others. While the investigation supports this assumption, it was found that the bulk of the supervisory effort was in directing the work of nonprofessionals. In the fourteenth career year, 90 percent of the Study Group members were supervising some personnel, with over half directing the work of at least five staff members. However, more than half of the 60 percent who supervised other professionals exercised control over fewer than five.

Men operated in a supervisory capacity more frequently than women and exercised greater control over the work of other professionals. The largest span of professional supervision, however, was that of women connected with armed-forces library services, with three women each reporting supervision of over 100 librarians.

For the Study Group as a whole, external mobility and supervisory role were related. Librarians with low mobility were not as likely as their more mobile colleagues to supervise professionals and those who were highly mobile were more likely than others to be directing the work of five or more professionals. When each sex was treated independently, it was found that a significantly greater number of women with EMR of 2 or more occupied positions supervising professionals. For males, findings were not as conclusive, but the data do suggest that men who moved three or more times were more likely to be supervising professionals, and that highly mobile males were more likely to direct the work of five or more professionals.

Information on salary of Study Group members pinpoints, perhaps more than any other element, the time frame of the investigation. The mean salary, $12,500, was consistent with figures reported in the 1970-71 salary survey for ALA members with 14-15 years' of experience (Manchak, 1971). Since, as was expected, considerable difference was observed in salaries for men and women, salary data were tabulated by sex. The average salary for women was $11,200, and for men, $14,200. No women were in the highest salary bracket ($20,000+), and no men were in the lowest range ($5,000-$7,000). However, since four of the six male respondents receiving the highest salaries held doctorates, it is conceivable that the salary differential was, in part at least, attributable to differences in educational achievement.

When EMR and salary were compared for each sex, it was found that the association between salary and external mobility was significant only in the case of the female librarians. The immobile woman was likely to be earning less than $10,000. Although, for this group, there appeared to be no association between external mobility of males and salary, there was an association between the salary received by the male and geographic mobility. Geographically immobile males tended to have lower salaries than males who made at least one move to another state.

EXTRAJOB CHARACTERISTICS

Employment histories reveal only partially the lives of these librarians as practicing professionals. To round out the depiction of career lifestyle for the Study Group, it was necessary to consider the extent to which its members had engaged in extrajob activities. The basic purpose here was to provide a foundation for identification of elements relating to professional involvement, with emphasis on activity closely related to librarianship. For purposes of comparison, attention was at times directed toward nonlibrary activity, though investigation of the full scope of individual interests—recreational, social, and familial—was, of course, beyond the scope of the study.

The extrajob characteristic most commonly exhibited by these librarians was membership in professional associations. All but six percent of the respondents belonged to one or more library associations; 74 percent belonged to at least two, and 8 percent held memberships in five or more library groups. The average number of memberships for the group as a whole was 2.5.

In part, the prevalence of library-association memberships is related to the multiplicity and diversity of existing "library" associations. It is not uncommon for a librarian to belong to associations that are national in scope and to regional, state, and local groups as well. The general associations (at every level) are open to the profession at large, but there are, also, at all geographic levels, organized groups devoted to special interests, such as "medical libraries" or "technical services."

For the Study Group, membership was strongest at the national level and least popular at the local level. Over 80 percent of the respondents belonged to at least one national association, 70 percent belonged to the American Library Association, and 29 percent, to other national associations, with 19 percent holding memberships in both ALA and one or more other national organizations. Seventy-five percent belonged to associations at the state and/or regional level. Only 36 percent held memberships in local library groups. At each level, the proportion of females holding memberships was greater than that of males,[6] but the difference was significant only at the national level.

While nearly all of the women and 90 percent of the men were dues-paying members of library associations, only a little over half of the respondents had held office or committee chairs in any of the professional groups to which they belonged. Sixty percent had been members of committees, and 75 percent indicated that they usually attended meetings. The proportion of active participation was seen to increase as the geographic span lessened. When only those claiming memberships at each level were considered, fewer than one-fourth of the national members held office or chairs, while over half of the local members had done so. For the group as a whole, greatest activity occurred at the state/regional level. A little over a third of all respondents had held office at this level, almost two-fifths reported some committee service, and over three-fourths usually attended state/regional meetings.

Membership in nonlibrary associations was almost as popular as membership in library groups. Eighty-three percent of the respondents indicated membership in one or more nonlibrary associations. One male and one female listed memberships in 14 different groups.[7] The average number of nonlibrary memberships for males was 2.4, and for women, 3.4. The proportion of women holding nonlibrary memberships was significantly greater than that of men. The nonlibrary organizations listed by respondents were extremely varied, ranging from international scholarly societies and national professional groups to local garden clubs, bird-watching groups, and church choirs. Professional or scholarly associations predominated for both sexes.

In many cases, there was an obvious relationship to the librarian's work; school librarians, for example, usually belonged to the National Education Association or some other teacher's group, while academic librarians were frequently members of the American Association of University Professors. Several public librarians noted that their affiliation with such local groups as the Chamber of Commerce or the League of Women Voters was job-related. However, no attempt was made to categorize nonlibrary memberships as to work-relatedness, since in many instances the categorization would be conjectural.

The extent of participation in nonlibrary professional or scholarly organizations was much less than in library associations, but some 30 percent of those in other professional groups did not report active participation in such groups. Among library-association members, only 13 percent of the women were inactive. For men, there was an even greater discrepancy in regard to active participation in professional and scholarly associations; 35 percent of those affiliated with such nonlibrary groups were inactive, compared to 14 percent of the males who were members of library associations. Men also joined library groups more readily than other professional or scholarly associations.

In contrast, female respondents were seen to be more active in the nonprofessional groups they joined than in library associations, while the male respondents, already noted as being more active in library associations than their female colleagues, were somewhat less active in nonprofessional organizations. Even though respondents infrequently noted that there was some connection between their professional work and some nonlibrary memberships, by and large, such nonprofessional associations represent outlets of nonwork-related interests—civic affairs, community- and family-service groups, church-related activities, and social and recreational clubs. Thus, these can be considered as not competitive with the work-related library associations.

Other extrajob activities, identified as components of professional development in librarianship, include part-time work, part-time study, research, and publication and other writing activity. These were scrutinized in relation to the career period and also from the standpoint of "current" activity (i.e., in the last twelve months preceding the survey).

Almost half of the Study Group indicated that at some time during the professional career period they had held part-time jobs or assignments supplementary to their primary employment. The librarian holding a nine-month appointment sought temporary employment during the summer months, and some others found it necessary or desirable to undertake part-time assignments concurrent with regular, full-time work. Almost all extra work was library-related, though a few respondents did work in other fields.

In the early days of the career, supplementary work usually consisted of employment in another library, frequently in another type of library but seldom in another type of work. For example, it was customary for an academic librarian to moonlight in a local public or special library, but a technical-service librarian rarely undertook part-time public-service work, and vice versa. Some respondents reported supplementary assignments as consultants or as library-school teachers. These assignments were seen to occur with greater frequency at later stages in the career, presumably as the librarian developed expertise and became known as an authority (albeit within a limited area). In all, 36 percent of the Study Group held such "prestigious" part-time assignments during the career period. A larger proportion of men than women held prestigious part-time assignments, but the difference was not statistically significant.

Data in regard to volunteer work supplement those on part-time work, in providing an overall picture of the life style of the librarian. Women were found to be more involved in volunteer service than men, and women's volunteer activities were more diverse than those of men. Nonlibrary volunteer service was considerably more popular than voluntary library-related work. Possibly those volunteering their services were seeking an escape from the work situation, but it is equally possible that such voluntary work was considered a function of community responsibility. The nonlibrary volunteer service mentioned most frequently by women was fund raising; Sunday-school teaching and other church-related activities came second; political campaigning, hospital-aide work, and social-service work were also mentioned by women. For men, volunteer service was largely limited to church-related activity or to scouting and similar work with boys. Library-related volunteer work was generally in church libraries, with a few women reporting volunteer work in libraries of hospitals or similar institutions. A small number of respondents reported current service as library-board members. Six women and 14 men were on boards of other community agencies—churches, social-service agencies, and the like.

The pursuit of learning is a frequent concomitant of librarianship. Only about a third of the Study Group failed to report some form of study during the career period. Women were more prone than men to engage in part-time study, but women frequently enrolled in individual courses rather than degree programs and, more frequently than men, undertook study that appeared to have no direct relationship to their work. A larger proportion of women than men (49 percent and 27 percent respectively) participated in less formal study.

It was impossible to make a meaningful distinction between work-related and other part-time study. Most part-time study during the career period was related to librarianship, and undoubtedly much of the nonlibrary study should be considered work-related. It would be appropriate, for example, for a fine-arts librarian to study foreign languages. In reporting current activity, respondents were asked to identify work-related and other study. In the 12 months preceding the survey, 13 percent had undertaken study that was not considered work-related. Three times as many said they had engaged in work-related study.

Few of the librarians in the Study Group were involved in research activity during the career period. Examination of job histories and study data revealed that only seven women and nine men had done any kind of research work, and most of this was in connection with doctoral study. Three respondents reported involvement in library research projects. Other "research" was noted as bibliographical in nature or related to the gathering of information for use by authors. A number of respondents (13 percent of the women and 21 percent of the men) reported that they were involved in "research" during the year preceding the survey. Owing to the ambiguity of the term research, it was impossible to assess the nature of the involvement. In any event, it is evident that the Study Group as a whole had little interest in research.

Slightly more than half of the group (53 percent) had some material published during the career period. Somewhat less than half produced unpublished papers and speeches. More than a third (39 percent) did not report any writing activity during the period 1955-69. The article was the form of publication most frequently noted (38 percent), followed closely by such minor productions as reviews and letters to the editor. Fifteen percent authored books, and 17 percent did editorial work. While most writing was related to the profession, more than 10 percent of the respondents produced materials relating to other fields, or materials of a general nature, including some fiction and poetry.

Although little difference was seen in the proportion of men to women, with published books or articles, a much greater proportion of men reported minor publications. Data in regard to current activity indicated that men were more active than women in writing for publication. The proportion of men reporting time spent in the last year in such activity was significantly greater than that of the women. In respect to time spent currently in preparing and giving talks, women outnumbered men, but the difference was not statistically significant.

MOBILITY AND PROFESSIONAL INVOLVEMENT

In assessing the relationship between external mobility and professional involvement, "professional involvement" was not viewed as a single, unique measure but was understood to consist of a complex of elements or indications of professionalism. Certain extrajob characteristics, together with two work-related ones (salary and supervisory capacity), were selected for analysis as indicators of professionalism, because they reflect professional attitudes and interests in one or more of the following ways:

1. as indications of commitment to development of the profession;
2. as indications of self-development within the profession;
3. as indications of prestige or status in the profession.

Specific elements considered to be positive indications of professionalism as identified in the survey data,[8] are listed below:

1. Membership in library associations, especially at the national level;
2. Participation in library associations (holding office or commitee chairmanship; serving on committees; attendance at meetings);
3. Production of works relating to librarianship (books and articles; editorial

work; minor items such as reviews, letters to the editor; unpublished materials);
4. Prestigious part-time work (consultation and evaluation; library-school teaching);
5. Part-time study, especially in degree programs;
6. Salary;
7. Supervision of professionals.

In contrast, other elements tending to reflect local interest and manifestation of nonprofessional activity were considered as negative indications of professionalism. These include volunteer work and affiliation with nonlibrary associations (chiefly at the local level.)[9]

The data collected on extrajob activities are largely concerned with "actions" of Study Group members, based on the observation that the respondent did or did not participate in an activity. No criteria can be stated for determining that a particular "action" is a precise measure of professional or nonprofessional behavior, but it can be postulated that the nature of an "action" implies a greater or lesser degree of professional interest and commitment and therefore provides a relative measure of professionalism. For example, involvement in library-related associations, in contrast to involvement in nonlibrary groups, would seem to imply greater interest in the library profession. Furthermore, participation in national library assocations can be assumed to indicate a higher level of professional interest and commitment (and prestige) than participation in local library groups. Similarly, formal academic study, particularly in a degree program, can be considered to indicate a higher level of interest in self-development within the profesion than participation in less formal modes of study (i.e., nonacademic study in workshops, institutes, in-service training, and the like). Admittedly, the distinction between "academic" and "workshop" study is not precise; in some instances academic credit can be obtained for workshop participation. The awarding of credit was not, however, customary in the period covered by the study.

Although the qualitative and quantitative measurement would have added to the validity of the investigation, it was not feasible in this limited, exploratory investigation. Except for the kind of broad qualification discussed earlier, no attempt was made to weight the quality of an individual's involvement. For example, no one national library association was considered more prestigious than another. Also, with few exceptions, no distinction was made on the basis of quantity. In most cases, examination of an element was based on dichotomization between action and nonaction. The element most affected by this treatment was that of publication: an individual was considered "active", whether credited with a single publication or many. Distinction was made according to the nature of published materials, by separate categorization of books and articles,[10] editorial work, and minor items such as reviews and letters.

The determination as to whether or not the mobility of librarians is indicative of professionalism is expressed in the following hypothesis: There is a relationship between rate of external mobility and professional involvement, with least involvement being associated with the extremes of mobility—the immobile and the highly mobile. Statistical testing of the hypothesis revealed that, while the immobile were indeed less involved in professional activities than the mobile, librarians designated as highly mobile proved to be more active than all others. Therefore, the hypothesis as stated cannot be accepted. On the other hand, test results provide sufficient evidence to warrant the statement that external mobility and professional involvement are associated. Corroborating evidence was found in all but one[11] of the areas of positive and negative indications.

Greater mobility was found to be directly associated with membership and participation in library associations at the national level, with production of materials relating to librarianship, with part-time study, particularly in degree programs, and with salary and supervision. Greater mobility was inversely associated with elements that are expressive of local concern: local library-association activity, membership in nonlibrary groups, and volunteer work. Taken as a whole, these findings support the conclusion that greater mobility reflects a higher level of prestige and self-development within the profession and a subordination of local concerns to professional commitment.

Significant findings relative to external mobility and professional involvement of females and males indicated that although there was an association between mobility and involvement for each sex, the pattern of association differed. Among women, there was a noticeable contrast in professional activity of those with low mobility and those with moderate to high mobility. Females with lower mobility were less active professionally and least likely to achieve status in the profession in terms of salary and supervisory duties. For men, there was a divergence in behavior of both the highly mobile and those with low mobility. The professional commitment of males with lower mobility appeared weak; the highly mobile males seemed disinterested in local concerns and more committed to the profession at large than all other males.

Almost half of all immobile females librarians were "unattached" women, either single or SDW. Although some of these, particularly the SDW, may have had familial ties that inhibited movement, it seems clear from the data that professional commitment and/or career aspirations of these women was low.

Marital status patterns of immobile and highly mobile male librarians varied slightly: More of the married men were immobile (26 percent, as compared to 18 percent who were highly mobile); more single men were highly mobile (30 percent, as compared to 22 percent who were immobile). These data hint that for the married male, family responsibility may inhibit change in employment, perhaps fostering the development of local attachments to the detriment of professional interests.

Although no attempt was made to test relationships between age and professional-involvement indications, it can be speculated that the inactivity of immobile women was due, at least in part, to their greater age. Difference in age, seemingly, was not a factor in the lesser activity of immobile males.

IMPLICATIONS

A case has been made for recognition of external mobility as an indication of professionalism in librarianship, on the grounds that greater external mobility is associated with increased professional involvement. Statistical validation of the association does not, however, explain the casual relationship. Does mobility result from involvement? Or does mobility stimulate professional action?

Mobility has both an active and passive mode. The passive mode reflects a willingness to move, should the opportunity arise, while the active mode indicates a desire to move. The active mode is, in large measure, equated with strong career aspirations, since, given the organizational structure of librarianship, the professional librarian may see little chance of advancement within an organization. The library field is composed of numerous autonomous units, few of which are large organizations, and even in relatively large library systems, openings at the upper level are scarce. To be sure, in some instances the desire to move is motivated by dissatisfaction with the present environment. Conversely, present satisfaction inhibits mobility under the passive mode, since any opportunity to move must be weighed against the values attached to the existing situation.

In view of the haphazard structure of library placement mechanisms at the time of the study (and, unfortunately, today as well), the librarian who wished to move had to be aggressive in seeking out appropriate positions. Furthermore, under the collegial system that characterized much of the library marketplace in those days, especially at the upper levels, job opportunities were more available to the librarian who became "known." The more career-minded librarians, then joined associations, attended meetings, sought to get into print, and engaged in other professional pursuits as a means of self-promotion. It follows that those whose involvement stemmed from professional commitment rather than a desire for self-advancement also became more visible in the marketplace and probably were presented with more job opportunities. Thus it can be said that in the active mode, mobility leads to involvement, while in the passive mode, mobility may be induced by involvement.

In sociological studies of librarianship (and other semiprofessional occupations), it is generally asserted or implied that a predominance of women in the field results in a low level of professional commitment. The lack of professionalism is usually attributed to the higher career aspirations of men and to the greater constraints on and inhibitions of women. While the present study does not refute this assertion, the findings do suggest that the indictment against female librarians may be too severe. The data indicated that librarians whose professional commitment is strong are less apt to be constrained by local and personal relationships or to develop attachments to a particular institution or locality. Hughes's (1958) delineation of the itinerant is compatible with this view (pp. 135-6). The applicability of this description to the highly mobile male librarians in the Study Group is inescapable, and undoubtedly reflects the strong career goals of some males. On the other hand, the less mobile females and males are aptly depicted by Hughes's term *homeguard*.

The immobile, less active women were generally older, late entrants in the profession. It is reasonable to expect that, for this group, local and personal attachments would be of greater importance than professional commitment. But what of the less mobile, less active males? Is it possible that some males view library employment as a sinecure? If so, the immobile male may be as great a deterrent to professionalization as the immobile female, if not a greater one.

It is probable that the seeming complacency of the immobile male was, in part, related to differentiation between the sexes in employment practices in librarianship. Although the less mobile woman was least likely to achieve a position of status in the profession, status of the male was not affected by external mobility. Apparently, preferred employment was available to the male even when he did not move. Undeniably, some male librarians have higher career aspirations and are more mobile and more active than the "typical" female, but this study shows that, except for a core of older women, female librarians were also both mobile and involved. The inference can be drawn that differentiation in employment of men and women because of the seemingly lower career aspirations ascribed to all women is unwarranted. Simpson and Simpson (1969) speak to this point as a "vicious circle," noting that "discrimination against women and the sometimes valid basis for it reinforce each other. Their competing family roles and the expectation that they will be discriminated against reduce women's performance and aspirations. They are then discriminated against partly because they are thought to lack ambition" (p. 230).

On the other hand, findings of the investigation indicate that at least some of the apparent discrimination against women, particularly in regard to salary, stems from the action (or inaction) of women. In the first place, a possible association exists between educational level and salary. While no women in the Study Group held doctorates, most men earning the highest salaries had doctoral degrees. More importantly, there is a definite relationship between low salary and immobility of women. Over half of the immobile females earned less than $10,000 a year; 19 percent received less than $7500 a year. Since a substantial majority of these immobile women were not married, the low salary would not, as a rule, represent a secondary source of family income. While it may be that the males were seldom asked to work for low salaries, the likelihood is that the male librarians insisted on reasonable remuneration. Some women, on the other hand, for one reason or another, seemed willing to accept a low rate of pay even after 14 years of professional experience. Unless more women, especially the older, late entrants, become adamant in demanding respectable salaries, the average salary of women librarians will continue to be low.

NOTES

1. For the most part, master's theses and the like.
2. Three categories of persons who otherwise met the selection criteria were excluded: Canadians; members of religious orders (whose movement might be assumed to be involuntary); and those already holding first professional (bachelor's) degree in library science.
3. The "leave" designation was generally specified by the respondent. In a few instances, it was assumed that a "leave" was implied by the nature of the intervening employment (e.g., work overseas or as a visiting teacher in a library school).
4. The designations "high mobility" and "highly mobile" refer to the upper range of mobility that could be tested with validity (by chi-square) with the data on hand. It should be noted that use of these terms to describe the mobility exhibited by the Study Group does not imply their general applicability to librarianship.
5. The point must be stressed that the Study Group did not include married women who left the profession for three or more years. Furthermore, marital status is not a stable variable; no attempt could be made to determine at what point (or points) in the employment history change in marital status took place.
6. Except international and foreign. The few cases here, however, did not warrant generalization.
7. Only one woman and five men claimed membership in no associations whatsoever. Three others (two women and one man) reported only alumni associations and collegiate or honorary fraternities.

8. One element, research, had to be omitted from the analysis, since data were not sufficient to permit valid testing.
9. A third negative indicator, production of nonlibrary publications, could not be tested, because of the small number of observations.
10. Limited data precluded testing of these two forms separately.
11. Prestigious part-time work.

Geographic Mobility and Career Advancement of Male and Female Librarians

JUDITH SCHIEK ROBINSON

SINCE THE LATE 1960s there has been increasing concern about the status of women in librarianship. Although women librarians outnumber men four to one, they are poorly represented in administrative positions and consistently lag behind men in earnings. Documentation of this salary and position gap between men and women has been plentiful; yet the reasons for this phenomena have remained evasive. One factor that has frequently been blamed for this discrepancy is women's lack of mobility.

Men have been perceived as more mobile, using frequent job changes to advance their careers. Women, on the other hand, have been presumed to be largely immobile. Seen as tied down by family responsibilities, they were thought to remain longer in the same libraries, limiting their opportunities for career growth. Existing research on librarians' mobility has tended to support these assumptions, although mobility has rarely been the sole focus of any of these corroborative studies.

There is indeed a wealth of evidence that job mobility can influence career growth. In a 1973 U.S. Department of Labor longitudinal study, for example, those respondents who had changed jobs fared better than nonmovers in terms of salary and job satisfaction. Research has also indicated that MBA's who are frequent job changers have a greater tendency to move into administrative positions than those who remain in their initial jobs (De Pasquale and Lange, 1971, p. 10). Cammack's research indicated that university faculty members who changed jobs were more rapidly promoted and enjoyed higher salaries than those who did not move (Blackburn and Aurand, 1972, p. 12). Similarly, a study of special librarians revealed that both those who had moved to accept their jobs and those who claimed the flexibility to move in the future received higher salaries than those who did not or could not move geographically ("A Study of 1967 Annual Salaries", 1967, p. 246). As a matter of fact, the study described in this chapter also corroborated the popular assumption that career advancement accompanies mobility, by indicating that mobile librarians enjoy higher salaries and positions than their immobile counterparts.

In this study, the mobility and career advancement of both male and female academic librarians in nine southern states were investigated, to determine the impact of mobility on the women's careers, as related to similar data for men (Braunagel [Robinson], 1975). The major research question posed was: can mobility patterns account for the differences in career advancement between men and women librarians? Research results indicated that the answer to this question was a resounding "no". While the results of this study reinforced the position that mobile librarians reap greater career gains than immobile librarians, no significant differences in career-long mobility rates were found between the two sexes. In other words, women were shown to have been as mobile as men throughout their careers.

Instead, the significant differences found between men and women related to their reasons for changing jobs, their expectations of future moves, and interruptions in their careers. However, further analysis revealed that these factors could not explain the extent of disparity between the sexes. Even when men and women with similar mobility patterns were compared, men came out on top in terms of salary and position.

DIMENSIONS OF MOBILITY

Research on labor mobility has tended to focus upon three categories of movement: (1) aptitudes and skills necessary to move into specific jobs, (2) propensity to move, and (3) actual movement (Parnes, 1954, p. 11). The first of these categories, aptitudes and skills required for certain types of jobs, was not analyzed in this study. The second two categories, propensity to move and actual movement, were used as a framework for this analysis, and are discussed in this section.

The quality often described as "propensity to move" deals not with actual past movement, but with an individual's perception of the flexibility to move in the future. An individual's propensity to move involves willingness, ability, or expectations of leaving a present job for another if a favorable opportunity were to arise. A person's claim of future propensity to move may not always be reflected in his or her actual mobility history. Nor can propensity to move always be accurately inferred from data on actual movement. If alternative job opportunities are limited or absent, propensity toward mobility may be high, without any actual movement. As a matter of fact, contradictions between a person's perceived propensity to move in the future and actual mobility history may reveal conflicts affecting a person's work patterns in general.

In a second approach to analyzing mobility, data on actual job shifts are collected. Individuals are asked to report job changes they have actually made in the past. Most empirical data on mobility have been gathered using this approach. Actual mobility can involve several dimensions:

1. Interlibrary movement, from one library employer to another.
2. Geographic movement, from one town or city to another.
3. Movement from an unemployed to an employed status.
4. Movement from an employed to an unemployed status.
5. Movement into and out of the labor force (Parnes, 1954, p. 1).

Since these are not mutually exclusive categories, several kinds of mobility may be involved in a single job change.

In this study, mobility has been analyzed as both actual job movement and as stated propensity to move. Actual movement has been defined as a job shift that involved a change in employing library. Assessment of actual job changes provided a measure of the average frequency of moves throughout each individual's career while propensity to change jobs provided perspective on respondents' attitudes toward future job shifts.

REVIEW OF RELATED RESEARCH

Introduction

This review focuses upon previous research related to both mobility and work patterns in general. Since one dimension of mobility is movement into and out of the labor force, work patterns such as career interruptions can be studied as components of mobility. Factors such as job satisfaction can also be considered, since this can be an influence in job-change decisions.

In this discussion, related research has been grouped into five categories. The first category concerns the mobility and career patterns of women, and includes research on women workers in all segments of the labor force, as well as data on the relationship between marital and family responsibilities and work patterns. Next, research concerned with variables involved in a worker's decison to move or remain in a job is discussed. The third section is concerned with mobility research in professions other than librarianship, and the fourth summarizes some basic trends that emerge in the diverse data that have been accumulated on mobility. The final section deals with mobility research directly related to librarians.

Mobility and Career Patterns of Women

Difficulties do exist in the attempt to combine family and work. And though the presence of such complications does not invalidate the contention that women should be seriously involved in work, it does impose the necessity of recognizing these problems for what they are, if they are to be dealt with intelligently (Bailyn, 1964, p. 701).

Bailyn refers to the complexity of the situation facing many women who attempt to combine the roles of wife, mother, and career woman. The fact that most married women have careers as homemakers in addition to their careers in the work force means that their career decisions are likely to reflect more complex sets of variables than those of men or unmarried women. In the past, mobility and career patterns have been examined in relation to numerous variables, including marital and family responsibilities and differences in sex. Several studies have investigated effects of marital and family status on women in the general work force and in librarianship. Differences in mobility and career patterns have been found between men and women, as well as between married and unmarried women, and between women with varying family responsibilites.

Garfinkle (Kievit, 1972, p. 22) found that a woman's pattern of work is less continuous than that of most men. Women tend to enter the work force for a few years after completing their education, leave work to raise a family and return to work when their children have reached school age or have left home. Garfinkle's study indicated that the largest portion of a woman's work life occurs after her children are grown.

The impact of family responsibilities on a woman's career and mobility may be complex, however, since Garfinkle also found that women in professions had smaller families and longer work-life expectancies than other women. Ross's (1964) investigations concerning timing and spacing of births also indicated possible variations from the norm by professional women. Her data showed that more-highly-educated women have a shorter interval between the births of their first and last children, are more likely to work after childbearing, and return to work sooner after their last births. Therefore, the professional woman who leaves work to bear children may reenter the labor market more quickly than other women, in addition to showing a strong tendency to return to work in the first place.

Women between 18 and 64 were surveyed by the Bureau of the Census in 1964, to detemine why women start and stop working. The most frequently mentioned reasons were family obligations and pregnancy. Women between 35 and 44 and those with children between 6 and 17 listed ill health and family obligations most frequently. Ill health was the reason most often mentioned by women over 45. Most of the women who had actually left the labor force in 1963 and had not returned by the time of the study were married. The reasons given for leaving work by those women who had actually stopped working verified the hypothetical circumstances that employed women had stated would cause them to stop working: women under 35 had most frequently ceased working because of pregnancy; those between 35 and 64 because of illness.

Both Mattila (1974) and Harrison (1964) corroborated the Bureau of the Census data on the reasons women leave employment. Mattila (1974) showed differences in the reasons men and women leave jobs (p. 3). He found that women are more likely than men to leave employment for nonwork reasons, while men are more inclined to leave for better jobs. Harrison's (1964) data were based on studies of the federal work force, where only a small proportion of women workers have middle- or upper-level managerial or professional positions—most hold lower-level, white-collar jobs. Harrison found that about one-half of the women who left their jobs did so because of marital or family responsibilities. The other 50 percent left either for job-related reasons or because of health and retirement. Men in the federal work force were more likely than women to leave jobs for increases in salary.

Family variables were again shown to have a relationship to women's career patterns in the Special Libraries Survey ("A Study of 1967 Annual Salaries," 1967). In this case, the women for whom data were gathered were members of a sample of special librarians, and one of the several career variables analyzed was their mobility. The data collected showed that 47.2 percent of the married men had moved to accept their current jobs, compared to 24.5 percent of the married women. Married men also indicated greater propensity toward mobility than married women, with 68.6 percent of the married men claiming ability to move, compared to 14.5 percent of the marrried women. Disregarding sex, the percent of married librarians and the percent of those single, widowed, or divorced who had moved to take their current jobs was almost identical: 34.6 percent and 32.6 percent. The unmarried respondents of both sexes claimed greater propensity to move than the married respondents: 59.8 percent, compared to 38.6 percent.

These data showed that marital status alone was not a reliable indicator of actual mobility, the sex of the married individual being a much more important indicator. Close to twice the number of married men had moved to accept their jobs than married women. The differences in propensity to move between married men and women were even greater. The survey questionnaire did not attempt to ascertain the reason behind the differences in mobility between married men and women, because this was not an objective of this particular study. Other studies of men and women in the work force, however, indicate that differences in family obligations between married men and women may be responsible for such differences in mobility.

Schiller also found differences in family commitments related to career patterns between married male and married female librarians employed in academic libraries. She found that 28 percent of the women and 17 percent of the men had left library work for six months or more. The reason for absence given by 53 percent of the women was marriage and family commitments, while less than 1 percent of the men cited this as the cause. The other major reason given for temporary absence from the field was to obtain additional education, cited by 44 percent of the men but only 28 percent of the women.

Mobility was one of the variables examined in a five-year study concerning the labor-market behavior of women between the ages of 30 and 44, conducted by the U.S. Department of Labor (*Dual Careers*, 1970). The first report of the study revealed that married women have lower labor-force participation than divorced, separated, widowed, or single women, even when the presence of children is controlled, and that women with no children under age 18 are more likely to be part of the labor force than those with children at home.

Sweet (1970) also found that the ages and number of her children influence a woman's work pattern. Using 1960 U.S. Census data, he investigated the employment patterns of married women in relation to the ages and numbers of their children. Investigating the proportion of mothers working as related to age of youngest child, Sweet found work participation increased continuously as the age of the child advanced from infant to early teens. The number of children under 18 was also a factor. Of those women with no children under 18, 43 percent were working. The percentage of women working was negatively correlated with their number of children under 18: 33 percent of the women with one child under 18 worked; 20 percent of those with three children under 18 worked. Sweet concluded that "women with more children are less likely to work than women with fewer children" (p. 198).

Sobol's (1973) conclusions were similar when she interviewed married women of childbearing age during a 10-year longitudinal study. She identified expected family size as one of the two most important influences on a wife's labor-force participation. Her findings indicated that the larger a woman's expected family size, the less likely she was to work.

Career interruptions were also examined by Linn (1971) and Simon, Clark, and Galway (1967) in their studies of highly educated married women. Their findings substantiate Garfinkle's data (Kievit, 1972) which showed married women to have discontinuous career patterns, greatly influenced by marriage and family commitments. Assessment of the impact of such trends upon female academic librarians is complicated, however, since only about 40 percent of female academic librarians are married (Schiller, 1969a, p. 24). In addition, Schiller found that three-fifths of those women were widowed, separated, or divorced (comprising 14 percent of all female academic librarians) had children, many of whom were under age 18 (p. 26). While the U.S. Department of Labor study showed that women with no children tended to be the most firmly attached to the labor force and to have the greatest job seniority, it is not clear whether women who are heads of one-parent families show career and mobility patterns similar to those of unmarried women, to men , or to married women.

Educational attainment has also been shown to affect a woman's labor-force participation (Sobol, 1973; *Dual Careers*, 1973; Spencer and Featherstone, 1970). Investigations concerning single women in the work force have indicated that the career patterns of women who have never married differ from those of other women. In his study of male-female differences in aspects of labor market behavior, Fuchs (1971) found that while the average woman earns 60 percent as much as a man, women who have never been married have an age-to-earning profile very similar to that of men (p. 10). The U.S. Department of Labor study (*Dual Careers*, 1970) of women between 30 and 44 years of age also showed that women who had never married had the highest mean rates of pay among thse studied (p. 115). Similarly, in her analysis of 1960 census data, Havens (1973) found that unmarried women earned more than those who were married.

Ferber and Loeb (1973) studied faculty members and concluded that higher salary and rank were slightly but significantly more likely to be given to single than to married women. Simon, Clark, and Galway (1967) also found that unmarried women Ph.D's were much more likely to have achieved professorial rank than were married women, who tended to stay at the instructor level.

Higher salaries earned by single women may relate to the fact that they tend to experience fewer career disruptions than married women. Suter and Miller (1973) have hypothesized that the total number of working years explain a large part of the difference in median income between single and married women. They found that married women with children earned about 75 percent as much as single women. Among women with a lifetime of work experience, however, the married women with children had salaries that averaged 94 percent of single women's salaries. Thus, married women earned almost the same amount as single women with similar work experience and education.

Linn (1971) found that women dentists who had never married were less likely to interrupt their careers than married women. Simon, Clark, and Galway (1967) made a similar discovery concerning female Ph.D.'s in the sciences, social sciences, humanities, and education. A Canadian study (Spencer and Featherstone, 1970) of working women gave further support to the more consistent work pattern of single women.

It showed work-force participation rates to be higher for single women than for widowed or divorced women, and lowest for married women.

The study of Special Libraries Association members ("A Study of 1967 Annual Salaries," 1967) found that, while more of the unmarried women had moved to take their present positions than had married women (31.3 percent, compared to 24.9 percent), the mobility of unmarried women was more similar to that of married women than to that of men. No differentiation was made between women who had never married and those who were widowed, separated, and divorced, which may be an important distinction, since some investigators have found distinct differences between these two groups. Hamel (1963) investigated job tenure as one aspect of mobility in the general work force and found single women over age 25 had longer job tenure than married women, while among widowed, divorced, or separated women, job tenure was similar to that for married rather than single women (p. 1146).

In terms of propensity toward mobility, the Special Libraries Association study ("A Study of 1967 Annual Salaries," 1967) revealed little difference between married and unmarried men in terms of ability to move, while unmarried women claimed considerably more ability to move than married women. Again, no differentiation was made between single and widowed, divorced, or separated individuals.

A review of the literature concerned with career patterns and job mobility of women in relation to marital and family variables provides no simple generalizations about women in academic libraries. While, in general, women tend to have intermittent career patterns, variables such as marital status, number of children and their ages, educational attainment, and occuption combine to make prediction difficult.

The Decision to Move

Research on the mobility of workers has included investigations of variables involved in decisions to remain in a job or to change jobs. The literature reviewed in this section has attempted to identify factors, both inside and outside the work environment, that influence workers toward patterns of mobility or immobility.

Job mobility can be viewed as a function of both occasion and of choice. The concept of occasion involves those factors that are outside workers' control and determine their potential for a job change. There are two types of occasions: opportunities (a job offer from another institution, for example), and necessities (such as the termination of an individual's job). Choice, a second, functional element of mobility, involves an individual's decision to change or not to change jobs, given the occasion to do so (U.S. Dept. of Health, Education and Welfare, 1971, pp. 53, 68).

Both the research of Balyeat (Blackburn and Aurand, 1972) and that of Flowers and Hughes (1973) has indicated that the attraction of a potential new job is not as strong an impetus toward mobility as dissatisfaction in a current job. Findings of a national study of social workers indicated that individuals were prone to leave jobs because of professional frustrations, such as work content and institutional practices (U.S. Dept. of Health, Education and Welfare, 1971, p. 88). Once the decision was made to leave, however, new jobs were chosen on the basis of salary and benefits. Actual job mobility of respondents seemed to result from both dissatisfaction with a former job and high expectations of satisfaction for a new job. The researchers determined that for a worker merely to contemplate a job change required less perception of difference between satisfaction at a present job and expected satisfaction at a new job than did an actual job change.

Flowers and Hughes (1973) found that reasons for remaining with an employer can relate to both external or internal environments. External environmental factors that can affect mobility include perceived job opportunities with other employers as well as nonwork factors, such as financial or family responsibilities, or friends. Internal factors that can affect mobility are job satisfaction, the institutional atmosphere, and the degree of comfort the worker feels within that atmosphere. Workers with less than five years tenure at an institution tend to remain with that institution for internal reasons. After working five years for the same employer, the worker who stays tends to remain more for external than internal reasons. In terms of job satisfaction, the very dissatisfied worker who continues to remain with an employer tends to stay for external reasons—financial reasons, family responsibilities, lack of outside opportunities, or age limitations.

Mobility in Other Professions

Trends in mobility and career patterns in professions other than librarianship have already been mentioned in this literature review. The following discussion of mobility research in other professions is an attempt to supplement this coverage of mobility literature in other fields. As these studies of other professions illustrate, it is difficult to generalize about the mobility of women without identifying their particular environment and occupation. While some characteristics of mobility seem to prevail regardless of the profession being studied, research findings in various fields have also revealed trends unique to the populations under investigation.

A study of faculty mobility (Kimmel, 1973) at the University of South Florida for the years 1965-70 indicated that women faculty were slightly (but not significantly) less mobile than men.

Similar to Kimmel's findings in psychology, De Pasquale and Lange's

(1971) investigation of the job turnover of MBA graduates indicated turnover for both sexes to be the same over a five-year period, with no relationship between the turnover of respondents and their ages or marital status.

Studies of federal workers have shown turnover to be higher for women than for men (Harrison, 1964). The greatest variances, however, were not between sexes, but between different age groups, occupations, and grade levels in the federal career structure. The turnover rate dropped for both sexes as they achieved more responsible positions or increased in age.

Turnover rates of teachers in Iowa, studied by Costa (1972), were highest among those with less than four years' experience. Married women under 30 had the highest turnover rates, followed by married males, and, finally, unmarried males. Reasons for moving given by teachers in Idaho were investigated by Orlich (1972). Although economic factors were prime in teacher mobility for both sexes, women had a greater tendency to change jobs or leave the profession for personal reasons, such as family or marital considerations. Men tended to consider salary more important than did women in deciding to move.

Previous research on the mobility of professionals cited in this section illustrates the difficulty of making generalizations about women's mobility without considering elements unique to the occupations involved. Studies of women in the professions have alternately shown their mobility to be greater, less than, and equivalent to, that of men. Variations in research findings make it impossible to confidently predict the mobility patterns of librarians from data gathered in other professions.

Summary

Research on job mobility has been diverse, and has included investigations of many occupations and varied segments of the work force. The following is an attempt to summarize basic trends identified in previous research (Wiens, 1973; Ladinsky, 1967a). Variables commonly found to affect mobility are listed, along with the type of relationship between each variable and mobility. A positive relationship indicates that as the variable increases, mobility also increases. In an inverse relationship, mobility decreases as the variable increases.

A. Demographic Factors
1. Educational level—positive relationship
2. Age—inverse relationship
3. Sex—males are more mobile than females
4. Marital and family status—married people are less mobile than single; school-age children in a family reduces mobility.

5. Occupation—young, married, professionals have the greatest mobility and move the furthest
6. Region—West and South have greatest mobility; Northeast has the least
7. Past mobility—positive relationship
8. Preference for geographic area—inverse relationship
9. Home ownership—inverse relationship

B. Job-related Factors
1. Salary—inverse relationship
2. Job satisfaction—inverse relationship
3. Tenure—inverse relationship

While certain trends can be identified using previous mobility research, as was done here, the research is too diverse to utilize as a basis for generalizing about mobility patterns of librarians. Mobility research results vary as the particular environments and occupations under investigation vary. In order to analyze and predict the mobility of librarians, it is necessary to utilize a research design focused upon this particular population. The final section of this literature review summarizes previous research on librarians' mobility.

Mobility of Librarians

The argument that women librarians tend to be less mobile than men has not been an unreasonable one. Earlier analyses of librarians' job mobility repeatedly testified to the fact that men change jobs more often than women. In all but two previous mobility studies, the resounding conclusion remained the same: men are mobile; women are immobile. These research results cannot simply be ignored, and will be discussed before presenting the results of this study.

Most of the data concerning job mobility of librarians have been gathered during investigations that focused primarily upon other areas of interest, and in which mobility was examined as one of several variables. Harvey (1958), however, focused specifically on the career mobility of librarians. His analysis was based on examination of career patterns of chief librarians of public and college libraries who had been included in the 1943 edition of *Who's Who in Library Service*. Harvey concluded that sex was the most important variable distinguishing mobile librarians from immobile librarians, and that women were less mobile than men.

Morrison (1969) also found male librarians to be more mobile than females, when he investigated career patterns of heads of academic libraries in 1958. He hypothesized that women tend to emphasize educational attainment rather than mobility in order to progress in their careers. Both Schiller (1969a) and Blankenship (1967) examined job mobility in two separate studies of college and university librarians, and both found female librarians to be less mobile than males. In her survey of professional librarians in colleges and universities, Anita Schiller found more than one-fourth of the women had worked in their current institutions for 11 years or more, compared to only one-sixth of the men. Similarly, in Blankenship's study of college and university head librarians, 69 percent of the females had remained at the same jobs for 16 or more years, compared with only 30 percent of the men.

Carpenter and Shearer (1972) identified a similar trend in a different library environment, public libraries serving populations of 100,000 or more. Using job tenure as an indicator of mobility, they found the relationship between sex and years worked in a single library to be statistically significant, and concluded that men were "far more likely" than women to change positions.

Two surveys of librarians in specific types of libraries, special libraries and health-sciences libraries, have also indicated that men are more mobile than women. Responses to a question about job movement in the 1967 salary survey of members of the Special Libraries Association ("A Study of 1967 Salaries," p. 246) showed that 16 percent more men than women had moved geographically to accept their current positions. The Survey of Health Sciences Libraries (Rothenberg, Rees, and Kronick, 1971) revealed that 69 percent of the male professionals had served in three or more positions, contrasted with 50 percent of the females.

Taylor (1973) examined mobility in order to measure the relationship between a librarian's job movement and professional involvement. She concluded that, while men moved slightly more often than women, there was no statistically significant difference in mobility rate between the two sexes. Schlachter and Thomison's (1974) examination of library-science doctoral recipients included an analysis of their mobility, and revealed no significant relationship between sex and mobility, women proving no less mobile than men.

METHODOLOGY

Research Objectives

The objective of this study was to collect and analyze data concerning the mobility of male and female academic librarians in the South, in relation to their career advancement. Respondents' mobility was determined through analysis of the number of job moves made during their professional careers, as well as their stated propensity to move.

Career advancement was determined by comparing an individual's present salary and position level with the salary and position maintained in the job immediately prior to his or her current job. No attempt was made to collect salary and position data for all job moves in each individual's career, since this could have involved problems of long-term recall for many respondents.

Research Instrument

The questionnaire was designed to gather three basic types of data: demographic data, mobility data, and data concerning career progress. Demographic data collected included sex, marital status, age, number and ages of children, number of dependents other than children, education, and years' of experience.

Mobility data collected concerned mobility history and propensity for future mobility. To obtain a measure of actual mobility, respondents were asked to report their total years' of professional work experience, as well as the number of libraries in which they had worked. The ratio between year's of experience and number of employers yielded an average for the frequency of job moves.

This ratio was used as a "mobility measure," and indicates the average time spent working for each employer, or tenure. For example, an individual with 10 years' of work experience who has been employed in two libraries would have a mobility measure of five. In other words, this person moved on the average of every five years. The same person's average tenure with each employer is also five years. This mobility measure allowed analysis of career-long mobility history.

Reasons behind job moves were also explored, to test several hypotheses relating motivations for job changes with career advancement. To accomplish this, respondents were asked what prompted them to make their last job move. In addition to an "other" category, two basic types of motivations were provided on a checklist. One set of reasons included those in which the primary consideration was career-oriented: better salary and/or position, continuation of education, and dissatisfaction with former job. In contrast, the second set of reasons included those for which the primary consideration was personal or family-oriented rather than career-oriented: spouse's relocation, personal health, health of family members, better geographic location, and a general category labeled "other marital and family-related reasons."

One additional type of mobility that was explored was that of career interruptions. Respondents were asked to note absences from library work for six months or more, the length of such absences, and their reasons for taking them. Propensity to move was assessed by asking respondents whether they would be willing and able to move in the future to accept a better position and/or salary. Those who predicted that they would not move were asked why, providing data concerning their reasons for expecting to remain immobile in the future. To relate propensity for mobility to job satisfaction, respondents were also asked to rate their satisfaction with their current jobs on a five-point Likert-type scale.

Data on career advancement were also gathered, and assessed in terms of two components: salary and position. Present salary and position was compared with that in each respondent's last job, to determine changes that accompanied the last job move.

Population

To make the study manageable, the study population was limited geographically and by library type. The geographic region chosen for the study was the South, specifically nine southern states: Alabama, Florida, Georgia, Kentucky, Louisiana, Mississippi, North Carolina, South Carolina, and Tennessee. Within these nine states, only academic librarians were sampled.

Sampling

Before a random sample could be drawn from the total population, a list of professional librarians currently employed in academic libraries in the South was needed. Unfortunately, no such composite list of personnel was available. Rather than rely upon incomplete or unrepresentative lists (such as the membership list of the Southeastern Library Association), as complete a list as possible was compiled by directly contacting the libraries in the population. Using *Library Statistics of Colleges and Universities*,(Smith and Williams, 1972) 260 private and public libraries in universities and four-year colleges were identified. The directors of each of these libraries were asked to submit lists of their professional staff. In the second phase of sampling, 530 libarians were randomly selected from this population (about 25 percent of the estimated total of professional librarians employed in the 260 academic libraries). Individuals in this sample were sent the survey questionnaire, and usable questionnaries were returned by 462 librarians, or 87.6 percent.

Research Hypotheses

Eight hypotheses concerning mobility and career progression were chosen for investigation, and are listed below in their positive form.

1. Male librarians are more mobile than female librarians.
2. Male librarians claim greater propensity to move than female librarians.
3. Single female librarians claim greater propensity to move than married or formerly married female librarians.
4. The greater the mobility of a librarian, the higher the librarian's salary.
5. The greater the mobility of a librarian, the higher the librarian's position level.

6. A move made for career-motivated reasons results in greater salary increases than a move made for personal reasons.
7. A move made for career-motivated reasons results in greater position advancement than a move made for personal or family reasons.
8. Female librarians take leaves from the field more frequently than male librarians.

Definitions of Terms

1. *Job mobility*—movement from job to job throughout a librarian's career; an overall pattern of job mobility is determined by the frequency of individual job moves.
2. *Job move*— a job shift that involves a change in employing library.
3. *Propensity for mobility*—an individual's stated willingness or ability to move from his or her present job to another position.
4. *Mobility measure*—the average frequency of job moves throughout an individual's career; also expressed as the mean tenure with each employer.
5. *Tenure*—continuous period of employment with a single employer.
6. *Mean tenure*—the average length of employment in each library throughout an individual's career.
7. *Career advancement*—the level of salary and position achieved by a librarian.
8. *Academic library*—a library in a public or private university or four-year institution that is listed in *Library Statistics of Colleges and Universities,* Fall 1971.
9. *Academic librarian*—an individual employed on an academic-library staff in a position classified as professional.
10. *South*—includes the states of Alabama, Florida, Georgia, Kentucky, Louisiana, Mississippi, North Carolina, South Carolina, and Tennessee.
11. *Single*—an individual who is not and has never been married.
12. *Formerly married*—an individual who has been, but is not presently, living with a spouse, who may be widowed, legally separated, or divorced.
13. *Leave from the field*—an interruption of professional work for a period of six months or more.

DATA ANALYSIS

In this section the results of data analysis are presented in two parts. The first describes the sample in terms of personal and professional demographic characteristics. The second and major discussion concerns the results of hypothesis testing and implications of the findings.

Demographic Characteristics

Sex, Age, and Marital Status Of the total respondents, 71.7 percent (331) were women. The average age for female respondents was 42.6 years, while men averaged 40.8 years, a difference that was not statistically significant (t-test, p = .157). Although average age was similar, chi-square analysis demonstrated a significant difference in distribution of age between men and women (p = .003). There were greater numbers of women in the categories representing the older age groups, with 13.3 percent aged 60 or over and 22.1 percent between 50 and 59, compared to only 6.1 percent and 15.3 percent of the men. A larger proportion of the women were also grouped in the younger age category, with 19.4 percent of them between 20 and 29 years, compared to 14.4 percent of the men. Men predominated in the 30-49 range.

A little more than one-half of the respondents were currently married, and about one-third were single. Those divorced, legally separated, or widowed (formerly married) comprised 13.0 percent of the sample.

There was a significant difference across sex (chi-square, p = .000) between men and women respondents in terms of marital status. While only about one-half of the females were currently married, approximately two-thirds of the males were. Conversely, more women than men were unmarried: the single and formerly married categories contained 52.1 percent of the female respondents, but only 33.6 percent of the male respondents.

The largest proportion of total respondents, 18 percent, had worked professionally for 21 or more years, while the smallest group was comprised of those who have worked as librarians for less than a year, 5.2 percent of the total. The mean number of years of experience for the total group was 10.2, and 41.7 percent of the respondents had worked 11 years or more.

Women had worked slightly, but significantly, longer than men (t-test, p = .430), their averages being 10.4 and 9.8 years, respectively. Chi-square analysis (p = .660) indicated no difference in the distribution of men's and women's professional work experience.

Tenure in Present Library The greatest proportion of the respondents, 17.5 percent of the sample, had spent between three and four years working with their current employers. The average tenure with their current employers for all respondents was seven years.

Differences between men and women were indicated by the t-test (p = .025), which showed a significantly longer tenure in present library for women than for men: 7.4 years, compared to 6.0 years, or 1.4 fewer years for men. The distributions of tenure between men and women showed differences that were not as statistically strong. Chi-square analysis showed a weak difference (p = .140) between the distributions of men's and women's tenures. Much of the difference between men and women in terms of distribution and mean tenures occurred at high tenure levels; 13.6 percent of the women had worked 16 years or longer at their present jobs, versus only 6.1 percent of the men.

Present Position Over two-thirds of the sample currently hold middle- or upper-managerial positions: departmental or unit supervisors, assistant directors, or head librarians. The remaining respondents are employed largely in nonadministrative positions.

Statistical analysis demonstrates an extreme difference in the position levels held by men and women (chi-square, $p = .000$). Women dominate in the lower position levels, with 37.5 percent of them holding nonadministrative posts, while only 18.3 percent of the men occupy nonadminisrative positions. Men, on the other hand, dominate the upper-level positions, especially directorships. Although men comprise only 28.3 percent of the entire sample, they represent 56.1 percent of the directors in the total sample. As a result, only about 9 percent of the women in the sample have achieved directorships, as compared to 28 percent of the men.

Job Titles in Present Library The average number of job titles respondents have held with their current employers was 1.7. Women have averaged more job titles in their current libraries than men, 1.8, compared to 1.6. The t-test demonstrates that this difference is significant ($p = .018$). Similarly, chi-square analysis shows significant differences between men and women in the distributions of number of job titles with their present employers. Men occupied fewer job titles than women, 62.5 percent of the men remaining in only one job title, as compared to only 49.2 percent of the women. At the highest level, five or more job titles, there were three times as many women (2.4 percent) as men (.8 percent).

Number of Library Employers Throughout their careers, the librarians sampled have worked in an average of 1.36 different libraries. No significant difference was found between the two sexes in terms of their average number of library employers (t-test, $p = .655$), with women having worked in 2.3 libraries and men having worked in 2.2 libraries. The chi-square statistic showed a significant difference ($p = .084$) between men and women in the distributions of the number of library employers. The distributions at the lower levels were similar, 43 percent of the women having remained in one library, a figure only 2.8 percent less than than for men. On the other hand, the percentage of women employed in three or more libraries was 3.0 percent less than that of men, 37.5 percent of whom had worked with three or more employers. Therefore, while men and women had worked in the same average number of libraries, differences were exhibited between them in the distributions of number of employers.

Educational Attainment While a majority of the librarians sampled, 81.7 percent, held a master's degree in library science, a significant difference (Mann-Whitney U test, p = .097) was found in educational attainment between men and women. Men were twice as likely as women to hold a library degree above the master's level, 6.9 percent, compared to 3.6 percent. Women dominated at the lowest educational levels, with 14.8 percent of them holding a bachelor's degree or less, versus 10.8 percent of the men. The great majority of both sexes, 82.3 percent of the men and 81.6 percent of women, held a master's degree.

The Mann-Whitney U test and chi-square analysis indicated that men also had overwhelmingly more education in subject fields other than librarianship. Men were 19 times as likely as women to hold doctorates in other fields (11.5 percent, compared to .6 percent) and also had more master's degrees in other fields, 26.9 percent, as compared to only 17.4 percent of the women. Women predominated at lower educational levels, with 22.1 percent of them holding no degree in additional subject fields, while only 15.4 percent of the men lacked other subject degrees.

Children and Dependents Overall, 45 percent of the respondents reported having children. There was a significant difference in the frequencies of men and women who had children (chi-square, p = .077). Women reported having children only 42.3 percent of the time, while over half of the men, 51.9 percent, reported having children. In addition, men averaged significantly more children (t-test, p = .016), with 1.18 per family, compared to .85 for women.

Only about one-tenth of the respondents reported dependents other than children. Both men and women reported having other dependents with about the same frequency, 9.3 percent and 10.6 percent, respectively (chi-square, p = .800). Over three-fourths of the respondents who had dependents reported only one, and statistical testing showed no difference between men and women in terms of dependents.

Hypothesis Testing

In this section, the results of hypothesis testing are discussed in detail. Hypotheses are presented in their null form, for statistical applications. When the null hypothesis has been rejected, it indicates differences between men and women for which chance alone cannot account. When the null hypothesis has not been rejected, then there is, of course, no support for the premises originally offered.

Hypothesis 1: There is no significant difference in mobility between male and female librarians.

Failed to Reject

Table 1 provides a mobility measure based on each individual's average tenure in individual jobs, or average frequency of job changes. The results of the t-test (p = .377) showed no significant difference in the mean mobility rates of male and female librarians. In addition, chi-square testing indicated no difference in distributions of mobility rates between sexes (p = .543).

On the average, women changed jobs every 5.2 years, while men moved slightly, but not significantly, more often, every 4.8 years. In addition, no significant differences in mobility rate were found between men and women even when marital status was held constant. Married, formerly married, and single men and women changed jobs at similar rates.

Obviously, these results conflict with previous research on librarians' mobility, and provide no support for the original research hypothesis that men are more mobile than women. The conflict emanates from differing definitions of mobility. In this study, mobility was defined in terms of career-long trends rather than as tenure with current employer. Relating total years' of experience to total number of employers provides a means for analyzing career-long mobility rates, not just a portion of an individual's career. Such a long-term view of mobility was not applied in earlier studies, where mobility was viewed as a short-term variable, often as equivalent to tenure with the current employer.

Although Schiller (1968) counted both the years of work experience and the places of employment, her definition of mobility was based on the length of time respondents had worked in their current libraries. Carpenter and Shearer (1972) did the same, using tenure in the current library as an indicator of mobility. Blankenship's (1967) discussion of mobility was also based on the length of time respondents had remained in their present positions. In the 1967 Special Libraries Association survey, ("SLA Salary Survey"), mobility was assessed by determining whether respondents had moved geographically to accept their current positions. Schlachter and Thomison (1974), who found no difference in mobility related to sex, defined mobility in yet another way. They compared each respondent's place of current employment with the location of the university granting the Ph.D.

For the 1969 Survey of Health Science Libraries, (Rothenberg, Rees, and Kronick, 1971), mobility was defined more broadly. Rather than limiting it to tenure in present library, mobility was calculated on the basis of the number of job changes made during the preceding decade. yet, for many librarians, a 10-year period represents only a portion of total career experience. In this study, for instance, 42 percent of the respondents had 11 or more years of work experience. Thus, a 10-year mobility history would not adequately reflect their career-long mobility patterns.

TABLE 1
Frequency of Job Moves, by Sex

Mean Number of Years Per Job	Total Sample		Male			Female			Total
	Number	Percent	Number	Percent[a]		Number	Percent[a]		
0 — .9	35	7.6	7	5.3	(20.0)	28	8.5	(80.0)	(100.0)
1 — 1.9	70	15.2	22	16.9	(31.4)	48	14.5	(68.6)	(100.0)
2 — 2.9	46	10.0	12	9.2	(26.1)	34	10.3	(73.9)	(100.0)
3 — 3.9	92	19.9	30	22.9	(32.6)	62	18.8	(67.4)	(100.0)
4 — 4.9	38	8.2	9	6.9	(23.7)	29	8.8	(76.3)	(100.0)
5 — 5.9	53	11.5	18	13.7	(34.0)	35	10.6	(66.0)	(100.0)
6 — 6.9	23	5.0	6	4.6	(26.1)	17	5.1	(73.9)	(100.0)
7 — 7.9	23	5.0	10	7.6	(43.5)	13	3.9	(56.5)	(100.0)
8 — 8.9	14	3.0	2	1.5	(14.3)	12	3.6	(85.7)	(100.0)
9 — 9.9	14	3.0	2	1.5	(14.3)	12	3.6	(85.7)	(100.0)
10 — 11.9	15	3.2	5	3.8	(33.3)	10	3.0	(66.7)	(100.0)
12 — 14.9	20	4.3	5	3.8	(25.0)	15	4.5	(75.0)	(100.0)
15 — 22	19	4.1	3	2.3	(15.8)	16	4.8	(84.2)	(100.0)
Total	462	100.0	131	100.0		331	100.0		
	Mean = 5.1 years		Mean = 4.8 years			Mean = 5.2 years			

[a] Percentages in parentheses relate to mean tenure per job and are read horizontally.

(T-test, t = -.88, p = .377)
(Mann-Whitney U Test, Z = -.292, p = .770)
(N = 462, X^2 = 10.84, df = 12, p = .543)

There is value in research examining tenure in a single institution, or mobility during a decade of an entire career. However, the resulting data should not be considered an indicator of career-long mobility trends, or used in analysis of long-term salary patterns. Short-term mobility may not duplicate long-term movement patterns. The data gathered in this study, for example, demonstrated that the two variables can differ significantly. While career-long mobility was similar for both sexes, statistically significant differences were demonstrated for tenure in present library, relative to sex. Females had remained with their current employers for an average of 7.4 years, compared to 6 years for males. In addition, 14 percent of the women had worked in their present libraries for 16 or more years, versus only 6 percent of the men. It is important to note that, had mobility been analyzed in terms of years employed at the present library, the present research results would have corroborated previous research findings, indicating men to be significantly more mobile than women.

Previously, research has provided evidence for the argument that it is a woman's immobility which restricts her career growth. In the present study, this has not been shown to be the case. The statistically significant differences between men and women in this study were exhibited, not in terms of actual mobility rate, but in propensity to move, reasons for changing jobs, and their career interruptions. The hypothesis testing that follows describes these differences in detail.

Hypothesis 2: There is no significant difference in propensity to move between male and female librarians.

Rejected

Table 2 indicates a significant difference between male and female respondents in propensity to move (chi-square, $p = .000$). When asked whether they would be able and willing to move geographically to accept better positions and/or salaries, the responses given by men and women were almost exactly opposite. Approximately two-thirds of the men expected to have enough flexibility to move, while about two-thirds of the women did not.

Lower expectations of future job moves did not appear to have a negative effect on women's mobility, however, since their actual mobility patterns duplicated those of men. Although women expected to be less mobile than men, they actually changed jobs with similar frequency. This apparent contradiction was resolved when their reasons for predicting immobility were explored.

As Table 3 shows, when males and females who lacked propensity were asked why they did not expect to change jobs in the future, a significant difference was found in their reasons (chi-square, $p = .000$).

TABLE 2
Propensity to Move, by Sex

Propensity to Move	Total Sample		Males			Females		
	Number	Percent	Number	Percent[a]		Number	Percent[a]	Total
Yes	198	43.3	81	62.3	(40.9)	117	35.8 (59.1)	(100.0)
No	259	56.7	49	37.7	(18.9)	210	64.2 (81.1)	(100.0)
Total	457	100.0	130	100.0		327	100.0	

[a]Percentages in parentheses relate to category of propensity to move and are read horizontally.

(N = 457, X^2 = 25.59, df = 1, p = .000)

The majority of women who lacked propensity to move (30.6 percent) stated that they planned to remain in the same geographic area because of the location of their husband's jobs. In fact, almost half the reasons given by women (47.3 percent) were related to marital and family considerations, while only about one-fourth of the men (24.5 percent) expected to remain immobile for these reasons. The explanation for lack of propensity given most often by men related to satisfaction or expectations in their present jobs (21.1 percent). Only 5.7 percent of the women cited this reason for lacking propensity.

TABLE 3
Reasons for Lack of Propensity to Move, by Sex

Reasons for Lack of Propensity to Move	Total Sample		Male		Female	
	Number	Percent	Number	Percent	Number	Percent
Retirement, Age	57	17.8	10	17.5	47	17.8
Spouse's Career	84	26.2	3	5.3	81	30.6
Family Considerations	56	17.4	12	21.1	44	16.7
Satisfied with Present Job	27	8.4	12	21.1	15	5.7
Home Ownership	22	6.8	3	5.2	19	7.2
Like Geographic Area	28	8.7	4	7.0	24	9.1
Other	47	14.7	13	22.8	34	12.9
Total	321	100.0	57	100.0	264	100.0

(N = 253, X^2 = 31.08, df = 5, p = .000)

The differing reasons given by men and women for their expected immobility indicates differences in the reasons they remain in their jobs. Males planned to stay in their current jobs for career-related reasons, while females' reasons for planning to remain in their jobs related to variables outside the work environment. This indicates that some women do not necessarily remain in their jobs because they want to, but often because they have to. In cases where their husbands and families are settled in a specific geographic area, these women must make the most of opportunities available within a limited geographic radius. Males, in claiming greater propensity to move, indicate a greater flexibility to seek jobs in terms of the opportunities they offer, rather than in terms of the geographic area in which they are located.

While they may remain in their jobs for different reasons than men, women did not exhibit more dissatisfaction with their current jobs than men, as shown in Table 4. Because previous research has indicated a relationship between propensity for mobility and satisfaction with one's present position, job satisfaction was analyzed for both sexes in relation to propensity to move. While a significant relationship was found between an individual's attitude toward his or her job and propensity to change jobs (see Table 5: Mann-Whitney U test, p = .000; chi-square, p = .000), no significant difference in attitude toward job was identified between men and women (see Table 4: Mann-Whitney U test, p = .420). It appears, then, that differences between men and women in propensity to move were not owing to differing levels of satisfaction in their jobs, but to other factors.

TABLE 4
Job Satisfaction, by Sex

Job Satisfaction	Total Sample		Male		Female		Total
	Number	Percent	Number	Percent[a]	Number	Percent[a]	
Like it very much	261	57.5	77	59.3 (29.5)	184	56.8 (70.5)	(100.0)
Like it fairly well	133	29.3	41	31.5 (30.8)	92	28.4 (69.2)	(100.0)
Neutral	16	3.5	3	2.3 (18.7)	13	4.0 (81.3)	(100.0)
Dislike it somewhat	33	7.3	5	3.8 (15.1)	28	8.6 (84.9)	(100.0)
Dislike it very much	11	2.4	4	3.1 (36.7)	7	2.2 (63.3)	(100.0)
Total	454	100.0	130	100.0	324	100.0	

[a] Percentages in parentheses relate to categories of job satisfaction and are read horizontally.

(Mann-Whitney U Test, Z = -.8054, p = .420)
(N = 453, X² = 4.39, df = 4, p = .356)

TABLE 5
Job Satisfaction, by Propensity to Move

Job Satisfaction	Propensity to Move		No Propensity to Move	
	Number	Percent	Number	Percent
Like it very much	92	46.7	168	66.1
Like it fairly well	65	33.0	66	26.0
Neutral	10	5.0	6	2.4
Dislike it somewhat	23	11.7	10	3.9
Dislike it very much	7	3.6	4	1.6
Total	197	100.0	254	100.0

(Mann-Whitney U Test, Z = -5.83, p = .000)
(N = 451, X^2 = 22.31, df = 4, p = .000)

An important factor in the low proportions of women with the ability or willingness to move is their role in the family structure. Almost half of the women who lacked propensity reported marital and family considerations as the reasons. Because their role in the family structure often predominated over their role as wage earner, many women would not be able to relocate to accept a better job, while most male librarians would have the flexibility to do so.

The influence of lower propensity on woman's actual mobility does not appear to be negative, however. Although women claimed less future mobility than men, they actually moved with similar frequency. Since the predominant explanation given by women for predicting immobility in the future was related to their marital and family responsibilities, it appears that the variables that work to keep a woman immobile also influence her frequency of job moves, and that marital and family considerations are much more prominent in the development of women's career patterns than is true of men.

The nature of the propensity measure is a factor in this dichotomy. Propensity refers not to actual past movement, but to a prediction of movement in the future. Thus, a woman who hypothesizes that family responsibilities will restrict her mobility may find, some time in the future, that these same responsibilities necessitate an actual move. This occurrence is difficult to predict in relation to career patterns, however, since it is determined by factors outside the work environment.

While analysis of propensity to move is valuable in gaining perspective concerning the dual roles of working women, it does not have a predictable relationship to their future mobility behavior. The fact that a woman expects to remain immobile in the future does not insure that she will actually do so. Therefore, analysis of propensity to move is less valuable than analysis of actual mobility patterns in understanding trends in female librarians' earnings or position patterns.

Hypothesis 3: There is no significant difference in propensity to move between single female librarians and married or formerly married female librarians.

Rejected

Table 6 indicates a significant difference (chi-square, p = .000) in propensity to move, between women who had never married and those who were presently married or had been married. More than half of the single women (55.2 percent) predicted that they could move in the future, compared to only one-fourth of married or formerly married women (25.1 percent). A significant difference was found between the two groups of women in terms of their reason for claiming no propensity (chi-square, p = .000). The greater propensity to move of single women can be partially accounted for by the mere fact that they are unmarried. Of the women in the sample who were either married or formerly married and claimed no propensity to move, 39.7 percent gave reasons that pertained to their husband's careers.

TABLE 6
Women's Propensity to Move,
By Marital Status

Propensity to Move	Married and Formerly Married		Single	
	Number	Percent	Number	Percent
Yes	53	25.1	64	55.2
No	158	74.9	52	44.8
Total	211	100.0	116	100.0

(N = 327, X^2 = 28.12, df = 1, p = .000)

While a significant difference was found in propensity to move between these groups of women, no significant difference in mobility rates between the two groups was demonstrated. Although single women claim more propensity to move than other women, they actually changed jobs with slightly less frequency than married and formerly married women, every 5.3 years, as compared to every 5.2 years.

This disparity is partly a result of the fact that married and formerly married women claim less propensity to move than their actual mobility rates would indicate. The predictions single women make about their future mobility patterns seem to be more accurate reflections of their actual mobility behavior than those made by women who have marital or family responsibilities to consider in addition to their careers.

Table 7 provides comparable data for single and married or formerly married males. When these groups of men were compared, they were found to be almost identical in terms of propensity to move, 62.4 percent and 63.2 percent, respectively, claiming willingness and ability to move (chi-square, p = .909). Thus, marital status is not a factor in the job flexibility of men, but severely inhibits women's capacities in this regard.

TABLE 7
Men's Propensity to Move, by Marital Status

Propensity to Move	Married and Formerly Married		Single	
	Number	Percent	Number	Percent
Yes	58	62.4	24	63.2
No	35	37.6	14	36.8
Total	93	100.0	38	100.0

(N = 131, X^2 = .013, p = .909)

Hypothesis 4: There is no significant relationship between a librarian's mobility and his or her salary.

Rejected

When data concerning present salaries of respondents were tested for correlation with mobility, using the Spearman correlation coefficient, a positive correlation was discerned (r = .37, p = .001). Results of this statistical testing indicated that the greater a librarian's mobility, the higher the salary. The same was found to be true when male and female librarians were examined as subgroups of the entire sample. A positive correlation was found between mobility and salary for librarians of both sexes (men: r = .32, p = .001; women: r = .41, p = .001).

As shown with respect to Hypothesis 1, statistical testing has demonstrated that rate of mobility is not significantly related to sex. Since mobility has been shown to be positively correlated with salary, it would be expected that higher salary levels would be distributed throughout librarianship. However, previous surveys of library salaries have repeatedly indicated higher salary levels for males than for females.

Statistical testing demonstrated the same to be true for the present sample, as shown in Table 8. Significant differences were found between the salaries of male and female respondents (t-test, p = .000). The average salary for males was $2,925 more than the average salary for females. In addition, women's salaries were $802 lower than the mean salary for the total sample. Females, on the other hand, had a mean salary 6.3 percent below that for the entire sample, resulting in a 23-percent difference in mean salaries between men and women.

TABLE 8
Mean Salary, by Sex

Total Sample	Male	Female
$12,687	$14,810	$11,885

(t-test, t = 7.83, df = 443, p = .000)

Tables 9 and 10 illustrate that in every age range and category of marital status, significant differences exist between males and females in terms of mean earnings. The greatest disparity occurred between males and females in the 60-or-over range ($4,682 difference). The smallest disparity was that between single males and single females ($2,026). Salary differences steadily increased as librarians' ages increased, for all age ranges but one (50 to 59).

TABLE 9
Mean Salary, by Sex and Marital Status

Marital Status	Male	Female	Significance Testing
Married	$15,270	$11,587	t = 7.06 df = 235 p = .000
Formerly Married	$15,851	$12,617	t = 2.33 df = 57 p = .023
Single	$13,613	$11,587	t = 2.84 df = 147 p = .005

TABLE 10
Mean Salary, by Sex and Age

Age	Male	Female	Significance Testing
20-29	$11,868	$10,038	t = 5.07 df = 81 p = .000
30-39	$13,444	$11,498	t = 3.27 df = 128 p = .001
40-49	$16,656	$12,135	t = 5.07 df = 88 p = .000
50-59	$16,692	$12,991	t = 4.22 df = 92 p = .000
60+	$17,902	$13,220	t = 2.92 df = 46 p = .005

A salary gap that widens with age may be accounted for by any of several reasons. The simplest explanation, but most difficult to systematically investigate, is that of discrimination. This explanation is based on a belief that males in librarianship receive greater remuneration because of their sex alone, and will continue to do so regardless of their career pattens or those of females. Another possible explanation for smaller disparities in earnings among younger librarians is based on the fact that attempts are currently being made to pay them on a more equitable basis, while older librarians are trapped in patterns of salary inequity that have been set over the years. A third possible explanation is that men tend to achieve greater salary increasees than women as they move from job to job.

Because this third possibility relates to patterns of mobility, it will be explored in the succeeding sections of this chapter. Since no differences in actual rate of mobility have been demonstrated between men and women, frequency of mobility alone cannot account for variations between their salaries. Therefore, in the hypothesis-testing that follows, other possible functions of mobility will be examined, to determine their influence on salary disparities between men and women in librarianship.

Hypothesis 5: There is no significant relationship between a librarian's mobility and his or her position level.

Rejected

When position levels were tested for correlation with mobility, using the Spearman correlation coefficient, a positive correlation was revealed (r = .14, p = .002). Results of this statistical test indicated that the greater a librarian's mobility, the higher the position. The same was found to be true when male and female librarians were examined as subgroups of the entire sample, revealing a positive correlation between mobility and position for librarians of both sexes (men: r = .13, p = .078; women: r = .17, p = .002).

Since mobility is not significantly related to sex, and higher levels of mobility are evenly distributed among males and females in librarianship, position levels would also be expected to be distributed evenly throughout the ranks of library professionals, regardless of sex. However, previous surveys have repeatedly indicated higher position levels for males than for females.

This situation was mirrored in the present sample, in which a significant difference in position levels was discerned between male and female librarians (chi-square, p = .000; Mann-Whitney U test, p = .000). Table 11 shows that, as with salary, higher positions in this sample tend to be dominated by males. Female respondents were represented to an extraordinary degree at the lowest position levels, with 38.4 percent of them holding nonadministrative jobs, while this was true of only 19.2 percent of the men. The proportions of women at the department and unit-supervisor levels was slightly greater than that of men, but at the assistant-director and director levels, the proportion of women decreased. A larger percentage of males than females occupied assistant-director status, 8.8 percent, as compared to 5.6 percent. In addition, men were three and a half times more likely to be library directors than were women, 30.4 percent of them achieving such status, as compared to 9.0 percent of the women.

The disproportionate presence of males in the highest administrative levels accounts for some of the disparity between men's and women's salaries, since higher administrative positions tend to provide greater remuneration than lower administrative or nonadministrative levels. The fact that males draw larger mean salaries than women, discussed in the previous section, is obviously concomitant with their simultaneous domination of higher position levels. While the disparity between the salaries of males and females may be accounted for by differences in administrative duties, however, such position variations have not been satisfactorily explained.

One possible explanation for this phenomenon is that men enter librarianship at higher position levels than women. While no data were gathered in this study to provide analysis of this possiblity, it was shown to exist in the University of California at Berkeley library system, and may be a common occurrence (Lipow, et al., 1971). An additional contributor to men's higher position attainment is the

TABLE 11
Present Position Level, by Sex[1]

Present Position	Total Sample		Male		Female	
	Number	Percent	Number	Percent	Number	Percent
Nonadministrative Professional	147	33.0	24	19.2	123	38.4
Department or Unit Supervisor	203	45.5	52	41.6	151	47.0
Assistant Director	29	6.5	11	8.8	18	5.6
Director	67	15.0	38	30.4	29	9.0
Total	446	100.0	125	100.0	321	100.0

[1] The category representing "other" types of positions has been deleted from this table.
(Mann-Whitney U Test, $Z = -4.90$, $p = .000$)
($N = 446$, $X^2 = 39.3$, $df = 3$, $p = .000$)

magnitude of the position advancements that accompany their job changes. When degree of position advancement accompanying mobility was examined (Table 12), a significant difference was found between men and women (Mann-Whitney U test, $p = .002$; chi-square, $p = .075$). Mobile men were found to obtain greater promotions than mobile women, thus progressing up the administrative ladder in larger leaps.

TABLE 12
Position Levels Lost or Gained as a
Result of a Job Change

Levels of Position Change	Total Sample		Male		Female	
	Number	Percent	Number	Percent	Number	Percent
-2	26	11.4	3	4.9	23	13.7
-1	22	9.7	3	4.9	19	11.4
0	93	40.8	24	39.3	69	41.3
1	59	25.9	19	31.1	40	24.0
2	22	9.6	10	16.5	12	7.2
3	6	2.6	2	3.3	4	2.4
Total	228	100.0	61	100.0	167	100.0

(Mann-Whitney U Test, $Z = -3.03$, $p = .002$)
($N = 228$, $X^2 = 9.99$, $df = 5$, $p = .075$)

In rejecting the null hypothesis on the basis of the data collected for this study, support has been provided for the predicted relationship between mobility and position level: the greater a librarian's mobility, the higher his or her position level. This predicted relationship cannot account for differences in position attainment between men and women, however, since no significant difference was found in their mobility rates. Since high and low frequencies of mobility are evenly distributed between males and females, high and low position levels would also be expected to distributed evenly among librarians, regardless of sex, unless other variables affect position attainment. In the sections that follow, data analysis related to several of the remaining research hypotheses provides additional perspective concerning disparities in career advancement as evidenced in salary and position variations between men and women.

Hypothesis 6: There is no significant difference in salary change resulting from career-motivated job moves and personally or family-motivated job moves.

Rejected

Calculation of the variables related to this hypothesis involved two steps. The motivations for each respondents's move from a prior to a present job were categorized as either: (1) career related, or (2) personal and family related. In addition, each respondent's former salary was subtracted from his or her present salary, to calculate salary change. This allowed comparison of the mean salary fluctuation resulting from each of the two types of stimuli for mobility.

Table 13 illustrates the difference in mean salaries achieved for the total sample as a result of career-motivated as opposed to personally or

TABLE 13
T-Test for Differences in Mean Salary Increase
Resulting from Types of Motivations
for Moving

Portion of Sample	Career Motivations	Personal and Family Motivations	Significance Testing
Total	$5,502	$3,829	$t = 2.67$ $df = 205$ $p = .008$
Male	$6,665	$6,328	$t = .17$ $df = 53$ $p = .870$
Female	$4,804	$3,586	$t = 1.86$ $df = 150$ $p = .065$

TABLE 14
Salary Increases for Males and Females Resulting From Types of Motivations for Moving

Salary Increase	Total Sample				Males				Females			
	Career-Motivated Moves		Personally and Family-Motivated Moves		Career-Motivated Moves		Personally and Family-Motivated Moves		Career-Motivated Moves		Personally and Family-Motivated Moves	
	#	%	#	%	#	%	#	%	#	%	#	%
$0	7	5.5	12	15.2	4	8.3	0	0.0	3	3.8	12	16.6
$1 —1,499	16	12.5	6	7.6	4	8.3	1	14.3	12	15.0	5	6.9
$1,500 —2,999	23	18.0	15	19.0	5	10.4	1	14.3	18	22.5	14	19.4
$3,000 —4,999	20	15.6	23	29.0	6	12.5	1	14.3	14	17.5	22	30.6
$5,000 —7,999	31	24.2	10	12.7	14	29.2	1	14.3	17	21.2	9	12.5
$8,000 +	31	24.2	13	16.5	15	31.3	3	42.8	16	20.0	10	13.9
Total	128	100.0	79	100.0	48	100.0	7	100.0	80	100.0	72	100.0

family-motivated job moves, a difference that was found to be statistically significant (t-test, p = .008). The overall difference in the mean salary increases resulting from moves made for career and for noncareer reasons was $1,673; the mean increases resulting from career motivated moves totaling $5,502, compared to a $3,829 increase for personally or family-motivated job changes.

Table 14 shows that, of those respondents who achieved salary increases as a result of their job moves, 64 percent cited career-oriented motivations for their moves. Only 5.5 percent of respondents who claimed career motivations for their moves did not receive subsequent increases in earnings, compared to over 15 percent of those who moved for personal or family reasons.

Moving on the basis of personal or family considerations did not negate the possibility that salary increases would occur, however. Of those respondents who moved at all, 90.8 percent experienced a resultant salary increase, regardless of their reasons for moving. This finding is consistent with the results of previous hypothesis-testing, which indicated that mobility alone tends to insure gains in salary. It is the motivation behind a job move, however, that influences the magnitude of the resulting salary increase. For instance, of those librarians claiming career motivations for job moves, 24.2 percent made salary gains of $8,000 or more, while those who moved for noncareer reasons achieved similar salary increases only 16.5 percent of the time.

In Table 15, motivations for mobility are examined in terms of sex, showing a significant difference in distribution of reasons for moving between men and women (chi-square, p = .000). Women moved four times more often than men for personal or family reasons (25.3 percent, as compared to 5.7 percent). When women were examined according to their marital status, however, a significant difference in motivations for moving was found between them. Table 16 shows that single women were significantly more likely to move for career reasons

TABLE 15
Motivations for Moving by Sex

Type of Motivation	Total Sample		Male		Female	
	Number	Percent	Number	Percent	Number	Percent
Career	349	80.2	116	94.3	233	74.7
Personal and Family	86	19.8	7	5.7	79	25.3
Total	435	100.0	123	100.0	312	100.0

(N = 435, X² = 20.21, df = 1, p = .000)

than were married or formerly married women (chi-square, p = .006; 84.8 percent, as compared to 69.6 percent). They were also half as likely to make moves for personal or family reasons (15.2 percent, as compared to 30.4 percent). Nevertheless, women as a group were much more likely to move for noncareer reasons than men. Similarly, of the men who changed jobs, 94.3 percent did so for career reasons, as compared to only 74.7 percent of the women (see Table 16). A logical consequence, therefore, would be mean salary increases which were lower for mobile women than for mobile men, since the positive relationship between magnitude of salary change and career related motivation for mobility has already been demonstrated.

TABLE 16
Women's Motivations for Moving, by Marital Status

Type of Motivation	Total		Married and Formerly Married		Single	
	Number	Percent	Number	Percent	Number	Percent
Career	233	74.7	144	69.6	89	84.8
Personal or Family	79	25.3	63	30.4	16	15.2
Total	312	100.0	207	100.0	105	100.0

(N = 312, X^2 = 7.72, p = .006)

Table 17 demonstrates a significant difference between men and women in terms of salary change resulting from job moves (t-test, p = .003). The mean salary gain for mobile women was $4,240, while men increased their earnings by $6,271 when they made job changes.

TABLE 17
T-Test for Difference in Mean Salary Increases, by Sex

Males	Females	Significance Testing
$6,271	$4,240	t = 3.04 df = 225 p = .003

Most important and most frustrating, however, are the facts revealed in Table 18, which show that salary increases attained by women were significantly lower than those of men even when both moved for the same reasons (career reasons: t-test, p = .045; noncareer reasons: t-test, p = .081). Thus, when women did move to further their careers, their salary gains were less than those of men who had moved for like reasons. A similar disparity occurred between women and men who moved for noncareer reasons.

TABLE 18
Mean Salary Changes for Men and Women
Who Changed Jobs for the
Same Reasons

Motivation for Moving	Males	Females	Significance Testing
Career	$6,655	$4,859	t = 2.02 df = 107 p = .045
Personal or Family	$6,328	$3,586	t = 1.77 df = 77 p = .081

When mean salary gains were compared for men and women who had moved for career reasons, as shown in Table 18, women's increases averaged $1,796 less than men's ($4,859 compared to $6,665). This is a figure that represents 32.4 percent of the mean increase for both men and women who moved for these same reasons.

When salary increases resulting from personally or family-motivated moves were compared, women continued to receive lower salary increases than men moving for the same reasons. Table 13 demonstrates the fact that males who move for other than career reasons can expect to receive salary increases similar to those of males who move for career reasons, since there is no significant difference in salary increases between the two groups of men (t-test, p = .87). Males who changed jobs for personal or family reasons had increased their earnings by $6,328, while women in the same motivation category made salary gains of only $3,586. This is a substantial difference of $2,742, which amounts to 55.3 percent of the mean increase for both men and women who moved for these reasons.

The magnitude of the men's salary increments is partially a reflection of the fact that their average salaries surpassed women's by almost $3,000, increasing their likelihood of reaping substantial gains when they changed jobs. A related factor was the concentration of men in higher administrative levels, with concomitant salaries. Of course, the fact that men dominate these levels has been frequently discussed but never satisfactorily explained.

Results of data analysis in this section have indicated that librarians who are mobile tend to receive salary increases despite their reasons for changing jobs, but that motivations prompting moves influence the magnitude of salary gain. And, although librarians of both sexes could expect smaller salary gains when they moved for noncareer reasons, a mobile man could expect a substantial salary increase regardless of his motivations for moving. For a woman, on the other hand, differences in reasons for moving resulted in significant differences in salary increases. In addition, women consistently received lower salary increases than men, regardless of their motivations for moving. However, this disparity in salary gains cannot be explained as a result of either mobility rate (which is the same for both sexes) or motivations for mobility.

Hypothesis 7: There is no significant difference in position advancement resulting from career-motivated job changes and personally or family-motivated job changes.

Rejected

Calculation of the variables related to this hypothesis involved two steps, the first being categorization of reasons for each respondent's last job change as either (1) career related, or (2) personally and family related. Secondly, the change in each respondent's position level was categorized as either (1) an advancement, or (2) no advancement, which included those instances in which position level either remained the same or declined.

Table 19 shows that, with application of the chi-square test, a significant relationship was evident in position advancement as a result of career-oriented, as opposed to personally or family-oriented, job changes (p = .053). Of those respondents who had experienced positive changes in position level, 71.3 percent had changed jobs for career reasons. A shift in jobs made for career reasons did not insure a higher-level position, however. More than half of the respondents who were motivated to move for career considerations received no resultant position advancement, although a move made on the basis of career considerations was more than twice as likely to result in position advancement as one made for personal or family reasons. Conversely, moving on the basis of personal or family needs resulted in more than a 50 percent greater likelihood that lack of advancement would occur. Of those respondents who moved for noncareer reasons, 70.1 percent experienced no position advancement.

Since a significant relationship has already been demonstrated between motivations for mobility and position advancement, it was not surprising to discover that women, four times more likely than men to

TABLE 19
Position Change Resulting from Types of Motivations for Moving

Type of Motivation	Total Position Changes		No Position Advancement		Position Advancement	
	Number	Percent	Number	Percent	Number	Percent
Career	128	62.4	71	56.8	57	71.3
Personal or Family	77	37.6	54	43.2	23	28.7
Total	205	100.0	125	100.0	80	100.0

(N = 205, X^2 = 3.75, df = 1, p = .053)

move for noncareer reasons, were also less likely to reap promotions when they moved. Table 20 shows that when position advancement was analyzed in terms of sex, a significant difference was discerned between men and women (chi-square, p = .026). More than two-thirds of the women who made job changes experienced no resultant promotions, while only about half of the men who moved failed to advance to higher administrative levels.

TABLE 20
Position Change, by Sex

Position Change	Total Sample		Male		Female	
	Number	Percent	Number	Percent	Number	Percent
No Position Advancement	141	61.8	30	49.2	111	66.5
Position Advancement	87	38.2	31	50.8	56	33.5
Total	228	100.0	61	100.0	167	100.0

(N = 228, X^2 = 4.95, df = 1, p = .026)

When men and women moving for the same type of reasons were compared, however, women's position advancement continued to consistently less than that of men. Table 21 shows the degree of position change in terms of number of position levels lost or gained as a result of motivations for moving. These data have been summarized in Table 22, which shows position changes in terms of advancement or no advancement. When all respondents who moved for carer reasons were compared, a significant difference was found between men and women in terms of position advancement (see Table 21: Mann-Whitney U test, p = .031). Lower percentages of women than men were found to have made positive gains, while a greater proportion of women were found to have declined in position status or remained at the same level. As Table 21 indicates, almost one-fourth (24.7 percent) of the women who changed jobs for career motivations saw no advancement or suffered a decline in position level, compared to only 8.5 percent of the men. Only 37.0 percent of these mobile women advanced to higher position levels following their career-motivated job shifts, while 57.5 percent of the men who moved for career reasons reached higher administrative levels.

When position changes resulting from personally or family motivated moves were compared, women continued to make smaller gains than men who had moved for the same reasons. As Table 22 shows, more women than men received no position advancement (71.3 percent and 57.1 percent, respectively). Similarly, fewer women than men advanced to higher position levels (28.7 percent, compared to 42.9 percent). The significance of these differences was not appropriate for statistical testing because of the small number of men in this category (seven).

Thus, in rejecting the null hypothesis, it has been shown that motivations for moving influence the position advancement achieved by mobile librarians. Career-motivated moves were more than twice as likely as personally and family-motivated moves to result in position advancement. Owing to the extraordinary proportion of women who move for family reasons, job levels would naturally be affected. Even so they are affected in an unnatural way.

Men are much more likely than women to improve their position status, regardless of their reasons for moving, and women receive advancements much less frequently than men. Even when women moved as a result of career motivations, they did not achieve the degrees of position advancement of men who had moved for personal reasons. Disparities in advancement, therefore, are partially explicable in terms of motivations for moving. However, degrees of difference in position advancement between males and females cannot be explained in terms of either mobility rates (which are the same for men and women) or motivations for mobility.

Hypothesis 8: There is no significant difference in the frequency of leaves from the field between male and female librarians.
Rejected

Table 23 clearly indicates a significant difference between men and women in terms of the frequency of their leaves from the field (chi-square, p = .001). When asked if they had been absent from professional work for a period of six months or more, 29.4 percent of the females answered affirmatively, as compared to only 13.7 percent of the males.

TABLE 21
Position Levels Lost or Gained Resulting from Types of Motivation for Moving

Levels of Position Change	Males				Females			
	Career-Related Reasons		Personal or Family-Related Reasons		Career-Related Reasons		Personal or Family-Related Reasons	
	Number	Percent	Number	Percent	Number	Percent	Number	Percent
-3	0	0.0	0	0.0	4	4.9	4	5.7
-2	3	6.4	0	0.0	8	9.9	4	5.7
-1	1	2.1	1	14.3	8	9.9	9	12.9
0	16	34.0	3	42.8	31	38.3	33	47.0
1	17	36.2	2	28.6	21	25.9	16	22.9
2	8	17.0	1	14.3	8	9.9	2	2.9
3	2	4.3	0	0.0	1	1.2	2	2.9
Total	47	100.0	7	100.0	81	100.0	70	100.0

(Mann-Whitney U test for differences in position levels lost or gained as a result of career-motivated moves, $Z = -2.16$, $p = .031$)

TABLE 22
Position Change Resulting From Types of Motivations for Moving, by Sex

	Males				Females			
	Career-Motivated Move		Personal or Family-Motivated Move		Career-Motivated Move		Personal or Family-Motivated Move	
Position Change	Number	Percent	Number	Percent	Number	Percent	Number	Percent
No Position Advancement	20	42.6	4	57.1	51	63.0	50	71.4
Position Advancement	27	57.4	3	42.9	30	37.0	20	28.6
Total	47	100.0	7	100.0	81	100.0	70	100.0
	(N = 54, X^2 = .10, df = 1, p = .751)				(N = 151, X^2 = .86, df = 1, p = .353)			

TABLE 23
Leaves from the Field

Leaves	Total Sample		Males		Females	
	Number	Percent	Number	Percent	Number	Percent
No Leaves	346	75.1	113	86.3	233	70.6
One or More Leaves	115	24.9	18	13.7	97	29.4
Total	461	100.0	131	100.0	330	100.0

($N = 461$, $X^2 = 11.45$, $df = 1$, $p = .001$)

Table 24 shows that the greatest percentage of women who reported leaves took them in order to continue their educations (25,8 percent), followed by leaves for pregnancy and child-rearing (25.1 percent), and leaves to accompany their husbands when they relocated (16.2 percent). Reasons relating to family responsibilities accounted for 56.7 percent of the women's absences, but only 5 percent of the men's. No men at all were represented in categories of reasons that had accounted for fully 46.4 percent of the women's absences (health of family members, pregnancy or childrearing, moves with spouse).

TABLE 24
Reasons for Leaves from the Field

Reasons	Total Sample		Male		Female	
	Number	Percent	Number	Percent	Number	Percent
Continue Education	46	29.5	11	55.0	35	25.8
Work in Another Field	15	9.6	3	15.0	12	8.8
Personal Health	5	3.2	1	5.0	4	2.9
Health of Family Members	7	4.5	0	0.0	7	5.1
Pregnancy or Child-rearing	34	21.8	0	0.0	34	25.1
Moved with Spouse	22	14.1	0	0.0	22	16.2
Marital or Family Reasons	15	9.6	1	5.0	14	10.3
Other	12	7.7	4	20.0	8	5.8
Total	156	100.0	20	100.0	136	100.0

In Table 25, reasons for leaves were divided into two general categories in order to analyze broad trends: (1) work related (continuance of education, employment in another field), and (2) personal and family related (personal health, health of family members, pregnancy or child-rearing, moving with spouse, marital or family reasons). Men had greater proportional representation than women in the work-related category of absences. Of the total leaves reported by men, 70.0 percent were taken for work-related reasons, compared to only 34.6 percent of women's leaves. On the other hand, women were over twice as likely as men to take leaves for reasons in the personal and family categories. These differences between men and women are extremely significant (chi-square, p = .001).

TABLE 25
Reasons for Leaves from the Field, Categorized by Type

Reasons	Total Sample		Males		Females	
	Number	Percent	Number	Percent	Number	Percent
Work Related	61	39.1	14	70.0	47	34.6
Personal or Family Related	95	60.9	6	30.0	89	65.4
Total	156	100.0	20	100.0	136	100.0

(N = 156, X^2 = 8.6, df = 1, p = .001)

Obviously, then, a woman's home and family responsibilities play a large part in the interruptions that occur throughout her career. Because a man's role in the family had traditionally been that of breadwinner, his career is often considered of primary importance in families in which both spouses work. A working woman must often combine the two roles of homemaker and worker, and conflicts between these roles may result in career interruptions that most men in the same profession do not have to face.

While the influence of work interruptions on women's careers has frequently been cited as an important contribution to their disproportionate salaries and position levels, such a relationship was not evidenced in this study. First of all, less than a third (29.4 percent) of all female librarians in the sample reported interruptions in their careers. Therefore, for the more than two-thirds of the female librarians in the sample who have experienced no career interruptions, leaves from the field cannot be held accountable for salary and position discrepancies.

Secondly, the contribution of such disruptions to women's professional status has not been demonstrated to be negative. While more than twice the percentage of women as men took leaves at least once in their careers, their length of time in the profession averaged slightly more than men's (10.4 and 9.8 years, respectively). Therefore, regardless of the time missed due to leaves women have professional library experience that more than favorably compares to that of men.

Tables 26 and 27 compare respondents who had taken career leaves with those who had not, in terms of salary, position level, and average tenure. Surprisingly, no significant difference was found between the two groups when the entire sample was analyzed. When respondents who had taken leaves were examined in subgroups by sex, however, some significant differences were evident.

TABLE 26
T-Test for Differences in Mean Tenure and Salary, by Leaves Taken

Category	No Leaves	1 or More Leaves	Significance Test
Average Tenure In Years	5.16	5.04	$t = .24$ $df = 445$ $p = .808$
Salary	$12,576	$13,020	$t = -1.08$ $df = 443$ $p = .279$

TABLE 27
Present Position Level, by Leaves Taken[a]

	No Leaves		1 or More Leaves	
Position Level	Number	Percent	Number	Percent
Nonadministrative Professional	117	34.8	30	27.5
Department or Unit Supervisor	146	43.5	56	51.4
Assistant Director	24	7.1	5	4.6
Director	49	14.6	18	16.5
Total	336	100.0	109	100.0

[a]The category representing "other" types of positions has been deleted from this table.
($N = 445$, $X^2 = 3.49$, $df = 3$, $p = .322$)

Tables 28 and 29 show these differences in tenure, salary, and position level within sex groups. Men who had taken leaves were not shown to be significantly differenct from men who had not taken leaves, in terms of their salaries (t-test, $p = .133$) and average tenure (t-test, $p = .676$). However, when position levels were examined, a

TABLE 28
T-Tests for Differences in Mean Tenure and Salary by Leaves Taken, by Sex

Category	Males			Females		
	No Leaves	1 or More Leaves	Significance Testing	No Leaves	1 or More Leaves	Significance Testing
Average Tenure in Years	4.89	4.26	t = .42 df = 127 p = .676	5.29	5.14	t = .26 df = 316 p = .793
Salary	$14,537	$16,615	t = -1.51 df = 120 p = .133	$11,665	$12,415	t = -.233 df = 321 p = .020

TABLE 29
Present Position Level by Leaves Taken, by Sex

Position Level	Males				Females			
	No Leaves		1 or More Leaves		No Leaves		1 or More Leaves	
	Number	Percent	Number	Percent	Number	Percent	Number	Percent
Nonadministrative Professional	24	22.2	0	0.0	93	40.8	30	32.6
Department or Unit Supervisor	44	40.7	8	47.05	102	44.8	48	52.2
Assistant Director	10	9.3	1	5.9	14	6.1	4	4.3
Director	30	27.8	8	47.05	19	8.3	10	10.9
Total	108	100.0	17	100.0	228	100.0	92	100.0

(Mann-Whitney U Test, Z = -.204, p = .042)
(X^2 not possible because of an empty cell for which collapsing was not appropriate)

(Mann-Whitney U Test, Z = -1.18, p = .237)
(N = 320, X^2 = 2.75, df = 3, p = .237)

significant difference was found between the two groups of men (Mann-Whitney U test, p = .042). The direction of the effect seems to indicate that men who took leaves benefited in terms of position. Unfortunately, the number of men who took leaves was relatively small, only 12.9 percent of all men in the sample, and additional data are needed before a strong statement can be made about this effect.

When women were analyzed as a subgroup, no significant difference was found between those who had interrupted their careers and those who had not, in terms of position (Mann-Whitney U test, p = .237) or average tenure (t-test, p = .793). There was, however, a statistically significant difference evident in their salaries (t-test, p = .020). The women who had taken absences exhibited higher mean salaries than those who had not. The difference in mean present salaries between the two groups of women was $750; $12,415 for women who reported leaves, and $11,655 for those who did not.

The analysis of data relating to leaves from the field reveals no evidence that the higher percentages of leaves taken by women are influential in depressing their salaries or position attainment. In fact, there is some indication that an absence favorably affects a woman's salary progression. It is the sex of a librarian, rather than the frequency of leaves taken or the reasons motivating them, that is the better indicator of career status.

Men who took leaves from the field had yearly salaries that averaged $4,200 more than those of women who also took leaves. This amounts to 32.3 percent of the mean salary for all respondents who reported absences, as shown in Table 26. When position level was examined, it was determined that none of the men who reported leaves presently occupy nonadministrative positions, compared to almost a third (32.6 percent) of the women who had taken leaves, and 40.8 percent of the women who had not. Conversely, almost half of the men who interrupted their careers (47.1 percent) are presently library directors. Only 10.9 percent of the women who experienced career interruptions are presently directors, while an even smaller percentage of women who worked steadily in librarianship hold directorships (8.3 percent).

CONCLUSIONS

In recent years, librarianship, typically characterized as a woman's profession, has welcomed greater numbers of men into its ranks. Recruitment of men into the profession has been enhanced by the fact that an ambitious man has the opportunity to rise to an administrative position and gain a higher salary. Some men who might otherwise hesitate risking the stigma of employment in a "feminine" occupation are attracted by the possibility of rapid advancement and the prestige that accompanies administrative responsibilities.

Until recently, this pattern of rapid and unequal advancement for male librarians was generally accepted as a means of enhancing the status of the profession (Schiller, 1974; Ginzberg and Brown, 1967). Since the late 1960s, however, the disparity in career progression between men and women in librarianship has been the subject of increasing concern. Recognition and discussion of the problem have prompted numerous explanations for such inequalities. One commonly accepted theory has been that women suffer because of their relative lack of mobility within the profession. Previous research, which has repeatedly shown women to be less mobile than men, has lent credibility to this argument.

The results of this study, however, indicated that the depressed status of women in librarianship cannot be attributed to differences in the frequency of their job moves compared to men. Nor is their situation explicable in terms of motivations that stimulate them to change jobs. First, fully three-fourths of the mobile women in the sample made their last job shift based on career considerations. Secondly, and more important, women who moved, whether for career or noncareer reasons, did not reap the benefits enjoyed by men who had moved for similar reasons. A woman who shifted jobs for either type of reason gained less than a man who had also changed jobs.

As a matter of fact, when men were analyzed separately as a subgroup, their motivations for moving were shown to have an insignificant effect on either their salaries or promotions. As a result, a man who moved for any reason could expect to move upward in his career. This, of course, was not true for women. Finally, men who had interrupted their careers earned higher salaries and occupied higher-level positions than all women, whether they had experienced interruptions or not.

In short, the results of this study indicated that frequency of job changes, and the motivations that prompt them, cannot be held responsible for the position and salary gap between men and women in librarianship. Further research is needed to thoroughly investigate other variables that may account for these professional variations between sexes.

An Analysis of the Study, "Career Paths of Male and Female Librarians in Canada"

ELIZABETH FUTAS

IN THE EARLY 1970s a group of sociologists and librarians[1] sought a grant from the Canada Council for funding a study on the career paths of male and female librarians in Canada. After receiving a moderate-size grant, four women designed a research project destined never to be completed. Why? There are all sorts of reasons why research projects are not completed: lack of funds, lack of interest, lack of time, problems of methodology, design, or implementation. In this study, all of these reasons are in part responsible. Perhaps there is one other—certainly an unprovable one (and one which the researchers themselves have denied) — political suppression. Why this may be so is not the reason for this discussion; that it may be so, is. The following discussion is on the methodological design and the analysis and findings that were completed before the project was dropped. It is one more attempt to release the work of this study to researchers in the fields of librarianship, sociology, and women's studies so that they may carry on the work begun by these four and build upon it. True scientific research is not complete until it is published in some form. With the publication of this chapter, the analysis and findings will come under public scrutiny, and the methodology and theoretical model constructed will be added to the scientific community. It will now be possible to build upon the conclusions and methodology of this study.

The objective of the research was to study the relationship between the causal variables of discrimination and motivation. In previous research, evidence showed that these two were significant reasons for the differences in achievement of males and females in the work world. What was new in this study was the attempt to tie these two variables together in a multivariate analysis, and using librarians as the population on which to do so. The significance of the findings of this study must be understood within these two parameters, since it will be the thesis of this discussion that a major explanation of the results (or lack of them) involved these two factors, especially the latter one.

Another objective of this study was to construct a complex theoretical model based on existing evidence, which would distinguish differences in motives between male and female librarians. These motives would be measured by both individual perceptions and life histories (qualitative, quantitative) of different types of librarians, the types based on demographic information (age, sex, education, current job status, and so on) and perceptual information (opportunities and abilities). A relationship was anticipated between motivation, aspiration, and action in seeking and applying for promotion. "Application for promotions as well as acceptance of promotions not applied for are paths leading to differential job histories which in turn lead to differences in current status" (Fischer, 1976).

To measure the second causal variable, discrimination, a matched sample of male and female librarians was drawn and a comparison made of their current status. Although work patterns upon which these comparisons were made were basically within male styles, the value judgment that the male work pattern of continuous employment was what should be aspired to was suspended for this research.

The use of librarians was seen as an advantage for several reasons. As a single professional category they are a fairly homogeneous group. This certainly helped in the design of the questionnaire. It is one of the few professions where women outnumber men to a considerable degree. This allowed enough female cases so that a smaller sample size might be taken. This latter reason was important, since a reasonable sample size coupled with a satisfactory response rate would, it was hoped, yield valid results. According to the researchers, the response rate may have contributed largely to the sampling problem encountered. Looking at the analyis and findings, another possible reason for these problems could be traced back to the use of librarianship as the population group to be tested. Those very factors that made it a useful group in this research may in fact have led to certain findings that could not be generalized to fit all men and women in the work world. Another possible problem was in the measurement of motivation and discrimination. This will be discussed later in the chapter.

As of 1981, very little had been done to publish or publicize the findings of this study. Only one article, in *The Emergency Librarian*, had appeared, concerning a small part of the findings of this study, having to do with the salary levels of female and male librarians in Canadian libraries (Fischer, Waysylycia-Coe, and Yaffe, 1978). Other than this article, and some notices in bibliographies, none of this research had been published. In fact, very little analysis of the data had been undertaken, other than for a report, which had never been published, submitted to the Canada Council in fulfillment of the grant.

THE STUDY

In 1973, four researchers, two sociologists and two librarians, decided that an in-depth social and psychological study of the career patterns of Canadian librarians was possible. Their reason for choosing librarians has already been mentioned. They singled out Canadian librarians because, for many decades, most of the research about this professional group concerned those who practiced their profession in the United States. Canadian social scientists would then generalize to the same professional groups in Canada. While there is no indication that this cannot be done, it was considered politically wise for Canadian researchers to work exclusively in their own country, particularly since they had obtained a grant from a Canadian foundation. Certainly, if studies made of United States professionals could be generalized to Canada, the reverse could also be done. That is, anything significant discovered about Canadian librarians could certainly be extrapolated to American ones.

This study concerns motivation and discrimination. It not only studies the differences between male and female librarians, but all differences among all kinds of librarians. In particular, it was designed "to investigate differentials which exist between males and females with regard to achievement in the work world (Fischer et al., 1976, p. 1).

Evidence of both discrimination and motivational differences does exist, but it has never been the kind that could be presented in a court of law or that would satisfy the research community. It is possible, of course, since the research community of both Canada and the United States is male-dominated, that such a study as this could never be accepted in the way it was intended. Few research studies that symbolize the first of their kind ever do. It is perhaps in that regard that this study, uncompleted as it was, failed the most. In order to gain acceptance in the social-science research community, many studies reaching basically the same conclusions will have to be done. By not completing this one, the researchers' groundbreaking will have to be repeated by the next investigator. Most feminists will say that there is no point to doing such studies, since they will not be accepted by the male-dominated community. This is a defeatist attitude. In fact, studies using the weapons of the male community are the surest way of proving what we already know—discrimination exists.

This study chose to use the tools of the traditional social scientist to examine what is essentially a feminist problem. In fact, because librarianship is a female-dominated profession, the results are more likely to be accepted because they show discrimination toward the whole of the profession, as opposed to only women. This shows that all who practice librarianship are discriminated against, regardless of their gender. In other words, all librarians might as well be women, since the discrimination affects all of the profession. Yet, this whole issue aside, women librarians may be doubly discriminated against, as males in the profession are paid more, have fewer role conflicts, and achieve more. What must be determined is why this is happening. The first step is to prove that this is indeed the case. This is what the Canadian study has done, to a degree, although the question, "Why is it so?" was abandoned.

The goal of the study was threefold:

1. To distinguish between types of people in several different dimensions (e.g., size of community, gender, and so forth);
2. To look at the differences in their perceptions (e.g., abilities and opportunities);
3. To note the effect this has on motivations and aspirations.

Although the data for all of these goals were actually collected, coded, and keypunched, the analysis of the first goal, the distinguishing of types, was barely begun, when the research group broke up. It is possible that the task they had so carefully laid out for themselves proved overwhelming for the group. Certainly that would be a reasonable excuse, since the task, as will be seen by the explanation of the model and the presentation of the hypothesis, was enormous. For whatever reason, these goals were not achieved, and what we are left with is an exceptionally well-planned study; its execution, perhaps not as well implemented (there were several reasons for this, including a mail strike of several months' duration in the middle of the sampling); and of the analysis, virtually nothing except one article on salary differentials (Cheda et al., 1978) and another one on the sex of chief librarians in Canadian libraries (Wasylycia-Coe, 1981).

With the three goals in mind, let us take a look at the most impressive part of the project, the conceptual design.

THE MODEL

The model used to organize variables at the conceptual level was adapted from Biddle and Thomas's (1966) role framework. Although their framework was used, the relationship between variables came from the findings and conclusions drawn from other studies. The result was a highly complex set of social and psychological variables, which the researchers divided into two groups; major and minor variables. In the diagram of the complete model, presented below, the major variables are enclosed in rectangular boxes, while the minor variables are underscored. The relationships among these variables is indicated by single-line arrows (minor variables with symmetrical relationships).

To make it easier to understand the model, the following symbols are used:

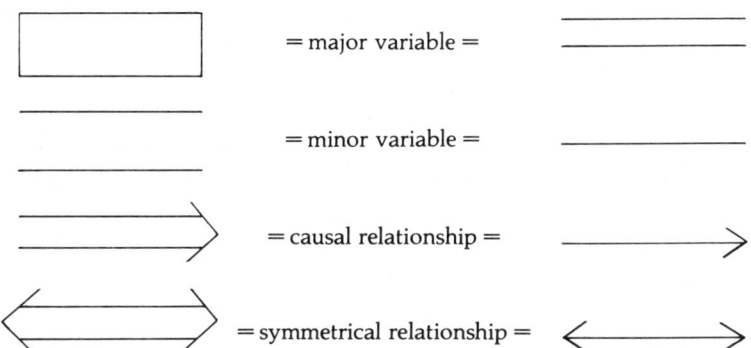

Although the study was originally to follow all paths indicated by the model indicated in Figure 1, it became apparent quite early in the design and implementation that this would not be feasible. Owing to limitations of money and time, only the major variables would be examined, and only the relationships that connect them to the one role component studied (current job status) could be researched through to the conclusion of the study. However, this small part of the large conceptual model really contains many parts. The final model can be seen in Figure 2. The symbols are the same as those used in Figure 1.

The two major variables studied were current job status and rate of advancement. Figure 2 represents the major facets of the study—what affects the current job status and degree of advancement of Canadian librarians? The researchers, contemplating an adjusted version of the full model, sought to remove some parts of it but at the same time to design a study that others could complete. For that reason, three role components are not studied:—the other position, family position, and everything other than those two. The role component of incumbent position was chosen for examination.

THE VARIABLES

There were nine variables in this study. The two major dependent variables were current job status and rate of advancement:

1. *Current job status* The prestige of a certain position in the library systems of Canada, as judged by librarians. These judgments are measured

FIGURE 1.
Diagramatic representation of social psychological model of variables affecting work careers and current job status. (Separate shaded areas define clusters of role components for positions.)

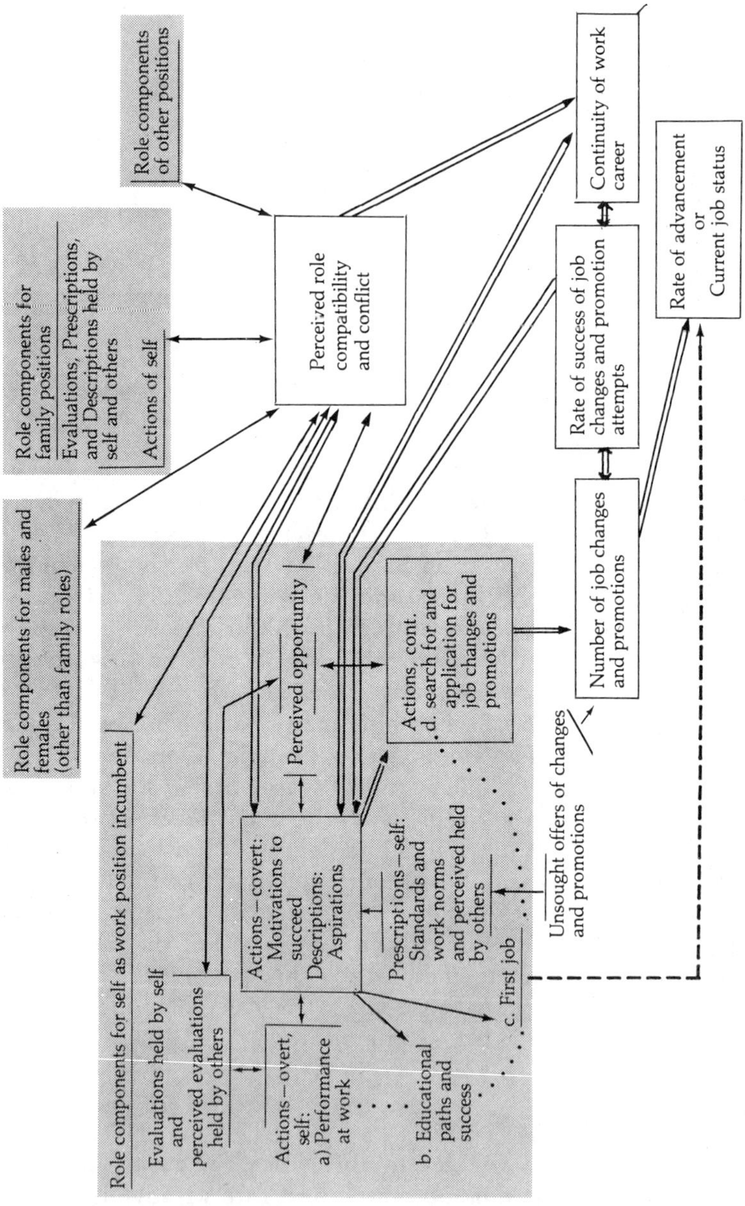

FIGURE 2

Role components for self as work position incumbent

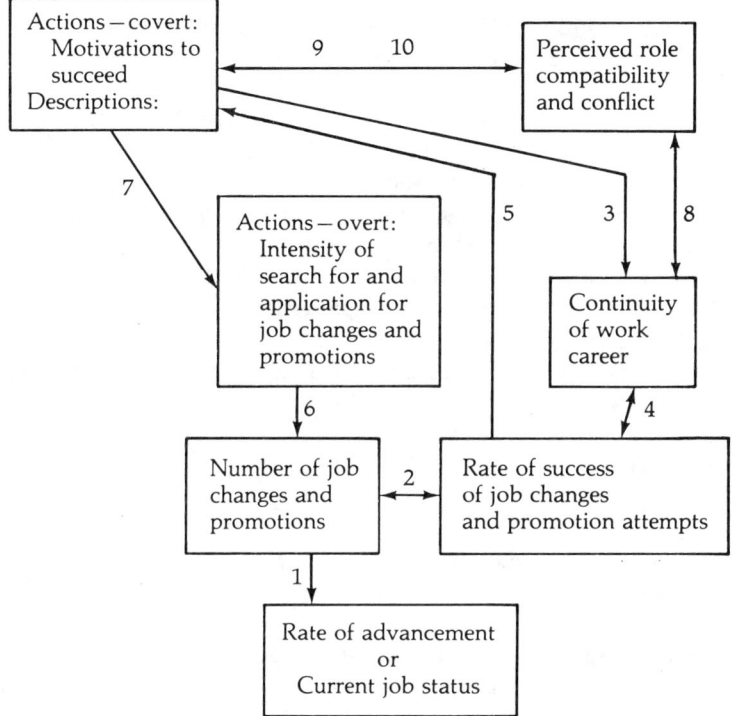

along a continuum that combines several aspects of the job, including title (e.g., assistant director), functions (e.g., supervision), and the prestige of the library or the systems represented (e.g., size of population served). Each person's job in the sample was given a score for this variable from a national panel. The score was in ratio data format.

2. *Rate of advancement* The rate of increase on a yearly basis of the job status (position prestige) from the status of the first position (in a set of positions held in the field) or the first professional position after the last educational degree that was relevant (e.g., library degree). These two (or one of them) are given in relation to the current job. Again, this is expressed as a ratio of the score assigned to the current job status and the years since the starting point.

It can be seen that there is a strong relationship between the major dependent variables. The current job status is the end product of the rate of advancement (when the starting point is controlled). For persons with the same number of years since their schooling ended, the greater the rate of advancement, the higher the current job status.

Variables that will be measured against them are seven in number. Only five of them are treated here:

3. *Continuity of work* A set of career patterns that are characterized by the nature of the nonjob-related activities that cause a full- or part-time interruption of a job (in the career pattern), as well as the number and lengths of these interruptions. There are many types of interruptions examined, the three most prevalent being reasons of family, education, and illness. Directly connected to this variable are three others: motivations and aspirations, role compatability and conflict, and rate of success of job changes and promotions. Variable 3 is an independent variable except when it is examined in the light of role compatibility and conflict.

4. *Number of job changes and promotions* The number of position changes within a set of positions held sequentially by an individual.

5. *Rate of success of job changes and promotions* The rate of successful job searches over a set of sequential positons.

Variables 4 and 5, while almost self-explanatory, are also closely-related measures of success.

6. *Motivation* Overt role action, measured by the performance of a position incumbent as a result of that incumbency. In less formal language, this means how well an individual does in a job in relation to the job's requirement. This will be measured, for the sake of this study, by the search and application for a new job and by promotions received. There is an underlying assumption that the success of getting new jobs proves performance in the job replaced. Some overt role actions are, of course, less important than others, e.g., first job.

Covert role action, another measurement of motivation (called motives by Biddle and Thomas) is really the history of actions by any and all sets of people concerning a certain position as well as a set of incumbents of that position and their actions.

Although it is difficult to examine motivation without the counterpart of aspirations (see Variable 7) the specific motivation in this research is distinguished from other motivations by the nature of the aspiration—in other words, here only the motivation toward upward mobility is examined. In this case, the motivation (or action, whether overt or covert) can vary, but the aspiration (where you are heading—up) can not.

The variable of motivation is, for this research, a key independent one. The motivation of being upwardly mobile is the individual's state of readiness to embark on a sequence of actions leading to a better position. These actions are what represents motivation and what is measured by this study.

7. Aspirations Role descriptions are behaviors in which persons represent events, processes, and phenomena without evaluative or affective accompaniments. They are known in two ways, by overt role descriptions (i.e., statements that may refer to role behaviors of the past, present, or future) and covert role descriptions, which, once they are made known to a researcher on the questionnaire, become overt, but which before then are covert (or unnamed).

Aspiration is, for this research, a key independent variable, and represents goals or plans to achieve them.

In the process of narrowing down the scope of the study, two unexplored relationships between these two key independent variables were dropped. Since they appear to very important to the future of such studies as these, it seems appropriate to mention them for future reference.

8. perceived role compatability and conflict

9. perceived opportunities

Motivations to succeed and high aspirations may cause conflict between two positions (or role components). An example is the possible conflict between work and family. If one is responsible for care for others, aspirations that lead to a perceived need for extra work hours in one's job may cause a conflict. This results in high aspirations' leading to greater conflict for some people. If conflict preceded the formation of expectations, the aspirations may be voluntarily restrained by way of diminishing the stress involved. In nontechnical language, those people who have two roles to play in their lives (work and family—as most women do) often find that when they feel they need to devote more time to one, stress is created, since they know that the other will suffer. In some cases, when one is brought up to take on responsibilities above or before all others, the best way to avoid conflict is not to perceive any need for aspirations in the other role. For example, if a woman does not aspire to get ahead in her work, she will never feel the stress of having to choose work over family.

Perceived role compatibility and conflict is the degree of felt conflict between role components (or positions). The most conflict is expected to be between family and work, although illness, second jobs, or school may provide temporary conflicts for anyone.

Sequencing is an important part of the descriptions of the foregoing variables and how they measure what they are supposed to. Much of the description of variables assumes a knowledge of their sequence. Without a longitudinal study, such information can only be secured by retrospective data from questionnaires that ask about how one was motivated, conflicted, and the like, at different time periods during the entire work career. There are varying degrees of validity for this method, depending on the nature of the information; e.g., successful applications are more likely to remembered and reported than unsuccessful ones, positions occupied even more likely to be remembereed and reported than are motivations and aspirations from long ago. For this reason, when the scope of the study was narrowed, it was felt that the least valid variables to be measured would be perceptions, and so they were dropped. To study them would require either a longitudinal study or a very large sample size, to be at all confident about the findings.

METHODOLOGY

This study was designed with two assumptions in mind. First, the data should be applicable to all librarians in Canada, and second, the expense of the study should be minimal. For these reasons, it is important to realize the difficulties involved. In order to generalize to all librarians, one group, school librarians, was not counted at all. In Canada this may not be of great significance, but of course it would be in the United States. A national sample of all other types of librarians was taken. This was not a random one, but a stratified cluster random sample.

First, all the academic and public libraries were treated as clusters, depending on their size and type. It is from these clusters that a random sample of librarians was chosen. Before the libraries were put into clusters, they were stratified as well by size. This reflected the number of staff members they had; therefore, the sample was taken so that no matter how small a library one came from, every librarian had an equal chance of falling into the sample. Several reference directories of types of libraries and numbers of librarians were available, and it was from these that the final sample was chosen. In all there are seven strata: small, medium, and large public libraries; small and large university libraries; community-college libraries; and special libraries. The method of drawing the sample was similar to the way in which the National Education Association samples teachers in the United States. Stratification was done by type and size, clusters sampled at different rates, and from each cluster, librarians were sampled. Therefore, it can be seen that the sampling rate for each cluster in the same stratum would be the same, but would vary between strata. The most appropriate sample size was estimated to be 1000. This was to insure a minimum of 200 in each cell.

There were two questionnaires created for this study. (See Appendix, pp. 414-23.) The first was sent to all those who fell into the stratified cluster sample. It was for the main part a demographic-type data collection, which asked for yes-or-no answers to questions, as well as some short answers to questions on background, current employment, previous work record, and so forth. The second questionnaire was sent to the same people. Several lengthier questions were asked that called for reactions to situations that could then be coded as to perceived status, worth, and the like.

The researchers consciously decided to emulate a rather successful methodology in sending out complicated and long questionnaires, by sending them out in two parts. A single questionnaire might have been too long for respondents, and this would have been reflected in the response rate. Instead, this two-step process was adopted and found to be an effective method of getting people to fill out a long, involved document. It appears that, once committed to a survey by answering the first questionnaire, an individual is more likely to fill out a second, more difficult one. In addition, a very long, involved, follow-up method was instituted, which consisted of four reminders to fill out the forms, each at two- (for the pretest) or three- (for the test) week intervals. "We received many positive and a few negative comments on our follow-up methods, but they did not work as well as we had thought they would or should" (Fischer et al., 1976, p. 37). In commenting on the low rate of return during the actual test, researchers said that during the pretest, a telephone call was made soon after the fourth reminder was sent out. During the actual survey, this call was made much later, and the response was much smaller. The one interesting aspect of the testing follow-up of nonrespondents versus respondents was that "nonrespondents were more likely to be reference librarians or cataloguers (Fischer et al., 1976, p. 39).

Certain criticisms can be leveled at the study very early in its implementation. School librarians were not counted, nor were library educators. As the researchers themselves are the first to admit, "We lost a disproportionate number of francophone college respondents this way" (Fischer et al., 1976, p. 33). In order to get the seven strata to have equal cell size, 200 in each, 2000 would be the correct sample size. For the sake of the entire population alone, without this stratified sample, 1000 would have been enough. Because of the Canadian mail strike, which came in the middle of the first mailing, in 1975, the response rate came to 831, even less than the 1000 needed to estimate on the entire population without going into the strata. The researchers were well aware of the problems faced with response rate to questionnaires in Canadian surveys. Along with the unfortunate postal strike, this meant that most of the significance (in a statistical sense) has been lost from these data. However, the model, the design, and some of the demographic data, although not totally conclusive, are certainly interesting. It is the control, the demographic data that will be discussed in this chapter, as well as the design, which is of the utmost importance.

There were 10 hypotheses developed for this study. Although many were not analyzed and some were not significant, the hypotheses themselves are valuable for further research.

HYPOTHESIS 1: The more job changes and promotions, the greater the degree of advancement from the first full-time job to the current one, and the higher the current job status.

This hypothesis results from analyzing the two major dependent variables, current job status and rate of advancement, and seeing their relationship. That relationship would seem almost a truism, since the definition of the two variables links them. The hypothesis is designed to detemine what that relationship is and if there is any difference between different types of librarians within the sample.

HYPOTHESIS 2: The greater the ratio of successful job changes and promotion attempts, the greater the number of such changes and promotions.

This hypothesis links the rate of success and the number of job changes. Once such a link is established, the researchers can then substitute, where appropriate, one for the other. As can be seen from the smaller model of the study, this hypothesis is of a symmetrical relationship, thus assuring the substitution once the relationship is proven.

HYPOTHESIS 3: The greater the search and application for job changes and promotions, the greater the number of such changes and promotions.

Some of the hypotheses in this study, including this one, could come straight out of *Poor Richard's Almanac*! This is one of them. It is a sort of cross between "If at first you don't succeed, try, try again," and "Nothing succeeds like success."

HYPOTHESIS 4: The greater the motivation and the higher the aspiration, the more intense the search and application for job changes and promotions.

When the applications are successful, the aspirations will rise, because the approval of others is perceived (an unmeasured variable in this study). The raised aspirations will lead to more search and applications (as in Hypothesis 7). If success continues (or as long as it continues), so does the cycle.

HYPOTHESIS 5: The greater the ratio of successful job changes and promotion attempts, the more the motivation to succeed, and the higher the aspirations.

HYPOTHESIS 6: The ratio of successful job changes and promotion attempts and career continuity are positively associated.

Hypotheses 3-6 are linked together in the cycle discussed concerning Hypothesis 4. If the ratio of successful job changes and promotions affects career continuity, then motivation and aspiration do also.

HYPOTHESIS 7: Motivations and aspirations of job (position) incumbents are positively related to continuous work careers.

This is the substitution of motivation and aspiration for the ratio of successful-job-change and -promotion attempts. Where job holders want to go and how they approach getting there is directly related and indirectly linked to continuous work. The rate of success of job changes and promotions is linked both directly and indirectly to continuous work, although it was expected by the researchers that there would be other variables (of a demographic nature) that would affect continuity more.

HYPOTHESIS 8: The fewer the role conflicts, the greater the work continuity.

Again, by definition (as in Hypothesis 1), this is assured. This hypothesis was to be tested using two different definitions of role conflict and compatability. First, conflict of other responsibilites with the demands of a continuous career would be judged by the researchers; in the second instance, the alternation of family and job responsibilities was to be determined by the way in which respondents filled out questionnaires, as when it was perceived to be easier to quit job responsibilities and carry out others, returning later to the workforce.

HYPOTHESIS 9: The greater the motivation and the higher the aspirations, the greater the perceived role conflict at present.

As can plainly be seen by the model, this hypothesis and the previous one are the symmetrical links between motivations and aspirations and perceived role compatability and conflict. They are, in fact, correlaries of each other.

HYPOTHESIS 10: The greater the perceived role conflict (past), the lower the motivation to succeed and the lower the aspirations.

Since the perceived role conflict and compatability were not measured (along with the last variable of perceived opportunities), these two hypotheses were incapable of being examined within the context of this study. However, they appear to be important to the overall objectives of a study such as this one. Given the questionnaire data collected (especially in part 2) these data presumably would have been collected and analysis possible.

In addition to the 10 hypotheses and the various variables defined here, several other variables were also collected. These were mostly demographic in nature, with no need for definition (e.g., age, family status, gender). A last group of variables was collected, because to do so meant no extra financial outlay. These include performance at work, self-evaluation, and other perceived evaluations. They were not, as far as could be determined, coded for this study, but they do exist on the work sheets. Most were on the second part of the questionnaire. (Both parts of the questionnaire are appended to this chapter.)

ANALYSIS AND FINDINGS

The findings of this study are divided into two parts— a detailed demographic look at the librarians who fell into the sample and a look at 8 of the 10 hypotheses. In fact, only a few of the hypotheses were provable.

There are many characteristics of the librarians in the sample that may be of interest to researchers. Certainly, if the sample is generalizable to the entire population of Canadian librarians, the characteristics are very interesting. Both English-and French-language librarians were sampled, although the French-language librarians (13.3 percent) were much fewer in number than their English (86.7 percent) equivalents. A majority of the librarians come from large public and large university libraries. The largest nonresponse rate came from these two groups as well. This means that even though they represent the largest two groups in the sample, they may still be underrepresented from the general population. The single greatest number of respondents come from the province of Ontario (44.5 percent). In Canada, the bachelor's and master's degrees are both acceptable as professional degrees. For that reason, 54.4 percent of the sample had bachelor's degrees, while 43.6 percent had master's. The majority of the librarians in the sample were between the ages of 30 and 39. Of these, 38.9 percent of all women were in this category, and 49.9 percent of all men. However, the chi-square value indicated this as a nonsignificant figure. A more significant figure was the marital status and parental status of librarians in the sample.

TABLE 1
Marital status of females and males in proportional sample

Marital Status	Females #	%	Males #	%	Total #	%
Previously Married	51	11.5	8	3.6	59	8.9
Currently Married	228	51.5	149	67.4	377	56.8
Single	164	37.0	64	29.0	228	34.3
Total	443	100.0	221	100.0	664	100.0

Chi-square value significant at .0001 probability level.
50 females (23.1%) reported ever being single parents while 4 males (2.7%) did.

Another significant figure is the number of children of married Canadian librarians (see Table 2).

Another set of interesting characteristics concerns the occupational levels of librarians in the sample. "If our respondents are representative of the distribution of librarians at different levels in Canada, almost 50 percent are in some supervisory or senior position" (Fischer et al., 1976, p. 53).

Among other significant characteristics was the income levels represented by the sample. They will not be addressed here, for two reasons. First, the only data published from this study concerned this particular characteristic (Cheda, 1978). Second, the data from this study are over six years old. By now, because of inflation during the last

TABLE 2
Parental status of ever-married females and males in the proportional sample (Respondents to Part I)

Number of Children	Females #	%	Males #	%	Total #	%
0	122	45.2	44	28.6	166	39.2
1-2	98	36.3	87	56.5	185	43.6
3+	50	18.5	23	14.9	73	17.2
No info.	9	—	3	—	12	—
Total	279	100.0	157	100.0	436	100.0

Chi-square value significant at .001 probability level.

few years, the salary figures themselves are meaningless. For the comparison of men's and women's salaries, Cheda's (1978) article tells it all.

One of the most interesting demographic features found in this study was the distribution by sex within language categories. The results were so unusual that the researchers went back to the sampling methodology to see if the French-language population was underrepresented. What they found, much to their surprise, was that, to the contrary, the French-speaking population was probably over represented. The following statistics, therefore, are perhaps even more significant than was originally acknowledged. "There are more male than female librarians who work in French libraries, while there are more women than men in English or bilingual libraries"(Fischer et al., 1976, p. 64).

TABLE 3
Sex distribution within language categories

Sex	French #	%	English #	%	Total #	%
Female	30	33.7	415	71.8	445	66.7
Male	59	66.3	163	28.2	222	33.3
Total	89	100.0	578	100.0	667	100.0

Chi-square value significant at better than .0001 probability level.

This complete reversal of both the English-language and American population figures of women to men was a cultural bias on the part of the researchers. There were probably reasons for this. Among the most probable are explained by Tables 4 and 5.

TABLE 4
Female and male distribution across strata

Strata	Females #	Females %	Males #	Males %	Total #	Total %
Small public	18	4.0	6	2.7	24	3.6
Medium public	64	14.4	13	5.9	77	11.5
Large public	112	25.2	44	19.8	156	23.4
Special	88	19.8	31	14.0	119	17.8
Small university	38	8.5	41	18.5	79	11.8
Large university	84	18.9	62	27.8	146	21.9
Community College	41	9.2	25	11.3	66	9.9
Total	445	100.0	222	100.0	667	100.0

Chi-square value significant at better than .0001 probability level.

As can be seen by Table 4, strata also seem to differ about the same way as sex and language do. In other words, there are many more men in large university libraries and a correspondingly low number of women in these libraries. There are also more French-speaking university libraries than French-speaking public libraries. The reason for this is probably historic, since the English-speaking world has had, in the past, a greater commitment to public-library service than any other culture.

The final step in determining the reasons for the foregoing variance was to determine if males of both language categories could be found in academic libraries.

Males and females who answered the French questionnaire are evenly distributed in large university libraries. Both sexes in both languages are even in college libraries. Males have the edge in small university French and both university categories for the English. Women have the edge in all public categories. These generalizations apply to the distribution of each sex across strata. Within each strata, men outnumber the women in French libraries and women outnumber the men in English libraries (Fischer et al., 1976, p. 67).

HYPOTHESIS 1: The more job changes and promotions, the greater the degree of advancement from the first full-time job to the current one, and the higher the current job status.

TABLE 5
French and English distributions across strata

Strata	French #	French %	English #	English %	Total #	Total %
Small public	2	2.2	22	3.8	24	3.6
Medium public	1	1.1	76	13.1	77	11.5
Large public	11	12.4	145	25.1	156	23.4
Special	5	5.6	114	19.7	118	17.8
Small university	23	25.8	56	9.7	79	11.8
Large university	29	32.6	117	20.2	146	21.9
Community College	18	20.2	48	8.3	66	9.9
Total	89	100.0	578	100.0	667	100.0

Chi-square value significant at better than .0001 probability level.

Basically, there are two comparisons in this hypothesis. One is the ratio of the number of job changes and promotions to the degree of advancement (from the first full-time job to the present job); the second involves the number of job changes and promotions and their relationship to the status of the current job.

In analyzing the data, the relationship, which was predicted to be causal, did, in fact, show a linearity. This, however, was very weak. In trying to strengthen it, only the first six jobs were counted (eliminating the seventh through ninth job changes listed on the questionnaire). A weak linear relationship was revealed. When trying to see if other demographic data would serve to indicate a stronger causal relationship, both sex and length of career were tested. Where gender was concerned, there was no improvement in the variation of degree of advancement explained by the six job changes. When examining length of career, this fell into two distinct stages; from 5 to 19 years in the career and from 20 to 34 years in the career. Each appears to be linear except for extremes. In other words, there was little variance in those librarians who had less than 5 years' experience or for those librarians with over 34 years'. Even with these changes, there was still only a slight degree of variance. "In other words, number of job changes does affect degree of advancement in the library hierarchy (as measured by prestige) slightly. The group whose careers are longer than 20 years but shorter than 34 are affected even more but there is less advancement for those with more than four job changes"(Fischer, 1976, p. 76).

The second relationship described by this hypothesis is that of the number of job changes affecting the level of status of the last (current) job. The expectation was that the more changes that were made, the higher would be the prestige of the position obtained last.

The researchers were trying, with this hypothesis, to determine which would be the better dependent variable—the prestige of this current position or the degree of advancement from first to last position.

In the second relationship, that of number of job changes and its effect on the current job status, from zero to six changes had a moderate positive linear relationship between the two. The background variables that appear to vary with the two include sex, age, and length of career, but the relationships were not all linear. When each sex was considered separately, these relationships were all linear for males.

In looking at the relationship between the two principal variables (number of job changes and current job status), we can say that the relationship is linear for the whole group. It can also be said that for each sex the relationship is linear; however, it is much more strongly linear for males than for females. While 8 percent of the variance is explained by number of jobs for females, 17 percent of the variance is explained for males.

The relationship between the two variables, when explained by use of age, length of career and prestige of first full-time position is more likely to be linear or approaching linearity for males than for females or for the entire group.

Other tests for linearity were done on the males of the group, since the pairs of variables with linear relationships were much stronger than the female equivalents. On the whole, however,

The conclusions that we come to as a result of this examination is that we should continue our investigations with women and men statistically separated considerably earlier than we had anticipated and with prestige of present job as the dependent variable. For women we still need to locate more salient variables which will explain the variance in their current prestige level. For men we will have the opportunity of pursuing a multivariate linear model in which we will control for age, length of career and prestige of first full-time job.

HYPOTHESIS 2: The greater the ratio of successful job changes and promotion attempts, the greater the number of such changes and promotions.

This ratio scale was shown to be not as valuable a continuous variable as had been anticipated. The highest and lowest values had to be disregarded in the examination of the hypothesis. The lowest value (less than .20) had too little variance in the other variables, and the highest (above 1) showed no pattern at all. The most useful were those grouped in the middle range, and three categories were created—.20 to

.39, .40 to .59, .60 to .99. With these groupings of values, the relationship between ratio of successful job changes and promotion attempts and the number of such was evident for the whole group of librarians. When the group was divided by gender, there was little change, the relationship between successful job changes, promotion attempts, and the number of jobs, although weak, was there for each separate group and for the whole group together.

Hypothesis 3 (see p. 404) proved to be only a weak curvilinear relationship and a nonexistent linear one.

HYPOTHESIS 4: The greater the motivation and the higher the aspiration, the more intense the search and application for job changes and promotion.

Again, this hypothesis deals with two separate variables: motivation and aspiration. Nothing worth noting was found in the relationship between search and application for job changes and promotion when linked to motivation. However, when these two were linked to aspiration, the variation in the current job's prestige is partially explainable by aspiration. Although as a whole this hypothesis is not supported, there does seem to be a definite link between aspirations and current job status, given the three variables of age, length of career, and prestige of first full-time position, especially for the males in the sample.

Although tests were made on four of the other six hypotheses, no strong links between variables and the hypotheses could be found. That could equally well have been said about the first four hypotheses. Nothing could be proven about any of these hypotheses, especially concerning females in the profession.

CONCLUSIONS

It becomes apparent, when the hypotheses are examined and the background characteristics are studied, that there is a very real problem with the research study, and it extends beyond the political ramifications or the fact that it was not published. These problems fall into two distinct categories. One is the problem of the findings; especially the fact that so few of them (if any) are statistically significant. There is little that can be said about any of the hypotheses that the study was designed to examine. The second problem concerns the implementation of the study.

If the timetable, the questionnaire, and the sampling technique and its corresponding response rate are looked into very carefully, the real problem of what went wrong with this study becomes evident. For whatever reasons, the sample was not capable of answering any of the questions for which the study was designed. There was, in general, a poor response rate and too few people fell into particular cells of the research design, thereby assuring the nonsignificance of much of the data.

The reasons for this were mentioned in passing in the beginning of this chapter: lack of money, time, and a loss of interest in the project. These probably contributed much to the failure of the research. But is it such a failure? In its findings and conclusions, certainly. But in its design, definitely not. It is a strong, high-quality, theoretical model of our profession, and this author would like to see other sociologists and librarians tackle a study like this of American librarians. It might be more successful in a country that doesn't have the problem of possible cultural bias, as does Canada with its French-speaking librarians, where the response rate would be better, as is usually the case in American surveys. Some of the hypotheses that were designed for this study, or perhaps some new ones, designed with the failures of this study in mind, should be analyzed. This author looks forward to sociological contributions such as this tightly designed study.

NOTES

1. Linda Fischer, Mary Ann Wasylycia-Coe, Sherril Cheda, and Phyllis Yaffe were the four researchers on the project. It is with their permission that this has been written.

Appendix—National Study of Career Paths of Librarians

[For purposes of clarity and space, these questionnaires have been reformatted—ed.]

QUESTIONNAIRE 1

Prior studies of librarians have revealed many different types of plans with regard to careers, or, in some cases, alternative activities. As this study will be charting the actual job histories in a more objective way through the questions on the following pages, would you explain your philosophy (plans and relevant assumptions) with respect to your own career? You might indicate if this has changed over the years and how.

Job and Family

1. What is your current position title? _____
2. Does your system classify librarians by levels?   yes _____ no _____
    a. If yes, how many levels are there? _____
    b. What is your level? _____
    c. What is the number of the highest level below the head librarian? ___
3. What is your specialty? (Check as many as apply to your current position.)   public service _____ technical service _____ administration _____ other (please specify) _____
4. With what age group in the population do you primarily work? (Check one.)   all age groups _____ children _____ college or university _____ adult _____ not applicable _____
5. In what type of library do you currently work?   public _____ special _____ college _____ university _____
6. What is the name of your library? Please include the (a) branch (if any), and (b) the system or parent organization names _____
7. What is the position title of your supervisor, or the person to whom you report? _____
8. How many professional librarians do you supervise directly (or who reports directly to you)? Full _____ part-time _____
9. How many non-professional staff do you supervise directly? Full _____ part-time _____

10. Do you consider your present position in line with your expectations for the future? yes _____ no _____ don't know _____
11. Your sex? Male _____ Female _____
12. Year of birth? _____
13. Current marital status? previously married or currently separated _____ currently married _____ single _____
    If you are now or ever were married, please indicate the duration(s) date (year) _____ to date (year) _____
14. Have you ever had or been responsible for any children? yes _____ no _____
    a. If yes, what year(s) were they born or did they enter the family? 19 _____ , 19 _____ , 19 _____ , 19 _____
    b. What year did the last child leave home or did your daily responsibility (contact) end? not yet _____ , 19 _____ , not applicable _____
    c. Were there any years in which you were a single parent? yes _____ no _____ If yes, what years were they? 19 _____ to 19 _____

Evaluations and Mobility

1. Compared to other librarians in your type of position, do *you* think that your work is...
   poor _____ satisfactory _____ good _____
   superior _____ don't know _____
2. How do you think your supervisor evaluates your work in your present position? poor _____ satisfactory _____ good _____
   superior _____ don't know _____
3. How do you think other people with whom you work evaluate your work in your present position? poor _____ satisfactory _____
   good _____ superior _____ don't know _____
4. Given your abilities and the qualifications required for your job, are you...
   overqualified _____ well suited _____
   underqualified _____ can not tell _____
5. If you consider yourself overqualified for your job, why do you think that you are in your present position? by my own choice _____
   do not care about positions in particular _____
   was discriminated against because (specify) _____
   no better position available _____ limited by my own ability _____
   limited by my family commitments _____ other _____ (please specify)
6. What is the average number of hours per week that you spend on library work including work at home, time spent at meetings, etc? _____
7. Does your schedule regularly include nights and weekends? yes _____ no _____
8. If not, would you take a job that did?
   yes _____ no _____ depends _____
   If "no" or "depends", please explain _____

9. Is your salary comparable with other people in your system doing similar work?   yes _____ no _____ don't know _____
If no, why not? _____

Past Higher Education

[The form given below was duplicated four times on the original questionnaire.—ed.]

Please fill in information about courses, degrees, etc.

Last grade completed in high school _____ Date of graduation (year) _____

Higher Education:

Name of school _____
Location _____
Field of study _____
Degree or diploma obtained _____
Dates attended: From 19 _____ to 19 _____
For which of the above years were you attending full-time?
From 19 _____ to 19 _____
For which years, part-time?   From 19 _____ to 19 _____

Occupational History

Please fill in your occupational history below—starting with your present job or first full-time (non-summer) job, whichever came first.

Position title _____
Primary job content _____
Department or division _____
Employer (e.g., library system or company) _____
Salary received   starting $_____ per _____; highest $_____ per _____
Dates worked   Fulltime, from 19 _____ to 19 _____; Part time, _____ from 19 _____ to 19 _____
How much effort on your part was required to obtain this job?
Less than average _____ average _____ above average _____
How did you obtain this job?   applied for it _____ It was offered without application _____ was asked to apply for it _____
after serving as acting position holder _____
Would you leave this job,

	Yes	Yes but (specify)	No
for a more challenging or interesting position	_____	_____	_____
for a better paying position?	_____	_____	_____
to go back to school?	_____	_____	_____
for a more prestigious position?	_____	_____	_____
to retire?	_____	_____	_____
for another reason? (please specify)	_____	_____	_____

[This form was repeated for prior jobs in the original questionnaire, except for the last question, which was changed to "Why did you leave this job," with the possible answer "to retire" deleted.—ed.]

Future Occupation

Do you expect to be working as a librarian *one* year from now?

O N E

    Yes _____ Do you have any ideas about what position you would *like* to hold one year from now?

        Yes _____ What position would that be? (position and type of library) _____
        Do you think this is a realistic goal?
        Yes _____ *(go to five-year question)*
        No _____ What position do you think you will be in and why? _____

        No _____ *(go to five-year question)*

    No _____ Why not? _____ *(go to five-year question)*

Do you expect to be working as a librarian *five* years from now?

F I V E

    Yes _____ Do you have any ideas about what position you would *like* to hold five years from now?

        Yes _____ What position would that be (position and type of library) _____

        Do you think this is a realistic goal?
        Yes _____ *(go to ten-year question)*
        No _____ (What position do you think you will be in and why? _____

        No _____ *(go to ten-year question)*

    No _____ Why not? _____ *(go to ten-year question)*

Do you expect to be working as a librarian *ten* years from now?

T E N

    Yes _____ Do you have any ideas about what position you would *like* to hold ten years from now?

        Yes _____ What position would that be? (position and type of library _____

        Do you think this is a realistic goal?

        Yes _____ What position do you think you will be in and why? *(go to last question)*
        No _____ What position do you think you will be in and why? _____

        No _____ *(go to last question)*

    No _____ Why not? _____ *(go to last question)*

Do you expect to be working as a librarian as long as you hold a job?

<pre>
          Yes _____ Do you have any ideas about what position you would
   L   like to hold at the height of your career?
   A
   S   Yes _____ What position would that be? (position and
   T   type of library) _____
                             Do you think this is a realistic goal?
                             Yes _____ (go to next page)
                             No _____ What is the highest position you will occupy?
                             _____
                             Why? _____
                      No _____ (go to next page)
          No _____ Why not? _____ (go to next page)
</pre>

QUESTIONNAIRE 2

Careers of Others

For each of the next six questions, there are two possible answers. Please choose the answer which describes the librarian who you think took the most appropriate action.

1. Some librarians want to become the best in their field, e.g., reference work, but are not anxious to move on to other more administrative posts. Two periodical librarians who like their respective work situations have been working part-time at tasks outside the periodicals section that do not appeal to them. They have gotten to the point where they would like to devote full time to periodicals but the position does not appear to be likely to be open for at least five years. Each notices that a position opens up in the only nearby system for a full time periodical librarian. It doesn't appear to be as pleasant a work situation. Which librarian do you think took the wisest action?

   _____ Librarian A tried for the position in the nearby system despite the risk of a less attractive work situation.

   _____ Librarian B decided to wait out the five years rather than risk letting his or her dissatisfaction show without being sure of a successful job application in the other library.

2. Which of the two people in the situation described below has made the most adequate adjustment to the situation?

   Two librarians have worked up from the bottom to responsible positions with a good income. Both like to be home with their families in the evening but both would like to reach positions which require further promotion. Any opportunity for this entails several years of advanced evening study at a nearby university.

_____ Librarian A decided for evening study to prepare for promotion. A realized that evening time spent with the family would be reduced and that his or her spouse would resent this.

_____ Librarian B decided against evening study to enjoy being with the family; his or her spouse was glad that the decision was to stay home evenings.

3. Two librarians have identical positions in a library system. Which is the attitude that best describes the librarian most likely to be doing a good job now?

_____ Librarian A has moved up about five steps from where he or she started in library work. A is proud of how far he or she has gotten ahead and thinks that past success is a good predictor of further promotion, so that an expectation of reaching the top of career before retirement is not unreasonable.

_____ Librarian B has moved up about five steps from where he or she started in library work. B is pleased with how far he or she has gotten ahead in the library and hopes to make a few more moves up to the highest promotion he or she can get in the library before retirement.

4. The satisfactions that people get out of their work differ for different people. Described below are two librarians who work effectively, but who have been bypassed for promotion. Which person has the attitude you would think is the most appropriate to the situation?

_____ Librarian A does not resent the lack of promotion and feels satisfaction in having gotten as far as he or she has in the library.

_____ Librarian B resents the lack of promotion. B continues to work effectively, but now gets less satisfaction from work.

5. Two librarians in similar positions are being considered for promotion to a high administrative position in a library. Which librarian do you think would be the best choice for the position?

_____ Librarian A began his or her career in a supervisory position and has had considerable experience and success in making decisions and supervising people.

_____ Librarian B has worked his or her way up from a low librarian position. B's career has given him or her experience and success in a variety of library positions of increasing importance.

6. Two librarians worked hard and effectively all their lives. Over the years both were able to attain respected and responsible positions in the library in which they worked. But neither of them reached the top. With which librarian would you sympathize the most?

_____ Librarian A felt that he or she had led a successful career because he or she had been able to reach an important position.

_____ Librarian B felt that his or her career had not been fully successful because he or she had not reached a top position.

Conflicts

1. Have your family commitments ever interfered with the fulfillment of job or school duties in your library career?
Yes _____ No _____
If yes, what years did this happen?   19_____ to 19_____;
19_____ to 19_____

2. Do your family commitments make fulfillment of present job duties...
very difficult _____ somewhat difficult _____ no problem _____

3. Do your family commitments interfere with desired or present schooling?
Yes _____ No _____

4. Has attendance at school ever interfered with the fulfillment of job duties in your library career?   Yes _____ No _____
If yes, considering your whole library career, during what years was there some degree of interference by your school with your job?
19_____ to 19_____; 19_____ to 19_____

5. If you are going to school right now, does it make fulfillment of job duties...
very difficult _____ somewhat difficult _____ no problem _____

6. Have job duties ever interfered with your attendance at school?
Yes _____ No _____ If yes, what years did this occur?
19_____ to 19_____; 19_____ to 19_____

7. If you are going to school *right now*, do your job duties make fulfillment of your school obligations...
very difficult _____ somewhat difficult _____ no problem _____

8. Has an illness or disability ever interfered with the fulfillment of job or school activities in your library career?   Yes _____ No _____
If yes, considering your whole library career, what years was there some degree of interference from illness or disability?
19_____ to 19_____; 19_____ to 19_____
If the condition is current, does this illness or disability make fulfillment of job duties right now...
very difficult _____ somewhat difficult _____ no problem _____

9. Has your job ever interfered with your family commitments?
Yes _____ No _____   If yes, what years did this happen?
19_____ to 19_____; 19_____ to 19_____

10. Does your present job make fulfillment of current family commitments...
very difficult _____ somewhat difficult _____ no problem _____

Current Position

1. When you were considered for your present position, what qualifications were stressed by those doing the hiring?

___ability
___personality
___experience
___personal characteristics
(please specify) _____

___training
___other (please specify)_____
___don't know

2. When being interviewed for a job in the last ten years, have any of the following been asked? If yes, check and indicate, for the last occasion, how many years ago it was asked.

	Has it been asked?	How long ago was the last time?
marital status	_____	_____
management skills	_____	_____
clerical skills, e.g., typing	_____	_____
number of children	_____	_____
provision for child care	_____	_____
availability for night and weekend work	_____	_____
future planned children	_____	_____
method of birth control	_____	_____
occupation of spouse	_____	_____
future of planned marriage	_____	_____
future career goals	_____	_____

3. Are there people around you who will probably advance more quickly than others in a library career? Yes _____ No _____ If yes, what characteristics do you think will affect their advancement?
_____

4. Is there a written job description for your position?
Yes _____ No _____

5. Do you have a contract? Yes _____ No _____

6. At your place of work, do any professional librarians have union contracts?
Yes _____ No _____ If yes, which positions are excluded?

7. Is information about salaries of individuals in your system public information? Yes _____ No _____ don't know _____
To some (please specify) _____

8. Do you have periodic evaluation face-to-face with your supervisor?
regularly _____ irregularly _____ rarely _____ never _____
haven't been on the job long enough _____

9. Do you have a peer grievance procedure? Yes _____ No _____

Opportunities

This question is designed to measure the extent of your opportunities for a change in position without a change in residence. Please give *numerical* estimates even when you are just guessing.

1. About how many librarian positions are there in an area which you would consider commuting distance from where you now live? _____

   About how many of them would you be qualified to hold (including the one you hold now?)
   _____

   About how many of these would you be willing to hold? _____

   About how many appeal to you as a position you might like to have?

   If your job was discontinued, how many of these positions would you consider seriously if an opening came up? _____

   About how many of those that you are qualified for are equal to or better than your present job by your criteria? _____

   About how many of these would you be willing to hold? _____

   About how many appeal to you as a position you might like to have?

   If your job was discontinued, how many of these positions would you consider seriously if an opening came up? _____

2. Here is a list of things which might stop some people from taking a new job. Suppose that you were offered an opportunity to make a substantial advance in your career. Check the appropriate box for each item in the list to show how important it would be in stopping you from making that advance.

	might stop me from making a change	would be a serious consideration but wouldn't stop me	wouldn't matter very much
learn a new routine	_____	_____	_____
move around the country a lot	_____	_____	_____
take on more responsibility	_____	_____	_____
leave your family for some time	_____	_____	_____
leave your community	_____	_____	_____
leave your friends	_____	_____	_____

Publications and Professional Associations

Have you written or edited any of the following that have been published? If so, how many? ____ books, nonfiction ____ articles in professional journals ____ other articles ____ bibliographies ____ poetry or fiction ____

If you belong to any professional organizations, would you indicate which ones? ____

The Reentry Professional Librarian

KATHERINE MURPHY DICKSON

TODAY MORE WOMEN WORK at paid employment than ever before:

A majority of women work because of economic need. Nearly two-thirds of all women in the labor force in 1978 were single, widowed, divorced, or separated, or had husbands whose earnings were less than $10,000 (in 1977).

Women accounted for nearly three-fifths of the increase in the civilian labor force in the last decade—13 million women compared with 9 million men.

The number of working mothers has increased more than tenfold since the period immediately preceding World War II, while the number of working women more than tripled. Fifty-three percent of all mothers with children under 18 years (16.1) million were in the labor force in 1978.

Women workers are concentrated in low paying dead-end jobs. As a result, the average woman worker earns only about three-fifths of what a man does, even when both work full time year round. The median wage or salary income of year-round full-time workers in 1977 was lowest for minority-race women—$8,383. For white women it was $8,787; minority men, $11,053; and white men, $15,230.

Fully employed women high school graduates (with no college) had less income on the average than fully employed men who had not completed elementary school—$8,462 and $9,332, respectively, in 1977. Women with 4 years of college also had less income than men with only an 8th grade education—$11,134 and $11,931, respectively (U.S. Department of Commerce, 1980).

BACKGROUND

Even after over a decade of intensive feminist activity, women today earn *less* than ever before. In 1955 women earned 64¢ for every dollar earned by a man; today they earn 59¢ (U.S. Department of Labor, 1980). This is partly due to the segregation of women in lower-paying, lower-status occupations, an issue that is currently being addressed by those fighting for comparable pay for work of comparable value (Grune, 1980).

For the older woman with professional skills, the problem is particularly acute, as Berkeley (1978) has pointed out: "Age discrimination is less evident in unskilled jobs, which pay the minimum—or less. Older women are rarely employed, even if they are qualified, in skilled jobs which pay better wages"(p. 29).

In this chapter, the problems of the "reentry" librarian are examined, in order to demonstrate the kind of research that is needed to enable the professional librarian who has left the workplace for family or other reasons to make the transition back to full-time, professional employment.

The term reentry librarian describes the woman who turned from her hard-won professional role to raise a family and now for various reasons seeks to reenter the labor force as a professional librarian. It applies to librarians separated from their husbands, divorcees, and widows—the rising number of women faced with discrimination in employment to whom support through Social Security (for those under 60), widows' benefits, and private-pension programs are unavailable. It applies to librarians whose husbands can no longer support the family. And it also applies to librarians who, in a decade of changing expectations for women, wish to resume their professional role. Often forced to attain financial self-sufficiency, frequently in the face of inflation, unemployment, no recent professional experience, outdated job skills, lack of knowledge of online data-base searching and computer skills, inadequate self-assessment skills, and inadequate sources of referrals, these librarians must often at the same time contend with their feelings of inadequacy and their lack of self-confidence about the world of work. Often jobless at the end of job-searching attempts, they are left with both the barest of financial resources and no prospects.

What are the problems confronting the reentry librarian? She is a person 35 years old or older who obtained professional credentials, worked, took time out to have a family, and then reentered or attempted to reenter the labor force. Why did she leave her profession in the first place? For many of the same reasons she is having difficulty returning (such as marriage, child rearing, moving to a different location, perhaps because of the husband's job). She was socialized to believe that she should give up her economic independence and become economically dependent on her husband, or perhaps she felt adequate day care was not available, or perhaps she expected that as a full-time housewife and mother she would be provided for by a husband. In the fifties, even most professional women became housewives. The whole society, the professions, the media, employers, high-school and college guidance counselors, encouraged women at that time to believe that husbands support their children and wives. They led women to believe that earning their own living was only short term (and therefore not important), and need not be a long-term concern. This social milieu was best described by Betty Friedan in *The Feminine Mystique* (1963). Women were encouraged by society to believe that they should suspend professional life for family, and most were encouraged to do this blindly, without any knowledge of the consequences:

> One of the most misleading myths in our society has been the idea that "women don't have to work for a living." Until the beginning of this decade and the advent of the women's movement, popular wisdom decreed that all women got married and were supported by their husbands.
>
> In spite of all the examples to the contrary—women who remained single by choice and women who lost their husbands through death, divorce, and desertion—the myth has prevailed. From the high school guidance counselor's office, from the vocational trade school, and from the medical school admissions office, the message has always been the same—you are a woman; ergo: you don't have to think seriously about a career! (Gibbons, 1979 pp. 1-3)

The situation of the reentry professional librarian is analogous to that of the "displaced homemaker"—only worse. Both have been encouraged to believe they would be provided for as wives and mothers. But such is often not the case. Through death, divorce, desertion, bankruptcy, or unemployment, both the displaced homemaker and the reentry professional librarian may be left without means of adequate support.

It is absolutely crucial that all women be able to earn a living for themselves and their children, in the event of disturbances, which may occur in even the most secure situations, and this is often a traumatic way to learn the importance of work. The plight of the professional woman who returns to work may be worse than that of the unskilled woman, because she does not have the benefits of the Displaced Homemaker legislation[1] and also because she is often older than her displaced-homemaker sister, having had her children later.

Curiously enough, not only does the reentry librarian face the social conditions of ever-rising divorce rates, longer life spans, inflation, unemployment, sexism, and ageism that all women face, she may also stand to face resentment from her younger-sister professionals who have *not* taken time out to have a family, as Williams (1978) pointed out in *American Libraries:*

> The tightness of the job market makes librarians reluctant to let go of their jobs. Women who in better times might have taken a few years off to raise a family are staying on the job. They want to be assured of having a position when they want it, and the best method is to keep the one they have (p. 469).

The professional librarian is often viewed as being either irresponsible for not taking her job seriously enough to hold onto it, or else as someone to whom the job is not an economic necessity but rather a kind of luxury or "personal-fulfillment" ego trip. In any case, she will have difficulty in being hired.

Although it is true that "this is a generation of women on whom the rules have been changed," it is a grave mistake to think of reentry professional librarians as temporary victims of social change. An American woman now has a fifty-fifty chance of being divorced, widowed, or single by the time she reaches middle age.

The U.S. Congress, House of Representatives, Select Committee on Aging's Subcommittee on Retirement Income and Unemployment (1979) held hearings on midlife women. The testimony (p. 1) included startling statistics:

—more than 1/3 of the women in the U.S. labor force today are 45 or over.
—women are 98% of the typists and 78% of the clerical workers.
—the mean income for women aged 45-64, working full-time in 1976 was $8800, for men, the mean income was $16,500.
—women aged 65 and over are 15% of the U.S. population but 22% of those living in poverty today.

The Director of the Women's Bureau stressed that it is *midlife women who bear the brunt of the changing expectations in this generation and the next*. She noted that women who reenter the paid labor force find employers unwilling to credit their previous experience; lack the skills sought today; lack recognition of the contributions they made as homemakers; lack access to a variety of jobs due to factors such as age limits for apprenticeships. The Department of Labor is working to increase benefits for homemakers and is conducting internal training to sensitize employers (prime sponsors) in the CETA program to displaced homemakers and the value of the homemaker [italics mine].

Ellie Smeal, President of NOW, called for a "Homemakers' Bill of Rights" based on the same premise as the Veterans' Bill of Rights—that homemakers have reordered their lives in order to serve their country and therefore are not "burdens" but deserving of benefits. NOW suggests that these benefits include:
—Educational Rights—deduction for education expenses, including child care; provision of education loans at modest interest; incentives to businesses to hire.
—Economic Rights—revision of income tax forms to assure all income on joint tax forms is co-owned not simply "co-liable," inclusion of homemakers'services in the GNP (gross national product), elimination of gift or inheritance taxes on interspousal transfers, increase in flexi- and part-time employment with full fringe benefits, availability of 24-hour child care.

Like the midlife women described at these hearings, the problems of reentry librarians are due, in large part, to the fact that they have had extended nonwork periods when they raised children and managed households. It is also due in part to society's changing expectations for women. In 1950, when middle-aged woman would have matriculated into college, the cultural belief that she would be provided for by a husband prevented her, and many like her, from completing an education and pursuing a career. Twice as many men as women enrolled in college in 1950, and only 60 percent of these women completed four years'. Although the reentry librarian completed her education at a time when this was unusual, obtained professional status and pursued a career, society's message at that time was that even career women who marry should become full-time mothers. The rules of the game have changed for women, and the most acute problems are experienced by women in the mid-forties and beyond.

The problem of the reentry librarian is a professional and social issue. We are all against unemployment. No one will deny that we pay a high price for unemployment today. Welfare, unemployment insurance, and food stamps run into billions of dollars, and the cost keeps rising. We cannot calculate the social costs of crime, disease, and neglected communities. This is to say nothing of what unemployment and underemployment does to the librarian herself and to her family. Who can calculate the cost to the woman and the profession in terms of the waste of her skills and a lessening of her sense of her own worth? None of us condones this waste. But that is not why the problem of the reentry librarian is a professional issue.

Why should the reentry professional librarian be hired? Because she is qualified for the job? Because she can humanize the workplace? We know that people live longer today. The average person works 40 years. Surely no one advocates spending 40 years doing exactly the same thing. We are told that more and more professionals become "burned out" and try to make a career change. The new and late entrant as well as the reentry professional brings skills from a different mode. Librarianship is often a late career choice or second or third career choice. Why penalize the professional who has taken time to have a family? All these things are true, but they do not make the problem a professional issue. The reasons why the reentry professional librarian should be hired are the very same reasons why this is a "women in librarianship" issue.

It is not only because the reentry professional librarian is a human being that she should be able to return to her profession. It is also because the obstacles to her returning to her former level are a denial of her *equal rights*. These obstacles are not only a denial of her rights; they also prevent her from full participation in the public/professional arena. They artificially restrict her activity and further trap her in the role of child-bearer and -rearer. It is still very difficult for a woman to rise again from child-raising to her chosen occupation, as Crystal Eastman (1978) observed:

But is there any way of insuring a woman economic independence while child-raising is her chosen occupation? Or must she sink into that dependent state from which, as we all know, *it is so hard to rise again*? That brings us to the fourth feature of our program—motherhood endowment. It seems that the only way we can set mothers free, at least in a capitalist society, is by the establishment of a principle that the occupation of raising children is peculiarly and directly a service to society, and that the mother upon whom the necessity and privilege of performing this service naturally falls is entitled to an adequate economic reward from the political government. It is idle to talk of real economic independence for women unless this principle is accepted. But with a generous endowment of motherhood provided by legislation, with all laws against voluntary motherhood and education in its methods repealed, and the feminist ideal of education accepted in home and school, and with all special barriers removed in every field of human activity, there is no reason why woman should not become almost a human thing (pp. 56-57, italics mine).

There are clear reasons why the needs and problems of the reentry librarian are a professional issue. Not only is the reentry librarian artificially restricted from full participation in the public arena and thus excluded from the power structure, further trapped in the child-raiser/homemaker role by the patriarchy, but she is also deprived of economic independence. She is economically subordinate and therefore deprived of her rightful economic status. This is a denial of her equal rights and therefore an important professional issue. It is possible that with the passage of the Equal Rights Amendment and eventual provision of adequate day-care facilities for children, some obstacles to equal rights will be removed for some librarians, at least for some of the time.

Reentry professional librarians are not a short-term phenomenon. Late motherhood is becoming increasingly popular. Up to 20 percent of women in urban areas are having their first children at 35 or older (Schultz, 1979; Fabe and Wikler, 1979). Among feminists, late motherhood is considered a *good thing*. A librarian who has had the chance to establish herself in a career, explore the world, and, above all, develop a strong sense of who she is, is going to be far less vulnerable to the pitfalls of motherhood. Although she is less likely to be trapped in the mother role, she is going to have a difficult time being as successful as she might have been as a childless woman. Whether she works full time, part time, or stays at home, she will find her career affected. That her career is affected by motherhood is abundantly clear from an unpublished pilot study done by Carol Learmont and Elizabeth Steltenpohl at the School of Library Service at Columbia University, not on reentrants, but on late entrants into the profession (Columbia University, School of Library Service [1974?]). Thus the problem of reentry is an issue for all librarians. For those who choose to leave the job market, the problems are the very real ones of retooling and being rehired. For those men and women who do not leave, the problem is more subtle, but the profession as a whole loses when the hard-earned skills of those who have temporarily left the work force are not made use of. Together all librarians must insist that options in life styles be open. A professional acceptance of the total life cycle, including having and raising children, needs to be made by the profession at large. As Deckard (1979) has pointed out:

In our society women have long faced a cruel dilemma: career or marriage. As a result, professional women were more likely to remain unmarried than other women. Some were driven to "choose" a career instead of marriage because of the rigid and sexist structure of the professions and of the traditional family which made it impossible to have both (p. 145).

Balancing the claims of work and family is one of the most pressing research issues of women in librarianship. At the present time the profession is structured on the male model of an uninterrupted career. It is rare that a librarian can take time out for a family and return at the same level as when she left. Nor is the traditional family structured to facilitate return to employment. Both work and family need to be restructured so that women do not have to suffer or forfeit other forms of participation and power while children are raised. Miller (1978) has observed:

Women find it difficult to believe they have the *right* to ask for so much [shared child care]. They are not irrational or immoderate demands. It is important to ask instead why the provision for such clear and obvious women's needs can still *seem* like so much to ask (p. 128).

The concepts of love (sex) and work (professionalism) must be redefined into a less divisive, more organic pattern, so that librarians may live more fully human and balanced lives.

There should be a sense of shared responsibility for the problems of the reentry professional librarian. What can be done? Research should be undertaken to determine the factors in reentry employment success. Journal articles on reentry should appear from time to time in the professional literature. Unions and professional associations can play an important role by providing workshops and seminars. There should be increased awareness of the identity of reentry librarians as a group with special needs. Perhaps professional associations and unions might have their round tables or committees on the status of women address the issue of the reentry professional. Professional associations or unions that have career or staff-development programs or internships should consider the special problems of the reentry professional, as should any library large enough to have staff-development programs.

Professional associations, staff associations, and unions should support consciousness-raising groups, hot lines, support networks, and counseling, and make available current literature on the subject. We barely have the conceptual framework for treating this issue, but if we do not deal with it, we continue to take power from the least powerful and give it to the most powerful.

NEEDED RESEARCH

There are only two articles on reentry librarians in the literature. One, by Patricia Lazell Ward (1966), is English[2] and the other, by Eric Bow (1972), is Canadian. Reentry librarians are discussed in only two American studies, one by the Bureau of Labor Statistics, on Library Manpower (U.S. Dept. of Labor, 1975) and the other in an article discussing this study, by Simon and Myers (1976) in *Wilson Library Bulletin*. Neither study reports any research done on reentry. The Bureau of Labor Statistics predicts that growth would account for only 25 percent of all job openings for librarians during 1970-80. The remaining 75 percent would result from replacement needs. This compares with a 50-50 growth/replacement ratio during 1960-70. Simon and Myers predict that replacement needs will continue to increase between 1976 and 1986, partly because of the large number of women in librarianship who quit upon marriage or pregnancy.

In its report the BLS projected that 9,000 librarians will be entering the labor market from library school annually to fill 11,200 jobs. The report suggested that the remaining jobs will be filled by librarians reentering the labor force and by people transferring from other occupations. It is not possible, however, to project how many people fall into these categories.... We need to know more about reentrants: who they are, why they are returning to the labor force, and whether they are being hired.... interrelationships of a number of a demographic, economic, and social factors are involved. Among the most important are trends in population, library services, level of government spending, and developments in automation and networking, causing changes in staffing patterns (pp.347-50).

The recent Conference on Reentry Women Scientists (Lantz, 1980) lists reentry issues needing research:

1. Trends in and determinants of reentry
2. Services that facilitate reentry
3. Government, employer, and trade union policies that affect reentry
4. Model programs (public and private)
5. Employment outlook and reentry prospects (p. 163).

A study by the Business and Professional Women's Foundation (1977), undertaken by Saroj Ghoting, suggested the following research on women's interrupted employment patterns: the causes, results, and possible alternatives to the pattern; the description and documentation of women's work patterns; analysis of the motivations of, facilitators of, and barriers to, continuous or resumed employment and recommendation for adjustment and acceptance of the pattern; organizational structure of the labor force; attitudes of employers as they impact on women; and employment policies that particularly affect women (pp. 3-4).

FOCUSING ON REENTRY LIBRARIANS

Adequate library positions are the primary need of reentry librarians. Unfortunately, little is currently known about their job-seeking experiences. Before policies responsive to the needs of this subpopulation of librarians can be developed, information on a number of questions needs to become available. For example, which female librarians seeking jobs are reentry librarians? What factors influence the decision to reenter the labor force? Further, what is the process of job-seeking? What informal systems and formal group supports are available and utilized, and further, what barriers to finding new jobs exist?

The importance of studying the job-seeking experiences of reentry librarians can be justified on two grounds. First, the results of the job-seeking experience in this cohort's middle years will affect the transition to, and experience in, old age. Second, from a social-policy perspective, the extent to which reentry librarians are able to establish financial independence is related to the demand they will place on societal services over the next several decades. This is not to mention the professional contributions to the society made possible by this group employed, as opposed to the waste of professional skills and services by this group unemployed.

The objectives of such research would be:

1. To obtain more knowledge about the characteristics of reentry librarians;
2. To specify the barriers that job-seeking reentry librarians confront as they seek preferred jobs;
3. To specify the types of informal support systems and formal support groups available to, and utilized by, this group;
4. To develop and disseminate materials to be used by library schools, libraries, professional groups, and other interested groups in assisting reentry librarians to find suitable employment.

Practically no information on the job-seeking process of reentry librarians, describing reentry librarians as a unique group with identifiable needs, exists. There is a clear indication that the librarian reentering the labor force in midlife faces a unique set of problems and needs. She often lacks structure and current information for her job search. She needs to update skills, become aware of existing resources, and present her abilities in a marketable way. She may need to understand, for instance, the impact of the computer on the profession. In conjunction with these are the need to develop self-confidence and to be aware that individual current employment difficulties are mainly a result of traditional social policy rather than of individual inadequacies. Women need help to work through the emotional and psychological stresses that accompany the loss of economic support. They need to obtain formal training and to update education in many instances. For librarians facing a period of great change in their roles and in their lives, support in coping with both the practical and emotional aspects of employment is equally important and equally needed. A program that can meet a range of human and employment needs (within an established profession) would be the most effective support to the reentry professional librarian.[3]

There must be research to detemine what factors contribute to employment success for reentry librarians. Exploratory research will provide information on the characteristics of job-seeking reentry librarians, their reasons for reentry into the labor force, and the process of job finding, including barriers and supports, in order to help these persons obtain new jobs after a period of work in the home.[4] Specifically, there should be a focus on identifying and describing that segment of the reentry-librarian population that has sought and found paid employment, characterizing its job-seeking patterns in order to develop professional/educational programmatic recommendations for enhancing the likelihood of others' obtaining suitable employment.

The reconciliation of professional and family responsibilities is not just a woman's issue; nor is it just an individual issue. It is a social issue. Men and women must be able to participate equally in employment and family life. Reentry is a very complex and deep issue, which calls the whole universe into question. Although we must take the state of the economy into consideration, we must not let economic issues prevent us from dealing with the issue.

If the profession accepts the challenges of the reentry professional, the future may perhaps appear as Kathleen Weibel (1976) describes it:

If librarianship accepted the feminist values of eliminating the dominant or single breadwinner per living unit and encouraged more people to work while balancing time for personal and community activities, the profession would be characterized by job sharing, serial, and part time work arrangements.

Individuals choosing these work styles would have the same benefits and career options as those who choose full time work. Continuing education not confined to job related subjects will be available for all levels of employees with adequate counseling time and general encouragement provided. Acceptance of the potential for individual contribution should result in creative job design possibly crossing current professional/nonprofessional lines as well as participatory decision making. Equal pay for equal work is, of course, a given; as are just payment for ability and effort accompanied by adjustment based on need (pp. 291-92).

The profession must have the courage to make these or similar changes. Women now live within a framework of beliefs and proscriptions that is destructive to their personhood. The scale of adjustment our society requires a woman to accept when she gives birth is enormous. In addition, the severity of the economic disadvantage with which she must cope is equally enormous. Why must women pay this price? If a community wants children, the entire community should share the responsibility. It is not only a problem for individual women to find individual solutions. How can the provision for such obvious needs seem like so much to ask? Reentry librarians should be restored their rightful economic status and assured equal opportunity. Otherwise the society not only wastes, but destroys, professional and human resources. This is an assault on human dignity. To insure its own vitality, the profession must make changes now, to attract capable librarians for the future.[5]

NOTES

1. Legislation that provides programs for displaced homemakers, administered by the Department of Labor through the Comprehensive Employment and Training Act (CETA) amendments of 1978, Titles II and VI.
2. Study undertaken in the 1960s to determine whether reentry might alleviate staff shortages in British libraries.
3. At the present time, there are no existing programs for reentry professional librarians. A review of the literature, and inquiries at the Library of Congress, the University of Maryland College of Library and Information Services, and Catholic University Department of Library and Information Science revealed no programs for reentry librarians.
4. Reentry success factors would probably be the same for any librarian with an interrupted career. The reason (education, military service, and the like) for absence may not matter to the outcome.
5. The author worked with the ALA Committee on the Status of Women in Librarianship to develop a proposal to explore reentry problems in the library profession. This proposal was awarded a 1982 ALA Goal Award.

Biographical Notes

compiled by

MARSHA KRAUS FULTON

Brand, Barbara Elizabeth
Barbara Brand received an M.A. in library science from the University of Wisconsin in 1965. She held a variety of public-service library positions, at Columbia University, the University of North Carolina, and the District of Columbia and Seattle Public Libraries, before earning a doctorate in higher education administration at the University of Washington in 1978. While at the University of Washington, Dr. Brand helped develop a grant to support a regional Career Development and Assessment Center particularly for women librarians. She is currently Head of the Reference Department in the Library of the State University of New York at Stony Brook.

Dickson, Katherine Murphy
Katherine Murphy Dickson has held a variety of positions in the library field. After receiving a B.S. in library science in 1954 from Simmons College in Boston, Ms. Dickson became a librarian at New York Public Library. In 1958 she received an M.A. in English literature from Columbia University. From 1958 to 1963 she held the position of Associate Reference Librarian at the Massachusetts Institute of Technology. During this time Ms. Dickson was Exchange Librarian (1961-62) at Associated Electrical Industries Ltd., Research Laboratory, Aldermaston, Berkshire, England. In 1963 she became the Rotch Architecture and Planning Librarian at MIT. Ms. Dickson also held several positions at the Library of Congress. She served as Bibliographer and Science Reference Librarian (1966-68), Cataloger (1977-78), and Librarian/Assistant Editor of Catalog Publications (1978-79). From 1979 to 1981 Ms. Dickson served as cataloger for the library of the American Federation of State, County and Municipal Employees, and from 1981 to 1982 was the librarian of the Business and Professional Women's Foundation in Washington, D.C. Ms. Dickson's publications include *History of Aeronautics and Astronautics: A Preliminary Bibliography* and *Reality: A Study of Katherine Mansfield's New Zealand Stories*. She is a Ph.D candidate in American Studies with concentration in Women's Studies at the University of Maryland. Ms. Dickson is a member of the American Library Association and the Special Libraries Association.

Fennell, Janice C.

Janice C. Fennell, Director of Libraries at Georgia College, received her Ph.D. from Florida State University. Prior to her present position, Dr. Fennell held positions at the University of South Carolina, the University of Central Florida, Florida State University, and the University of Georgia. She also served as a librarian in Florida and Virginia public schools. In May 1980 Dr. Fennell was elected to a three-year term on the SOLINET (Southeastern Library Network) Board of Directors. Other professional activities include membership in ALA, ACRL, SELA, and the Georgia Library Association. Dr. Fennell has served as a consultant for several Georgia private and public schools, has been a participant in an AALS workshop, "Simulation Techniques," has written several articles, and is a grant corecipient for her preparation of an index to the Milledgeville *Southern Recorder* 1820-1900.

Ferber, Marianne A.

Marianne A. Ferber is Professor of Economics and Director of Women's Studies at the University of Illinois, Urbana-Champaign. She received her B.A. at McMaster University, Hamilton, Ontario, Canada in 1944, her M.A. at the University of Chicago in 1946, and her Ph.D. at the same institution in 1957. From 1946 to 1948 she worked in the economics research section at Standard Oil (N.J.) and taught part time at Hunter College. Dr. Ferber joined the faculty at the University of Illinois in 1955. Her research has been concerned with various aspects of the economic status of women, focusing especially on earnings, job placement, the value of nonmarket time, and the economics of the household. From 1978 to 1981 she was a member of the Committee on the Status of Women in the Economics Profession of the American Economic Association, and is currently a member of that Association's Committee on Economic Education, as well as the Committee on Women in Statistics of the American Statistical Association. She is also a member of the editorial board of the *Journal of Consumer Research*.

Futas, Elizabeth

Dr. Futas is an assistant professor in the Division of Library and Information Management at Emory University, where she teaches in the areas of reference, literature of the social sciences, collection development, and adult materials. Other positions held by Dr. Futas include Cataloger of the Ford Foundation; Instructor at the Paul Klapper Library, Queens College; and Co-adjunct faculty member in the Graduate School of Library and Information Studies, Rutgers University. She received a B.A. in political science from Brooklyn College in 1965. In 1966 she received an M.A. in library and information studies from the University of Minnesota and she was awarded a Ph.D. by Rutgers University in 1980. Dr. Futas has been an active member of the American Library Association, and she is currently serving on the Council. In her capacity as a member of the Committee on the Status of Women in Librarianship, she has delivered speeches to a variety of groups interested in issues concerning women. Dr. Futas is also a member of the Association of American Library Schools, the Metro-Atlanta Library Association, American Society for Information Science, and the Atlanta Women's Studies Association. She has served on the Editorial Board of *Serials for Libraries* and *Collection Building*. From

1971 to 1973 Dr. Futas was the editor of the *SSRT Newsletter*, the official organ of the Social Responsibilities Roundtable. Her publications include *Library Acquisition Policies and Procedures* and *Library Forms* (available in 1982).

Grotzinger, Laurel A.

Dr. Grotzinger has contributed in vast measure to the library-science profession. Prior to her current position at Western Michigan University of Dean, the Graduate College, and Chief Research Officer, Dr. Grotzinger held positions as a faculty member, the Assistant Director and the Acting Director of the School of Librarianship. She was also an instructor and assistant librarian at Illinois State University and a university teaching fellow at the University of Illinois. In 1957 Dr. Grotzinger received an A.B. from Carleton College in Northfield, Minnesota. She holds an M.S. (1958) and a Ph.D. (1964) from the University of Illinois. Dr. Grotzinger's career is marked by diverse professional activities and memberships. She has served in a variety of capacities in the American Library Association, including service on the Committee on Accreditation. Dr. Grotzinger is also an active member of the Association of American Library Schools, the American Association of University Professors, and the Michigan Library Association. She is listed in several directories, including *The World Who's Who of Women* (1980). Dr. Grotzinger has participated in numerous conferences and has contributed to various professional publications. She has also served on the editorial or advisory boards of the *Journal of Education for Librarianship*, the *Dictionary of American Library Biography*, and the *Journal of Library History*.

Kathleen M. Heim

Kathleen M. Heim received a B.A. in English from the University of Illinois, an M.A. in English from Marquette University, an M.A in library science from the University of Chicago, and a Ph.D. in library science from the University of Wisconsin-Madison. Dr. Heim has held reference positions at Elmhurst College and the Rebecca Crown Library at Rosary College, where she was Director of Public Services. She is currently an assistant professor at the Graduate School of Library and Information Science at the University of Illinois at Urbana-Champaign, where she teaches library administration, government publications, and adult services. She is co-editor, with Kathleen Weibel, of *The Role of Women in Librarianship 1876-1976: The Entry, Advancement, and Struggle for Equalization in One Profession* (1979) and author of *ALA Yearbook* articles on the status of women librarians (1979; 1980; 1981). She has also contributed articles to *American Libraries, Library Journal*, the *Journal of Education for Librarianship*, and *School Media Quarterly*. With Leigh Estabrook she was investigator for the ALA study of career profiles of librarians. She chaired the ALA Committee on the Status of Women in Librarianship in 1980-82 and has been active in working for passage of the ERA.

Hildenbrand, Suzanne

Suzanne Hildenbrand, a native of New York City, received her B.A. in history from Brooklyn College of the City University of New York and an M.S. in library service from Columbia University. After several years as a high-school teacher and librarian in New York City and with the Department of Defense Dependents Schools, she served as Assistant Cultural Affairs Officer for libraries in French-language Sub-Saharan Africa with the United States Information Agency (now International Communications Agency). She received a Ph.D in education from the University of California, Berkeley. Dr. Hildenbrand is currently an assistant professor in the School of Library and Information Science at the State University of New York, Geneseo. Her areas of special interest include information resources in the social sciences, reference, cataloging and classification, and women in librarianship.

Irvine, Betty Jo

Since 1969 Dr. Irvine has held the positions of Fine Arts Librarian and part-time instructor in the Fine Arts Department at Indiana University. She served as the Assistant Fine Arts Librarian at Indiana University from 1968 to 1969. Dr. Irvine received an A.B. in 1966, an M.L.S. in 1969 from Indiana University, and a doctorate in 1982 from Indiana. She has contributed to a number of professional publications, including *College and Research Libraries, Library Trends*, and the *Art Libraries Journal*. She also authored the book *Slide Libraries, A Guide for Academic Institutions, Museums, and Special Collections*. As a member of the Special Libraries Association, the American Library Association, the College Art Association, and the Art Libraries Society/North America, Dr. Irvine has served in numerous capacities. She is included in *Who's Who In American Art* (1978) and *Contemporary Authors* (1979).

Martin, Jean K.

Jean K. Martin is currently Library Manager, Molycorp, Inc., Los Angeles, California. Her previous positions include Chief, Library Service, VA Medical Center, Des Moines, Iowa; Head, Russell Research Center Library, USDA, Athens, Georgia; and Head, Physics-Math-Astronomy Library, the University of Texas, Austin. She holds a master's degree in Business Administration from the University of Georgia, as well as an M.L.S. and a B.A. from the University of Texas, Austin. Ms. Martin has served as editor of *Library Management Bulletin* and as the book review editor of *Southeastern Librarian*. She has written articles published in *Science and Technology Libraries, Special Libraries*, the *Journal of the American Society for Information Science*, and the *Proceedings of the American Society for Information Science*. Ms. Martin is an active member of the Special Libraries Association and the American Society for Information Science.

O'Brien, Nancy Patricia

Nancy O'Brien is currently the Assistant Education and Social Science Librarian at the University of Illinois Library at Urbana-Champaign. After receiving an M.S. in library science from the University of Illinois in 1977, she served at the same institution as Serial Bibliographer until 1979, and as Social Science Bibliographer in Collection Development and Preservation from 1979 to 1981. Ms. O'Brien is currently coeditor of the "Media/Microforms" column in *Serials Review*. She is a member of the ALA/RTSD/RS Micropublishing Committee's Subcommittee to Monitor the Quality of Microforms. Her professional interests are in the areas of recruitment, the image of the librarian, library instruction, and microforms.

Reeling, Patricia

Patricia Reeling has been teaching library-school students and practicing librarians how to use government publications for some 15 years. Currently she is on the faculty of the Rutgers University Graduate School of Library and Information Studies, where she is Coordinator of the Library Services curriculum. Dr. Reeling is active in several professional groups advocating the promotion and use of government documents. At the state level, she is President of the Government Documents Association of New Jersey. Nationally, she is an active member of ALA's Government Documents Round Table (GODORT). Dr. Reeling is the immediate past editor of *Documents to the People* (DttP), GODORT's official journal, and she continues to write several columns for *DttP* on a regular basis. She is a frequent attendee at meetings of the Depository Library Council to the Public Printer, and she has recently completed visits to a number of depository libraries located throughout the country. Dr. Reeling also serves on the editorial advisory board of *The Index to U.S. Government Periodicals*. Her graduate library degrees are from Indiana University and Columbia University, and she has taught at both institutions. With her husband she is a partner in Reeling Associates, Inc., an educational and governmental consulting firm.

Rhodes, Lelia Gaston

Dr. Rhodes received a B.S. in education from Jackson State University, an M.S. in library science from Atlanta University, and an A.M.D. and a Ph.D from Florida State University. After serving as a library assistant at Jackson State University from 1945-1953, Dr. Rhodes held the position of Librarian of Hill High School, Jackson, Mississippi. In 1957 she returned to Jackson State University as the head of the Catalog Department. Dr. Rhodes has also held the positions of Associate Head Librarian and Associate Director, and she is currently Director of the Jackson State University Library. Among the numerous memberships she holds in professional organizations, she is active in the American Library Association and the Mississippi Library Association. In 1979 Dr. Rhodes was elected "Citizen of the Year" by the Beta Alpha Chapter of Omega Psi Phi Fraternity, and in 1980 she was elected "Citizen of the Year" by the Seventh District Omega Psi Phi Fraternity, Inc. Her publications include *Jackson State University 1877-1977: First Hundred Years* (1979).

Robinson, Judith Schiek

Judith Schiek Robinson received a B.A. in English and an M.L.S. and a Ph.D. in library science from Florida State University. Dr. Robinson has held the positions of Administrative Assistant to the Head of Departmental Libraries at Ohio State University Libraries, Young Adult Librarian at Monroe County Public Library in Bloomington, Indiana, and Cataloger at Florida State University Library. She is currently an associate professor at the State University of New York at Buffalo, where she teaches in the areas of reference, library management, government documents, and young-adult resources and services. Dr. Robinson is the coauthor, with Dr. Gerald Jahoda, of *The Librarian and Reference Queries: A Systematic Approach* (1980). She has also contributed articles to *American Libraries*, and the *Journal of Education for Librarianship*. Dr. Robinson served as Special Consultant for the Office of the Federal Register in Washington, D.C. from 1978-1979. As a consultant, she was contracted to present 10 workshops in the Northeast, entitled "How to Use the Federal Register." Dr. Robinson is a member of the American Library Association and the Association of American Library Schools.

Sukiennik, Adelaide Weir

Adelaide Weir Sukiennik received a B.A. from Otterbein College at Westerville, Ohio in 1961, an M.L.S. in 1965, and a Ph.D. in 1979 from the University of Pittsburgh. After teaching English at South Hills High School in Pittsburgh from 1961-1964, she became an assistant librarian. In 1966 she became the Humanities Bibliographer for the Ohio State University Libraries. From 1968-1970 Dr. Sukiennik was a Title II Fellow in the School of Library and Information Sciences at the University of Pittsburgh. She served as a part-time instructor at the University of Pittsburgh from 1970-1972, and she is currently Education Bibliographer/Women's Studies Bibliographer at Hillman Library. Dr. Sukiennik is the author of "The Teachers' Library," *Encyclopedia of Library and Information Sciences* (1980), and *Resources in Women's Studies, Hillman Library* (1980).

Taylor, Marion R.

Marion R. Taylor received an A.B. from Wesleyan College at Macon, Georgia in 1943, an M.A. in librarianship from Emory University in 1957, and a Ph.D. from Rutgers University in 1973. Her areas of expertise include cataloging and technical services. Dr. Taylor was employed as a cataloger and assistant serials librarian at Emory University library. For 12 years she served as editor of the *Atlanta-Athens Area Union Catalog*. Since 1964 she has been a library-school educator at Emory University, where she currently holds the title of associate professor. Dr. Taylor is active in the South Atlantic Chapter, SLA. She holds memberships in ALA, SLA, the Association of American Library Schools, the Southeastern Library Association, the Georgia Library Association, and the Metropolitan Atlanta Library Association. Dr. Taylor is also a member of Altrusa International and is the past president of the Altrusa Club of Atlanta.

BIBLIOGRAPHY

"ALA Policy Makers Set House in Order." *American Libraries* 7 (September 1979): 497, 503.

"Accredited Library School Histories." *Library Journal* 62 (January 1937): 24-35.

Acker, Joan, and Van Houten, Donald R. "Differential Recruitment and Control: the Sex Structuring of Organizations." *Administrative Science Quarterly* 19 (June 1974): 152-163.

Alberti, Robert E., and Emmons, Michael L. *Your Perfect Right.* 2nd ed. San Luis Obispo, Calif.: IMPACT, 1974.

———.*Stand Up, Speak Out, Talk Back.* New York: Pocket Books, 1975.

Allport, Gordon. *The Nature of Prejudice.* Cambridge, Mass.: Addison-Wesley, 1954.

Allport, Gordon W; Vernon, Philip E.; and Lindzey, Gardner. *Study of Values Manual.* Boston: Houghton Mifflin, 1960.

Alvarez, Robert S., "Let's Start Recruiting." *Wilson Library Bulletin* 15 (January 1941): 367-369.

———."Women's Place in Librarianship." *Wilson Bulletin for Librarians* 13 (November 1938): 175-178.

American Library Association. "Future Unlimited: What You Need to Be a Librarian." Demco Series no. 2, n.d.

———. "Proceedings, 1905." *Library Journal* 30 (September 1905): 164-176.

American Library Directory, 1976-1977. 30th ed. New York: Bowker, 1976.

Antin, Mary. *The Promised Land.* Boston: Houghton Mifflin, 1911.

"Are You Interested." n.p.: New York Library Association. Record Series 9/2/6, Box 3, Folder: Recruitment Literature ca. 1947-56. University of Illinois Archives, Urbana.

Armour Institute. "Announcement 1896-1897." Chicago: Department of Library Science, n.d.

Association of American Library Schools. *Recruiting for Librarianship.* Chicago, 1945.

———. "Why Library School Students Chose the Library Profession, A Report of the Committee on Recruiting and Personnel." Mimeographed, n.d.

Association of Research Libraries. *Minutes of the 89th Meeting October 20-21, 1976.* Alexandria, Va.: ARL, 1976.

Astin, Helen S. *The Woman Doctorate in America: Origins, Career, and Family.* New York: Russell Sage Foundation, 1969.

Astin, Helen S., and Bayer, Alan E. "Sex Discrimination in Academe." In *Academic Women on the Move.* Edited by Alice S. Rossi and Ann Calderwood. New York: Russell Sage Foundation, 1973, pp. 333-356.

Bailey, Louis J. "Legislative Reference Service." *Special Libraries* 21 (January 1930): 7-9.

Bailyn, Bernard. *Education in the Forming of American Society: Needs and Opportunities for Study.* Chapel Hill: University of North Carolina Press, 1960.

Bailyn, Lotte. "Family Constraints on Women's Work." In *Women & Success: The Anatomy of Achievement.* Edited by Ruth B. Kundsin. New York: William Morrow, 1974, pp. 94-102.

———. "Notes on the Role of Choice in the Psychology of Professional Women." *Daedalus* 93 (Spring 1964): 700-710.

Bancroft, Jane. "Occupations and Professions for College-Bred Women." *Education* 5 (May 1885): 590.

Banning, M.C. "Women as Administrators." *Library Journal* 63 (February 1, 1938): 569.

Bannister, John R. "Just How Is Mr. Munn?" *Library Journal* 75 (February 1, 1950): 141-142.

Bardwick, Judith M. *Psychology of Women: A Study of Biocultural Conflict.* New York: Harper and Row, 1971.

———, ed. *Readings on the Psychology of Women.* New York: Harper and Row, 1972.

Baron, Alma S., "Selection, Development and Socialization of Women into Management." *Business Quarterly* 42 (Winter 1977): 61-67.

Barsky, Lillian, and Ferlina, Rose. *Job Horizons for the College Woman.* Washington, D.C.: U.S. Department of Labor, Women's Bureau, 1967.

Bartol, Kathryn M. "The Sex Structuring of Organizations: A Search for Possible Causes." *Academy of Management Review* 3 (October 1978): 805-815.

Basil, Douglas. *Women in Management.* New York: Dunellen, 1972.

Bayer, Alan. "Teaching Faculty in Academe: 1972-73." *American Council on Education Report* 8. Washington, D.C.: ACE, 1973.

de Beauvoir, Simone. *The Second Sex.* Translated and edited by H.M. Parshley. New York: Knopf, 1968.

Bem, Sandra L. "The Measurement of Psychological Androgyny." *Journal of Consulting and Clinical Psychology* 42 (April 1974): 155-162.

Bem, Sandra L., and Bem, Daryl J. *Training the Woman to Know Her Place: The Social Antecedents of Women in the World of Work.* Harrisburg, Pa.: Pennsylvania Department of Education, 1973.

Bennet, Margaret. "Don't Give Us Your Tired, Your Poor." *Atlantic Monthly* (May 1965) [reprint] Record Series 12/1/5. Box 9, Folder: Recruiting, 1964-65. University of Illinois Archives, Urbana.

Berdie, Ralph F. "Factors Associated with Vocational Interests." *The Journal of Educational Psychology* 34 (May 1943): 257-277.

Berkeley, Joyce Maupin. "Older Working Women." In *Feminist Frameworks*. Edited by Alison M. Jaggar and Paula Rothenberg Struhl. New York: McGraw-Hill, 1978, pp. 28-29.

Bernard, Jessie. *Academic Women.* University Park, Pa.: Pennsylvania State University Press, 1964.

―――. *Women and the Public Interest: An Essay on Policy and Protest.* Chicago: Aldine, Atherton, 1971.

Beshurs, James B., and Nishiura, Eleanor N. "A Theory of Internal Migration Differentials." *Social Forces* 39 (March 1961): 214-218.

Biddle, Bruce J., and Thomas, Edwin, J., eds. *Role Theory: Concepts and Research.* New York: John Wiley, 1966.

Blackburn, Robert T., and Aurand, Charles H., Jr. *Mobility Studies on Academic Men: Some Methodological Concerns and Substantive Findings.* Bethesda, Md.: ERIC, 1972, ED 065 092.

Blankenship, W.C. "Head Librarians: How Many Men? How Many Women?" *College and Research Libraries* 28 (January 1967): 41-48.

Blau, Francine, and Hendricks, Wallace. "Occupational Segregaton By Sex: Trends and Prospects." *Journal of Human Resources* 14 (Spring 1979): 197-210.

Blaxall, Martha, and Reagan, Barbara, eds. *Women and the Workplace: The Implications of Occupational Segregation.* Chicago: University of Chicago Press, 1976.

Bloom, Lynn Z.; Coburn, Karen; and Pearlman, Joan. *The New Assertive Woman.* New York: Delacorte Press, 1975.

Boch, E. Wilber. "Farmer's Daughter Effect: The Case of the Negro Female Professional." *Phylon* 30 (1969): 17-26.

Bolino, August C. *Supply and Demand Analysis of Manpower Trends in the Library and Information Field, Final Report.* Bethesda, Md.: ERIC, 1969, ED 038 986.

Books and People: A Career in Library Service. American Library Association, Chicago, 1947. Record Series 28/50/6, Box 3. Folder: Personnel—Shortage of Librarians. University of Illinois Archives, Urbana.

Boordem, Curtis D., and Flowers, John V. "Reduction of Anxiety and Personal

Space as a Function of Assertion Training with Severely Disturbed, Neuropsychiatric Inpatients." *Psychological Reports* 30 (June 1972): 923-924.

Borko, Harold. *A Study of the Needs for Research in Library and Information Science Education, The Final Report.* Los Angeles: University of California, Institute of Library Research, 1970. (O.E. Bureau of Research No. BRITD-L & IS Contract No. BR-No. 9-0256.)

Bow, Eric. "Interrupted Careers: The Married Woman as Librarian." *Ontario Library Review* 56 (June 1972): 76-78.

Bowman, G.W.; Worthy, N.B.; and Greyser, S.A. "Are Women Executives People?" *Harvard Business Review* 43 (July/August 1965): 14-16; 19-20; 22; 24-26; 28; 164; 166; 168-170; 172; 174-176.

Bradley, Ben W. "A Study of Characteristics, Qualifications, and Succession Patterns of Large U.S. Academic and Public Libraries." Master's thesis, University of Texas, 1968.

Brand, Barbara Elizabeth. "The Influence of Sex-Typing in Three Professions, 1870-1920: Librarianship, Social Work, and Public Health." Ph.D. dissertation, University of Washington, 1978.

Braunagel, Judith Schiek. "Job Mobility as Related to Career Progression of Female Academic Librarians in the South." Ph.D. dissertation, University of Florida, 1975.

―――. "Job Mobility of Men and Women Librarians and How It Affects Career Advancement." *American Libraries* 10 (December 1979): 643-647.

Broverman, Inge K.; Vogel, Susan Raymond; Broverman, Donald M.; Clarkson, Frank E.; and Rosenkrantz, Paul S. "Sex-Role Stereotypes: A Current Appraisal." In *Women and Achievement: Social and Motivational Analyses.* Edited by Martha T.S. Mednick, Sandra S. Tangri, and Lois W. Hoffman. Washington: Hemisphere Publishing, 1975, pp. 32-47.

Bryan, Alice. *The Public Librarian.* New York: Columbia University Press, 1952.

Buchanan, Bruce. "Building Organizational Commitment: The Socialization of of Managers in Work Organizations." *Administrative Science Quarterly* 19 (December 1974): 533-546.

Buck, Vernon E., "Toward Professionals Managing Professionals: A Case Study of Career Development for Women Librarians." In *The Evaluation of Continuing Education for Professionals: A Systems View.* Edited by Preston F. LeBreton and Kathleen A. J. Murphy. Seattle: University of Washington, 1979, pp. 197-219.

Bundy, M.L., and Wasserman, P. *The Academic Library Administrator and His Situation.* Bethesda, Md.: ERIC, 1972a, ED 054 796.

―――. *The School Library Supervisor and Her Situation.* Bethesda, Md.: ERIC, 1972b, ED 054 798.

———.*The Public Library Administrator and His Situation.* Bethesda, Md.: ERIC, 1972c, ED 054 797.

———.*The Administrator of a Special Library or Information Center and His Situation.* Bethesda, Md.: ERIC, 1972d, ED 054 799.

Business and Professional Women's Foundation. *Work Force Entry by Mature Women.* Washington, D.C.: Business and Professional Women's Foundation, 1977.

Butler, Pamela E. *Teaching Women Not to Discriminate Against Themselves.* Bethesda, Md.: ERIC, 1973, ED 082 103.

———.*Self-Assertion for Women, A Guide to Becoming Androgynous.* New York: Canfield Press, 1976.

Buzenberg, Mildred E. "Training and Development of Women Executives: A Model." *Collegiate News and Views* 29 (Fall 1975): 19-22.

Cain, Glen. "The Challenge of Segmented Labor Market Theories to Orthodox Theory: A Survey." *Journal of Economic Literature* 14 (December 1976): 1215-1257.

Caplow, Theodore. *The Sociology of Work.* New York: McGraw-Hill, 1964.

Caplow, Theodore, and McGee, Reece J. *The Academic Marketplace.* New York: Arno Press, 1977.

Careers Ahead in Librarianship: Recruitment Program at the Queens Borough Public Library, Week of April 11-16, 1955. Record Series 90/21/6, Box 1, Folder: Joint Committee on Library Work as a Career, General correspondence, 1954-58, University of Illinois Archives, Urbana.

Carey, J.T. "Overdue: Taking Issue with the Issues." *Wilson Library Bulletin* 45 (February 1971): 592-594.

Carpenter, Raymond L., and Carpenter, Patricia. "The Doctorate in Librarianship and an Assessment of Graduate Library Education." *Journal of Education for Librarianship* 11 (Summer 1970): 3-45.

Carpenter, Raymond L., and Shearer, Kenneth D. "Sex and Salary Survey: Selected Characteristics of Large Public Libraries in U.S. and Canada." *Library Journal* 97 (November 15, 1972): 3682-3685.

———."Sex and Salary Update." *Library Journal* 99 (January 15, 1974): 101-107.

Carroll, C.E. *The Professionalization of Education for Librarianship.* Metuchen, N.J.: Scarecrow, 1970.

Cartter, Allan M., ed. *American Universities and Colleges.* Washington, D.C.: American Council on Education, 1964.

Chapman, J. Brad, and Luthans, Fred. "The Female Leadership Dilemma." *Public Personnel Management* 4 (May/June 1975): 173-179.

Cheda, Sherrill; Fischer, Linda; Wasylycia-Coe, Mary Ann; Yaffe, Phyllis. "Salary Differentials of Female and Male Librarians in Canada." *Emergency Librarian* 5 (January/February 1978): 3-13.

Clark, Linda. "Fact and Fantasy: A Recent Profile of Women in Academia." *Peabody Journal of Education* 54 (January 1977): 103-109.

Clarke, Edward H. *Sex in Education, or, a Fair Chance for Girls.* Boston: J.R. Osgood, 1873.

Cohen, Michael D., and March, James G. *Leadership and Ambiguity: The American College President.* New York: McGraw-Hill, 1974.

Cohn, William Loewy. "Factors in the Career Decisions and Position Choices by the Directors of Libraries at the State Supported Senior Colleges of Florida." Ph.D. dissertation, Florida State University, 1970.

———."An Overview of ARL Directors, 1933-1973." *College and Research Libraries* 37 (March 1976): 137-144.

Coker, Janis L. "Rating the Personality of Library School Students." M.L.S. thesis, Emory University, 1958.

College Entrance Examination Board. *A Description of the College Board Scholastic Aptitude Test.* Princeton, N.J.: CEEB, 1967.

Colman, Gould P. "The Oral History, Inc." In *The Third National Colloquium on Oral History.* Edited by Gould P. Colman. New York: The Oral History Association, 1968.

Columbia University. School of Library Economy. *Circular of Information.* New York: Columbia University [then College], 1884/85-1888/89.

Columbia University. School of Library Service. "Report on Pilot Study of Women Graduates in the Library Service Field." 1974?

Comeau, Reginald Alfred. "Recruitment Motivation: An Analysis of American Library Association Recruitment Literature: 1950 to 1965." Master's thesis, Southern Connecticut State College, 1967.

Conference of Librarians. *Transactions and Proceedings.* London: Charles Whittingham, 1878.

Cooper, Michael D. "A Statistical Portrait of Librarians: What the Numbers Say." *American Libraries* 7 (June 1976): 327-330.

Cook, Harry and Wessels, Helen E. "It's Up to Us." *Library Journal* 77 (December 1952): 2035-2039.

Costa, Crist H. *The Prediction of Teacher Turnover Employing Time Series Analysis.* Bethesda, Md.: ERIC, 1972, ED 063 336.

Cott, Nancy. *The Bonds of Womanhood; "Women's Sphere" in New England, 1780-1835.* New Haven: Yale University Press, 1977.

Cowper, Rena. "Not In Our Stars." *Library Association Record* 42 (June 1940): 166-167.

Cox, Martha Baldwin. "Recruiting for Librarianship: A Comparison of the Recruiting Programs and Materials in Library Work with Those Used in the Fields of Teaching and Nursing." Master's thesis, Carnegie Institute of Technology, 1953.

Crawford, Jacquelyn S. *Women in Middle Management.* Ridgewood, N.J.: Forkner Publishing Corp., 1977.

Crawford, Jim D., "Career Development and Career Choice in Pioneer and Traditional Women." *Journal of Vocational Behavior* 12 (1978): 129-139.

Cremin, Lawrence. *The Transformation of the School; Progressivism in American Education, 1876-1957.* New York: Knopf, 1961.

Creth, Sheila. "The Impact of Changing Life Styles on Library Administration." *Southeastern Librarian* 30 (Summer 1980): 74-81.

Cross, Patricia K. "The Woman Student." In *Women in Higher Education.* Edited by W. Todd Furniss and Patricia Albjerg Graham. Washington, D.C.: American Council on Education, 1974, pp. 29-50.

Crowley, Joan E. *Fact and Fiction About the American Working Woman.* Bethesda, Md.: ERIC, 1973, ED 074 235.

"The Crying Need for Librarians." *Changing Times: The Kiplinger Magazine* 18 (August 1964): 30-31.

Curby, Vicki M. *Women Administrators in Higher Education: Their Geographic Mobility.* Washington, D.C.: National Association for Women Deans, Administrators, and Counselors, 1980.

Cussler, Margaret. *The Woman Executive.* New York: Harcourt, Brace, & Co., 1958.

Cutler, Mary Salome. "What a Woman Librarian Earns." *Library Journal* 17 (August 1892): 89-91.

Dain, Phyllis. *The New York Public Library: A History of Its Founding and Early Years.* New York: New York Public Library, Astor, Lenox, and Tilden Foundations, 1972.

Davidson, Percy E., and Anderson, H. Dewey. *Occupational Mobility in an American Community.* Stanford, Ca.: Stanford University Press, 1937.

Davis, Earl F. *Attitude Change: A Review and Bibliography of Selected Research.* Paris: UNESCO, 1965.

Deckard, Barbara S. *The Women's Movement: Political, Socioeconomic and Psychological Issues.* 2nd ed. New York: Harper and Row, 1979.

De Fichy, Wendy. "Affirmative Action: Equal Opportunity for Women in Library Management." *College and Research Libraries* 34 (May 1973): 195-201.

De Pasquale, John A., and Lange, Richard A. "Job-Hopping and the MBA." *Harvard Business Review* 49 (November-December 1971): 4-12+.

Dewey, Melvil. "Librarianship as a Profession for College-Bred Women: An Address Delivered Before the Assocation of Collegiate Alumnae on March 13, 1886." Boston: Library Bureau, 1886.

Dick and Jane as Victims: Sex Stereotyping in Children's Readers. Princeton, N.J.: Women on Words and Images Society, 1976.

Douglas, Priscilla D. "An Analysis of Demographic Characteristics and Career Patterns of Women Administrators in Higher Education." Ph.D. dissertation, University of Connecticut, 1976.

Douglass, Robert R. "The Personality of the Librarian." Ph.D. dissertation, University of Chicago, 1957.

Downs, Robert B. "The Role of the Academic Librarian, 1876-1976." *College and Research Libraries* 37 (November 1976): 491-501.

Drennan, Henry T., and Darling, Richard L. *Library Manpower: Occupational Characteristics of Public and School Librarians.* Washington, D.C.: U.S. Office of Education, 1966.

Dual Careers, A Longitudinal Study of Labor Market Experiences of Women. Washington, D.C: Manpower Research Monograph, no. 21, vol. 1, 1970.

Dual Careers, A Longitudinal Study of Labor Market Experiences of Women. Washington, D.C.: Manpower Research Monograph, no. 21, vol. 2, 1973.

Duff, John C. "This Is It! D-Day for the Library." *Library Journal* 71 (September 15, 1946): 1182-1184.

Eastman, Crystal. "Now We Can Begin." In *On Women and Revolution.* Edited by Blanche W. Cook. New York: Oxford University Press, 1978, pp. 52-57.

Edwards, Allen L. *Edwards Personal Preference Schedule Manual.* New York: The Psychological Corporation, 1959.

———.*Statistical Analysis.* 3rd ed. New York: Holt, Rinehart and Winston, 1969.

Eisler, Richard; Hersen, Michel; and Miller, Peter. "Effects of Modeling on Components of Assertive Behavior." *Journal of Behavior Therapy and Experimental Psychiatry* 4 (March 1973): 1-6.

Englebarts, Rudolph. *Librarian Authors: A Bibliography.* Jefferson, N.C.: McFarland, 1981.

Epstein, Cynthia Fuchs. "Bringing Women In: Rewards, Punishments and the Structure of Achievement." In *Women & Success: The Anatomy of Achievement.* Edited by Ruth B. Kundsin. New York: William Morrow, 1974, pp. 13-21.

———."Encountering the Male Establishment: Sex-Status Limits on Women's Careers in the Professions." *American Journal of Sociology* 75 (May 1970): 965-982.

———."Encountering the Male Establishment: Sex-Status Limits on Women's Careers in the Professions." In *Woman: Dependent or Independent Variable?* Edited by Rhoda Kesler Unger and Florence L. Denmark. New York: Psychological Dimensions, Inc., 1975, pp. 751-772.

———.*Woman's Place.* Berkeley: University of California Press, 1970b.

Etzioni, Amitai. *Modern Organizations.* Englewood Cliffs, N.J.: Prentice-Hall, 1964.

———.*The Semi-Professions and Their Organization.* New York: Free Press, 1969.

Fabe, Marilyn, and Wikler, Norma. *Up Against the Clock: Career Women Speak on the Choice to Have Children.* New York: Random House, 1979.

Fairchild, Salome Cutler. "Women in American Libraries." *Library Journal* 29 (December, 1904): 157-162.

Farrington, Helen Seymour. "Daydreaming Will Not Bring in Any Recruits." *Library Journal* 73 (September 1, 1948): 1162.

Fecher, A.R. "Career Patterns of Women in College and University Administration." Ph.D. dissertation, Indiana University, 1972.

Fennell, Janice C. "A Career Profile of Women Directors of the Largest Academic Libraries in the United States: An Analysis and Description of Determinants." Ph.D. dissertation, Florida State University, 1978.

Fensterheim, Herbert. "Behavior Therapy: Assertive Training in Groups." In *Progress in Group and Family Therapy.* Edited by C.J. Sager and H.S. Kaplan. New York: Brunner Mazel, 1972, pp. 156-169.

Fensterheim, Herbert and Bauer, Jean. *Don't Say Yes When You Want to Say No.* New York: David McKay, 1975.

Ferber, Marianne A. and Loeb, Jane W. "Performance, Rewards and Perceptions of Sex Discrimination Among Male and Female Faculty." *American Journal of Sociology* 77 (January 1973): 995-1002.

Ferrari, Michael R. "Origins and Careers of American Business, Government and Academic Elites." *California Management Review* 12 (Summer 1970): 26-32.

Filbey, Mary Louise. "The Early History of the Deans of Women: University of Illinois, 1897-1923." Filbey Family Papers (unpublished), University of Illinois, Urbana, n.d.

Fischer, Linda; Wasylycia-Coe, Mary Ann; Cheda, Sherrill; and Yaffe, Phyllis. *The Career Paths of Male and Female Librarians in Canada: Report to the Canada Council.* Grant S74-1740, 1976. (unpublished).

Fishbein, Martin, comp. *Readings in Attitude Theory and Measurement.* New York: Wiley, 1967.

Fitzpatrick, Edward A. *McCarthy of Wisconsin.* New York: Columbia University Press, 1944.

Flowers, Vincent S., and Hughes, Charles L. "Why Employees Stay." *Harvard Business Review* 51 (July 1973): 49-60.

Ford, Oscar W. "Ask Any Woman." *Library Journal* 94 (May 1969): 1819.

Form, William H. "Popular Images of Librarians." *Library Journal* 71 (June 15, 1946): 851-855.

Form, William H., and Miller, Delbert C. "Occupational Career Pattern As a Sociological Instrument." *American Journal of Sociology* 54 (1947): 317-329.

Forsyth, Kenna, and Harvey, John F. "Drexel Library School Students, Where Do They Come From and Where Do They Go?" *College and Research Libraries* 26 (March 1965); 138-144.

Fox-Genovese, Elizabeth, and Genovese, Eugene. "The Political Crisis of Social History: A Marxian Perspective." *Journal of Social History* 4 (Winter 1976): 205-220.

Frankie, Suzanne, *ARL Statistics, 1976-77.* Washington, D.C.: Association of Research Libraries, 1977.

———*ARL Annual Salary Survey 1977-78.* Washington, D.C.: Association of Research Libraries, November, 1978.

Franklin, Christine Ladd. "Endowed Professorships for Women." In *Association of Collegiate Alumnae Publications.* Series III No. 9 (February 1904): 53-61.

Franklin, John Hope. *From Slavery to Freedom.* New York: Knopf, 1967.

Frarey, Carlyle J., and Learmont, Carol L. "Placement and Salaries 1972: We Hold Our Own." *Library Journal* 98 (June 1973): 1880-1886.

Freedman, Estelle. "Separatism as Strategy: Female Institution Building and American Feminism, 1870-1930." *Feminist Studies* 5 (1979): 512-529.

Freedman, Janet. "The Liberated Librarian?" *Library Journal* 95 (May 1, 1970): 1709-1711.

Fretwell, Gordon. *ARL Annual Salary Survey 1978-79.* Washington, D.C.: Association of Research Libraries, February 1980a.

———.*ARL Annual Salary Survey 1979-80.* Washington, D.C.: Association of Research Libraries, December 1980b.

Freund, John E. *Mathematical Statistics.* 2nd ed. Englewood Cliffs, N.J.: Prentice-Hall, 1971.

Friedan, Betty. *The Feminine Mystique.* New York: Norton, 1963; and New York: Dell, 1964.

Fuchs, Victor R. "Differences in Hourly Earnings Between Men and Women." *Monthly Labor Review* 94 (May 1971): 9-15.

Gambril, Eileen. "A Behavioral Program for Increasing Social Interaction." Paper presented at the Seventh Annual Meeting of the Association for the Advancement of Behavior Therapy. Miami Beach, December 7, 1973.

Garceau, Oliver. *The Public Library in the Political Process.* New York: Columbia University Press, 1951.

Garrison, Dee. "The Tender Technicians: The Feminization of Public Librarianship, 1876-1905." *Journal of Social History* 6 (Winter 1973): 131-159.

———.*Apostles of Culture: The Public Librarian and American Society, 1876-1920.* New York: Macmillan, 1979.

Garskof, Michele Hoffnung, ed. *Roles Women Play: Readings Toward Women's Liberation.* Belmont, Calif.: Brooks/Cole, 1971.

Gasser, May H. "Career Patterns of Women Administrators in Higher Education: Barriers and Constraints." Ph.D. dissertation, Southern Illinois University, 1975.

Gaver, Mary Virginia. "Women in Publishing and Librarianship." *AB Bookman's Weekly* 52 (November 26, 1973): 1819-1824.

Ghoting, Saroj, comp. *Business and Professional Women's Foundation: Work Force Entry by Mature Women.* Washington, D.C.: Business and Professional Women's Foundation, 1977.

Gibbons, Kathleen M. "The Single Working Mother." *Federal Jobs* 4 (September 24-October 7, 1979): 1-3.

Gilman, Daniel Coit. "University Libraries: An Address at the Opening of the Sage Library of Cornell University, October 7, 1891." In *University Problems in the United States,* edited by Daniel Coit Gilman. New York: Century, 1898, pp. 245-255.

Ginzberg, Eli. *Life Styles of Educated Women.* New York: Columbia University Press, 1966.

———.*Occupational Choices: An Approach to a General Theory.* New York: Columbia University Press, 1963.

Ginzberg, Eli, and Brown, Carol A. *Manpower for Library Service* (A report prepared for the U.S. Office of Education, Bureau of Research, Conservation of Human Resources Project, Columbia University, New York). Bethesda, Md.: ERIC, 1967, ED 023 408.

Ginzberg, Eli, and Yohalem, S.M., eds. *Corporate Lib: Women's Challenge to Management.* Baltimore: Johns Hopkins University Press, 1973.

Glass-Schuman, Patricia. "Women Marking Out Their Destiny." *Library Association Record* 78 (July 1976): 305 +.

Gleason, Eliza Atkins. *The Southern Negro and the Public Library: A Study of the Government and Administration of Public Library Service to Negroes in the South.* Chicago: University of Chicago Press, 1941.

———."The Atlanta University School of Library Service—Its Aims and Objectives." *Library Quarterly* 12 (July 1942): 504-510.

Goode, William J. "The Librarian: From Occupation to Profession." *Library Quarterly* 31 (October 1961): 306-320.

———."The Librarian: From Occupation to Profession." In *Seven Questions About the Profession of Librarianship,* edited by Philip Ennis and Howard W. Winger. Chicago: University of Chicago Press, 1962, pp. 8-22.

———."The Theoretical Limits of Professionalization." In *The Semi-Professions and Their Organization,* edited by Amitai Etzioni. New York: Free Press, 1969, pp. 266-313.

Gordon, Francine E., and Strober, Myra H. *Bringing Women into Management.* New York: McGraw-Hill, 1975.

Gornick, Vivian, ed. *Woman in Sexist Society: Studies in Power and Powerlessness.* New York: Basic Books, 1971.

Grimm, James W. "Women in Female-Dominated Professions." In *Women Working,* edited by Ann H. Stromberg and Shirley Harkess, pp. 293-315. Palo Alto: Mayfield Publishing, 1978.

Grimm, James W. and Stern, Robert N. "Sex Roles and Internal Labor Market Structures: The 'Female' Semi-professions." *Social Problems* 21 (June 1974): 690-705.

Grotzinger, Laurel Ann. *The Power and the Dignity: Librarianship and Katharine Sharp.* Metuchen, N.J.: Scarecrow Press, 1966.

Grune, Joy Ann. *Manual on Pay Equity; Raising Wages for Women's Work.* Washington, D.C.: Conference on Alternate State and Local Policies, 1980.

Gruzen, Joan. "The Relationship of Attitudes Towards Women's Liberation to Political Orientation and Sexual Sophistication." Paper presented at meeting of the American Psychological Association, Miami Beach, 1970.

Gummere, Richard. "Toward a New Breed of Librarians." *Wilson Library Bulletin* 41 (April 1967): 810-813.

Hackamack, Lawrence, and Solid, Alan B. "The Woman Executive." *Business Horizons* 15 (April 1972): 89-93.

Hacker, Helen Mayer. "Women as a Minority Group." *Social Forces* 30 (October 1950): 60-69.

Hall, Granville Stanley. *Adolescence; Its Psychology and Its Relations to Physiology, Anthropology, Sociology, Sex, Crime, Religion and Education.* New York: D. Appleton and Co., 1907.

———."Children's Reading: As a Factor in Their Education." *Library Journal* 33 (April 1908): 123-128.

Hall, Katherine Patterson. "Sex Differences in Initiation and Decision-Making Among Prospective Teachers." Ph.D. dissertation, Stanford University, 1972.

Hamel, Harvey R. "Job Tenure of American Workers, January 1963." *Monthly Labor Review* 86 (October 1963): 1145-1152.

"Hampton to Close." *Library Journal* 64 (May 1, 1939): 339.

Harper, W.R. "The Educational Progress of the Year 1901-1902." In *Annual Report of the Commissioner of Education 1902*, vol. 1, Washington, D.C.: U.S. Bureau of Education, 1903, pp. 647-666.

Harris, Michael. "The Purpose of the American Public Library: A Revisionist Interpretation of History." *Library Journal* 98 (September 15, 1973): 2509-2514.

Harrison, Evelyn. "The Working Woman: Barriers in Employment." *Public Administration Review* 24 (June 1964): 78-85.

Harvey, John F. *The Librarian's Career: A Study in Mobility*. ACRL Microcard Series, no. 85. Rochester, N.Y.: University of Rochester Press, 1958.

———."Advancement in the Library Profession." *Wilson Library Bulletin* 36 (October 1961): 144-147.

Havens, Elizabeth M. "Women, Work, and Wedlock: A Note on Female Marital Problems in the United States." *American Journal of Sociology* 78 (January 1973): 975-981.

Hazeltine, Alice Isabel. "Values in Library Work with Children." In *Library Work With Children*. New York: H.W. Wilson, 1917, pp. 111-155.

Heim, Kathleen M. "Professional Education: Some Comparisons." In *As Much to Learn As to Teach*, edited by Joel M. Lee and Beth A. Hamilton. Hamden, Conn.: Linnet Books, 1979 (a), pp. 137-169.

———."Status of Women in Librarianship." In *ALA Yearbook 1979*, edited by Robert Wedgeworth. Chicago, American Library Association, 1979 (b), pp. 294-299.

Heim, Kathleen M., and Kacena, Carolyn. "Sex, Salaries and Library Support." *Library Journal* 104 (March 1979): 675-680.

Heinen, J. Stephen; McGlauchlin, Dorothy; Legeros, Constance; Freeman, Jean. "Developing the Woman Manager." *Personnel Journal* 54 (May 1975): 282-286.

Helmich, Donald L., and Brown, Warren B. "Successor Type and Organizational Change in the Corporate Enterprise." *Administrative Science Quarterly* 17 (1972): 371-381.

Hennig, Margaret M. "Career Development for Women Executives."Ph.D. dissertation, Harvard University, 1971.

———."Family Dynamics and the Successful Woman Executive." In *Women & Success: The Anatomy of Achievement,* edited by Ruth B. Kundsin. New York: William Morrow, 1974, pp. 88-93.

Hennig, Margaret M., and Franklin, Barbara Hackman. "Men and Women at Harvard Business School." In *The Managerial Woman,* edited by Margaret Hennig and Anne Jardim. New York: Doubleday, 1977.

Hennig, Margaret M. and Jardim, Anne. *The Managerial Woman.* Garden City, N.Y.: Anchor Press/ Doubleday, 1977.

Herbert, Clara. *Personnel Administration in Public Libraries.* Chicago: American Library Association, 1939.

Hersen, Michel; Eisler, Richard M.; and Miller, Peter. "Development of Assertive Responses: Clinical Measurement and Research Considerations." *Behavior Research and Therapy* 11 (November 1973): 505-521.

Heyns, Barbara. *Summer Learning and the Effects of Schooling.* New York: Academic Press, 1978.

Higgins, Alice G. "Eighteen Thousand Librarians Wanted." *Library Journal* 70 (June 15, 1945): 551-554.

Hoage, Annette. "Job History of A Library School Class, 1937-1949." (May) Atlanta University, 1950. Mimeographed.

Hofstadter, Richard. *Anti-Intellectualism in American Life.* New York: Knopf, 1963.

Holden, Miriam Y. "The Status of Women Librarians." *Antiquarian Bookman* 36 (August 23, 1965): 647-648.

Holly, E.G. "Librarians 1876-1976." *Library Trends* 25 (July 1976): 177-207.

Holt, Louise Conrad. "A Study of Western Reserve University Library School Women Graduates, 1934-1953." Master's thesis, Western Reserve University, 1957.

Hooks, Janet. *Women's Occupations through Seven Decades.* U.S. Women's Bureau Bulletin no. 218. Washington, D.C.: Government Printing Office, 1947, p. 30.

Hooyman, N.R. and Kaplan, J.S. "New Roles for Professional Women." In *Libraries in Post-Industrial Society,* edited by Leigh Estabrook. Phoenix: Oryx Press, 1977, pp. 107-113.

Horner, Mattina. "Differences in Achievement Motivation and Performance in Competitive and Non-Competitive Situations." Ph.D. dissertation, University of Michigan, 1968.

———."The Motive to Avoid Success and Changing Aspirations of College Women." In *Readings on the Psychology of Women,* edited by Judith M. Bardwick. New York: Harper & Row, 1972, pp. 62-67.

Horrocks, Norman A. "A Few New Projects...The Annual Meeting of the Association of American Library Schools." *Library Journal* 102 (March 15, 1977): 688-689.

Hostetter, Anita M. "A Library School for Negroes." *American Library Association Bulletin* 33 (April 1939): 247.

———.To the Director of the Library School. April 21, 1942. Library of Education Board of Education for Librarianship Subject File, 1914-1956; Record Series 28/50/6, Box 3, Folder: Personnel-Shortage of Librarians, 1942-43, University of Illinois Archives, Urbana, 1942.

Howard, Suzanne. *But We Will Persist: A Comparative Research Report on the Status of Women in Academe.* Washington, D.C: American Association of University Women, 1978.

Hughes, Everett Cherrington. *Men and Their Work.* Glencoe, Ill.: Free Press, 1958.

Index of Opportunity in the Library and Information Sciences, 1971: A Directory of Career Opportunities for Qualified Librarians and Information Science Specialists with Public, Private, University and Special Libraries and Information Centers. Princeton, N.J.: G-W Resource Publications, 1971.

Indiana State Library. *It's Primary.* Record Series 9/2/6, Box 3, University of Illinois Archives, Urbana, n.d.

Institute for Research. *School and College Librarianship as a Career.* Chicago: (Research No. 159) 1947.

Jacklin, Carol N., and Maccoby, Eleanor E. "Sex Differences and Their Implications for Management." In *Bringing Women Into Management,* edited by Francine E. Gordon and Myra H. Strober. New York: McGraw-Hill, 1975, pp. 23-28.

Jakubowski-Spector, Patricia. "Facilitating the Growth of Women Through Assertive Training." *Counseling Psychologist* 4 (January 1973a): 75-86.

———.*An Introduction to Assertive Training Procedures for Women.* Washington, D.C.: American Personnel and Guidance Association, 1973b.

Jencks, Christopher, and Riesman, David. *The Academic Revolution.* Chicago: University of Chicago Press, 1977.

Jewell, Donald O., ed., *Women and Management: An Expanding Role.* Atlanta, Ga.: Publishing Services Division, School of Business Administration, 1977.

"The Job of the Librarian: What He Does, How He Qualifies, What He Earns, What Is the Employment Outlook." *Occupational Brief,* No. 29. Washington, D.C.: Government Printing Office, 1945. Prepared by the National Roster of Scientific and Specialized Personnel of War Manpower Commission for Use in the Education Program of the Armed Services. Record Series 28/50/6, Box 3, Folder; Personnel—Shortage of Librarians, 1942-43, University of Illinois Archives, Urbana.

Jones, Dorothy Scott. "Library Work is Exciting: A Study of Methods Used in Recruiting for Librarianship." Master's thesis, Pratt Institute Library School, 1951.

Josey, E.J. *The Black Librarian in America.* Metuchen, N.J.: Scarecrow, 1970.

Kagan, Jerome, and Moss, H.A. *Birth to Maturity.* New York: Wiley, 1962.

Kanter, Rosabeth Moss. *Men and Women of the Corporation.* New York: Basic Books, 1977.

Karier, Clarence J. "Testing for Order and Control in the Corporate Liberal State." In *Roots of Crisis: American Education in the Twentieth Century,* edited by Clarence Karier and Paul Violas. Chicago: Rand McNally, 1973, pp. 108-137.

Katz, Michael. *The Irony of Early School Reform: Educational Innovation in Mid-Nineteenth Century Massachusetts.* Cambridge, Mass.: Harvard University Press, 1968.

———. *Class, Bureaucracy and School: The Illusion of Educational Change in America.* New York: Praeger, 1971.

Kemp, Helen Lamon. "An Annotated Guide to the Literature of Recruitment for Librarianship, 1940-1953." Master's thesis, Western Reserve University, 1954.

Kenniston, Ellen and Kenniston, Kenneth. "An American Anachronism: The Image of Women and Work." *American Scholar* 33 (Summer 1964): 355-375.

Key, Ellen. *The Century of the Child.* New York: G.P. Putnam's Sons, 1909.

Key, Mary Ritchie. "The Role of Male and Female in Children's Books— Dispelling All Doubts." *Wilson Library Bulletin* 46 (October 1971): 167-176.

Kimmel, Ellen B. *Job Mobility of Men and Women Psychologists in the Southeast.* Bethesda, Md.: ERIC, 1973, ED 078 798.

Kievit, Mary B. *Review and Synthesis of Research on Women in the World of Work.* Columbus, Ohio: Ohio State University, The Center for Vocational Education, 1972.

Kitson, Harry. *Vocation for Boys.* New York: Harcourt Brace, 1942.

Klemmack, David L., and Edwards, John N. "Women's Acquisition of Stereotyped Occupational Aspirations." *Sociology and Human Research* 57 (1973): 510-525.

Komarovsky, Mirra. "Cultural Contradictions and Sex Roles." In *Readings on the Psychology of Women,* edited by Judith Bardwick. New York: Harper & Row, 1972, pp. 58-62.

Korb, George M. "Successful Librarians as Revealed in *Who's Who in America.*" *Wilson Library Bulletin* 20 (April 1946): 603-604.

Kraus, Joe W. "The Qualifications of University Librarians, 1948 and 1933." *College and Research Libraries* 11 (January 1950): 17-21.

Kronus, Carol L. and Grimm, James W. "Women in Librarianship: The Majority Rules?" *Protean* 9 (December 1971): 4-9.

Krucoff, Carol. "Money: The Question of Men, Women and 'Comparable Worth.' " *The Washington Post*, November 13, 1979, B 5.

Labb, June. "Librarians in *Who's Who in America.*" Wilson Library Bulletin 25 (September 1959): 54-56.

Ladinsky, Jack. "The Geographic Mobility of Professional and Technical Manpower." *Journal of Human Resources* 2 (Fall 1967a): 484-493.

———."Occupational Determinants of Geographic Mobility Among Professional Workers." *American Sociological Review* 32 (1967b): 253-264.

Lander, Joyce A. *Tomorrow's Tomorrow: The Black Woman.* New York: Doubleday, 1971.

Lange, Alexis F. "The Problem of Professional Training for Women." *School and Society* 3 (April 1916): 480-485.

Lantz, Alma. *Conference on Re-entry Women Scientists, Proceedings.* Denver, University of Denver, Denver Research Institute, 1980.

Larson, Magali Sarfatti. *The Rise of Professionalism: A Sociological Analysis.* Berkeley, Calif.: University of California Press, 1977.

Lasch, Christopher. "Breckinridge, Sophonisba Preston, " in *Notable American Women, 1607-1950; A Biographical Dictionary*, vol. 1, edited by Edward T. James, Janet Wilson James and Paul S. Boyer. Cambridge: Harvard University Press, 1971, pp. 233-236.

Lawrence, Philip. "The Assessment and Modification of Assertive Behavior." Ph.D. dissertation, Arizona State University, 1970.

Lazarus, Arnold. *Behavior Therapy and Beyond.* New York: McGraw-Hill, 1971.

Leigh, Robert. *The Public Library in the United States.* New York: Columbia University Press, 1950.

Leigh, Robert and Sewny, Kathryn W. "The Popular Image of the Library and the Librarian." *Library Journal* 85 (June 1960): 2089-2091.

Leonard, Ruth S. "Recruiting for Librarianship Literature Sadly Inadequate." *Library Journal* 72 (September 1947): 1181, 1183.

"The Librarian-Idea Consultant." Demco Production File, Record Series 9/2/6, University of Illinois Archives, Urbana.

The Librarian—Merchant of Ideas. Demco Production File, Record Series 9/2/6, University of Illinois Archives, Urbana.

"Librarianship as a Profession." *The Illini* 26 (May 28, 1897): 1041-1043.

Library of Education, Board of Education for Librarianship Subject File, 1914-1956; Record Series 28/50/6, Box 3, Folder; Personnel—Postwar Library Personnel, 1947, University of Illinois Archives.

Lightfoot, R.M. "Further Discussion." *Library Journal* 63 (June 1, 1938): 438.

Linn, Erwin L. "Women Dentists: Career and Family," *Social Problems* 18 (Winter 1971): 393-404.

Lipow, Anne. *A Report on the Status of Women Employed in the Library of the University of California, Berkeley, with Recommendations for Action.* Bethesda, Md.: ERIC, 1971, ED 066 163.

Lipset, Seymour M., and Bendix, Reinhard. "Social Mobility and Occupational Career Patterns, I., "Stability and Jobholding." *American Journal of Sociology* 57 (January 1952): 366-374.

———.*Social Mobility in Industrial Society* Berkeley: University of California Press, 1967.

Little, Cecily. "Librarianship: A Female Profession?" *Michigan Librarian* 38 (Autumn 1972): 10-11.

Livingston, J. Sterling. "Myth of the Well-Educated Manager." *Harvard Business Review* 49 (January/February 1971): 79-89.

Lomont, James F.; Gilner, Frank H.; Spector, Norman J.; and Skinner, Kathryn K. "Group Assertion Training and Group Insight Therapies." *Psychological Reports* 25 (October 1969): 463-470.

Loring, Rosalind, and Wells, Theodora. *Breakthrough: Women into Management*. New York: Van Nostrand Reinhold, 1972.

Lowen, Walter. *How and When to Change Your Job Successfully*. New York: Simon and Schuster, 1954.

Lowenthal, Helen. "A Healthy Anger." *Library Journal* 96 (September 1, 1971): 2597-2599.

Lydon, Christopher. "Role of Woman Sparks Debate by Congresswoman and Doctor." *New York Times*, July 26, 1970: 35.

Lynch, Beverly P. "Women and Employment in Academic Librarianship." In *Academic Libraries by the Year 2000*, edited by Herbert Poole. New York: Bowker, 1977, pp. 119-127.

McAnally, Arthur, and Downs, Robert B. "The Changing Role of Directors of University Libraries." *College and Research Libraries* 34 (March 1973): 103-125.

McCann, Eleanor. "Let Them Come In." *Library Journal* 74 (December 1949): 1802.

McClelland, David C. "Wanted: A New Self-Image for Women." In *The Woman in America*, edited by Robert J. Lifton. Boston: Beacon Press, 1967, pp. 173-192.

Maccoby, Eleanor E., and Jacklin, Carol Nagy. *The Psychology of Sex Differences*. Stanford, Calif.: Stanford University Press, 1974.

McCord, Bird. "Identifying and Developing Women for Management Positions." *Training and Development Journal* 25 (November 1971): 2-5.

McDiarmid, E.W. "The Place of Experience in Developing College and University Librarians." *Library Quarterly* 12 (1942): 614-621.

McFall, Richard M., and Lillesiand, Diane B. "Behavior Rehearsal with Modeling and Coaching in Assertive Training: Assessment and Training Stimuli." *Journal of Abnormal Psychology* 77 (June 1971): 313-323.

McFall, Richard M., and Marston, Albert R. "An Experimental Investigation of Behavior Rehearsal in Assertive Training." *Journal of Abnormal Psychology* 76 (October 1970): 295-303.

McFall, Richard M. and Twentyman, Craig T. "Four Experiments on the Relative Contributions of Rehearsal, Modeling, and Coaching to Assertion Training." *Journal of Abnormal Psychology* (June 1973): 199-318.

McGowan, Frank M. "The Association of Research Libraries, 1932-1962." Ph.D. dissertation, University of Pittsburgh, 1972.

MacLean, Malcom S., and Lanier, R. O'Hara. "Negroes, Education and the War." *The Educational Record* 23 (January 1942): 35-43.

McMahon, Anne. *The Personality of the Librarian, Prevalent Social Values, and Attitudes Toward the Profession*. Adelaide: Libraries Board of South Australia, 1967.

MacPherson, H.D. "Report on Recruiting." *American Library Association Bulletin* 42 (March 1948): 112-114.

Manchak, Barbara. "ALA Salary Survey: Personal Members." *American Libraries* 2 (April 1971): 409-417.

Manderino, Mary Ann. "Effects of a Group Assertive Training Procedure of Undergraduate Women." Ph.D. dissertation, Arizonal State University, 1974.

Marchant, Maurice P. *Participative Management in Academic Libraries*. Westport, Conn.: Greenwood Press, 1976.

Martin, Jean K. "Factors Related to the Representation of Women in Library Management." Master's thesis, University of Georgia, 1978.

———."Academic Library Management: A Comparison of Females and Males." *Library Management Bulletin* 2 (Spring 1979): 9-11.

Massman, Virgil F. *Faculty Status for Librarians.* Metuchen, N.J.: Scarecrow, 1972.

Mattila, Peter J. *Labor Turnover and Sex Discrimination.* Bethesda, Md.: ERIC, 1974, ED 096 497.

Meacham, Colquitt L. "The Law: Where It Is and Where It's Going." In *Bringing Women into Management,* edited by Francine E. Gordon and Myra H. Strober. New York: McGraw-Hill, 1975, pp. 59-76.

Mednick, Martha; Tangri, Sandra; and Hoffman, Lois, eds. *Women and Achievement, Social and Motivational Analyses.* New York: Wiley, 1975.

Metcalf, Keyes. "Six Influential Academic and Research Librarians." *College and Research Libraries* 37 (July 1976): 342-345.

Metz, Paul. "Administrative Succession in the Academic Library." *College and Research Libraries* 39 (September 1978): 358-364.

Milam, Carl H. "To a Few Librarians." Library Education. Board of Education for Librarianship Subject File, 1914-1956; Record Series 28/50/6, Box 3, Folder: Personnel-Postwar Library Personnel, 1947, University of Illinois Archives, Urbana.

Miller, A.E. "Professional Education." In *Annual Report of the Commissioner of Education, 1893-1894.* Washington, D.C.: U.S. Bureau of Education, 1896, pp. 973-1018.

Miller, Jean B. *Toward a New Psychology of Women.* Boston: Beacon Press, 1978.

Miller, Joanne; Schooler, Carmi; Kohn, Melvin L.; and Miller, Karen A. "Women and Work: The Psychological Effects of Occupational Conditions." *American Journal of Sociology* 85 (July 1979): 66-94.

Miner, John B. *The Human Constraint: The Coming Shortage of Managerial Talent.* Washington, D.C: The Bureau of National Affairs, 1974.

Moore, Anne Carroll. "Special Training for Children's Librarians." *Library Journal* 23 (August 1898): 78-80.

———."Training for the Work of a Children's Librarian." *American Library Association Bulletin* 82 (July 1914): 238-243.

Morlock, Laura. "Discipline Variation in the Status of Academic Women." In *Academic Women on the Move,* edited by Alice S. Rossi and Ann Calderwood. New York: Russell Sage Foundation, 1973, pp. 255-309.

Morrison, Perry D. *The Career of the Academic Librarian: A Study of the Social Origins, Educational Attainments, Vocational Experiences, and Personality Characteristics of a Group of American Academic Librarians.* (ACRL Monograph, No. 29). Chicago: American Library Association, 1969.

Munn, Ralph. "It Is a Mistake to Recruit Men." *Library Journal* 74 (November 1949): 1639-1640.

Myers, Margaret, and Scarborough, Mayra, eds. *Women in Librarianship: Melvil's Rib Symposium.* New Brunswick, N.J.: Rutgers University Graduate School of Library Service, 1975.

National Science Foundation, Bureau of Social Research. *Two Years After the College Degree: Work and Further Study Patterns.* Washington, D.C: U.S. Government Printing Office, 1963.

Newland, Kathleen. *Women, Men, and the Division of Labor.* Washington, D.C.: Worldwatch Institute, 1980.

Neuman, Donald. "Using Assertive Training." In *Behavioral Counseling: Cases and Techniques*, edited by John D. Krunhiltz and Carl E. Thoreson, New York: Holt, Rinehart and Winston, 1969, pp. 433-441.

Niebor, N.S. "The Administrative Woman in Higher Education." Ph.D. dissertation, U.S. International University, 1975.

Oboler, Eli M. "Men Librarians." *Library Journal* 75 (January 1950): 66, 98.

O'Keefe, Beth Egan. "Attitudes Towards Women's Liberation: Relationship Between Cooperation, Competition, Personality, and Demographic Variables." Ph.D. dissertation, St. Louis University, 1971.

Olcott, Frances Jenkins. "Rational Work with Children and the Preparation for It." *Library Journal* 30 (September 1905): 74-75.

⸻."The Public Library: a Social Force in Pittsburgh." *Survey* 23 (March 1910): 849-861.

O'Leary, Virginia. "Some Attitudinal Barriers to Occupational Aspirations of Women." *Psychological Bulletin* 81 (1974): 809-826.

Olsgaard, John N., and Olsgaard, Jane K. "Authorship in Five Library Periodicals." *College and Research Libraries* 41 (January 1980): 49-53.

Oltman, Ruth M. *Campus 1970, Where Do We Stand?* Ann Arbor, Mich.: University Microfilms, 1969. (Cited in text as ERIC item 1970, ED 046 366.)

Oppenheimer, Abraham. *Questionnaire Design and Attitude Measurement.* New York: Basic Books, 1966.

Oppenheimer, Valerie K. "Demographic Influence on Female Employment and the Status of Women." *American Journal of Sociology* 78 (1973): 946-961.

*Opportunities for Constructive Giving Through Library Service.*Chicago: American Library Association, 1945.

Opportunities for Women in Higher Education: Their Current Participation, Prospects for the Future, and Recommendations for Action. A Report and Recommendations for Action. New York: McGraw-Hill, 1973.

"Oral History Association Guidelines for Interviewing." In *Guidelines for the Interviewee.* Oral History Association (25 November 1968).

Orlich, Donald C. "An Analysis of Teacher Mobility." *Journal of Teacher Education* 23 (Summer 1972): 230-236.

Orth, Charles D. III, and Jacobs, Frederic. "Women in Management: Pattern for Change." *Harvard Business Review* 49 (July/August 1971): 139-147.

Ory, John C., and Poggio, John P. *The Development and Empirical Validation of a Measure of Achievement Motivation.* Bethesda, Md.: ERIC, 1976, ED 124 567.

Osborn, Richard N., and Vicars, William M. "Sex-Stereotypes: An Artifact in Leader Behavior and Subordinate Satisfaction Analysis?" *Academy of Management Journal* 19 (September, 1976): 439-449.

Osborne, Susan M., and Harris, Gloria A. *Assertive Training for Women.* Springfield, IL: Charles C. Thomas, 1975.

Osmond, Marie W., and Martin, Patricia Y. "Sex and Sexism: A Comparison of Male and Female Sex-Role Attitudes." *Journal of Marriage and the Family* 37 (November 1975): 744-758.

Panek, Paul E.; Rush, Michael C.; and Greenawalt, James P. "Current Sex Stereotypes of 25 Occupations." *Psychological Reports* 50 (1977): 212-214.

Parker, Garland G. "Statistics of Attendance in American Universities and Colleges, 1964-1965." *School and Society* 93 (January 1965): 5-18, 20.

Parnes, Herbert S. *Research on Labor Mobility.* New York: Social Science Research Council, 1954.

Parrott, Shirley. "An Analysis of the Biographies of Librarians Listed in WHO'S WHO OF AMERICAN WOMEN 1958-1959." M.L.S. thesis, Atlanta University, 1962.

Parsons, Jerry L. "Characteristics of Research Library Directors, 1958 and 1973." *Wilson Library Bulletin* 50 (1976): 613-617.

Parsons, Talcott. "Implications of the Study." In *The Climate of Book Selection: Social Influences on School and Public Libraries,* edited by J. Perriam Danton, pp. 77-96. Paper presented at a symposium held at the University of California, 1959.

Parsons, Talcott, and Bales, R.R. *Family: Socialization and Interaction Process.* London: Routledge & Kegan Paul, 1956.

Patterson, Michelle. "Sex and Specialization in Academe and the Professions." In *Academic Women on the Move,* edited by A. Rossi and A. Calderwood. New York: Russell Sage, 1973, pp. 313-332.

Petros, John G. "The Search for a Code of Ethics." *American Libraries* 2 (July/August 1971): 743-746.

Petty, M.M., and Miles, Robert H. "Leader Sex-Role Stereotyping in a Female-Dominated Work Culture." *Personnel Psychology* 29 (1976): 393-404.

Pfaender, Ann McLelland. *Miss Library Lady.* New York: Julian Messner, 1954.

Pfiffner, Virginia T. "Women as Leaders in Higher Education in These Changing Times." *The Delta Kappa Gamma Bulletin* 41 (Spring 1975): 5-10.

Phelps, Linda. "Is There Equal Opportunity for Women in Public Library Management?" *West Virginia Libraries* 27 (Spring 1974): 10-12.

Phelps, Stanlee, and Austin, Nancy. *The Assertive Woman*. San Luis Obispo, Calif.: IMPACT, 1975.

Plate, Kenneth H. "Letter in Response to 'The Disadvantaged Majority.'" *American Libraries* 1 (July-August 1970): 644.

Pollard, Frances M. "Characteristics of Negro College Chief Librarians." *College and Research Libraries* 25 (July 1964): 281-284.

Presthus, Robert. *Technological Change and Occupational Response: A Study of Librarians*. Bethesda, Md.: ERIC, 1970, ED 024 129.

Rainwaters, Nancy Jane. "A Study of the Personality Traits of Ninety-Four Library School Students as Shown by the Edwards Personal Preference Schedule." M.L.S. thesis, University of Texas, 1962.

Randall, William M. *The College Library*. Chicago: American Library Association and the University of Chicago Press, 1932.

Rathas, Spencer. "An Experimental Investigation of Assertive Training in a Group Setting." *Journal of Behavior Therapy and Experimental Psychiatry* 3 (June 1972): 81-86.

Rathbone, Josephine Adams. "Library Work". In *Vocations for the Trained Woman: Opportunities Other Than Teaching*. Edited by Agnes Frances Perkins. Boston: Women's Educational and Industrial Union, 1910, pp. 215-220.

Ravitch, Diane. *The Revisionists Revised: A Critique of the Radical Attack on the Schools*. New York: Basic Books, 1970.

Reagan, Agnes Lytton. "A Study of Certain Factors in Institutions of Higher Education Which Influence Students to Become Librarians." Ph.D. dissertation, University of Illinois, 1957.

―――."Southeastern Colleges and Universities: A Source of Supply for the Library Profession." *The Southeastern Librarian* 8 (Fall 1958a): 86-94.

―――.*A Study of the Factors Influencing College Students to Become Librarians*. Chicago: Association of College and Research Libraries, 1958b.

Reece, Ernest. *The Task and Training of Librarians*. New York: King's Crown Press, 1949.

Reeling, Patricia A. "Undergraduate Student Characteristics as an Aid in Early Identification of Potential Librarians." New York: School of Library Service, Columbia University, 1965. Unpublished.

Reeling, Patricia Ann. "Undergraduate Female Students as Potential Library Recruits." Ph.D. dissertation, Columbia University, 1969.

Reeves, Nancy. *Womankind, Beyond the Stereotype*. Chicago: Aldine, Atherton, 1971.

Reif, William E.; Newstrom, John W.; and Monczka, Robert M. "Exploding Some Myths About Women Managers." *California Management Review* 17 (Summer 1975): 72-79.

Reiss, Albert J. Jr. "Occupational Mobility of Professional Workers." *American Sociological Review* 20 (1955): 693-700.

"Report of the Committee on the Proposed School of Library Economy". *Library Journal* 10 (September-October, 1885): 291-294.

"Report on Pilot Study of Women Graduates in the Library Service Field." New York: Columbia University School of Library Service, 1974? Mimeographed.

"Report on Recruiting." *American Library Association Bulletin* 42 (March 1948): 113.

Reubens, Beatrice and Reubens, Edwin. "Women Workers, Nontraditional Occupations and Full Employment." In *Women in the U.S. Labor Force*, edited by Ann Foote Chan. New York: Praeger, 1979, pp. 103-126.

Reynolds, Judy, and Whitlatch, Jo Bell. "Salary Equity." San Jose, Calif., 1978. Typewritten.

Rhodes, Lelia Gaston. "A Critical Analysis of the Career Backgrounds of Selected Black Female Librarians." Ph.D. dissertation, Florida State University, 1975.

Robinson, Joseph A. "Women Managers: Aids, and Barriers in Their Career Paths, Performance and Advancement." Ph.D. dissertation, University of California, Berkeley, 1974.

Rosen, Benson, and Jerdee, Thomas H. "The Influence of Sex-Role Stereotypes on Evaluations of Male and Female Supervisory Behavior." *Journal of Applied Psychology* 57 (1973): 44-48.

―――."Sex Stereotyping in the Executive Suite." *Harvard Business Review* 52 (March-April 1974): 45-58.

Rosenberg, Morris. *Occupations and Values*. Glencoe, Ill.: Free Press, 1957.

Rosenfeld, Carl, and Perrella, Vera C. "Why Women Start and Stop Working: A Study in Mobility." *Monthly Labor Review* 88 (September 1965): 1077-1082.

Rosenfeld, Rachel A. "Women's Intergenerational Occupational Mobility." *American Sociological Review* 43 (February 1978): 36-46.

Ross, Sue G. "The Timing and Spacing of Births and Women's Labor Force Participation: An Economic Analysis." Ph.D. dissertation, Columbia University, New York, 1964.

Rossi, Alice S. "Equality Between the Sexes: An Immodest Proposal." In *The Woman in America*, edited by Robert J. Lifton. Boston: Beacon Press, 1967, pp. 247-266.

Rossi, Peter H. "Discussion of 'The Librarian's Search for Status' by Harold Lancour." In *Seven Questions About the Profession of Librarianship*, edited by Philip H. Ennis and Howard W. Winger. Chicago: University of Chicago Press, 1962, pp. 82-83.

Rothenberg, Lesliebeth; Rees, Alan M.; and Kronick, David A. "An Investigation of the Educational Needs of Health Sciences Library Manpower: IV Characteristics of Manpower in Health Sciences Libraries." *Bulletin of the Medical Library Association* 59 (January 1971): 31-40.

Ryan, Mary Jane "Librarian's Perceptions of Librarianship." Ph.D. dissertation, University of Southern California, 1967.

Ryan, William. *Blaming the Victim*. New York: Pantheon Books, 1971.

"SLA Salary Survey 1976." *Special Libraries* 67 (December 1976): 597-624.

Safilios-Rothschild, Constantian, ed. *Toward a Sociology of Women*. Lexington, Mass.: Xerox Publishing, 1972.

Salter, Andrew. *Conditioned Reflex Therapy*. New York: Creative Age Press, 1949.

Savord, Ruth. "Men vs. Women." *Library Journal* 63 (May 1938): 342-343.

Sayers, Frances C. *Anne Carroll Moore, a Biography*. New York: Atheneum, 1972.

Schein, Edgar. "The Individual, the Organization, and the Career: A Conceptual Scheme." In *Organizational Psychology: A Book of Readings*, edited by David A. Kolb, Irwin M. Rubin, and James M. McIntyre. Englewood Cliffs, N.J.: Prentice-Hall, 1974, pp. 333-349.

Schein, Virginia E. "Relationships Between Sex Role Stereotype and Requisite Management Characteristics Among Female Managers." *Journal of Applied Psychology* 57 (April 1973): 95-100.

―――."Sex Role Stereotyping, Ability and Performance: Prior Research and New Directions." *Personnel Psychology* 31 (Summer 1978): 250-268.

Schick, Frank L. "Meet the College Librarian." *Library Journal* 74 (June 1950): 1017-1019.

Schiller, Anita R. *Characteristics of Professional Personnel in College and University Libraries*. Springfield: Illinois State Library, 1969a.

―――."The Disadvantaged Majority: Women Employed in Libraries." *American Libraries* 1 (April 1970a): 345-349.

―――."Response to letters on 'The Disadvantaged Majority.'" *American Libraries* 1 (July/August 1970b): 644-645.

———."Sex and Library Careers." In *Women in Librarianship: Melville's Rib Symposium*, edited by Margaret Myers and M. Scarborough. New Brunswick, N.J.: Rutgers University Press, 1975, pp. 11-22.

———."The Widening Sex Gap." *Library Journal* 94 (March 1969b): 1098-1100.

———."Women in Librarianship." In *Advances in Librarianship*, vol. 4, edited by Melvin J. Voight, New York: Academic Press, 1974, pp. 103-147.

Schlachter, Gail, and Thomison, Dennis. "The Library Science Doctorate: A Quantitative Analysis of Dissertations and Recipients." *Journal of Education for Librarianship* 15 (Fall 1974): 95-111.

Schneir, Miriam, editor. *Feminism: The Essential Historical Writings*. New York: Vintage Books, 1972.

Schultz, Terri. *Women Can Wait: The Pleasures of Motherhood After Thirty*. New York: Doubleday, 1979.

Schuman, Patricia Glass. "Women Marking Out Their Destiny." *Library Association Record* 78 (July 1976): 305 +.

Schwartz, Eleanor. *The Sex Barrier in Business*. Atlanta: Georgia State University, 1971.

Sharp, Katharine. Letter to Andrew Draper, 1 December 1902. Draper Papers, Faculty Correspondence 1901-12, University of Illinois Archives, Urbana, 1902b.

———."Library School on a Graduate Basis." *Association of Collegiate Alumnae Publications*, Series III, no. 5 (February 1902a): 24-33.

———."University of Illinois State Library School." *Library Journal* 23 (August 1898): 63-66.

Shera, Jesse. "Little Girls Don't Play Librarian." *Library Journal* 87 (December 1962): 4483-4487.

Sherif, Carolyn W. "Dreams and Dilemmas of Being a Woman Today." In *Women in Librarianship: Melville's Rib Symposium*, edited by Margaret Myers and M. Scarborough. New Brunswick, N.J.: Rutgers University Press, 1975, pp. 23-48.

Shetty, Y.K., and Peery, Newman S. Jr. "Are Top Executives Transferable Across Companies?" In *The Applied Psychology of Work Behavior: A Book of Readings*, edited by Dennis W. Organ. Dallas, Tex.: Business Publication, 1978, pp. 481-488.

Shockley, Ann Allen. "Negro Librarians in Predominantly Negro Colleges." *College and Research Libraries* 28 (November 1967): 423-426.

Simon, Barry E., and Myers, Margaret. "Supply and Demand: Old Law Trips Up New Grads." *Wilson Library Bulletin* 51 (December 1976): 346-353.

Simon, Rita J.; Clark, Shirley M.; and Galway, Kathleen. "The Woman Ph.D: A Recent Profile." *Social Problems* 15 (Fall 1967): 221-236.

──────."The Woman Ph.D: A Recent Profile." In *Readings on the Psychology of Women*, edited by Judith M. Bardwick, pp. 83-92. New York: Harper and Row, 1972.

Simpson, Richard L., and Simpson, Ida Harper. "Women and Bureaucracy in the Semi-Professions." In *The Semi-Professions and Their Organization: Teachers, Nurses, Social Workers*, edited by Amitai Etzioni. New York: The Free Press, 1969, pp. 195-265.

Smart, Anne. "Women—the 4/5 Minority." *Canadian Library Journal* 32 (February 1975): 14-17.

Smith, Betty. *A Tree Grows in Brooklyn, A Novel*. Philadelphia: Blakiston, 1943.

Smith, Elva S. "The Carnegie Library School—A Bit of History." *Library Journal* 46 (October 1921): 791-794.

Smith, Manuel J. *When I Say No, I Feel Guilty*. New York: Dial, 1975.

Smith, Stanley V., and Williams, Joel. *Library Statistics of Colleges and Universities*. Fall, Part B Washington, D.C.: U.S. Government Printing Office, 1972.

Sobol, Marion. "A Dynamic Analysis of Labor Force Participation of Married Women of Childrearing Age." *Journal of Human Resources* 8 (Fall 1973): 487-505.

Special Libraries Association. *Putting Knowledge to Work: The Profession of a Special Librarian*. New York: Special Libraries Association, 1956.

──────.Recruitment Committee. *Special Librarianship: Information at Work*. New York: Special Libraries Association, 1962.

Speider, Virginia. "Image of the Librarian as Seen in Eight Career Novels." Master's thesis, University of North Carolina, 1961.

Spencer, Byron G., and Featherstone, Dennis C. *Married Female Labour Force Participation: A Micro Study*. Ottawa, Ontario: Dominion Bureau of Statistics, 1970.

Spring, Joel H. *The Sorting Machine: National Educational Policy Since 1945*. Chicago: Rand McNally, 1976.

Squires, Gregory. *Education and Jobs: The Imbalancing of the Social Machinery*. New York: Transaction, 1979.

Starr, Kevin. *Land's End*. New York: McGraw-Hill, 1979.

Stead, Bette Ann. *Women in Management*. Englewood Cliffs, N.J.: Prentice-Hall, 1978.

Stein, Aletha, and Bailey, Margaret M. "The Socialization of Achievement Orientation in Females." *Psychological Bulletin* 80 (November 1973): 345-366.

Stevenson, F.B. "Women Administrators in Big Ten Universities." Ph.D. dissertation, Michigan State University, 1973.

Stone, Elizabeth W. *Factors Related to the Professional Development of Librarians.* Metuchen, N.J.: Scarecrow Press, 1969.

Strober, Myra H. "Bringing Women into Management: Basic Strategies." In *Bringing Women into Management,* edited by Francine E. Gordon and Myra H. Strober. New York: McGraw-Hill, 1975, pp. 77-96.

"A Study of 1967 Annual Salaries of Members of the Special Libraries Association." *Special Libraries* 58 (April 1967): 217-254.

Sukiennik, Adelaide Reno Weir. "Training Women Library School Students for Greater Career Achievement." Ph.D. dissertation, University of Pittsburgh, 1978.

Suter, Larry E., and Miller, Herman P. "Income Differences Between Men and Career Women." *American Journal of Sociology* 78 (January 1973): 962-974.

Sweet, James A. "Family Composition and the Labor Force Activity of American Wives." *Demography* 7 (May 1970): 195-209.

Talbot, Richard J. and von der Lippe, Ann. *Salary Structures of Librarians in Higher Education for the Academic Year 1975-1976.* Chicago: American Library Association, 1976.

Tangri, Sandra S. "Determinants of Occupational Role Innovation Among College Women." In *Women and Achievement: Social and Motivational Analyses,* edited by Martha T.S. Mednick, Sandra S. Tangri, and Lois W. Hoffman. Washington, D.C.: Hemisphere Publishing, 1975, pp. 255-273.

——.*Occupational Aspirations and Experiences of College Women.* Bethesda, Md.: ERIC, 1971, ED 060 470.

——."Role Innovation in Occupational Choice." Ph.D. dissertation, University of Michigan, 1969.

Tarr, Susan A. "The Status of Women in Academic Libraries." *North Carolina Libraries* 31 (Fall 1973): 22-32.

"Task Force on Women." *Social Responsibilities Round Table Newsletter* 41 (October 1976): 3.

Taylor, Marion Ruth. "External Mobility and Professional Involvement in Librarianship: A Study of Careers of Librarians Graduating From Accredited Library Schools in 1955." Ph.D. dissertation, Rutgers University, 1973.

Taylor, Sydney. *All-of-a-Kind Family.* Chicago: Wilcox and Follett, 1951.

Terborg, James R. "Women in Management: A Research Review." *Journal of Applied Psychology* 62 (1977): 647-664.

Terborg, James R., and Ilgen, Daniel R. "A Theoretical Approach to Sex

Discrimination in Traditionally Masculine Occupations." *Organizational Behavior and Human Performance* 13 (1975): 352-376.

Terborg, James R; Peters, Lawrence H.; Ilgen, Daniel R; and Smith, Frank. "Organizational and Personal Correlates of Attitudes Toward Women as Managers." *Academy of Management Journal* 20 (March 1977): 89-100.

Tessler, Sharlene. "Profiles of Selected Women College Presidents Reflecting the Emerging Role of Women in Higher Education." Ph.D. dissertation, Boston College, 1976.

Thornton, Luanne E. "A Scale to Measure Librarians' Attitudes Toward Librarianship." *Journal of Education for Librarianship* 4 (Summer 1963): 15-26.

Times Herald 22 May 1897, President's Office Scrapbook, 1868-1897, University of Illinois Archives, Urbana.

Tingley, Sherman, and Inskeep, Gordon. "Job Satisfaction and Mobility Among Scientific and Engineering Personnel." *Journal of College Placement* 34 (December 1973-January 1974): 58-64.

Toren, Nina. "Semi-Professionalism and Social Work: A Theoretical Perspective." In *The Semi-Professions and Their Organization*, New York: Free Press, 1969, pp. 141-195.

Trautman, R. *A History of the School of Library Service*. New York: Columbia University Press, 1954.

"Ulveling Interview on Librarianship." *American Library Association Bulletin* 39 (November 1945): 457-459.

U.S. Army Service Forces, Office of the Adjutant General. *Informational Bulletin*, no. 24. University of Illinois Archives, Urbana, 1944.

U.S. Congress, House of Representatives, Select Committee on Aging, Subcommittee on Retirement Income and Employment. "Policy Proposals on Midlife Women." (hearings). May 7-8, 1979. As summarized in *Women's Action Coalition Newsletter*. Prince George's County, Maryland.

U.S. Department of Commerce, Bureau of the Census. *Census of the Population: 1970*. Washington, D.C.: U.S. Government Printing Office, 1972.

———.*Occupation of Persons with High Earnings*. Washington, D.C.: U.S. Government Printing Office, 1973.

———.*Statistical Portrait of Women in the United States: 1978*. Current Population Reports, Special Studies Series D-23, No. 100. Washington, D.C.: U.S. Government Printing Office, 1980.

U.S. Department of Health, Education, and Welfare. *National Study of Social Welfare and Rehabilitation Workers, Work and Organizational Contexts, Research Report No. 1: Overview Study of the Dynamics of Worker Job Mobility*. Washington, D.C:

Department of Health, Education, and Welfare, Social Rehabilitation Service, 1971.

———.*Taking Sexism Out of Education. The National Project on Women in Education.* Washington, D.C.: U.S. Government Printing Office, 1978, pp. 50-63.

———.National Center for Education Statistics. *Digest of Education Statistics 1979.* Washington, D.C.: U.S. Government Printing Office, 1979.

———.*Earned Degrees Conferred, 1962-1963: Bachelor's and Higher Degrees.* Washington, D.C.: U.S. Government Printing Office, 1965a.

———.Library Services Branch. *Library Statistics of Colleges and Universities, 1963-1964, Institutional Data.* Washington, D.C: U.S. Government Printing Office, 1965b.

U.S. Department of Interior, Bureau of Education. *Public Libraries in the United States of America: Their History, Condition, Management, Special Report, Part I.* Washington, D.C: U.S. Government Printing Office, 1876.

U.S. Department of Labor, Bureau of Labor Statistics. *Occupational Outlook Handbook.* Washington, D.C.: U.S. Government Printing Office, 1959.

———.*Library Manpower: A Study of Demand and Supply, Bulletin No. 1852.* Washington, D.C: U.S. Government Printing Office, 1975.

———.*Perspectives on Working Women: A Data Book, Bulletin 2080.* Washington, D.C: U.S.Government Printing Office, 1980.

———.Women's Bureau. *Background Facts on Women Workers in the United States.* Washinton, D.C.: ERIC, 1970a, ED 048 438.

———.*Fact Sheet on the Earnings Gap.* Washington, D.C: ERIC, 1970b, ED 050 253.

———.*Handbook on Women Workers.* Washington, D.C: U.S. Government Printing Office, 1975.

———.*20 Facts on Women Workers.* Washington, D.C: U.S. Government Printing Office, 1979.

University of Illinois Library and Library School Reference File, 1892-1912, Box 16, University of Illinois Archives, Urbana.

"Up 2%—But Still Only 7% of Total." *Comment* (American Council on Education) 11 (July 1979): 2.

U'Ren, Marjorie B. "The Image of Women in Textbooks." In *Women in Sexist Society.* Edited by Vivian Gornick and Barbara K. Moran. New York: Basic Books, 1971, pp. 318-328.

Van Alstyne, Carol; Mensel, R. Frank; Withers, Julie S.; Malott, F. Stephen. *Women and Minorities in Administration of Higher Education Institutions: Employment Patterns and Salary Comparisons.* Washington, D.C: College and University Personnel Association, 1977.

Vance, Carmen Lee. "Comparison of the Career Development of Women Executives in Institutions of Higher Education with Corporate Women Executives." Ed.D. dissertation, Indiana University, 1978.

Vann, Sarah K. *The Williamson Reports: A Study.* Metuchen, N.J.: Scarecrow Press, 1971.

Veiga, John F. "Women in Management: An Endangered Species?" *MSU Business Topics* 25 (Summer 1977): 31-35.

Walsh, Mary Roth. *Doctors Wanted: No Women Need Apply. Sexual Barriers in the Medical Profession, 1835-1975.* New Haven, Conn.: Yale University Press, 1977.

Walsh, Patricia A. "Career Patterns of Women Administrators in Higher Education in Institutions in California." Ph.D. dissertation, U.C.L.A., California, 1975.

Ward, Patricia Lazell. *Women and Librarianship: An Investigation Into Certain Problems of Library Staffing.* London, England: Library Association, 1966.

Warner, Lloyd W. "The Careers of American Business and Government Executives: A Comparative Analysis." In *Social Science Approaches to Business Behavior,* edited by George B. Strother. Homewood, Ill.: The Dorsey Press, 1962, pp. 99-123.

Wasylycia-Coe, Mary Ann. "Profile: Canadian Chief Librarians By Sex." *Canadian Library Journal* 38 (June 1981): 159-162.

Watson, Paula De Simone. "Publication Activity Among Academic Librarians." *College and Research Libraries* 38 (September 1977): 375-384.

"The Weaker Sex?" *Library Journal* 63 (March 1938): 232.

Weibel, Kathleen. "Toward a Feminist Profession." *Library Journal* 101 (January 1976): 263-267.

Wells, Sharon B. "The Feminization of the American Library Profession, 1876-1923." Master's thesis, University of Chicago, 1967.

White, Carl M. *A Historical Introduction to Library Education: Problems and Progress to 1951.* Metuchen, N.J.: Scarecrow Press, 1976.

Who's Who in Library Service, 4th ed. Edited by Lee Ash. Hamden, Conn.: Shoe String Press, 1966.

Wiebe, Robert. *The Search for Order, 1877-1920.* New York: Hill and Wang, 1967.

Wiens, A. Emerson. *The Characteristics of "Mobile" and "Stable" Occupational Educators by Specialty and Type of School.* Urbana: Bureau of Educational Research, University of Illinois, 1973.

Wilensky, Harold L. "Work, Careers, and Social Integration." In *Comparative Social Problems,* edited by S.N. Eisenstadt. New York: Free Press, 1964a, pp. 306-319.

Wilensky, Harold. "The Professionalization of Everyone?" *American Journal of Sociology* 70 (September 1964b): 137-158.

Willey, Laura M. "Recruitment for Librarianship." Master's thesis, Southern Connecticut State College, 1965.

Williams, Janet. "Librarianship/Working Mother." *American Libraries* 9 (September 1978): 469-470, 477.

Williamson, Charles C. *Training for Library Service.* New York: Carnegie Corporation, 1923.

———."Essentials in the Training of University Librarians—II." *College and Research Libraries* 1 (December 1939): 30-32.

———. *Training for Library Work: A Report Prepared for the Carnegie Corporation of New York.* reprint edition. Metuchen N.J.: Scarecrow Press, 1971.

Wilson, Eugene Holt. "Preprofessional Background of Students in a Library School." Ph.D. dissertation, University of Illinois, Urbana, 1937.

Wilson, Louis R., and Tauber, Maurice F. *The University Library.* Chicago: University of Chicago Press, 1945.

Winship, Barbara Jean. "Effects of the Comprehensive Model of Assertiveness, When Used in a Systematic Training Program to Develop Assertive Behavior." Ph.D. dissertation, Georgia State University, 1974.

Woerdehoff, Frank. "Selective Recruitment Practices and Ideas." *Wisconsin Library Bulletin* 49 (July/August, 1953): 149-154.

Wolpe, Joseph. *The Practice of Behavior Therapy.* New York: Pergamon Press, 1969.

———.*Psychotherapy by Reciprocal Inhibition.* Stanford, Calif.: Stanford University Press, 1958.

Wolpe, Joseph, and Lazarus, Arnold. *Behavior Therapy Techniques.* New York: Pergamon Press, 1966.

Women in Administration 1978. Washington, D.C.: Office of Communication Services National Association of State Universities and Land-Grant Colleges, 1979.

"Women in Administration: Wisconsin Meeting." *Library Journal* 100 (April 1975): 718.

"Women Library Workers." *Social Responsibilities Round Table Newsletter* 41 (October 1976): 2.

Wood, Mary S. "Sex Discrimination: The Question of 'Valid Grounds'." *Protean* 1 (December 1971): 32-40.

"Young Man, Be a Librarian." *Esquire* 69 (April 1964): 8.

Zimmerman, Lee F. "The Academic and Professional Education of College and University Librarians." Master's thesis, University of Illinois, Urbana, 1932.

INDEX

ALA World Encyclopedia of Library and Information Services, 145, 148, 149, 170, 172
academic librarians
  administrators, 103-104, 207-241, 243-282, 287-290, 292-302, 317-320, 345-391
  education, 245-246
  Fennell study, 207-241
    career profile, 239-241
    education, 217-219
    personal background, 211-217
    professional background, 219-234
  Martin study, 243-282
    highest degree in library science, 263
    highest degree in subject field, 263
    personal and family, 264, 270, 272-273
    position level, 258-259
    professional development activities, 261, 269-270, 272
    salaries, 259-260, 266
    work continuity and experience, 265-267, 269, 271-272
  marital status and/or children, 246-248
  mobility, 248, 345-391
  professional development, 251-252
  Robinson study, 345-391
    demographic characteristics, 359-362
    salary, 371, 378, 379, 387, 388, 389
  work continuity, 248-249
Acker, Joan, 307
Advances in Librarianship, 141
affirmative action, 208, 223
Ahern, Mary Eileen, 170, 171, 180
Akers, Nancy M., 186
Allport, Gordon, 11
Allport-Vernon Study of Values, 69, 73, 87, 88, 103

Alvarez, Robert S., 292
American Association of University Women, 209, 290, 303
American Council on Education, 217
  Office of Women in Higher Education, 290
American Library Association, 33, 38, 56, 75, 143, 147-148, 167, 229, 234
  Association of College and Research Libraries, 244, 288-289
  Board of Education for Librarianship, 54-55
  Committee on the Status of Women in Librarianship, 435
American Library History: A Bibliography, 140-142, 145, 146, 152
American Library History: 1876-1976, 141
American Library Institute, 22
American Library Pioneers Series, 145, 148
American Society for Information Science, 229
American Women, 142
Anderson, E.A., 41
anomie, 110
Armour Institute School, 37
Askew, Sarah, 170
Asplund, Julia Brown, 155, 158-159
assertiveness training, 114-138
Association of American Library Schools, 55, 56, 70
Association of American Universities, 292
Association of Collegiate Alumnae, 32, 39
Association of Research Libraries, 4, 207-208, 255, 256, 288, 292, 299, 300, 301, 302, 309-310, 318, 319 (fns 4, 5)
Astin, Helen, 212, 214, 215, 302, 304

Atlanta University School of Library Service, 192

Bailey, Margaret N., 253, 254
Bailyn, Bernard, 8, 348
Baker, Augusta, 198, 200, 201, 203
Baldwin, Clara F., 153
Bales, R.R., 30
Banks, Kalani, 164
Banning, M.C., 53, 57
Bannister, John R., 57, 60
Bardwick, Judith M., 253, 254
Barnard, Henry, 35
Barrette, Lydia Margaret, 181
Barzun, Jacques, 151
Batchelder, Mildred L., 150, 156, 162
Bayer, Alan, 211, 304
Becker, Margaret, 167
Bennet, Margaret, 51, 64-65
Berdie, Ralph F., 195
Bernard, Jessie, 302
Beshurs, James H., 321
Biddle, Bruce J., 396, 400
Billings, John Shaw, 34, 41
A Biographical-Bibliographical Directory of Women Librarians, 145, 147
Biographical Cyclopaedia of American Women, 142
biographical research (general), 4, 139-140
  on women librarians, 139-190
Biography: The Craft and the Calling, 139
Blankenship, W.C., 297, 355
Boaz, Martha, 153, 173
Bogle, Sarah, 144, 170, 171, 173
Bolden, Ethel, 159
Booth, Mary Josephine, 150, 156-158
Bowen, Catherine Drinker, 139
Bowman, G.W., 310
Brand, Barbara Elizabeth, 3, 437
  "Sex-Typing in Education for Librarianship: 1870-1920," 29-49
Braunagel, Judith. See Judith Schick Robinson.
Breckinridge, Sophonisba, 32
Bryan, Alice, 61, 65, 68, 101-102, 293, 294
Buchanan, Bruce, 316
Business and Professional Women's Foundation, 433
Butler, Nicholas Murray, 35
Butler, Pamela E., 116-117

Butler, Susan Dart, 155, 159

Caldwell College for Women, Caldwell, New Jersey, 72
Campbell, Mildred M., 161
Canada Council, 393, 394
Caplow, Theodore, 107-108, 302
career orientation, 321-322
Career Paths of Male and Female Librarians in Canada, 393-423
Carnegie, Andrew, 12
Carnegie Corporation, 45-46, 47, 292
Carpenter, Patricia, 194
Carpenter, Raymond L., 194
Catholic sisters, 6
Century of the Child, 17
Cheda, Sherril, 393, 394, 396, 403, 407, 408, 409, 410, 413
children's librarians, 12, 16-17, 21, 23, 42-45
Civil Rights Act of 1964, 208
Coffey, Katherine, 170
Cohen, Michael D., 308-309
Cohn, William L., 196, 319 (fn 5)
Coker, Janis L., 101
College and University Personnel Association, 289-290
College Entrance Examination Board Scholastic Aptitude Test, 73, 85, 86, 88, 89, 103
Collings, Dorothy W., 198, 200, 201, 203
Colson, John, 173
Columbia University (Library School), 19, 20, 33, 34, 35, 36, 40, 299. *See also* New York State Library School.
Comeau, Reginald Alfred, 64
comparable pay. *See* pay equity.
Conference on Reentry Women Scientists, 432
Coolbrith, Ina, 154, 173
Cooper, Michael D., 245
corporate management, 287-288, 291, 306-317, 317-319
Cott, Nancy, 24 (fn 5)
Coulter, Edith, 173
Countryman, Gratia Alta, 153, 156, 159
Cowper, Rena, 54
Cox, Martha Baldwin, 61
Crawford, Jacquelyn S., 313

Index 477

Cremin, Lawrence, 8
Cross, Patricia, 218
Cummings, Cynthia S., 145, 147
Curby, Vicki M., 305
Cussler, Margaret, 319-320 (fn 12)

Dain, Phyllis, 170
Dale, Doris, 171, 173
Danton, Emily Miller, 148
Danton, J. Periam, 172-174, 184 (fn 59)
Darling, Richard L., 68
Davis, Donald G. Jr., 171, 173
Dewey, Annie, 16, 19, 20
Dewey, Melvil, 9, 12, 13-14, 16, 18, 19, 20, 22, 25 (fns 11, 12), 26 (fns 18, 19, 20), 33-37, 46, 153, 178, 179, 207
Dickson, Katherine Murphy, 5-6, 437
  "The Reentry Professional Librarian," 425-435
Dictionary of American Biography, 142, 143, 147, 173
Dictionary of American Library Biography, 145, 148, 149, 158, 159, 160, 167, 170, 171, 172-174
Doe, Janet, 153
Doren, Electra Collins, 178
Douglas, Mary Peacock, 149
Douglass, Robert, 68-69, 101, 102
Downs, Robert B., 141, 298-299
Draper, Andrew Sloan, 38-39
Drennan, Henry, 68
Drummond, Donald, 161
Duff, John C., 56
Dyste, Mena C., 159

Eastman, Crystal, 429-430
Eastman, Linda Anne, 144, 155, 159, 160, 165
Edge, Sigrid A., 170
Edgecliff College, Cincinnati, Ohio, 71-72
education for librarianship. *See* librarianship—education
Edwards Personal Preference Schedule, 69, 72, 85, 87, 101, 103
Elmendorf, Theresa West, 144, 148, 171
The Emergency Librarian, 394
The Emerging Woman (film), 125

Encyclopedia of Library and Information Science, 145, 148
Englebarts, Rudolf, 142
Epstein, Cynthia, 30, 36, 222, 305, 313
Equal Employment Opportunity Act of 1972, 208
Equal Pay Act of 1963, 208, 316
equal pay for comparable work. *See* pay equity.
Executive Order 11246, 208

Fain, Elaine, 171
Fair Standards Act of 1938, 208
Fairchild, Mary Salome (or Fairchild, Salome Cutler), 173, 209
Farrington, Helen Seymour, 51
female-intensive occupations. *See* occupational segregation.
The Feminine Mystique, 427
Fennell, Janice C., 4, 301, 438
  "The Woman Academic-Library Administrator: A Career Profile," 207-241
Ferber, Marianne A., preface, 304, 351, 438
Ferrari, Michael R., 307-308, 309
Field, Sister Mary, dedication
Fischer, Linda, 393, 394, 396, 403, 407, 408, 409, 410, 413
Flexner, Jennie Maas, 170, 173
Form, William H., 322
Franklin, Barbara Hackman, 212
Franklin, Christina Ladd, 32
Franklin, Louise, 155, 160-161
Freeman, Marilla Waite, 173
Friedan, Betty, 427
Fulton, Marsha Kraus, acknowledgments, 437
Futas, Elizabeth, 5, 438
  "An Analysis of the Study, 'Career Paths of Male and Female Librarians in Canada,'" 393-423

Gambee, Budd, 171, 173
Garrison, Dee, 7, 9-14, 16, 20-23, 24 (fns 5, 7), 25 (fns 10, 11, 13), 30, 40, 141
Geller, Evelyn, 177
Ghoting, Saroj, 433
Giffin, Eta Josselyn, 154
Gillis, Mabel Ray, 176-177

Gilman, Daniel Coit, 40
Gilroy, Marion, 171
Ginzberg, Eli, 15, 220-221, 302
Gleason, Eliza Atkins, 198, 200, 201, 203
Goode, William J., 109
Graham, Bessie, 155, 161, 173
Greene, Belle de Costa, 171
Grimm, James W., 13, 250, 318
Grothaus, Julia, 155, 161-162
Grotzinger, Laurel A., 4, 49, 173, 439
  "Biographical Research on Women Librarians: Its Paucity, Perils, and Pleasures," 139-190
Gruzen, Joan, 121
A Guide to Research in American Library History, 145, 146, 155
Guilford-Martin Inventory of Factors (GAMIN), 68, 101
Gummere, Richard, 64
Gunter, Lillian, 155, 162

Hacker, Helen Mayer, 24 (fn 4)
Haines, Helen, 144, 148, 171, 173, 179
Hall, G. Stanley, 44
Hall, Katherine Patterson, 117-118, 138
Hall, Mary Evelyn, 144, 173
Hampton Library School, 192
Harper, William Rainey, 32
Harris, Gloria A., 123-125, 138
Harris, Michael, 24 (fn 1), 140, 145
Harrison, Alice S., 155, 162, 163, 176
Harrison, Evelyn, 349
Hart, Hillary, 180
Harvard Business Review, 310
Harvard Business School, 212
Harvey, John F., 246, 294-295, 296, 355
Hasse, Adelaide, 142, 148, 173
Heim, Kathleen M. (editor, this volume), 27 (fn 21), 57, 65, 439
  "Introduction," 1-6
Hennig, Margaret W., 212, 253, 310, 311, 313, 314, 315-316
Herbert, Clara, 53
Herring, Billie Grace U., 186
Hersey, Frederick Earnshaw, 167
Hester, Goldia, 163

Hewins, Caroline Maria, 35, 143-144, 154, 155, 164-165, 170, 171, 173
Hewitt, Vivian Davidson, 198, 200, 201, 203
Heyns, Barbara, 23, 27 (fn 22)
Higgins, Alice G., 55
higher education (general), 31-32
  for librarianship, 33-48
higher education administration, 287-288, 290, 302-306
Hildenbrand, Suzanne, 2, 439
  "Revision versus Reality: Women in the History of the Public Library Movement, 1876-1920," 7-27
Holley, Edward Gailon, 140, 141, 149, 173, 175
Holt, Louise Conrad, 100
home economics, 144
Hooyman, N.R., 249
Horner, Mattina, 107
Hughes, Everett Cherrington, 321-322, 323, 342
Hunt, Clara Whitehill, 44-45
Hutson, Jean Blackwell, 198, 200, 201, 203

Ideson, Julia Bedford, 155, 162, 164
Index of Opportunity in the Library and Information Sciences, 106
intraoccupational segregation, 1
Irvine, Betty Jo, 5, 440
  "Women in Academic-Library, Higher-Education and Corporate Management: A Research Review," 287-320
Isom, Mary Frances, 142, 179

Jacklin, Carol N., 29
Jacobs, Alma S., 198, 200, 201, 203
Jardim, Anne, 212, 253, 311, 313, 314, 315-316
Jencks, Christopher, 13
Jerdee, Thomas H., 250-251
Johns Hopkins Medical School, 34
Jones, Clara Stanton, 198, 200, 201, 203
Jones, Dorothy Scott, 60-61, 70
Jones, Mary L., 179
Jones, Virginia Lacy, 159, 198, 200, 201, 203

Josey, E.J., 197

Kanter, Rosabeth M., 316
Kaplan, J.S., 249
Kaplan, Justin, 180-181
Karier, Clarence, 8
Kaser, David, 141
Katz, Michael, 8
Kelso, Tessa, 147, 149, 177, 179
Kemp, Helen Lamon, 64
Kidder, Ida Angeline, 180
Koehler, Julia Hansen, acknowledgments
Kraus, Joe W., 292
Kroeger, Alice Bertha, 173, 179, 180
Kronus, Carol L., 250

Ladner, Joyce A., 195, 199
Lake Placid Club, 19, 20, 25 (fn 12), 36
Larson, Magali Sarfatti, 48 (fn 1)
law, 31
Lawrence Assertive Inventory, 120, 126, 127, 129, 133, 135, 136, 138
Lawson, Richard W., 158
Lazarus, Arnold, 115
Lee, Mollie Huston, 177
legislative reference service, 41-42
Librarian Authors: A Bibliography, 142
librarians—general. *See also* specific types, e.g., academic librarians; children's librarians.
  administrative positions, 1, 2, 51, 52, 53, 54, 55, 56, 57, 60, 61, 62, 63, 66, 107, 96, 207-241, 243-282, 287-290, 292-302, 317-320, 333, 373-374
  Australia, 102-103
  black (female), 191-205
  Canada, 5, 301-302, 393-423
  career commitment, 252-253
  careers, 103-104, 294-296
  employed in U.S. (1940-1970), 65
  employment projections for 1947-1960, 58
    postwar library service, 59
  Great Britain, 101
  mobility, 5, 248, 321-344, 345-391
  personal achievement motivation, 253-254
  personality of, 68-69, 101-103, 138

  personality of potential librarians, 85-89
  professional development, 251-252
  recruitment of
    men, 51-67
    undergraduates, 67-98
  reentry, 425-435
  Rhodes study, 191-205
    birthplace and date of birth, 200
    careers, 203-204
    education, 200-203
    education of parents, 199
  salaries, 54-56, 64, 103, 259-260, 266, 301-302
  sex roles, attitudes toward, 249-251
  Taylor study, 321-344
    background, 325-326
    career mobility, 326-328
    extrajob characteristics, 334-338
    functional mobility, 329-332
    geographic mobility, 328-329
    professional involvement, 338-341
    salaries, 333-334
    vertical mobility and career patterns, 332-334
librarianship
  attitude toward by undergraduates, 78-84
  demographic peculiarities, 1
  education for, 29-49
  feminization of, 13, 14, 45-46, 176
  image of, 9, 14, 51, 65, 70, 93-94, 322
  marginal profession (see general heading occupational segregation)
  Marxist view of, 20-21
  "women's sphere" view of, 20
libraries (by type). See specific type, e.g., public libraries.
library school students, 118-138
Lightfoot, Robert Mitchell Jr., 53
Lindquist, Jennie D., 165, 170
Lipscomb, Ernestine Anthony, 198, 200, 201, 203
Livingston, J. Sterling, 310
Loeb, Jane W., 304
Logasa, Hannah, 173
Loring, Rosalind, 315
Louisville Free Public Library, 192

Ludington, Flora Belle, 142, 173
Lydenberg, Harry Miller, 41
Lynch, Beverly P., 244, 246, 247, 252

McAnally, Arthur, 298-299
McCann, Eleanor, 57
McCarthy, Charles, 41-42, 47
McClelland, David C., 29, 30
Maccoby, Eleanor E., 29
McDiarmid, E.W., 293
McGowan, Frank M., 300
McMahon, Anne, 101, 102-103
McMullen, Haynes, 171, 173
MacPherson, Harriet D., 170
male-intensive occupations. *See* occupational segregation.
Mallory, Mary, acknowledgments
Manderino, Mary Ann, 118, 120, 135
Mann, Margaret, 39, 142, 145, 146, 148, 169, 173
March, James G., 308-309
Martin, Allie Beth, 173, 175
Martin, Jean K., 4-5, 301, 440
"Salary and Position Levels of Females and Males in Academic Libraries," 243-282
Martin, Mary P., 156
Martin, Patricia Y., 250
Mattila, Peter J., 349
medicine, 31
men
  in academic libraries, 243-285
  predominance in top positions, 2, 207-208
  recruitment to librarianship, 51-67
Metz, Paul, 300-301
Mickey, Melissa Brisley, 169, 173
Millam, Carl H., 57
Miller, A.E., 31
Miller, Herman P., 351
Mills, C. Wright, 18
Milum, Betty, 171
Minnesota Multiphasic Personality Inventory, 103
Miss Library Lady, 62
mobility, 346-355
The Modern Researcher, 151
Monti, Minnie Sweet, 155, 167
Moore, Anne Carroll, 42-43, 48, 144, 148, 155, 165-167, 173
Morris, Effie Lee, 198, 200, 201, 203
Morrison, Perry D., 103-104, 138, 196, 245, 246, 250, 252, 295-296, 355

Morsch, Lucile M., 148, 173
Morton, Elizabeth H., 171
Mudge, Isadore, 39, 144, 147, 148, 150, 156, 157, 158, 170, 173
Munn, Ralph, 57, 60, 293
Myers, Margaret, 432

National Association of State Universities and Land Grant Colleges, 290
National Cyclopedia of American Biography, 142, 144
New York State Library School, 36. *See also* Columbia University.
Nishiura, Eleanor N. Beshurs, 321
Noel, Jacqueline, 174
Notable American Women: 1607-1950, 142, 143, 147, 170, 171, 172
Notable American Women: The Modern Period, 142, 144, 170
nursing, 2, 22, 52 (table), 61, 79, 144

Oboler, Eli, M., 60
O'Brien, Nancy Patricia, 3, 440-441
"The Recruitment of Men Into Librarianship, Following World War II," 51-67
"obsessive compulsive" personality, 11, 13
occupational segregation, 1, 13, 21, 22, 23, 24 (fn 6), 29-30, 99-100, 104-114, 311, 320 (fn)
O'Keege, Beth Egan, 121
Olcott, Frances Jenkins, 43-44
O'Leary, Virginia, 312
Oral History Association, 197
oral history technique, 193-194, 197
Ory, John C., 256, 283-284
Osborne, Susan M., 123-125, 138
Osmond, Marie W., 250

Parrott, Shirley, 100
Parsons, Jerry L., 299, 308
Parsons, Talcott, 30, 110-111
pay equity, 22, 27 (fn 21), 48, 425-426
Pettigrew, Claudie, 160
Phelps, Linda, 208
Phenix, Katharine, acknowledgments
Phillips, Cecil, 160
Phinazee, Annette Lewis, 198, 200, 201, 203

Pierce, Cornelia Marvin, 155, 169, 173, 179
Pioneering Leaders in Librarianship, 171
Pittsburgh Survey, 43
Plate, Kenneth H., 105
Plummer, Mary Wright, 141, 143, 144, 171, 173
Poggio, John P., 256, 283-284
Pollard, Frances M., 196-197
Poole, William, 35
Poor, Anne, 166
Porter, Dorothy Burnett, 198-200, 201, 203
Post-War Library Personnel: A Report from the American Library Association on Post-War Educational Opportunities for Service Personnel, 58
Powell, Lawrence, 173
Power, Effie Louise, 144, 145, 156, 167, 168
Pratt Institute, 37
professionalism, 11, 12-13, 22, 24 (fn 7), 25 (fn 10), 48 (fn 1), 104-113, 322-323
public libraries, 8, 9, 12, 13, 14, 17, 18, 19, 20, 21, 22, 23, 32, 64

Rainwater, Nancy Jane, 69, 101
Randall, William M., 292, 319 (fn 2)
Ratchford, Fannie Elizabeth, 177-178
Rathbone, Josephine Adams, 180
Reagan, Agnes Lytton, 62, 69-70, 95
recruitment to the library field
 of men, 51-67
 of GIs, 54-55
 of undergraduates, 67-98
Reece, Ernest, 60
Reeling, Patricia, 3, 103, 441
 "Undergraduate Women as Potential Recruits to the Library Profession," 67-98
reformism, 14-15
Reubens, Beatrice, 24 (fn 6)
Reubens, Edwin, 24 (fn 6)
revisionist history, 7-9
 in education, 8
 in librarianship, 9
Rhodes, Lelia Gaston, 4, 441
 "Profiles of the Careers of Selected Black Female Librarians," 191-205
Richardson, Cora, 168
Ricking, Myrl, 63
Riesman, David, 13

Robinson, Carrie Coleman, 198, 200, 201, 203
Robinson, Judith Schiek, 5
 "Geographic Mobility and Career Achievement of Male and Female Librarians," 345-391, 441-442
Rogan, Octavia, F., 156, 162, 164
role models, 231-232, 312-313
The Role of Women in Librarianship, 1876-1976: The Entry, Advancement, and Struggle for Equalization in One Profession, 150
Rollins, Charlemae, 198
Rosen, Benson, 250-251
Ross, Sue G., 348
Rossi, Peter, 13, 106
Rothstein, Samuel, 171
Russell Sage Foundation, 43
Ryan, Mary Jane, 195

salaries, 60, 62, 64, 103, 259-260, 301-302, 371
Sasse, Margo, 143, 144
Saunders, Minerva, 12, 143, 144
Savord, Ruth, 53, 55
Schein, Virginia E., 250, 311
Scheubar, Jennie Scott, 156, 162, 179-180
Schick, Frank L., 294
Schiller, Anita, 51, 68, 103, 104, 105, 138, 207-208, 209, 243, 244, 245, 246, 247, 248, 252, 297, 298, 300, 350, 351, 355, 356
schools (public), 8, 17, 26 (fn 16)
Schwartz, Eleanor, 248
Sears, Minnie, 148, 149, 173
segregation of blacks, 200
Seligman, Edwin R.A., 35
semiprofessions. *See* occupational segregation.
Seymour, Evelyn, 173
Sharp, Katharine, 3, 4, 37-40, 46, 47, 48, 142, 150, 154, 156, 163, 173, 178, 180
Shaw, Dorothy R., 169
Shera, Jesse, 64, 139, 173
Shockley, Ann Allen, 198, 200, 201, 203
Shortess, Lois F., 156
Simon, Barry E., 432
Simpson, Richard L. and Simpson, Ida Harper, 29-30, 51, 59, 105, 111-113, 138, 342

Smeal, Ellie, 428
Smith, Jessie Carney, 198, 200, 201, 203
Smith, Katherine Wells, 179
Sobol, Marion, 350
social work, 99, 112, 145
Special Libraries Association, 63, 229, 349, 352
Speider, Virginia, 64
Spofford, Ainsworth, 35
Spring, Joel, 8
Squires, Gregory, 26 (fn 15)
Stallman, Esther, 176
Starr, Kevin, 25 (fn 9)
Stearns, Lutie, 144
Stechert, Gustav, 35
Stein, Aletha, 253-254
Stevenson, F.B., 305
Stone, Elizabeth, 149, 251-252
Strober, Myra H., 315
Sukiennik, Adelaide Weir, 304, 442
 "Assertiveness Training for Library School Students," 99-138
Sullivan, Peggy, 149
Suter, Larry E., 351
Sweet, James A., 350

Tangri, Sandra S., 314
Tarr, Susan A., 245, 250
Taylor, Marion R., 5, 356, 442
 "Mobility and Professional Involvement in Librarianship: A Study of the 'Class of '55,'" 321-344
Taylor, Robert N., 162
teachers, 1, 22, 32, 52 (table), 61, 99, 117-118
Terborg, James R., 249, 251, 257, 264, 285
theology, 31
Thomas, Edwin J., 396, 400
Thomison, Dennis, 171
Thornton Scale to Measure Librarians' Attitudes Toward Librarianship, 120, 121, 126-128, 132, 133, 134, 136, 138
Tomorrow's Tomorrow: The Black Woman, 199
Turman, Barbara, 174
Tyler, Alice Sarah, 156, 163, 167, 168, 173

Ulveling, Ralph A., 56
undergraduate women
 of Edgecliff College, Cincinnati, Ohio
  class standing, 76
  demographics, 90-91
  education, 89
  extracurricular activities, 70
  goals, 91-93
  intelligence, 85
  personality, 86-89
  preference for library science as graduate major, 76
  reading habits, 90
  undergraduate major, 76
  work experience, 90
 recruitment to librarianship, 71-98
Understanding History: A Primer of Historical Method, 151
U.S. Dept. of the Interior, Bureau of Education report of 1876, 32
University of California at Los Angeles
 librarians, 245
University of Chicago, 32
University of Chicago, Graduate Library School, 192, 299
University of Illinois at Urbana-Champaign, Graduate School of Library and Information Science, 38-40, 68, 299
University of Maryland, School of Library and Information Services Manpower Studies, 288
University of Michigan, School of Library Science, 299
University of Pittsburgh, Graduate School of Library and Information Sciences
 students, 121-138
University of Texas, Austin, 162
University of Wisconsin-Madison, Library School Women's Group, 147
university teaching, 32

Van Houten, Donald R., 307
Vann, Sarah, 170
Veiga, John F., 253
Vormelker, Rose L., 156, 163, 167, 168-169

Waddell, John, 157, 173
Wadleigh, Harriet, 179
Walton, Genevieve, 149
Ward, Patricia Lazell, 100, 432
Warner, Lloyd W., 307, 308, 309
Warren, Althea, 153, 179
Wasylycia-Coe, Mary Ann, 393, 394, 396, 403, 407, 408, 409, 410, 413
Weibel, Kathleen, dedication, 434-435
"Wellesley half dozen," 16
Wells, Sharon B., 138
West, Elizabeth H., 162, 163-164
West, Mary Howard, 156
Who's Who in Library Service (1966), 324
Wiebe, Robert, 14
Wilensky, Harold L., 108-109
Williamson, Charles C., 21, 41, 42, 45-46, 293
Williamson Report, 3, 21, 45-46
Wilson, Eugene, 68
Winchell, Constance, 174
Winser, Beatrice, 170
Winsor, Justin, 33, 207
Wisconsin Legislative Reference Library, 42-43
Wolpe, Joseph, 115, 116
Wolpe-Lazarus Assertive Inventory, 120

"woman's place" rhetoric, 11
women
  in corporate management, 287-288, 292, 306-317, 317-319
  in higher education administration, 287-288, 290, 302-306
  pioneering of reform careers, 14, 15-17
  treatment in historical and social science writing, 10
  in the workforce, 1870-1940, 52
Women and Achievement, 137
Women as Managers Scale, 257, 264, 285
Women in Library Administration (University of Wisconsin-Extension conference held in 1975), 208-209
Women in the Library Profession, 147
Women's Liberation Scale, 120, 121, 126, 127, 131, 133, 134, 136
Wood, Raymund, 173
Woodworth, Florence, 176
World War II
  recruitment of librarians following, 51-67
Wright, Alice, 160

Yaffe, Phyllis, 393, 394, 396, 403, 407, 408, 409, 410, 413